KT-475-543

'A strenuously researched, carefully written and intelligent book' Francis King, *The Oldie*

'Excellently written – Clarke's biography apparently received the subject's co-operation but, commendably, this does not blind him to his defects. Clarke's biography is on a grand scale, matching Cooke's own career' Tim Yeo, *Country Life*

'It was a bright idea ... of Nick Clarke's to seek to examine the life behind the legend. This is a meticulous and methodical biography' Anthony Howard, *Sunday Times*

'Nick Clarke's assiduous and respectful – but a couple of steps short of entirely enthusiastic – biography' Andrew Billen, *Evening Standard*

'Clarke's book will be welcomed by Cooke's legion of fans and will be a useful work of reference' David Chipp, *Literary Review*

'[Cooke's] legacy will be enriched by this biography, which does [him] the courtesy of being well written and balanced' Brian Viner, *Hampstead and Highgate Express*

'It took Clarke many attempts to persuade Cooke to co-operate in this biography, but the results are more than worthwhile. *The World at One* presenter has left few stones unturned in his research into the man popularly claimed to be the most successful broadcaster of the century – and by some as the most knowledgeable man of our times. Yet Clarke, like Cooke, wears his learning lightly and the result is a most readable work' Richard Hopgood, *Yorkshire Post*

Nick Clarke is the son of a journalist and read Modern Languages at Cambridge. After three years at the *Yorkshire Evening Post* he joined BBC TV News in Manchester in 1973. He spent five years on BBC TV's *The Money Programme*, three years with *Newsnight* on BBC2 and since 1989 he has been a BBC Radio presenter, first on *The World This Weekend*, and since 1994 on *The World at One*. He may also be heard as question-master on *Round Britain Quiz* and he regularly chairs *Any Questions?* He is married and lives in London.

ALISTAIR COOKE

THE BIOGRAPHY

~

Nick Clarke

An Orion paperback
First published in Great Britain
by Weidenfeld & Nicolson in 1999
This paperback edition published in 2000 by
Orion Books Ltd,
Orion House, 5 Upper St Martin's Lane
London, WC2H 9EA

Fourth impression 2002

A CIP catalogue record for this book
is available from the British Library.

ISBN: 0 75283 709 5

Printed and bound in Great Britain by
Clays Ltd, St Ives plc

For Barbara.
And in memory of my father
and mother, John and Ruth.

CONTENTS

ILLUSTRATION ACKNOWLEDGEMENTS

The majority of photographs come from AC's voluminous – if haphazard – collection with the following additions:

Between pages 36 and 37
I am grateful to Kathleen Turner (née Cooke) for a number of the family groups and to William Whalley for the victorious Blackpool rugby team. David Curnow provided the splendid Old Blackpoolians dinner.

Between pages 180 and 181
A number of the Cambridge photos, especially those celebrating *The Granta* magazine and the Mummers, came from Eddie Wiltshire, Hugh Stewart and the late Norrie Davidson.

Between pages 276 and 277
I was delighted to have the shot of Ruth Cooke in Ibiza, and the Southold Sunday Lunch, from John B. Cooke. Ruth herself unearthed the evidence of her modelling career.

Between pages 356 and 357
John Cooke found the post-war shot of Cooke's parents and brother. The David Low cartoons hang in the Bunker at Nassau Point and the *Omnibus* sequence comes from the extensive archives of Roy Stevens in New York.

Between pages 452 and 453
Several of the photographs in this section were taken by Leonard McCombe in the early 1950s: he very kindly allowed me the pick of his portfolio. The shot of AC in his study was taken by John Cooke.

Between pages 596 and 597
Pictures from the making of 'America' are from the BBC Stills Library in London. John Cooke caught his father playing golf in the hallway of his Manhattan apartment. Colin Clark provided the shot of AC with Prince Charles, and Freddie Hancock entrusted me with her prize photo – Bernstein and Galway in concert. Thanks also to *Masterpiece Theatre* for the farewell party, to Heather Maclean for 'Bedside Broadcasting' and to the Huntington Hotel, San Francisco, where Jane's portrait of AC hangs. Some of the later snaps are my own.

Caricatures

The caricatures which appear at the beginning of each part were drawn by AC himself and correspond roughly to the relevant period of his life. The hangman drawing (Part Three) was used to decorate his wedding invitation.

INTRODUCTION

One Thursday afternoon in the summer of 1994, I waited anxiously outside a BBC Radio studio at Broadcasting House in London, where Alistair Cooke was recording a *Letter from America*. From the corridor, it was possible to catch the rise and fall of the familiar voice, but not to hear the words. I had been warned that Cooke disliked being overlooked or overheard while he was delivering his script: the producer and sound engineers were allowed to listen, but only under sufferance. Critics and reviewers had often noted this insistence on the intimacy of his art – the art of speaking directly, and without distraction, to each individual listener. None of which was much help to the would-be biographer, pacing the faded carpet-tiles, and wondering how to broach what was likely to be an unwelcome subject.

Cooke, I had read, was a private man with a tendency to prickliness, but when we were finally introduced, he was courteous to a fault. We exchanged conversational niceties – about golf and the prospects for Wimbledon – until the moment could be deferred no longer. What did he think about the suggestion that I should write about his life? Cooke did not think much of it, and was not afraid to tell me so. I should choose somebody more interesting, or dead, or both. Einstein might be a good subject, or the golfer, Bobby Jones.

Later that week Cooke did agree to meet me at his rented apartment in Mayfair, where he plied me with absurdly strong gin – being a whisky-drinker himself – and regaled me with tales of politics, publishing and the BBC. The anecdotes whetted my appetite, and emboldened me (after more than two hours) to ask my question again. Cooke smiled sympathetically, gently informed me how often he had deflected such advances in the past, and let me know that he had no intention of being more compliant this time. I retired, slightly shakily, with a vague promise of some 'conversations' on specified topics at some unspecified future date. I was still sufficiently in possession of my faculties to recognise that I had been turned down.

That might have been that, if it hadn't been for the determination of Richard Cohen, whose idea the book was, and John Coldstream, Literary Editor of the *Daily Telegraph*, who had proposed my name as the writer. Cohen believed that it was worth persisting, and encouraged me to delve into Alistair Cooke's roots in the North of England. In due course, I began to unearth fragments of his early life before, during, and after the Great War: a Salford Sunday School picture, an old classmate from Blackpool, a long-lost niece. I kept Cooke informed of my progress, and after six months he finally cracked: if the book was going to happen anyway, he concluded, it might be better to ensure – as far as possible – that the biographer had his facts straight.

From that time on, I had access to all Cooke's papers, photographs and archives, and I was able to speak freely to his family and friends on both sides of the Atlantic. Without that co-operation, this book would not have been possible. What's more, Cooke made no effort at any time to influence the course of my work: indeed, he always claimed that he had no intention of reading it. I am properly grateful for his initial act of faith, which – as he often told me afterwards – he immediately regretted.

Nick Clarke
June 1999

PROLOGUE

Alistair Cooke is his own invention.

The voice of the *Letter from America*, purveying word-pictures of his adopted home back to the land of his birth, is deceptive. So, too, is the elegant figure of an archetypal Englishman, which so many Americans recognised in the host of *Masterpiece Theatre*. Neither image of the man tells the whole story.

To begin with, he wasn't even Alistair Cooke, having been christened – in November 1908 – plain Alfred. The 'Alistair' came later, part of a long and slow process of osmosis.

The first concrete evidence of this process appears on the inside cover of a moth-eaten history textbook – *Pages of Britain's Story, AD 597–1898*. A book-plate with a school motto and crest bears the name of its owner, neatly inscribed: 'A Cooke, Form IV x.' But just above, in bold capitals, a fourteen-year-old hand has doodled a more extravagant signature: 'Alister Alfred Cooke.'

A decade later, on his twenty-second birthday, the boy's tentative change of identity was confirmed by deed poll. He would henceforward be known as Alistair A. Cooke. His elder brother Sam might have resigned himself to a life as a butcher's assistant, but young Alfred had no intention of following in those humble footsteps.

PART ONE

THE
EARLY
YEARS

1

A RESPECTABLE CHILDHOOD

A child's horizons, in the industrial north of England before the Great War, were severely circumscribed. The narrow, grey streets were not designed to encourage a small boy to raise his eyes beyond his immediate surroundings. Row upon row of terraced houses reinforced notions of conformity and submission to the *status quo*. The sprawling complex of docks, the mills, the chemical works – these were the landmarks of Salford, which Cooke remembered as a bleak suburb of Manchester. They defined the lives people led and the lives their children could expect to lead. 'An appalling place,' Cooke called it once in an unguarded moment.

It was a community which discouraged affectation. So when Mary Elizabeth Byrne Cooke gave birth to a second son on 20 November 1908, she and her husband Samuel chose a solid, no-nonsense Lancashire name. Alfred it would be, after the Wesleyan minister Alfred H. Lowe, who had helped Samuel himself acquire an education when his own father died young. The birth certificate, giving the father's occupation as 'iron fitter', underlined the family's place in the Edwardian scheme of things. Number 7 Isaac Street wasn't at the bottom of the heap, but it was not a place, either, for the nurturing of great ambitions.

Many years later, Cooke's niece Kathleen was taken to see the place where her Uncle Alfred had been brought up. She was astonished by the murky meanness of the neighbourhood, where the sun rarely reached the densely packed streets. Eventually, in an excess of civic zeal, these streets were condemned as slums and bulldozed. But in 1908 Salford, although poor, was relentlessly respectable. 'That was the word – respectable,' Cooke reflected from a comfortable old age. 'My God, you never saw anybody hanging about on street corners.' The artisan class kept its doorsteps scrubbed or whitewashed, and protected its armchairs with antimacassars. And Methodist families like the Cookes tried to ensure that this outer show was matched by the inner order of their lives. No alcohol, therefore, no gambling or swearing, and no cards on Sundays.

His father helped establish the Wood Street Mission for deadbeats, drunks and derelicts, which acted as a shelter for runaways and battered wives, as well as carrying out voluntary work amongst the very poor. Only as an old man did Samuel Cooke reveal the full seaminess of life at the Mission, blushing as he related to his son tales of roaring drunks and whores, and children abandoned outside pubs. In Cooke's recollection, 'my father never tried to convert them. They could be the foulest human beings alive, but they wouldn't be turned away.'

Isaac Street must have felt a secure, if somewhat cheerless, place for a child growing up – and Newport Street, too, close to the park across Langworthy Road, where the family moved. Alfred was dispatched to Seedley Communal School at the age of four. It had only been open for seven years, and there were constant complaints about overcrowding and staff shortages, especially during the disruptions of war.

Alfred took his pleasures where he could find them. As he grew older, he would make his way to the local shop each Monday for a copy of *The Magnet*, with its slapstick public-school adventures of Billy Bunter, Harry Wharton and Bob Cherry. What can a Salford boy have made of these absurd antics of the idle rich? Once his teacher caught him reading *The Magnet* in class. 'I was devastated with shame,' he recalled, 'and having always been a law-abiding type, I never did it again.' For a time, he chose girls as his playmates – an oddity to which a kindly parson thought it wise to draw his parents' attention. As a result, 'care was taken that I should meet and play, for a change, with boys. I took to marbles, then to flipping cigarette cards against the pavement.'

The other highlight of the week was a Saturday afternoon visit to the Langworthy Picturedrome where, despite the reservations of his mother, he discovered the wonders of cinema: the one-reelers, and then, when he was five or six, full-length features. The films with their urgent piano accompaniments were a delightful distraction, and a first glimpse of what things might be like beyond Isaac Street: they sowed the seeds of an obsession which in time would influence the course of his life. His mother's antipathy to the cinema was complete. She thought the whole concept irredeemably vulgar, an impression not helped when she was finally tempted through the doors of the Picturedrome in 1914 to see the much-vaunted Chaplin six-reeler called *Tillie's Punctured Romance*, the first full-length feature film. Alfred, aged five, was entranced. Mrs Cooke found it boring, nonsensical, rowdy and worthless.

Yet life was sweet enough:

> We used to be told, about once a year, to write an essay on the relative advantages of living in the town and the country. Since we lived in a big city, we knew the answers beforehand. Though we were scrawling away in a grey class-room, in a forest of red brick, under Manchester skies about as dramatic as blotting paper, we never for a moment doubted that we were living the only bearable life... We thought of country boys as simple-minded clods who must long to move to the city and marvel at the tram-cars, the dense and endless horizon of the slums, not to mention the high-toned tootling of the Hallé Orchestra.

Apart from such musings in a *Letter from America*, Cooke's recollections of this period in later life are strangely insubstantial. He thinks he remembers a visit by the King and Queen in 1911 or 1912: in this hazy picture, his first claimed memory, he is sitting on his father's shoulders, decked out in tight new bonnet and the unisex skirt of Victorian infants, complete with petticoats. The anecdote, even if overlaid with the detail of a much-told family story, is vivid – the heat of the day, and the cheers breaking over the crowd like a wave as the royal couple went by.

Otherwise, it is as if the sepia photographs of Salford, his home until the age of eight, had faded almost beyond recognition, stored in an album whose pages he preferred to leave unturned.

The war provided the sharpest images – his father interrupting his sandcastle-building on a seaside summer holiday, to announce, on 4 August 1914, 'We're at war with Germany!' Or the dark shadow of a German Zeppelin drifting slowly across the Manchester sky, attracting more curiosity than fear among the children who rushed into the streets to see it. And then, in June 1916, turning up after school to meet his mother at the laundry where she was doing her part-time warwork. Instead of the normal cheerful atmosphere, the women were silent and glum, and he knew immediately that something was wrong. His mother took his hand and said, 'Kitchener has been drowned.' This time, the recollection has the ring of authenticity. 'It was one of those typical Manchester days when the sun slants through the coal-dust after heavy rain. We walked home hand in hand, and I thought the bottom had dropped out of our world.'

At least the Cookes were spared the personal tragedies that afflicted so many of their neighbours. A densely populated urban area like Salford provided much of Kitchener's cannon-fodder, and the Lancashire Regiment was heavily involved in the Battles of the Somme and the Dardanelles campaign of 1916. Before long every street had its quota of widows' weeds and black armbands, as wives and mothers mourned their loss. As far as Alfred and the other children were concerned, this was nothing special. It was the way things were – like the shortage of food, rationing and the partial black-out at night. And often at night he would dream of being chased by Germans in spiked helmets, like those in cartoons and posters, in a nightmare which long outlasted the war.

Alfred's elder brother Sam was just young enough (born in 1902) to avoid being called up. Their father was, at the start of the conflict, just too old. Eventually even men in their mid-forties were needed to make up the numbers, but Samuel failed the army medical. The conscription board judged him unfit for active service because of his varicose veins (a condition he passed on to his younger son) and he was graded B2, suitable for non-combat auxiliary service only. The skills which until then he'd deployed on decorative iron-work were redirected to building aeroplanes at the Avro factory in Manchester. The varicose veins probably saved his life and he survived into his eighties.

In due course the war did begin to impinge directly on Alfred's existence. His mother, like so many others enduring a poor diet and polluted atmosphere, suffered increasingly from bronchitis. A visit to the doctor confirmed the bad news. In a judgement which entered family folklore, Cissie Cooke was told that if she continued to live in Salford she was unlikely to survive. 'You need a change of air,' the doctor said. 'Egypt would be ideal. But failing that, I suggest Blackpool.' Her younger son had grown used to her bronchial coughing each morning – 'like a pack of wolves'. Strangers found it alarming, but he took it in his stride, as he did 'the endless dark mornings, the blanket of smog, the slippery veil of mud on the streets, which only later did I discover were not typical of life on this globe, but only of life in Manchester'.

In April 1917, then, the Cookes left Salford for the bracing air of the seaside. Alfred was eight and a half years old, and ready for anything. Did Salford leave any impression on him at all? He was asked the question once, as an old man – thought for a moment – and chose to identify not a sight, sound or smell, but the Northerner's distaste for affectation, and the certainty that those given to showing off would surely be cut down to size. Both precepts remained with him, but otherwise nothing much – or nothing obvious – survived from his Salford days. Cooke showed no interest later in re-examining these roots, let alone returning to them. Indeed he consistently played down the idea that he was in any sense a humble boy made good. He wanted at all times to be accepted for what he was, and not compared to something he might have been.

It wasn't that his family life was unhappy. He liked to refer to the words of his mentor H.L. Mencken, American journalist and master of the *bon mot*, who insisted that 'teams of psycho-analysts working in shifts like coal-miners' wouldn't find anything untoward in his relationship with his parents. But whether he knew it or not, Alfred Cooke was marked by his childhood, if only in his determination not to be bound by it. Thirty years later he would write in one of the earliest of his BBC *Letters*: 'I never remember hearing anyone in America, however snobbish, say that somebody didn't know his place. It is a deep almost unconscious belief of Americans, that your place is what your talent and luck can make it.'

~

In Blackpool, the Cookes moved first into a large house in Vance Road, which was to be much more than merely a home. It was what the locals called a 'company house', not quite a private hotel, but with a number of extra bedrooms to be let out to holiday-makers in the summer. Such establishments were rather looked down upon and in wartime Blackpool theirs was not exactly a thriving business.

But the Cookes probably needed the money. Samuel immediately disappeared back to the Avro factory in Manchester for three or four weeks at a time, and Sam junior, at the age of fifteen, was looking for work. Alfred himself, installed in the Palatinate Central School, must have found it hard to concentrate on his studies. In the very month the family reached the seaside, huge headlines blared from the newspaper billboards. 'The Yanks are Coming!'

The American declaration of war on Germany on 6 April 1917 seemed a momentous event, a turning-point in Britain's fortunes, but the promise of salvation was premature. In the coming months Alfred heard and absorbed the growing volume of complaints from the adults around him. Where were the Yanks? Hadn't they waited long enough to get their hands dirty? Why was it taking so long to get their troops into Europe? The rancour could well have been infectious, fed by the evidence of the boy's own eyes. The Vance Road house, like all its fellows, had been commandeered by the War Office for the billeting of soldiers under training. Throughout the summer the residents grew younger and younger, more and more infirm. The B2s (fit for non-combat duties) were succeeded by the C3s, whose unsuitability for active service was no longer any protection from a front line in France which was insatiable for young men. Even the 'bluejackets', men already wounded in battle, had to be re-drafted into the fray. Anglo-American relations reached a low ebb as the delays dragged on.

In Alfred's mind, the Yanks who were coming were not so much part of a complex military or diplomatic process, as fantastical creatures from another world, as portrayed in books and films:

> The early films of Douglas Fairbanks gave a wonderfully vivid picture of American cities as being inhabited by big pompous fathers and fusspots who tried to keep the bounding Fairbanks busy with his books or his bank-clerking. He always eluded them, since his delightful gift was to convert the walls and counters and turnstiles of the city into a gymnasium. So I expected that when the Americans came into town, they would bound and vault and leap all over the place. This was my complete picture of America.

It was a charming misconception, as Alfred would discover soon enough – an early example of the mutual incomprehension between these two nations which became his stock in trade.

His first summer in Blackpool was spent settling into a new routine. Or rather variations on an old routine, dominated by cinema, school – and chapel. His father was a lay preacher, who performed regularly at the pulpit of the Adelaide Street Wesleyan Chapel. Alfred himself was enrolled in the morning Sunday School, as he had been in Salford, and now he was compelled to attend the evening service, too. He admired his father's abilities, but that didn't prevent the development of 'a child's healthy distaste for sermons'. Sundays were uniformly miserable. The boys weren't even allowed to play cards – whist or the American stockmarket game, Pit. Bagatelle, on the prized mahogany and baize board his father had bought him for Christmas, was banned. Even the piano was under curfew.

The only exception to this Sunday music embargo was sacred music, particularly the music of Handel. Every Christmas, at Methodist Chapels across the North of England, the strains of Handel's Messiah rang out. Cooke claims to have known the entire work off by heart from the age of four, so often had he been exposed to it. And he recalls a telling conversation with the local grocer, the day after an early radio broadcast, relayed from Manchester. 'Did you hear the Beethoven symphony from Manchester?' Cooke inquired. 'Aye, lad. I did. But as far as I'm concerned, there's nowt wrong with 'andel.'

Alfred's eight-year-old life had its memorable moments. A maid called Emily was engaged to help at Vance Road. She was pretty, elegant, and the proud possessor of an officer boy-friend. One afternoon she took Alfred to the Blackpool Grand Theatre to see a musical comedy by P.G.Wodehouse. This would have been entrancing enough, but her military connections allowed them to occupy a box – something far above the aspirations of either of them. The play was called *Old Boy*, and at one point an upper-class character uttered the phrase: 'Do you think I'm a bloody scooper?' The boy was horrified, never having heard such a dreadful word spoken in public. It was only much later that he realised what the actress had actually said – in tribute to one of the great pin-ups of the moment – 'Do you think I'm Gladys Cooper?'

Swearing was simply a sin too awful to contemplate. Indeed the Cooke household was hemmed in by the rules strictly enforced by his mother. Once his father returned from a walk on the beach in glowing good humour. 'The air,' he remarked to his wife, 'was like wine!' Cissie blanched. How could he possibly know? His father hastened to revise the analogy. 'I mean . . . I mean, like Wincarnis.' This being a celebrated temperance tonic, and therefore acceptable in the Vance Road sideboard.

During the summer of 1917, a decision had to be taken on the future of Sam Cooke, then aged fifteen. He fell ill, and the doctor's diagnosis was grim. If he continued with his studies, he would become a likely candidate for tuberculosis, a judgement reached by study of the patient's neck. Until this time Sam had been hoping to go to college in Manchester, sponsored by the English Velvet and Cord Dyers Union, but the health warning meant a change of plan. The doctor advised him to choose some healthy physical occupation and Sam became a butcher's apprentice. He was quite unlike his precocious younger brother. Physically they were worlds apart – Sam stocky and heavily built, Alfred tall, thin and graceful. And where Alfred was sharp and intelligent, Sam had, at best, some manual skills, which enabled him build his own wireless set before they were available in the shops. Somehow their parents had produced two offspring of very different talents.

When Cooke looked back at his relationship with Sam, he was always protective, uncomfortable about the gulf between his good fortune and Sam's humdrum fate. It's impossible now to tell whether the TB scare was simply a story spun to an eight-year-old child so as not to damage his esteem for his brother. But the truth seems to be that the butchery business was the best that Sam could hope for.

All the while, the Vance Road company house observed a succession of young men come and go, frequently to their deaths. On afternoons through the summer and early autumn, Alfred watched their training exercises on the beach, designed to ensure that they could at least march in step towards the sound of enemy gunfire. Until, one day shortly before his ninth birthday, the Yanks finally came.

～

Cooke always claimed that the arrival of American troops in Blackpool was a decisive moment in his life. Whether this is mere romantic rationalisation, this period etched itself in his memory in vivid detail, no doubt because seven of these exotic creatures were garrisoned at Vance Road – the 'doughboys', named after their boy-scout hats. Until then, he had 'loved America through films', but this was the real thing.

He described in *Alistair Cooke's America* his puzzlement at the colour of the soldiers' skin: 'They were taller than ours and uniformly paler, almost yellow.' Most, he discovered subsequently, came from the cities of the Eastern Seaboard, or from the South, where the burning sun was to be avoided. At the time he was inclined to believe his father's explanation – that their biscuity complexions came from living in the shadow of the famous skyscrapers.

Alfred's confusion was multiplied as these 'palefaces' (so that's what it meant!) settled into Blackpool life. In his short experience there had never been any difficulty, whether by accent, manners or behaviour, in identifying an officer from a regular soldier. But now, suddenly, Alfred found he couldn't tell them apart. He couldn't understand, either, the Americans' lack of respect for the social niceties of English middle-class existence. Professors, plumbers, school-teachers and businessmen treated his mother with equal New World courtesy, dealt with children as equals, and even helped the maid with the washing-up. And their accents ... For a child brought up on silent films this was the first opportunity to hear Americans speak, and he was intrigued and delighted by the variety of voices, from southern drawl to the clipped vowels of New England.

Alfred was star-struck. The Vance Road residents adopted him as an unofficial mascot and, with his father away for so much of the time in Manchester, he looked up to them as unofficial parents.

His inclination to warm to Americans, he noted, was incontrovertibly determined during these final months of the war. He watched them going through their paces on the sand, cutting fine figures – especially compared with the miserable local contingents of C3s. And he had his own first taste of Anglo-American tensions. An English bluejacket was strolling back along one of the piers that jut out into the Irish Sea. Coming in the other direction was a newly-arrived young American. The bluejacket looked him up and down and said, 'So what are you doing over here?' 'Me?' he replied. 'Come to win the war, of course.' At which point he found himself unceremoniously dumped into the sea. The town was instantly in uproar, and all Americans were confined to barracks.

Cooke often related this story, largely because of the moral he believed could be drawn from it. From his point of view the interesting thing about what must have been a run-of-the-mill event was the identity of the two unnamed combatants:

I learned much later that the Bluejacket was a Lancashire man and the American, a Texan. They are two races who share a tradition which caused this little tragedy. They both have a high regard for what we now call deadpan humour. The Texan thought the Lancashireman was solemn. The Lancashireman thought the Texan was in dead, and offensive, earnest. A little more knowledge and they could have been fast friends – swapping their best stories with a chuckle or even a smile.

His school lessons had done nothing to raise the level of his own Anglo-American understanding. 'American history stopped abruptly with the outbreak of the Revolutionary War, on the principle that if they didn't need us, we didn't need them.' Yet all the while, Alfred was being exposed to important influences much closer to home which served to counter the prejudice of the age.

Samuel Cooke was an unusual Methodist preacher, with an ineradicable liberal streak – a sense that the other man's point of view might, after all, be right and should in any case be respected. This tended to undermine his effectiveness as a promoter of the Bible message. His younger son watched and listened, and picked up a distrust of dogma which he never lost:

> Forgiveness was all. It was something in those days, in a strict Methodist chapel, to go on acting as if there were as many good people outside the church as in it. He felt the same way about politics. He was a staunch Manchester Liberal (to the constant grief of my mother – she always voted Conservative) but even there you never knew who, from any party, he'd decide was a good man. I think – I hope – his habit of mind passed over to me.

All Cooke's memories of his father are warm and respectful. But Vance Road was not a household given to public displays of affection, and much of the potential warmth between the two remained unstated – something which was to have a profound impact on Cooke's own later relationships. This certainly had much to do with Cissie, as his mother was always known.

Mary Elizabeth Byrne Cooke was of Irish Protestant stock. Her forebears emigrated to Britain some time in the miserable mid-nineteenth century when the potato famine was rife. She was a stern and often forbidding mother. Her grand-daughter, (Sam's daughter Kathleen) described later being petrified of this Victorian figure with Victorian attitudes to children. Cooke himself always strove to be more generous, describing her as 'very intelligent and sensible'. It was she who organised the family Bible-readings and ensured that Alfred's first efforts on the piano, picking out the tune of 'Drink to Me Only', were suppressed on the Sabbath. Cooke believes he inherited her toughness. But she also passed on a diffidence about the outward expression of emotion which returned to haunt him.

∼

Alfred had followed the progress of the war with intense curiosity – about everything from the way a tank worked to why the Tsar had been murdered. When peace came, he rose at dawn, and spent hours inscribing the terms of the armistice on cartridge paper. He then rolled it up into the sort of scroll which statesmen clutched in official portraits, and marched into the streets of Blackpool, playing at being Lloyd George, or Clemenceau, or President Wilson. Looking back on 'that memorable jog around the town,' his most lively memory is of a confectioner's window, which was bare 'except for one glittering jewel of an object, bang in the middle. It was a bun. We'd had buns of various dark, coarse meal, but I'd never seen a bun like this. It had on it a circular coating of snow. "That," said my mother, "is not snow, it is icing." It was a marvel, a symbol that happy days would soon be here again.' Radio listeners came to know that bun well, especially when the *Letter from America* coincided with Remembrance Day.

The arrival of peace meant that Samuel could give up his factory-work. He, too, had trouble with his lungs, and decided on a less physically demanding occupation. He became an insurance salesman for the Britannic company, collecting payments from door to door. He thrived in a job which exploited his personal charm, eventually rising to be National President of the salesmen's union. His new career and Cissie's hard work at home paid dividends. From Vance Road, the family steadily moved up-market and up Blackpool's North Shore until they reached Ormond Avenue, in those days a more salubrious corner of the town away from the rowdiness of the seafront. This was not a company house: there was no room, nor any longer the need, for lodgers.

Samuel evidently realised that he had an exceptional child on his hands. He bought Alfred an engraving of Charles Dickens, showing him as a benign figure with his celebrated characters floating around him. This was hung in the boy's bedroom, and reflected his voracious appetite from the age of about ten for the entire Dickens canon; not just the novels, but more obscure works like *My Father as I Recall Him* by his daughter Mamie. The letter 'k' in Cooke's own signature was modelled on the way that Dickens signed his name. 'For a time,' he confessed, 'my life was Dickens. I can remember the books far more clearly than what was happening around me.' Samuel Cooke also had a weakness for prints and paintings. He acquired a water-colour painted by a trainee preacher, featuring a cow staring morosely across the bleak, flat landscape of the Fylde coast – and several pre-Raphaelite prints which showed 'languid ladies, with necks like giraffes, taking a bath'. These unlikely adornments of a Methodist drawing-room were judged to be 'art' and therefore immune from censure. And the ladies were, at least, draped with robes in the classical style.

Only after the war did the family start to explore beyond the town itself. One of the first expeditions, in the spring of 1919, took them inland for a picnic in rural Lancashire and Alfred was overwhelmed by the greenery. 'Perhaps because of the sea-breezes, it seemed to me that Blackpool had no trees higher than a privet-hedge. Suddenly there were trees and leaves all over.' He came home and composed a piece of music – the melody of a typical Victorian ballad with Mozartian overtones. He called it 'Spring Song', and still remembered it well enough thirty-five years later to be able to perform it on a gramophone record.

Although he never learned to read music he would sit for hours at the piano, copying what he'd heard at the cinema. Try as he might, he could not make the music on the page resemble anything other than 'flies on telegraph poles'. Sam, by contrast, worked his way methodically through a five-volume set of popular tunes, from hymns and love-songs to extracts from *Carmen*. Alfred, with a highly receptive ear for the music of the nascent film industry, managed perfectly well without such aids.

Yet the glow of post-war optimism in the Cooke household nearly came to an abrupt end. In that same spring of 1919, Britain, the United States and many other countries were stricken by the pandemic of influenza which killed more people than the Great War. Blackpool did not escape unscathed. A number of children from Alfred's school were among the victims, and at least two from his class succumbed, including a boy called Sutliffe. 'We were taken to see his body laid out. I was absolutely terrified.' Then Alfred himself became sick. For a while his fever was so high that he floated in and out of consciousness, scarcely aware of what was happening. At last, weakly, he opened his eyes to be greeted by the unconcealed relief of his parents – his mother, for once, sweet, gentle and concerned. Gradually it dawned on him that he himself had been in danger of ending up like Sutliffe, displayed in an open coffin in the front-room while relatives and friends filed past.

2

YOUNG ALFRED

Alfred's education really began in September 1920 when he was enrolled at the Blackpool Secondary School, the best for miles around and not ashamed to proclaim the fact, even at the risk of acquiring a reputation for snobbishness. It could hand-pick its pupils, and it was blessed by the presence of a headmaster of real stature. Joseph Turral – known variously, behind his back, as JT, Joe, Plug or simply 'The Boss' – made an indelible impression on all who passed through his hands, and became a 'tremendous figure' in Cooke's life.

This was the picture he drew of JT in honour of the school's Golden Jubilee in 1956: 'A small, dapper man with a handsome Roman profile and blue eyes as alert as gas-jets; a bald head glistening like a billiard-ball, cushioned by two pads of silver hair and decorated by a whitening moustache burned yellow at the fringes by cigarettes that sometimes went on smouldering long after they disappeared from sight.'

The impression never grew fainter. Years afterwards, JT resurfaced in Cooke's writing as 'a man of many cryptic utterances, most of which he delivered impromptu – to uncomprehending small boys – with alarming emphasis on unexpected phrases, as if the listener had just dared him to make a point. Thus he would seize a boy going along a corridor minding his own business and bellow: "D'you know what a bounder is, boy? You *do not* know what a bounder is?! A bounder is a man who walks along Piccadilly wearing a Guards' tie and *doesn't even know* it's a Guards' tie!!!" In Cooke's eyes, Turral was the one great Dickensian character that Dickens forgot to invent. 'He regarded the school as an oasis of gentility in the desert of the North Country, a fortified town holding the siege against the surrounding Philistines,' a reference to the hordes of visitors who invaded the town each summer.

Turral was also, incidentally, the author of that dog-eared

textbook – *Pages of Britain's Story* – in which Alfred Cooke first toyed with a name of more distinction.

The school's motto, inscribed in that book, was *Meliora sequamur*: Let us follow better things. And to that end Turral gathered around him masters who subscribed to his ambitious ethos – the search for excellence, the maintenance of an open mind, and the eschewing of all things common or mean. Since many of the masters were imported from the South of England, there was clearly also a specific plan to eradicate from his school the coarse northern accent. In Cooke's case it worked. No one subsequently can remember him talking with anything resembling a Blackpool twang.

The rules of the school debating society provided an example of Turral's principles in practice. Each boy was honour-bound not to accept an assignment which coincided with his own prejudices: thus anyone in favour of capital punishment had to speak against it. The debate, in other words, was the thing and any idea, however unfashionable or inconvenient, deserved at least to be heard.

In this atmosphere Cooke flourished. He was always near the top of the class, though frequently thwarted by a studious youth called Alan Vickerman, who went on to become the youngest town clerk in British municipal history before being drowned in the Solway Firth at an early age. Cooke would tell this story with just a hint of 'it served him right'. Unlike Vickerman, who never wasted time on games, he was a keen sportsman. Space also had to be found for music, books and cinema – or as JT scathingly pronounced it, following the Greek, *Kineemah*: 'JT deplored the movies till the day he died. But he thought he'd better see everything that might corrupt his pupils... He considered it his duty to look them over as a police sergeant must stoop to search every suspect.'

Turral's reputation attracted a strong batch of speech-day dignitaries, including Bishop William Temple (then of Manchester, later Archbishop of York and Canterbury). The idea of having to listen to a bishop was not initially appealing to Cooke and his friends. 'We snuggled into our seats and dreamed of cricket. And then he walked on. He was a big, round, spectacled, jolly man in black gaiters – like Mr Pickwick taken to Holy Orders,' he told a BBC audience in 1948, soon after Temple's death. 'He said he'd just had the experience of getting on a weighing machine that told you your weight through an invisible voice. When he got on, he said, the machine sang out, "One at a time please!" ' It was an old joke, but his audience lapped it up. They loved him even more when he managed to avoid, while handing out the prizes, any mention of the 'rewards of industry'. And more still when he sympathised with those who had won no prize because – like him – they couldn't spell. 'Spelling,' he declared, 'is just a form of low cunning.'

By the time Alfred was fifteen, he was already being warned by teachers about the dangers of spreading himself too thinly. But he was having too good a time to worry. Doubtless in the hope of becoming the second Douglas Fairbanks, he regularly attended the gymnasium under the tutelage of another of his heroes – Hal Gregory, a renowned Alpine climber. Basing his instruction on a skimpy recollection of some Swedish exercises and the routines he'd learned in the army, Gregory inspired the young Cooke to a high level of skill, especially on the horizontal and parallel bars. He also caused his doting pupil to change the way he gripped a pen: his teacher clasped the instrument between his second and third fingers. Cooke, for a while, imitated him slavishly, greedily assimilating influences from every conceivable source.

Pictures of him at the time show an angular-faced boy, with a mop of dark hair ending in a widow's peak, always with an air of slightly condescending self-confidence. The hair was a constant source of anxiety, particularly when he attended the folk-dancing classes which also took place in the gym: Hal Gregory was a versatile instructor. Attendance meant risking the disapproval of the stalwarts of the Methodist chapel, but Cooke was more worried about the effect of strenuous activity on his unruly locks, which flopped around uncontrollably. 'After consultation with an older boy, who had some connection with a pharmacist, we compounded all sorts of glues and lotions which were supposed to fix your hair to the consistency of cement. It did no good.' He still performed the dances with enough style to catch the eye of the girls watching from the balcony above. One, Phyllis Dunkerley – a future classmate – confessed that she and her friends used to arrive early for their own tuition in order to admire the talent from on high. Another contemporary, Hilda Unsworth, remembers her first sight of Alfred, in the bizarre setting of a chemistry lab, where a school society called 'Literific' was meeting. 'Suddenly this quiet boy got up and started reciting poetry. He read so well, I thought, "What's someone like that doing in Blackpool?" '

Yet he remained comparatively shy. One younger girl called Muriel Stopford used to ride with him on the tram to school, and found that when she and her friends flirted with him, Cooke buried his head more deeply in his books: 'We used to call him "Still Waters". '

~

By the autumn of 1924, Alfred Cooke, approaching sixteen years old, had floated through the School Certificate exams, though he managed to fail geography – a feat regarded as practically impossible. He was still a prime candidate for the recently established sixth form and Blackpool Borough offered grants to those who would otherwise be starting work. From thirty-five children in a class, suddenly there were only nine in Modern Studies One: and – wonder of wonders – five of them were girls. Blackpool Secondary was a mixed school, but until the sixth form, the sexes were studiously separated. All amorous contacts had to be by surreptitious note, although stories of illicit dalliance occasionally surfaced, scrawled in chalk on a blackboard. Boys and girls weren't even allowed to walk home together.

The sixth form offered liberation, with only a token row of empty desks between the two groups to act as a *cordon sanitaire* against the depredations of teenage desire, though Alfred was not by nature an experimenter. In the Christmas of that year, the school held a dance, which all were expected to attend. When Alfred failed to buy a ticket – from shyness, he suggested later, and because his mother was likely to object to the idea of such public displays of licentiousness – he was confronted by the history master, William Iggulden Curnow ('Billy Wick' from his initials), who demanded a reason for this inexplicable lack of school spirit. 'This is a social occasion,' he expostulated, 'and you are part of this society. ' A feebly muttered excuse was brushed aside: 'I will not stand, boy, this Manchester attitude!'

Whatever Curnow meant – Cooke was never sure why his birthplace should be so vilified – the message was clear enough. He duly paid up one shilling for the dance card with its little pencil attached – '(1) Foxtrot, (2) One-Step, (3) Valeta, (4) Polka' . . . each with a gap for the lucky girl's name and before long Phyllis Dunkerley, Ennis Garstang and the rest had taken him in hand. 'From then on, life was bliss.' Yet somehow the strictures of his upbringing never quite deserted him. One dance at the Norbreck Hydro Hotel found him partnering a particularly voluptuous girl. When the band struck up a romantic ballad, 'Yearning', Cooke suddenly felt a ghostly sense of his mother's disapproving presence at his shoulder, and withdrew in confusion, feeling that his partner's delightful proximity was not quite right.

This was the first of many golden periods in his life. Billy Wick was just one, though probably the most significant, of a group of masters who conjured up a remarkable atmosphere of academic enterprise. Many of these men were damaged survivors of the Great War. Curnow himself had suffered shell-shock and used to bare his teeth in an alarming fashion; J.K. Starkie looked twice his thirty years as a result of a bullet-wound in the neck; a geography master called Gastall wore a leather brace to protect a spinal injury. The Secondary School's bright children, who were there through ability and ambition, not privilege or social position, represented the future of which they themselves had been robbed.

Sixth-form boys and girls were exhorted to read widely and well beyond the school syllabus. It was a competitive environment which often meant spending all weekend immersed in literature in order to score vital points. Alfred, with Dickens already under his belt, had a head start, and went on to consume Chesterton, Shaw and Arnold Bennett, H.G. Wells and Henry James, Hazlitt and Lamb and much more besides.

W.I. Curnow, deputy headmaster and history teacher, was one of the main promoters of this intellectual steeplechase. He was a theatre-lover and something of an aesthete, certainly by the standards of Blackpool in the 1920s, and was quite likely to give up all pretence of teaching history in the 'lazy twilights' in favour of a rambling reminiscence about the actress Mrs Patrick Campbell. He proceeded to gather around him a group of the most promising boys, creating a charmed circle which often met outside school hours, sometimes at his own house on a Saturday evening. There the boys would be encouraged to think, to ask questions, and to put the world to rights. One of his specialities was a Friday afternoon diversion – a game whose winner was allowed to leave school half an hour early. It was designed as a corrective to the popular notion that on any important issue people can be classified into simple opposing camps: in the English Civil War, for instance, it was wrong to think that everybody was either a Roundhead or a Cavalier when most citizens bided their time and hoped to back the winner. The prize in Curnow's game went to the boy who could think up the most ridiculous yet plausible example of an unhelpful label.

Cooke recalled one of his own successes – that 'the world is divided into people who prefer Greta Garbo to Marlene Dietrich, and those who prefer Dietrich to Garbo.' The whole exercise had taught him a lesson he said. Labelling people is a natural impulse to make a contradictory and complicated world more manageable, but it is an impulse to be avoided.

Curnow exerted a powerful influence over his flock, and the reading began to pay dividends. Alfred had already marked himself out by winning a school essay prize, beating several candidates from higher forms. Turral used the opportunity to lecture his older pupils on their shortcomings: how had they allowed themselves to be put in the shade by such a youthful scholar? Afterwards he took the winner on one side to issue what turned out to be a prophetic word of congratulation: 'All I have to say, Cooke, is this: if you go on like this, one day you will write for the *Manchester Guardian*! Dismiss!' For an academic of liberal bent, this was the very apogee of praise. As a more immediate prize Cooke asked for – and was given – Max Beerbohm's collection of parodies, *A Christmas Garland*. He wolfed it up, and digested it so thoroughly that seventy years later he could still quote accurately from the take-off of Arnold Bennett's sagas of the Five Towns ('Scruts'). This inspired him to do his own parodies of Chesterton, Shaw and others, several of which appeared in the school magazine, along with the first examples of another new skill – small caricature portraits of school friends and staff, like the portly English master Harry Duguid, whose ash used to dribble from his cigarette and commingle with the egg on the flap of his waistcoat.

Yet Cooke's activities were not confined to the scholarly and artistic: he was just as likely, at the end of a long school day, to wander down the promenade to the Kardomah Café, which had been condemned by the local police as the dangerous haunt of 'lounge lizards', to drink coffee, listen to the jazz trio, and watch the girls go by.

By his last year, Alfred had taken over the editor's chair for the school magazine, which was classically and cheekily entitled *Virginibus Puerisque*, (for girls and boys). His reputation as an all-rounder was enhanced by his sporting achievements. As a member of the school rugby team, his height ensured that he played as a forward: 'wiry, strong and tough', according to one of his team-mates, Bill

Whalley, 'though not particularly fast'. Cooke's own recollections were fond, coloured by the memory of one particularly nasty knee wound, which, he believed, returned to plague him in later life. Soccer had been banned by JT on the grounds that it was a plebeian sport, but watching was a different matter. Through the mists of Blackpool winter afternoons long ago the names of some of the town's star players drift back: Cooke would stand on the terraces with his father, cheering on the infuriatingly inconsistent Mingay – 'a glum little man with ping-pong-ball eyes, and lids as heavy as Sherlock Holmes got up as a Limehouse lascar'.

If his interest in football faded, he maintained a much greater affection for cricket, becoming vice-captain of the team, with bowling his main strength. He claimed to have modelled his action on the great Lancashire and England player Cecil Parkin. Just as important, he perfected the Parkin trick, now used by all bowlers, of flicking the ball up with his foot as it rolled towards him rather than bending down to pick it up. Although the school did not possess a permanent sports field until after Cooke's departure, the peripatetic cricket team had Turral's fanatical support. One location was next to the town's abattoir. 'On Saturdays,' Cooke says, 'JT guided his lawn-mower like a regimental pony, and paused only to flick that nostril in silent tribute to the cattle who were passing out in droves in the nearby abattoir and emitting their abominable funeral odours over his beloved cricket-field.' In the annual staff match, the head would turn out in a starched dress-shirt, and would never neglect a graceful word of praise for the boy who got him out.

Cooke followed Cecil Parkin's career with intense interest, rushing after school to discover Lancashire's latest score in the Stop Press column of the evening paper. He was also a fervent collector of cricket autographs, one of his prize exhibits being the signature of the *Manchester Guardian* correspondent Neville Cardus. His greatest disappointment was to have missed the chance of seeing the great Jack Hobbs play for Surrey. In the summer of 1924 his father took him to London for the first time, but on the overnight sleeper Alfred, fired up with adolescent anticipation, was unable to sleep. Consequently he dozed through the match at the Oval, and managed to miss his hero's – unusually short – innings.

This London visit had its compensations. Samuel Cooke did not share his wife's conviction that the theatre was as worthless as the cinema, and after the match took his fifteen-year-old son to see *The Punch Bowl Revue* at the Duke of York Theatre, featuring a twenty-year-old heart-throb called Enid Stamp Taylor. The following year, they were in London again, watching Shaw's *St Joan*, and fixing for ever in the boy's mind the riffling flag at the back of the set at Joan's words, 'The wind has changed!' Afterwards, in the Lyons Corner House, he and his father would have earnest debates about the comparative merits of actors – and cricketers – of the moment, compared with those on whose fame his father had been nurtured.

Inevitably Alfred was involved in any theatrical performance the school had to offer – notably the 1926 production of Goldsmith's *She Stoops to Conquer*, in which he played young Marlow, and Roland 'Jack' Robinson (the future governor of Bermuda) took the part of his father. Another choice was a tear-jerking Edwardian morality play, *The Bishop's Candlesticks*, inspired by Victor Hugo's *Les Miserables*. It ends with an act of human kindness which transforms the life of a convict bent on stealing the eponymous candlesticks. Cooke played the melodramatic role of the convict: 'I dare not ask for work,' he proclaims to the bishop. 'I dare not go into a town to beg, so I stole, and they have made me what I am, they have made me a thief! God curse them all!' At which point the convict hurls a bottle to the ground, and Cooke, in doing so, managed to extinguish all the footlights.

As with theatre, so with music. Brought up on hymns, Handel and the crepuscular tinkling of the cinema pianist, Alfred was exposed at the Secondary School to a whole new musical world. Turral's public disapproval of the cinema was matched by his huge enthusiasm for music, starting with Gilbert and Sullivan. He introduced the idea of 'mass singing', in which all the children were required to perform extracts from *The Pirates of Penzance* having memorised the obscure lyrics of the 'Ta-ran-Tara' chorus. This doubled with 'Jerusalem' as the school song.

Alfred's Grandmother Byrne was a music buff, too, and when she visited from Fallowfield in Manchester she would take the boy to the Sunday evening concerts at the Tower. There they listened to such stars as the violinists, Jan Kubelík and Fritz Kreisler, or the mighty contralto Dame Clara Butt. Some shows were slightly less culturally correct – one featured 'the strongest man in the world' who appeared in a leopard-skin jock-strap and could lift a grand piano with two blondes on top.

That was the public side of Alfred's musical appreciation. Privately, among themselves, the pupils were much more inclined to devote themselves to the great influx of music and popular culture from the United States, with its enticing vision of an existence far removed from the dowdiness of an English seaside resort. The transatlantic influence on the young Cooke was powerful and insidious: 'America called the tune of our leisure. However much the bishops and magistrates (and JT) might bemoan it, we wallowed like kittens in the novelties that poured across the Atlantic: bobbed hair, and crossword puzzles, the yo-yo, fresh slang, jazz, electrical recording, the nights leaping with all the best tunes of Irving Berlin, Jerome Kern and Vincent Youmans, Rodgers and Hart, Ray Henderson and Gershwin.'

In the new Memorial Hall, opened in 1924, there was a grand piano on which Alfred started to develop his considerable talent for improvisation. He continued to play purely by ear and was soon in great demand as an accompanist for dancing, as these provincial teenagers lapped up the latest American fashions. Younger children used to eavesdrop on his impromptu recitals.

For something as *risqué* as the Charleston, subterfuge was required. 'We mastered it behind closed doors, while a look-out listened for the imperial warning of the headmaster's cough, which at a corridor's length sent us vaulting back to our desks and a deep preoccupation with solid geometry or the seven-years' war.' Turral was famed for not wishing to catch his sixth-formers *in flagrante*: his long-distance cough was specifically designed to avoid awkward confrontations. Hilda Unsworth, who had joined Alfred in the sixth form, persuaded him to play for the informal dancing-classes she'd arranged for her friends on a Friday evening. In return, she thought she should make an effort to entice him onto the dance floor, but always found him happier to stay at the keyboard.

Thus he was admired and in demand, for instance by 'the brunette who hung over the piano' while he played 'Blue Skies'. And in his second sixth-form year, the Christmas Soirée, with its formal dance-band, became a source not of nervousness but of intense delight. The 1925 dance-card somehow survived into his old age, hidden at the bottom of a heap of mementoes – and this time the card is complete: Foxtrot – Phyllis Dunkerley; Valetta – Ennis Garstang; and so on through to the last waltz.

~

Much of the raw material out of which Alistair Cooke constructed himself was provided by those seven years at Blackpool Secondary School, soon afterwards elevated to the status of Grammar School: cinema, theatre, sport and music, literature and history, a bedrock of North-Country liberalism with its conservative respect for manners and convention, a love of writing and language, a rigorous training in objectivity – not to mention a lively awareness of America and an ability to match his accent to the needs of the moment.

His college magazine at Cambridge, honouring him three years later as one of its finest, listed his Blackpool achievements with a breathless reverence: 'He was vice-captain of cricket, a rugger colour, editor of the school magazine, head of house and senior prefect. His first play was produced in his first year at school. His first appearance on stage was as Valentine in Shaw's *You Never Can Tell*: at midnight at the annual school dance, his arrangement of "It ain't gonna rain no more" as a Beethoven symphony was performed by the school orchestra.'

As with other mentors still undiscovered, Cooke was generous in his acknowledgement of his teachers and what they achieved, particularly JT:

> He helped poor, promising boys without any show of sentimentality [he wrote in 1956], and he treated their parents with the simplest chivalry and understanding. He set the standards – of the curriculum, of dressing, of plain English writing, of what was allowed as necessary fun and what was thought to be intolerable . . . We were in fact swathed and suffocated by his peculiar form of affection. In the beginning he inherited just another town school and made it, in his own image, into our own world.

Turral put it in his own words when he retired in 1933, decrying the difficulty of maintaining high standards in unfashionable state schools: 'The world is crying out for well-educated men with poise, able to think for themselves, able to take charge of awkward situations, and to drag others out of the pit of despondency and indifference in which so many are floundering.'

The school had already established a strong stream of candidates to Oxford and Cambridge. Alfred was duly awarded a Blackpool Borough Scholarship of £86.50. (today almost £3000) per annum for four years, enough to allow him to set out on the adventure, but not much more. His admission papers to Jesus College, Cambridge, confirm one choice which caused him some regret in later life: that he would not read history, but English. They also include this revealing entry: 'Profession contemplated (if any) – Schoolmaster.'

It was not unusual for boys from relatively humble backgrounds to opt for a career in teaching. In Alfred's case as in many others, there was one overwhelming incentive: the opportunity of an extra grant to attend the teacher training college – £69 in the first year alone – and the assurance of steady employment thereafter. Did Alfred Cooke ever believe that he was destined for a life of scholastic endeavour? Perhaps, however fleetingly, he really did – predisposed by the example of Turral, Curnow, 'Billy Bumps' Heythornthwaite and the rest – regard this as the profession he genuinely intended to pursue. If so, the allure of the blackboard soon faded.

Alfred had already abandoned one putative calling, as a minister of the church, as he confessed to Roy Plomley on *Desert Island Discs*. To be a clergyman, he said, had been his first ambition, 'and some people say I've never really abandoned it.' For a brief period, during which he was clearly dazzled by the histrionic possibilities of the pulpit, he had indeed become a Sunday School teacher. This phase lasted long enough to earn him a going-away gift of a Bible from the Westfield Methodist Church in Blackpool – to the intense gratification of his father. One of the young women in the congregation expressed the pious hope that he would 'blaze a trail' at Cambridge, presumably for the Lord. It wasn't to be. When Alfred returned from Cambridge, he was bold enough to negotiate an opt-out from the Sunday service. He stayed at home and read the papers instead, thus taking the first steps towards a secondary career as an active agnostic. Naturally he could always see both sides of the greatest argument of them all.

On 17 November 1925, in St Paul's Church on the outskirts of Blackpool, the younger Sam Cooke married Elsie Stirzaker. He was twenty-three, she twenty-six. His profession was recorded as 'butcher', and his father's as 'insurance agent'. Alfred, just short of his seventeenth birthday, was one of the witnesses. The wedding day photo, like most pictures of the two brothers, shows Sam standing up and Alfred seated, or propped against the furniture, to avoid accentuating the difference in height between the two.

They seem to have got on well enough, despite the ever-increasing divergence of their lives. Long afterwards, when Sam was dead and

Cooke was famous, he looked back on the relationship with a mixture of guilt and respect. 'Sam,' he declared, 'was devoid of malice, like our father. He never expressed the slightest glint of envy about what happened to me. Maybe he stifled it, but I don't remember having a single bad word with him.' One letter survives to show the concern that he felt – from a distance. In January 1931, he wrote from Cambridge to sympathise with Sam's 'simply infuriating dismissal' from his latest job. He was as full of advice as any twenty-two-year-old undergraduate could be to an older sibling: 'I suppose there's no point in losing one's temper, but really I could willingly strangle some of the employers of Blackpool. I hope with all my heart you'll soon get a job with a little more security. Is it possible to get something in which you can learn a specialised job, where hard work will mean continuous promotion? What I mean is, after all, you can only run a shop – that's the end. I often think it a thousand pities your health compelled you to leave the English Velvet and Cord Dyers. I know you feel desperate and anxious, but keep your wits about you – don't plunge into slavery – and keep up some dignity before an employer.' As a postscript, he offers to write to anyone he knows if there's a chance of a job for Sam.

Cooke insists that he did not, in any sense, have a deprived childhood. The family's Ormond Avenue house had no pretensions, but it was quiet, neat and respectable. The street survives to this day. It may not have aged well, but in the 1920s it marked a distinct improvement in the family fortunes. Cooke liked to quote the great jazz critic Otis Ferguson, who became a friend in the 1940s: 'He told me once he couldn't stand people who became famous, and then made out that they'd risen from a poverty-stricken background. I never felt any such need myself.'

As evidence, he pointed to the twenty-one-volume set of Ruskin's work given to him by his father. The books cost at least ten guineas – the equivalent of two weeks' income for an insurance agent. His parents were unquestionably proud of their younger son, particularly when – in the autumn of 1926 – he travelled to Cambridge to sit the University's scholarship exams. His teachers warned him not to be deflected by the competition, however daunting. Boys from Winchester and Eton might look and sound as if they owned the place, but how many of them would have read so widely in the philosophy of history – Acton, Brice or Benedetto Croce? Once he had overcome the shock of how tawdry the back streets of Cambridge looked, compared with the red-brick sparkle of Blackpool, he settled down to the exams, and passed in the Exhibition Class.

Did Samuel and Cissie have their doubts about sending him to the effete south and life as a feckless student? It would have been understandable if his parents had followed their lower-middle-class instincts that a boy should be settled in a good job, rather than being seduced by the frippery of further education. If they had such reservations they did not communicate them to their son.

Whatever else may have been in his eighteen-year-old mind as he stepped onto a train bound for Cambridge in October 1927, the most important thing was to be leaving Blackpool behind. He carried with him a ragbag of parental injunctions, schoolmasterly advice and such well-worn pieces of Blackpool folklore as 'never sit on wet steps, or you'll get piles,' and 'never cast a clout till May is out,' which meant persisting with warm underwear until June. But his eyes were on the future, not the past.

3

BLACKPOOL BOY MAKES GOOD

Cambridge must have felt like an alien city. Boys from state schools were still very much the exception, and to make matters worse Cooke was a Northerner, for all the efforts of Turral and Curnow to soften the rough edges and modify the tell-tale accent. He was allocated digs in Jesus Lane under the unwelcoming eye of a landlady named Miss Germany. For two terms he had to endure grim Victorian furniture and spartan conditions, and students wishing to take a bath had to cross the road to the college. The only consolation was the gentle playing of jazz records in the rooms above, which helped to pass away the long winter nights.

The reason for the choice of Jesus College was a properly academic one. Cooke had been introduced at school to the writing of 'Q', Sir Arthur Quiller-Couch. And Q, who had founded the University's Department of English Literature and become its first professor, was based at Jesus. He had fought long and hard to persuade the entrenched University establishment that Literature was worthy of study in its own right, and not just an element in the Anglo-Saxon Tripos. The book which had so impressed Cooke was *On the Art of Writing*, a selection of lectures including one dealing with the scourge of jargon. Q was dedicated to the elimination of pomposity, verbosity and obfuscation and the 'Jargon' lecture includes, as a dreadful warning, this re-formulation of Hamlet's soliloquy: 'To be, or the contrary? Whether the former or the latter be preferable would seem to admit of some difference of opinion . . .', and so on.

The lecture concludes, 'If your language be jargon, your intellect, if not your whole character, will almost certainly correspond. Where your mind should go straight, it will dodge: the difficulties it should approach with a fair front and grip with a firm hand it will be seeking to evade and circumvent. For the Style is the Man, and where a Man's treasure is there is his heart, and his brain and his writing will be also.'

Whether Cooke was drawn to these principles unaided, or steered towards them by JT, the notion of studying at Q's feet seemed to him 'like some scraping amateur fiddler going to live next-door to Beethoven.' But there was one saving grace in this unequal relationship: Q, too, was a man from the provinces. He never attempted to conceal his Cornish origins and, for all his eminence, treated the Blackpool boy with special understanding.

Nevertheless, the Professor was sometimes alarmingly eccentric. Cooke described his impressions half a century later in a BBC programme called *Three Heroes* (the others being two Americans – H.L. Mencken, and the golfer Bobby Jones): 'Q had a countryman's creased face, and in the mornings he dressed as though he was going to look over the horses – riding-breeches, checked waistcoat and stock. The Master of Magdalene College once said, "This new Professor of English Literature dresses like a racing tout." ' The Blackpool boy, desperate to please, began his university studies with all the dedication which his old schoolmasters would have expected. He was naturally anxious to demonstrate to Q the precocity of his talent – to prove that he was as good as his public-school rivals. The rich literary diet on which he had been fed produced an exotic flowering of purple prose, and one essay on Romantic Poetry seemed to him to be unusually fine. Cooke set out in the early evening to deliver it to Q's rooms where, disconcertingly, he found the Professor dressing for dinner. He had not expected his masterpiece to be perused by a man wearing a shirt but no trousers. Q took the first page and studied it, mumbling as he read, and then returned to the bedroom to fetch his white tie. He was securing the suspenders on his socks while reading the second page, still mumbling, and disappeared again bearing the final page.

This, Cooke knew, contained his finest passages – perhaps the most brilliant ever written by a Cambridge undergraduate: 'Eventually he came back, this time pulling up his trousers. He buttoned them very slowly and wrestled with his braces as he went through it. Then he turned his great brown eyes towards me and said, "Cooke, you must learn to murder your darlings." With which he turned away to fetch his tail-coat.'

Cooke was bitterly disappointed and hurt by the rejection of his brilliance. He wasn't used to it. He only realised in retrospect how important Q's advice had been – to strip away the verbiage and concentrate on the vital core of a piece of writing.

At the time, he was already being seduced by the rival forces within the School of English. I.A. Richards, the guru of the Cambridge English School, had just published (with C.K. Ogden) *The Meaning of Meaning,* and *Principles of Literary Criticism.* His radical approach to the subject, rooted in science and psychology, seized Cooke's imagination. He found Richards a charismatic speaker, whose Wednesday lectures proved to be a chic place for an aspiring intellectual to be seen. Cooke discovered that he had a real talent for Richards's 'protocols', in which students were invited to examine an unattributed piece of verse or prose, to date it and to assess its literary value.

Cooke's time at Cambridge was just before the real rise to prominence of Richards's alter ego, the lowering figure of F.R. Leavis: but the seeds of the New Criticism, and the Deconstruction movement which flowed from it, were already being sown – not least by the work of the undergraduate poet, William Empson. Empson was only two years ahead of Cooke, but had already begun to establish a national reputation. His work was ruthlessly modern, applying the language of mathematics and science to subjects steeped in the classical tradition. (One piece, described as a metaphysical seduction poem, includes the lines, 'Lucretius could not credit centaurs;/ Such bicycle he deemed asynchronous./ Man superannuates the horse;/ Horse pulses will not gear with ours.')

The audacious use of language, the refusal to accept conventional imagery, the minute attention to linguistic detail – these characteristics marked Empson out. His cerebral approach – and Richards's encouragement of the mechanistic analysis of works of art – were impossible to reconcile with the relaxed, rather romantic, attitudes of Sir Arthur Quiller-Couch. Q's 'appreciative criticism' could be summed up in a phrase Cooke frequently heard from his lips: 'This is beautiful, gentlemen.' Q, in other words, was an appreciator and that, in the mouths of his enemies, became a term of vitriolic abuse.

Cooke was caught in the middle of these two distinct forces whose clash created such ferment in the Cambridge academic establishment. It was a heady, adversarial atmosphere and Cooke himself, whose style until then had been mainly derivative and ironic, expressed most successfully in parodies, was stimulated and enthused by every aspect of wordmanship.

There was no doubt, though, about which was the dominant influence on him in his undergraduate years. Richards, Empson and Leavis were busy proving that criticism was a crusade to discover the truth about literature, which in turn had the power to improve society. Acolytes were taught that nothing was as simple as it seemed, and that novels and poems were simply constructs which could be taken apart and reassembled like a Swiss watch. Once he'd left the University Cooke's enthusiasm waned. He took to quoting the critic James Agate: 'I don't want to see a Swiss watch in pieces, I want to hear it tick.' In the end he came to despise Leavis and the Deconstruction movement and to see in Quiller-Couch 'a superior human being'. But that did not mean that he had swung back to Q's view of literary appreciation. In fact he'd reached the conclusion that English Literature as a field of study was essentially worthless. 'The curse to me of the whole literary school is that it's so hopelessly subjective. There's no way of testing anything, and ultimately it's a waste of time. You will read what you want to read, not what you're told to read, and you will develop your own tastes.'

His own mature writing, he claimed, drew from both competing traditions. From Q he had imbibed the journalist's art of a lively style without florid over-elaboration, direct in its appeal but rooted in literary tradition; while Richards fed his fascination with language itself and the duty of the honest observer and critic. In the short term, at least, the techniques he learned at Richards's feet were of far more immediate importance in guiding him into fields which proved fruitful for his own intellectual development.

~

His supervisor during the first two years of study was another great figure of English criticism, Eustace Mandeville Wurtenbaker Tillyard, who went on to become Master of Jesus College. After Cooke's first term, Tillyard recorded in the college records the following assessment: 'Well-read, quick, keen, industrious. I doubt if he has any real originality.'

This decidedly faint praise was reflected in the first-year exams – the Mays – in 1928. Cooke's results were less than dazzling. In four papers he accumulated just 201 marks out of 350, and was graded 2.2.

In the following winter's report, Tillyard's approval was still muted. His comment this time: 'Satisfactory, but a journalist's mind.' That was, at least, prescient. But clearly Cooke's confidence grew rapidly, as any residual Blackpool inferiority evaporated, and by the time he sat Part One of the English Tripos, in June 1929, he was firing on all cylinders.

The award of a first-class degree, even at this preliminary level, was a milestone. It marked Cooke out, both with the academic authorities, and with his peers. The college tutors, as if realising the need to justify their earlier scepticism, offered a brief explanation: 'Tillyard writes that Cooke got his first by an exceptionally good original composition.' At the time, nothing more was said, but thirty years later Cooke had the opportunity to hear from the horse's mouth how he'd scored his triumph.

He had been invited back to Cambridge to give a lecture, and was the guest of another of his old tutors, Basil Willey. 'Willey told me I should call round and visit E.M.W. Tillyard before leaving town. I was appalled. Even at the age of fifty-four, I still had in my mind the picture of that nineteen-year-old boy who once a week had to present himself at the great man's house to read an essay. Call on Tillyard! I would no more think of dropping in on Tillyard than of going to Rome and calling on the Pope.' Willey told him that Tillyard was a regular listener to *Letter from America*, and that he was very sick. Cooke gathered up his courage:

> He was wearing a dressing-gown, and he was as sweet as could be. He told me that in that exam, I'd been right at the top of the second class, and there'd been a debate about whether I deserved a first. He'd pointed out to the University Senate that in my thesis on Katherine Mansfield, I'd quoted the work of a critic called A.R. Orage. Orage was a frightful phoney who started something called the *New English Weekly*, but Tillyard told them it was the first time any student had ever mentioned him.'

On the strength of this obscure citation the Senate was moved to elevate Cooke to a first, and many things followed from this homage to Orage: Jesus paid its respects with a 'Prize of Three Guineas to be spent on books at Deighton Bell's,' and more importantly awarded him a Minor Scholarship which boosted his finances by some £40 a year. Samuel Cooke was required to complete an application form to determine the level of the college contribution: it reveals his income from insurance commissions to be just £284 (today just under £10,000) a year – not a sum which left much leeway to help his younger son, who, compared with his well-heeled contemporaries, was permanently penniless. Yet a shortage of funds was never likely to deter a young man whose character and personality were adapting rapidly to their new surroundings: the emergence of Alistair from the chrysalis of Alfred.

~

On the personal and social side, it would have helped his swifter integration into university life if his first two terms – in the winter of 1927 – hadn't been spent with Miss Germany, a quintessential Cambridge landlady, in dank, gloomy rooms so susceptible to the bitter Fenland winds. After the pleasures of a mixed school, he found the monastic discipline of the University disconcerting, too. 'You had to be in at 10 p.m., and the other half of the human race was not only ignored, it was nowhere in sight. You should have seen us sitting there under Tudor beams, in rooms steaming with damp, moping over warm beer on frosty nights.'

Potentially, Cooke had many interests and skills which might offer an *entrée* into student society – theatre, cinema, music and sport. But it took him some time to find his feet. Among the first and firmest friends he made was a fellow toiler in the department of English Literature, Erik Chitty:

> Up to that moment, I – a raw boy from the north country – had been pretty nervous in the presence of so many nonchalant public schoolboys. But once inside the study of Mr Tillyard, with Chitty teetering on the edge of an armchair, I felt as blithe as Noël Coward. If Tilly was the shyest teacher I ever knew, Chitty was the most trembly human being in the presence of any stranger. He literally sweated anxiety, mopping his forehead and hands with a handkerchief.

Chitty and Cooke shared a common aim. They both thought it would be a fine thing to seek fame on the stage. Chitty's ambition was so well-developed that he had brought with him a scrapbook of photographs and reviews from all his school plays, religiously catalogued and indexed – a dedication which would bring him a successful stage and television career. The obvious step would have been to join one of the established drama clubs, but they were deterred by the unpalatable fact that all the University's dramatic societies were single-sex, which they found weird and embarrassing.

Tentatively, Cooke tried out other distractions. He was inveigled into college athletics, and found himself taking part in trials for the University team as a long-jumper. There was even talk of his competing in the Olympics. He and another Jesus man, A.C. 'Ghost' Williams – one of many New Zealanders at the college – would traipse down every Tuesday afternoon to Fenners, which doubled as athletics track and cricket field. This soon lost its charm, and Cooke's most strenuous physical activity at Cambridge thereafter was at the end of a punt-pole.

Possibly the most comforting experience of Cooke's first year was to be befriended by another alumnus of Blackpool Secondary School, Ernest Done, known to most people as Joe or Joey, but – always to Cooke – as Eddie, for reasons that no one can remember. There was a strong Blackpool network at the University, but Cooke and Done were still an unusual combination.

Eddie Done was nearly four years older, and reading science at a different college, Magdalene. He had few of Cooke's interests and none of his intellectual pretensions, but when the eccentric Old Etonian who shared his Chesterton Road digs left abruptly, Done offered the younger man a room for the summer term of 1928. In order to escape the gloom of Miss Germany's establishment, Cooke would probably have agreed to move in with anyone who'd asked; in fact he found in Eddie a solid, down-to-earth and long-lasting friend. The two men continued to correspond sporadically until Done's death at the age of ninety – a friendship which prefigured many others in Cooke's life, with no obvious basis beyond the time and place from which it stemmed.

Eddie Done's invitation set the seal on Cooke's new existence, and ushered in what he called his magical years. The sun must have shone throughout that first Cambridge springtime. Even if it hadn't, Cooke would hardly have noticed. He was doing just enough work to get by ('industrious if unoriginal'), and had no real cares in the world. Blackpool seemed like another country, so far removed from his present existence that he could scarcely bear to write home. One old friend, who had become a runner on the Manchester Cotton Exchange, wrote to him from time to time: couldn't he please drop a line to his mother? She had to get used to his long silences. 'I think I was inconceivably callous at that stage,' he said in old age. 'Eventually I made myself write, but it was always a chore. There was no common language.'

Samuel and Cissie Cooke, pictured in the 1890s – ten or fifteen years before the birth of the child they named Alfred.

Sunday School at the Wesleyan Methodist Chapel in Blackpool, *c* 1918: Alfred looks very pleased with his position on the teacher's left hand. Corporal Beckett was a dedicated lay-preacher.

Alfred spent much of his adolescent life worrying about his hair. Sideways on you can see that the patent gel is just beginning to lose its potency.

The Blackpool Secondary School rugby team was undefeated in the 1925–6 season. Cooke is at the back, fifth from the left. Next in line is William Whalley, who treasured this picture for seventy years.

The evidence of a youthful commitment to cricket. But Cooke (with a sweater artfully draped round his neck) was not one of those expatriates who clung to a sporting obsession in a foreign land.

Harry Duguid, teacher of English, was a favourite master at Blackpool. Cooke started sketching at school, but this caricature was done at Cambridge, and presented to the school magazine during a 1929 vacation.

To H. DUGUID, Esq.

Baleful his look,
But if you think his passions so,
Take down this book
And bid him read.
Then pardon beg for having thought
That he could harbour ought
But guilelessness and wisdom, he
Who slender once to Merton went
Returned not one but all mankind's epitome.

A. C.

Jones, Warburton and Cooke, three of Blackpool's finest.

Sam Cooke's wedding to Elsie Stirzacker in November 1925. His younger brother Alfred, as usual, is propped against the furniture, so as not to emphasise his height.

This family group was sent by Cooke's mother to her daughter-in-law, Elsie, to celebrate Christmas, probably in 1925.

Cooke (front row, second from right) as Valjean, the miserable convict in *The Bishop's Candlesticks*. The play's producer (top left) is J.K. Starkie, one of the war-damaged masters at Blackpool Secondary School.

Cooke as an operatic extra for the Carl Rosa company: in the wake of the show, he fell briefly for Harry Duguid's American niece.

The Old Blackpoolians' reunion, Christmas 1929. W.I. Curnow (Billy Wick) is second from the left, and the headmaster J.T. (with a moustache) in the centre. Cooke is fourth from the left.

His mother certainly wouldn't have understood the wonder of punting, which he and Chitty had just discovered. They would take to the River Cam once a week with a wind-up gramophone perched precariously in the middle of the boat. This required the operator of the punt-pole to develop a smooth and regular stroke: Cooke became an expert, while the less athletic Chitty concentrated on the music – Edythe Baker or Paul Whiteman and the Rhythm Boys – as they cruised along the Backs.

Girls, in these austere times, were not invited on board. But every now and again Cooke would call round to Newnham, one of the two women's colleges, to see Hilda Unsworth who'd been with him in the sixth form at Blackpool. This was a complicated business. A note had to be sent to her Newnham tutor to announce that she would be having a guest for tea, and giving the name of an approved chaperone. When the visitor arrived, he would be kept in a waiting-room until all these details, vital for the avoidance of lascivious lapses, had been checked. Whatever happened, the sexes were required to separate before dinner. The only exceptions were formal college dances or May Balls; Hilda would find herself in demand whenever a member of the Blackpool brigade was short of a dancing-partner.

Hilda, however, could not solve the one abiding irritation of Cooke's Cambridge life: how to pursue his dramatic interests in the uncongenial atmosphere of all-male societies like the well-established Amateur Dramatic Club – the ADC. Serious plotting began with like-minded malcontents and gradually a radical plan began to crystallise.

~

What followed was one of the greatest acts of rebellion of Cooke's life. He was not a natural rebel. Rebels need a cause, a commitment to one side or another, a certain blindness. They must be impervious to criticism and counter-argument. Cooke, by instinct, was a chameleon who could blend unostentatiously into different surroundings, a conciliator who preferred to build bridges rather than dynamite them. In this sensitive business of sex and the stage, was he perhaps provoked? Did the ADC spurn his advances? He certainly wasn't accustomed to failure, and if there had been some expression of public-school snobbery towards a grammar school boy from the north, or even an unsuccessful audition, it might help to explain what happened.

He was helped, no doubt, by the contacts he'd made in another sphere. The caricatures and cartoons which he'd developed in Blackpool came to the attention of the staff of *The Granta*, one of the University's leading undergraduate magazines and the predecessor of today's *Granta*. Broadly it covered culture and the arts: in the late 1920s its style veered between high-flown criticism of theatre or cinema, and straightforward student satire. It attracted some of the intellectual heavyweights of the moment, including the poets Empson and James Reeves as well as Michael Redgrave and Jacob Bronowski. Into this illustrious company Cooke was adopted as one of the regular artists, whose sharply observed pen-portraits of cultural luminaries became a regular feature.

The Granta was by no means anarchic in its approach, but it did take risks. At the regular staff gatherings, there was certainly seditious discussion of the ban imposed by the University Vice-Chancellor on mixed-sex stage performances. How could you take seriously a male Portia, Ophelia, or Juliet in the modern theatre? Cooke recruited like thinkers to his cause, men, in some cases, who'd never been involved in the theatre, but who liked the idea of challenging the system.

Throughout the summer of 1928, with Cooke comfortably installed in Eddie Done's digs, the idea germinated. Erik Chitty was an obvious ally, and there was no shortage of women from Girton and Newnham anxious to break the masculine mould. Planning spilled over into the Michaelmas term. Cooke took up residence in the main Jesus buildings, where each student was entitled to occupy rooms for one of his three undergraduate years. Eventually, shortly before the end of 1928, the idea finally took shape. As *The Granta* put it in a tribute to Cooke at the end of his tenure, 'Alistair had cocked an observant eye at the plight of Dramatics at Cambridge. It appeared strange to him that Newnham and Girton were not *de rigueur* in 'Varsity productions. For six sleepless months he pondered and sweated. Then shattering the canons of Cambridge drama, he founded the Mummers.'

The new group started work in earnest the following term. The local paper greeted the maiden performance – a triple bill staged at the Central Hall – with considerable warmth:

The first production of any dramatic club must of necessity be somewhat of an ordeal, since it is then that the reputation of the club is made or marred. This is even more the case when the club, like the Mummers, is of a revolutionary nature in that it is the first dramatic society in the University to admit women members. On Monday evening the Mummers passed through such an ordeal, and their performance surpassed the most sanguine hopes of those who had seen the rehearsals. But for two slight hitches, only one of which was noticeable to the audience, the whole of the rather difficult production ran on oiled wheels.

The programme included a miracle play, Chekhov's *The Wedding* and the centrepiece of the evening, *Tom Thumb the Great* by Fielding, for which Cooke composed the music. The newspaper reviewer was especially enthusiastic about the Fielding, which included in its cast Chitty, Empson and Cooke – who 'as Lord Grizzle played and looked the part equally well.' Another of the performers that night was Eddie Wiltshire, a first-year student at Jesus who had met Cooke through *The Granta*. Sixty years later, he remembered vividly the cast's sense that they had scored a decisive victory against the forces of reaction.

The ADC crowd was not impressed. They made sure that the eminent *Cambridge Review* took proper revenge and sent along none other than Michael Redgrave to cast his patrician eye over this upstart production. 'Mr Cooke knows all the tricks,' Redgrave wrote, 'but I regret to say can perform none of them.'

Cooke's self-confidence was by now solid enough to resist such predictable barbs. But he had missed one trick – when another first-year student trekked across Jesus Common, one bitter winter's day, to take part in an audition. The test piece was from R.C. Sherriff's First World War drama, *Journey's End*, which had opened in London during the autumn. The aspirants were required to act out one of the emotional trench scenes with Cooke playing the hero, Raleigh. When it was over, Cooke asked the young man what subject he was reading.

'Architecture,' he replied.

'If I were you,' said Cooke, 'I should skip acting and stick to architecture.'

The name of the rejected applicant was James Mason.

~

Cooke had begun to collect friends like pebbles on a beach. Eddie Done, a trainee teacher, had nothing in common with Ghost Williams and the rest of the Antipodean enclave at Jesus – many of them rowers – in whose hearty company Cooke was perfectly at home. Likewise there was no very strong connection between an actor-friend like Chitty – the highbrows and aesthetes who populated the columns of *The Granta* – and Hugh Munro-Fraser, the rather dim young man on an army scholarship who became one of Cooke's main allies. And what would Humphrey Tillings, the Peterhouse rugby captain, have found to talk about to the poet James Reeves?

Yet all these disparate figures became Cooke's familiars, stored in discrete compartments to be picked up and relished at his leisure. Was it the unconscious indecisiveness of a butterfly mind? Or a more calculated attempt to keep all options open, maintaining control because he was the point of contact between so many differing circles, part of each yet committed to none? This eclectic approach, he said, was both 'instinctive and temperamental' and it became a hallmark of his life.

In this social whirl, and with his Part One exams triumphantly completed, Cooke was able to enjoy the summer of 1929. Some of the time was spent in Blackpool, one of the last long holidays he spent in the town. It was during such a home visit that Cooke volunteered to help the grocer's son, Charlie Jackson – recuperating from scarlet fever – with his algebra. Jackson remembers looking up at the lean undergraduate sporting a college scarf – and the shock of realising that this was the younger brother of Sam, the small, dumpy butcher and the son of Mr Cooke, who called round each week in trilby and wing collar to collect their insurance payments.

During this summer, too, the old school connection brought Cooke and Eddie Done a pleasant diversion from their studies. JT's fascination with opera, and Curnow's love of the stage meant that touring companies frequently asked the school to provide extras during the summer season. While Cooke was still a pupil, the venerable Sir Frank Benson, one of the last great actor-managers, took a production to Blackpool and played the title role in Julius Caesar at the age of almost seventy. Cooke was one of the boys chosen to take part in the crowd scenes.

Then, in the spring of 1929, during the Cambridge vacation, he acted with the Carl Rosa light opera company as a gypsy in dashing bandanna and earring. The musical was unmemorable, though he did fall for a girl in the gypsy chorus – the American niece of his old schoolmaster, Harry Duguid. He pursued her for some months, with music, theatre-visits and trips on the river, until she announced without warning that she was returning home.

While those wounds were still healing, Cooke heard that a new production was starting a provincial tour ahead of a London opening in September. He and Eddie again succeeded in signing up as extras. This time, the actor-manager was Matheson Lang, and the play – an adaptation of the novel *Jew Süss*, a melodrama set in eighteenth-century Central Europe. It was unashamedly a vehicle for Lang, noted for his 'magnificent presence and stupendous bass voice'. But the critics were also struck by the performance of an ambitious young actress, who had been struggling to emerge from the repertory shadows, playing Naemi, the daughter of Süss.

Her name was Peggy Ashcroft, and her career was about to take wing. The part of Naemi is not a long one: its climax comes when the evil Duke comes to her father's castle and tries to seduce her. Being a girl of ineffable purity, given to the reading of scripture, she chooses to hurl herself from the battlements rather than bring dishonour on herself and her race. Years later, Dame Peggy recalled her death-scene. 'I backed away from the wicked Duke, went up to the window-sill and then fell backwards onto a conveniently placed mattress. It probably looked more dangerous than it actually was. What I also remember is that I was caught and helped to my feet by one of the young supporting actors, who was none other than Alistair Cooke.'

The experience made a deep impression on the twenty-year-old Cooke: he fell in love instantaneously and, as it turned out, hopelessly. 'It was very nice, breaking her fall,' he reported. 'She was twenty-one years old, not beautiful but very sexy.' For some time he was too nervous to speak to her, but when the provincial tour moved from Blackpool to Manchester, he finally plucked up the courage to invite her to tea at the Midland Hotel. 'Oh I'd love to,' she said, 'but my fiancé is coming up to see me so I'm afraid it won't be possible'. And that was almost that, except that the fiancé, Rupert Hart-Davis, went on to publish Cooke's first books and to become one of his most enduring friends.

~

Jew Süss, however, wasn't just a chance for Cooke to display his theatrical talents and amorous aspirations. He also demonstrated his enterprise by contacting the *Manchester Guardian*, and suggesting that the paper could steal a march over its rivals by running a review of the play during its Blackpool trial, rather than waiting until it arrived in Manchester where most of the critics would see it. This turned out to be Cooke's first contribution to the paper he was later to serve for a quarter of a century. It also exposed him to considerable risk.

The review, headlined THE NOVEL AS PLAY, discourses in learned fashion on whether the adaptation of the original book could be counted a success. But the reviewer reserves his firmest opinions for the performances – which he had, after all, seen at somewhat closer quarters than most critics enjoy. And he does not feel the need for deference in dealing with the star of the show, Matheson Lang. 'Only the very innocent could expect Mr Matheson Lang to tread his way through the insinuating, wily paces of Feuchtwanger's Josef. These were never Mr Lang's graces . . .' Maybe a sense of self-preservation and balance dictated that he should go on to note that there is 'no actor on our stage with a finer presence.' But the praise is decidedly faint. Of Peggy Ashcroft, by contrast, the tyro critic enthuses, 'she resists every temptation to be coy' and 'has the courage to play Naemi with the strictest integrity. Her implied passion for purity is con-sequently genuinely moving.' Then, after nodding at the qualities of other stars of the show, he signs off : 'A.C.'

The review provoked a furore. When Cooke arrived at the theatre that evening, he was cornered by the stage manager, Arthur Rooke, who told him to keep out of sight. 'Normally,' according to Cooke, 'this man liked nothing better than to impart the latest stage gossip. This time was different. He hustled me into a dressing-room and said, "If Mr Lang finds out it was you, he'll slaughter you." ' For the rest of the run, Cooke kept his head down, uncertain whether Lang, his colossal ego severely dented, had made the connection between 'A.C.' and the tall young man with a one-line part in his play. (The line was, 'The Stuttgart courier is here, sir.')

In the event he escaped detection. When the play moved on to Birmingham, Cooke and Eddie Done tagged along, and stayed with Eddie's aunt and cousins in the unfashionable surroundings of Walsall. The cousins, Millicent and Aida Nowell, recalled how the two young men were an exotic curiosity, spied on and peered at by all the local youngsters. And that Cooke was still laughing over the stories of Matheson Lang, stamping round the theatre, endlessly fulminating about the unidentified critic from the *Manchester Guardian*.

By the time *Jew Süss* moved into the West End at the start of a successful run of more than 200 performances, Done had left to begin his teaching career in Bristol, and Cooke was back at Cambridge. And now he could call himself a critic for the *Manchester Guardian*.

4

THE CONCEPTION OF ALISTAIR COOKE

For the winter term of 1929 Cooke decided not to take up the option of a further year in college, to which his Minor Scholarship entitled him, but to return to 69 Chesterton Road where another unlikely friend had taken up residence. Hugh Munro-Fraser was no intellectual high-flier, no critic, no actor (although he was roped in to act as secretary to the Mummers). He had begun by reading law, but having delivered what was described as one of the worst papers in the history of the law qualifying examination, he transferred to a course known as Military Subjects 'A'. This, according to undergraduate mythology, was a course designed for duffers – especially those for whom an army career was the only feasible option.

While Cooke was immersed in William Blake, Munro-Fraser would return to the digs in the evening weighed down with American Civil War texts, demanding to know why these should form the basis of the strategy and tactics of military training in the late 1920s. Drifting into soldiery by accident, he began to behave as if he'd already joined up, growing a moustache, throwing open windows at every opportunity, and generally 'banging about'.

None the less, like so many others, this odd character struck a chord with Cooke: he discovered that Munro-Fraser, despite being otherwise an aesthetic philistine, had acquired through his upper-class upbringing an informed taste for eighteenth-century furniture. It soon became a shared passion and laid the basis for Cooke's own tastes in furniture, art and architecture. Whenever his father replenished his funds, Munro-Fraser would organise an expedition to Colston's, a rambling antique shop behind Christ's College, although for the impecunious Cooke, trailing in his wake, the hunt for bargains had to remain a vicarious pleasure.

Cooke – at the start of his third undergraduate year – was a prominent figure. Not only was he doing theatre and film criticisms, as well as caricatures, for *The Granta*, he had also begun to act as the local reviewer for periodicals such as *Theatre Arts Monthly*, and the *Athenaeum*, taking a special interest in covering Terence Gray's new Cambridge Festival Theatre. This was in addition to his role as President of the Mummers, leading the group into its first full year of operation. Little time was left for study. Indeed, there is some tetchy correspondence with the English faculty in the Jesus College records, in which Cooke argues that he should not be charged for lectures because he 'went to no lectures in the term (my supervisor knows).' Cooke insisted that his supervisor Tillyard had positively encouraged him to skip lectures and work on his own in the University library.

As well as frequent play readings among the Mummers and what were called 'Trial Productions' of short plays, Cooke also continued to arrange visits and talks by theatrical luminaries: his greatest coup was to tempt to Cambridge the actor Cedric Hardwicke, a figure of distinction, fresh from a triumphant performance in Shaw's *The Apple-Cart*.

The main event of the Mummers' year in 1930 was, once again, to be a full-scale commercial performance in February and as late as December no play had been chosen: Cooke's efforts to promote Noël Coward's *The Vortex* had fallen foul of the University authorities, still dubious about the whole unpalatable idea of men and women on stage together. Coward's tale of incest and drugs was unceremoniously vetoed. It was not, the Vice-Chancellor wrote to Cooke, a suitable play for 'undergraduates and members of women's colleges'. Finally Cooke chose a less weighty, if still challenging, alternative, *At Mrs Beams*, a comedy with a serious edge. The play is set in a respectable boarding house whose occupants are shocked by the arrival of an enigmatic couple of unknown marital status – one played by Cooke, the other by a glamorous Girton student, Sybil Hawkey. Things went well enough to encourage the planning of a tour which would take three short plays to Munro-Fraser's home in Jersey, at the end of June.

In the midst of this frenetic cultural activity Cooke – like so many other students before and since – neglected his studies. The time loomed for his final exams, Part Two of the English Tripos. He was certainly expected to repeat his triumph of the previous year and claim a first-class degree, but it was not to be.

~

There was nothing shameful about his upper second, a 2,1, although it was manifestly a blow to his self-esteem. Its real impact was of the delayed-action variety. Hard though it must have been for him to remember, he was still supposed to be working towards a career in education: under the terms of his Blackpool scholarship he was about to start a fourth year at Cambridge to complete his training, including a spell of work experience in a local school. Any enthusiasm he may have had for the profession had long since drained away and he had already begun to angle for ways to wriggle off the educational hook. What he really wanted was a research fellowship, which would enable him to perpetuate his delightful Cambridge life, his income topped up with a little light tutoring of undergraduates. But there was intense competition for such posts, and Cooke had – in effect – scuppered his chances. The training college for schoolmasters beckoned uninvitingly.

It wasn't just the degree itself – it was the manner of its achieving. As he would discover in the coming months, his Jesus College mentors had become disenchanted with Cooke's progress and regarded his failure to get a first as an affront. Cooke himself heard the news just before leaving with his friends for the Channel Islands. He went to see the intimidating head of the College of Education, Charles Fox, in the hope of a release from his obligations. But he was told, baldly, that he could not apply for a research scholarship at Christ's College, which would have offered an escape-route.

The Jersey sunshine must have helped to ease the pain, along with congenial company: his friends were sure that he had a particular soft spot for one of the actresses, Joan Charles, although according to Eddie Wiltshire it was not the sort of trip on which virginities were mislaid. On 20 June Cooke wrote to C.A. Elliott, his college tutor, from the Demi-des-Pas Hotel: 'I have had my result. I am sorry I could not establish Jesus in unchallenged superiority as Laing has done for Pembroke. Still, I am not unduly depressed.' Photographs from the tour seem to bear out this assertion, and his friend Miles Mayall, writing in *The Granta*, added, 'There, with the Atlantic at his feet, a well-tanned Alistair matured the finer instincts as director of communal sunbathing.'

None of his friends thought for one moment that Cooke was likely to go through with the teaching business. Eddie Wiltshire was convinced that they had in their midst a new Noël Coward in the making, equally at home in greasepaint or at the piano. Cooke himself – as at many other times in his life – had no clearly defined plan, apart from the general, comfortable sense that there would be a place for him somewhere in the theatre, as performer, director, writer or critic. In the meantime, a year at teacher training college would at least mean that Cambridge life could continue.

In that spirit, he and Miles Mayall, instead of returning to England with the others, took a boat to Granville on the Normandy coast. For two weeks they walked through Normandy and Brittany, covering more than twenty miles a day, cooking on a primus stove and sleeping in a tent. Apart from the blazing heat, the trip had two memorable features. First, they decided to aim for what looked on the map like an interesting spit of land, just west of St Malo, called St Jacut-de-la-Mer: this, they fondly believed, would be an exclusive discovery, a place to which none of their friends would have been. They followed the sand-dunes northwards, savouring the isolation, until they breasted a final rise. There, laid out below on the beach, was a huge hotel full of English tourists.

Of longer-term importance was a chance encounter with a police-man in a rural backwater called Villedieu: out of this Cooke conjured the first of a number of pieces of fiction which he sold to the *Manchester Guardian*. Under the title *Alarm in Normandy*, it told the story of how his British passport, with its direct request from the Foreign Secretary of the day to give the holder free passage, transformed them in the eyes of the local constabulary (who had never seen such a thing before) from suspicious aliens cowering in a tent on private land, into VIPs. This – and a handful of other pieces for the same paper such as *Prelude with Applause*, a tender tale of love and music which involves the humiliation of an amateur pianist – were almost his only attempts at fiction in a lifetime of writing.

Cooke returned from France, in the gnomic words of the College magazine, 'after three weeks' idyll in which the name of Mlle Pot mysteriously figures'. Sixty years on, Cooke had no idea what this referred to, though it smacks of student humour – and there is a reference to an ex-Folie Bergère performer, Popo or Pot-Pot, in Selina Hastings's biography of Nancy Mitford. This ageing courtesan who 'did a dance and took her jersey off' was the star turn at a night-club in St Briac, not far from St Jacut-de-la-Mer.

The Cooke who took up residence in new digs at number 3 Pretoria

Road at the start of the Michaelmas term was a very different figure from the provincial schoolboy who'd left Blackpool three years earlier. As if in recognition of the fact, he began to grow an artistic moustache and chose his twenty-second birthday to give formal blessing to this new persona.

On 20 November 1930 he changed his name by deed poll to Alistair Cooke. It was, in any case, the name by which most of Cambridge knew him. Those early history book doodlings, inspired by a Scottish aunt, showed an incipient dissatisfaction with his given name. When the men he admired on *The Granta* indicated that 'Alfred' wasn't quite the thing, the choice of an alternative was easy. He kept the 'A' of Alfred as an initial, perhaps for sentimental reasons, but it was used only by those who'd known him in Blackpool – at the occasional reunions, for instance of the Cambridge Old Blackpoolians, attended by Turral and Billy Wick. The transmuting of Alfred into Alistair had been more by evolution than by calculation, but it included a strong element of denial of his past. It was said that he scarcely ever mentioned Blackpool: if anyone asked, he said he came from Manchester, which at least had a metropolitan, rather than small-town, ring to it.

There was no question that, in the eyes of his contemporaries, he had become something of an icon. Founding a radical new drama group, hobnobbing with famous actors, at ease on the piano, and with a string of articles under his belt in serious, national publications... it was an enviable record. One Blackpool youngster, William Whalley, newly arrived on another teaching scholarship, remembers the awe and trepidation he felt when summoned by Cooke to share a breakfast of sausages and toast.

In that Michaelmas term, Eddie Wiltshire became editor of the Jesus College magazine, the *Chanticlere*, and chose Cooke as one of the term's 'Cocks of the Roost'. Next to a picture of Cooke in a dashing, theatrical pose from the opera production in Blackpool (complete with gypsy moustache), Wiltshire's encomium ends with this breathless catalogue of his lifestyle: 'When he is not talking, playing squash, making new friends, writing poetry, composing music, fretting before the footlights, sitting in stalls not paid for, charming Lancashire lasses with his touch on the piano, writing theses, drawing caricatures, reading Katherine Mansfield, furnishing other men's rooms, entertaining, studying sexology, or writing essays on cider in the college kitchen suggestion book, you will find him wasting somebody's time, probably your own.' And it adds, 'Pet abominations: Punctuality, spirits and the English gentleman.'

This enthusiasm is the mirror image of the ominous rumblings of disenchantment in the Jesus College Senior Common Room. Cooke's easy acceptance of a 2,1 had exacerbated his tutors' natural disappointment and, although he didn't know it, they set about undermining his reputation. The first evidence comes in a letter from his college tutor, C.A. Elliott, dated 18 November, in reply to a request for information from the University Appointments Board, the body responsible, among other things, for placing putative teachers in the best posts.

> I do not find it easy to assess his personality for you. He undoubtedly has ability, though I think he has an exaggerated idea of it. He obtained a First Class in Part I of the English Tripos owing to an excellent original composition. His supervisor [Tillyard] was doubtful if he would obtain a first in the second Part and Cooke, I think, made certain that he would not by giving a great deal of his time to acting. He undoubtedly has a great deal of drive and he was, I believe, the leading spirit in founding the Mummers. In spite of his abilities and initiative and general wide awakeness I cannot say that he is really a first class man. I think the trouble is that he lacks proportion, takes himself and his interests too seriously and has little use for views which are not his own, and for those who hold them.

Elliott had at least realised that Cooke might not be ideally suited to teaching.

> I imagine that his scheme of things would totally exclude the low-brow and the sans-brow and the world being what it is, this means that he will be a little difficult to place. I think he would be hopeless in the ordinary Public School but he might get on perhaps in a school like Manchester Grammar School or in a coeducational school. I doubt if he has any real interest in schoolmastering for his ultimate ambition certainly is to write plays.
>
> He might have been saved by a sense of humour but in this he seems totally to be lacking. I am afraid I write unsympathetically about him but he is one of the only undergraduates I have ever come across who have stayed up their full three years and with whom I feel I have quite failed to make contact.

It was an unattractive portrait, fuelled no doubt by incomprehension and frustration. A steady scholar had been diverted from the straight and narrow – in the eyes of an academic – into essentially sterile byways. To make matters worse he was not only unapologetic, but also popular and successful. Elliott's failure to advance his school-mastering future was of no great moment for Cooke. In reality he was going through the motions, attending a minimum of lectures at the training college, and preparing to subject himself – without any real sense of urgency or conviction – to a spell of teaching practice at Ely Grammar School. But there was a more serious aspect to this neglect of the University establishment. He had lost potential allies – and there would be a price to pay. The newly remodelled Alistair Cooke was now just a few months away from being catapulted reluctantly into the real world. His original Blackpool scholarship had been offered on the explicit understanding that the graduate would repay the community by deploying his talents as a teacher. Something had to be done to avoid this depressing outcome.

∼

Through the winter of 1930 and the following spring, there were plenty of reminders for Cooke of the benefits of Cambridge life. He was still heavily involved in the Mummers, whose season reached its climax in February with a performance of Congreve's comedy of seventeenth-century manners, *The Way of the World*. Cooke played the part of the scoundrelly Fainall.

He was also increasingly busy on *The Granta*, which was now being edited by J.N.G. (Norrie) Davidson, known to all by the pseudonym 'Heb' (Hebdomedary), borrowed from weekly columnists of earlier times. In fact most members of its staff adopted a *nom de plume*: Cooke was Moke, an obscure reference to the donkey in the (theatre)-stalls. Under Heb's guidance, *The Granta* liked to play things for laughs. In November, for instance, a special spoof edition appeared, purporting to be the parish magazine of St Mary-Down-the-Drain. In an age of burgeoning interest in Moral Rearmament, some of the copy was considered downright scurrilous. Brownie Notes wondered 'how many of my little Cub friends know that they can qualify, (and pass out) with a Fathercraft Badge. I am sure the Rev. W. Wicklyffe-Smythe will be only too pleased to take a little group of boys in hand.' When this edition appeared in villages around the city, there was a chorus of indignant complaint. Davidson and his fellow authors came close to being sent down, and he cherished for years one letter cancelling a long-standing subscription. 'Is this judicious mixture of dullness and dirt, so generously encouraged between your covers,' it expostulated, 'typical of undergraduate "wit" today?'

Davidson's recollection was that Cooke was less than wholehearted about this kind of levity, concentrating his own efforts on high-minded reviews and carefully constructed caricatures. He produced an entire page of cartoons to celebrate the Mummers' performance of Congreve, with his own self-portrait in the corner – the nose aquiline and eyes slightly protruding, in a self-deprecatory style which he was still using years later on letters and cards.

His reviews are full of a slightly laboured cleverness, especially those covering the output of the Festival Theatre with its reputation for austere modernism and intellectual rigour. Indeed, the atmosphere at The Granta's gatherings seems to have been aesthetically high-flown, but laced with that strain of erudite silliness. Group photographs included unlikely props – a donkey, or a brick on a tripod, although when Cooke took over the editorship in the autumn of 1931 these were abandoned in favour of a more classical college pose. The artistic moustache, nurtured during his formative years on the magazine, was also banished. The staff certainly regarded themselves as the University's cultural cream – with some justice, as it turned out: Cooke himself and Redgrave (specialising in theatre and film), Empson, Reeves and Bronowski, usually as book critic, the novelist T.H. White, Lionel Gamlin, heading for the BBC, and Norrie Davidson, who became one of Ireland's leading documentary filmmakers.

Throughout this period, conversation at the staff tea was always more likely to be on art and culture, rather than politics or international affairs; but it might just as well be about nothing in particular. Looking back, Cooke reflected on the way he was able to move so easily between the Cambridge cultures. 'In the downright, and hideously unfair, way of confident young men, we made a black and white distinction between what were called the "toughs" and the "aesthetes".' Most, he believed, were neither wholly one nor the other, but some – and he was one – 'had always enjoyed the best of both worlds, alternating a chapter of Thomas Hardy with a game of squash, or a deep draught of Beethoven with a chaser of Louis Armstrong'. It was a time for the attaching of labels: high- middle- or low-brow. Lowbrow men were supposed to have no interest beyond beer, skittles and the farces of Ben Travers, while highbrows had 'an almost trade union obligation to look on cricketers as "flannelled fools" and footballers as "muddied oafs". '

Hugh Stewart joined *The Granta* two years after Cooke, and was instantly in his thrall. Stewart, who went on to become a noted film-editor working for Hitchcock and many others, was struck by Cooke's unusual ambition and sense of purpose, while in Eddie Wiltshire's assessment he was a man with an eye for any opportunity to make a mark or advance his cause – and a natural leader, too. That impression was reinforced during the Easter vacation of 1931.

Cooke led a group of friends, including Wiltshire, on a reading party to Winchelsea, an unfashionable backwater on the East Sussex coast near Hastings. The four young men rented a cottage called Whipsyderry, with the idea that isolation from society might be conducive to intensive pre-exam study. However successful the theory, there was evidently plenty of time for extra-curricular activities.

Wiltshire's photographs depict an unusually warm April on the chilly channel coast. One shows Cooke and the other two members of the party stretched out on a shingle-beach: another records a remarkable piece of seaside art. In a niche in the sand Cooke has sculpted an elaborate female figure, a girl kicking her leg in the air. Wiltshire's album marks this ephemeral creation, 'Heteros find sublimation in seaside sculpture.' Sex was on their minds.

In the evenings, when the walking, sightseeing and sunbathing were over, the four would relax by speculating, and fantasising a little, about the girls who had caught their eyes. Harry Townsend was known to be sweet on Margaret Hodgson, whom he later married. Eddie claims to have made up his amour, while poor Jasper Frankenburg, with no demonstrable attachment, was awarded an imaginary girl-friend called Nesta. His friends hung a notice, 'Nesta's Nook', on his bed. Alistair alone escaped the teasing, saved by his age and comparative eminence, and offering the caricature in the sand as his contribution to the game. On the strength of their seaside deliberations, Eddie remembers Cooke and Townsend delivering a talk at Jesus (to a select, and presumably trustworthy, group – considering the *risqué* nature of the topic) on the benefits of coeducation, and enthusing about an experimental institution called 'Coonsend' which preached the Platonic principles, up to and including free love. Sitting in the audience, Eddie found himself presented with the shocking idea that boys and girls at this school of the future would be issued with free contraception. 'Then I went back to Jesus in 1990,' he recalled, 'and found it had all come true.'

Cooke also had those other, more pressing educational matters on his mind. A letter to his tutor, Elliott, at Jesus, dated 13 April, asks for permission to return from Winchelsea a day after the start of term. It concludes with this plea: 'Is Mr Brittain in charge of English super-vision, now that Mr Tillyard is away? I am rather anxious next term to do something in the way of coaching and I should like to know who may be wanting some intensive coaching or supervision for the Tripos or for English Specials.' The time had come for urgent action, if he was to perpetuate his Cambridge career into a fifth glorious year.

Behind the scenes the tide was moving against him. Cooke, approaching the end of his teacher training, had applied to various colleges for research posts or fellowships. To be fair Elliott did his best to help his wayward star-pupil, despite his reservations:

22 MAY 1931 – I can strongly recommend my pupil Mr A. Cooke for a Goldsmiths Senior Studentship . . . I have little doubt he would have obtained a 1st Class in the second part of his Tripos if he had not been largely occupied with other interests . . . he is certainly a man of first-rate ability and original views and in my opinion deserves every help and encouragement in order that he may develop them.

25 MAY 1931 – Cooke is a remarkable man . . . while working for his Teachers' Diploma (which he should obtain this summer) he has been collecting and preparing material for a book on the History of Dramatic Criticism . . . I believe there is a reasonable chance of him producing some good work.

10 JUNE 1931 – A pupil of mine, A. Cooke, has asked me if it would be proper for him to send in an application for one of your bye-fellowships . . . Cooke is an able man and Q is prepared to back him.

The doubts and lack of warmth permeate the words of praise. Elliott was well aware that these research awards attracted the University's highest achievers, and he was wary of recommending a man with a propensity for non-academic distractions. The carefully phrased letters told the recipients all they needed to know. Cooke would be a risky prospect. And one by one the rejection slips came through.

By July Cooke was writing to Elliott for help and advice. 'I am desperately anxious to undertake the work I had planned. It remains to discover the means.' He mentions that Mr Fox, of the teacher training college, is 'surprisingly genial' about his plan to stay on . . . 'Will Jesus help me, do you think?'

With no immediate reply, there was nothing for it but to hope for the best and to pass the summer as agreeably as possible. The second Mummers tour took the twenty-three-year-old Alistair and his friends to Devon to perform an ambitious revue, Book, Music and Production by Alistair Cooke. The programme drew on his talents as a parodist, re-working scenes from *The Rivals*, but there was 'straight' singing as well, with what was claimed to be the first performance of an oratorio attributed to Handel, and a popular one-act play. In between times Cooke played the piano, while Hugh Stewart, Eddie Wiltshire and others sang and played the fool. Stewart remembers Cooke's extraordinary facility for dreaming up tunes, and where necessary, lyrics. Stewart's girl-friend and future wife, Frances Curl, asked for a match, and one of the company replied, 'Little girl, I'll light you up.' This set Cooke off, and within moments the chance phrase had grown into an impromptu ballad:

> Little girl, I'll light you up
> When the shadows fall.
> Little girl, you won't have to call.
> I'll be the lamp to your path
> At the close of day.

A large cast was involved – almost two dozen people in all – traipsing contentedly from theatre to beach, photographing each other along the way. By the time the group reached Paignton, they were able to reproduce as a handbill this glowing testimonial from a local celebrity, the actor-manager Cyril Maude, who had seen the opening night in Dartmouth: 'MR CYRIL MAUDE – DELIGHTED WITH THE CAMBRIDGE MUMMERS: Sir, Last night I had the great happiness of witnessing a really good, amusing and witty performance by a young and most talented body of players from Cambridge, all undergraduates and "ettes". I went, I must own, quite prepared to be bored, but it remained for me to laugh heartily and enjoy practically every moment.' He goes on to praise the 'particularly talented young man of much charm called Mr Alistair Cooke, who wrote the "book" as well as the music it appears! I advise everybody in Paignton to patronise these young people.'

This was high praise from an important theatrical figure. Maybe encouraged by this success, and certainly spurred by the lack of news from Cambridge, Cooke sat down on Friday 3 July in his room at the Esplanade Hotel in Paignton and penned a letter of impressive bravado to the Talks Director of the BBC.

> I am trying to obtain permission and the opportunity of giving a series of talks. May I put down my qualifications: B.A. Jesus College, Cambridge – First Class, English Tripos, 1929 – Editor-elect of *The Granta* – Cambridge Dramatic Critic of the *Manchester Guardian* and *The Nation and Athenaeum* – Ex-President, Cambridge University Mummers – College Prize for English, 1929 – Staff Artist for *The Granta* since 1928.

Astutely sliding over the degree he finally achieved, he rushes on to his proposal:

> I am prepared to talk on:
> - (a) The Theatre – criticism and comment – a short history of English Acting or Drama
> - (b) Literary Criticism – a history of Modern English Criticism – Eliot, Richards etc.
> - (c) Read Fiction or Poetry
> - (d) Write Revue Sketches
> - (e) Write songs
> - (f) Help on the *Radio Times* with caricatures, articles etc.

His offer is backed by references from Q, the literary editor of the *Manchester Guardian*, the Cambridge Festival Theatre director, Terence Gray, and Ashley Dukes – editor of *Theatre Arts Monthly*. He has the grace to conclude, 'Please forgive the immodesty of my application, but I take it you want definite paper qualifications rather than vague longings.'

The reply politely informs him that the BBC already has both theatre and literary critics, and is going through a glut of 'talks of this kind'. As for other ideas, he should submit scripts to the appropriate departments.

Soon after this setback, Cooke set off on his second great foreign adventure.

5

LOVE AND LONGING

For the second half of July, Cooke had organised a visit to Germany by a group calling itself the Oxford and Cambridge Players. This impressive nomenclature concealed the fact that all but one of the Players came from Cambridge and the whole enterprise was designed to tie in with Cooke's own teaching job, later in the summer, at a school in Silesia. Their repertoire was mostly mainstream European theatre, including scenes from Shaw and Shakespeare, but they also decided to perform a modern short play which was almost certainly unknown to a Munich audience, and probably incomprehensible, too.

Young Woodley, written by John van Druten in 1925, deals with the doomed passion of a romantic pupil and a master's wife at a minor public school. Cooke played the part of Vining, a fellow pupil and cad ('rather coarse and too well-dressed', according to the stage direction) whose goading of the hero leads to his expulsion from the school. The script is full of references to the peculiar practices of an English boarding-school, using language inaccessible to a German audience. One line stuck in Cooke's mind: as a prefect catches sight of a junior boy peering through the window, he utters the phrase, 'Scrim-shanking, the little tic!' The actors felt the theatre humming with incomprehension. '*Was ist eine scrimshankinger Tick?*' The choice of play, Cooke concedes, was misguided, but the trip still left an indelible mark.

As well as the actors, he had persuaded Lionel Grunbaum, *The Granta*'s music critic, to come along for the ride and act as stage-manager. After rehearsals one day they drifted across the road to a beer-garden and waited to be served. Nothing happened. The waiters ignored them. Cooke cried 'Hierüber!' from time to time, but with no success. Grunbaum looked more and more morose. 'I don't think they like my face,' he said eventually.

'What do you mean?' Cooke inquired.

Grunbaum told him that there was a new political party whose main policy plank was to throw the Jews out of the country. Cooke was flabbergasted. Years later he still felt embarrassed at his utter naïveté, which left Grunbaum to explain, patiently, about a Munich-based politician called Adolf Hitler who was building a national reputation.

As they talked, they noticed a stir of activity beyond the trees at the edge of the garden. Grunbaum pointed out that Hitler's headquarters, the Braunhaus, was next door: it had become something of a tourist attraction to hear the leader of the National Socialist Party addressing his faithful followers in the grounds on a Thursday afternoon. They decided to take a look.

'When we got there, we found a small crowd, no more than 35 people, gathered round a podium that was really just a soap-box. There was a Red Cross van with a nurse, and after a few minutes Hitler himself appeared.' Cooke retained a vivid image of the scene.

He spoke for about twenty minutes on a theme of the corruption and rottenness of the old order in general and the Jews in particular. He kept warning his audience that it was five minutes to midnight – 'Fünf Minuten vor zwölf!!' He never explained what would happen at twelve, he simply repeated the same phrase over and over again, gently at first, quiet and explanatory, then increasingly furious, and finally shouting at the top of his voice. He played with his audience. He had pathos, tenderness, decisiveness, frightfulness. I thought, 'Wow! Who is this guy?'

Oblivious to the political importance of what he was witnessing, he found himself 'hypnotised by this powerful and subtle man'. At the end of his oration, Hitler retired and the crowd of office workers and pimply women dispersed, watched over by unsympathetic-looking policemen. The Red Cross van, they learned, was always on hand to treat women who fainted in breathless admiration of the Führer. For Grunbaum, a German-speaker whose family had fled to England from an earlier Central European pogrom, it was a chilling occasion; for Cooke it was a memorable oddity.

This wasn't the end of the learning process. When the Oxford and Cambridge Players dispersed, Cooke boarded a train and headed north-east to Silesia. He was met at the station in Dresden by a teacher from the school where he was to spend the next few weeks. 'I was taken to a restaurant and the waiter, against the manager's instructions, seated us at a table by the window. At the first appearance of a plate of soup, children tottered along from nowhere and glared through the window: small children with black circles under their eyes, rib-cages as well-defined as in an X-ray, and bellies swollen like balloons. Then the cops came swarming and beat them off.' The Blackpool boy had never seen anything like it, but he still drew no particular conclusions about what it might mean.

His friend Eddie Wiltshire, who was in Vienna to learn German during the same summer, also saw the signs – the young men ranting about the jobs the Jews had stolen, the swastikas chalked on walls – and confessed to the same lack of political awareness. When the two met up afterwards to compare notes, their talk was more of romance than rumours of oppression. Wiltshire became convinced that Cooke, during his time trading English lessons for German tuition at the Hochschule at Bunzlau, had stolen a march in the race towards manhood. This suspicion seems to be borne out by a nod and a wink in the *Granta* valedictory article: Alistair, having wended his way to Silesia to study German stagecraft, 'acquainted himself with the Scandinavian Theatre, character and blonde'.

On more mature reflection, however, the exposure to some of the petty cruelties of Nazism proved to be a formative experience which helped to shape Cooke's journalistic philosophy. In particular, he developed an antipathy towards sweeping political generalisation. From the desperate faces pressed against the glass of a Dresden restaurant he drew a moral: that even the most horrific events and attitudes are likely to have a rational explanation, and that the explanation is worth pursuing. It was an attitude of mind which caused him trouble over the years. To explain something is to understand, and to understand can sometimes look perilously like forgiveness. In a 1980 lecture to young soldiers at West Point Military Academy, Cooke described the atmosphere at the German school where he'd taught fifty years earlier:

> I was surrounded by country people, so ground down by depression and hunger, and the vengeful conditions imposed on them by the Allies (after the First World War) that the best they could do was scrape for food and dream of the dignity of a job and a half-way decent home. It would have been an insult to the facts of their life to talk to them about such rosy

abstractions as civil rights or freedom. Survival was all. Then came Hitler, pointing to two scapegoat villains. He told them they were a fine, upstanding people cheated by the Allies and swindled by the Jews. And in relief and thanksgiving they rallied to him. It was my first political lesson in the frailty of freedom.

Freedom, he concluded, is provisional and pragmatic.

~

Throughout the German trip, he was waiting for news from Cambridge. On 2 August, he dictated (having been stricken by food poisoning) a letter giving the Bunzlau School address, so that 'I could quickly hear of any decision of the College Council.' The decision was going against him. His tutor, Elliott, consulted his supervisor, Tillyard, in unpromising terms:

> Our friend Alistair Cooke has been asking me if (a) the College could make him a grant to enable him to stay up a (further) year to research the History of Dramatic Criticism and (b) if the college would help him by giving him some supervision work for the English Tripos.
>
> Personally I feel very doubtful if it is worth spending any considerable sum of money on encouraging him to research, and I am equally doubtful as to whether he is up to supervising or coaching for the Tripos.

Tillyard agreed: from his holiday hotel in France he wrote that he wasn't keen on Cooke's extra year: 'There are better men about. I doubt his aptitude for research'.

The bad news was conveyed to Cooke on 15 August. 'I am afraid that this will be a great disappointment to you,' wrote Elliott, 'but we have used up as much scholarship money as is justifiable for the coming year . . . you will know that I do not find this a pleasant letter to write . . . please let me know if I can in any way help you to obtain a job.' And he added, 'I am sorry to hear that you have been poisoned.'

The same letter acknowledged the nature of Cooke's financial crunch. His one stroke of good fortune was to have acquired, from Norrie Davidson, the editorship of *The Granta*: this, in principle, offered the chance of a modest income. However, as Elliott pointed out, a graduate in digs for a year would probably need £250 to live on.

By 3 September, Cooke was still writing from Germany that he 'hoped' to be up in Cambridge for a fifth year, and making sure that the residence list recorded his name correctly as Alfred Alistair Cooke. On his return home, he even roped his old headmaster into the quest for funds: JT duly sent a telegram to Elliott asking him to recommend Cooke for a research loan from Blackpool Borough Council. But even that didn't help. At a time of general economic hardship, Blackpool was trying to cut back its own educational expenditure.

When he returned to Cambridge in the first week of October, Cooke's finances were in a parlous state. His old accommodation in Pretoria Road had been taken over by Eddie Wiltshire, and he moved into the spare bedroom. One bonus from this arrangement was that, as well as being a passionate butterfly-collector, Eddie was the jazz critic of *The Granta*, and the possessor of a notable collection of modern American music. At first, Alistair didn't show more than a passing interest, but Eddie's enthusiasm for jazz and the blues proved infectious.

Cooke started to accumulate his own favourites: Ethel Waters singing 'Miss Otis Regrets', Duke Ellington's 'East St Louis Toodle-oo' and Jelly Roll Morton and his Red Hot Peppers, with numbers like 'Shoeshiners Drag' and 'Shreveport Stomp'. Gradually he developed his own expertise in the music of Black America, with a particular affection for piano-players such as Morton. He would take his passion home to Blackpool, too, to the horror of his mother. In a *Letter from America* of 1971 he told how a yearned-for record – 'St James's Infirmary' – finally reached the local store:

> It began with a shattering chord and a trumpet taking off like a supersonic jet. Long before it was over, I took it off the machine because I saw that my mother was sitting there in tears. She was not moved by the beauty of the piece, or the artistry of the mad trumpeter. She was frightened by it, and aghast that her son could listen to this jungle music without a blush. To her, in those remote days, it was as if today a mother had seen her son nonchalantly take out a needle and give himself a shot of heroin.

The new preoccupation with jazz and the blues complemented his love for the American popular music of the 1920s, the young Richard Rodgers, Irving Berlin, and above all George Gershwin, whose fame had swept across Europe with the ragtime number 'Swanee'.

∼

In this October of 1931 Cooke didn't have much spare money for buying records. Indeed he didn't have much spare money for anything. His main source of income was supposed to be from running *The Granta*. The editor who had originally employed Cooke as a staff-artist was reputed to have made as much as £300 from his year at the top. If so, he was a phenomenon. Cooke's predecessor and benefactor, Norrie Davidson, with a tally of £60, was a much more realistic comparison. And in the event, even £60 would have been a triumph. *The Granta* plunged into an economic crisis. It was probably less to do with Cooke's move up-market and consumer rejection of his campaign of high-seriousness, and more a result of the gathering Depression which made advertising in student magazines an unaffordable luxury. His first term produced an income of £13 (about £500 today), but in the New Year *The Granta* recorded a loss of £12.

His friend Miles Mayall wrote that he piloted *The Granta* through the crisis, 'an exacting but not unkind editor.' His own affairs required a hand just as steady. He was able to earn something from freelance contributions to the American periodical *Theatre Arts Monthly*, and he had another short story accepted by the *Manchester Guardian* – a curious tale of an English boy having nightmares while on a 13-hour journey on a German train. Usually he wrote reviews, but one oddity was a light-hearted piece for the *Daily Sketch* on the prospects of the Cambridge rowing eight in the University boat-race. Not, in this case, their prowess on the river, but their attractiveness to young women in general and 'flappers' in particular.

Despite such journalistic forays, Cooke was growing desperate for funds, as he confessed in a *cri de coeur* to Eddie Done: 'I have about twenty pounds in the bank,' he wrote on New Year's Eve, 'with which to pay my landlady, my college bill, to live during the vac. and to make allowances for next term. Somehow I've got to earn some money. Otherwise I can't move . . . *Que faire*?? Haven't you one wretched boy whose parents will pay me an odd fiver for coaching their infant during the vac? Really I've got you beaten hollow over privation and suffering, so far as the economy ramp's concerned. Make a few suggestions. Quick!' Desperation eventually drove Cooke to borrow money from better-placed friends to keep going. 'I hated doing it. I knew my parents would be appalled if they found out, but I had no choice. When I tried to pay the money back, one of them told me: "Don't worry – do the same for somebody else some time." '

Somehow he made it through the winter, though the Jesus archives give a hint of the endless niggling awkwardness over comparatively small amounts of money. The College was still trying in March to recoup an unpaid winter-term bill for £23. Through this period of uncertainty, he ploughed away at his 'researches into the history of dramatic criticism' without a firm commitment that anyone would ever publish them. And he prepared for his last major outing with the Mummers – Aldous Huxley's *The World of Light*, in which he was both producer himself and leading actor – and which, unsurprisingly, received a rave review in *The Granta*. Even the less biased local paper was friendly, hailing 'excellent team work of a kind not usually seen in amateur performances', with Cooke's acting displaying 'feeling and vigour'. It was the first time the Mummers had performed in the much-derided ADC Theatre and the paper commented that Cambridge would be missing a good thing if the theatre wasn't full for the run of the play.

None of which helped to pay the bills. But although Cooke didn't know it, financial salvation, and much more, was just around the corner. For the spring of 1932 changed Alistair Cooke's life and defined its final shape.

~

At the time, he himself could have misread the omens. He may well have concluded that the most significant event was a chance meeting over a glass of sherry at Clare College on 13 March which was, as luck would have it, a Friday. His host, a would-be novelist called Lionel Birch, was proudly showing off his glamorous girl-friend, Hetty. Cooke, having come for a cocktail, left with an aching heart.

'Bam! That was it,' he recalls. 'A month later, on her 19th birthday, we were engaged.'

Henrietta Riddle was an entrancing creature with an exotic pedigree: her mother was a romantic novelist of renown, and a woman with a chequered personal history. Bettina Riddle was born in Pennsylvania and became famous with her first novel *Pam*, published in the late 1890s, following this with a string of successful sequels. But her own life-story – which included marriage to a German baron – was just as compelling as the books she wrote. She tired of the feudal

atmosphere at her husband's *Schloss*, and retreated to England until –
as Baroness von Hütten – she was interned as an enemy alien during
the First World War. Thereafter, she lurched between bankruptcy and
high society until her death in 1957.

Her obituarist was clearly captivated. 'Her beauty, her charm, dis-
armed the most fault-finding ... She was a unique being, with the
power of making all who came within her orbit love and excuse her.'
This paean of praise hints at elements of a racy life-style which,
even in 1957, weren't usually mentioned in newspaper tributes. In
particular, it fails to mention that Bettina became the mistress of one
of the great actors of the age, Henry Ainley. He, in due course, became
the father of Henrietta.

Cooke may not have been altogether inexperienced, but he was
certainly ill prepared for the rapid onset of this amour. His friends
were simply bemused. Miles Mayall's farewell article in *The Granta* a
few weeks later describes the affair in these cryptic terms:

'Our last note is, as he (Cooke) would say, "appallingly fragrant".
It seems that last vacation was a landmark, crisis, heart-attack, what
you will. Till then he had stayed the course, riding with a stiff upper
lip. Now at his last fence he hesitated, took thought, and willingly fell.
The result is our solid congratulations on his engagement.'

The passion was grand and almost all-consuming. Almost, but not
quite. For at long last one of his grand schemes to extricate himself
from a lifetime of classroom drudgery was beginning to bear fruit.
He told the story in a Fulbright Address in 1982:

On a dank, dark late winter's day in Cambridge, (of the sort John Milton
had in mind when he wrote about 'not light but darkness visible') I saw a
printed notice on my college bulletin-board. It was a darker day than most
for me, because the approach of the last term of a five-year languishing in
the cloisters reminded me cruelly that it was time to move out into the
real world. The notice announced that something mysteriously called the
Commonwealth Fund invited applications from graduates of British and
Commonwealth Universities for two years of study in the United States.

The Fund had been set up by the American philanthropist Edward S.
Harkness, its original aim being to finance medical research in Central
and Southern America. But in 1925 the Fund's remit was extended to
encourage British students to continue their research in the United
States – a tradition which continued until 1996.

Cooke did not hesitate. On 18 February his tutor gave him a letter of recommendation, and this time there were no real caveats from Elliott – or at least none that an outsider would recognise.

> I think there is no doubt that Cooke is a remarkable man. He was the leader of a group of undergraduates who formed the Mummers Dramatic Club in the University, and he is a prominent figure among the junior members of the University who are interested in modern literary tendencies and the more serious aspects of Drama. It is quite clear that he possesses an exceptional degree of initiative and a personality which is capable of impressing itself upon others.
>
> I believe he would be an admirable representative of the type of young Englishman who is interested in the development of the theatre and in modern literature. His character and conduct have throughout his residence at Cambridge been excellent, as has also his health.

It was cleverly and carefully written: 'an admirable representative of the type of young Englishman who is interested in the development of the theatre' is particularly subtle. Elliott's true feelings about Cooke had not changed one jot. The evidence came in an exchange of letters at the start of May 1932 with the University Appointments Board about the possibility of offering Cooke some teaching work. This time the tutor's response, to an insider, is nothing short of vitriolic, with a tinge of personal animosity which is hard to account for. Elliott refers back to his earlier letter – the one that speaks of Cooke's exaggerated sense of his own talents. His view hasn't changed, he says, but it has been modified:

> [Cooke] has even more drive and more of a certain kind of ability than I gave him credit for before. I still believe that he is not really a first-class man but there is no doubt he has an extraordinary capacity for impressing himself on others who are really much sounder and solider than he is. For example he has achieved a very strong and most mysterious influence over Snell, last term's President of the Union, who though he is not really clever is much sounder than Cooke. Also several men of the highbrow type at this college, one of whom is certainly much cleverer than Cooke, appear to regard him as a sort of demi-God.

Elliott accepts that teaching is no longer an option. 'He is, I am sure, very much out for himself and I should sum him up as a very clever careerist. I believe he has done well as Editor of *The Granta*, and he certainly has brains of a sort. I think it is relevant to add that I found that on 20 November 1930 he took the christian name of Alistaire (sic) by Deed Poll.'

Solidity and soundness – those were the true virtues in the eyes of a Cambridge don. The last straw for his college seems to have been Cooke's change of name to something so palpably unsound, so redolent of artistic unreliability: Alistaire (the final 'e' is an invention of Elliott's). Why did Elliott take such a keen dislike to an evidently talented student? Nothing in Cooke's record seems to justify the vitriol of those memoranda and there must have been a real personal antipathy at work. State school entrants were still in a small minority at Cambridge and perhaps Cooke was simply encountering the innate snobbery of the time against a boy from a secondary school in the North of England: not many Jesus men had fathers in insurance and mothers who had once kept a guest-house in a plebeian seaside resort.

Having heard Elliott's views, the Appointments Board presumably did not offer Cooke any vacation work. Within days it ceased to matter. Along with twenty-four others, he was awarded a two-year Commonwealth Fund Fellowship and became overnight a rich young man. Successful applicants qualified for an immediate payment of $200 (£50) for 'equipment' with the promise of $150 a month on top of tuition fees for twenty-four months. There would also be an extra allowance for travel during each Christmas recess and a further lump sum to finance a three-month tour of the United States in the summer break. No limitation was imposed on the course of study to be chosen and there were two dozen of the country's best universities from which to choose.

The offer of this largesse, in the words of the official memorandum, was 'impelled by a belief in the value of international opportunities for education and travel, and by a conviction that mutual amity and understanding between Great Britain and the United States will thereby be promoted'. In 1932 each was still a very foreign country to the other.

Cooke's plan was to study theatre production at Yale. It was a risky choice. Solid subjects like physics or mathematics or history were the norm. The generosity of the deal ensured the strongest possible competition and candidates faced a daunting selection board chaired by Lord Halifax, later Foreign Secretary in Neville Chamberlain's government. 'Do you mean to say,' he had inquired of Cooke, 'that if

you get this you'll come back and revolutionise the English Theatre?'
Cooke looked him in the eye: 'That's right.' Halifax let it be known
that Cooke's confidence had been an important factor. 'What's more,
he's from the North Country, and they're always the best types.' The
Blackpool Gazette and Herald soon picked up the story, with the
headline, £1,600 FELLOWSHIP: COMMONWEALTH AWARD FOR
BLACKPOOL MAN. It quoted the proud mother (suppressing her
suspicion of all things dramatic): 'He has always been tremendously
interested in theatre, and particularly the critical side of it. He has
worked very hard for this scholarship.' Cooke told Eddie Done later,
'Did you see the local rag about our Mr Cooke? Disgraceful. They
descended on Mother for information and she hadn't the foggiest
idea I'd been awarded a Fellowship.' If so, Mrs Cooke performed nobly
in concealing the fact that she'd been kept so completely in the dark.

His selection raised just two awkward issues. The first was the small
matter of his teacher training. He was told he would have to write to
the Board of Education in London to inform them of his imminent
departure and his letter included this postscript: 'Though in the
present economic situation it is impossible to make promises, I shall
hope, when circumstances permit, to come to some arrangement
with the Board by which it will be possible to make some return to
them either in service or in kind.'

The Board replied by return: there would be no objection to his
accepting the Fellowship: nevertheless, 'if you should eventually
abandon your intention of teaching in State-aided schools, it is understood that you hope, as soon as your circumstances permit, to make
an offer of repayment in respect of the grants paid towards your
course at Cambridge. The amount of the grants was £348.5s.0d.'

The other awkward issue was contained in a five-word section of
the Conditions of Tenure. 'Fellowships are vacated by marriage'.

For the newly engaged Cooke, this stipulation must have caused
more than a tremor of anxiety. The arrangement was now public
knowledge: he wrote to Eddie Done at the end of June, using the
exaggerated argot he often affected with his friends: 'Naturally you
will realise the engagement has long ago ceased to be a secret – in fact
we bought the ring at Blarckpooool [sic]. We spotted a shop called
Mr Hyman and thought that would be an appropriate place. But
unfortunately Mr Hyman refused to yield and we went elsewhere.'
Hetty lived and worked in London, and with her Bohemian

background was unlikely to sit at home sewing samplers for two years. Yet the offer could not be refused and the couple had to face the prospect of deferring their wedding until after Alistair's return.

By the time all this happened, Cooke was in the throes of his last term at Cambridge. *The Granta* turned the corner into profit again, though only to the tune of £13, and Cooke was contributing both caricatures and theatre reviews, which were self-assured if over-worked, never using one sub-clause where two could be devised. It was a way of writing which, in retrospect, he grew to loathe. 'The trouble was, I'd read everything in sight and became very pretentious. A lot of it was absolute junk.' Doubtless it was much admired at the time by his contemporaries, as were (with more reason) his drawings: a selection of five years' work was republished in a special 'Alistair Supplement' to *The Granta* in June, including the cartoon of Q which had been his first success, along with depictions of actors, fellow students and academic staff like G.M. Trevelyan and Maynard Keynes. There's a '(Self-)Portrait of The Artist as a Young Man' on the gallows which he later used to decorate a wedding card. And an elaborate illustration framing a poem by James Reeves, which pokes gentle fun at American tourists surveying Kings College.

The Granta days were drawing to a close. Jesus College continued to pester Cooke for unpaid bills, but he was blithely unconcerned. (The last £15.10s.0d. was only recovered by the college in May 1935, while the Board of Education continued to pursue him for longer still, over the repayment of grants which had been 'for the purpose of assisting you to qualify as a regular teacher in a State-aided School'. There is no evidence they were ever finally settled.) He would travel to London, or Hetty to Cambridge: there were plays and films to see, and clothes to buy. He was floating through the summer in the first flush of a new love and on a wave of comradely affection from his friends.

Miles Mayall's tribute in the May Week issue of the *Granta* ended, 'So we leave him to his summer of solace. We do not predict. We know that, if he can manage to catch the boat, greatness awaits him in the States. We have his legacy of the Mummers. But when there is a play to produce, or a song to compose, or drawings to be done, or an odd 1400-word compact criticism of the Festival to write, or a tea to miss, we fear we may scour the streets and find them empty.'

~

Two formalities awaited the twenty-five new Fellows. The first involved a visit to Harley Street, where the royal physician gave them an eccentric medical inspection. His name, which caused much student mirth, was Sir Farquhar Buzzard and he did little more than check each man's height and weight, wave his stethoscope vaguely across each student chest, and peer unenthusiastically into mouths and ears. In Cooke's case the only flaws he could find were 'a couple of teeth quite capable of stopping', in other words in need of filling. The Yale School of Dentistry later found that Sir Farquhar had missed twelve more teeth capable of stopping.

The more dignified occasion came on a sunny morning in late June, when Cooke was summoned to the headquarters of the Commonwealth Fund in Portman Square, just off Oxford Street. From there the Fellows were ferried in a fleet of taxis to St James's Palace to meet the Fund's Honorary Chairman, His Royal Highness the Prince of Wales. For the Prince, Cooke wrote in his book *Six Men*, this ceremony was 'yet another of the tedious chores that hobble the days and nights of royalty'. For 'the small band of scientists, historians and English scholars bowling down St James's Street' it was an occasion to relish. They were 'high on the waggishness with which young college types cover up their self-consciousness on state occasions and, in this instance, their child-like awe at the prospect of coming face to face with the legendary Prince Charming'.

The Fellows were led into a reception room in the private residence of the future King Edward VIII, where the bearing of the royal aides pulverised their poise and reduced them to 'the timidity of a country cousin being presented with his first wine-list'. Nervously they eyed the huge pair of gilt-encrusted doors, decorated with the *fleur de lis* as the aides made small talk in the strangulated accents of the aristocracy.

At last they heard the 'choirboy babble' of the Prince's voice. 'We adjusted our neckties and I recall shooting a cuff, since on the advice of an undergraduate friend of mine, a young man of deafening poise and the son of a West End actor, I had acquired his tailor and encased myself, for this royal occasion, in a brand-new double-breasted, hound's-tooth suit. When the two doors opened and the Prince came in, I was amazed and comforted to see that he was wearing a suit of the identical material and cut.'

Cooke thought the prince looked older than the newspaper pictures had led him to expect. He seemed nervous, too, as he looked each graduate in the eye and asked about his speciality. Physics and molecular chemistry left him cold, but he perked up as he reached the man immediately ahead of Cooke in the queue. He was off to the Pacific Coast to learn how to rehabilitate English oyster beds damaged by submarine activity in the Great War.

Then he turned to Cooke, whose appearance produced a sudden raising of the royal eyebrow: 'My God, my brother!' Cooke, often teased for his supposed royal resemblance, was less startled. But 'for all its ridiculous triviality, it was a moment of odd intimacy'. And what, the Prince inquired, was his field of study?

When Cooke mentioned American theatre direction, the Prince's eyes bulged even more than usual. 'Visions, I felt sure, of the Ziegfeld and Vanities choruses floated before him. He wanted to know what the Americans had to teach about directing plays that "our own fellahs" didn't know, and he was willing, even eager, to believe that there was a great deal. Would I, he asked tugging at his cuffs, and lowering his voice a little, expect to direct musicals?'

It was a shocking suggestion to an earnest student who had spent the summer studying German techniques of theatre direction. Cooke wishes that he'd had the wit, or mischief, to say 'Of course.' Instead 'the Prince drooped visibly, and rightly, at my earnest exposition of the superior discipline of the German and American directors.'

The fellowship, the princely presentation and his upper-class engagement ensured Cooke of celebrity status back home in Blackpool. The local paper, the *Gazette*, printed on 19 July a half-column item headed ENGAGED TO BARONESS'S DAUGHTER – MR A.A. COOKE OF NORTH SHORE. 'There is considerable local interest in the announcement of the engagement of Mr Alfred Alistair Cooke, younger son of Mr and Mrs S. Cooke of 55 Ormond Avenue, and Miss Henrietta Mary Jeanne Riddle, daughter of Baroness von Hütten, the well-known woman novelist.' And in August the same paper secured new studio portraits of the two young people, while noting that, under the terms of the Fellowship, 'they may not marry for two years'.

This cruel stricture meant that there was no time to lose. By the end of July Alistair and Hetty were taking the bold step of setting up home together, unmarried, in London. They rented a room in Chelsea, where such modern behaviour would attract little attention, and tried not to upset the fearsome, and (despite her personal history) fiercely conservative, Baroness. Early in their relationship, Cooke told Norrie Davidson, he had brought Hetty home later than expected. The Baroness was fuming and insisted on sending her daughter upstairs to fetch a Bible: Cooke was made to swear that he'd never do it again. To no avail.

The rooms they took in Thistle Grove belonged to an eccentric couple called Anderson. Before long, the household was joined by Eddie Wiltshire who was preparing to sit the Civil Service exams nearby. It was a steaming hot summer and the Andersons had decided that the only way to keep cool was to sleep on the lawn. Consequently, except when it rained and he was banished to the sofa downstairs, Wiltshire was able to use one bedroom, with Alistair and Hetty in the room next door. In the evenings this odd fivesome would sit around drinking and talking. Anderson was an engineer with a yen for the paranormal: Wiltshire remembers being entranced by the conversations on such obscure subjects as the possibility of an astral universe parallel to our own.

Then at night the three young people would snoop guiltily from the windows and watch their landlords on the lawn, carrying on as if in the privacy of their own bedroom, apparently oblivious to the possibility of prying eyes.

In the flush of new romance, Alistair and Hetty went everywhere together. Cooke had acquired a thrice-weekly film column for *John O'London's Weekly*, so they sat though three movies a week. So great was Hetty's devotion that she even appeared to enjoy a day watching cricket at Lords. With his studies at Yale in mind, Cooke also tried to concentrate as much theatre-going as possible into the few short weeks that remained before his departure. Nothing left a stronger impression than the evening of 7 August when they went to see Hetty's father, Henry Ainley, in a performance of *Tobias and the Angel* by the Scottish dramatist, James Bridie. It was Ainley's last role before illness drove him from the stage for six years, and afterwards they chatted with him in his dressing-room, and then wandered homewards through the West End.

~

September crept up on Alistair and Hetty. There were long evenings in cafés and pubs, and countless plays, and the Andersons in their Chelsea garden and Eddie Wiltshire, known to them all as 'James'

because of the part he'd played in one of the Mummers' productions... And suddenly it was time to go.

On 16 September, they attended one last show, the first night of
Noël Coward's *Words and Music*, with its memorable hit song 'Mad
About the Boy'. Then they boarded the boat-train for Liverpool. On
17 September Alistair Cooke waved goodbye to his fiancée and
climbed the gangway of the S S *Laconia*, bound for New York.

PART TWO

THE DISCOVERY OF AMERICA

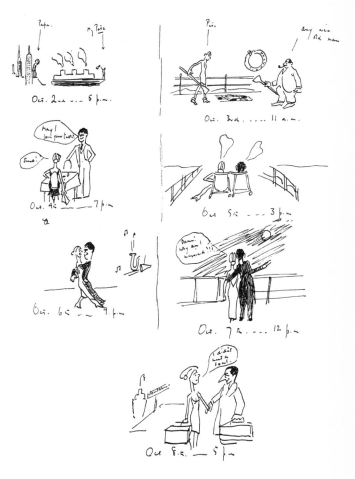

A series of drawings from a love-lorn Cooke to
his new wife on her journey to England.

6

IVY LEAGUE

Did the young man's self-confidence wane even briefly in the ten days of the crossing? Did he wonder, perhaps, about the wisdom of abandoning the cosy, comfortable Cambridge set which had so cherished him? Or was he so buoyed by belief in the character he had created for himself that doubts remained buried?

For comfort, in that late September of 1932, he brought along some of the records he had enjoyed with Eddie Wiltshire – a foretaste of the blues he expected to hear at first hand, oozing from every corner café in New York. He had money, too, to enjoy the trip and an elegant wardrobe generously provided by the Commonwealth Fund: a tail-coat, a dinner jacket, two suits and a heavy overcoat. All students were warned in apocalyptic terms of the need to protect their clothes from the attentions of the voracious Buffalo Moth.

The Cunarder *Laconia* was the first of many whose transatlantic comforts Cooke learned to appreciate. He travelled free from political anxiety, with no sense of the mounting misery of the Depression, only dimly aware of an American election campaign which would soon sweep Franklin Delano Roosevelt to power for the first time to pursue his New Deal. He was much more absorbed by matters cultural, noting with interest the linguistic pitfalls signalled by American passengers: not 'tram' but 'streetcar' or 'trolley'; not 'pavement' but 'sidewalk'; and never 'biscuit' – always 'cookie' or 'cracker'.

This last point was stressed by one young American passenger, who insinuated himself into everyone's conversations with well-meaning, if irritating, advice. The English called him the Scoutmaster. He explained patiently the difference between a cracker, a cookie and a biscuit: 'Look, a biscuit is hot – almost a scone – you'll never come across it except in Southern fiction. Forget about it. A cracker, that's a dry biscuit but the thing to remember is the cookie: that's kinda like the sweet biscuit you have at home.'

In due course the Scoutmaster stood with his new friends at the rail as the Cunard liner nosed her way into his home-town harbour. It was one of the rare occasions in each year when the tide required by the big ships coincided with twilight. The result was the picture-postcard spectacle of office buildings ablaze with lights, etched against a dramatic sky. Twenty years later, in September 1952, Cooke recalled in a *Letter From America* his first view of Manhattan.

> Since it was Fall, the upper air was cool and clear, and this always brings on skies of great purity in the evening. The downtown skyscrapers were soaring and black but the sky behind them was a sheet of almost metallic blue. They were piled up like the ramparts of some medieval city. And this, too, seemed right, for American spectacles – from the Grand Canyon to a night baseball crowd – are always (to a European, at least) bigger than life.

The young Cooke suddenly caught sight of something totally unexpected. 'Suspended high off to the left was a huge scarlet neon sign, gasping on and off like an expiring dragon. It said, "NATIONAL BISCUIT COMPANY". We stammered our protests to the New Yorker and he put his head on one side and said, "Yeah, I know, but stick to cookies just the same." ' And the moral of this tale? 'It was my first warning that English and American differences were not merely gross – my first suspicion that the American language, like any other, was subtle and perilous to the stranger. You learn the idioms and the rules and then you have to learn where they don't apply.'

Those conclusions were for later. As Cooke and his fellow-students decamped from the *Laconia* and set foot on American soil for the first time, they were plunged into a turmoil of impressions: the subway, 'smelly and full of naked girders, like a London tube in the second week of construction'; the view from the top of the Empire State Building, with 'the endless honeycomb of buildings miles below'; the 'new and breathless span' of the George Washington Bridge, itself completed just twelve months earlier.

The real shock, however, was the abject human misery spawned by the Great Depression. 'In Times Square there was a curling queue of shabby men, lining up in the glimmer of a big electric ad for a Harold Lloyd picture. They were not, however, going to the movies. They were, like many another shambling line all the way from Harlem to The Battery, lining up for free bread and soup.' The shock was intensified by the ignorance of the newcomers. As the bellboy showed Cooke to his room on his first night in town, he asked politely, 'So you're from England. How're conditions there?' Even though his home country, too, had been plunged into the same economic mire, he had no idea: 'I was abysmally non-political.'

The contrasts were melodramatic. The elegant young Englishman with his well-cut suit and bulging wallet found his progress round the sights of New York haunted by a chorus with a monotonous refrain: 'Buddy, can you spare a dime?'

～

Before long, Cooke was on his way to Yale, an island of upper-class excellence largely insulated from these dismal realities and the place he came to call his American Alma Mater. Unknowingly, as he travelled north from New York, he began that mental process of comparison and contrast between the old world and the new – and between his preconceptions and the reality of what he saw – which would become his stock-in-trade, the very stuff of his journalistic career, aided by a phenomenal memory for detail. He watched the scenery of New England in the fall roll by, wondered at the preponderance of wooden-built houses – such minutiae would one day inform and colour countless broadcasts and articles.

At the station in New Haven, Connecticut he summoned a taxi and asked for 'Harkness', which turned out to be the name of his hall of residence. Room 953 was a revelation. It had wood panelling, a bed, a desk and bookshelves inlaid into the wall. There was no ceiling light, but a series of lamps – and a bewildering number of doors. A Baltimore man from the floor above showed him round, demonstrating with some amusement the wonders of the walk-in wardrobe complete with rods and suit hangers and a sloping rack for shoes. And as for the bathroom . . . 'It glimmered, to my naïve European eyes, like a jet-bomber: tiled floors and walls, enclosed radiator (goodness, a warm bathroom!) – all this was my very own, quite a change from the communal bathhouse I had been used to on shivery winter mornings at Cambridge.'

He ventured out onto the campus with its restful green lawns and wide-open spaces. 'A London tailor had fortified me against what he told me was the Arctic American winter by selling me a coat that looked like something that might be worn by the foreman of a retired railroad gang in Siberia. It was lamb or sheep or some brown woolly monster, it came down to my ankles and added about fifty pounds to my appearance.' Two little shoeshine boys sitting on a wall saw this spectacle and yelled, 'Get that coat!' Cooke, aware from films of the omnipresent gangster threat, took to his heels. It was a while before he discovered that 'Get that coat!' was simply a way of expressing surprise.

The same coat, and the furled umbrella that went with it, caused some hilarity among the students, too. Misinformed by British movies, they saw him as the quintessential toff, to be greeted with such stage-English salutations as 'Top of the morning, old top', or 'By Jove, what?'. He tried to plead his humble upbringing and to protest that he knew nothing of grouse shooting or drilling a platoon – to no avail; the stereotypes were deeply ingrained.

It was all good-natured enough. Younger men like Jerome Hartz, his neighbour from Baltimore, did their best to make him feel at home. Their first meeting was ingrained in Hartz's memory:'I heard someone playing a piano in another room. He was playing very good jazz,' he told a newspaper reporter forty years later, 'and then started playing something by Poulenc. I thought to myself, anyone with musical tastes as diverse as that might be an interesting person to know. So I went to his room. It was bare except for the essentials: bed, desk – and this piano which he had moved in.' The two struck up an easy accord.

Despite the friendliness of the natives, Yale delivered one early disappointment. Cooke had sold himself to the Commonwealth Fund as a serious student of the history of dramatic criticism, but that was only part of the story. He also planned to immerse himself in the University drama scene, carrying his triumphs with the Cambridge Mummers to a new audience. It soon became clear that opportunities to direct plays would be strictly limited, probably until the end of his two-year tenure. To make matters worse, he rapidly concluded that the Dean of Studies in the School of Drama was a 'bonehead'. This was a serious blow. None the less, as a twenty-three-year-old with a world-weary, Cowardesque air and an impressive catalogue of con-tacts in theatre and films, he had no trouble in building up a circle of younger friends and admirers. He moved seamlessly into a student society that knew a kindred spirit when it saw one.

One of the first and firmest of friends was Eugene Rostow, who –

like his younger brother Walt – was to hold a number of US Government posts from the 1940s onwards. Gene Rostow was reading history and was part of Yale's intellectual élite – the sort of people who didn't have much time for the noisy camaraderie of the fraternity houses or sports teams. These literary and Bohemian types used to gather at the Elizabethan Club, an Anglophone establishment with a fine collection of first folios and a reputation for serving a rather good afternoon tea. Cooke felt at home, although his first experience of the string and paper contraption known as a tea-bag (invented in San Francisco in 1919) sent him and his English friends into gales of condescending laughter.

There may have been no stage to strut, but he soon became a regular contributor to the Yale magazine, the *Harkness Hoot*. The name was an irreverent reference to the university's main benefactor, the same Harkness whose Commonwealth Fund was subsidising Cooke's decadent lifestyle. Despite the flippant title, the *Hoot* was a slick and well-produced monthly, carrying serious student writing on culture and politics along with some original literary pieces. One item in the December issue is a poem by the future film-ghoul, Vincent Price, whom Cooke remembers as 'a very large, fat and amiable boy, good-natured and rather lazy, who was rich enough not to have to do much work.'

His own first contribution to the *Hoot* came in February 1933 – a review of Coward's *Design For Living*, which had just arrived in New York. And he was also trying his hand at poetry. 'A Close Prospect of War' was a tribute to the 'powerful obscurity' of writers such as William Empson, while 'Hitler' was even more elaborate and obscure. A sub-heading quoted one of the Führer's Munich speeches: 'There is too much education. Henceforth we must have instinct – instinct and hatred.' There follows a twenty-seven-line piece of blank verse, opening with an extended metaphor of larks rising from under the feet of the poet and ending with this peroration:

> [For] when a similar onset of unwavering blunderers
> Shall shock you to forced wheeling,
> Drunken appropriations of crest and sword,
> Not humour then but gravity
> Will straight prescribe your course.

William Empson would have been proud of it.

As a demonstration of the *Hoot*'s radical pretensions, 'Hitler' was placed strategically next to an article by a German student, Friedrich Franz von Papen II, denouncing the Treaty of Versailles, explaining the malign and overweening influence of the Jews and expressing Germany's desire for peace and friendly relations with all other countries. Gene Rostow, acknowledging the risk he was running in printing such a piece, added an editorial note that much might be learned from this apologia for Nazism about its true nature and purpose.

Rostow, as committed as Cooke was unconcerned, was always ready to stick his neck out. Throughout the autumn of 1932 he wrote fervently about the forthcoming presidential elections and recommended his readers to vote not for Roosevelt ('disarmingly glib'), but for the Socialist leader Norman Thomas, whose manifesto called for such Communist remedies as central economic planning and nationalisation of the banks.

Despite living in this atmosphere of political ferment, Cooke's interest was still not seriously engaged. Rostow has no recollection of his taking part in their discussions, nor any sense of which party he might have supported.

Cooke acknowledged (in *Six Men*) that it was, for him, a period of political and literary innocence. At every opportunity he would race down to New York to see the latest plays, taking advantage of a free rail pass thoughtfully provided by the Fund: he courted the writers who came to the University, like Thornton Wilder, and he soon became a popular figure, known for his cartoons and impromptu piano sessions in the evening.

With Prohibition still in force, there was no alcohol to lubricate these affairs, but Cooke was soon initiated into the mysteries of the student distillery: 'They thought I ought to learn as soon as possible how to make my own gin, since the stuff that was smuggled to you by the campus bootleggers was expensive and sometimes made you blind.' For Cooke, the idea of such lawlessness was horrifying – what would his mother have said? – but there were young men to impress, and girls to meet if all went well. 'So I took my first step along the primrose-path of a gin-maker.'

The ingredients were simple enough: distilled water, juniper drops from the chemist, and some grain alcohol – although this was only available through a bootlegger. Slosh the whole lot together in a bath, and you were ready for the fray. 'Whether imprisoned in a bottle, or at liberty on the berries of juniper trees in the Nevada desert, it takes me back with great speed, clarity and nostalgia to my first days at Yale.'

The female company was not immediately available, of course, in these single-sex establishments but arrived in hordes, to widespread rejoicing, to watch the big sporting events. Cooke, looking back, regretted the loss of such innocent pleasures and rued the advent of such liberal ideas as 'married student quarters'. 'In those days,' he wrote, picking his words carefully,

> girls were a periodic luxury. The idea was that you went to college – if you were lucky – and spent half your time studying, the other half playing games, joining societies, and just generally mooching around with your buddies. During the holidays you enjoyed, (and because they were scarce in college, all the more), such things as movies, girls, reading novels, going to parties. At that time, the sight of an undergraduate walking along the street clutching the hand of his girl-friend would have been as odd and hilarious as the sight of the football captain with his hair done up in curlers.

By the time he reached Yale, of course, he himself was the proud possessor not just of a girl-friend, but a fiancée. Several of the under-graduates, too, had long-term liaisons at neighbouring women's colleges, even if they didn't flaunt them in public. Smith College, a mere ninety minutes away by road at Northampton, Massachusetts, was particularly popular, and easily accessible to the richer young men with fast cars.

Gene Rostow introduced Cooke to his fiancée, Edna, a student at Smith who became a close friend in her own right. So stern were the social conventions that Gene and Edna took the considerable risk of marrying in secret before Gene disappeared to Cambridge on a reverse transatlantic fellowship in September 1933. If they'd been found out, Edna would have been thrown out of college and her husband would have lost his Fellowship. They took the risk because they were terrified that their relationship might not survive a year's separation: Edna in particular was being pursued by unwelcome suitors and wanted a reliable way of fending them off. She had, after all, evidence of the risks before her eyes.

～

Cooke's relationship with Hetty Riddle had, from the start, been impetuous: their one-month courtship – setting up home together in defiance of the usual niceties – the dramatic farewell on the eve of his departure. He'd known her, in all, for less than nine months. As they stood on the Liverpool quayside, they'd vowed to write constantly. The transatlantic postal service was extremely reliable. A young lover simply marked a letter 'via *Majestic*, departing New York 5 November', and five days later the letter arrived. Through October and November, Alistair and Hetty bombarded each other with messages of love and reassurance.

Then, without warning, Hetty's letters dried up. A week passed, then another. Cooke's missives became increasingly anxious. What was going on? Had something happened? The silence grew longer and more deafening. He began to be haunted by the fear that he'd lost her. At Christmas he travelled north to Toronto to spend the holiday with his aunt Ada, his mother's sister, but nothing could distract him from the disorientating experience of being so inexplicably let down. He was lonely, far away and helpless. He longed to be able to play for her the song they'd heard on their last night together, 'Mad About the Girl', which he'd been practising ever since.

All through January he waited, unable to concentrate on anything. Finally, he cracked. He sent a cable to Hetty demanding an explanation and shortly afterwards it came – in the most unwelcome form. Cooke called it a 'Dear Alistair' letter and it calmly informed him that she was breaking off their engagement.

That would have been bad enough, but Hetty had a further humiliation to deliver. She offered as consolation her view that it was all for the best, because they'd 'never been very good together, anyway'. This was something of a shock for Cooke, who had floated through the whole brief relationship in a haze of happiness and excitement. He rushed to the cable office again and fired off a last, desperate plea: 'DON'T DO ANYTHING STOP I'LL GIVE UP FELLOWSHIP STOP READY TO SAIL FOR LONDON STOP LET'S MARRY SOONEST STOP'

Back at Yale, he wandered disconsolately among his friends, waiting for a reply. Jerry Hartz from the rooms above did his best to help, but the delay was agonising.

At last the cable from London arrived. Cooke ripped it open, expecting the worst. He was right. Hetty's reply was simple: 'No, stay in America and make good.' Rejection and condescension in one unpalatable gobbet.

Hartz took a firm line. 'The best way to deal with this', he told Cooke, 'is to wash your hands of her. Good riddance, I reckon.' His friend's misery turned to fury. What right had this nineteen-year-old girl to treat him like a wayward child? It didn't take much imagination to realise what had happened and a letter duly followed, admitting that Hetty had found another man.

The blow to Cooke's self-esteem was acutely painful and probably reinforced an unwillingness to express emotions which he'd learned at his mother's knee. The experience left deep scars, too. Hetty's apparent betrayal continued to pain him long after the conscious memory of the affair had subsided. Cooke took a Freudian view of such traumatic experiences: being jilted, he came to believe, can be rationalised away by the intellect, but without touching the source of the pain. He felt himself permanently damaged by the sense of not being quite good enough: perhaps, subconsciously, this fell into the same category as the disapproval of his Cambridge tutors – a punishment for not being out of the top social drawer.

True relief had to wait more than half a century in a curious sequel to the saga of Henrietta Riddle. Cooke was watching television one day, when he saw the name of Anthony Ainley slide past in a list of credits. It suddenly occurred to him that this was surely another of the old rogue Henry Ainley's impressive brood. Tentatively, he wrote to inquire whether Anthony might be related to Hetty and discovered that she was indeed a half-sister – with a different mother. But the reply went much further. Ainley said that Hetty had often spoken of her former fiancé 'with great warmth and pride'.

Cooke felt as if a great weight had been lifted from him. All those years he'd suffered from a private fear of failure and suddenly he'd been purged of the repressed anxiety of being rejected again. He wrote back to Ainley, thanking him for the emotional service that he had unwittingly supplied. Such stories, of course, are never quite so simple. Other members of Hetty's family later offered an alternative explanation for her abandonment of Cooke – not the rival attractions of a new lover, but a creeping realisation that she could not cope with his possessiveness.

~

The spring of 1933 was haunted by Hetty – his sense of loss helping to keep him in continued ignorance of the world about him. If he picked up the *New York Times*, it was only to catch up on the latest Broadway reviews; he didn't listen to the radio because he regarded it as little more than audio advertising. There was a brief – and painful – distraction in February when he was diagnosed with a grumbling appendix. It was removed at the expense of the Commonwealth Fund. And three weeks later, taking further advantage of his sponsors' munificence, he had his tonsils out, too.

It took the extraordinary events of 4 March, the day of Roosevelt's inauguration, to impinge, finally, on his consciousness of the wider world. Cooke had arranged to act as guide to an English girl arriving in New York on her first visit. She was an acquaintance rather than a friend, a grand-daughter of Sir Johnston Forbes-Robertson, patriarch of another great stage family. At least this duty provided a distraction from his woes. On the Saturday morning in question he took the familiar train trip, and met up with his guest as she disembarked.

As a veteran New York visitor of almost six months' standing, he probably relished the idea of showing off his easy familiarity with the city. But there was one small chore before he could begin the tour. With the girl in tow, he strode confidently up to the desk at the Tudor Hotel on 42nd Street where he always stayed and knew he'd be recognised. The clerk watched with a sullen air as this elegant young man, in his natty Harkness Fund suit, leaned against the desk and wrote out a cheque for $30.

'What', said the clerk, 'is this?'

'Why, is there something wrong?'

'I'll say there's something wrong, sonny. I can't cash this.'

In his best imitation of a Noël Coward hero, Cooke replied sarcastically, 'D'you know if there's a bank somewhere in the United States that might have the kindness to cash this cheque?'

'No,' said the clerk. 'Go and read the papers, my friend.'

Clutching his failing credibility around him, he led the girl out into the street. There on a newspaper billboard was the awful truth: 'ROOSEVELT TO BE INAUGURATED AT NOON – DECLARES MORATORIUM ON ALL BANKS'. And then another, more starkly: 'NO MONEY FOLKS!'.

While FDR in Washington was issuing his great rallying cry to the American people – 'The only thing we have to fear is fear itself' –

Alistair Cooke was scratching his head on 42nd Street in New York wondering how to extricate himself from the fall-out of the President's first executive action. 4 March 1933 had been declared a national banking holiday, allowing Congress to rush through emergency legislation to stem the torrent of withdrawals, which threatened the country's financial system with collapse. Cooke wasn't much interested in the intricacies of this bold and controversial plan. He needed funds and he needed them without delay.

He raced to the station and headed back to Yale to hunt out his friends. Most were away, but he finally caught up with Gene Rostow. Rostow had no spare cash, but as Cooke bemoaned his fate, his friend had a brainwave. 'Wait a minute! You are *an* editor of the *Hoot*, and I am *the* editor!' It was a defining moment, as he went on to explain in his Yale lecture.

'Rostow gave me a merry look and said the sentence that turned me from a theatre director into a foreign correspondent. "Do you know," he said, "what a due bill is?" I didn't but I soon learned.'

At this time of financial crisis, it was customary for advertisers in the student magazine to settle their bills not in cash, but in promissory notes, which could be used to claim payment in kind – due bills. And one of the outstanding bills was from the St Regis Hotel – in return for its advertisement:

Dancin' with Anson

THE SEAGLADE

Have you danced to Anson
Weeks' music yet? Better
reserve a table now before
somebody really important
asks you that again. Special
dinner $3 . . . supper $1.50

Ask about us at the St Regis College Club

HOTEL
ST REGIS

5th Ave at E 55th
New York

Armed with $100 of credit, Cooke set off for the city again. 'We must have been the only new guests that day, and the reservations clerk was suspicious enough to call the manager. A dapper, grey-haired man appeared and looked in amused contempt at these two innocents. "Can I help you?" he asked with the tone of a cop turning his light on a burglar. I said we should like two nice rooms on the top floor. He reeled, but only for a moment.' The due bill transformed the scene: at $8 a night, Cooke and his guest were rich in a land of the suddenly poor. The city lay at their feet.

He already had tickets in advance for the first night of *Strike Me Pink*, a musical starring Jimmy 'Schnozzle' Durante. It had evidently been adapted to reflect the national crisis. The chorus girls leaped to the front of the stage and tapped out a routine, chanting in unison. 'We depend on *Roo*sevelt, We depend on *Him!*' The audience, in white tie, tails and evening gowns, cheered their delight. It was the start of a long night for Cooke, who must have been grateful for the chance to banish for a while the pervasive gloom of Hetty's loss. 'We danced all night. We dispensed carefree – 25 cent – tips,' he remembered with glee. Even cab drivers broke the habit of a lifetime and accepted cheques from cashless customers. 'I spent the next three months going through the cheques in my depleted bank account and came on the reckoning – by way of taxi rides, a nightclub supper, a ride through Central Park, the whole mad whirl. "Antonio Colucci, 65 cents"; "Connie's Inn, $1.95", and so on.'

It took him ages to pay off his debt to the *Harkness Hoot*, but it was worth it.

~

One of the less onerous obligations of the Commonwealth Fund was Item VI: 'A fellow is required to travel for three months within the United States at the end of the first academic year.' After submitting a plan 'in connection with his work, to visit, for example, libraries, laboratories or universities,' he would be given advice, letters of introduction, and 'sufficient allowance for comfortable travel.'

In the introduction to his book *Alistair Cooke's America*, he wrote, 'It was more of an outrageous luxury than an obligation, at a time when bankrupt stockbrokers were pulling their sons out of Yale, and this first safari through America, in the midst of Roosevelt's Hundred Days, shook me out of my deep ignorance of politics.'

At the time, Cooke interpreted his instructions in liberal fashion. He would buy a car and simply travel to places that interested him, before winding up in Hollywood. Not many libraries or laboratories featured on his itinerary. He wanted to see real life, American-style. His masterstroke was to dream up a way of making the trip doubly worthwhile. Throughout his Yale year he had been filing occasional reviews for London papers and magazines, including the *Observer*. In the spring of 1933 he wrote to that paper's editor, J.L. Garvin, offering a series of interviews with Hollywood's finest: simultaneously, he contacted a number of leading figures in the film business, explaining that he'd been commissioned to write a series for the *Observer*. The bluff worked. Garvin told him that his regular film critic, Miss C.A. Lejeune, was intending to take a long summer break and the interviews would fill the gap nicely. And Hollywood took the bait, too. It was quite a line-up. The most famous British resident, (Sir) C. Aubrey Smith, the director Ernst Lubitsch, a leading cameraman, Lee Garmes and the biggest name of all – Charlie Chaplin. All agreed to see him during July and August.

That was after the grand tour. One of Cooke's friends from the Fund was a Scot named Alexander (Sandy) Honeyman, a student of Biblical languages. He was doing a Ph.D. at the University of Chicago and Cooke planned to fly out from New York to meet him. First he called at the Kodak shop on Fifth Avenue to buy an 8mm camera. The assistant showed him a $22.50 model and invited him to take it onto the street to see how it felt. 'He told me to shoot whatever I saw. A cab was pulling up, so I panned round and through the view-finder I saw a lady step out, wearing a comic hat. As I lowered the camera I realised I was actually filming Eleanor Roosevelt. The only time I'd ever seen her before was at the newsreel cinema, with the homeless or down a coal mine.' Unfortunately, his unique footage came out as an impenetrable blur.

The trip to Chicago – his first experience of air travel and his last for many years – took five bone-shuddering hours. Once safely landed, he and Sandy bought themselves a second-hand Model A Ford for the modest sum of $60 and set off, on Monday 19 June, in a roughly westerly direction, after acquiring a tent from Sears and Roebuck. This was unfurled for their first night on the road in Wisconsin; then they discovered how cheap it was to stay in newfangled motorcabins and the tent was never troubled again.

The journey which followed was the first of more than a dozen such odysseys that Cooke undertook over the next two decades. With a variety of companions he criss-crossed the country, from familiar beauty spots to rural backwaters, from smart city clubs to the seediest of small towns, collecting all the while impressions and characters to be stored away for future use. Few Americans can ever have known their own country as intimately as Cooke came to know it.

He and Sandy Honeyman drove through Minnesota and the Dakotas, down to Nebraska and then, via Wyoming – taking in Yellowstone National Park – and Montana, they crossed into Canada under the impression that it was the only way to see the Rocky Mountains properly. On the way south again, there was a change of personnel. At the Glacier National Park, on the Washington-Montana border, they met up with another English graduate, Charles Spencer, researching into education in Chicago. Cooke and Spencer continued west towards Seattle and the state of Oregon, while Honeyman made his own way south – to join Cooke again later, in San Francisco.

In retrospect Cooke offered this assessment:

> The trip was an absolute eye-opener. First there was the discovery of a land and a people infinitely more varied than anything I had imagined or been taught by the British newspaper stereotypes. But 1933 was also the first year that the American people were beginning to crawl out of the pit of the Great Depression. To see what the depression had done to them, and how Roosevelt was rousing them very slowly but positively to assert their old vitality: all this was far more dramatic, and moving, and – to be cold-blooded about it – more sheerly interesting than anything that was happening on Broadway. I did not realise for another year or two that that trip, and the undimmed memory of it, were to mark the twilight of my life in the theatre and the dawn of the idea that a foreign correspondent's was a better trade for me.

Oddly, the most memorable part of the trip wasn't in the United States at all, but across the border in Mexico. Cooke and Honeyman found themselves in Tijuana, an undistinguished, dusty little town at that time, with dirt roads and one passable hotel, the America. At the bar they were offered a concoction described as a 'Frisco Punch' and Sandy had several: he was still drinking when Cooke retired to bed.

The next morning Cooke was woken by a tentative knock at the door. A small boy thrust a grubby piece of paper into his hand. On the reverse of a handbill for a bullfight was a scrawled message: 'Come and get me! I'm in prison!' Cooke dressed hurriedly and followed the boy to the local jail. There he found his friend languishing on the floor of a cell with six Mexican miscreants. 'With his reddish-gold hair and unshaven chin he looked as though he'd been dipped in breadcrumbs,' Cooke remembers. 'I handed over the appropriate fine and they brought him out.' The fifty dollars which had been in Honeyman's pocket the night before had disappeared, but he was otherwise undamaged. 'I asked him what he'd been up to, and he told me he'd been charged with disturbing the peace: they'd found him walking up and down the street swearing in Yiddish.'

That wasn't the end of this unlikely day. As they wandered back to the hotel, Cooke noticed that what he'd thought was an advertisement for a bullfight was in fact promoting a performance of *Carmen* in which (in the rudimentary Spanish of his memory) the audience was promised '*un toro positavamente a muerte*'. Could it seriously mean that a real bull would be slaughtered in the course of an operatic entertainment? It did.

One other encounter remained in Cooke's mind from this visit across the Mexican border. They strolled past a smart club, the Embassy, offering 'Lunch and Cabaret'. Neither had ever dreamed of attending a cabaret in the daytime and decidedly never on a Sunday. 'We sat in this rather charming place with a dance-floor, and eventually the MC announces: "Will you please welcome – Los Cansinos!" This stunning-looking creature came out and danced with a much older man, right in front of us.' The girl's face stuck in his mind, so much so that he felt sure he recognised her later in the features of a famous film actress of the 1940s and 1950s.

It was a full thirty-two years before Cooke was able to confirm face to face what he'd always suspected. The girl on the stage of the Embassy Club on that August day in 1933 was Margarita Carmen Cansino, then just fifteen years old and dancing with her father – and somewhat better known by her adopted name, Rita Hayworth.

Hollywood marked the parting of the ways with Sandy Honeyman. While his friend drove home towards a rather more sober career as Professor of Hebrew at St Andrews University, Cooke stayed on the West Coast – and within a month he had been befriended by the most famous man in the world.

7

PANACEAS

The movie industry was barely twenty years old, but that had been long enough to transform Hollywood into a place of legend. The stars who had populated Cooke's childhood were all here, lodged in palatial splendour in the hills above the city; along Sunset Boulevard lay the film lots whose magical transformations had captivated him at the Langworthy Picturedrome. Here, too, were the great directors and cameramen whose work Cooke had studied so earnestly at Cambridge, and the moguls whose millions made the system tick.

Into this fantastic world, Cooke – not yet twenty-five – stepped with astonishing assurance. He was a stranger. He knew no one. All he possessed were the letters of acceptance from his prospective interviewees. There was no guarantee that the stars would honour their commitments: the place was seething with hopeful hangers-on trying to break through the cordon protecting the dream factory from the real world. Yet Cooke affected blithe unconcern for the boldness of the enterprise, as he trundled up the Boulevard in his battered Model A. That, at least, is the impression left by the finished articles, mostly in the form of extended conversations, which appeared in the *Observer* a few weeks later. Here was a man prepared to quibble, debate and, where necessary, to disagree with the rich and famous, always ready to express his own point of view or demonstrate his own prejudices.

There is a strong element of journalistic bravado here, not to mention a tendency to pretentiousness. Cooke's true feelings were more mundane. As he planned his grand tour, he had marked down two places in California of special interest, one inspired by a popular song – 'Home in Pasadena,/ There where the grass is greener,/ I wanna go,/ Where humming bees,/ Sing melodies.' It turned out to be an uninspiring suburb of Los Angeles, where the grass was burned browner than desert sand.

Hollywood was the other target, partly because of the *Observer* project, but also because (as he put it in a 1969 *Letter from America*) 'in the minds of even the most intelligent and high-minded people, Hollywood was a free foretaste of the more attractive aspects of Babylon'. Having spent much of the previous month in 'the evergreen forests of Western Canada, the State of Washington and Oregon', California in general, and Hollywood in particular, beckoned enticingly. Never mind the pursuit of journalism:

> when I came under cross-examination from the prosecuting attorney I should have to say simply that I was wildly in love with Loretta Young. I had one secret and raging ambition – to meet Miss Young, preferably on the set, amid the lakes and cages and pepper trees of her latest movie, which is a forgotten opus called *Zoo in Budapest*. Sure enough I wangled my way into the studio. I padded my way around the carefully contrived zoo. And I was even taken out to lunch by the cameraman, who had just won the Oscar for his work on the movie.

But, to his deep disappointment, not a glamorous actress in sight.

There is only the barest hint of all this in the finished interview with the cameraman concerned, Lee Garmes. 'The "fan" magazines', he writes, 'may ask their public to remember *Zoo in Budapest* for Miss Loretta Young. But the industry remembers it for a man who has been behind a camera for seventeen years . . .' There is not a hint of raging ambition or hopeless desire, indeed there is remarkably little colour in any of the seven *Observer* articles which appeared, through September and October, under the generic title 'Hollywood Prospect'. Cooke was determined to use the opportunity to crystallise his own views of the cinema as a developing art-form and, for a serious readership anyway, starlets were not the point.

The tone throughout the interviews is one of easy familiarity with the genre and its masters. It must, in reality, have been nerve-racking, not least because Hollywood was in the midst of a strike of stagecrews and the studios were in turmoil. The meeting with Ernst Lubitsch, for instance, took place on the set of *Design for Living* where Cooke overheard an assistant director warning one of the temporary stagehands drafted in to cover for the strikers that he'd better learn the studio's signalling system by the following day. While the great German director, cigar clenched between his teeth, brought the interview to an abrupt end when the next scene was ready – a scene requiring sixteen takes of the actress Miriam Hopkins slamming an office door and pressing an elevator button.

The final article ('Whither the Movies? – Survey and Estimate') concludes that Hollywood had fallen prey to a damaging tyranny: 'It's a tyranny of the story-conference, of the mundane hierarchy of the producer (the man with the money), associate-producers (the men with not quite so much money), and "supervisors" (the men with an unflattering sense of "what the public likes") over the men who make the films.' In other words, crass commercialism, blind to the real potential of the movies and uninterested in developments outside California.

Only one man is exempted from this critique: Charles Chaplin.

∼

Chaplin, according to Cooke's plan, was just one more *Observer* profile – though admittedly the most exciting of the Hollywood prospects. The arrangement was for a morning meeting at the Chaplin studio but that formal interview was just the start, as Cooke described in his book of autobiographical sketches entitled *Six Men*.

> On a still and brilliant midsummer morning in 1933 I sat on the deck of a yacht, anchored twenty-odd miles south-west of Los Angeles harbour, looking across the shimmering water to the small mountainous island called Catalina. There were five of us on board. Chaplin, then forty-four. Paulette Goddard, an enchanting twenty-two-year-old brunette, as trim and shiny as a trout, whom Chaplin had known for little more than a year. Andy, the skipper, (a former Keystone Cop) was a gnarled, good-natured man of few words. And Freddy a Japanese cook. And there was I, a lean, black-haired twenty-four-year-old Englishman on a fellowship at Yale.

After a little while, sitting alone and smelling the bacon odours drifting up from the galley, he felt like 'a fortunate nobody immersed in a glow of vanity wondering how I got there.'

The answer to that rhetorical question was both simple and improbable. Chaplin, who had suffered terribly at the hands of the press, seems to have found Cooke, the journalist, an unthreatening adjunct to his circle – attractive and respectful, yet thoughtful and knowledgeable about his business. An amanuensis in the making, in fact.

Approaching the Chaplin studios a few days earlier, Cooke had at least admitted to some nervous anticipation as he drove up and down, gathering his courage. He was met by one of Chaplin's old retainers, and taken into an unlikely office: 'It had worn oilcloth on the floor and if it was ever wall-papered, the paper had rotted in the fungi of mildew. There was one small window, three straight-back chairs, an old table, about half a dozen books with peeling spines, and an ancient upright piano hideously out of tune.' After a few minutes Cooke was led into the Little Man's presence.

> You expect a small man to have a small hand, but it was not until you doubted for a moment whether it was flesh you were holding or some ivory knick-knack, that you looked up at its chuckling owner and said to yourself, he certainly is a tiny man. His feet were in scale, peeking out like mice from high-held trousers. Above the trousers was a white angora sweater, and above that a tanned face, small ears set behind the cheek bones, grey eyes of dancing mobility, and above them a monumental forehead and hair piled like a melting snowball.

The interview went well. It touched on some of Cooke's obsessions of the moment: and Chaplin confided that, although he was intrigued by the talkies, he would not be giving a voice to 'Charlie', the hero of so many silent films. 'Who is to write my dialogue if I allow that little man to talk? I'm not sadly rejecting a desirable novelty. I don't want it. I like, I enjoy, the limitation of the non-talking film.'

The conversation was in full flight when lunch-time came: Chaplin swept him off to a restaurant and thereafter back to his home in Beverly Hills. Cooke was introduced to 'my friend, Miss Goddard' and the interview continued by the side of a swimming pool, empty because of an outbreak of polio. He left eventually at sundown, promising to return for dinner the following day.

He did secure one critical scoop for the paper: Chaplin's confession that he'd made a terrible mistake in the final scene of the celebrated 1931 film, *City Lights*. In the story 'Charlie' the tramp falls in love with a blind flowerseller. He manages to raise enough money for an eye operation, but she never discovers the identity of her benefactor. The film ends with Charlie peering through a flower shop window at his lost love. Chaplin told Cooke that, instead of playing the scene as a simple, blank and puzzled figure, as he'd intended, he'd succumbed to the temptation to play up the tragedy and to invest Charlie with profound feelings of despair. 'It was really immoral,' he explained. 'It was bad, bad and cheating.'

Certainly that first day of their acquaintance demonstrates a remarkable level of trust on the part of a man who had more or less cut himself off from the press. Having exacted an oath of secrecy from Cooke, Chaplin even revealed the details of his next film, playing out the characters on the lawn around the pool. Cooke informed the readers of the *Observer*, tantalisingly, that the subject matter would have to remain a secret. He could only say that he expected it would be 'as palpably funny as anything Chaplin has done'.

For the time being this film had no title and Cooke was one of those drafted in to search for inspiration. His suggestion was 'Commonwealth' – the word, no doubt, being on his mind. It appealed to Chaplin momentarily, but was then dropped in favour of the final choice, *Modern Times*, in which the tramp faces the perils of factory machinery, poverty, starvation and the Depression. This more serious approach was very much in tune with Cooke's own predilections. From a series of meetings with Chaplin over the next few days, he had no trouble eliciting the material for a second *Observer* article in which he was bold enough to wonder whether the Little Man might be in danger of tipping over into sentimentality – becoming, as he put it, 'Everybody's Little Ray of Sunshine'. Chaplin admitted to sharing the concern. 'Nobody's told me. But it's a spook that's haunted me for two years.' Perhaps, weary of acolytes and simpering admirers, he found it refreshing to hear the truth, however tentatively advanced. He said frankly that the familiar clown with his bowler hat, moustache and walking-stick might be pensioned off after two or three more outings.

A few days later came the invitation to spend a weekend aboard the yacht, *Panacea*, and Cooke crossed the boundary between casual contact and friend. In *Six Men* he writes of Chaplin opening himself up in the most natural and revealing way. 'The impression I picked up then . . . was that when Chaplin took to anyone he was wide open from the start, spontaneous, generous, gabby, confidential, as if taking up again where he had left off with a favourite, long-lost brother.' Cooke was being 'collected', rather as he himself liked to gather chance friendships along the way. It was a flattering experience, but also comforting for a young man so far from home.

So they bathed and lounged on the deck of the *Panacea* together: Chaplin performed charming dumb-plays for him, once appearing silently with a napkin over his forearm in the frozen pose of a butler indicating that a meal was served as Cooke deployed his new 8mm camera. 'With his extended thumbs touching and his palms at the parallel Chaplin would fix the frame for me and retreat to mime a range of characters he picked up from the only newspaper we had brought aboard' from the actress Jean Harlow to the Prince of Wales. This unique footage – to Cooke's distress – was lost after an extract had been used in the making of the *America* television series.

There was one story that Cooke did not include in his published portrait: it concerned Hetty. Not unnaturally in this relaxed and unreal environment, he unburdened himself of the story of his lost love. Chaplin proved to be a sympathetic listener and, when the tale of Hetty was done, he looked at Cooke and said, 'Don't go back!' The vehemence of this injunction surprised Cooke, but Chaplin proceeded to tell him about his own Hetty, whom he'd known and loved when he was a young man. And then, he said, he'd made the mistake of going back – only to find that a divine and adorable creature had turned into an ordinary, and rather stupid, woman. That's what Cooke needed to hear from a man of Chaplin's experience.

One morning, when 'Miss Goddard' was still in bed, Chaplin took him ashore in a dinghy and thence for a two-hour stroll. It must have been a diverting sight: Chaplin, scarcely five-feet tall; Cooke, a lanky six-footer, trailing in his wake; and all the time, Chaplin talking, as if to some latter-day Boswell, about his life, philosophy and politics. In this last area, the acutely apolitical Cooke was struggling. Chaplin presented himself as a radical and a socialist, unaffected by the time he spent with princes and socialites. He attacked Ramsay MacDonald for forming a National Government and thus betraying his Labour roots. He had strong views about budget deficits and the gold standard, on which he expounded his half-baked theories while squeezing the sand between his toes.

Even an unusually dumbstruck Cooke detected that many of Chaplin's views were homespun and unsophisticated, little more than sentimental preferences for peace, humanity and 'the little man'. Tentatively, he ventured the evidence of the trip he'd just taken across America, and mentioned how he'd been roused by the impact of Roosevelt on a listless nation. It was the right thing to say. Chaplin enthused about FDR, and held up the New Deal as a useful half-way house on the way to 'true socialism' as exemplified by – Joseph Stalin. Cooke also noted that this fierce critic of capitalism was happy to boast about the way he'd shifted his money to safer markets just in time to miss the 1929 Wall Street crash.

All in all, over a period of several days, Cooke absorbed this stream of Chaplin consciousness – rambling stories about his childhood, anecdotes about the days he used to share digs with Stan Laurel on provincial tours, tedious sermons about the anachronism of hereditary monarchy in the twentieth century. He found him charming, alluring and sometimes unworldly.

After total immersion in the deep waters of such a dominant personality, it's not surprising that Cooke should have been favourably inclined. But even at this early stage he can be seen flexing his instinct for fairness – an observer always more ready to quarry out what was positive in a subject than to carp on about shortcomings; or where those shortcomings were too glaring to omit, to put them at least in comforting context.

When he was back in New York he wrote a card to his mother (via *Aquitania*) to apologise for failing to respond to her letters. Guilt haunts the lines: 'I was very angry you paid a doctor's bill. Pay *no more.* But I'll send you a cheque to cover the guinea in my letter. If you paid Eaden Lilley [the store] tell me *without fail* in your next letter.'

~

This was not the end of the Chaplin story, but for now Cooke had to return to the East Coast. After selling the car, he headed for the station, clasping the notes from his interviews and his Corona portable typewriter. One stop on the return trip proved particularly instructive. He broke his journey at Amarillo, Texas, checking into a hotel where he intended to spend a day working on his articles. He noticed – but paid no real attention to – the attractive young women lounging in the lobby and accepted the clerk's smirking suggestion of a room on the fourth floor. Even the offer of a bucket of ice (at 9 a.m.?) failed to rouse his suspicions and before long he was so absorbed in his work that the knock on his door scarcely distracted him.

The girl on the landing was doe-eyed and dramatically made-up. She sauntered in with a knowing smile, simpering through purple eye-liner, bounced on the bed, and noted with approval the ice-bucket awaiting its consignment of champagne. It was a B movie moment. 'Lonely?' she inquired, with rising inflection.

'Not particularly, ma'am,' replied the confused and blushing Cooke.

Panic began to claw at his soul and the girl was looking puzzled, too. She wandered over to the typewriter and caught sight of the title page of *Form and Content in the Cinema*. By now alarm messages were flickering across Cooke's brain: advice to Harkness students about the rampaging Buffalo Moth had been accompanied by other, more terrifying edicts. There was something called the Badger Game, when an angry 'husband' would burst in on a chance sexual encounter demanding money with menaces. And what about the Mann Act, whereby innocent males could be inveigled into taking girls across state borders, with the direst of consequences? Desperately he made his excuses and the girl departed. But Cooke was sure that he had already exposed himself to some unspecified threat. He left the hotel at high speed, and spent much of the day holed up in Amarillo's movie theatre. Late at night he crept back to his room and bolted the door. By 6.30 a.m. the next day he was on the first train out of town.

Before leaving Yale in June, Cooke had come to a decision: disenchanted by the drama studies he was supposed to be pursuing, he asked the Commonwealth Fund if he could switch to a graduate course being offered at Harvard – 'The History of the English Language in America', under the tutelage of Professor Miles L. Hanley, a noted linguistic scholar. The Fund accepted, and Cooke set off for his new university and a new obsession.

Hanley himself turned out to be a dogmatic and charmless man, but he was a demon when it came to tracking down the derivation of dialect and regional accent. The course was nothing to do with literature or written language, except where crude phonetic spelling in the records of colonial town meetings might offer clues to the way people spoke in the seventeenth century: it was pure linguistics, and apparently of minimal interest to the locals since Cooke was in a class of just three – one of whom was away doing field work much of the time, researching 'New England words for the poached egg'. There were, it came out, two of them and his fellow-student pin-pointed them with great accuracy on a map showing white circles in all the places that called it a poached egg and black circles where it was known as a dropped egg.

Cooke spread his own researches a little more widely. The linguistic particularities of American English had been a source of interest even before the Scoutmaster's impromptu lessons on board the *Laconia*. Cooke entered into the game with a will and began to listen out for, and record, examples of his own. Hanley was involved in the creation of a linguistic atlas (hence, doubtless, the poached egg research), but he also encouraged his new pupil to send off his findings to the other great etymological guru of the age – none other than the redoubtable H.L. Mencken.

Mencken as a political thinker was rapidly falling out of fashion. Throughout the Twenties he had been a popular radical, launching devastating attacks in his *Mercury* newspaper against what he called the 'booboisie' – the monied Establishment which ran the country. But he had done so not on behalf of the common man, but rather from what Cooke called 'the fortress of an older conservatism'. He decried democracy as being the mere impulse of envy. It was the subject of one of his favourite *bons mots*: 'Democracy is the theory that the common people know what they want, and deserve to get it good and hard.' Instead, in the words of Thomas Jefferson, he yearned for an 'aristocracy of talent and virtue'. The clinching argument against Mencken was that he despised the New Deal, loathed the aristocratic Roosevelt and was prepared to say so at length. He remained, according to Cooke, fixated by his old enemies: 'In the awful silence of unemployment and poverty, Mencken's salvoes against the prostrate bankers sounded gratuitous, against the genteelism of American writing irrelevant, against the chicanery of labour leaders, tasteless.'

If his political thinking had been overtaken by events, Mencken's academic reputation was intact. His monumental work *The American Language*, a unique study of the special characteristics of his mother tongue, was still evolving: two full volumes of supplementary material were in preparation and all contributions were gratefully received. Each time Cooke sent off a nugget of information to Baltimore, a polite acknowledgement duly followed. It emerged that he, and a correspondent in San Francisco, were competing to supply Mencken with different names for cuts of meat: English *sirloin* = American *porterhouse*; American *sirloin* = English *rump*; American *ribchops* = English *best end*.

The small blue notebook in which Cooke kept track of his discoveries became something of a legend among his new Harvard friends. Some thirty years later a Harvard contemporary dropped in to see him and although they hadn't met in the intervening period, the book was the first thing he mentioned. As they reminisced, they both recalled an hilarious discussion late one evening at an all-night cafeteria in Harvard Square. His friends started to debate the precise difference between 'haywire', 'flooey' and 'kaput' and when they were all agreed, Cooke inscribed the details in his precious book. He was well placed to deal with the final linguistics exam, with questions like: 'What peculiarities of your own pronunciation would be striking to an Englishman, a New Englander, a Middlewesterner, a Southerner?' or 'Describe briefly in tabular form the movement of the glottis, velum, tongue and lips in the utterance of the word "switching"' or again, 'From what part of the USA did the author of the following schoolboy howler come? "A haberdasher is one who washes out harbors."'

Life at Harvard proved highly congenial. It had a reputation for attracting blue-chip families whose sons had attended expensive prep schools, at a time when Yale, and other establishments, were casting their nets more widely to include the brightest high-school students. Young men at Harvard tended to be endowed with comfortable parental allowances and enjoyed luxurious accommodation. Breakfast was served from freshly starched tablecloths, for instance, by respectful young waitresses.

Cooke, as a temporary resident, took digs in Garden Street, Cambridge, and discovered this time a welcoming theatrical scene. The Harvard Dramatic Society latched on to him with enthusiasm and before long Cooke had established his own experimental group known as the 'Un-named Players': a public reading of W.H. Auden's *Paid on Both Sides* was followed by a performance of a Japanese Noh play; the climax of the season came with a modern-dress *Cymbeline*, transmogrified into a scandal among Rome's diplomatic corps. It included a cameo performance by Cooke, as the villain of the piece, playing Poulenc on stage. This travesty – Shakespeare à la Coward – is said to have caused the drama critic of the *Boston Evening Transcript* to suffer a fatal seizure. *Cymbeline* also brought him to the attention of one of Harvard's most venerable institutions, the Hasty Pudding Club.

The club, founded in 1770, was dedicated to a single elaborate production each spring, although its premises on Holyoake Street had an important social function, too. The Hasty Pudding's President in 1933 was a young science student, Francis Moore, whose ambition to follow a medical career was matched only by his enthusiasm for jazz and amateur dramatics. Moore had dreamed up the outline for his 1934 show: it would be a fantasy-revue based on the absurd notion of a co-educational Harvard. This unthinkable scenario would be given added savour because all the women's parts would, naturally, be played by men. He had managed to acquire a Broadway reject to train the troupe in its dance steps and he himself had written much of the music. What he lacked was an overall director for the enterprise. Cooke was the solution.

Cooke was four or five years older than most of the cast and he came (in student terms) with a wealth of experience. Moore's first impressions were of 'an elegant, highly educated, perceptive and artistic British gentleman'. He seemed more sophisticated than any of them, with the patina they associated with Cambridge – and none of that which might have conjured up a northern seaside town. Moore took his accent to be 'Mayfair and West End' and he was soon a regular part of the Hasty Pudding circle. The new director was in on the final decision to call the show *Hades, the Ladies* and by Christmas he was deeply involved in refining the script, casting and early rehearsals. 'It's a much more glorified [Cambridge] Footlights', he told Eddie Done, '. . . the snootiest Harvard club, very wealthy and pleasant.'

Another social commitment was to fulfil an undertaking he'd given to his Yale crony, Gene Rostow. Before leaving on a fellowship to study Economics at Kings College, Cambridge, Rostow asked Cooke to look after his illicit bride Edna, who was in her final year at Smith College. This task he carried out assiduously, with frequent visits and lunch outings. Edna remembers his attentions with gratitude: her marriage had been carried out by a justice of the peace doubling as the local butcher in a rural backwater of New York state, and the fear of discovery proved perpetually traumatic. Cooke was one of the few who shared the secret, and she found him far more attentive and sympathetic than the strongly male-bonded group of Gene's American friends. Cooke, in return, felt able to share his own unrelieved pain over the Hetty affair.

It was a pleasant period, a period for marking time. The winter months were enlivened by weekend skiing trips to New Hampshire, sometimes requiring a 150-mile round trip for just a day on the slopes. One outing coincided with a particularly vicious cold snap and, confined to his farmhouse lodgings, Cooke amused himself on an upright piano. There was no music to hand, simply a hymn book – words only. He flipped idly through the pages, and came across one hymn whose words sounded strangely like the chorus of a twelve-bar blues: 'In the midst of earthly pleasure,/ In the fight for earthly treasure,/ Mid your blessings without measure/ Have you forgotten God?' He began to sketch out a tune. 'You give welcome to the stranger,/ From the palace or the manger/ And the weak you seize from danger / – Have you forgotten God?'

'I remembered', he wrote later, 'how the Salvation Army used to put its own words to the latest song hits, on the principle that the devil had no right to all the best tunes. Applying this in reverse it occurred to me – maybe the churches shouldn't have all the best words?' The resulting song, complete with a whistled refrain, subsequently found its way into *Hades, the Ladies* and later still featured in Cooke's extremely brief career as a recording artist.

Yet it's clear that he was still brooding about Hetty. When he heard that Eddie Done was intending to get married, he sent him a warning message about the risks, jokey in tone, but deadly serious in intent. 'Well, what can I say? One thing fairly decisively . . . don't go to Siberia on a Frozen Fellowship for two years. Get used to, nay insist on, being away from her for days, odd weeks at a time. But not for years. By this means you may steer clear of, to me, the two ever-present obsticholes of marriage – selfishness through being possessive, or irresponsibility through absence. . . . Lesson Three, don't wait several years before you marry.'

~

As 1933 drew to a close, there came the first of a series of striking developments, prefiguring a new year in which Cooke would acquire his first job, a wife and the chance to be a movie star.

This token of things to come was a letter from Charlie Chaplin. Would he be free to return to Hollywood in the summer? The Little Man intended to start work on a film about Napoleon and wondered if Cooke might be available to do research and to help him with the script. Cooke wrote back, accepting the invitation.

The next approach was from H.L. Mencken. Impressed by the flow of verbal oddities from his Harvard correspondent, the Sage of Baltimore asked him to call by, to enjoy 'the gorgeous crabs that infest the protein factory of Chesapeake Bay'. This was another unmissable opportunity. The appointment was for lunch at Schellhase's Restaurant and when Cooke arrived he found Mencken sharing steins of beer with a colleague from the *Baltimore Sun*:

> What I saw was a small man so short in the thighs that when he stood up he seemed smaller than when he was sitting down. He had a plum pudding of a body and a square head stuck on it with no intervening neck. His brown hair was parted exactly in the middle, and the two cow-licks touched his eyebrows. He had very light blue eyes small enough to show the whites above the irises; which gave him the earnestness of a gas jet when he talked, an air of resigned incredulity when he listened and a merry acceptance of the human race and all its foibles when he grinned.

After a discussion of no great moment, they parted with a request from Mencken for further notes and suggestions and an invitation for him to call in whenever he was passing through Baltimore.

This acquaintance with two of the great names of the age, and his readiness to gossip knowingly about them, improved still further his standing among his younger friends. But the biggest break of all came when his long campaign to find a niche in the BBC finally showed signs of bearing fruit. The story has taken on the characteristics of legend: Cooke, as he told interviewers for years afterwards, was wandering along a Boston Street one March morning when he caught sight of a headline in the *Globe*: 'BBC FIRES PRIME MINISTER'S SON'. The story concerned the BBC's decision to part company with Oliver Baldwin, its film critic, adding that a search had already begun for a replacement. Cooke, by his own account, immediately telephoned the Director of the Commonwealth Fund in New York who confirmed that, if a student was placed on a shortlist for gainful employment, he would be offered free passage to Britain for an interview. A cable to the BBC followed, explaining that he was ready to travel, but on the strict understanding that he would be a shortlisted candidate. The reply came back from the Director of Talks, Charles Siepmann, assuring him in best diplomatic fashion that he would certainly be granted a final interview but 'with no obligation on our part'. That was good enough. He sailed on the *Aquitania* on 12 April, arriving in Southampton eight days later and within twenty-four hours had been given the job.

The story is true enough as far as it goes, but it omits a vital element or two. First, Baldwin was not immediately sacked in March, as Cooke always asserted, though he did have a serious falling-out with his employers that was widely reported. In fact, he was one of the first recorded critics of BBC bureaucracy and he launched his attack in sensational fashion. In a speech in London he spoke of his contempt for the headquarters staff, the philistinism of the Director-General Sir John Reith and the snootiness of senior members of the board, many drafted in from the armed services ('. . . then there is Vice-Admiral Sir Charles Carpendale, who knows all about quarter-decks, and Colonel Dawnay, late of the Brigade of Guards,' Baldwin thundered). He complained that staff, preparing for a visit by the King to Broadcasting House, had been made to rehearse 'like school-children' the singing of the National Anthem. He poured scorn on a memo directing that paper had to be torn into smaller shreds before being deposited in waste-paper baskets. And he was supremely vit-riolic about the censoring (on air) of a talk by another contributor. 'The whole attitude is ridiculous, stupid and fatuous,' he told a bemused audience of trades unionists. 'It can only be produced in Prussia and in England. The whole of our militarism was learned in Prussia and that is why we have *Prussianism* in the BBC.'

That was the word upon which the headline-writers seized. 'PRUSS-SIANISM IN BBC' (*Daily Telegraph*); 'RADIO CRITIC CALLS BBC PRUSSIAN' (*Daily Express*). The *Evening Standard* applied to the Corporation for a response, and was told by an unnamed source that 'Prussianism' was an exaggeration, though there had to be strict discipline to ensure the smooth running of an organisation with 1000 employees. (The paper gave a few examples: no inter-departmental telephone instruction could be accepted unless followed by a typed memorandum; being the guilty party in a divorce meant instant dismissal.) Other press coverage noted that Baldwin's contract ran out in June, with the possibility of a three-month extension. The fulminating critic himself admitted that he might be disciplined for his outburst.

The message was clear enough – and all the prompting Cooke needed, since he had applied for Baldwin's job less than two months earlier in an unsolicited letter. If the BBC was still in the habit of changing its film critic quite regularly, he had written, he would like his name to be considered. As usual, this letter bristles with self-confidence. Cooke mentions his plan for a book entitled 'A Preface to Theatrical Criticism' and for another based on the 'Hollywood Prospect' articles in the *Observer*. (Neither ever saw the light of day.) He notes that he has done a little work for the WBZ station where he was told 'that my voice was perfectly clear and [I hope] quite intelligible, pleasant and inoffensive to Americans . . . "especially for an Englishman" '.

By now he is well into his stride: 'I believe that the cinema is in urgent need of serious, unsolemn propaganda rather than analysis – active, crusading journalism rather than criticism.' Radio, he reckons, is the place for this to happen. 'The radio film critic should not be chosen as a journalist but as a critic, so that whether he vigorously declares them or not, his standards may be implied as not less rigorous, not less human, than they would be for criticism of books, plays, paintings.' He concludes this opening assault, ' . . . and I am formally applying for a try-out as a film critic on my return.'

Cooke must have been disappointed by the reply which arrived three weeks later. An executive named Lionel Fielden wrote that 'the position at present about film criticism is that Oliver Baldwin is doing the talks extremely well, but will probably be going abroad next winter, and will have to be replaced at the beginning of October'. The best he could offer was a try-out as a critic when Cooke returned to England in the autumn. Unabashed, Cooke responded on 1 March with an offer to make himself available in late September when, even if he hadn't seen any recent films, 'a first talk could very easily be about more general topics, about Hollywood, about English and American audiences, about one of a score of related topics on the difference in film-making in England and America.'

Then came Baldwin's broadside . . . and Cooke's equally rapid manoeuvring to replace him as the presenter of the fortnightly 'Cinema Talks'.

When he reached the BBC's new headquarters in Broadcasting House, on Monday 23 April, he was met by Fielden, a tall, languid figure who informed him rather sniffily that he should have been there earlier and had very probably missed his chance. Cooke muttered something about not being able to legislate for the vagaries of the boat train, although in fact he'd spent an evening near Southampton with Lionel Birch, in whose rooms at Kings College he'd first met Hetty Riddle. And where, Fielden inquired, was the review he would read for his recording test? Cooke said that if he could have a typewriter he would write one and proceeded to dash out a critique of the last film he'd seen before leaving the States, *Blonde Bombshell* with Jean Harlow and C. Aubrey Smith. This was hardly normal procedure, but when he'd finished Fielden led him to a studio with a closed-circuit link to Charles Siepmann's office. When he'd finished the talk, Fielden's demeanour had changed: would Mr Cooke please come straight round to Siepmann's office? The Director of Talks told him that the job was his, and Cooke claims that the assistant was dispatched to 'inform the other 200 candidates that they'd been unsuccessful.' Allowing for a certain measure of exaggeration on the part of the ecstatic candidate, this was still a considerable coup.

Thus, at twenty-five, he was about to become a paid employee for the first time, although admittedly on a three-month contract. All the gags he'd endured about becoming a 'foundation bum' – a perpetual student constantly seeking cosy, academic byways – could be laid to rest. He headed straight for Blackpool to share the good news with his family, whom he hadn't seen for nearly two years and then, after the most fleeting of stays, hurried south again.

∼

One of Cooke's appointments in those frenetic few days was with T.S. Eliot. He had been in correspondence with Eliot ever since leaving Cambridge, for two very good reasons: Eliot edited the quarterly review, the *Criterion*, to which Cooke had contributed occasional articles – and he was also a director of the publishers, Faber & Faber. The exchange of letters suggests that Eliot was impressed by Cooke's passion for theatre and film criticism, and although none of the projects which Cooke brought to him reached fruition, Eliot was always supportive. Cooke's first idea was a volume to be entitled *A Preface to Theatrical Criticism*, based on his work for *The Granta*. But more serious discussions began the following year over a book based on the *Observer* articles, *Hollywood Prospect*.

AC to TSE, 9 October 1933: 'I should try to keep it light and alternate the subjective, whimsical accounts of Hollywood . . . with serious discussion of film technique . . . It would not be a heavy book, nor a profound one; but thoughtful enough for cinema people to get something, quite apart from allaying their thirst to know the personal "human" feel of Hollywood.'

Eliot, unfortunately, mislaid Cooke's lengthy letter for some months, and wrote an apologetic reply in December, offering to help to place the book if Faber and Faber decided it was not suitable. Then Cooke sought Eliot's help in finding an outlet for a review of the latest Eugene O'Neill play, *Days Without End*, which he believed would be too controversial for most newspapers and magazines. 'I have just seen a very, very bad play,' he explained, 'and unfortunately an importantly bad play.' Once again, Eliot agreed to contact likely editors, or alternatively to offer the article to an agent. In due course, he kept his promise by writing to the literary agency, Curtis Brown:

'There is a young man from Cambridge named Alistair Cooke ... who is devoting himself to dramatic criticism. He has not yet produced anything, but I have some hopes of him, and I think he is worth getting hold of.' He accepted that the O'Neill review might be too obscure for an English audience, but added, 'What I have in mind is not so much this article, but the possibilities of future books from him.' The firm responded that it would, naturally, be interested in any writer recommended by so distinguished a figure.

Eliot made a special effort to fit in a meeting with Cooke, who was *en route* from Blackpool to Cambridge. They took tea at the Oxford and Cambridge Club in London, and discussed the pictures that might be used to illustrate *Hollywood Prospect*. But the strongest impression left in Cooke's mind was nothing to do with his ambitions as a writer. In the course of their conversation, he was bubbling over about how exciting it was to be in the land of President Roosevelt, while Europe was 'slinking around, saying "yes sir, no sir" to Hitler.' Eliot – speaking as an American who had taken British nationality – declared with clerical gravity, 'There's only one reason why I would feel the need to go back to America now – it's to buy my shoes.' Cooke looked down at Eliot's feet, decked out in canary-yellow, and understood.

Immediately after this encounter, Cooke repaired to Cambridge to meet some old college friends, and also to make contact with Gene Rostow, languishing at Kings College far from his bride. Through Rostow's good offices, Cooke then borrowed a large and impressive Chrysler from another visiting American student and after some trouble with a left-hand drive vehicle on English roads, set off for London. He had decided there was one more essential duty to be carried out before recrossing the Atlantic.

Baroness von Hütten was delighted to invite her daughter's former fiancé to dinner, and Hetty was there too. The welcome was warm enough, but Cooke soon began to detect that he might have made a fatal mistake: as he tapped out melodies on the piano from *Words and Music* – the show he'd seen with Hetty on their last night together – he felt uncauterised wounds opening up. 'The dinner turned out to be quite early, quite brief and quite awful,' as he remembered it, although he had the impression that the Baroness was sympathetic to his plight and perhaps preferred him to the usurper of Hetty's affections – a Scot who remained an unmentioned, and unmentionable, presence at the feast. 'I felt myself beginning to fall in love all over again.'

And Hetty? When the dinner was over, he offered to drive her in the Chrysler to her own flat in Gloucester Road. He parked outside. Hetty turned to him and asked, 'Would you like to come up for a nightcap?'

It was a classic screen moment. Cooke in sharp profile, wrestling with his re-awakened desires before finally turning away: 'Thanks awfully,' he replies, 'but I'm afraid I've promised to meet some friends later, and I can't let them down.' Hetty, Cooke believed, must have been impressed by his self-restraint. It was also a way of reimposing his own control over a relationship which had slipped away from him. The couple said goodbye and never had another formal meeting. The image of his Hetty did not suffer such rapid degradation as Chaplin had predicted: much later he caught sight of her on a boat train and found her as gorgeous as ever. 'I found myself thinking of H.L. Mencken's cruel line: "A man always remembers his first love. After that, he bunches 'em."'

~

At the end of these interesting few days in his homeland, Cooke set sail for New York and when he finally reached Harvard turned his attention to the final stages of rehearsal for *Hades, the Ladies*. He was still in a febrile emotional state. He always claimed that he had had no serious girl-friends from the day he left Liverpool for the first time – though opportunities must certainly have presented themselves. Yet within weeks of the encounter with Hetty, at a birthday party for the wife of Professor Manley O. Hudson, he met – and immediately became besotted by – a beautiful girl.

Ruth Emerson was twenty-four years old, and the great-grand-niece of the essayist and poet, Ralph Waldo Emerson. On this particular occasion she was also decidedly merry, something of which her father would sternly have disapproved. As Cooke put it, 'She was feeling no pain.' He was bowled over not only by her beauty, but by her unconventional background.

Despite coming from one of the most respectable, and respected, of all New England families, Ruth had dropped out of college and left to spend a year in Vienna, training to be a dancer. More radically still, she and a friend had then abandoned their first dance-school, which was full of Americans, and signed up with a creative Austrian teacher called Gertrud Kraus. As well as five hours' dancing each day, Ruth found time to win diving competitions and to study Italian from a German-Italian grammar book, with occasional help from a Hungarian tutor. At the end of the summer term, the two girls travelled together round Italy before returning home.

Ruth had always felt like the odd one out in the family. Her father was one of the country's leading epidemiologists, Dr Haven Emerson, and her sister and three brothers were all academically or technically gifted, destined to work in various fields of medicine or research. Ruth, by contrast, was taught at home for some years, struggled at school and was soon overtaken by her younger brother Ralph. Her mother would say to her, 'But they can't dance and you can.' It didn't really help. 'Everyone else was scientific,' she felt. 'I wasn't about to compete intellectually. In fact I always thought I was pretty dumb and that all the brains had gone to my brothers.' Hence her abandonment of formal studies. The Emerson household was sufficiently libertarian to issue each child with a college allowance – whatever they decided to do with the money.

When Cooke met her, Ruth had established her own small studio in Boston where she taught dance and pre-skiing exercises. She was also a member of a professional dance group run by Jaan Veen, a German émigré with a national reputation. Her home, she admitted, was 'behind the hospital, on the wrong side of the tracks.' After the Hudson party she stayed the night with her hosts. The next morning Cooke reappeared on the pretext of having left something behind.

Their mutual needs were obvious: he wanted to reassure himself that he could still sustain a relationship – she was looking for a way of expressing her individuality, thus regaining the respect of her family and her peers. Neither could recall any formal moment of

engagement. They simply started to live together in the certain knowledge that marriage would follow.

Before long Cooke was taken to see her father at his country seat
at Southold at the end of Long Island's North Fork. Haven Emerson
was an imposing and – to a stranger – an intimidating and terrifying
figure. He came from Puritan stock, and it showed. Cooke recalled
his early impressions in a 1966 *Letter*:

> The world, outside the world of microbes, hygiene and medical research,
> was not only a stranger to him – it was a very disreputable stranger. It
> drank. It smoked. It was full of luxury and stupidity and politicians. He
> was against all these things.

He had begun his working life as a medical doctor but gave up
his practice because he 'couldn't abide sick people' and turned his
attention to public health. While still in his thirties he'd become New
York's Health Commissioner and, when America joined the First
World War, he was drafted by General Pershing to oversee the health
of the American Expeditionary Forces in Europe. In the years that
followed he became an adviser to the Greek Government too. Scurvy
was rife among the ill-nourished population and he made a series of
recommendations to the King which helped wipe out malnutrition.
He was hailed as a national hero. Back in the United States he became
Professor of Epidemiology at Columbia University – and when Cooke
appeared on the scene, he had also been elected President of the
American Public Health Association. The family's favourite anecdote
about him came when he was summoned back to Athens, many years
later, to receive an award for his services to the Greek people. On the
morning of his departure he appeared in an ancient suit going slightly
green with age, carrying nothing but a small Gladstone bag. Ruth
said, 'Papa, where are the rest of your things? What about your tails
for the banquet?'

He replied, 'If the King of Greece wants a guest with tails, he'll have
to find himself another epidemiologist.' When Ruth said she'd call
him a cab, he brushed the idea aside. He would go, as always, by
subway to Grand Central Station, then by bus to the docks. 'Public
transportation,' he informed his family, 'is for the transportation of
the public OF WHICH I AM ONE.'

Privately, Dr Emerson took some precautions to reassure himself
about Cooke's credentials. He contacted his brother-in-law, an

English architect living in London, and asked him to make discreet inquiries about 'the man Cooke'. The brother-in-law, Harry Fletcher, was amused by the request and put it down to a touch of Emerson snobbery. 'What am I supposed to do?' he asked his wife: 'Consult the police records?' He did manage to unearth the fact that Mr Cooke senior was some sort of tradesman, and that his mother had run a Blackpool boarding house – which indicated a respectable, if not top-drawer, family.

Dr Emerson was wise enough not to inquire too closely into his children's lives, and Cooke must at least have struck him as a nicely mannered and intelligent escort for his younger daughter. Certainly the young man did not feel totally inhibited by this austere presence behind the scenes. Edna Rostow told one story which demonstrates the way Cooke and his circle were prepared to flout normal convention. Towards the end of the summer term, he gathered a group of half a dozen friends and headed off for a picnic in the country. As they ate and drank, he produced his cine-camera and invited the company to devise a story-line which they could perform and he could film. In the end, it was Cooke himself who suggested a plot requiring the entire company to strip off and act in the nude. His friends duly shed their clothes and ventured, for some spurious artistic reasons that Edna could not recall afterwards, into a brook. She had the feeling that Cooke had engineered the whole affair and she found the experience embarrassing, believing her own body compared badly with the others on display – particularly Ruth's.

The final great event of the academic year was the Hasty Pudding tour of the East Coast. *Hades, the Ladies* had become a pulsating love story between a male student (Francis Moore) who, when Harvard goes co-ed, falls for one of the new intake of women, played, naturally, by a man. The humour was often somewhat scabrous, but only in a heterosexual sense. Despite the scenario, none of the jokes hinted at the possible homosexual overtones of men serenading men and men dressed as girls.

It was a glamorous and complicated trip, taking in Boston, Providence and New York. Not only was there a large cast; there were stagehands and business managers, a pianist and a jazz combo. In Washington, President Roosevelt – a former Hasty Pudding performer himself – invited the students to dinner in the East Room of the White House. Cooke and Moore performed a short medley of songs from the show with the revered and ancient figure of Chief Justice Oliver Wendell Holmes in attendance.

Moore remembers long conversations with Cooke as they travelled between venues. The latter amused himself by identifying the origins of other members of the party from their accents and language: even among students who'd gone through Harvard homogenisation, he could reputedly differentiate between a North Carolinan from the hill country and another whose home was by the coast. He talked about Charlie Chaplin and his summer's work ahead. And he also shared his musings about the state of the world. Moore's recollection was that Cooke was deeply pessimistic, and not just about the Depression and the risk of social breakdown in the United States. The ominous rise of Hitler and Mussolini, threatening Europe with fascism, in Cooke's prognosis, heralded the approach of another terrible war. They had all better enjoy themselves while they could, because there might be no tomorrow.

The climax of the tour was a four-day stay at the Homestead resort in North Carolina. As they approached these final performances, Moore was suddenly taken ill with a virulent fever: the only person capable of taking over the lead-role at short notice, naturally, was the director who had coached the players in their parts. Cooke duly stepped into the breach. Moore felt that his friend was in his element – the centre of attention – as they acted before audiences drawn from the state's finest families. The prep schools, and the girls' private schools like Miss Porter's and Miss Fitch's, had just broken up for the summer and the Harvard group was invited to a series of post-production parties. 'Many a matron at the Homestead "with a beautiful seventeen-year-old daughter according to Moore" was only too glad to meet Mr Cooke. He cut a fine figure,' although in these genteel circles there was no overnight impropriety. In any case, Ruth was waiting back in Boston.

8

DOMESTICITY?

Cooke had to report for duty to the Chaplin studios by mid-June; Ruth's father was giving the presidential address to the American Public Health Association at Pasadena at about the same time; why not drive to California and get married there? The only slight fly in this ointment was that Cooke had already agreed to make the trip with a Harvard classics assistant, Charles Farwell Edson. Edson would just have to come too. Ruth wrote to her father with details of the plan. In the circumstances – Cooke feared the news of their Bohemian escapade might cause him to suffer a heart attack – he cabled a reply of considerable equanimity: 'Pasadena in midst of polio epidemic. Good place for young folks to avoid. Going by car you run many risks and save no money. Shall welcome your return rather than cheer your departure.'

His warnings about road travel turned out to be prescient: the car they purchased was 'an absolute lemon', which broke down at regular intervals. None of the three had the remotest idea how an engine worked, which meant paying exorbitant, and probably unnecessary, repair bills at a string of rural garages. They were also blighted by minor mishaps. They drove in rotation, a hundred miles in each session, and often at night to avoid the heat. Ruth remembers how she was dozing in the back seat at dusk with Edson at the wheel when the car suddenly skidded and slammed sideways into a solid object, ending up on its roof. The object was a cow, which left its imprint on one side of the vehicle. On the other side, Cooke was trapped by one elbow and one foot, upside-down, until passers-by managed to free him: he spent the night in hospital. On another occasion he was holding his camera out of the car window when, through the view-finder, he watched one of his own wheels detach itself and spin off into a field. And later still, after passing through Arizona's petrified forests, he managed to impale his arm on a pineapple cactus as he danced by moonlight, foolishly, with Ruth filming him.

Accidents apart, the trip provided a dramatic survey of a wide swathe of the Southern states, taking in Missouri, Oklahoma, Texas, New Mexico and Arizona. They covered tourist sites *en route*, such as the Carlsbad Caverns in New Mexico and the Grand Canyon. In St Louis Cooke claimed to have taken lunch (in the first air-conditioned restaurant he'd ever experienced) alongside Cary Grant on his honeymoon with Virginia Cherrill – star of Chaplin's *City Lights*. Ruth's main problem was persuading the two men to eat properly: a shortage of food, she discovered, tended to 'break down people's dispositions'. A tiny notebook survives from this epic journey. Much of it is simply a record of all financial transactions, however petty: '5 gallons – $1.32. $1 for repairs, Ruth. Edson owes Ruth $1.50. Front wheel, 30 cents. Brakes tightened, 75 cents.' The notebook also tracks their stay in a series of hotels across Texas – Dallas, Abilene and El Paso, with rooms at $2.50 a night. The total mileage, from Boston to Hollywood, was 3214 miles. Across the final pages are scrawled a few lines in Cooke's hand, written in pencil while Ruth or Charles was driving. He is clearly musing about his new job: 'practice of a critic is the achievement of an idiom – to diagnose, to identify, not to judge – increasingly embarrassed by the civility of our theatre – have felt that something earthy and exaggerated could redeem it – explain American plays.'

As soon as they arrived in Hollywood the trio checked into the Mark Twain Hotel. While Ruth luxuriated in her first Pacific Coast holiday, Cooke prepared to report for work as part – this time – of Chaplin's professional entourage.

Cooke spent the first couple of weeks passing on information about Napoleon, gleaned from the public library. Only then did work start on the script: 'The first thing he taught me was that you don't begin at the beginning. "We look," he said, laying down the law with a firm index finger tapping the table, "for some little incident, some vignette that fixes the other characters. With them, the audience must never be in any doubt. We have to fix them on sight."

If they were stuck, Chaplin paced round the room, mimicking all the parts and trying out variations on a line Cooke had written. And if all else failed they would plod off to lunch, always taken at the same restaurant, Musso Frank's. Despite his famed moodiness, Chaplin never fell out with his young collaborator. Far from it. In breaks from work he was happy to invite Cooke and his fiancée to spend time on board *Panacea* and Ruth sunned herself as Chaplin and Cooke traded stories.'They were both great raconteurs,' she says. She also remembers Paulette Goddard slipping out to the bathroom after dinner to replenish her drink out of Chaplin's abstentionist sight. So warm did the relationship become that Cooke was moved to invite the star to be best man at his wedding. Chaplin accepted with alacrity, and started to act out comic scenes of imagined disasters during the ceremony.

Cooke's attitude to life during these halcyon weeks can be summed up in one anecdote recounted by Ruth. 'One day we were driving along Hollywood Boulevard when we saw this beautiful dress in a shop window. We went in and asked how much it cost, but they told us it was just a piece of material draped on the mannequin. Alistair said, "But surely you can make it up?" They said they could, and that was the dress I chose for my wedding.' Impulsive and self-assured – and careless of cost: Cooke had taken on the colours of a Hollywood creature.

The wedding itself was fixed for 24 August, but things did not go as planned. When they arrived at the Pasadena Register Office Ruth's father was already there, deep in conversation with the magistrate, and her brother Bob and his wife were also in attendance. But where was Chaplin? They waited until the magistrate would delay matters no longer: after almost an hour, Cooke had to ask Charles Edson to stand in as best man. It did not make for a comfortable occasion and for several days Cooke didn't dare to call the Chaplin house. When he did so, the servants told him simply that 'Mr Chaplin had gone with Miss Goddard to Arrowhead'. There was no message. The following evening, he risked one more call.

'Chaplin came on as blithe as a robin,' Cooke wrote later. 'When was he going to see the bridal couple? Where and when should we hold the wedding party? We must come up to the house at once.' When they arrived, not a word was spoken about his non-appearance. 'He walked up and down in bubbling spirits, setting the date – we'd dine and dance at the Coconut Grove, and nothing would do but white tie and tails.' Paulette's ears perked up at the idea of a rare outing to a night-club. A day or so later, they took in the midnight show. Chaplin was in fine form, and the two couples posed for a picture which duly appeared in the movie magazine, *Motion Picture*.

Towards the end of the evening, however, a sugary crooner named Gene Austin took to the stage. His speciality was to slip into the register of a boy soprano for the final notes of each song. Chaplin was appalled, and decreed that he would never again expose himself to such horrors. The drive home was dismal, as Paulette contemplated the crumbling of her vision of a life of music and dancing. 'A tear ran down her enchanting face and her eyes fairly popped in frustration as she said, "What are we going to do evenings – stay at home and *write theses*?!"'

"Well,' Chaplin replied, 'one night a year is enough of that rubbish.' And he proceeded to offer his guests a nightcap served from a pitcher of water. Cooke observed wryly: 'Our wedding party ended on a scene that would have warmed the heart of a Southern Baptist. We sat there yawning slightly, throwing in the odd monosyllabic response to Chaplin's elegy on the modern world, and took long, meditative draughts of pure cold water.'

As well as a night out at the Coconut Grove, Chaplin made further amends with the gift of some expensive luggage. But if his failure to turn up at the register office was a shock to the bridegroom, it may not have been such a surprise to the bride. As the date drew nearer, Ruth had begun to panic at the idea of a wedding wrecked by the explosive pairing of the sensuous and uninhibited Paulette Goddard and her strait-laced, teetotal father. In her own, rather more humdrum, version of the story, she warned Cooke that, although Chaplin himself would be welcome, Paulette would have to be left at home; Chaplin, she went on, had been understanding, but regretted that he couldn't possibly come without his friend – though the couple were welcome to say that he'd been in attendance anyway.

The ceremony was thus a low-key affair and from Ruth's point of view, rather depressing, too. At dinner, her father only wanted to talk about the impending marriage of his other daughter whose prospects, because she was older, had been much less certain. While, on the other side of the table, she says she was aware of the antagonism of her brother Bob: when she'd first introduced her fiancé, Bob had remarked, 'Surely you're not going to marry him? He's a four-flusher.' She wasn't sure what it meant, but she recognised the tone well enough.

This, none the less, was the way the event was reported back home in the *Blackpool Gazette*:

Mr Charles Chaplin, the world-famous comedian, was the best man at the wedding of Mr Alistair A. Cooke, the new film critic of the BBC, who succeeds Mr Oliver Baldwin . . . The wedding took place at Los Angeles, where Mr Cooke has been the guest of Mr Chaplin for the past few months. Also among the guests was Miss Pauline [sic] Goddard, Mr Chaplin's new leading lady.

Cooke's working association with Chaplin that summer came to an unexpected climax, too. The Napoleon script seemed to be progressing well and one evening they were sitting at the piano together playing duets. 'After a break,' Cooke says, 'he came back into the living-room, took out a toothpick, sucked his teeth, and calmly announced, "By the way, the Napoleon thing. It's a beautiful idea – for somebody else. They wouldn't take it from the Little Man." He said no more, and we never wrote another word or referred to the project again.' Cooke failed to discover why Chaplin changed his mind. The research notes still lie, unused, in the Chaplin archive.

There was one further shock to come. Just before Alistair and Ruth were due to return to the East Coast, to prepare for their journey to England, Chaplin came down to their hotel and offered them dinner. Before they ate, he led Cooke onto a balcony overlooking the hills and asked, out of the blue, if he'd like to stay and act as his assistant director on *Modern Times*. Cooke was flattered, but stuttered that he was required, under the terms of the Commonwealth Fund, to return to a job somewhere in the British Empire for at least two years. Chaplin said politely that he thought it was a pity. 'If you stay with me, I'll make you the best light comedian since Seymour Hicks.' Cooke describes his breathless reaction: 'Hicks was then as adroit a light comedian as any on the English stage. But a comedian still. We thanked the maestro warmly for all his kindness, and I went to bed still marvelling that an artist of Chaplin's sensitivity and lightning perceptions could offer to cast the next Eugene O'Neill as a light comedian.'

Did Cooke ever regret the missed opportunity? He discovered soon afterwards that the Commonwealth Fund would certainly have waived its requirements at the mention of Chaplin's name. Perhaps, in any case, it was an excuse: he would have had to throw up the certainty of his BBC job, with all its promise, for the chance of fame and fortune in a business where he would be a very small fish indeed.

He said goodbye to Chaplin and only saw him two or three more times in his life.

~

Even while he worked on the Napoleon script, Cooke's mind was buzzing with ideas for his new role as a film critic. One letter to Lionel Fielden suggests that the fortnightly talks should be supplemented with a series of shorter broadcasts, lasting seven to ten minutes, alternating reviews with discussions based on ideas from his audience. Cooke is decidedly sniffy about the populist approach to films. 'The sort of topic I do <u>not</u> intend to indulge in is polite discussions with literary critics, politicians, film-producers, famous boxers, on "Are the movies worthwhile?" or "Should film stars marry young?" Forgive this apparent flippancy, I am only hoping to reassure you that I shall always consciously resist falling into more easy and banal approaches, and it is desperately easy to do.' Fielden's reply to this outpouring is sympathetic, with the proviso that a large and slow-moving organisation like the BBC wasn't likely to shift from its traditional format of fifteen- to thirty-minute programmes.

Cooke's last letter to the BBC before sailing for London in September was on his favourite subject of language – and a plea not to be banned from all Americanisms:

> It will be difficult, but possible, for me to warm again to those ingratiating little (British) idioms like 'ripping', 'in the soup' and 'perfect heaven'. . . I'm not interested in transporting slang, excellent and racy as it may be, but as we've been shamelessly borrowing American words for a hundred years, and confessing the theft about fifty years later, I see no harm in helping the process to be speedier and more accurate. Please don't think I propose to *hand in my checks* or *lose out* or *make the grade* or *pass the buck* or *bawl anyone out* but I see only good in gradually calling the Cinema *movies* and even in good time calling a trick *phoney* instead of our slangy *fraudulent.*

He was quite ready, even as an incipient disciple, to speak up for the vigour and value of the American language in the face of Old World disdain. Cooke went on tell Fielden that he had written most of his first talk – a personal statement of his attitude to film criticism – and tried it out, successfully, on Chaplin. Finally he inquired whether speakers had to follow any particular dress code.

Rather surprisingly in an organisation so vilified by Oliver Baldwin for its hidebound ways, Fielden replied that Cooke could come in pyjamas if he pleased, and that there were no rules about American slang . . . 'in fact, no rule about anything. We are ready for you to set the pace as you think fit.' It would not, however, be possible to record the first talk and send it to Chaplin in Hollywood since EMI charged 9 guineas for each four-minute wax record which, with shipping costs, would mean a prohibitive £50 for a single talk.

~

In mid-September Cooke and his wife returned from Hollywood to the East Coast by train. They were to travel separately to London, so that Ruth could say her goodbyes to relatives in Philadelphia and Boston. Cooke sailed from New York on the 29th aboard the German liner *Bremen*. He travelled with a sense of imminent loss: there was Ruth, of course, for the moment, and some more practical regrets. He told Eddie Done about them, in the traditional argot of their exchanges:

> The more I think of the return to England, several Characteristic Phantoms depress and disturb my dreams . . . one is the painful ghost called 'English Food'; another is English Sanitation; a very floppy Woollen Droopy Ghost is called English Men's Underwear. I can do only one little service to my Cerntry. I can't bring over a whole flock of diners, dog-wagons, excellent and ubiquitous cheap restaurants; twenty-seven kinds of pie; I can't give every Englishman an efficient bathroom, a clean hairbrush; but I can humbly discover the measurements of some friends whose domestic bliss I value and bring two or three extra underpanties, a shirt or two. Here, men in underclothes look like gay, rational, sensible human beings. And considerably less pansy than the Englishman in silk.

Armed with these emergency supplies, he was off to London, staying a few days with Norrie Davidson, and awaiting Ruth's arrival.

In these early days of radio, performers – especially new performers – were severely tested by the requirement to broadcast everything live. One Friday afternoon, Cooke stepped into Broadcasting House to take up his new job, and by 6.45 p.m. on the following Monday evening, 8 October, he was sitting in front of a microphone preparing to deliver a twenty-minute address to the nation. Timing was critical. The announcer for the evening (for whom formal evening dress certainly was *de rigueur*) read the news at 6.00 p.m., and was then charged with keeping the rest of the programmes on schedule: in case of an overrun, he simply contacted the studio engineers and told them to fade out the sound, even if it meant ending a programme in mid-sentence or mid-symphony. The announcer also had to improvise if a broadcast ended early. In extreme cases he resorted to a gramophone record or called on the services of the stand-by pianist Aunt Sophie. There are no reports of Cooke having suffered any such indignity in the course of his first series of talks. One of the young announcers, Harman Grisewood, was immediately struck by the new critic's demeanour: his first impression was of a tall, thin, attractive man crouching over the microphone, very eager and full of humour.

Cooke's inaugural 'Cinema Talk', as promised, took the form of a lengthy statement of personal intent. The transcript reveals much about the sort of broadcaster he was to become. The tone is light and conversational, but with the slight sense of a new teacher confiding in a group of willing pupils – mildly self-deprecating, humorous, but with a clear and serious purpose. Cooke, the writer for radio, seems to have arrived almost fully formed, ready for a 65-year stint at the microphone.

He begins by describing his last day in New York, which he'd intended to spend wandering through the coolness of Central Park and enjoying a ferry trip to Staten Island. Instead, he stayed in bed late, spent the afternoon checking his luggage and by tea-time was trying to find an excuse for taking in one more movie. His audience had to understand, in other words, that they were dealing with an addict. In the end, he tells them, because he was feeling hard-up, he spent 25 cents for a last fix at a newsreel theatre. He then offers his own declaration of independence:

> I declare that I am a critic trying to interest a lot of people in seeing, and a few ambitious people into making, interesting films. I have no personal interest in any company. As a critic I am without politics and without class. I swear I am committed to no country, no director, no star, no theme, no style ... My malice extends only to those who have a dull talent and continue to exploit it, whether they live in London, Hollywood, Moscow, the African jungle, or behind the sets of a musical comedy.

Strip away the specific references to film – and substitute politics, music, literature or sport – and that might serve as a credo for Cooke's entire journalistic career, driven as it was by an almost obsessive commitment to objectivity and detachment. Finally, Cooke confesses a few of his own whims and prejudices – in particular, in dealing with women:

> Even a critic has a heart. Or had one before he became one. And though I solemnly swear to take no new lights of love, I can't abruptly get rid of all my old flames. I believe it my duty to tell you, for instance, that until very recently I was in love with Miss Loretta Young. Now please . . . there's no point in snorting, or saying tut-tut, or even, I'm sorry to say, in applauding loudly. It just happens that my chemistry and Miss Young's peculiar chemistry seem to click. I hope. And I shall probably be abominably unfair to the rest of the cast in her pictures.

Afterwards he wrote to Lionel Fielden to report that he had 'just heard from an MP, a schoolmaster, a farmer's daughter, a butcher and a man in a boot factory – they all "understood" and felt it was said specially for them.' This was yet another token of things to come: the same universality of appeal lay behind the concept of the *Letter from America* which was meant to be equally accessible to 'shrewd bishops and honest carpenters.'

It was certainly refreshing stuff and set the tone for a series successful enough to ensure that there was no doubt about the granting of a second contract in the new year. The day after the maiden BBC broadcast he set out to follow two of his father's most fervent pieces of advice: that as soon as he secured his first job, he should (a) open a bank account and (b) take out a life insurance policy. He duly walked round the corner to Barclays Bank in Edgware Road and deposited his cheque for 15 guineas – an account which he never gave up.

Two days later he was back in Blackpool for another brief parental visit, and gracing the *Evening Gazette and Herald* with an exclusive interview. 'CHAPLIN IN A NEW LIGHT', says the headline – 'BLACKPOOL MAN REVEALS A SECRET'. Cooke confides to the paper that Chaplin may soon appear for the first time without his moustache, bowler hat and baggy trousers. But the title, the story and the part to be played by Chaplin cannot be revealed. 'Another secret about the film was whether it would be a silent or a talking picture. "Sorry," said Mr Cooke, "but . . .". '

Back in London, still awaiting Ruth's arrival, he found temporary accommodation in Oxford Terrace, in what amounted to theatrical digs. His old friends were delighted to have him back in town. Heb

(J.N.G. Davidson), who was making films for the Empire Marketing Board, was given privileged access to the first programme: by telephoning a special number in Broadcasting House he was able to listen directly to the studio output, although he was warned not to cough or speak in case of a cross-over of the circuits.

Cooke found plenty of other distractions. He was invited to the Harvard Club in London to listen to a World Series baseball game on an inadequate radio circuit from New York. The commentary 'came at us in whimsical gusts, like showers of autumn leaves. Sometimes a blizzard, sometimes a patter, sometimes one leaf.' Since he still had only the haziest idea of the rules of the game, even crystal-clear reception wouldn't have helped much, but at least the company was congenial and comfortingly American. On another occasion he breakfasted with Jacob Bronowski, who reckoned there might be a market for an anthology of writing from *The Granta*. The matter had been discussed by transatlantic mail and Bronowski had even gone so far as to paste together a mammoth compilation of what Cooke (looking back) believes was certainly a homage to pretension – with William Empson's writing an honourable exception. The idea came to nothing.

The frenetic activity alleviated – but could not eradicate – twinges of doubt about being separated from his bride. Leaving a woman on the opposite side of the Atlantic could be a risky business. The insecurity is evident in the messages with which he presented her before he left, sealed in separate envelopes – one to be opened on each day of her voyage. Seven touching sketches show Ruth first playing shuffleboard with a harmless old man, but on the next day meeting a handsome stranger, then sharing deck-chairs with him, dancing, and finally, on the last night, strolling arm-in-arm by moonlight. In the last frame, Alistair, with his aquiline nose in profile, greets Ruth at Southampton. She is saying, 'I didn't meet a soul.' (See p. 73)

~

All Cooke's friends seemed to be bowled over by Ruth when, six weeks later, she arrived unmolested to join her husband, first in Oxford Terrace, and after Christmas in Devonport Street close to Paddington Station – a street subsequently wiped out by wartime bombing. It was not a large flat, but Ruth, at Cooke's firm prompting, set about decorating it in a resolutely modern manner. At night they launched themselves into a round of night-clubs and jazz-spots after the theatre or cinema – sometimes Cooke had to see five films a week. They also developed a list of favoured eating-spots, recorded for posterity in a list drawn up for a country friend spending his honeymoon in London. Among the recommendations: 'Café Royal – moderate lunch for 3/6. Very good cooking, especially grills and fish. Don't go downstairs for lunch, it's 1/6 extra.' Martinez, serving Spanish food, is singled out for its chicken and rice dish and exquisite sherry, poured out of tiny barrels. Martinez is easy to find, he adds, by asking a bobby. Finally, Cooke tells his friends that for a blow-out, expensive but worth the money, they should go to the Ivy, 'the pleasantest restaurant in London to sit in. Packed with celebrities. But you'll not get away with less than 6/6 each.'

He and Ruth constantly hob-nobbed with those celebrities – movie people, actors and writers. Ruth investigated the possibility of taking up dancing again, but was deterred by the grim state of the facilities at the London schools where 'you couldn't even take a shower after class'. Cooke wrote articles for anyone who would take them. Between times, he even had tennis lessons on top of Selfridges store in Oxford Street with a man who claimed to have coached the Wimbledon champion Suzanne Lenglen, but gave up when he was told that he'd have to unlearn the game and start again.

The first trips to Blackpool passed off well enough. Ruth recalled Cooke's parents being determinedly kind to her – and the odd sight of her new brother-in-law, Sam, behind the counter of the butcher's shop. On one visit she fell sick and was confined to bed. The doctor opined that she was obviously a 'bit nervy', which she thought might be taken amiss in the Ormond Avenue household, run as it was on the principles of bracing air and healthy living. In fact, as she realised later, confined in a hideously uncomfortable bed with its lumpy kapok mattress, it was probably a simple case of nervous tension at being in such unaccustomed surroundings. Another odd encounter was with Grandmother Byrne, who took her on one side and offered the confidential view that birth control was a great blessing. She herself had had five children to contend with.

~

While Ruth was adjusting, Cooke was thriving. He wrote to the Director of Talks, Charles Siepmann, about his plans for the spring series on 'The Cinema', pointing out that eighty-five per cent of his correspondents were 'unequivocally For' his approach, and only five per cent 'unequivocally Against'. When he posed a particular question to his audience, 200 people had written in. 'The working-class letters, especially, show they have understood, that they are often unbelievably interested in film-making, that they prefer some sort of personal, flippant or intimate comment rather than impersonal description of plots.' There was also, apparently, an irresistible public demand for more Cooke broadcasts: 'Many listeners beg for a weekly talk.'

On a more serious level, he says that he's discussed, with the documentary film producer John Grierson, running sound-track from films: 'About the most important novelty one could experiment with on the radio . . . Grierson believes that such a use of film talks would be the first practical step to examining together talkies and television . . . with a careful choice of track it can be very exciting to hear a picture and not see it.' Among his other ideas is to invite guest speakers such as the actor Robert Donat. But most significantly, he was anxious to sell the BBC a special one-off programme on language, and a separate set of programmes on American life.

The latter gradually took shape as a 13-week series under the banner *The American Half-Hour.* The concept was positively avant-garde. The series would set out to offer to an English audience a word picture of the United States by the use of commentaries, music, interviews and dramatic scenes – acted out, for the most part, by Cooke's friends. This was one of the most innovative aspects of the plan and it allowed Cooke to establish a thread of continuity across the series. A young actor took the part of an Englishman abroad: this imaginary character, christened Speaight, was heard week by week, apparently travelling across the United States (and, naturally, following routes already covered by Cooke himself the previous two summers). *En route* Speaight met interesting people who offered him titbits of information on the local scene in Chicago or Charlotte or Santa Fe. Naturally, all these exchanges took place in a Broadcasting House studio.

Nothing like this had ever been tried before and it says much for the courage of Charles Siepmann that he was prepared to take the risk. His main concern is expressed in a letter on 17 February: 'I was very glad that you agreed with me that what we want for this programme is something which avoids sensationalism of all sorts; which makes it primarily a talks feature, and which avoids treatment of a kind to suggest to the public that this is mere light entertainment.' Finally, a contract was signed offering Cooke 25 guineas to 'devise, act as producer and compere' for each programme. The broadcasts were scheduled for Saturday evenings from April to June and the prestige of the enterprise was greatly enhanced when the American Ambassador to London, Robert Bingham, agreed to supply a few introductory remarks. 'I believe there is nothing so important and so vital to the welfare of our countries,' he said, 'as understanding and co-operation between your country and mine. I should like to repeat that we really know more about you than you know about us.'

Thus launched, the first programme touched on such fundamental oddities as the autonomy of individual states and the language of the menu in a New York restaurant. Speaight (he was never given a first name) is heard in conversation with Ben Weldon, an American actor Cooke had met in London, playing the part of a typical New Yorker.

WELDON: Soup – Gumbo in Jelly – Clam Chowder?

SPEAIGHT: I haven't the vaguest idea what a clam is...

WELDON: A clam? It's a mollusc.

SPEAIGHT: I'll have it ...

WELDON: Then for dessert?

SPEAIGHT: What about a sweet?

WELDON: I'm saying – what you call a sweet we call dessert. The choice is apricot pie, peach shortcake, strawberry shortcake à la mode, lemon meringue pie, cheese pie, Boston chocolate, cherry pie, apple, blueberry ...

At which point the English listener presumably starts to salivate, goggle-eyed, at the cornucopia of an American sweet-trolley.

The highlight of the first *American Half-Hour* was to be the portrayal of a Broadway first night, done with nothing more exotic than a phonograph record, a sound effects disc of a theatre audience, and the actors, Weldon and Speaight. The show he chose was Cole Porter's *Anything Goes*, featuring Ethel Merman singing *You're the Top*.

'The show had not yet arrived in England,' he explained years later, 'but the London impresario, C.B. Cochran, was eventually prevailed upon to let us give the hit-song this single promotional fling. But where to find a bootlegged copy of the record?' As part of the build-up to the series, Cooke had got to know the London representative of the NBC network, Fred Bate, who – he guessed correctly – would know how to solve the conundrum. Cooke was told to report to a flat in Bryanston Court at 6 p.m., and was shown into a sumptuous sitting-room:

> Presently there appeared a middle-aged brunette, clipping on the earring that would give the last touch of elegance to an impeccable production. She had coiled braids pinned above her ears, darting black eyes and a determined square jaw. She also extended to me the brief courtesy of a drink chased with enthusiastic small talk about the talents of Cole Porter and the endearing brashness of Ethel Merman. Then she handed me the record and I was on my way out. For another year or more I would have had to make an effort to recall her name from this hasty encounter. She was a Mrs Simpson.

The subsequent *Half-Hours* ranged from travelogue to earnest consideration of social issues. The pervasive feel of the series is Cooke's wonderment at the country he's discovered. He makes use of visiting Rhodes scholars (including Walt Rostow, Gene's younger brother) to proclaim to the mythical Speaight the marvels of a cowboy life in Wyoming, herding cattle in Texas or the spectacular scenery provided by New Mexico and Arizona. One erstwhile travelling companion, Charles Spencer, makes a cameo appearance to applaud the principles underlying American education, while another, Charles Edson, is Speaight's guide to California.

Perhaps the most intriguing programme is number nine, entitled 'The Negro', in which Speaight wanders through the cotton fields of Mississippi to Memphis, Tennessee. The *Radio Times* billing gives a fair idea of the spirit of the piece.

> The Negro plays no inconsiderable part in the American scene, and his activities go further than many people in this country realise. Tonight we are to look at the Negro as orator, poet, preacher, writer, composer and singer ... We shall hear on special records compositions by Duke Ellington and his predecessor W.C. Handy, composer of the 'Beale Street Blues'; a fragment of the remarkable sermon, 'The Black Diamond Express to Hell'; and spirituals sung by the Hall Johnson choir.

The text of the accompanying article in the *Listener* magazine is positively pastoral. The hard-working black man (humble, poor, always at work) is heard singing in his unrefined voice, all the better for 'its own folk purity'. Speaight peeps inside a cabin in a clearing, where the cotton pickers are eating their fat back pork and maize porridge bathed in molasses ('One meal of this would put you and me in hospital. Three meals a day keep the Negro at work'); he watches a game of crap, played on Beale Street in Memphis; he has a history lesson from a black economics graduate.

The realities of segregation make only fleeting appearances: there are references to the economic plight of the black residents of Harlem and Speaight is made to discuss the long aftermath of the Civil War with a character in Virginia. Yet even that discussion focuses on the desire of the South not to be lectured by the city dwellers of the North about the way the black population lives. As revealed in these pieces, Cooke is certainly no romantic, seduced by the stability of social life in Alabama or Tennessee, but nor is he the liberal that his background might have suggested, ready to question the inequalities he observed. Everyone, including the cotton barons of the deep South, must be allowed a point of view.

~

The other significant project of the first half of 1935 was a broadcast entitled *English on Both Sides of the Atlantic*. This essay, based on his Harvard researches, made a number of bold assertions on the premise that English as spoken in America derives from the speech of the seventeenth-century settlers: 'People who have observed that the North of England today has many sounds superficially like American sounds wrongly concluded that what Americans carried to the New World was an English dialect. It was not. It was the socially accepted standard of the South of England.' The implications of this were startling. 'Not only is American speech historically an older speech, but it means that if Geoffrey Chaucer were alive today, he would have much more difficulty understanding the pronunciation of his very-great-grandson in Hampstead than he would have in understanding a cousin in Milwaukee.' Cooke notes in passing that Boston speech, with its similarity to modern English, is perhaps the only artificial and 'created' form of speech in America.

As well as pronunciation, Cooke also covers the differences in vocabulary and idiom between the two countries, and launches a crusade for cheerful acceptance of what – in Britain – is dismissed as transatlantic slang, but which – in America – has no social status and is used by all classes. 'As a new language, the American language is now where ours was in the reign of Elizabeth I. Its vocabulary is rich, practical and untidy. It is ready to invent new words for new events. It has never lost its vitality and its lively gift of metaphor. And this vitality and invention is so irresistible that for a hundred years now the pendulum has been on the back-swing; and I suppose England has been absorbing American words at an unbelievable rate.' Instead of fretting about this phenomenon, he argues, the English should accept and celebrate it.

Much flowed from this piece of work. First, it established what was to be a highly significant relationship between Cooke and Fred Bate of NBC, who arranged to have the broadcast transmitted across the United States. The message was seized upon by large numbers of newspapers, the *Hartford Courant* in Connecticut devoting an editorial to the subject, expressing surprise and delight that an Englishman should take up the cudgels on behalf of the much-maligned American language, and reporting Mr Cooke's conclusion that 'not American, but English is the bastard language'. The publicity provoked by the broadcast even reached Mencken, and helped to bolster Cooke's reputation, in his eyes, as a researcher with genuinely radical credentials.

The second consequence of *English on Both Sides of the Atlantic* was an invitation to sit on the BBC's Advisory Committee on Spoken English. It had been set up in 1926 to provide an authoritative guide on pronunciation and the use of language for BBC announcers. The results of its deliberations were also published in a pamphlet, *Spoken English*, available to the public. The committee was dauntingly high-powered with an average age somewhere in the late sixties. At various times it boasted Dr William Temple, who had been elevated to Archbishop of York since his speech-day appearance in Blackpool; C.K. Ogden, linguistic collaborator of I.A.Richards at Cambridge; Professor Lascelles Abercrombie; the literary critic Lord David Cecil; the actor, Sir Johnston Forbes-Robertson; the scientist, Julian Huxley; and, always in the chair, the imperious figure of George Bernard Shaw, now nearly eighty years old.

The minutes of one meeting show the members discussing how various words should be uttered on the airwaves – acoustic, aerated, decorous, disputant, garage, ordeal, and ukulele. In many cases the crucial issue was to protect the English tongue from foreign interlopers.

To this end, members were provided in advance with extracts from all the leading English and American dictionaries: in the words of the committee's moving spirit, Professor Arthur Lloyd-James, 'the BBC very definitely concerns itself with checking ultra-modern tendencies in the language, and carrying out the injunctions of the Committee with regard to the so-called purity of English vowels.'

It was by no means a straightforward task. Often the committee was split, and had to make its decisions by majority vote. Shaw himself commented at one stage, 'The committee so far is a ghastly failure. It should be reconstituted with an age-limit of 30 and a few taxi-drivers on it. The people *won't* pronounce like the old dons. And then, are we to dictate to the mob or allow the mob to dictate to us? I give it up.' That turned out to be a temporary fit of pique, and when Cooke arrived (representing not just youth – he was twenty-six years old – but the dreaded American tongue) GBS was still firmly installed in his seat.

Cooke had been a Shaw enthusiast throughout his Cambridge days, though on the same basis as the critic James Agate – that Shaw's plays were the price you had to pay for the prefaces. He also admired him for his political stance, equating Shaw's socialism with his own avowedly naïve liberal ideas. This was how he described their first meeting in a *Letter from America* written in 1953 and the shock of discovering that he was far from being the socialist firebrand of popular repute, but rather, 'A grave and very delicate old gentleman, given to the more courtly forms of address, who certainly lived up to his own prescription that the only proper behaviour for a democrat was not to treat a duchess as a charwoman, but to treat every char-woman as a duchess.'

Cooke soon found that the chairman's democratic instincts were selective. If he disagreed with a vote of the committee, he simply overruled it. But he treated the young man kindly, remarking that it was a fine idea to have acquired an expert in American linguistics and speech. Sometimes Cooke, or the American writer Logan Pearsall Smith, would point out a particularly glaring difference between the two tongues, and Shaw would ask for a note to be added to the final report – 'Lieutenant (Am. Loo-tenant)'. Proper names were a particular bugbear for the announcers. Cooke recalls a lengthy debate over 'Conduit Street' in the West End of London. Should it be Cundit? Con-doo-it? Con-dwit?

But one exchange in particular stuck in his mind.

The word was canine. Shaw went round the table – should the 'a' be short or long? Opinion was mixed, though Pearsall Smith forsook his native 'cay-nine' for the 'can-ine' preferred by the classicists – and by Shaw himself. It looked as though the majority favoured 'can-ine', but Shaw insisted on a vote. There was a heavy pause. 'Gentlemen,' said Shaw, 'somebody has voted twice.' Cooke, wondering why he was behaving so ostentatiously in such distinguished company, confessed. 'I felt I had no choice but to vote for both versions,' he explained. 'There's no doubt how the Americans say the word, and apparently the English way is different.'

There was a pause, before Shaw declared, 'Very good! Quite right!' and delivered a short homily: 'I believe in recommending the pronunciation of people who use the word in their daily trade. And my dentist always says, "Cay-nine".'

At which Pearsall Smith suggested, 'I think your dentist must be an American.'

'Of course,' Shaw replied. 'Why do you think I have all my teeth at the age of 78?' He vouchsafed Cooke a small smile as he stalked from the room at the end of the meeting.

The only member of the committee with whom Cooke became friendly was the man who had invited him to join, Arthur Lloyd-James, the Professor of Phonetics at the School of Oriental Studies in London. The two men shared a fascination with the more arcane corners of linguistic research – but they also met socially, sometimes with Ruth and the Professor's wife Elsie. Only five years later, Lloyd-James was in the dock of the Old Bailey, charged with bludgeoning and stabbing his wife to death after suffering a mental breakdown. He was spared the gallows, after being found guilty but insane.

~

For their first summer holiday, the Cookes were invited to spend a month in Ibiza with friends, a trip which Ruth remembers as one of their happiest times together. On their return to London, the social cycle resumed, with Cooke busier than ever. Ruth did not sit idly at the Devonport Street flat. She started to work as a model, and soon began to figure prominently in magazines such as *Harpers* and *Vogue*. Her greatest stroke of good fortune was to be taken up by a young photographer who had just opened his first studio. Norman Parkinson was beginning to make his name with elegant and romantic portraits for fashion magazines, frequently shot in the open air. Ruth found herself tearing round the countryside in a sports car with Parkinson, seeking out locations on beaches or at golf clubs. Occasionally she travelled to Paris, too, to work with one of the best-known French photographers, Horst. The only drawback was that the couple's lives began to suffer a certain disconnection. Ruth was often out of the house early in the morning, so that Parkinson could make maximum use of the daylight – Cooke was decidedly a late riser. And for some reason she wasn't even present when, on New Year's Eve of 1935, her husband acted as best man for his old Blackpool friend Eddie Done, who was getting married in Bristol.

Done's widow Esme remembered the occasion vividly. It was a High Church occasion, with candles bristling and the air heavy with incense. 'When Alistair walked into the church for the first time and saw what was going on, he immediately dropped down on one knee and put his head in his hands: he was play-acting as usual.' He contrived to miss the wedding photos and, because he took so long changing out of his morning suit, he was partly responsible for the couple missing their train to London. Then he travelled with them and when they reached Paddington Station, began an elaborate charade (à la Chaplin?) in which he acted the part of a second bridegroom. The other passengers were duly confused as he, Eddie and Esme all boarded the same taxi. Esme was entranced, recalling his thin figure and his dramatically black hair. 'He was very entertaining, and all my friends fell for him.'

9

FOUNDATIONS

The BBC film critic's job was still going well. Among the films he reviewed: Greta Garbo in *Anna Karenina* ('Acting doesn't often go to the head. It hits you in the pit of the stomach. And when a woman is acting it strikes most of us, heaven help us, hard on the left side of the chest'); H.G. Wells's *Things to Come* ('The acting doesn't help at all, being performed by three actors who on the stage have grace and power and possibly even delicacy, but here look and move like the latest additions to Madame Tussaud's').

In November 1935, just before his twenty-seventh birthday, Cooke was busy trying to extend his broadcasting empire, this time through the new Director of Talks, J.M. Rose-Troup, Charles Siepmann having fallen foul of power struggles in the upper echelons of BBC management. Cooke's letter suggests that there could be a strong case for a daily film service, 'with the firm provision that we remained committed to no company, that we talked always about the things that interested us and not about the films which the distributors are anxious to sell'. More realistically, he still hoped to be given a weekly, rather than a fortnightly, slot. He also produced detailed statistics to show that more people visited cinemas in the three summer months – July to September – than in the spring, which he believed was a compelling argument for giving him yet more air time. Each of these ideas was patiently rebuffed by an organisation locked into long-term planning of programmes.

As a testament to Cooke's independence, though, the BBC received a formal complaint from two film distribution companies about a remark in one of his talks. In the words of an internal memo, 'The statement was to the effect that listeners should stay home and save their money for the next fortnight as there was not a single film worth seeing.' The same companies reacted badly when approached by the BBC to buy advertising space in a special television supplement to the *Radio Times:* 'Fortunately the Film Industry does not take Mr Cooke very seriously but even so they object to being asked to pay for advertising and then made the victims of unfavourable and unnecessary criticism.'

Try as he might, he could not persuade the BBC to offer him a weekly slot. Films had to alternate with books and that was that, but it did mean that there was time for excursions. At the end of November, he and Ruth were back in the North for a visit to his old school – which by now had become Blackpool Grammar. Cooke agreed to give a talk to the boys on 'The Cinema in England, America and Russia'. Whether or not this rather ponderous title was to the taste of his young audience, it certainly seems to have enraptured 'Jane', who reviewed the event for the local paper.

'Almost the first thing you notice are his long, thin expressive fingers, used so skilfully to illustrate as he talks,' she cooed. 'In fact everything Mr A.A. Cooke, BA, film critic for the BBC, says and does is vital.' Cooke apparently talked about his subject in enormous detail, while 'in the front row, his attractive wife Ruth . . . watched his every movement, but hardly moved a muscle.'

'Jane' enthused over the speaker's carefully sculpted metaphors, tinged with wit, and was moved by one passage in particular: 'There must have been many young hearts that revolted and yet rejoiced with Mr Cooke as he spoke of the new British film which shows some of the most dreadful slums in London.' These sensitive schoolboys then heard Cooke make a plea on behalf of such socially conscious cinema, in particular a gritty piece entitled *Housing Problems*, made by his friend Edgar Anstey. 'It is one of the most heart-rending films I have ever seen in my life,' he told them. 'But it is time that more of this type of film was produced in England . . . so that everyone in the country should see for themselves the horrors of the housing problem.' 'Jane' is utterly won over. 'Here is the type of brain that does not stoop to the pettiness of social fame, but sees beyond the acclamation of the crowd. We should be glad to own him as a Blackpool man who has gone far, and intends to go further.' The younger listeners, when they'd finished revolting and rejoicing at the portrayal of the plight of the poor, might have preferred some anecdotes about Charlie Chaplin.

The BBC management may not have been quite as dazzled as 'Jane' but they were sufficiently pleased with his work to waive their usual rule – that critics should be changed each year. A memo of 15 January 1936 notes that 'the standard set by Alistair Cooke is so high that the finding of a successor to carry on after him will be very difficult'. What's more, 'Mr Cooke is not what we call "in the racket". He has a high standard of taste and thus fulfils one of the most important requirements for a BBC Film Critic.' And the writer, Rose-Troup, having paid tribute to Cooke's 'really good broadcasting personality', recommends a further extension to his contract. This idea is enthusiastically taken up by another executive, Lindsay Wellington (the man who, in 1946, would commission the first ever *Letter from America*).

Wellington's comments say much about the struggle taking place within the BBC about the corporation's role in the mid-1930s. 'It is all too rare', he writes on 29 January,

> to find someone with personality and charm whose qualities are undimmed by microphone and loudspeakers. More relevantly, I would say that it is particularly important that the BBC should enable its listeners to hear vigorous, intelligent (but not Bloomsbury) appreciation of the cinema, because it is a popular art which is normally swallowed whole, uncritically and unintelligently. The Cooke approach to the subject is the very influence one would wish to bring to bear upon the man who 'just goes to the pictures'.

The upshot was the offer of a further contract, stretching through into the autumn of 1936, which gave him the space and confidence to develop other ideas. In March, for instance, he put together a programme of American 'hobo' songs called *New York City to the Golden Gate* which was kindly reviewed by the *Star* newspaper: 'Mr Cooke is never dull, always provocative and original.' The reviewer described the programme, with its recordings of the music of itinerant workers trekking round the country by train, as 'brilliantly arranged'.

Cooke reported to his bosses that he received more enthusiastic correspondence over this musical half-hour than from any other single broadcast he'd given. Naturally, his instinct was to propose without delay a full series on similar themes and he even offered a detailed thirteen-week programme plan, but was once again brushed off with vague expressions of interest. At the same time he was trying to sell the idea of a small booklet with recommendations for the pronunciation of American place names, which he hoped might justify an expenses-paid trip to the US, but which was turned down by the Director-General, Sir John Reith, and contributing reviews to magazines such as the *Spectator*. One of these was a rather dismissive account of a new book, *America Came My Way*, by Sir Anthony Jenkinson. Cooke, swiftly spotting an interloper on his territory, accuses Jenkinson of making sweeping statements based on a highly superficial experience of the country.

On top of all that, he accepted gleefully a proposition from Fred Bate, who had been cultivating him assiduously ever since the success of *English on Both Sides of the Atlantic*. Bate commissioned a special NBC programme for the centenary of Mark Twain's birth in 1835: and in due course suggested that Cooke should write a weekly *London Letter* – to be transmitted to New York each Sunday evening. Cooke's gentle survey of the cultural highlights of the week was a direct precursor of the *Letter from America* ten years later.

~

The summer of 1936 brought a visit from Ralph Emerson, Ruth's youngest brother and the one Cooke liked best. They spent time with Bate (who had an exotic black-walled bathroom) and another American, Dick Simpson, who ran the Commonwealth Fund in London. There were further trips to Blackpool, where Cooke was inveigled into adjudicating at the Northern Music Festival and where Ruth shocked the staid folk of the town by appearing in public wearing slacks. David Curnow, the son of Cooke's erstwhile history master, remembers women gaping at her in the street and muttering disparaging remarks as she passed. When he himself was first introduced to her at the age of ten, he stammered out, 'Are you a film star?' She laughed the notion aside, but then produced a copy of *Vogue* which showed her in a Parkinson pose, sporting an aviator's suit complete with goggles. The Cookes must have been a phenomenon, a whiff of high society amid the whelk stalls and beach huts, but at least, with their own unconventional background, they would have been untroubled by the irregular marital status of Curnow himself.

It was a scandalous open secret that, although he was still married with two young sons, 'Billy Wick' was involved in a long-term relationship with one of his former pupils – and Cooke's one-time dancing coach – Hilda Unsworth, more than thirty years his junior. She had fallen in love with Curnow on her seventeenth birthday, when he called round to give her a book as a present. She kissed him on the cheek, as she did all adults who needed to be thanked, but this time it was different: she vowed to herself that she would marry this trim and respectable figure, however long it took. True to her promise, she waited patiently until he was finally ready to divorce his wife more than twenty years later. In the meantime they wrote to each other every day and spent time together whenever they could. This became easier when Hilda returned to Blackpool to look after her dying father. Although this tender love-story remained a taboo subject in polite Blackpool conversation, it seemed quite natural that the Cookes should agree to go for a day's outing to York as a foursome with Curnow and Hilda. It was Ruth, as usual, who managed to raise eyebrows in the prim tea-room beside the Minster by asking for a glass of milk – an outlandish request which caused some panic among the waitresses who had no idea what to serve it in.

Having failed to secure an extended run of BBC film talks for the summer, Alistair and Ruth made alternative arrangements for a trip back to the United States. Cooke's finely honed freelance instincts secured him a commission from the *Observer* for two pieces on the tercentenary of Harvard University. The first, a preview of the event published on 13 September, is an extended history lesson. (As time went on, and aware of his weakness for pedagogy, he would often refer to himself self-mockingly as 'teacher', and his audience as 'the class'.) The second Harvard article is a colourful portrayal of a great gathering of academic eminence as 'blustery wind sprinkled rain from the trees'. The celebrations took in exhibitions, symposia, speeches and church services, but the highlight came with the unexpected visit of FDR, who commanded Harvard to stand for the freedom of the human mind in an age of modern witch-burning. Cooke was moved by the experience, but not just because of the President's powerful speech. As an old Harvard man himself and equipped with a press pass, he had found himself earlier wandering beyond the public areas into an alleyway he'd never seen before. With the rain sheeting down, he was looking for shelter when he was suddenly confronted by a secret-service man, who leaped from a car and demanded to inspect his pass. Having established his *bona fides*, he told Cooke to stand still and wait, because the President was about to arrive.

'The car pulled up about 10 feet away from me. Another secret-service man got out, along with Roosevelt's son, Elliott. Together they lifted the President out of the car and propped him on his feet, and then supported him, with a cane in each hand, towards a special ramp. It was a tremendous shock. Until that moment I had no idea that Roosevelt was crippled.' It was an unnerving revelation, especially for a reporter. Like most Americans, Cooke had been ignorant of the extent of the President's disability, since newsreel pictures were always shot to disguise the fact. But confronted with the reality – and the possibility of a minor scoop – he opted for the traditional reticence, which in any case appealed to him. When he started work as a journalist in New York, he continued to subscribe without demur to the convention that no mention should ever be made of a politician's physical frailty. It was a convention which survived for a further twenty years – until the day of the open recognition that Eisenhower's Secretary of State, John Foster Dulles, was suffering from cancer. This became one of Cooke's favourite topics for historical reflection: was the public good really well served by open discussion of the medical condition of its leaders? Would Roosevelt, for instance, ever have been elected if the truth had been known? Truth, in other words, was not – for Cooke – an absolute force for good. He was in all things a relativist, a trait which did not necessarily endear him to his fellow journalists.

Apart from his Harvard commission, Cooke spent most of this summer at the Emerson family home on Long Island. It was universally known as 'Southold', although strictly speaking that was the name of the township in which the house lay. The real name, Bayside Farm, was in any case a poor description of the hundred-acre spread, overlooking Richmond Creek and Little Peconic Bay beyond. Although New York City was only ninety miles away to the west, Southold was still rooted in the nineteenth century, in a flat and fertile land populated by immigrant farmers, especially Poles. At the heart of this rural community, Dr Haven Emerson had created an island of sophisticated (if uneconomic) self-sufficiency.

The terrain has survived comparatively unscathed to this day, dominated by a large brick-built mansion. A farmhouse lies to one side and dotted around the grounds there are smaller wooden dwellings, where members of the Emerson tribe would bring their families for the summer. Each house bore an affectionately disparaging name – the 'Hut' or the 'Shack'. Back in 1936, all the fields around the house were cultivated, growing grain to feed the milking cows and the pigs. Fruit trees and bushes abounded – peach, pear, cherry, raspberry, blueberry. There were formal gardens surrounded by neat box hedges, a croquet lawn, walkways through alleys of trees, and lawns on which children could run barefoot. It was designed less as a business enterprise, and more as a refuge from the health hazards of the city (like infantile paralysis) and as a place where Emerson could indulge in the pleasures of physical labour.

Most of the money for this idyll came from Ruth's mother's side of the family, Emerson himself being too busy improving other people's lives to accumulate any wealth of his own. But there was no doubt about who was in charge. Guests were supposed to attend the evening meal with Dr Emerson at the 'Big House', and many did not find it a relaxing experience. After a day working at his trees and shrubs, he could be tired and crabby. He would push aside all the cutlery and plates from his place, retaining only a bowl and a spoon which he used for the whole meal – insisting that it was a waste of time to generate a pile of washing-up. In addition, Ruth's brothers and sister were all alarmingly brilliant in their own scientific fields. Bob (the one who called Cooke a four-flusher) was a biologist, Ralph became a distinguished botanist, while Jack was credited with perfecting the modern iron lung.

For Cooke, however, this was not the most problematical aspect of a visit to Southold. Indeed he had a jovial relationship with his mother-in-law Grace and soon established a decent rapport with the great man himself, based largely on a genuine interest in the latter's field of study. Dr Emerson, like all obsessives, enjoyed nothing better than relating his favourite epidemiological investigation to an attentive audience. He told them like detective stories: why, for instance, had a large number of American soldiers serving in the South of France during the First World War suddenly gone down with acute food poisoning? Emerson noticed that most of the sufferers had Italian names, and a hunch led him to the discovery that in their home state of Connecticut they were accustomed to eat a particular wild mushroom. They thought they'd found the same plant in France, but instead they'd been eating poisonous toadstools. Emerson was also instrumental in establishing that the miners' disease, silicosis, was caused by the conditions in which they worked, rather than simply being a type of tuberculosis.

Cooke found the subject fascinating, so much so that he speculated openly one day about whether he might give up his career for the study of medicine. Emerson was dismissive. 'My dear boy,' he said, 'you are 27 years of age and you have lost all your intellectual flexibility. Einstein made his greatest discovery at the age of 26. For you, it is too late.'

Yet although Ruth's mother and father were able to overcome their misgivings about having a feckless writer in the family, Cooke's sojourn at Southold was still uneasy. It was, after all, a place for outdoor pursuits. All the Emerson children had been brought up to feel at home both in and on the water, sailing over to the great sandy bluffs across the sound, canoeing, or enjoying the beaches, coves and marshland that were overlooked by the house. This was in line with Haven Emerson's favourite dictum: 'If we left the automobile in the garage a little oftener and took to our legs, we'd most likely have fewer coronaries and need fewer laxatives.' Cooke, seditiously, was very much happier with a good book.

Ruth felt that he was often discomfited by the healthy heartiness of the Emersons *en masse*: 'It was hard on him, because he had none of the skills that my brothers had. If he did come out in a boat, he never knew what to do.' It was a relief when the couple were able to move into the comparative privacy of one of the outbuildings. In the summer of 1936, this meant the Bungalow, a rambling wooden structure built thirty years earlier in the Indian style, with a cool and spacious screened porch along two walls. Even in this peaceful spot Cooke seems to have been irked by a sense of isolation from the city life on which he'd come to rely. The movie theatre in the nearby town of Greenport was hardly a substitute for the West End of London, but they visited it none the less, and finished these evenings in the local bowling alley. Fortunately, at least part of the trip was spent in the reassuringly urban surroundings of an apartment next to Central Park. That was quite enough nature for Cooke.

It was from here in New York, by special dispensation, that he broadcast to London the first film talk of the autumn season. Such long-range contributions were rare enough to cause consternation back at the BBC headquarters in London. Memos and messages fluttered back and forth, until Felix Greene, recently appointed as the Corporation's first North American Representative, finally snapped. Somebody cabled, asking him to 'Confirm you have seen Alistair Cooke'. In a note to 'Whoever sent the attached cable', he wrote, 'This is the silliest message I've yet received.' He listed everything that had been done to ensure that nothing would go wrong and finished in a fine fury: 'It reminds me of the classic War Office telegram to Hamilton at Gallipoli, sent three days after his desperate S.O.S. messages for more munitions – "Your messages are under consideration. Please inform us of the state of your ammunition and how much you require – if any!" And has our friend Alistair Cooke *ever* been known to produce his script seven hours in advance, let alone seven days?'

$\sim$

If Cooke sometimes irritated his employers, he continued at the same time to be widely respected as a performer. In September 1936 Cecil Lewis – a veteran of the BBC's earliest days – was given the task of seeking out speakers who might be suitable for the new medium of television. He consulted the radio management and asked for possible contributors under three headings: those who had achieved a 'personality' through broadcasting, rather than celebrities who happened to be good broadcasters; those who could be trusted to speak fluently without a script, but still with discretion (as defined by the BBC); and those with a 'charm of manner and personal appearance' likely to give them a head start over other less attractive personalities. Lewis acknowledged that the illustrated talks he had in mind were still ill-defined, but asked his correspondent to 'fling the net wide'.

The response is certainly frank. While Malcolm Sargent (music) is said to qualify in both classes 1 and 3, the writer warns that Mrs Arthur Webb (subject – cookery) would, once she started talking without notes, have to be stopped with a hammer. Miss Arnot Robertson (literary subjects and an anti-feminist) might do, 'if you can televise red hair!', but Julian Huxley should be 'kept off pseudo-scientific subjects which have a political angle'. Of Alistair Cooke, the survey reports: 'Class 1 and 3; also 2 so far as easy talking is concerned, but needs watching on policy. Chief interests films and the United States. Will talk about United States manners and customs, hobo songs etc.' Despite this recommendation, the caveat raised over his ability to stick to the BBC rules might – had he seen it – have given him pause for thought.

He may not have been helped by a flurry of press interest in a lunch-time speech he gave (in November 1936) to the Film Exhibitors' Club in London. An open letter in the journal *Cinema Today* attacked him for peddling his own prejudices. 'It is easy enough to pooh-pooh a film because it does not achieve the heights of Frank Capra or Walt Disney, just as it is easy enough for a child to take the four nuts off a piece of clockwork and watch the wheels fall out over the floor. But is either activity really constructive?' The correspondent of the *Daily Film Renter* was even more corrosive:

> For nearly an hour this guy roved all over the face of the hemisphere and dilated on every conceivable topic under the sun, whether it be political, military or what have you. He then informed us that he went to bed at 3.30 and rose at 12.30 – and for my part, after listening to his speech I am bound to confess he could have overslept!!

This infuriated scribe was finally driven to walk out when Cooke launched an attack on double-feature bills. 'He advocated that the perfect program would be a feature with Clark Gable – and a documentary, preferably Anstey's *Housing Problems*. Blimey!! That was enough for me – I had to flee!'

For a man 'not in the racket', this speech was probably sailing close to the wind: after all, some of Cooke's best friends were those makers of documentaries whose interests he was so keen to promote. In his own eyes, however, he was probably doing no more than telling a few home truths to a cinema industry where crass commercialism and culture had already begun their long battle for supremacy. There is certainly no evidence of any decline in his professional self-confidence as 1936 drew to its climactic conclusion – though, as it turned out, there should have been.

~

The evening of the first day of December produced a classic London pea-souper – a fog as impenetrable and atmospheric as any whipped up by a Hollywood film studio for a Sherlock Holmes movie. In the 'stew of grey mist', as Cooke wrote, 'a landmark such as the Tower or the Houses of Parliament loomed up like the prow of an oncoming liner'. Cooke himself was in the company, that evening, of learned and thoughtful men meeting under the auspices of the English Speaking Union to develop ways of improving the British view of the United States. At one point the chairman, Sir Frederick Whyte, asked the cartoonist David Low whether he could adjust his portrayal of the typical American, always shown as 'a moon-faced man with horn-rimmed spectacles and belted trousers hitched high above his ankles.'

Low protested that national stereotypes were what his readers wanted and could not be eradicated overnight.

Despite the broad range of backgrounds represented – apart from the journalists, there were a soldier, a lawyer, a Conservative MP and a number of academics – one topic was never raised in that night's conversation, a topic that was certainly on the minds of all present and assuredly the most explosive aspect of Anglo-American relations of the hour. For several months the American press had been speculating about 'the dire consequences of a royal episode that no more than a few hundred Britons at most had ever heard of: namely, the King's affair with Mrs Simpson'. A Democratic Congressman in Washington had even announced publicly that he would introduce a resolution forbidding American representatives to attend the coronation of a king 'who proposed marriage to an American divorcee'. Yet so far, not a word had appeared in the British press, bound as it was by the self-denying ordinance enforced by the Newspaper Proprietors Association.

In the strange and artificial silence which held Britain in its thrall, Cooke, like most of the others in that Mayfair meeting, was among the minority in the know. Thanks to his friendship with Ferdinand Kuhn of the *New York Times* (one of the contributors to *The American Half-Hour*) he had read all that paper's dispatches over the previous two weeks. On 26 November, for instance, the *NYT* inferred correctly that the King had threatened to abdicate when he summoned the Prime Minister, Stanley Baldwin, to Buckingham Palace. (The British press recorded the visit in a perfunctory paragraph as a procedural formality.) Two days later, New Yorkers read that the British Cabinet had held an emergency session to discuss the King's implacable determination to step down. (In Britain, the 'emergency' discussed was supposed to be the Spanish Civil War.)

It was on that murky December evening that the dam of silence finally burst, and Cooke was one of the very first to reap the journalistic benefits. He described the moment of truth – heralded by a knock on the door as the meeting drew to an inconclusive end – in *Six Men*:

> A prune-faced butler glided to the chairman's side and announced, 'There is a telephone call from New York for Mr Cooke.' It is hard today to convey the sinister prestige implicit in such a line at such a time. Long before the

transatlantic cable, when the radio circuits had to go from New York to exotic places like Tangier, telephone calls between London and the United States were placed only by such as the Rockefellers, Presidents of the United States, and export-import millionaires. The meeting was chilled into silence by the news that I was wanted on the phone, and Sir Frederick gave me an alarmed but kindly look as if I, a young film critic with a known bee in my bonnet about the United States, had been suddenly unmasked as an informer. Flushed with embarrassment heavily tinged with self-importance, I excused myself and was taken into an adjoining office.

The voice on the other end of the line, faint but excited, was that of Fred Bate, who had just returned to America on a Christmas holiday. The timing of his trip was unfortunate. To his intense frustration, he had arrived home just in time to hear that a radio station in upstate New York had forecast the King's imminent abdication. Cooke queried why a small-town radio station should be paid such attention and added that, in any case, no one in Britain had heard of Mrs Simpson. Bate replied that the American papers were full of the dramatic news that the Bishop of Bradford had broken the voluntary censorship of the British establishment and castigated the King. 'It was vital', Cooke was told, 'to get to Broadcasting House, do a five-minute talk, six minutes – anything! – as long as it was finished by midnight.' Bate promised they would break into any programme on the air to accommodate him. 'Nothing will be believed in America from now on,' he said, 'except what comes from London.'

Cooke knew that one reason for Bate's insistence on the timing of his broadcast was that his rivals at CBS had a circuit booked at midnight. That left him less than two hours to gather reaction to a story almost no one in London had yet heard. Fortunately David Wills, one of his Harvard friends – by now a journalist with the *News Chronicle* – was sitting next door with the rest of the English Speaking Union's Research and Discussion Committee. With minimal explanation, he scooped him up and together they rushed to Fleet Street, where the newsroom was awash with rumours about what Bishop Blunt had had to say. In cold print, those words scarcely amounted to a head-on attack, but their message was judged to be clear, especially the prayerful hope that the King, with God's grace, should do his duty: 'We hope that he is aware of his need. Some of us wish that he gave more positive signs of his awareness.' It emerged later – too late – that Blunt was not referring to Mrs Simpson, of whom he'd never heard, but to a veiled suggestion that changes in the coronation service might lead to the disestablishment of the Church. But the blue touch-paper, once lit, could not be extinguished.

Cooke heard that a number of regional papers were going to press with stern editorials which – although they did not name the King's lover – made their feelings about his predicament abundantly clear. The *Birmingham Post*, for instance, decided that the Bishop must have been fully satisfied that 'the gossip, rumour and highly circumstantial tale-telling as to one particular phase of His Majesty's private life is not without its base of solid truth'. It warned the King that, in the eyes of his people, 'the private and public life of the King-Emperor are inseparable'. This was bold stuff and the *News Chronicle* was preparing to take the same line in its own coverage of the story. Cooke grabbed a smudged proof copy of the article and set out to fulfil the second part of his brief – to relay the palpitating scenes of national excitement unleashed by the news.

There were none, of course. He wandered aimlessly around the streets before repairing to Broadcasting House with only a matter of minutes to go before he was due to perform. He ad-libbed as best he could, 'recounting for an American audience the amazing sustained silence of the British press, and hoping that the Bishop knew what he was doing in breaking it'. When it came to describing the reaction of Londoners, Cooke came to the conclusion that the *lack* of a reaction was itself the story and that 'understatement in behaviour is the very pith of English living, with a dramatic quality all its own – the most authentic local colour'.

The BBC was not impressed. The moment the red light went off, the announcer, a retired major with an arrogant air, bounded into the studio. 'Blue with rage, and flexing his jaw-muscles like pistons, he said very deliberately, "I have *never* heard anything like it. It is *absolutely mon*strous that an Englishman should use a BBC circuit to denigrate His Majesty the King before a foreign audience. You may be *quite* sure that I shall report this to my superiors." '

Even if the threat was carried out, it was instantly overtaken by events, as the British press tumbled over each other to make up for lost time. Cooke was quick to quote Mencken's view that this was 'the greatest story since the Crucifixion' and he himself set off on an unprecedented broadcasting marathon. In the twelve days between

Bishop Blunt's pronouncement and the final capitulation of the King to the reality of his situation, Cooke delivered a non-stop stream of commentary to an NBC audience across the United States. While CBS brought in a range of distinguished British voices, from H.G. Wells to Harold Nicolson, to pad out their coverage, NBC kept faith with Cooke. 'I found myself putting New York to bed at four in the morning London time, doing the same for California three hours later, then waking New York at noon, the mountain states at two, California at three, and so on.'

Sometimes there were real news developments to report: the Cabinet meetings at which the Baldwin government steadfastly refused to contemplate the possibility that Edward could marry and remain King; the ebb and flow of dignitaries to the King's private residence, Fort Belvedere, a few miles south of Windsor Castle; and the denouement, as Edward boarded the destroyer *Fury* in the small hours of 12 December and slipped away into exile. But for much of the time, Cooke had to fall back on anecdotes, potted versions of British constitutional history and, in desperation, the recitation of undigested chunks of newspaper articles.

There were news reports of four or five minutes, and longer, more reflective pieces, like the (rather short) history of abdications. It wasn't easy for the reporters. As a special edition of the magazine *Weekly Illustrated* – (THE ROYAL CRISIS: EXCLUSIVE PICTURES) – put it, 'Crowds gathered at all points of interest – outside the Palace, in Downing Street, near Mrs Simpson's home in Regent's Park, and on the roads around Fort Belvedere. They had to be content, for the most part, with occasional glimpses of closed cars and barely recognisable occupants.' In those circumstances Cooke was lucky to have a good leg man, prepared to peer into those closed cars, traipse round pubs and clubs, and infiltrate the crowds at Downing Street and the Palace. The leg man – a blond, bespectacled twenty-year-old – was Walt Rostow, eventually Chief National Security Adviser to Lyndon Johnson during the Vietnam War.

Cooke himself quite soon contracted an infection which caused flu-like fever, and warned Bate that he might have to retire to bed. NBC promptly organised a Post Office line to be run into Cooke's house, linked to a microphone in his living-room, and told him to keep up the good work. In *Six Men*, Cooke claims to have broadcast 400,000 words over the ten days of the abdication crisis. This is one of those impossible estimates which has varied over time and with constant re-telling of the story. If he spoke at an average speed of two or three words a second, he would have had to broadcast for almost five hours a day to reach such a total. The evidence of the fee he was eventually paid (which was to become an important issue in its own right) produces a figure somewhere nearer to 150,000 words, or just over one and a half hours a day. It may not sound so gruelling, but the crucial fact was the way the speaking-time was dispersed across twenty-four hours, never allowing for proper rest. That probably constitutes some sort of record.

A few recorded examples survive of this epic endeavour. What strikes the listener immediately is the slight mid-Atlantic twang of the voice, the flattened 'a's (a characteristic of American speech, but also a throwback to his North of England origins), the distinctive lengthening of the stressed syllable of 'ex*hau*sted' and '*clothe*s' – and yet at the same time, elements of upper-class (Jesus College) English accentuation, reminiscent of Noël Coward. It's as if he was trying to make himself accessible to an American audience, while letting them know that he spoke from the well-informed heart of the British Establishment.

On the last night of the crisis – between 10 and 11 December – Cooke broadcast via short-wave link at great length and with almost nothing to say: the scratchy recording survives in New York's Museum of Broadcasting. He read out all the various movements of the leading figures in minute detail: 'At 10.50 Sir John Simon, the Home Secretary . . . At 4.19, the Premier and Mr Monckton [Attorney-General to the Prince of Wales] left on what some people say was an historical journey to Fort Belvedere . . . 10.00 p.m. After dining with the King, Mr Baldwin left . . . ' This section of his talk ends with the honest admission, 'That's all the news of the day.' It wasn't, however, the end of his broadcast. For a man who always eschewed idle speculation, Cooke was stretching the available facts thinly, as he improvised through the night.

'It was said in London that Mr Baldwin, on his way home, knew the final decision and was troubled by the word "abdication". If Mr Baldwin pondered on that word as his car rumbled along the damp Surrey roads, if he thought it was an ugly or alien word, he could reflect with a shadow of comfort that it was all too familiar to English kings and English ministers, though it has not been used in an official document since 1688.' There followed an exhaustive history-lesson, before Cooke launched into a critical survey of the British character when faced by a crisis; it was based, he suggested, on the ostrich principle: burying the head in the sand allows the pleasant picture of the *status quo* to remain unsullied.

Next, Cooke read out the entire line of succession after the King's younger brother, the Duke of York, taking in such unknowns as the Earl of Macduff (number thirteen) – and ending with the distant prospect of Queen Maud of Norway or her son, Prince Olaf, succeeding to the British throne. Finally, as the end of the slot approached at an agonisingly slow pace, he reached his peroration. His voice weary and downbeat, the pauses long drawn-out – he gazes from the window of his studio and offers this surreal picture of the capital city:

> It's four o'clock just striking in the London streets, the long empty streets, and the only animation is the meaningless regular winking of green and red lights along an Oxford Street without a car in sight. No! Sorry, there goes one square taxi now, waiting to reach the top of a small gradient so he can move into second gear. And at this dead hour of night, there's no more rumour and conjecture. A nation sits over fire and stove and waits, and almost unanimously hopes, that Mr Baldwin crawling back through the fog knew the answer, and that tomorrow it will be the right one. Good night.

It is a minor miracle of bricks without straw.

The following day, along with the reports of events in the House of Commons and the confirmation that the King was indeed stepping down, Cooke offered a personal view of the man as he himself had found him – a small, neat figure who preferred small rooms filled with personal photos and pipes. The portrait is polished and lovingly drawn. Cooke was moved by the human predicament, while respecting the predominant view in the country that Edward should have known from the start that he could be King, or married to Mrs Simpson, but not both.

Over the years, however, the generosity of Cooke's assessment wore off. In *Six Men*, he quotes extensively from the biography of Edward by Frances Donaldson, which is frank about the shortcomings of the King. 'Edward comes out of it all as one of the least enlightened of British monarchs – a charming, spoiled, woefully ill-educated man, painfully simple-minded and ferociously acquisitive.' And Cooke ends this chapter with a chilling epitaph, one from which 'all comfortable people should cower from deserving: he was only at his best when the going was good'.

10

A NATURAL THING TO DO

At some time between 12 December 1936 and 21 January 1937, Alistair and Ruth decided to pack up and leave for America – as it turned out, for good. Although it wasn't immediately clear how much NBC would pay for Cooke's abdication endeavours, it was bound to be a substantial sum – and almost certainly enough to fund a transatlantic move. Asked to submit a bill, Cooke did his best to tally all the words he'd spoken, and computed the final figure at the BBC rate of a guinea a minute: it came to £1100 – roughly equivalent to two years of his BBC salary. With grave misgivings, he dispatched this unlikely demand to head office in New York, hardly daring to believe in such largesse.

But even before the reply arrived, he began to prepare for his departure. Looking back from old age, he brushed aside the significance of the decision. It was 'something we always intended to do': he was 'just waiting for the opportunity'. He was married to an American woman and expected to have American children. It was 'no big deal': he remembered his father telling him after the Great War that, in the ensuing peace, all men would become 'citizens of the world', travelling freely without passports.

Cooke certainly had good reason to expect that there would be an appetite for articles and broadcasts about the United States. As he told a magazine interviewer in 1980, 'I developed a strong yen to get back to America. England was sort of grey, cowed and dreary. The only thing people were reading from America was drivel about gangsters and movie stars. I saw real potential.' He had already started casting around for possible sources of employment, contacting – among others – his old linguistics professor at Harvard, Miles Hanley. The professor mentioned the possibility of a Fellowship in 'American English' at Wisconsin and the nascent university radio station, but added, 'I have no idea whether such a thing would be attractive or sufficiently lucrative for you.'

There was another reason for his decision, when it came, to walk away so abruptly from a successful career and an absorbing lifestyle – a sudden dip in his popularity at Broadcasting House. Even if he was unaware at the time of the depth of the displeasure he'd occasioned, he must have detected the cooling of the atmosphere. In fact his boss Rose-Troup sat down on 17 November, just before the abdication drama, and wrote the stiffest of stiff memos. 'I propose to take immediate steps to get possible successors to Alistair Cooke to record specimen talks, and at the same time to tell Alistair Cooke that we wish to discontinue his talks at Easter.' What had caused this intemperate outburst? Rose-Troup hastened to explain:

> Cooke has become increasingly difficult about sending in scripts and conforming to normal procedure, but I get the impression that his talks are not quite as good as they were. It is just possible that when he knows that he is not going to go on after Easter, he will go all slack or make so many difficulties that he becomes impossible to handle. In that case, I am quite prepared to drop him immediately, and to put in another man at two days' notice. If I am actually in a position to do this, the threat will, I think, be enough to keep him straight until Easter.

The coincidence of the NBC cheque meant that he saved the BBC the trouble – and awkwardness – of sacking him. It was presumably a relief for Rose-Troup to be able to inform his colleagues, towards the end of January, that Cooke was intending to quit the country in early April. At Easter, in other words.

Could Ruth, perhaps, have been home-sick? She had been away from home for the best part of two years and may well have been lonely: she certainly remembers the anxiety of being apart from her husband for so much of each day. But in her recollection those feelings were never strong enough to prompt the dramatic step they planned to take. A more immediate spur was the enthusiasm of NBC for more Cooke offerings. Fred Bate was full of praise for his efforts during that frenetic fortnight, and told him that there would be plenty of work in New York. It wouldn't, to be sure, be a staff job, but Cooke must have calculated that he'd have no trouble building up a portfolio of outlets for his work. To reassure him still further, there was the evidence of a poll (conducted among 620 radio station editors) for the American magazine *Fame*, in which he was placed twelfth in a list of the best commentators of the year. The intriguing question remains: did he regard it as a temporary or permanent migration? The question arises because in April 1937, just before sailing from Southampton, Cooke gave an interview to the *Blackpool Gazette*: he would be away, he told the paper, 'probably eighteen months'.

The *Gazette*, describing Cooke's plans as a 'big American adventure', adopted its usual breathless style. Cooke would be – in his own words – a 'modern Columbus'! This pretentious claim was supported by his intention to 'travel 12,000-odd miles in an old "flivver" [a cheap car] to discover odd corners, odd people and odd jobs'. More mundanely, the article explains that Cooke will 'broadcast regularly from New York on the theatre, films, books or personalities' and 'relay talks from New York to England for the BBC on big national events'. It adds that, if time allows, he will write a book of short stories for an English publisher – one of many unfulfilled literary aspirations.

Could the *Gazette* have exaggerated or elaborated on these views? Or misquoted the proposed absence of just eighteen months? As it happens, it's possible to demonstrate that Cooke was perfectly happy with most of the report because he took the trouble to demand a correction, in a letter to the editor, over one particular passage – a passage which referred to the opportunities for a freelance journalist in a country where 'the average American knows far less about his country than the average Englishman can tell him'.

This, Cooke complains, is 'doubly unfortunate because it says exactly the opposite of what I have, for several years now, in interpreting America to England, tried to make clear.' Namely, that it is the English who suffer from a knowledge deficit. 'We are taught nothing of American literature, history, art, architecture; there are only two universities in the British Isles which maintain chairs of American history; and our newspapers give neither the same space nor the same seriousness to the reporting of American affairs.' The English, consequently, he finds to be ignorant and misinformed about America, its people, its habits, thinking and traditions. He ends with another of his periodic attempts to write himself a job description: 'It will need many years of disinterested study of a continent, and much more humility from all visiting Englishmen, before even the most extraordinary of them can tell Americans anything that is valuable or relevant to the land and the problems that confront the "average American".'

The inference of the article, reinforced by the reply, is clear: this might turn out to be a provisional emigration, with all options kept open. It adds to the sense that, although Cooke had a clear idea of the sort of journalistic niche he might be able to fill, he had no specific strategy to achieve his ambitions – except for the abiding hope that the BBC might one day appoint him their 'man in America'. To complicate matters he had spent most of the winter going through the rigmarole of applying to the American Embassy for an immigrant visa, which was the first step to becoming a fully-fledged citizen.

Perhaps, after all, the mention of eighteen months was designed to placate an anxious mother, who didn't need to be told immediately that her son might be leaving for good.

One other idea was planted in his mind during this restless period. He had a farewell dinner with his friend John Grierson, the documentary filmmaker, who had himself spent time in the States on a Fellowship in the 1920s. Grierson questioned whether Cooke really would return to Britain: 'What about being a Foreign Correspondent?' he suggested. 'There's a real job to be done, reporting from America.' And to underline his view that most commentators were rooted in the sterile stereotypes of Hollywood, he went on: 'What we need is someone who'll tell the English what's good about Babbitt.' The eponymous anti-hero of Sinclair Lewis's satirical novel had come to represent the philistinism of small-town America: any correspondent who could persuade his readers to sympathise with Babbitt . . .

At the time, Cooke dismissed the notion of becoming a news reporter as preposterous. He saw his future as an observer on cultural and social affairs, and in his last few weeks as a film critic, he spent much of the time bending the ear of anyone at the BBC who might commission him to make the sort of programmes he'd been making in London. On 5 April, for instance, he went to see Cecil Graves, Controller of Programmes. Graves noted afterwards that he'd told Cooke that he could be 'very useful to us as commentator or presenter of certain special programmes which we took from the other side'. But it was a time of considerable flux at Broadcasting House. While serious policy disagreements were being fought out at the highest level, there were no guarantees to be had – and still, in some BBC quarters, that indefinable sense of dissatisfaction about Cooke. A memo from one of his senior producers, Malcolm Brereton, summed up the spring series of film criticism with a rather weary finality. Although there would, at first, be many who regretted losing Cooke's 'scintillating style and manifest knowledge of the subject', Brereton asserted that the new man would have no difficulty letting the public know just as much about the cinema.

Newspaper reports at the time were more generous. 'There will be much regret throughout a large audience . . . his cinema talks have achieved what few, if any, other speakers on films have achieved, by combining an appeal to intelligence with an appeal to the widest range of tastes and interests . . . no broadcaster has so successfully or sympathetically presented American ways of living and thinking to an English audience.'

The Cookes' final few months in England continued much as before, although he took some time to recover from the sickness he'd contracted during the abdication crisis. He was sufficiently worried to visit his doctor, who advised a chest X-ray. The result was to produce the first of many medical eccentricities which Cooke was to collect, cherish and chew over for the rest of his life. He never had a simple complaint. Others might have a fever or a lung infection, but Cooke's X-ray discovered something much more interesting: the doctor was fascinated by the level of costal calcification – a natural build-up of calcium deposits on the rib-cage.'Such levels', he opined, 'are those to be expected in a man of fifty-nine'. Cooke, who was twenty-eight, was bewildered by the precision of the diagnosis – fifty-nine seemed such a curious age to choose. Was the condition dangerous? 'We attach to this fact', the doctor went on, 'no pathological significance whatsoever.'

He was to demonstrate – and enjoy discussing – several other such quirks of medical science to which he seemed unusually prone. In the early 1940s for instance, he went for a medical examination in New York and found himself confronted by two doctors. One, a Cuban, asked him to take off his shirt – and went white when he saw that Cooke's body was completely covered in a rash of tiny red pin pricks, like scarlet fever. Naturally, neither doctor had ever seen anything like it and it was left to the patient to explain that it was an exceptionally rare condition, urticaria pigmentosa. It had been diagnosed earlier by a woman in New England who charged him $50 for the depressing advice that the only solution was to avoid sunlight and soap. The Cuban dimly remembered reading about the disease in medical school. 'We were told that a dermatologist could go through his whole career and never see a case! And if he did, it was nearly always a child!' Cooke's fascination with the subject eventually developed into a full-blown passion. He was never happier than befriending (and bending the ears of) doctors and never more delighted than when he could amaze them with the rarity of his condition: 'Pseudo-gout – no, not the ordinary kind with a build-up of uric acid crystals: *Pseudo*-gout – calcium pyrophosphate. Same symptoms as gout, but actually a form of arthritis. How many cases have you seen in your life? Not many, I bet.'

~

At some time during the spring Cooke went to see Fred Bate's secretary to hear about the final fee for his abdication broadcasts. He discovered that NBC had done its own rough calculation about what might be appropriate – and come up with a figure of $20–25,000, at least five times more than the bill he'd submitted. There was some joking about whether they should split the difference, but he ended up with precisely what he'd asked for – £1,100. Somehow, it didn't seem so much any more.

~

In the second week of April 1937, the Cookes closed up the Devonport Street flat and headed for Southampton – setting sail aboard the American liner, *Manhattan*, on the 16th, for a journey that almost ended in a New York police cell. The couple struck up conversation on board with a former American army officer, a distinguished figure in late middle age, who informed them that he was also a member of the Catholic lay order, the Knights of Columbus. Cooke was delighted to talk about his work as a film critic. What sort of films did he cover? Well, all sorts – for example, the newly released thriller *A Marked Woman*, based on the career of the Mafia godfather, Lucky Luciano, who had finally been arrested a year earlier for running a New York prostitution racket. This led the young journalist to discourse on the Mob's hold on Manhattan Island. 'I once did a talk on the subject in London,' he told his new friend, '. . . about how New Yorkers have to pay protection money to get fresh vegetables brought onto the island – and to stop their laundry being burned with acid. The rackets have got a real grip on the place.'

The army veteran seemed fascinated. What Cooke didn't know was that his cocktail-bar acquaintance was making a mental note of everything he said, ready to rush off with a report of the conversation to the ship's purser. Once the alarm had been raised, a radio message was sent ahead to the docks, with a request for an interview to be conducted with whoever had acted as referee (and guarantor of his good behaviour) on Cooke's immigration papers. This, it transpired, was none other than the supremely respectable Dr Haven Emerson, who was amused by the idea that his son-in-law might be a seditious rabble-rouser. He delivered the appropriate reassurances and, by the time the couple stepped ashore on 24 April, the trouble had evaporated. The first Cooke knew about it was when Emerson regaled him with the story.

~

A new freelance career in a foreign land was bound to require a good deal of groundwork, but first things had to come first – and that meant travel. Back in the winter, Cooke had come to a complicated arrangement with Charles Siepmann, the executive who'd given him his first BBC break. Siepmann had subsequently found himself shifted sideways into an unwanted job and had spent most of 1936 traipsing round the British Isles, preparing a lengthy report on the regions' broadcasting needs. As an escape, Cooke helped him secure a three-month study-tour of the United States to investigate educational radio.

The tour was timed to end in mid-April, just as the Cookes arrived from London, and the three agreed to meet up in Tennessee. Alistair and Ruth took the train from New York and, as they rolled into Memphis station, they spotted their friend strolling up and down the platform. 'It was a hot day for April,' Cooke remembered. 'Most of the Southerners were in shirt-sleeves, or seersucker suits if they were going to work. Yet there was Charles, immaculately turned out in a double-breasted suit and a black Homburg. And he was carrying a rolled umbrella in case of rain.' Siepmann – BBC man incarnate. The first thing they did was to find him a new lightweight suit, before buying a car for $100. Siepmann was provided with an American driving licence by the simple expedient of stating his age. They were ready for Cooke's third great American odyssey.

Memphis and New Orleans represented Mecca for a true disciple of the blues. As Cooke put it later, 'Back home in England, we hankered after these places the way Americans yearn for Loch Lomond and the Taj Mahal.' And elsewhere, on the disc which represented his musical autobiography: 'Memphis was a compulsory stop, like Athens to a classical scholar: as I came out of the station for the first time, I saw two big, dark, angular men squatting on the sidewalk, beating a piece of metal with a hammer. They were most likely fixing somebody's fender, but I thought it was some all-American voodoo, because one of them was singing to himself, "Going to the country, Baby bird – I can't take you … ".'

Their hosts in New Orleans, however, did not fully understand that Cooke was ready for a religious experience. 'They were nice, indulgent people and asked if I wanted to see the Cathedral and a grove of trees President Andrew Jackson had once brooded under. I'm afraid that all I wanted to see were the prostitutes' cribs in Storyville, and the transoms of the old gay houses on Basin Street. They were slightly petrified, but they took me anyway.' The reality was something of a disappointment. Basin Street was still there, of course, with the names of legendary inhabitants engraved on the transoms above the doors: Lulu White, in ornate script, appears in one photograph he took. But the place had been robbed of its atmosphere and its soul. It was New Orleans, but not as he'd imagined it.

The trio then turned west, aiming for California: a visit to Chaplin in Los Angeles, and then, often by the back roads, north through the Sequoia National Park to San Francisco. There, the car was sold for $25 (it had been a hard journey) and Siepmann took his leave. The Cookes stayed on with an Emerson uncle for a while before taking a train back to the East Coast. They occupied themselves by filming each other with the 8mm camera: in the middle of the prairies, Cooke panned away from his wife onto the passing scenery and suddenly noticed in his viewfinder a flag flying at half-mast. It marks the day as 23 May, when the nation was informed of the death of one of its financial father figures – John D. Rockefeller.

In New York Alistair and Ruth had found themselves a small apartment at 166, East 78th Street, between Third Avenue and Lexington. It was a new 'walk-up' building next to one of the familiar old blocks with an awning leading out onto the street: in other words, they were three floors up and there was no elevator. It suited them well enough, even after they discovered that the elevated railway (the 'el') ran dispiritingly close to their bedroom window. From this base, Cooke proceeded to link up with any contacts who might nurture his freelance future. The BBC's North America Representative, Felix Greene, was an early port of call. Greene was in the process of expanding the number and range of programmes to be broadcast from the United States, and doing so more or less single-handed. Although, left to himself, he might have welcomed contributions from Cooke, he didn't have much to offer.

Long negotiations with Broadcasting House in London had just determined that the main commentator for the coming year would be
Raymond Gram Swing.

Swing was a remarkable character. He'd spent years as a correspondent in Germany and other European countries, writing under
the byline of plain 'Raymond Swing'. On his return the latest of his five
wives, Betty Gram, insisted that if she was going to take his name, he'd
have to take hers in return. The result was an unforgettable combination, which seemed to transform his desirability as an employee.
Cooke was a great admirer: 'Swing was the son of an Ohio preacher
with a marvellous voice. He could take a subject like agricultural appro-
priation and make it sound as if the world was coming to an end – all
the drama of Lady Macbeth.' From the BBC's point of view, Raymond
Gram Swing had the advantage of maturity (he was in his fifties) and
familiarity with Europe, as well as that memorable voice and a name to
match. The only problem was that he was asking for £2000 to com-
pensate him for giving up a contract to write for the *News Chronicle* in
London. The compromise Felix Greene had just reached was that Swing
should be employed on a week-by-week basis, in the hope that he could,
in time, be weaned away from the *Chronicle*. The programme would be
called *American Commentary*.

For Cooke this must have been a blow. Raymond Gram Swing was,
in effect, being given the very project he'd cherished above all others.
There was to be no formal place for him in the BBC scheme of things.

It didn't matter too much, because NBC were as good as Fred Bate's
word. On Bate's instruction, Cooke called on the corporation's New
York supremo, an Irishman called John Royal. 'I was summoned into
his office,' Cooke explained, 'and he simply asked me what I'd like to
do.' After some discussion they settled on a weekly broadcast of fifteen
minutes, scheduled for Wednesday evenings. It would, in effect, be the
London Letter transposed to New York – reviews, criticisms and personal musings, but eschewing politics. 'Then he wanted to know how
much I would charge, but I had no idea what to ask.' Royal called in his
secretary, a Miss O'Connor, and inquired how much NBC were paying
another popular commentator, Hendrik van Loon. Miss O'Connor
made a signal behind Cooke's back. He still didn't know what to expect.
'Do you think you're as good as van Loon?' Royal said.

'If I wasn't', Cooke replied, 'I'd jump out of that window.' Royal then
informed him that they were prepared to pay him $100 per programme

and Cooke accepted with alacrity: it was far more than he could have expected. The *Letter* would be broadcast on NBC's Red Network on Wednesday evenings, immediately after the news.

Job security thus restored, he could concentrate on building a social life to match what he and Ruth had enjoyed in London. It had its comforting routines. He soon became friendly with the unlikely figure of Herbert Wiener, Mrs Emerson's doctor. Every week, Wiener would meet him after he'd delivered his talk from NBC's Radio City studios, having taken care to park his car (illegally) beside a fire hydrant with the sign 'Medical Emergency' prominently displayed. They shared supper and went ten-pin bowling in the building's elegant alley. But music was the key to the period. It was the start of the great flowering of jazz in New York and the Cookes became regulars at the clubs and (comparatively respectable) strip-joints along 52nd Street on either side of 6th Avenue: Jimmy Ryan's, The Onyx, Leon and Eddie's, the Samoa, The Hickory House. It was no passing fancy. Cooke made a point of seeking out the company of the great musicians of the moment – Joe and Marty Marsala, Jack Teagarden, Art Tatum, Buddy Rich and Benny Goodman.

On some Sunday afternoons there would be long, informal jam sessions for aficionados, or he took Ruth to Harlem instead, where blacks and whites shared the experience of Fletcher Henderson playing at The Apollo, or Duke Ellington at the Cotton Club, known as 'Harlem on Times Square'. (Ellington's 'Clarinet Lament', written for Barney Bigard, was one of Cooke's eight Desert Island Discs in 1962.) As a jazz practitioner, however modestly, Cooke watched, listened and learned, particularly from the pianists: and in the process, he laid down a rich seam of experience and knowledge to be mined for programme ideas, on and off, for the next fifty years.

As a musical sideline, he also found himself giving intermission talks for NBC's regular relays from the Metropolitan Opera. Another long-established NBC figure provided the plot details between acts, but Cooke was given the task of filling five or six minutes while the patrons were at the bar. During a performance of *Don Giovanni*, for instance, he conjured up for the first time what became one of his favourite analogies – the iceman, the ubiquitous adulterer of American suburban legend. If Don Juan had been around in the late 1930s, he suggested, he would have been an iceman, delivering relief to over-heated housewives in the days when refrigerators were still a rarity. *La Traviata* enabled him to expound on his medical theories about tuberculosis in the modern age. Decades afterwards, in 1994, Cooke was sitting in the back of a yellow cab in New York giving directions to the driver. The man listened politely and then said, 'You're the guy who used to do those opera talks, arencha? I use-ta enjoy those. What you been doing since then?'

Cooke renewed his interest in the words business, too. The BBC broadcast his latest diatribe – *The Impact of America* – in June and the accompanying article was duly forwarded to Mencken in Baltimore. It struck all the chords which Mencken had come to appreciate in his young disciple, hammering home his message that English was so full of unsuspected Americanisms that there should be an end to all linguistic hostility. Who remembered in 1937 that 'wallpaper' was once regarded by purists in England as a barbarism? Was the same not likely to happen to hundreds of other more recently imported words – 'worthwhile, highbrow, or antagonise', for instance?

It must have warmed Mencken's heart. This was, essentially, the theme of his immense tome *The American Language*, revised and republished as recently as April 1936. Indeed, the book contains three extracts from Cooke's earlier writing.

Despite the scope of Mencken's work – 325,000 words of text covering 800 pages – he was already working on lengthy supplements to accommodate all the extra information which poured in from correspondents like Cooke, several of whose gleanings appear in the First Supplement, eventually published in 1945 – 'fender' and 'windshield' for the English 'mudguard' and 'windscreen': 'hood' instead of 'bonnet': the 'notion counter' in a New York store, as opposed to London's 'haberdashery': 'race-track' and its English equivalent 'race-course'.

~

One project, however, dominated this first year of Cooke's American life: his first book, or to be strictly accurate, the first book to carry his name on its cover. It came about through his renewed acquaintance in London with the man who'd cut short his wooing of Peggy Ashcroft. Rupert Hart-Davis, the lanky and much resented fiancé, had married his star and been divorced in short order. Soon afterwards he abandoned his own theatrical career and, in 1932, joined the publishers Jonathan Cape as a junior director. Years later neither he nor Cooke could be certain exactly how the book came about and who approached whom, but Hart-Davis remembered his struggle to persuade his firm to publish *Garbo and the Night Watchmen*.

The book was simply a collection of film reviews by writers whom Cooke judged to have matched his own independence of mind, ready to risk the wrath of the studio publicity machines. It was based on the principle that film criticism was still an art in its infancy and would benefit from the respectability bestowed by a hardback volume. Cooke had first discussed the idea of such a book three years earlier with T.S. Eliot, though his original plan was simply to reprint a number of his own BBC film-talks. He told Eliot that he had been toying with a title like *Talking of Garbo* which would be 'genial, inviting and popular'. He had even sketched out a design for the title page, showing 'Chaplin and Garbo linking arms and leading Mickey Mouse behind'.

Eliot, as a director of Faber & Faber, had encouraged the enterprise, but eventually felt that the scripts were 'too scrappy and discontinuous'. 'I really feel that the material should go back into the melting-pot', Eliot went on, 'so that a real book may eventually be made.'

Garbo and the Night Watchmen was the result. Cooke's introduction explains the philosophy. 'This is a book about the movies by people who earn their bread and butter by dashing from meals to movies. It is probably the first book about the movies by writers who are so busy seeing them that they have no time to write books.' It had no pretensions to definitive analysis of trends in the modern cinema. Each piece was the work of a 'night-watchman who must rush away at midnight to state a heartache or a preference against the dawn's deadline.' The dustcover shows the honest toiler seated by the watchman's brazier, from which the wispy face of Garbo floats into the night air.

From the moment he became a full-time critic himself in 1934, Cooke was an avid consumer of his competitors' output. Every Saturday morning in London he would stroll down Oxford Street to Selfridges, to pick up copies of the *New Yorker* and the old *Vanity Fair*. This exposure to American writing meant that he could offer a proper transatlantic selection covering the first ten years of the talkies. The line-up of contributors to 'Garbo' is impressive, drawing partly on his personal contacts and partly on cold-calling of those he admired: there are fifteen pieces, for instance, by Graham Greene (whom he'd never met), already an established author but also film critic for the *Spectator*

₁ᴄ₋₋ᵢₑ. All of those approached, not surprisingly, expressed satisfaction at having their ephemeral offerings captured for posterity.

The book ends with an enterprising idea of Cooke's: to print side by side reviews of the same film by each of the nine critics. For this experiment he chose Chaplin's *Modern Times*. Most of the writers, while questioning the work's validity as a piece of social commentary, still found Chaplin's performance dazzling. Cooke begged to differ and used his article to summarise his doubts about a movie in which he'd so nearly been intimately involved. *Modern Times*, Cooke sighed, 'is like Chaplin the actor directed and produced by MGM.' He felt that the Little Man had sold out to the brash sophistication of the big studios. Searching around for someone to blame for the sorry state of the finished product, Cooke singles out the censor and possibly 'the assistant director, for the unexpected, and fatal, flaws in structure, lighting, sound and style.' Was there a hint of *Schadenfreude* in this denigration of his unnamed replacement?

Garbo and the Night Watchmen won a few plaudits in the cultural press, but it did not make anyone rich. Cooke's inscription, in the copy he gave to Hart-Davis, reads, 'To Rupert, patron, mentor and kindliest backer of the wrong horse.' But at least this was one literary project which did see the light of day.

Cooke's NBC broadcasts weren't making him rich, either, but they were at least making him new friends. One particular tribute survives – from a New York academic who wrote in January 1938, praising Cooke's forthright criticism and expressing the pious hope that his words would be preserved for posterity as 'a permanent contribution to our letters and our times.' (Sadly, they weren't. The weekly NBC radio programme survives only in a few faint recordings in the Library of Congress.) But the object of the listener's adulation knew that his NBC contract was unlikely to last indefinitely.

Cooke had not given up hope of building a new relationship with the BBC, and in those early months of 1938, he plied Felix Greene with ideas for entertainment programmes. He was even on hand at the unaccustomed hour (for a reporter) of 6.30 a.m. on 12 March – to meet the BBC executive Lindsay Wellington, arriving in New York from Broadcasting House on his first transatlantic visit. Wellington was a BBC veteran, who in due course would become the wartime head of the BBC's American Operations, before returning to Britain to take up the post of Controller of the Home Service. In a 1950 *Radio Times* profile, Cooke described the relationship which developed from that first March meeting.

> From then until the invasion of France, Lindsay and I were together, or in a telephone's reach, at most of the intervening crises. The proper midwife is a necessary condition for getting out of a broadcaster the kind of thing he's best able to do. Lindsay Wellington was an accomplished midwife. He knew me in the studio. He knew me at the typewriter. He knew me at meals, at play, in times good and bad. Best of all he knew me at home – which is the only sensible place to look for good broadcasters because there a man is the only human being he can ever hope to be.

For the time being, Felix Greene was still in charge and he was at last on the verge of helping Cooke sell a new series to the BBC. It was to be a musical extravaganza, tracing the history of American folk-song back to its roots. The seeds of this idea had been sown two years earlier with the successful programme of hobo songs. Now Cooke began some serious research. The dominant figures in the field were John Lomax and his son Alan, who had spent years touring the country, particularly the prison camps of the South, collecting material which was lodged in the music section of the Library of Congress. Cooke duly travelled to Washington, met the younger Lomax and persuaded him to part with a number of recordings which had never before been broadcast. These would form the bedrock of the series.

The visit threw up one startling encounter. Alone and at a loose end one evening, Cooke followed his musical nose into a black quarter of the town. 'I went into this saloon. It was a real dive, a smoky room with four or five people propped up against the bar. There at the piano was this guy with gold, and even a diamond, in his teeth.' He knew immediately who it was: Jelly Roll Morton, pianist, composer and bandleader of the Red Hot Peppers – one of the great heroes of his student days. Morton was forty-eight years old, and almost a forgotten figure picking up pin-money in seedy bars. Cooke recalled the occasion, with suitable romantic gloss, on the record he made in 1952, 'An Evening with Alistair Cooke'.

'He was a gangling, wide-mouthed, flat-faced man with big wrists. He was playing a sour piano in a really smelly café – the sort of place where they never serve a meal, just a neon sign with two bulbs missing and a cab-driver leaning up against a glass of beer. It was like meeting the President in a shoe-shine parlour. "London?" he said. And he fell around my neck. "Why sure, I was through that section in nineteen and thirteen [1913]".'

Cooke was emboldened to test out his own technique on that sour piano. Morton listened and then declared, 'If you want to play the blues, boy, just take it easy. Stick to the chords, and cut out that picture-show right hand.' The old purist didn't like the ornamentation of the pianists at the silent-movie theatres. 'Let me play for you,' he went on, 'the first blues I no doubt heard in my life . . . "If you can't spare me a dollar, give me a lousy dime / I gotta feed that hungry man of mine." '

As the evening wore on Cooke discovered that Jelly Roll had been approached by Alan Lomax, who planned to record his illustrated reminiscences of the early days of jazz. Cooke sat in on some of these sessions and persuaded Lomax that, when he transcribed the musician's words, he should allow them to keep their natural eccentricity, rather than sanitising 'I was through that section in nineteen and thirteen' as 'I was in London in 1913'. And he kept in touch with Morton, even visiting him on his deathbed in 1941. 'He was babbling away that he'd invented jazz. Maybe he didn't, but he was still a great man.'

The deal with Lomax was a coup, but it still left much ground for Cooke to cover with anyone who could possibly help. This research was a time-consuming and costly business for which Cooke was receiving no advance payment or expenses. Ruth's family income became an increasingly important part of their budget. On 5 April Greene sent a memo to London suggesting that the agreed fee for the series should be twenty-five guineas per programme, rather than twenty. 'Cooke has drawn to my attention that the cost of the recordings might be more considerable than we had in mind. Many of the records he will play may have to be specially prepared from historical copies, or being unusual in themselves, may cost more than those in normal commercial circulation.' He added pointedly that Cooke 'is not in a financial position to make his trip to England unless he can manage to get the cost covered by work while he is there. He told me, in a perfectly frank way, without any suggestion of blackmail, that he would not be able to undertake the series if the fee were not raised, for he would have to cancel his plans of going to England.' This was eventually agreed, although it caused a great deal of tetchy correspondence with accounts departments, who pointed out that the maximum fee for a music programme was usually twelve guineas.

Greene worked tirelessly to find other ways of boosting Cooke's BBC exposure and, in the face of stout resistance from London, he secured him a high-profile theatre talk in May. He also made yet another attempt to sell the notion of a weekly Cooke Letter. He pointed out that Raymond Gram Swing had tapped a powerful latent interest in things American. 'If such an astonishing number of people are willing to listen to a weekly commentary on American politics, I cannot help feeling that a far larger number would listen eagerly to a series on everyday American happenings.' Cooke, he said, was a commentator who had shown himself to be liked by listeners. 'He could handle such a series admirably.' London remained unmoved.

The final preparations for the folk-music series caused the usual anxious transatlantic interchanges. The series had finally gained a title: *I Hear America Singing*, but Cooke's arrangements were still a matter for conjecture as May gave way to June. The BBC in London was appalled to learn that he was not intending to arrive until the day of the first broadcast in July and that it might even be necessary to present the programme from Plymouth, the first port of call for the liner *Manhattan*. The very idea was 'chancy' verging on the 'improper'. What would happen if the records he was carrying were held up by Customs? The legendary American correspondent Ed Murrow, 'who presumably has some experience', had informed them that it was extremely unlikely that such material would be released quickly. Some at Broadcasting House were in favour of cancelling the first programme altogether, rather than risk being 'left in the cart'. Even Cooke's friend Charles Siepmann, back in harness as a programme planner, wrote rather plaintively, 'He can't really just walk across the Atlantic and fire straight off without a word to any of us.'

11

THE CHARM OF CORRESPONDING

Cooke did not trouble himself with such tedious details. He was already proving a hard man to manage, reluctant to the point of resentment if anyone tried to interfere with his work in progress. Later in his career, when his reputation was fully established, he could afford to adopt such an offhand approach to notions of editorial control. In the summer of 1938 he still needed friends and he tested their patience. On this occasion he left it to Greene to sort things out and the North American Representative had to apply 'endless persuasion and pressure' to get a berth for Cooke on the *Georgic*, sailing two days earlier. Greene also managed to extract publicity material, billings and photographs, to be dispatched some days in advance aboard the *Queen Mary*. In a letter to Siepmann he makes soothing and reassuring noises about the project, but adds, 'You and I know our Alistair well enough to know that he needs pinning down and that careful discussion of his intentions is necessary if his exuberance and optimism is not to run away with him.'

It's hard to see how much – if anything – could have been done by way of careful discussion of *I Hear America Singing*. Cooke was back and forward to Southold before leaving for Britain, and by the time he reached London there remained less than 48 hours before the broadcast of the introductory programme at 9.30 on the Tuesday evening, 5 July. He did at least arrive with a clear idea of the themes for the following eleven weeks: 'The Melting Pot' covering the music imported by the first waves of immigrants – 'The Lone Prairie' with cowboy songs – and 'Go West Young Man' including ballads of the prairies and the great westward migration. Subsequent programmes would be devoted to the music of the railroads and the big cities, the sophisticated East Coast and the black community, the Civil War and the Depression. Even with Cooke installed in London, there was little opportunity for Siepmann and others to exercise any real control over the finished products. Not only were they broadcast live, but Cooke did not work to a pre-written script.

His engineer for the series was a young man named Charles Chilton (who went on to arrange the music for *Oh! What a Lovely War*). He had worked his way up from Broadcasting House messenger boy to 'assistant to the gramophone assistant', in which capacity he was required to trace and compile records for music programmes. The normal procedure was to hand them to an announcer who would construct his own links, but Chilton soon discovered that there was a market for fully scripted programmes and even documentaries. In addition, no one else in the department was interested in jazz, and he set about becoming the resident expert – qualifications which made him a sensible choice for *I Hear America Singing*. Chilton never forgot the haphazard way in which the programmes reached the public:

> Alistair used to turn up at about 6 o'clock, when most people were going home. It was only then that he started writing the script, with me playing the discs in between. When we went to the studio at 9.30, he wouldn't necessarily have finished the script, and while one record was playing he'd be searching in a book for some reference or other. Then, when it was time to speak, he'd say, 'As John Lomax says . . .' and he'd read a section straight from the book.

It may have been risky, but it seems to have created a distinctive tone which appealed to listeners. Did the critic who said that 'Mr Cooke has a way of making you feel that he has, at that moment, thought to tell you this and that' know how close he was to the truth? The same writer continues, 'A quietness of manner, coupled with refreshing and vivid use of the English language, makes his talks so acceptable.' While *The Times* remarked that the only problem was the way tunes were not played in full: 'his half-hour should be longer.'

Chilton says that he learned a huge amount from the series, with its use of popular songs to illustrate the social history of the nation. Many of the discs Cooke had acquired from Alan Lomax had never been heard anywhere before, and certainly not in Britain. The first programme alone included six tracks from this private collection, with titles like 'Blackberry Cry' (performed by a Negro 'huckster' – a street-trader or peddler), 'Po' Farmer' and 'Old Abe Lincoln'. New York's *Variety* magazine was so impressed that it suggested the series be recreated in

America. In fact, in the absence of copyright clearance for the Library of Congress material, no recordings of the programmes were made.

~

Throughout their summer stay in London the Cookes were the guests of Siepmann and his wife Gwendolen at their home in Primrose Hill. The experience led them to realise how unhappy Siepmann had become with a much older woman, whom he'd married out of sympathy – believing her to be suffering a terminal illness. Eventually, after he moved to the United States to take up the inaugural Chair in Communications at Harvard, they indulged in a little matchmaking to bring him together with his second wife Dolly. For this summer, however, the Cookes simply picked up their social life where they'd left it eighteen months earlier. One newspaper report noted that 'before they had been two days off the boat, they had discovered what is probably London's only American bowling alley. Ever since, Cooke has been rioting in strikes and spares.'

Having brought Cooke, temporarily at least, back into the fold, Siepmann helped him boost his fragile finances by commissioning six more programmes, called *The Day and the Tune*. He and a co-host, Marianne Helweg, read out listeners' letters linking personal memories to record requests: fee – five guineas a time. For this, Cooke was supposed to deal with all correspondence arising from the show and he soon incurred the wrath of the Rev. D.C. Hoey, chaplain to Cornwall Mental Hospital in Bodmin, whose three letters had gone unanswered. As the series drew to a close this situation deteriorated rapidly. Hundreds of people who had filled in a form printed by the *Radio Times* bombarded the Corporation with complaints that their requests had not even been acknowledged. 'Because Cooke has no secretary,' a BBC memo whined, 'listeners have written to us direct accusing us of discourtesy and inconsideration.' It was agreed that, in future, presenters would not be expected to deal with such experiments in audience participation.

Before the Cookes headed back for New York, arrangements were also made for them to appear together in an early television broadcast at Alexandra Palace, speaking about the differences between living in London and New York. In the simplest of studio formats, contributors to *Speaking Personally* were given ten minutes of airtime: the invitation letter explains apologetically that 'in the present stage of development, television fees are not as high as those for sound broadcasting'. Would ten guineas be acceptable? The script of Cooke's first serious effort in front of camera did not survive.

At least once during this long summer sojourn, from July to September of 1938, Alistair and Ruth went to Blackpool. In Ruth's case it was the last visit she would ever make and Alistair did not see his family again until 1946. His father, now aged sixty-two, was approaching retirement – doubtless calmer and more philosophical than his wife, who had never ceased to fret at the idea of her son living in the lawless anarchy of the land where Al Capone was king. Cooke's brother Sam was still behind the butcher's counter, all ambition extinguished: and his daughter Kathleen, who was just four years old, pin-points this visit by her Uncle Alfred and Auntie Ruth with clarity because the next time she saw Cooke she was twelve years old. None of them, of course, had any notion of how long the parting would be, despite the grimness of the news from across the Channel. But it is possible to get a hint of how Cooke himself felt.

Before one of their sessions on *I Hear America Singing*, he invited Charles Chilton to eat fish and chips with him at Sherrifs Restaurant in Regent Street. As they travelled back by taxi, Cooke suddenly turned to him and said, 'Why don't you think about emigrating to America?' Chilton replied that he was quite happy where he was. 'Well, I can tell you there's going to be a terrible war. Now really is the time to get out.' It was hardly a dazzling insight, but it struck enough of a chord with the young technician that he never forgot the moment. The advice was perfectly consistent with what a well-meaning expatriate might have volunteered to any single man with no family ties. Yet there is no question that people – particularly in Blackpool – watched Cooke go, and wondered about his patriotism. David Curnow remembers his father telling him that older members of staff at the school, especially those who had seen service in the Great War, thought Cooke's behaviour 'bloody outrageous'.

When war finally broke out, Englishmen abroad were expected to rally to the flag. Mitigating circumstances or complications – and there were plenty in Cooke's case – tended to be brushed aside as irrelevant excuses. It was his bad luck that, as he came close to completing his two-year residence qualification in the spring of 1939, the American immigration system was being swamped by 120,000 European Jews fleeing Hitler. Understandably, Cooke's papers kept being pushed to the bottom of the pile. By the time he finally achieved citizenship in the winter of 1941 (after four and a half years), Britain's war fortunes were at rock-bottom. However unfairly, the message that reached Blackpool was that Alistair Cooke had deserted his country when it needed him most. It was a stigma that never quite went away. Ironically, Cooke's last broadcasts before sailing were two pieces for NBC on the Czechoslovak crisis and Hitler's annexation of the Sudetenland.

~

The return crossing was eventful. They boarded the French liner, *Normandie*, on 17 September, and almost as soon as they reached the open sea, the winds started to blow. Cooke recounted his mariner's tale in a 1952 *Letter from America*. By the third day,

> twelve of us – from a total passenger list of two thousand – came down to dinner, and had about eight waiters each. I say twelve of us not to imply, in a nauseatingly casual way, that I am braver than my fellow men. I am terrified of all forms of movement not circumscribed by a motion picture screen. But I happen to belong to that tenacious brand of hypochondriac who can never get sick even when I feel the gravedigger at my elbow.

The ship arrived unscathed but the East Coast of the United States suffered serious damage. The hurricane had turned inland and devastated huge areas from New York, Connecticut and Rhode Island, up into New England. 638 people died in its wake and hundreds of acres of trees were destroyed. Long Island had been in the eye of the storm – one South Shore movie theatre had been picked up and tossed into the sea with thirty-five film-goers still inside. When Dr Haven Emerson greeted the couple at the dockside in New York a few days later, he was in sombre and reflective mood. As he guided them through the painstaking Customs clearance, Cooke asked how badly Southold had been affected by the storm.

'I'm afraid we have lost some trees,' Emerson replied. But then he rapidly changed the subject, and muttered that his domestic problems were trivial compared with what families must be thinking and fearing in Europe, where Chamberlain was on his way to Munich. Two days later, after unpacking at their apartment, the Cookes took the train to Southold and were shocked by what they found. 'I can describe it best,' Cooke wrote,

> by recalling pictures of the Western Front as it appeared in 1918. The house

stood, with a single chimney down. But that was all. Boat piers were crumpled up and deposited on the broken roofs of nearby houses. Giant oaks that were planted soon after Captain John Smith sailed into Peconic Bay (in 1607) had been ripped away from yards of gaping soil. And a drive of thick woods Dr Emerson had planted a quarter of a century earlier was beaten and thrashed to matchwood.

It had taken the family three days to extricate themselves from the wreckage.

~

Cooke had returned from his British trip with a prized opportunity for alternative employment – and it was just as well. His contract with NBC had run its course, with his career as critic for American radio almost ending in disaster. He had already drawn attention to himself by mentioning the sensitive subject of lesbianism in a film called *Love of Women* – and been censored for his pains. Then, true to his belief that a reviewer should say what he thought, he had passed on to his listeners an acerbic appreciation of the latest Paramount western starring Joel McCrea: *Wells Fargo*. 'This', Cooke opined, 'is the longest teaser in the history of motion pictures – a ninety-minute trailer to a film that was never made.' Paramount did not get the joke and they suspected film-goers might not get it, either. The film, after all, *had* been made. If the public got the wrong idea . . . Within days, the magazine *Hollywood Reporter* bore a blaring headline – 'PAR PLANS TO SUE CRITIC FOR KNOCK ON WELLS FARGO', while *Variety Weekly* chipped in with, 'ALISTAIR COOKE DRAWS PARAMOUNT "FARGO" SQUAWK.' In splendid journalese, the article explained, 'Par [Paramount] on the Coast was apprised of Cooke's comments by exploding exhibitors. NBC, in settling the matter amicably, promised close watch-dogging on the commentator's copy.'

One supporting letter from a listener in Connecticut survives: 'What you said about *Wells Fargo* hit the spot with me . . . The men who control the money-bags dictate the policies and they can't get it out of their heads that they think they know what the American public wants – or doesn't want. They think a regular diet of boudoir plots and négligé close-ups will do the trick.' But it was a serious business. Cooke learned that the studios were talking of a million dollars in damages and it required intensive Hollywood lobbying by NBC's John Royal to pacify them. This hiatus in Cooke's relations with NBC made it even more important to find other sources of income. In the nick of time the BBC finally relented sufficiently to allow him to try his hand at a regular – personal – assessment of American life.

The breakthrough was limited in scope. The programme was given the title *Mainly About Manhattan*, which was a reminder to all and sundry (including Cooke) that he was not to stray from the narrow confines of life and culture in New York City. Above all, he was not to venture onto the ground so imperiously occupied by Raymond Gram Swing, nor anywhere near the southern tip of Manhattan from where Herb Elliston delivered *Wall Street Week*. (Elliston, the financial journalist soon to be plucked from his comfortable billet to edit the struggling *Washington Post*, was a blunt Yorkshireman whom Cooke had known since his Harvard days.)

The first *Mainly About Manhattan* went out live on 13 October 1938, at 5.20 local time – 10.20 in London. It continued, fortnightly at first and then weekly, for about six months. There were nineteen broadcasts in all: they encapsulate much of the spirit of what he hoped he might achieve as a radio journalist, as well as prefiguring many of the themes and obsessions, techniques and verbal trickery which he continued to deploy for the following six decades.

The listener was offered small, intimate glimpses of the Cookes' life, and introduced to his gentle, self-deprecating sense of humour. The sound of a New York fire engine siren, he suggests, will be a 'tuning note for this series, and also, if you like, a warning siren – Look out! There goes Alistair Cooke! Time to turn off the wireless!'. The opening programme locates him in a four-room apartment in 78th Street: it mentions 'Carolyn, our Negro maid' and Rittler, 'a dirty black cat who sleeps in the gramophone'; and it tells the story of the destruction of the Emersons' Southold estate, though cautiously describing the landowner as 'a friend', rather than his father-in-law. This leads on to a more general discussion of the weather, partly because of the British preoccupation with the subject and partly because climatology was one of the disciplines in which he had begun to take an enthusiastic amateur interest. The effect is direct, accessible, sometimes verging on the folksy, with well-sugared snippets of history or social commentary, always understated.

Week two, for students of Cooke's canon of the essential America, provides a gem: the first of very many descriptions of New England in the fall. Throughout his writing life, nothing was more certain to activate his creative juices than trees in their autumn uniform. 'As far as you could see there was not a speck or hint of green – mountains, fuzzy to their tops with foliage, shone yellow and gold; and rushing through them like a bright blood stream went the scarlets of the maples.' The death of the inventor of the traffic light enabled him to expound on the phenomenon of urban parkways – newly appearing around New York – and he drew, too, on a recent biography of Benjamin Franklin and a play about the history of New York. The junctions between these disparate ideas are sometimes quite awkward: 'thinking about ships and the nature of Americans, I went along to see a play which also had its mind on the same matters.' As he honed his techniques over the years, the fifteen-minute talks would become much more seamless, with threads of ideas delicately interwoven and neatly finished off.

He did, however, try to stick scrupulously to the rules of his engagement, under which the mid-term elections were strictly off-limits. Cooke was in Times Square to see the results being flashed up on giant screens, but his commentary was confined to a description of the complicated, multi-levered voting-machines, while the 17 November talk begins: 'It is not my business in these weekly letters to talk to you of the political life of this country, or even of this town; you wisely wait for Saturday night to receive an illumination which would anyway completely obliterate the pocket flashlight that I try to throw up the back streets of Manhattan.'

Cooke's brief did give him ample excuse to pursue his musical preferences. In a newspaper interview of the period, he traced his obsession with jazz back to the influence of his old Cambridge room-mate, Eddie Wiltshire. It was Wiltshire's 1932 shopping list which had started him rummaging in junk shops for old numbers and rarities on his first visit to America. 'I became interested in the social background of this music,' he explained. 'I found that the lyrics of these simple blues tunes of coloured folk, originating from the deep South, all had some well-defined meaning with some linguistic significance, though most of the crazy-sounding jargon of jazz is generally thought to be meaningless. I began to realise that the study of linguistics was very closely mixed up in all this.' He told the reporter, 'I'm planning to write a whole book on the subject of blues singing and lyrics.' This was another project that never made it past the planning stage.

There may have been no book, but Cooke's 52nd Street contacts eventually gave rise to a remarkable piece of live broadcasting. The BBC agreed to take a relay of a jam session performed on the roof garden of the St Regis Hotel, with Cooke providing an informal running commentary. The impetus came from the band leader Joe Marsala, who convened a high-powered group of jazz musicians – his brother Marty, Yank Lausen, Bobby Hackett, Max Kaminsky, Carmen Mastren, Bud Freeman and Dave Tough on the drums. The event gathered a considerable crowd, including a bevy of journalists and the composer, W.C. Handy, the 'father of the blues'. It went without saying that visitors as distinguished as this had to be treated with proper respect, but unwisely, the gold-embossed invitations advertised champagne all round. Handy had no compunction in bringing his entire family to share in this unexpected largesse. The St Regis Hotel was not cheap and the result was a bar bill of catastrophic proportions. This caused another hiatus in Felix Greene's relations with his masters in London. The BBC, according to Cooke, raised holy hell. Subsequent recordings were in the less salubrious surroundings of the bar at the Hickory House or at the BBC's own studio.

Although no official BBC copy was made of the St Regis event, news emerged after the war that the session had not been altogether lost in the New York mist. Across the Atlantic in Sweden, a jazz fanatic was crouching over a primitive piece of recording equipment, capturing the band's performance. It was released on a bootleg record, copies of which eventually turned up in the United States, complete with Cooke's voice overrunning the music.

These experimental broadcasts did not produce universal acclaim. One newspaper critic in Blackpool wrote, 'Am I wrong? It seems to me that except for the wailing of cats on the tiles at midnight there is no noise as hideous as a jam session. I have heard only one session and I will not hear another unless I am bound and gagged in a chair close to the loudspeaker.' Jazz was still a minority taste in the English provinces and the imprimatur of the town's favourite son did not make the music any more acceptable.

To help in his proselytising Cooke had also been working on his voice. A contemporary profile includes a snide reference to 'what might best be called Cooke's mid-Atlantic accent'. He was still only six years out of Cambridge and ten years or so away from Blackpool, but the accent was evolving all the time, taking on new and subtle colorations.

A few revealing words in the abdication broadcasts had by now given way to a wholesale remodulation of his broadcasting style. In a flash of frankness, Cooke explains his motives in another *Mainly About Manhattan*, recalling that he had once been informed by a pretty girl at a party that the consonants of an English speaker were like a man falling through a plate-glass window. As he began to study phonetics, he became sensitive to American inflections which he first mimicked, then found himself emulating unconsciously. 'I had to find for myself – as an effort of goodwill merely – a voice which would not hurt the English, and which would also not cause the Americans to sing quietly to themselves the song which goes, "Bang! Bang! Here come the British!" ', as they had during his first days at Yale. The studied tones of the Englishman abroad, therefore, were no accident.

~

At the start of 1939, Cooke – having just enjoyed his thirtieth birthday – was about to launch himself into another new career. Although he'd done nothing much about it, he had at last begun to mull over the possible benefits of the foreign correspondent's trade to supplement his income. Shortly before leaving London the previous summer, he and Ruth had dined with his publisher Rupert Hart-Davis, an aspiring young revue artiste called Joyce Grenfell and the travel-writer Peter Fleming – elder brother of the creator of James Bond. Fleming had good contacts at *The Times*, and those connections were about to pay off.

Cooke had applied to *The Times* before leaving Britain in 1936 and had been told that not only was there no vacancy, but that any opening that occurred would necessarily be filled from London. The Fleming connection made the difference. *The Times* was one of only three or four papers which maintained permanent correspondents in the United States and its man in Washington was the revered and autocratic figure of Sir Wilmott (Bill) Lewis. Lewis was exactly twice Cooke's age and coming to the end of an epic journalistic journey which started in the Far East and included a spell running American propaganda in France, before he was picked by Lord Northcliffe to represent *The Times* in the United States. There, his distinction and long service brought him a knighthood and led many (up to and including presidents) to regard him as Britain's *ex officio* ambassador.

In appearance he was an archetypal Edwardian Englishman – tall, straight-backed, with 'eyebrows like Gothic arches' and a voice 'more like an archbishop's than any archbishop' – and he had a weakness for marrying rich American widows. Cooke offered a warm tribute in a *Letter from America* when Lewis died in 1950:

> Deep below his worldly, sophisticated surface was a quite unruffled, almost scornful integrity. If this was ever threatened, there was nothing he would not say, for he had enormous, almost heroic, gall. He could enjoy confidences as well as the next man, but nobody could seduce him into retailing them, not even a President.

It was to this alarming figure that Cooke reported early in 1939, ready to start work as a junior correspondent for *The Times*, to be paid (pitifully) by the piece. Despite his lack of experience, he came with his own ready-made ideas about what the job should entail and how it might fit in with his wider purpose. Indeed, he had already passed on these ideas to the audience of *Mainly About Manhattan* in the first programme of the New Year, regretting the fact that so few American stories made an impact in Britain apart from 'the matrimonial woes of Hollywood's blondes, and the mental condition of Al Capone'.

> The time, I think, is long overdue for a new kind of foreign correspondent – one who does not take it for granted that we will all live and think alike; one who will take the word 'affairs' to mean the American world of science, literature, social life, music, the condition of the press; the very things which, when the political control is changed, come to life – or droop and die.

Presumably Cooke did not unburden himself of these musings to Bill Lewis, nor to the New York bureau chief, Lou Henricks, who was his immediate superior. There was work to be done and Henricks was perfectly happy to have an extra pair of hands to do it. 'He was too sensible to show me the ropes,' according to Cooke. 'He just indicated where the ropes were, and it was up to me to get the feel of them.' Nobody niggled over the new boy's copy and he was well enough regarded to be given a special task which drew on his knowledge of the cinema.

The Times had commissioned an early version of an in-house documentary featuring the paper's most famous names. The director's plan was to end one sequence with the Berlin correspondent being frog-marched out of the country: the last shot dipped down to show a pair of civilian shoes being hustled along between two pairs of jackboots. Cooke was to pick up the theme with a shot starting on Sir Wilmott's feet and panning upwards to reveal him in all his splendour climbing onto a shoeshine stand. The scene then moved to Lewis's office which grew progressively steamier under the lights.

With the filming still incomplete, Lewis turned to Cooke and said, 'I'm sorry, my boy. I'm afraid we'll have to break now. I've got to go and get married.' As he descended from his office, he was spotted through the lattice-work door of the elevator by a messenger boy from Western Union. 'Hi, Sir Wilmott! I hear you're getting married again. Is she rich?' As his head disappeared from sight, the reply could be clearly heard: 'You know my record . . . '

Apart from these extra-mural activities, Cooke was soon thrust into one of the biggest stories of the day – the trial of James J. Hines. Hines was a Tammany Hall stalwart – in other words, a member of the New York Democratic Party aristocracy which had run the city for as long as anybody could remember. Tammany had long been associated with corruption and other forms of skulduggery, but it was usually only the lower-grade officers who ended up in court. Hines was different. He controlled New York's 11th District, a position which should have guaranteed him immunity from legal interference. Yet in March 1939 he found himself in the dock, charged with organising illegal lotteries and graft – using his political clout to pervert the course of justice. His accuser was the Republican District Attorney Thomas Dewey, whose performance in court helped to establish his credentials as a front-runner for the next presidential primaries. Hines was found guilty on thirteen counts and Tammany's remaining influence suffered accordingly.

It was on this sensational case that Cooke cut his teeth, and it was also his first opportunity to exercise that economy of effort whereby one story could be used to serve two masters. His 1000-word 'turnover' article in *The Times* was mirrored by an account of the same case in *Mainly About Manhattan* a week or so earlier. Even at this early stage, Cooke demonstrates considerable artistry in reworking the same details for the formal requirements of a newspaper of record and a conversational radio essay. Thus, for the radio:

On Sunday morning, I flipped my finger along the bookshelf and stopped at that classic chronicle of American life written eight years ago: it bears the simple title, *The Great Mouthpiece.* Now a mouthpiece has nothing to do with a telephone or a football – a mouthpiece is the criminal lawyer for a gang. He knows enough policemen and crooked judges to see that gang sentences are short and not played up too much in the papers . . .

While for *The Times*, the chatty background details have been stripped away:

No trial since that of *The Great Mouthpiece*, William J. Fallon, in 1924, had so caught the imagination of the city. And no revelations of graft in high places have so shocked and angered the conscience of the Democratic Party throughout the country.

There are clear differences of tone and language – between words to be heard and read. This instinctive feel for the use of words in different settings, developed with no special training or guidance, would serve Cooke in good stead.

~

Those listening back at Broadcasting House still found time, despite the worsening problems in Europe, to quibble with Cooke's coverage of the Hines trial: not surprisingly, Raymond Gram Swing had chosen the same topic and the overlap was glaring. The BBC were much happier when Cooke discoursed on such topics as the subtleties of New York's social structures, highlighting the Social Register – the commercial booklet confirming the status, schooling and income of a city's élite. Cooke explained the American way: 'Of course we have social stratification, based more or less on economic status. But the classes and titles are not hereditary. Individuals rise and fall with wholesome alacrity. The poor are always with us, but not the same people are poor today as yesterday. Similarly, the rich have their reverses.' The idea of classlessness appealed to him as much as it had done when he first experienced it seven years earlier.

He did his best to stick to the constraints imposed upon him. Yet the constant strain of resisting the drag of history is increasingly evident. On 2 February 1939, Cooke enters a plea of mitigation about 'a wholly political topic' which 'in a few days you will hear discussed that way by Mr Swing'. The issue is the uproar in Congress over the sense that Roosevelt (who had just delivered a coruscating speech attacking the new European dictators) might be ready to challenge – or even abandon – the Neutrality Acts. Cooke quotes a Senator from California demanding a public inquiry into FDR's foreign policy: 'Good God, do you not, gentlemen, think the American people have the right to know if they are going down the road to war?' Openly acknowledging this trespass on Swing's territory, Cooke veers off just in time into a reflection on the way Americans conduct their public life.

Deep down he knew that the issue of neutrality was likely to present a disciple of Anglo-American friendship with a stern test. American foreign policy during the 1930s, according to the historian Hugh Brogan (the son of one of Cooke's long-time friends, Denis Brogan) was built upon unilateralism – the conviction that America must remain a free agent as she had since the French Revolution – and a long tradition of pacifism. The result was to create the isolationist ethos which made it hard for Roosevelt to follow his instincts and to put America's might behind the Allied war effort.

So hamstrung was the President that he found himself powerless even to apply more liberal immigration rules to German Jews. Latent anti-Semitism was fed by the activities of the German-American Bund, known at the time as the Nazi Bund. Cooke reported on one of their rallies on 23 February: he supported the decision by the (Jewish) Mayor La Guardia to allow the meeting to go ahead in the name of free speech and dissented from other commentators who took a far more apocalyptic view. Strong democracies, he maintained, could easily cope with the strident propaganda of a noisy minority, even one as ill-intentioned as the American Nazis. This was, in a way, a little bit of propaganda of his own. He wanted an English audience to accept that – whatever might appear in their morning newspaper – the activities of a few thousand fanatics did not define the policy of the government or the spirit of the people.

The problem for Cooke was that he was swimming against a tide of British public opinion, which, in the face of FDR's unconvincing pleas for peace on just principles, tended towards the view expressed by Neville Chamberlain: 'It is always best and safest to count on nothing from the Americans but words.' It was not a good time to be a salesman for transatlantic amity.

The final *Manhattan* programme ended with an unashamedly self-promoting on-air message from the broadcaster to his bosses:

> Your knowledge of a foreign country may depend on stories that you hear, but it's liable always to be in point of time behind the reality; and it's the glory and duty of radio to keep you posted on the changes. It is the duty

of radio. . .to keep on checking and denying and explaining, and turning corners quickly on an untruth, and smashing it down. That's only one reason why, although this series is ended and I say to you 'good night', I hope that it is not 'goodbye'.

For some time it looked as though his message would go unheeded. Apart from the occasional one-off assignment, eighteen months were to pass before he was offered regular employment again by the BBC.

12

THE LULL

The BBC's coolness still did not herald a serious crisis in Cooke's affairs, financial or personal. Social life in New York was absorbing, in a period during which a number of important friendships were established; Herb Elliston, for instance, soon to be elevated to editorship of the *Washington Post*, became a regular dining-partner and Long Island house-guest. He and Cooke teased each other about their backgrounds: Cooke would relay some gory tale dredged up from his youth in a stage Lancashire accent – at which Elliston would shake his head and say in his genuine Yorkshire brogue, 'Ee, lad, I'd love to tell yer some Yorkshire stories, but I've forgotten the accent.'

Among occasional visitations from English friends, Eddie Wiltshire, by now working as a diplomat in the Middle East, stayed for a fortnight in the New Year of 1939. They toured The Hickory House and other jazz haunts, and Cooke was manifestly delighted to be acting as host and guide to the man who had once been his musical mentor.

Another caller was the one-time Broadcasting House announcer Harman Grisewood, now on his way up the BBC management ladder. He rang Cooke from the St Regis Hotel in a linguistic panic when his efforts to order a 'whisky and soda' had met with incomprehension. Cooke advised him to order 'whisky in a tumbler and soda on the side' and then to mix his own. 'It's no good trying to get it any other way.' Grisewood, with an ear attuned to voices, noted with interest a discernible change in Cooke's intonation since they'd last met in London. 'The change was subtle,' he thought, 'and certainly not yet a full-scale conversion to an American accent.'

One way and another, Cooke was evidently too busy to reply to much of the family's mail and it fell to Ruth to try to keep up. In March she wrote apologetically to her brother-in-law Sam and his wife: 'Sending our news to Mother as near once a week as we can manage seems to be about all we can manage in the way of letters to the other side. We've only written to about three of our friends over there which is terrible, because the others will think we've forgotten all about them and we haven't.' She regrets, too, that Sam had to pay duty on the Christmas gifts she'd sent – cigars, a frock, bedsocks and a toy. To make up for it, she encloses two 10-shilling notes ('dirty ones, I'm sorry to say'). There was some helpful advice for her sister-in-law, too. 'I meant to tell you when we sent the toy . . . the paint can be tasted freely and with no ill effects because it is harmless on purpose. It is one of a line of "educational" toys . . . the funny thing is that from what I have seen of children who have them, they seem to have more fun and to enjoy these toys over a longer period of time than the more usual varieties.'

Ruth ends by reporting that she and Alistair 'are both in fine health'. As for the coming summer, 'We can't say definitely what we'll be up to yet, but we have hopes.'

~

As that summer of 1939 approached, the news from Europe showed no sign of improving. Yet the new opinion polls developed by Dr Gallup showed that only a tiny minority of Americans were ready to enter the war. Cooke, still a British citizen, must have wondered about his own position, robbed of his weekly opportunity to pursue his 'ministry' by mediating between a neutral America and a sceptical British public. He still had his job at *The Times*, but did he begin to wonder whether he should return home? There was still plenty of time. Instead, on 26 June, he set off on another of his continental tours. Ever helpful, Felix Greene cabled London about Cooke's plans: 'If interested might be able to arrange weekly talk in co-operation NBC: BBC paying fee, NBC covering lines; believe would make entertaining summer series.' A BBC memo, signed rather surprisingly by Cooke's friend Charles Siepmann, gives the tersest of answers to the question, 'Do we want to pay for another Cooke's tour?': 'No!'.

Three times, Alistair and Ruth had spent the summer touring the States – and three times they had taken a companion. There were practical reasons: on such interminable journeys it clearly made sense to have a third driver available. Yet these holidays might have been an opportunity for the couple to spend time alone together, something which didn't always prove easy in New York. There was so much

Right Sir Arthur Quiller-Couch – 'Q' – demonstrating why he was not regarded as entirely reliable by the Cambridge academic establishment.

Below right Cooke's vacation trips to Blackpool were a trial, and the company of Cambridge friends, like Desmond Armstrong, probably helped to ease the excruciating unease at being back in the provinces.

Below A shot taken at a demure tea-party in 1928. The love-lorn Hilda Unsworth is on Cooke's left, and Zelda Caplan on his right – one of the Jewish school contemporaries whose easy acceptance in Blackpool explained Cooke's shock when he first became aware of anti-Semitism.

Erik Chitty, Cooke's first Cambridge friend, starting young in his habitual acting role as an elderly man.

The moustache flourished briefly in Cooke's second and third years at Cambridge. He, Eddie Done (from Blackpool) and Desmond Armstrong referred to themselves as the 'Three Musketeers'.

The staff of *The Granta*, 1930. The photograph came from Hugh Stewart (second from left at the back). Norrie Davidson carries his trademark umbrella. Nobody (including Davidson) could remember how the umbrella tradition arose.

High jinks at Jesus. It appears to be a rag-day scene, recorded in 1930 by an official Cambridge photographer. Michael Redgrave is declaiming in the top left-hand corner. The poet James Reeves is between Redgrave and Cooke.

More student jollity: Eddie Wiltshire, Cooke (who had no idea how to play the cello), Norrie Davidson and Lionel Grunbaum.

Lionel Grunbaum in a Munich beer-garden in the summer of 1931 – the occasion of the loss of Cooke's political virginity.

Cooke's editorial year on *The Granta*, 1931–2: now firmly established as Alistair (rather than Alfred), he has dispensed with the undergraduate moustache.

Two examples of Cooke's drawings for *The Granta*. His caricatures
for the Mummers' production of *The Way of the World* (1931) with the artist
in the bottom right-hand corner, are typical; the Cambridge punting
scene (1929) is part of a page illustrating a humorous verse by James Reeves.

Admiring friends in *The Mummers' Revue* were sure that
their writer/composer/pianist/director/performer would be the
next Noël Coward.

A scene from Aldous Huxley's *The World of Light*, performed by the
Mummers. The other actor is Lionel Birch, later a journalist and editor
of *Picture Post*.

Above No doubt the cast were properly impressed by this further evidence of their director's talents.

Top left The Paignton tour of 1931 left plenty of time for lounging on the beach. Cooke's companions here are Hugh Stewart and his girlfriend Frances Curl.

Left The girl in the middle is Joan Charles, 'romantically linked' with Cooke, without any evidence at all.

The Winchelsea Reading Party. Although they could be discussing literature, it might just as well be sex.

Hetty Riddle

Hetty and Cooke
in Cambridge in the
painfully brief summer
of 1932.

socialising in the city, so many films and plays to see, and Cooke's work so often caused him to keep strange hours – while Ruth's life gravitated increasingly around home and family: the contrast was beginning to prey on her mind. But instead of throwing them together, their seven-week holiday, locked in the peculiar intimacy of a small car and an empty road, was shared with an outsider. The 'third man' on this occasion was Dr Jerome 'Jerry' Hartz, now a fully-fledged psychiatrist and keen amateur photographer, who'd become a regular weekend visitor to Long Island.

The general route was predictable: first south to New Orleans, where Hartz took some striking photographs, including a shot of a row of prostitutes' cribs, like neat rows of beach huts, and a passing whore gesticulating to her dog. 'She was talking to the creature,' Cooke remembered. ' "You get back here, hound-dog, man come all the way from New York to take your picture." ' Then the great trek to the West, choosing new routes wherever possible, in what turned out to be a steaming Southern summer. As they ploughed across Texas and Oklahoma – 'The Rodgers and Hammerstein musical, by the way,' he wrote in a 1976 *Letter*, 'is pure propaganda. Where do you think Rodgers and Hammerstein lived? Not Oklahoma, I can tell you.' – the temperature stayed stubbornly above a hundred degrees Fahrenheit, and rarely fell below eighty at night. There was no relief. Into New Mexico, then Arizona with its Painted Desert – America's heartland was gripped in a particularly remorseless heatwave.

To survive the cauldron they relied on salt tablets, dispensed in machines outside every station and drugstore. While in New Mexico they rediscovered the great Gold Rush invention of a small bag of ice in a thin canvas bag: 'By day you shut all the car windows, since the air outside was as hot as a branding iron, left a little chink on the driver's side, and set the bag dangling beside this chink. It worked even better at night when you hung the bag against the bedroom window that faced west, where the prevailing wind (if any was prevailing) came from.' The relief on reaching the Californian coastal range, and dropping down towards the resort of La Jolla was beyond describing.

Like its forerunners, the 1939 trip was enlivened by at least one adventure. Ignoring the stringent instructions to all visitors, Jerry Hartz was trying to film a brown bear as they drove through Yosemite National Park. With deceptive speed the bear lumbered towards them, placed a huge paw on the side of the car and grabbed Hartz's arm between its teeth. Cooke accelerated and the creature released its prey, but Hartz spent the next twenty-four hours undergoing repairs at a local hospital.

Also like its forerunners, this journey ended with another historical conjunction: on their long return journey across the Great Plains and the Mid-West they stopped for the night in London, Ohio. After a night in a motel they picked up a paper in the coffee-shop over pancakes and coffee: the Foreign Ministers of Russia and Germany, Molotov and Ribbentrop, had signed (on 23 August) the non-aggression pact which enabled Hitler to turn his full attention to Poland without risk to his Eastern flank. By the time the Cookes reached New York, war was only days away.

~

What was Cooke to do? He was thirty years old, able-bodied (apart from an obscure skin-ailment) and British. His job as a freelance foreign correspondent for *The Times* confined him to matters of general interest with all the serious political coverage in the hands of Sir Wilmott Lewis.

In November 1972, a *Radio Times* profile noted that it was Cooke's wartime broadcasts which had first brought him to public attention. He was quoted as saying, 'I had wanted to return from America to England when the war came, but I was told to stay. This was before the BBC had a permanent correspondent and I began to do a couple of talks a day. Without sentimentality, I think they did give people some hope. It reminded them that America had not forgotten them.'

There is, in fact, no documentary evidence at all of any attempt by Cooke to return to London, nor of his being advised by the BBC to stay where he was. Indeed the *Radio Times* account, thirty years on, skates over a year of growing difficulty and frustration – a year during which it was he himself who was in danger of being forgotten.

That reality emerges first, and most strikingly, in a letter Cooke wrote on 8 September. Marked 'Personal' and handwritten, it is addressed to his friend Peter Fleming, the travel-writer who helped him secure his post on *The Times*. In the interim, Fleming had disappeared into the bowels of the War Office and the letter was forwarded by the newspaper to the BBC executive Cooke named as another possible contact – Sir Stephen Tallents, who had been seconded to the Ministry of Information.

Cooke starts by mentioning an article he has written 'on spec' for *The Times*: 'In spite of my assumption that the background and *habits* of Am. neutrality would have been covered, I am taking the risk of sending a piece meant to clarify – for British readers – neutrality *as Americans see it*. In view of several tactless and mildly reproachful public statements by travelling Britons here, it is most urgent that Britons should know in what ways Ams. will and will not exercise neutrality.'

There follows a lengthy PS, in which Cooke's anxiety about his own future is only too obvious. He reports that he has been listening to short-wave radio broadcasts and comparing the 'excellent subtlety of the German service' with 'British propaganda designed to satisfy the national attitudes of the sender (i.e. the British) and not the psychology of the receiving end (i.e. the US)'. Such pitfalls, he goes on, can be avoided by 'observations at this end'. The question is, how can he be found a role in restoring the balance? He confides in his correspondent that he has mentioned his thoughts neither to Felix Greene, nor to Sir Wilmott Lewis – nor, indeed, to the Ministry of Information or the British Consulate, 'who would naturally know my possible usefulness a good deal less than you or the BBC'.

He concludes, 'I <u>have</u> written to F.W. Ogilvie, the BBC Director-General offering to do what I can there, though this is really separate, because it would be talking from here for the entertainment or peace of mind, for instance, of British audiences: this is quite distinct from what I might do <u>here</u> for the Ministry of Information, for Tallents, for Intelligence, or whatever it is to be.'

What Cooke was seeking was a role which would allow him to stay in the United States while making a contribution to the war effort. Sir Stephen Tallents was not going to give him that lifeline. On 22 September he offered a courteous, but cool, reply.

'I very much wish that I could see some way that would bring us into wartime association, for there is nothing I would enjoy more.' He informs Cooke that, regretfully, he has relinquished the post of Director-General Designate of the Ministry of Information and returned full time to the BBC. 'I therefore spoke personally to Sir Frederick Whyte, who is head of the American Department at the Ministry. He enquired if you were nowadays a British or American citizen and this I could not tell him.' The best Whyte could do – despite the fact that he presumably remembered Cooke from the English Speaking Union on the eve of the abdication – was to offer some Ministry contacts in New York and Washington. Tallents's letter ended, 'I am afraid that this is as much help as I can give you. I can only add that I shall always be delighted to hear from you and wish that I was better placed to advise you than in fact I am.'

The dismissive tone must have been a shock to Cooke and a reminder of the awkward position of a man, in wartime, caught between two nationalities. There were financial implications, too. *The Times* was not exactly a goldmine for its freelance staff, who might only be paid two or three guineas even for a substantial article. Working for the paper was, as Cooke would jocularly explain, an occupation for gentlemen: 'They kept you in cigarettes but otherwise expected you to have a private income.' This genteel arrangement was Cooke's main source of funds in the early months of the war and it soon became clear that it wasn't enough to maintain his habitual lifestyle.

Far above Cooke's head (and beyond his hearing) the BBC was in the process of reconsidering all aspects of its overseas broadcasting. Almost as soon as war broke out, programmes from the United States were suspended – apart from a reduced quota of talks by Swing. Felix Greene, in the New York office, was reduced to firing off letters and cables to London. In October he wrote that 'it is of the greatest importance that the British people be not misled by false hopes and that they be accurately and frankly informed week by week as to the course of American opinion'. Cooke's voice is clearly audible, as Greene gave vent to his frustration that his office was becoming 'irked by idleness'. What would happen, he fulminated, if America were to enter the war and the BBC found itself without an office in the country? At the very least, it would be an 'aggravating embarrassment'.

In Cooke's recollection, Greene had in any case been infected by a great sense of gloom about the war and, in an access of pacifist zeal, had found religion. Not surprisingly, the decision was taken to replace him. In one of his last letters to the Deputy Director-General, Sir Cecil Graves, Greene begged that his successor should not be 'afflicted by the British upper-class manner which is taken here (quite often mistakenly) as insufferable arrogance.' In the circumstances, there was little point in Cooke hanging round the BBC offices in the last few months of 1939. His thirty-first birthday, on 20 November, can hardly have been a joyous or optimistic affair. He was desperate for a basic income – and was prepared to settle for as little as $20 or $25 a week. It was quite a come-down from the heady days of NBC's lavish, $100-a-programme treatment of their new recruit just two years earlier. Times were so tight that he agreed to do some trial programmes for the local radio station WQXR, one of the progenitors of National Public Radio. One talk a week would be on politics, and the other a film review. There was only one drawback: there would be no pay. 'I had an assurance from the station that sponsors would leap at me. No sponsors leapt. I was really very strapped.'

The Cookes were never in danger of going hungry. Ruth's money ensured that life went on more or less as usual and at Christmas there was a grand (Emerson) family reunion. Her brother Ralph travelled over from California for the first time in several years, and another brother (the mistrustful Bob) had only recently returned from Europe. Cooke was able to renew his animated discussions on medical matters over dinner at Southold or at the Emerson home in New York. So preoccupied were they that Cooke neglected to send even a Christmas card to his brother Sam in Blackpool. His niece, Kathleen, preserved another letter from Ruth written on 3 March 1940, in which she apologises to Sam and Elsie for their failure to be in contact. Recognising the name by which her husband was still known in Blackpool, she wrote: 'Alfred and I sent hardly a card by way of Christmas greeting, this year or last year. Not on purpose, but just as it happened. We feel very much amiss.' Ruth goes on to remark how glad they were to hear about Sam's new job at the Co-op butchers' shop. 'What you said about all the turkeys and other meat you sold at Christmas time certainly sounded good. All the letters we get from England are most wonderfully cheerful and chin-up, for a country at war. Where will it all end? How long will it continue?'

The same letter also reinforces the picture described so vividly by Felix Greene: 'We heard again recently from the BBC office over here that they might take some talks by Alfred. So perhaps you will hear his voice again soon. But I must say there has been so little broadcasting from here to England that the office has been very quiet, and very different from last year.' Ruth encloses a belated Christmas cheque – £1 each for the two children, Kathleen and Sheila, and £1 for them to spend on 'something you would like as a present from us'.

The only hint of positive news in the letter is that Cooke had at least found one new source of employment, if not of fame or fortune.

It came about thanks to his reputation as a film critic, culminating in *Garbo and the Night Watchmen*. Film critics still formed a small clique in which such a book was bound to attract a level of specialist interest out of proportion to its sales figures. In the year that Cooke set up home in New York the Museum of Modern Art (MOMA) established a new film library, whose benefactors included Nelson Rockefeller. The library's curator, Iris Barry, was another expatriate, who had once worked as the reviewer for the *Daily Mail*, and she was interested to meet the man who had done such service to a youthful art-form.

It was Iris Barry's idea that, in order to give the new library a certain academic standing, it should publish a series of monographs on the industry's great figures. She launched the process with a study of the director D.W. Griffiths, many of whose early prints were lodged in her archives. But she turned to Cooke to supply a second volume in the series and he chose as his subject his youthful hero, Douglas Fairbanks. Cooke was provided with a small office in the museum next door to Barry's, and spent his time rerunning the much-loved films of his childhood. While he was still engaged in the research, Fairbanks died, at the age of just fifty-six, on 12 December 1939: thus the monograph became a tribute as well as an academic exercise. A slim volume appeared the following year in an edition of 8,000 copies: *Douglas Fairbanks – The Making of a Screen Character*, billed as 'Museum of Modern Art Film Library Series No.2'. (There never was a number three.)

The book chronicled the early years of Fairbanks' life, in which he dabbled extremely briefly in the worlds of finance, the law and manufacturing industry before settling on a successful Broadway career. This led in turn to his adoption by Hollywood in 1915 at the age of thirty-one. The following year he made no fewer than eleven movies, mainly 'melodramas decorated by acrobatics'.

Cooke was moved to invoke the shades of his own past: Hal Gregory putting him through his paces at the gymnasium in Blackpool and the admiring girls waiting for their dancing classes. With the insight of a practitioner, he notes that Fairbanks' gravity-defying agility was rooted in basic athletic disciplines: 'There is not a leap, a turn or a change of terrain which cannot be precisely named in the gymnastic jargon. It is simply that these things are normally done on a horizontal bar, or on parallels, or on a trapeze.'

This exercise in nostalgia even brought to Cooke's mind a vision of his disapproving mother: 'To many an anxious parent at this time, "Doug" stood for the film industry's total respectability. He was not merely inoffensive, which is what parents were looking for: he was a positive ideal worthy of any small fry's adulation.'

~

Cooke's hours in the projection room, reviewing *The Thief From Baghdad* and *The Three Musketeers*, were pure escapism. While Europe waited uneasily through the early months of 1940 for Hitler's next move, resentment grew at America's quiescence and Cooke felt isolated and unable to help. The only extra work he was able to eke out of the BBC was a news item describing the arrival of the *Queen Elizabeth* in New York harbour after her maiden voyage. He watched from the vantage point of the Staten Island Ferry as the new liner – dressed out in drab camouflage grey – approached the dockside. 'There are no crowds,' Cooke reported, 'no bands, no airplanes, no ticker-tape. One New York paper says "it's as if an Empress had arrived incognito, with a grey veil over her face."'

This sort of work was not what he had in mind when, on 22 January 1940, he had made another attempt to browbeat the BBC into taking him back into the fold. He wrote to the Deputy Director-General, Sir Cecil Graves, ruing the 'sad day indeed when the news tells us of rising friction between Great Britain and the US'. What better reason for commissioning more talks from New York? Cooke confessed that he was writing without the knowledge of Felix Greene (who was on his way out, in any case) and made two – familiar – suggestions. The first:

A regular talk, a sort of diary of a country at peace, in style and form like *Mainly About Manhattan*, but spanning a wider field: taking in two or three topics each time, touching on life away from the East Coast; on democratic festivals or celebrations it might be good for Britons to know about; on a new invention; a great man dead; on a new writer; on American experiments in democracy – the country teems with projects that are gallantly run.

To be called, say, – *A Letter From America*.

The baptism of a broadcasting institution? Not yet.

The reply, this time, was couched in terms more disheartening than ever before – and for reasons which say much about the deeply troubled state of UK-US relations. The man who penned the deadly rejection was Harman Grisewood, now acting as Assistant Director of Programme Planning. 'Whilst I think there is need for the USA to understand the British, and indeed the European, situation, *I do not feel that at this stage there is an equivalent need for us to understand the American point of view*' [author's italics]. This blatant snub was not sent to Cooke himself : it was circulated among senior managers, along with Grisewood's assertion that the reduced number of talks by Raymond Gram Swing was quite enough of an American point of view. Years later the Grisewood memo became the star turn at a BBC dinner celebrating one of the frequent Cooke anniversaries: the incredulous guests found it hard to imagine that Alistair Cooke had ever been treated with such disdain.

Grisewood was just as unenthusiastic about Cooke's second idea – for a series of talks on new writing, followed by a reading from the work in question, whether in books, magazines or newspapers. The key, Cooke reckoned, would be an attractive title which avoided book-ishness: 'I timidly suggest "*American Nights* with AC" or "AC reading *Between The Lines*" or "*You Must Relax*" but *not* "Readings From American Writers of Today"'. Grisewood found the whole thing 'a bit recherché', and doubted whether listeners would even have heard of most of the writers on Cooke's list of potential subjects: 'I think AC has become a good deal more Americanised than in the *Mainly About Manhattan* days. Those programmes were fairly successful because in those days he was able to take up the standpoint of an Englishman.' It was a damaging perception – the sense of Cooke's statelessness at a time of patriotic intensity.

There's no doubt that these opinions were widely held. Another executive who was shown Cooke's letter was even more direct. Robert MacDermot, a Programme Organiser, was evidently a student of transatlantic affairs and he didn't like what he read. 'AC seems to have become very Americanised and has adopted the rather irritating American attitude whereby the US is regarded as being the sole guard-ian of democracy, an attitude which is apt to puzzle the average Englishman who has been nurtured on American-manufactured films and stories of gangsters and proto-nazi police methods.' Mac-

Dermot concedes that some explanation of American institutions might be useful, but that it would have to be done very brightly to avoid 'the almost inevitable impression of traditional American superiority complex'.

Unlike Harman Grisewood's internal memo, the formal reply dispatched to Cooke by Sir Cecil Graves is scrupulously polite and blames changes in the wartime transmission system for the restrictions on overseas programmes. There is no hint of the underlying reasons for rejecting his ideas, and the letter includes an undertaking that he will be kept in mind for 'proposals more suited to our present needs', to be channelled through the North American Representative.

On this count fate continued to smile on Cooke, providing him with another ally and future friend. Greene's replacement was a man who had already made a considerable name for himself as the BBC's first Director of Television, Gerald Cock, described in the Corporation's official history as 'highly energetic and imaginative' and 'a man given to bold initiatives'. It was he who had identified at an early stage, and in the face of considerable corporate scepticism, that television would be 'the greatest medium for communication the world had ever seen'. Now, on 3 March, he arrived in New York to help develop the BBC's new wartime relationship with the United States. It was still not regarded as a high priority. What's more, Cock's masters judged that the more important aspect of the relationship by far was to ensure that Britain's voice was clearly heard in America, not the other way round.

None of which was of much immediate help to Cooke, who had just discovered that Ruth was pregnant.

~

It was not an ideal time to be starting a family. The news coincided with Hitler's Blitzkrieg and the fall of Denmark, Norway, Belgium, Holland and France. Closer to home, Cooke's bank balance was in a shaky state, and he was about to be given wider responsibilities by *The Times*, requiring him to spend more time away from home.

Ruth had plenty to keep her occupied. She had, for instance, joined the board of a Community Centre whose aim was to engage youngsters from a deprived part of the city in worthwhile projects promoting citizenship. But Cooke's new brief, combined with her own approaching role as a mother, would hasten the process of detaching her from the mainstream of his life. These developments were to have serious implications for the marriage.

Cooke's new position did not come about from anything as simple as promotion or a job interview. It was a sudden, unexpected transmogrification which took place when Cooke arrived, one sultry May day, in the un-air-conditioned offices of Sir Wilmott Lewis. There was a glint in the old man's eye: 'My boy,' he said, reaching into an inner pocket, 'I have something for you.' He took out a business envelope with what Cooke described as 'the air of a rich man who'd decided to pass on his worldly goods to a favourite orphan'. Inside, there was a set of cards. They included Lewis's White House pass, his State Department pass, his Washington police card and his passes to the press galleries of both the Senate and the House of Representatives. That wasn't all. Cooke realised that he'd also been handed the newspaper's accreditation to the nominating Conventions of both the Democratic and Republican parties which were due to take place in July.

'Sir . . . ' he stuttered.

'Not a word,' Lewis declared. 'They are all yours.'

'Do you mean that you're not even going to cover the Conventions?' Lewis had been one of the few foreign correspondents to attend every significant political gathering since the early 1920s.

'My dear boy, nothing that happens today has not happened yesterday, and will not happen tomorrow.'

Cooke was momentarily dumbstruck. The great Wilmott Lewis was throwing in his hand. It was an act of renunciation and an unparalleled opportunity for a novice correspondent in a field where there was little competition from British journalists. The Conventions were expected to be more than usually interesting: would Roosevelt really break with tradition and stand for a third term of office? And whom could the benighted Republicans find to oppose him?

At about the same time, a small chink of light appeared in the darkness of Cooke's relations with the BBC. Towards the end of May there was a suggestion that Swing might not be able to continue his *American Commentary* much longer. His main radio job was for the American WOR Network, for whom he did a weekly talk sponsored by the General Cigar Company. This involved not only commercials at the beginning and end, but also a half-way break (in a fifteen-minute show) to allow the sonorous voice of an announcer to intone,

'More men smoke White Owl cigars than any other cigars in the world!' Swing loathed this interruption, and the row came to a head in the week of the German invasion of the Low Countries. He told his paymasters that he would refuse to broadcast unless he could do so without interruption. They gave in, and Swing renewed his commitment to the station. His autobiography, *Good Evening*, gives a telling insight into the comparative status of the two broadcasters. The sponsorship deal alone reached $87,000 by 1941, and it was by no means his sole source of income. Cooke, at about the same time, reckoned that $10,000 constituted a good year's work.

With only a hint of Swing's departure to work on, Cooke rushed off a letter to Sir Stephen Tallents, raising what he called this matter of first-rate importance. There's a strong whiff of *Schadenfreude* in the language: 'It must be sad news for you, as it certainly is for me, to hear that Raymond Swing will do no more regular talks for you.' In Cooke's opinion, Swing had in any case been finding it difficult to get across the 'complexity of the American position" precisely because he was American himself. Now if an English voice were to be used instead . . .

To help out, and after consultation with Gerald Cock, Cooke was ready to do a recorded test talk which London could review before commissioning a regular series, 'for continuity is essential and it can never be established by three or four speakers'. He promises 'a simple, vivid and watchful summary of the progress of American opinion and American policy'. Perhaps, he mused, the BBC might be unaware that he was no longer a mere commentator on social oddities: he had become a well-informed correspondent for *The Times* and a journal called the *Fortnightly*, filing newspaper clippings each day from 'all over the place'. He would not be resorting to the ubiquitous (and untrustworthy) 'confidential reports', but would chart public attitudes according to the scientific principles of Dr Gallup and his Institute of Public Opinion.

Cooke then made his personal pitch: his uncertain national status could, he suggested, be a positive advantage.

It appears that the BBC is anxious not to have an Englishman; this seems to be a good point, since most Britons I have met here are naturally committed to a cause, but also to a 'wish' for American policy, which blurs the accurate vision of American attitudes.

> At the same time, I fall into a curious, and dare I say useful, category. Namely one who knows something of English psychology, an Englishman and an American citizen (I am awaiting my final call these next two weeks). I believe I could give objective fact without having to writhe with regretful apology – because the British are much tougher at accepting a situation than I think most Americans know.

This was a bold and subtle stroke. Bold, because his naturalisation wasn't nearly as imminent as he claimed: he would not become a citizen for another eighteen months. And subtle, because his argument rested on persuading the BBC that only a man with American knowledge and awareness of British sensitivities would meet the bill, whatever kind of passport he happened to carry.

With a parting word of regret for Raymond Gram Swing ('we are agreed, I hope, that he is irreplaceable'), he assured Tallents that his letter implied 'no more or less' than it said. This may have seemed a necessary precaution at a time when so many furtive initiatives were underway, with the participants often in ignorance of each other's activities. In Cooke's case, however, Tallents was undoubtedly the better informed of the two, thanks to his Ministry of Information connections: he may already have known that Cooke was in danger of becoming *persona non grata* with the British authorities in the United States.

PART THREE

DARK DAYS:
AMERICA
AT WAR

13

NEW ALLEGIANCES

Official suspicion was not the immediate reason for the BBC's continued reluctance to take Cooke to its bosom. *American Commentary* was one of the most popular programmes on radio, with an average audience of almost six million, and Swing already had an understudy, in the figure of Elmer Davis, a newspaperman and novelist of note. Cock none the less advised London to reconsider, because Davis had a habit of expecting too much background knowledge from his British audience: 'Believe Cooke after investigation excellent with intimate knowledge of situation. Recommend trial.'

The pressure was to pay off, but not before Cooke's first real exposure to American politics in the raw – at the Republican Convention in Philadelphia at the end of June 1940. As if there wasn't enough inherent tension in such an open fight for the right to challenge Roosevelt, news came through on the eve of the gathering that France had fallen. 'Philadelphia', Cooke wrote in the *Fortnightly*, 'was stunned into a sense of responsibility no Republican National Committee could ever have urged on them. Out of a denouement staged in Europe came the *deus ex machina* – Wendell Willkie.' This business magnate, who had made his fortune from the electricity industry, was a political unknown – and that, it transpired, was what appealed to the delegates. At a moment of crisis the Republicans chose a fresh face, although only after a series of desperately close ballots and a great deal of vigorous horse-trading. For Cooke, it was a gripping and invigorating introduction into the way America did its political business. Few of the fifteen conventions he covered over the next thirty years could match it.

His instinctive tendency to approve the Democratic cause was certainly not betrayed in his coverage of that party's Convention in Chicago three weeks later. He disliked the Machiavellian manoeuvring to achieve a vote by acclamation for Roosevelt and the apparent artifice of the President's reluctance to run for a third term: 'Many very case-hardened political writers were moved by the voice of the galleries at Philadelphia, as they were sickened at Chicago by the electrical amplification of a single voice to imitate a united cry for Roosevelt.' In the event, 950 of the 1100 delegates opted for FDR after a long and bad-tempered delay punctuated with 'growls and hoots as the nominating speeches and the balloting dragged on'.

Once the Conventions were over, Cooke took an extraordinary decision. Leaving behind his five-months pregnant wife, he drove off with Ralph Emerson on a three-month holiday to California, where his favourite brother-in-law was about to take up his first academic appointment. 'If you had asked me then what was the state of my marriage,' Cooke wrote when he sat down more than half a century later to try to make sense of what happened, 'I should have thought it a very odd question. I had been happily married to the beautiful and gentle-tempered Ruth for six years.' It never crossed his mind that he was doing something perverse: after all, he expected to be back for the birth.

While he was staying in Berkeley, however, there came out of the blue a call from Gerald Cock: could Cooke take over the *American Commentary* – at least for a week? It meant that the holiday would have to be unceremoniously curtailed, but Cooke didn't care. Before hurrying back to the East Coast, he wrote to Sir Stephen Tallents,

> This is not to be a harangue or a pamphlet like my last. Simply to say to whomever was responsible – thank you for the chance of doing the scheduled 7 September talk. I am resolved to make it a humdinger and, however the BBC looks on it, I cannot help but regard it as a trial in the hope of an unceasing series . . .
>
> I know it is an assignment of maximum delicacy. But the alternative to the attempt is something that makes me lie awake nights — it is the miserable, and by no means impossible, prospect that from silence may develop a habit of recrimination between the two countries. After the recrimination that was manufactured between Britain and France, this would be the worst tragedy, the best invitation to Hitler to do as he chose with the last cocky remnants of democracy.

Fortune smiled on the enterprise, in the form of a strong, solid piece of good news about America's intentions which formed the basis of the broadcast. Roosevelt's decision in August – to exchange fifty ageing destroyers for six strategic air and sea bases belonging to Britain – was the first and most concrete sign of a new era of active US involvement in the war effort. But Cooke was well aware of the danger of exaggerating this optimistic picture: 'We have seen the greatest of Hitler's tactics has been the planting of doubt between friends. There are now only two great powers that remain to be divided by recrimination – they are Great Britain and the United States. To achieve that would be Hitler's greatest conquest.' He stepped down from the pulpit with a quiet 'Good night'.

London liked it and he was offered a short series of four further programmes in the run-up to Christmas, alternating with Swing each fortnight. The following month he even attracted admiring references in the British press:

What has happened to the BBC? Usually its official speakers are tongue-tied. Yet Alistair Cooke, a BBC employee, suddenly blurted out in his broadcast a few words of truth. Was the Ministry of Information taking a weekend off? . . . Cooke made the frank statement that, virtually, Britain and the States were now allies. His broadcast was generally more forthright than is Raymond Gram Swing's, whose place he took.

~

The highlight of the presidential campaign for Cooke came with another act of renunciation by Sir Wilmott Lewis. On a sweltering Washington day, Lewis summoned him into his office and handed him an invitation to one of the monthly lunches held at the White House for senior members of the press. Cooke was to take his place and listened as Lewis rang the relevant official: 'If it's all right with you, I'm sending my young friend'. Cooke was among the dozen guests who arrived on the appointed Thursday. They were shown into a room in which the heat was oppressive: there was no air-conditioning in the White House. The scene remained etched on Cooke's mind:

Roosevelt was at the head of the table, and a butler approached with a great silver tray of lobsters. The butler, we learned, was Duke Ellington's father. The President inspected the tray, with his great, long cigarette holder angled from the corner of his mouth. He would lift up a lobster, inspect it, replace it and pick up another. All the time he was talking through his cigarette, until finally he found the one he wanted. 'That's the baby!'

Cooke was impressed by this display of confidence and humanity. One part of the lunch-time conversation in particular stayed with him. The journalists raised the question of Willkie's marital problems: might these play a part in the campaign? Contemptuously, Roosevelt brushed the idea aside. 'Let it rest,' he told them.

The campaign developed in such a way that the President hardly needed to concern himself with his opponent's love life. Although the election may have started as a referendum on the New Deal, it rapidly became a question of choosing the right man to defend America in an uncertain world. Roosevelt let it be known that he would not be conducting the normal campaign tour of the country: it was essential for him to remain within striking distance of Washington in case of emergencies. His vast new defence programmes offered the prospect of jobs for all and who could question the need? As Cooke wrote,

> The campaign, which since Mr Roosevelt had cleverly renounced any intention to make one, meant the campaign of Wendell Willkie, slithered anticlimactically on to the shelf of national memoranda, at the very moment when Mr Willkie's trans-continental train was pulling into New York for a speech on the third term, which the Republicans had resolved to make 'the issue', and which popular sentiment now cared less about than the cut of George Washington's trousers.

With good reason, Cooke eventually came to despise and fear psephology, but in this case he was prepared to write an early epitaph on the 'brave, unlucky and mishandled career of Wendell Willkie'. For once he was right. Roosevelt won thirty-eight states – although the Republican share of the popular vote was well up on 1932 and 1936.

Cooke's initial respect for Willkie grew in the years after the election – a man whose genuine distaste for the economics of the New Deal might in other times have brought him success. It appealed to Cooke – as a matter of principle – that, in America, an outsider could come from nowhere and run the President close: and he took a strikingly open-minded view of the political theory behind Willkie's campaign. 'As a person, what Willkie has done has been to unite behind him all the best opposition to the New Deal – all those honest people who are against the pressure of Government bureaux, who are against the liability of a huge dole poured from the nation's Treasury, who are against the New Deal's open alliance with the most ruthless political bosses in this country.'

The presidential election was a strong formative influence on Cooke's own political thinking. His early, naïve enthusiasm for Roosevelt had rapidly been tempered and, whereas he might once have been in general sympathy with the liberal, leftish views of his friends at Yale, he was beginning to develop the sense of distance from any politician – and, just as important, from any political label – that would define his journalism.

~

On Saturday 5 October 1940, in the heat of the election campaign, Ruth gave birth to a son at the Harkness Pavilion of the Columbia-Presbyterian Medical Center. He was christened John Byrne Cooke, his middle name taken from his paternal grandmother. In advance of the birth, the Cookes had moved from East 78th Street to a third-floor apartment at 1078 Madison Avenue just a few blocks further north – cheek by jowl with a funeral parlour. The building had a lift. Ruth did not intend to carry a child and accoutrements up three flights of stairs, especially when her husband was so often unavailable to help.

One of the first people to hear that Cooke was a father was a fourteen-year-old English boy who had just arrived in New York after an unnerving Atlantic crossing on board the British liner *Samaria*. David Curnow was the younger son of Cooke's Blackpool history master, W.I. Curnow – Billy Wick. The fall of France had persuaded Curnow that David, whose elder brother had already joined up, ought to be moved to a place of safety. Under a special evacuation scheme funded by benefactors, families prepared to risk the crossing could send children to homes in the United States. David was destined to spend the war with an unconventional academic in Boston – Samuel Lothrop Thorndike 3rd – a professor of astronomy at Wellesley women's college.

The *Samaria* docked in New York on 4 October and David's first act, as he'd been instructed, was to ring the Cookes. Instead of the warm welcome he was expecting, the call was answered by Alistair in a flap. 'I'm terribly sorry,' he explained. 'I'd love to come down and meet you at the dock but I can't. Ruth's about to have a baby.' The boy was left to make his own way to Boston, where he was soon installed as a pupil at the local high school, although the Cookes moved quickly to make up for this disappointment by inviting him to spend Christmas in New York with the Emerson tribe. David was fussed over, and even Dr Haven Emerson took the trouble to give him a pen as a Christmas present, with a bit of advice thrown in for good measure. 'Never waste your money on toothpaste,' he told the boy. 'Ridiculous modern invention, toothpaste. Carbolic soap and salt. That's what works best.'

After Christmas lunch, Dr Emerson retired for a nap and the rest of the family breathed a sigh of relief. Curnow couldn't believe it: 'All these very sophisticated people, including Alistair, started muttering, "Quick, he's gone!" They produced packets of cigarettes, and we all huddled round the fireplace blowing our smoke up the chimney. Nobody dared risk it when Dr Emerson was in the room.' In this, and many other ways, it was not like a Blackpool Christmas holiday.

Despite the boy's tender age, Cooke would take him to jazz clubs and even to burlesque shows: his parents might well have been shocked to learn that he had become a regular visitor to Minsky's – a dive subsequently closed down by Mayor La Guardia. 'By today's standards it was terribly innocent – feeble, low-down comedians and then a pudgy, rather overweight chorus', Curnow recalls. 'The high spot came with the arrival of the stripper, strutting round and removing her gloves to the music. If you were frightfully lucky, you might get a glimpse of half a breast.'

It was a curious way for Cooke to treat such a young and inexperienced visitor. It's tempting to see it as an early manifestation of the difficulty he always had relating to children, including his own. He simply found it easier to regard David as a young version of the adults with whom he spent the rest of his time.

~

The first few months of 1941 marked another of the low points in Cooke's professional life. He'd been beset for a year or more by unfamiliar (and thus disconcerting) bouts of self-doubt – making do with a pittance from *The Times*, and dribs and drabs of occasional work from elsewhere. Perhaps the most curious of these part-time occupations had come by way of the film maker Edgar Anstey, who moved to New York to work on the monthly newsreel film, *The March of Time.* After its creation in 1935 it had become an institution in cinemas across America and the English-speaking world. It consisted of serious documentary films on domestic and international issues, though it owed something of its celebrity to the voice of the narrator – the deep, rich and resonant voice of Westbrook van Voorhis – who invested the words 'The March . . . of Time' with the solemnity of a papal blessing. Each episode ended with a similarly portentous phrase: 'Time . . . Marches . . . On!' It was a wonderful way of grabbing the audience's attention and the same – trademark – voice was also used for film-commentaries within the newsreel. It soon transpired that the voice did not appeal to British cinema-goers. Anstey had asked Cooke to provide a less melodramatic alternative, by re-recording the *March of Time* film commentaries – excluding, of course, the magnificent opening and closing words.

This was still not the sort of work which was going to end Cooke's financial worries, though this period entitled him to say with some justification (long after the event) that everybody should be unemployed once in their lives. Years later, when his own son was trying to carve out a new career in impecunious circumstances, he wrote, 'When you were a tiny baby, I recall walking in the park and thinking, "If only I could write a column or get some steady job that would guarantee me $25 a week – then I'd be all set!!!!" ' So bad did things become during the year that Ruth had to make him a substantial loan – of several hundred dollars – out of the money her father had settled on her.

In these depressing circumstances, New Year's Day saw him at his typewriter, pounding off another lengthy missive to the BBC, complaining to Sir Stephen Tallents about the irregular scheduling of *American Commentary.* His friends, he said, could hardly believe it: 'They fall into silent awe of a nation that can still regard the United States, not as a world power, but as a sort of Martian vitamin factory from which, twelve times a year, a stimulating dose is pumped.' He even inserted a public protest into the broadcast of 11 January: 'If this dispatch seems to hop around a little desperately from item to item, I should like to remind you that these commentaries on the American news come to you only once every fifteen days.'

He ended his New Year letter to Tallents with a question: 'just what sort of commentary does the BBC want from *American Commentary*?'. The depressing answer was that the BBC wanted a commentary which reflected more accurately the policies and prejudices of a nation at war. Cooke was not prepared to concede that the only propaganda which mattered to the authorities in London was the dissemination of their point of view by whatever means and to anyone who would listen. Occupied Europe was the priority, but the Empire was of high importance. Consequently, the emphasis in dealing with the United States was on journalism which demonstrated to the enemy that they were dealing with an immensely powerful potential ally. Cooke's obsession with keeping the British audience informed was so low a priority as to be off the radar.

In any case, despite the vocal protests of the isolationist minority, it was increasingly obvious that America under a re-elected Roosevelt would not leave Britain in the lurch. The passing of The Lend-Lease Act (under which ships and guns were provided in return for payment, later, in kind) proved the point – as did the build-up of American naval activity in the Atlantic. It was no longer necessary to indulge in minute textual analysis of Presidential speeches to find encouraging news for a British audience.

And when the chance did arise for Cooke to convert the sceptics at Broadcasting House, something always seemed to go wrong. Early in 1941 he was asked to do a five-minute weekly talk for the Empire Service, to be broadcast across the Pacific. In the eyes of his masters, this could have been just as significant as the *Commentary* since it made Cooke part of the real propaganda war. Yet within weeks, his work was being described by one of his critics as 'of low quality'. The judgement was damning. 'If Cooke is not any better next time, I would propose to get an American journalist in London to give a weekly review for the Pacific, and would you ask Cock to find someone else to take Cooke's place from New York.' Then at the end of January, his Pacific transmission was adjudged to have given 'disproportionate weight' to the views of Charles Lindbergh (the air pioneer who had become a noisy advocate of neutrality) and Senator Joseph Kennedy.

On 2 February, Gerald Cock sent a long memo to London, bowing to the inevitable. 'I am sorry that Alistair Cooke, who is such a good broadcaster, is for the moment at least out of favour for *American Commentary* on account of the now rather long succession of blunders which he has made from lack of considered political judgement.' This memo crossed with one from London cancelling Cooke's commitment to the *Pacific News Reel* as well. 'His piece on Wednesday, even after the warning sent last week, was if anything worse than the two previous pieces.'

The demand for Cooke's suspension arrived too late for Cock to find an instant replacement. Consequently, there was one more Pacific transmission on 5 February – and it caused another row. In the course of what seems a rather reassuring account of the growing acceptance of Lend-Lease, Cooke indulged in some analysis of US relations with Australia. The text was referred to the Foreign Office who demanded that the broadcast be withdrawn. 'The FO say we should on no account use the Cooke statement which they consider extremely ill-advised in every point of view.'

That, for the time being, was that. The *News Reel* managers were adamant – 'It is a waste of money to go on taking these weekly pieces, and from our experience now it seems unlikely that we shall want to revert to Cooke again.' They were wrong about that. And in a hand-written addendum to the memo, Sir Cecil Graves wondered whether all the criticism was fair. 'Is it a case of "give a dog a bad name?!"'

The immediate result, however, was to reduce Cooke to a handful of non-political items like descriptions of shipyards or military manoeuvres. Not surprisingly, the letter Cooke received on 7 March from Sir Stephen Tallents, in reply to his long shopping-list of suggestions two months earlier, was non-committal verging on the apologetic: 'I agree personally with the points you make, but I am not personally in charge of our Home Service and find some of my colleagues less ready to be convinced.' He could scarcely offer Cooke more than a feeble invitation to drop him a line some time.

Although he would have sporadic commissions from the BBC over the succeeding months – including a reprieve for his monthly appearance on *American Commentary* until September – he was not taken back into the Corporation's full confidence for more than two years. He was already thirty-two, and most of his reporting triumphs still lay some way in the future.

Part of the problem was that, in the course of 1941, Cooke's ill-paid work from *The Times* dried up, although acquiring a weekly column in another British newspaper, the *Daily Herald*, was some compensation, especially since the *Herald* believed in paying market rates to freelance contributors – sometimes five or ten times what was offered by *The Times*. On New Year's Day Cooke launched a series which the paper called '12 Riddles of 1941...The *Daily Herald* begins a momentous series of articles, written by outstanding experts, on subjects which vitally affect every man, woman and child in the country.' Cooke, 'famous transatlantic broadcaster whose voice is known to millions of listeners', set out to answer the question: 'Will America Enter the War?' Cooke's answer, naturally, was yes, though he wasn't prepared to wager when it might happen.

Working for the *Herald* was not the proudest experience of Cooke's journalistic career. Looking back, he admitted that it involved too much of the slap-happy punditry from which he subsequently recoiled. 'It was sincere enough,' he reflected, 'but you knew you didn't have to be as careful about checking your facts.' Under this carefree regime, he was bold enough to pass on a piece of gossip he'd picked up from a Korean traveller on a train journey; its message was that the South Pacific 'could blow up in the first week of December.' He thought no more about this casual prediction, but when news of Pearl Harbor came through on 7 December, the *Daily Herald* emblazoned Cooke's clairvoyant words on placards all over London.

As the weather warmed up, Alistair and Ruth decided to give up their Madison Avenue base for the summer and move to Southold. At least, Ruth and Johnny (as the baby became known to all) would live at Southold and Alistair would share an apartment in town with Walt Rostow, younger brother of his Yale friend, Gene. Most weekends the Cookes would entertain their friends at the Bungalow on the Southold estate. Walt Rostow was a frequent visitor, and the two would drive back to New York on Monday morning. On one such occasion – Monday 23 June – they stopped at a gas station, where the attendant was muttering into his beard: 'Oh boy, oh boy, oh boy. You know what? Hitler's invaded Russia.' Cooke and Rostow shrugged the idea aside: 'We said, this guy must be a moron. He doesn't know what he's talking about.' The man made them accompany him to a radio set to prove his point.

Frustratingly, this was not the sort of event which he was encouraged to cover for the BBC. Come August, Cooke was telling Britain how 'Mr and Mrs America' were tightening their belts, and ruing the President's decision to clamp down on the joys of the instalment system – hire purchase – 'perhaps the most attractive American invention of the century.' He recalled how his 'negro maid' had been able to acquire an immense combination radio-gramophone, which turned itself into a cocktail bar complete with ice box. Now, the consumer party was over.

There were only rare exceptions to this bland and undemanding diet. One was a five-minute talk entitled 'The President's Day', which he read live from a hand-written script on notepaper from a Washington hotel – a quirky view of Roosevelt's working habits. Another notable piece of writing was a *Commentary* on the appearance before a Senate Committee of General George Marshall, the Army Chief-of-Staff, explaining the need for a huge increase in military spending. Cooke was deeply impressed by Marshall, long before he became associated with the plan for the post-war reconstruction of Europe. The General is also the subject of an anecdote which reveals much about Cooke's approach to his work. Towards the end of the war Cooke was invited to take tea with Eisenhower's second-in-command, Air-Marshal Sir Arthur Tedder, at a time when the liberal press was full of stories about the possibility of a second front in Europe. Cooke asked Tedder if he could arrange a meeting with General Marshall. The trouble was that Marshall was notorious for never talking to journalists, but Cooke promised – remembering the nostrum by which Sir Wilmott Lewis had lived and worked – that the interview would not just be off the record, but that no direct reference to it would ever be made: 'The whole point would be to stop me writing nonsense.' On that basis agreement was reached.

On the due day, he visited Marshall in Washington to ask why there was no sign of a second front. The General explained that there still wasn't enough spare capacity for the task despite the fact that Henry Kaiser's 'Liberty Ships' were being churned out of California docks at the rate of one every six days. 'It's very simple', Marshall told him. 'You cannot mount an invasion across the Channel unless you can guarantee a continuous line of supply. We risk losing a million men.' Cooke was left with the clear impression that it was only a matter of time, but that Marshall would not be rushed. He never reported the interview, but felt that he was far better able to offer serious commentary on events because of his private knowledge.

This was a technique he used with other dignitaries. Lord Halifax, the British Ambassador to Washington from 1941, gave him regular private briefings. Indeed Cooke made his own small contribution to the new Ambassador's acclimatisation. With his acutely tuned class antennae, Cooke felt that the appointment of a British toff was a diplomatic risk – especially when one of Halifax's first actions was to be seen, very publicly, riding to hounds with a traditional hunt in Virginia. He suggested to a press attaché that there should be some immediate PR counter-balance – something self-evidently demo-cratic: why not arrange for the Ambassador to be seen enjoying a coffee and sandwich in a popular cheap restaurant, like one of the White Tower chain? It was an image every American would imme-diately recognise – and Cooke believes that the resulting photographs helped to redeem Halifax's reputation.

A prohibition against divulging sources – following the principles upheld by Sir Wilmott Lewis – may have prevented Cooke from registering dramatic scoops about Halifax or anyone else, but he felt it was a price worth paying. His approach was always the same: 'Trust me, and you can be sure that the arrangement will work to our mutual benefit, I will be better informed, and you will have less misleading coverage of important matters.' This did not mean that he set out to befriend the great and the good. Friendship with news-makers, he came to believe, was distracting and dangerous to the business of journalism. He even struck a deal with a newly acquired friend and fellow journalist, James 'Scotty' Reston, never to indulge in the cosy habit of familiarity with politicians.

Cooke's good contacts were about to become even more of a main-stay as information from conventional sources started to dry up. He had his own explanation for this, looking back: 'I was very unpopular with the British Information Service because I preferred not to deal with them. I went to the top people instead, with a pledge not to quote them.' But that was not the whole story.

In many respects Cooke was his own worst enemy, driven by the compulsion to beat the American drum at every opportunity, noisily and often tactlessly. 'The American Government,' he told readers of the *Daily Herald* one day, 'knows its own welfare better, and in more detail, than any amount of visiting British officials. Washington and other cities of the eastern seaboard are plagued with a flock of well-meaning do-gooders.' As if the general invective wasn't brutal enough, Cooke decided to name a few names. 'Colonel Wedgwood's New York meditations were superbly tactless, and Baron Vansittart's speculation was brilliantly ill-timed.' Abusing well-connected diplomats was not the done thing, however wrong they might be.

The deterioration of his reputation in official circles was accelerated by a piece of bad luck and inauspicious timing. The interminable process of his conversion to American citizenship was finally drawing to a conclusion at the worst possible moment – when, from the Mediterranean to the Russian steppes and the Atlantic, the Germans were rampant. It was an awkward moment to say, 'I am no longer an Englishman.' No matter that his decision had been made, and his application lodged, four and a half years earlier – when war still seemed a decently distant prospect. The message was clear. Cooke was opting out. Some who came to know him well spoke of a battle fought with his conscience, but it was a while before he himself realised what effect his decision would have.

Among those who knew before he did was a young BBC manager, Leonard Miall, who spent two years in Washington from October 1942. 'Some people thought that [Cooke] had deliberately chosen that moment to renounce his British heritage,' Miall wrote in his book *Inside the BBC*. 'The British Information Services were instructed not to offer him any help. He was officially cold-shouldered.' Miall had every reason to know how seriously Cooke's act of 'desertion' was taken: he had been seconded to the Political Warfare Executive as German Talks Adviser and was thus at the heart of the secret propaganda effort in the United States. Even though he reached Washington a year after the event, he found that the British establishment was still prepared to make Cooke's life difficult. Cooke himself never accepted that his action had been controversial: he had acted purely on his father's dictum that all would become citizens of the world. 'We never anticipated that after the war the world would go into a frenzy of nationalism,' he was quoted as saying in 1980. 'There was never an emotional conflict in my mind. And I don't regret being an American citizen now. In fact, I'm quite proud of it.'

~

On 1 December 1941, Cooke was summoned to a downtown office to undergo the final act in the immigration process – a personal examination, followed by the swearing of a solemn oath of allegiance. There were queues of aspirants, waiting to be directed to one of a line of tiny cubicles. Snatches of conversation drifted out. One man, having been asked a question about the role of the Supreme Court, was corrected by the official – who got his own facts wrong. 'I knew more about the Constitution than he did,' Cooke remarked, 'but I wasn't going to argue.' On the other side, he overheard an old lady grappling with the questions in a thick Central European accent. Her interrogator was making life as easy as possible for her: 'Who appoints the Supreme Court of the United States?'

A pause . . . 'President Roosevelt?'

'Quite right, lady. Now, who is in charge of the armed forces?'

'President Roosevelt?'

Cooke himself was not unduly stretched by his interview and was then corralled into a large group for a mass swearing of the oath – offering allegiance to the United States and renouncing all ties to foreign princes, potentates and powers, most especially George Edward Albert David – King George VI. A joker at the BBC office sent him a telegram saying, 'Please, No! – signed George Edward Albert David.' The deed was done.

Six days later Japan attacked Pearl Harbor, and for a few days at least any tension between Cooke and the BBC was set aside. On the day of the attack he was called in at short notice to provide the BBC in London with its first full report, cabled from Washington. 'Just after lunch on brilliant sunny Sunday afternoon people of Washington were thunderstruck by news hastily read before regular Sunday radio symphony concerts of Japanese attack Pearl Harbor.'

The following day came a second dispatch, timed at 2.02 in the afternoon, read live into the BBC news service from scribbled notes, and describing the scenes in Congress: 'It is impossible to over-dramatise the overnight change of spirit in the ordinary American. The taxi driver who took me over to the House said to me, "I've been against any war and against any boys being sent abroad, but by jeepers, this is our war. Lindbergh better not open his trap from now on!"'

Reservists appeared on the streets in uniform, crowds thronged around the White House and dustmen noticed that the Japanese Embassy was throwing out the ashes of burned documents. Cooke gave a graphic picture of the Congressional proceedings:

As the clock moved on to twelve-thirty, the talking dropped like a breaking wave. The whole house rose, the newspapermen dropped their pencils and stood. Up the ramp that leads to the dais came, with his infinitely slow tread, the President of the United States – one arm on the rail, the other held by his son James Roosevelt in the uniform of the Marines. Those 500 fated words, you have heard. And the phrase that brought the House to its feet – that about America's 'Righteous Might'. The Speaker began a roll-call – Douglas, Downs, Duncan ... Sykes, Simpson, Smith of Maine, Smith of Ohio ... Each replied, 'Aye' like a chapter from the Old Testament. It was the signal and the tune of a great nation going into battle.

Forty minutes later, Cooke was broadcasting these momentous events to Britain and the Empire.

America was at war. An initial flurry of work for Cooke included a portrait of Washington DC on the 'first day of total war' – 11 December. Yet ten days later he was back on his non-political beat, giving special talks about the history and ethnic mix of his home town: 'Hello children, I'm speaking to you from New York City ...'

~

Much of Cooke's working week, inevitably, was spent in Washington. Ruth, with their one-year-old son, was stuck in New York, where the couple had acquired a new apartment on the Upper East Side, at 1150 Fifth Avenue, on the very edge of Spanish Harlem. It was hard enough for Alistair and Ruth to find time together, and even harder because Cooke soon proved to have no instinct for the messy and time-consuming business of looking after a baby. He liked the idea of having a son more than the reality of the associated chores. It was a weakness which he never managed to overcome, and extended to a lack of interest in any grandchild until it was old enough to converse on an adult basis.

Nor was the BBC quite ready to relent in its campaign of coolness, although for the third time running Cooke was about to acquire a boss in New York who admired him unreservedly. Lindsay Wellington, having spent several months touring North America during 1941, was posted to New York in September to co-ordinate a new integrated propaganda approach – dedicated, as always, to impressing occupied Europe with the potential strength and invincibility of the American armed forces. Gerald Cock was moved aside and eventually sent to set up a new office in San Francisco. Less than two weeks after America's entry into the war, Wellington was doing as all his predecessors had done: selling Cooke to London. The job he had in mind was 'the BBC's reporter in America', or something corresponding to the brief of Ed Murrow in London. Not at all, Wellington stressed, for 'the political field,' but 'live interest stuff, going out and getting recordings, etc.' Cooke, he reckoned, was the only suitable person for the job.

This memo ended up on the desk of the Deputy Director-General, Sir Cecil Graves, who commented: 'Wellington believed that in some quarters here there was prejudice against Cooke and I thought very possibly this was so.' Despite the continuing suspicions in London, there were important differences this time. Wellington was in charge of a rapidly expanding empire: by January 1942 the new BBC offices in the Rockefeller Center already boasted a staff of twenty-three – a figure which would rise to seventy over the next two years. With America committed to the war effort, many of the old transatlantic sensitivities had become far less relevant.

This did not mean that Cooke could immediately be assigned to anything as important as Churchill's visit, which began in December. But he and Wellington did dream up the idea of a grand tour of the country with the whimsical objective that Cooke would cover 'all 3000 counties' of the United States. The plan had many attractions. Cooke would be well away from politics, reporting on how the war affected ordinary people from every walk of life. From Wellington's point of view, the image created would be of a common purpose uniting two peoples. But the project had implications for Ruth and Johnny. If Cooke was to be away for several months, could they really justify the upkeep of a Manhattan apartment? And wouldn't it be less lonely for Ruth if she were to settle with her family at Southold until her husband's return? The decision was eased by the arrival in New York of a young couple, appointed by the BBC to join Wellington's staff.

John Salt had been nominated Deputy Director of the American operation, while his wife Olive Shapley – a veteran of *Children's Hour* – was planning a fortnightly Newsletter for the programme which she called, coincidentally, 'Letter from America'. They had arrived in January, and after several weeks in hotels were keen to find a more permanent base. 1150 Fifth Avenue was the ideal solution. Ruth retreated to Long Island, and Cooke handed over the keys of his apartment to his new tenants. Shapley was overwhelmed by the level of luxury: 'New York kitchens looked magnificent to us,' she wrote, 'with neat and efficient storage, large refrigerators and electric appliances like toasters which we had never seen before.' Ruth had less to shout about. The arrangement might be saving money, but she felt rather as if she was being sent away to the country to keep her out of the way.

~

The plan was for Cooke to travel with the (supposedly) portable recording equipment using 16-inch glass records: all the modern materials, like shellac – a hardened resin – had been requisitioned by the armed forces. He would compile two or three special programmes on America at war with the possibility of filing separate news reports as the opportunity arose. Even by the standards of his previous adventures, it was a huge undertaking and it started badly. Although he had acquired without difficulty a war correspondent's pass from the Defence Department – giving him the right to visit a number of sensitive locations – this did not cut any ice with the Office of Price Administration.

The Office was in charge of rationing strategic items. Tyre rubber was placed on the restricted list soon after Pearl Harbor and Cooke was compelled to apply to the New York Ration Board for four tyres for his journey. He explained his case to the weary-looking officials, who sat behind a table laden with pleading letters. It was the first such case they'd had to deal with and after some debate they informed him that, unfortunately, he did not fall into any of the categories entitled to new tyres. After the meeting, he bumped into one of the Board's lawyers in a bar. 'In Britain,' he explained soothingly, 'you have what we call ad hoc committees: that's to say, you set up some rules, but if the rules don't cover your case then it's judged on its merits. Over here we look up the law on paper, and if the law has overlooked your particular position, or never anticipated it, you're simply out of luck.'

In the end, through judicious tweaking of strings he got his tyres though, as it turned out, most of the trip was by train anyway. Regardless of the means of transport, this was one of the most extensive and exhaustive journeys in journalistic history, covering swathes of the country from Florida to Oregon and New England to southern California. It lasted almost five months, providing Cooke with a patchwork of impressions and experiences, all jotted down religiously in a succession of small notebooks.

He was on the look-out for optimism, in whatever form, to offset the pervading gloom. Singapore fell to the Japanese in the first week of his travels and the Germans were threatening to overrun the Atlantic shipping lanes. America suddenly felt exposed on both flanks, and Cooke was determined to demonstrate that a sleeping giant was stirring. It might seem late in the day to a British audience, but they should be aware of the resilience and fortitude of ordinary people, ready at last to rally to the cause. One of his very first encounters set the tone for the whole enterprise. He sat in on the negotiations for the Air Force to billet troops in the glossy hotels of Miami Beach, and savoured the dismay of the hoteliers when they heard that rent would be paid at the rate of one cent per cubic foot – which meant $2 a day for the $35-a-day suite in which they sat. 'The managers staggered out in low dudgeon,' Cooke recorded, 'though happily their patriotism got the better of them and they decided, on the whole, it was better to survive on a few funded dollars a day than to prosper under the Nazis.'

The stories he gathered were eclectic, with a single uniting thread: that they should illustrate how the war was changing everyday life. On this first leg of the trip, he and the engineer met a research chemist in Miami working on the crazy idea that orange juice could be reduced to a concentrate – to which water could then be added in a ratio of five parts to one. In this compact form it would be feasible to ship the vitamin-packed liquid to Britain, thus boosting the grim wartime diet. Little did he (or Cooke) realise what future concentrated orange juice might have as a drink in its own right.

He visited Irish orchid growers in Oregon, steel factories in Pittsburgh and fields of long-staple cotton in Phoenix, destined for the manufacture of parachutes. He watched scientists with infra-red lamps crawling through the mountains of Arizona at night, trying to spot strategic minerals 'embedded in the rocks like petrified tropical fish'. And he revealed that the most popular request from sailors wanting tattoos in San Diego was for the single word 'mother', whereas in the First World War, girl-friends' names had been the rage.

With the help of his notebooks and a prodigious memory Cooke stored up far more information and anecdotes than he could ever hope to use in BBC talks or articles for any newspaper at the time. The level of detail, which survives in the typewritten manuscript of a long-planned book of his travels, is exceptional.

The night closes in and extinguishes Kentucky, pushes the war reeling away into memory, leaving you with the special timeless intimacy of driving at night. You have no goal, only a ploughing shaft of light on white cement and, to remind you happily of your own warmth, you hear far away the lonely call of a train. The little dead towns tick by like tombstones of a pioneer's past – Munfordville, Rowletts, Horse Cave, Bear Wallow, Good Night – and then you see a string of lights coming up above your headlights. It is Glasgow, and as good a place as any to stay the night.

Some of the characters he stumbled upon during his travels resurfaced much later in a memorable talk entitled 'Six Typical Americans' – pen-portraits of a pale and modest priest who shared the lives of reservation Indians in Arizona; an Oregon lumber merchant who refused to chop down princely Douglas firs for ships' bottoms; a Chicago meat-packer who fell in love with fine painting and filled his home with the work of French Impressionists. These 'typical' Americans are essentially unremarkable, decent people, just as capable of noble instincts as any Briton, and unrelated to their filmic compatriots. They are the life-blood of an America which Cooke hoped that his listeners far away would come to recognise as the real thing.

14

THE PSYCHIATRIST'S COUCH

Throughout the trip, he was 'in constant touch' with Ruth, but when he finally returned to New York in June, Olive Shapley and John Salt were still in possession of his apartment, while Ruth and Johnny remained at Southold. There seemed no pressing reason for ejecting their tenants, who were providing them with a useful supplementary income. But the decision not to do so had fateful consequences.

Although Cooke could spend the weekends on Long Island, he needed a working base in the city and he did what all New Yorkers did – he turned to the *New York Times*. The paper's classified section threw up the perfect solution – a two-room office-cum-apartment in the Croydon Hotel, overlooking 86th Street, at $40 a month, with maid service. He learned that the owner was a psychiatrist who had just joined the army: he and a partner had used one room to see patients and the other as a bedroom if either needed to stay in town overnight. Cooke moved in almost immediately.

It was a little while before he met his landlord, Major Whitfield (Whit) Hawkes, but only a matter of days before his first encounter with the Major's wife Jane. Hawkes was undergoing training at Fort Devens in northern Massachusetts, and asked Jane, who was working in the city as a nursing aide, to collect some files which he'd left in his old office. She duly rang Cooke and arranged to meet him at the Croydon Hotel at 7 p.m. It was a humdrum arrangement which was to change all their lives.

Cooke was forty minutes late, having lost none of the distaste for punctuality to which he'd confessed at Cambridge. Jane waited for a while but with a dinner appointment looming she began to grow impatient. The desk manager recognised her, and allowed her to go upstairs to the office on her own. She retrieved the files and pressed the down button on the iron-grilled elevator, which creaked and trundled its way up to her floor: when the doors were drawn back, they revealed what she described afterwards as 'this foreign-looking man'. She realised it must be the new tenant and introduced herself.

In the Cooke family legend it was love at first sight – a moment of blinding passion in the corridors of the Croydon Hotel. That would have been quite understandable. By general agreement Jane Hawkes was stunningly beautiful, a dark-haired Texan belle with just a hint of continental glamour, inherited from French ancestors. But the words exchanged during that first meeting were unremarkable in the extreme. In Cooke's version of the story he had been showing photographs of his trip to a friend and lost track of time. He rushed to the hotel, and when he bumped into Mrs Hawkes, could only mutter his apologies. She explained that she'd been into his apartment, said she was sorry that she hadn't been able to wait and headed for the lift. Before he had time to engage her in conversation, she was gone – so brisk and business-like that the entire encounter lasted no more than a minute or two. Was he left by the lift-shaft, transfixed by what he had seen? If so, he did nothing immediately to pursue the matter.

Some time later, Whit Hawkes came home on leave and took Jane for a celebration lunch, after which they took the train to their weekend house – a house which, fatefully, was also at the eastern end of Long Island. Because it was a special occasion, they sat in the parlour car with its luxurious swivel seats – and there, just across the aisle, was Cooke, on his way to the Emerson house for the weekend. Jane walked up to him and said, 'Mr Cooke – this is Major Hawkes, your landlord'. Her own view is that Cooke seemed not to remember who she was, but as the journey progressed her husband set off down the train to look for a friend and the two were left together.

'Alistair started telling me about how his wife lived at Southold,' Jane recalled, 'and how beautiful she was and how she'd been a model and had been such a sensation in London. He was very voluble.' It transpired that her younger child, Stephen, was almost the same age as Johnny. Cooke also let slip that Ruth had heard about the house the Hawkeses had just built at the end of Nassau Point – almost visible across the bay from Southold: it had caused something of a stir in the local community – its avant-garde Bauhaus design, with geometric shapes formed from redwood planks, was regarded either as an eyesore or as the last word in architectural fashion. In no time the two families started visiting each other, and Ruth and Jane became friends.

The course of events thereafter followed a familiar course. If first sight had not done the trick, Cooke found every excuse to see more of Jane, who in turn confessed that she had begun to find him 'a very interesting-looking man'. There were practical considerations for Cooke, too: 'Jane only had the usual "A" ration card for petrol, whereas I had a "C" card – unlimited supplies – provided for a War Correspondent. What could be more gallant, more obviously gentlemanly, than for me to offer to drive Mrs Hawkes to her house by the Bay at weekends?' During one such act of gallantry, he contrived to make the hundred-mile journey last six hours, taking in the newly built La Guardia airport and every other possible attraction *en route*. Every now and again, he would stop the car and ring Ruth to let her know that they'd be a little bit later still.

Despite these contacts, it was a while before the evident attraction between the two went beyond the bounds of propriety, although Jane guessed what would happen, and dubbed the self-deluding Cooke 'Mr Unconscious of 1942'. He was no womaniser and he had enough of the north country Methodist in him to feel growing guilt at the neglect of his family. But the guilt could not turn him into the home-loving father he'd never really been. The drifting apart was hastened by Ruth's reluctance to bring matters to a head: her upbringing – and sense of inferiority among her brothers and sisters – made her temperamentally unsuited to standing up for herself.

Edna Rostow, who had been working in psychiatric research, was a close friend of the couple from the start and she had seen it coming. Ruth, she felt, had been riding for a fall: she remembers sitting with her at a drugstore counter in New York and begging her to confront her husband for the sake of their marriage. Ruth simply wouldn't fight back, feeling the whole thing was somehow her fault. Edna construed this as Quaker quiescence, even though Ruth's family had been, at best, lapsed Quakers: 'Despite all the modelling and glamour, she never really felt comfortable about indulging herself. Once she became a mother she reverted to type and expected Alistair to become a father, hoping that he would change his working schedule and give up his late nights. The trouble was, he simply didn't want to be confined to the house and had no interest in feeding the baby, diapers, burping and the rest.' Looking back, Edna Rostow sees something of

Pygmalion in the relationship, except that Cooke's efforts to create a wife in his own stylish image were ultimately thwarted. She also believes he was seduced by the mystique of the Emerson name and the distinction it bestowed on a boy from Blackpool.

It wasn't particularly difficult or risky for Cooke to pursue Jane. Both were based in New York, while Whit Hawkes was safely tucked away in the depths of rural New England and Ruth similarly immured in the backwaters of Long Island. But, deeply smitten as he was, he also contrived more complicated opportunities to spend time with a woman who was not only beautiful, but also a talented artist with the Bohemian streak that Ruth had renounced. David Curnow, the Blackpool evacuee now finishing his High School studies at Wellesley, found himself caught up in one such amorous exercise.

Curnow had been well looked after by the Cookes throughout his time in the country. In the holidays he would take the train from Boston to Connecticut and cross over to Long Island by ferry for weekend visits, during which Cooke taught him to fish. It was in 1943, when Curnow was about to go up to Harvard, that Cooke announced his intention of picking him up in Boston and taking him on an outing to explore New Hampshire. His timing was meticulous. Jane, uncoincidentally, was visiting Whit at the training camp for the 9th Federal Hospital Unit. She and a fellow army-wife had put up at a hotel in Groton – which just happened to be on the New Hampshire border.

It seemed quite natural for Cooke to drop in on his way north. Jane remembers a maid knocking on her door at the Groton Inn and informing her that there was a gentleman waiting in reception. She discovered Cooke – with young Curnow in tow – expressing his delight at bumping into her and promising to call by again on his return, purportedly for a chance to meet Whit. Even though he was not yet seventeen, David Curnow felt sure there was something in the air between his unofficial guardian and this exotic army wife.

In his own considered reflection on the development of the relationship, Cooke said that he been horrified by the dawning realisation that he was in love with Jane. 'This was not me. I didn't play around. I'd never had any adventures outside marriage. It was a bad year for my conscience.'

~

As Cooke began to pay court to Jane in earnest, the work on offer from the BBC – apart from the briefest of pieces for *News Reel* programmes – was confined to sporadic reports of his grand tour. Lindsay Wellington was far too busy conducting delicate discussions with London about great matters of policy to have much time to spend on the interests of his protégé. In the summer of 1942 the BBC was grappling with what were described, in a memo of 6 July, as 'deep misunderstandings' on both sides of the Atlantic. In the words of the Corporation's official historian, 'American propaganda to Europe was both too distant and too brash, too unsophisticated and too contrived to challenge the propaganda forces already at work on the Continent.' The BBC, by contrast, felt that it was bending over backwards to respond to the sensitivities of an American audience. Because of the persistent misunderstandings, Wellington had advised London that no reciprocal exchange of broadcasting facilities with any of the US networks was feasible. 'We are,' the 6 July memo proclaimed, 'at the parting of the ways.'

The upshot was the decision to go ahead with a substantial investment in the BBC's American operation: a secret memo was dispatched from New York to the new joint Director-General, Robert Foot, via Foreign Office channels on 31 August. It confirmed Wellington's expansion plans and gave a figure of £100,098 for his next year's running costs.

Yet Alistair Cooke's reputation was still so firmly lodged in the groove of corporate criticism that he was in no immediate position to benefit from this largesse. Robert Foot himself took the trouble to inquire about Cooke's recent record and received a depressing document which recycled all the old complaints and cited one or two new ones besides. Foot was told that Cooke had only done two *News Talks* in the previous six months; and that in one appearance on *Radio News Reel* he had been accused of 'speaking too fast, breathing so hard he sounds like a race-horse... and sounding childish alongside other British commentators'. The most positive thing anyone could find to say was that 'Cooke's forte is personality sketches of people in the news'.

Cooke's newspaper employers did not feel so constrained. Some of his columns were trenchant in their comments on British – and American – society:

'Only a drooling idiot will cite Great Britain or the US as model societies,' ran one Cooke piece picked up by the American press:

> Let us cheerfully admit that we are ashamed of some old practices of the
> British Empire, but are proud of the Commonwealth system, that we
> revere the American Constitution and are only too sorry we never brought
> it up to date to include poor immigrants and Negroes . . . If we don't admit
> to them, as well as to ourselves, the beam in our own eye, it's unlikely they
> will allow us the privilege of curing the mote in theirs. Let us tell the truth
> as we see it and be damned to him who twists it.

It was strong stuff. Cooke clearly knew what was likely to strike a
chord with his *Herald* readers, though in some cases the diet was too
rich for the American censors. All correspondents were suffering, but
Cooke had a long-running feud with the Office of War Information
in Washington. The OWI, having bowed to a wave of suspicion about
all foreign-born Americans, told Cooke he would have to sign up
under the Aliens' Registration Act. While other foreign correspondents reluctantly obeyed the edict, Cooke held out against
it: he had no wish to be lumped in with employees of the British
Information Services as a potential purveyor of British propaganda.
In extremis, he telephoned H.L. Mencken in Baltimore: '[Mencken]
raised his voice to a piping tenor: "Who are the people who want you
to do this? The OWI? A gang of draft-dodgers! Tell 'em you won't
sign and tell 'em to go to hell." ' When the time came for his final
interview, Cooke toned down the language, but did pass on the fact
that 'my friend Mr Mencken had told me mine was a special case, and
that to declare myself a British propagandist would be an affront both
to my trade and my status as an American citizen.' By great good
fortune the official was – in Cooke's words – 'a heavy-lidded New
York socialite' and therefore of an age to be impressed by the great
man's name. 'I'm afraid', the official said, 'his argument is unanswer-
able.' The case was dropped.

Back at the BBC, such defiance probably produced a shudder of
relief that Cooke had found other outlets for his more outspoken
views. It's hard to imagine that a man who became known as one of
the most consummate broadcasters of all time should have been held
for a while in such low regard. He never gave up trying: 'I wish we
could do more', he wrote in another anxious appeal to London, 'to
show that Chicago and Seattle and El Paso and Baltimore and Detroit,
and a hundred other cities, are "capital" cities of American life that

are just as necessary for Britain to know about as New York and Washington. I have masses of material on hand from my nine months' tour of the country...' Setting aside the minor exaggeration of the length of his trip, the rest was true enough, but still the BBC would not bite.

Over the following months, therefore, Cooke had time to work that material up into a full-length tome entitled 'Face of the Nation – America at War'. Sadly, by the time it was due to be published in November 1945, the bottom had dropped out of the market for books about the war. He'd even got as far as plotting what should be on the dust jacket – Jane's first portrait of him, sitting at the wheel of a car. It never saw the light of day and eventually Jane decided the painting didn't deserve studio space, either.

~

Cooke's tenants finally moved out of his apartment in October of 1942, leaving behind – to their great regret – the black maid, Mabel. Alistair and Ruth returned before Christmas and stayed there until their marriage finally broke up. One visitor who noticed the signs was Leonard Miall, who was invited to dinner soon after taking up his post with the Political Warfare Executive in Washington. 'It was to be a formal dinner, and the dining table was set with cutlery and glasses. The Cookes' little boy climbed up onto the table and started kicking the spoons onto the floor – and neither Alistair nor Ruth did anything to reprimand him.' Miall's assessment was that this was a family with serious problems.

At no stage was there a formal rupture in the relationship, nor do there seem to have been rows and disagreements. From Ruth's perspective, it looked more like a drifting apart, until one day Cooke suggested that they should try a period of separation. Ruth's response was, 'but that's just what we've been doing all along.' She found it hard to understand what had gone wrong: they had a good home, a baby and many friends: she pressed him to try again, and after one period of temporary reconciliation, Ruth found that she was pregnant. To her distress, she lost the baby and didn't tell Cooke what had happened.

For much of the time after the parting, Cooke shared an apartment with his friend Bill Burrows, whose marriage was also going through an awkward stage. But Burrows went back to his wife and Cooke couldn't bring himself to do so. Matters were certainly hastened and probably brought to a head by events thousands of miles away. In the summer of 1943 Whit Hawkes was posted to a remote corner of the South Seas – Goodenough Island, off the eastern tip of New Guinea. The island, recaptured from the Japanese after a few months of occupation, had been chosen as the location for a military airstrip. Before long, the American forces there were stricken by a mysterious sickness which baffled their doctors: within months, a third of the 9th Federal Hospital unit were dead – among them, Whit Hawkes. The disease was identified too late as Tsutsi Mangui fever, a variant of typhus left behind by the retreating Japanese. If it had been correctly diagnosed, many of the lives could have been saved, but as it was, Jane Hawkes found herself, in December 1943, a war widow with two children under five.

~

At about the same time, with the Battle of the Atlantic more or less over, President Roosevelt was able to travel to Cairo and then Tehran for meetings with Churchill and Stalin. As they discussed the shape of the post-war world, Cooke found himself at long last back in BBC business. Wellington's enthusiasm had overwhelmed London's doubts, allowing Cooke to resume a share in the *American Commentary* for the remainder of the war. It was a decent distraction from his growing emotional turmoil.

Cooke also became master of ceremonies (for a few weeks) of a regular discussion show called *Answering You*, in which 'ordinary' members of the public had the chance, in a stylised format, to question experts on the other side of the Atlantic. The programmes were gentle, easy-going and informative. Each began with an announcer in New York: 'This is New York calling the BBC in London,' to which his counterpart replied, 'This is the BBC in London answering you.' 'Ladies and Gentlemen, through short-wave facilities we span 3000 miles of ocean to bring you the BBC's transatlantic discussion programme.' The episode of 12 December must have brought a special *frisson* to the spine of the master of ceremonies. The London guest was none other than Caroline Lejeune, the *Observer* film critic, whose timely holiday in 1932 had opened the way for Cooke's first Hollywood experience.

Cooke's output was being closely monitored by the BBC for signs of slippage into areas of suspected unreliability. Some *Commentaries* teeter on the brink of serious political analysis, before veering off into the safety zone of social observation. On 18 December, for instance, a description of Roosevelt's return from Tehran elides into a survey of how Americans are likely to spend a wartime Christmas. This piece caused a tremor of delight in his old home town: the *Evening Gazette* carried a report entitled 'WE ARE FAMOUS' – 'Evidence of the Growing Fame of Blackpool', it remarked, 'is that probably no town is mentioned so often on the wireless. On Saturday night Mr Alistair Cooke, in the broadcast from America, said, "New York is no more America than the Pleasure Beach at Blackpool is England." '

As usual, however, Cooke's most pointed observations were reserved for the printed page. In London the *Daily Sketch* of 7 January 1944 proudly promoted 'the first of a series of *American Commentaries* specially written by Mr Alistair Cooke, latest recruit to our brilliant staff of special correspondents. Mr Cooke's broadcasts,' the blurb continues, 'have made his voice known to millions, and have been a valuable contribution to Anglo-American friendship.'

In such small ways, and after all the disappointments, the myth of Cooke's special role was beginning to gather substance. He seemed to be able to take on the political colour of each separate audience, like a journalistic chameleon. *Daily Sketch* readers, for instance, were treated to the diatribe to one of Cooke's English friends, dejected about 'the present state of feeling between Britain and America as he had sensed it in England'. '[Cooke's friend] is an earnest man, who believes unwaveringly that this war will clean out the dirt from some of the dark places of our society and will secure the privileges of good food, healthy bodies and equal education to the mass of the peoples.' The BBC would hardly have tolerated such socialist rhetoric. Cooke pursued his friend's uncomfortable impressions: instead of active companionship between soldiers of the two allies, he found no curiosity 'to know and respect the motives of the Americans who work in factories and man the railroads and pour the steel. He found grumbling suspicion and impatient indifference.'

Cooke's obloquy is not confined to the grumbling and impatient British. Americans, he said, were so blinkered that their opinion was likely to rise or fall according to 'the exploits of the RAF, the reports of India's famine, the oratory of Mr Churchill, and other easy incitements to a dramatic attitude of admiration or distrust': and that

American soldiers persisted in forming 'little Americas' wherever they happened to be.

Was this polemic really justified? Was it reasonable to expect that two peoples thrown together in such strange and alarming circumstances should immediately warm to each other, abandoning all prejudices? For the purposes of his argument, Cooke is not prepared to consider the alternative: that American soldiers, far from home, might understandably wish to stick together and surround themselves with the comfort of the familiar. Or that the British might therefore be forgiven for treating them as stand-offish and peculiar.

At a political level, there was by now more general acceptance that American efforts should be concentrated on helping to win the war against Hitler and Cooke's *Commentaries* during the spring of 1944 were full of news about how the draft was being widened to include previously exempted groups. And, as always, there were personal touches to add to the tone and texture of the piece – none more personal than this: 'I remember a friend of mine – a doctor in the Army – who said last summer that he was getting ashamed to go home every weekend and be seen working in his garden. People said, "What sort of soldier are you anyway?" But he went out to New Guinea and he's been dead these many months.'

~

The break-up of Cooke's marriage to Ruth was inevitable well before Major Whit Hawkes died on Goodenough Island. Jane had been discussing her feelings for Cooke with her psychiatrist. It was the fashion of the moment – the first, rather than the last, resort of prosperous New Yorkers. Hawkes himself had undergone sessions as part of his training – and Jane, according to her daughter, Holly, had followed suit at her husband's instigation, long before she met Cooke, so that she would better understand their relationship. Holly joked later that she sometimes felt she came 'pre-shrunk'. After the major's death, Jane grappled with her emotions for some time before announcing to Cooke, in February 1944, that she was sure of herself. 'I'm ready to marry you,' she informed him. Now it was Cooke's turn to seek refuge in analysis. Both Ruth and Johnny would follow him into the psychiatrist's chair as the family unravelled.

In Cooke's case the guilt was a severely inhibiting force. 'The divorce was my fault,' he admits candidly. 'I fell violently in love with Jane. But I was such an upstanding creature, it seemed a terrible thing to do. It produced such a turmoil inside me, and that was the time when if you had turmoil in New York, you got analysed. Almost all my friends were doing it.' He took one of the Rorschach 'ink-blot' tests, which confirmed the presence of deep-seated neuroses that might benefit from analysis. A leading psychiatrist – a German immigrant – who happened to live in the same apartment block, directed him to the consulting rooms of Dr Sidney Kahr on 86th Street. It was the start of a long, sometimes painful experience – and not just for Cooke's love life.

He was expected to attend five days a week whenever he was in town, and kept it up for almost two years – a strict regimen, with no possibility of casual visits as a cushion for sudden crises. Kahr's first instruction was that Cooke should stop seeing Jane, on the grounds that the meetings relieved the very anxiety which was the daily raw material for analysis. It also became clear to Cooke that there was no future for his relationship with Ruth. 'The sad moment came – which she'd been expecting – to ask for a divorce. I hated it. Divorce is defeat, and I sensed at once that it would have an effect, as such things always do, on Johnny. To be frank, I don't think I ever quite got over the distress of having caused Ruth such pain (for she was not – I gathered – by any means ready to leave me).' For about four months, however, Cooke didn't see Jane, either, and was probably kept sane by being sent away on a lecture tour with the ATC – the Air Transport Command. He returned at the end of September 1944 and phoned Jane, who told him that the psychiatrists now agreed: the forcible parting hadn't worked, and they might as well get together. They did.

Cooke began to sketch out the harsh logistical details of his new life, with the aim of ensuring that Johnny was damaged as little as possible. 'Making the best of a bad job meant, in part, taking Johnny and Jane's son, Stephen, to the movies together and trying to praise or scold them equally.' Installed in Jane's apartment, this proved no easier for him than for any other step-parent and perhaps less easy, because of his difficulty in relating to young boys. He was certainly anxious about what the effect might be on Johnny of being brought up in the Emerson household, which he perceived as a place governed by strict rules and intolerance towards self-expression. At Southold, he felt, children were expected to behave like small adults and at the back of his mind was the fear that his son would grow up as he had done, repressed and emotionally insecure.

Even after being reunited with Jane, he continued to report to Dr Kahr, and gradually the analysis moved beyond the immediate problems in Cooke's life to a wider and more probing examination of his character. It started to change the way he thought, not just about himself, but about his work. The gentle coaxing of the psychiatrist, drawing out the inner man through free association, dream study and plain talk – this was what Cooke felt had been suppressed by a childhood in which emotions were never displayed in public, and by a young adulthood in which so much acting was required (on and off stage). 'This takes time, patience, the rocketing through many moods (on your part) and <u>pain</u> – when you discover that some of the time, perhaps all the time, human motives are child<u>like</u> and simple: wish to be liked, envy, fear, wanting to impress, masking self-interest as altruism – and there's always a period when you discover, to your distress, that you are not quite as splendid or complicated a character as you thought.'

Kahr taught Cooke that there was no way of imposing external explanations upon his dreams – it was his own interpretations and associations that mattered. Since, in the Freudian unconscious, opposites were the same, there was nothing to be frightened of. Cooke claimed that he later adopted these principles in his broadcasts – letting his unconscious lead him from one thought to the next, without trying to enclose it in an intellectual strait-jacket. In these terms, the *Letter from America* would become the first (and perhaps only?) avowedly Freudian radio talk.

More immediately, in February 1946, he told Dr Kahr that two years was enough: he had done all he could and now knew his own mind. Kahr said he'd been wondering how long it would take Cooke to realise the treatment was over. 'From all the signs,' he told his grateful patient, 'it has succeeded.' Cooke was wiser, poorer and twenty pounds lighter than when he'd started. 'You can never <u>cure</u> neurosis,' he commented later, 'but you learn to recognise it, where it distorts your conduct and judgement – in other words, you learn to <u>cope</u> with your neurosis. In a nutshell, you learn the truth of Freud's remark that "intellect is the great rationaliser, the great excuser." '

If Cooke was at ease with his ego, it had fallen to Ruth to go through the wretched business of formalising the split. There was only one place to go for a swift separation – Reno, Nevada. When other states had cottoned on to the commercial potential of the quickie divorce,

Nevada outflanked them (in 1931) by reducing the period of residence required from three months to six weeks. Six weeks, for Ruth, was still quite long enough. She had no intention of leaving her son behind, so John, still not four years old, found himself shipped off to the desert – though after a distressing spell in an impersonal boarding house, they were at least able to stay with Ruth's brother Bob and his wife who lived nearby.

Cooke himself wrote about the system in a curiously dispassionate *Letter from America* a mere seven years later. In his capacity as a social historian, he sketched for his listeners the unique qualities of the laws of Nevada, where divorce was possible simply on the word of the injured party that he or she had suffered mental cruelty. 'You stay six weeks in a boarding house, or a dude ranch, or in various hotels, and you stay put for forty-two days and nights. The next morning, you go along to the county courthouse with a local lawyer, to whom you have paid a fee of not less than 150 dollars. The judge asks your name and the State of which you are resident. You say, having been well coached, "Nevada". Cause? Mental cruelty. You may have to make a little speech but on average it's all over in about five minutes.' Put like that, it sounds quite painless. Ruth didn't find it so. For her it was a 'ghastly and humiliating' experience.

In the meantime, Jane's two children – Holly and Stephen, born in 1938 and 1940 respectively – saw a good deal of their future stepfather, starting well before the divorce. Holly has a particularly vivid recollection of her first encounter, which took place when she was having tea in the kitchen of their New York apartment with the nanny. Her mother rushed in and announced that 'Mr Cooke' had brought her home from lunch, and that his car had caught fire in the street outside. The idea of a blazing automobile caught their imagination, but when they discovered the fire was out they had to make do with the rather less thrilling vision of a strange man prostrate on the sofa in the living-room. 'We were allowed to go and look at him,' Holly remembers, 'but perhaps he was traumatised by the fire. He certainly wasn't very friendly – this pale figure lying on the sofa, very elegantly. Once we'd looked, we were sent back to the nursery.'

Jane's apartment was on East 71st Street – a faded, but chic nineteenth-century building complete with its own wrought-iron cage elevator and a liftman who smoked cigars without ceasing. The smell of his smoke, in Holly's memory, competed with the acrid reminders of the cats belonging to the German bachelor who acted as the building's superintendent. Yet No 114, full of mahogany and mosaic floors, had retained a measure of Victorian elegance, too.

Like the Cookes, the Hawkeses had always divided their time between Manhattan and Long Island, where their Bauhaus creation had been built almost at the end of the narrow spit of land known as Nassau Point. Jane's best friend, Marcella Burrows, already had a new house at the Point in the grounds of a much larger mansion occupied by her parents. There remained a small patch of unoccupied land – and it was here that Jane and Whit had paced out their own new property on the edge of a steep sandy bluff. It was a spectacular spot, if somewhat exposed to the vagaries of the Atlantic weather: and although the design was modernistic, it relied on local materials – mainly wood. Cooke described it as 'the grand-daddy of the hundreds of modern beach-houses at the end of the island.' Once the divorce came through, Cooke's life began to revolve between these new poles, while Ruth stayed with the Emersons for a time before finding herself an apartment in 92nd Street and trying to adjust to life as a single parent.

~

Cooke's gradual rehabilitation within the BBC was hastened by the Corporation's burgeoning presence in the United States. In April of 1944 Cooke was asked to host a new light entertainment show – *Transatlantic Quiz* – which used the same short-wave circuits as *Answering You* and was a co-production with NBC's Blue Network. A chairman and two team-members traded questions between London and New York, with the idea of testing one team's knowledge of the other's country. Some of the questions were cryptic, but many were plain general knowledge and over the following two and a half years it gained a nice competitive edge: in particular, it became a matter of honour for New York to find ways of outwitting the Scottish historian, Professor (later Sir) Denis Brogan, whose encyclopaedic memory for matters American was virtually unassailable. It was Cooke himself who set the questions for the London team and he took particular pleasure in exposing his friend's few weak spots.

The hosts remained the same until the programme was finally dropped in December 1946: Cooke in New York and Lionel Hale in London. There were, however, frequent team changes. Colonel David

Niven, already a leading Hollywood actor, had joined up at the out-break of war and had to leave the show, without explanation, just before D-Day – only returning after the Normandy landings at the end of July. Among many other players were the crime writer Eric Ambler, Sir Thomas Beecham and Peter Ustinov, who recalls a feeling of abject ignorance beside the all-knowing Brogan. 'The first question I was asked was, "What is a greenback?" I hadn't a clue, so I said it must be an inexperienced football player. I didn't get any points and it all seemed very unfair.' Brogan, the polymath, remained the unchallenged star – a man who could identify the most obscure political quotations, or plumb the shadiest depths of American literature. There were more than a hundred editions of the show in all before it gave way – in 1947 – to a purely domestic version of the game *Round Britain Quiz*.

~

When D-Day arrived, Cooke had to wait ten frustrating days for his next *Commentary*. Newspapers had abandoned their advertising space, he said, to allow more room for reports from the front. 'These racy, and often finely written, accounts of the landings have told the millions of America's newspaper readers that what the bank-clerks from Sheffield, and the drug-store waiters from Chicago, have had to meet and pass was the best that German military skill and planning could offer. They passed. They have made us humble – and very proud.' The Anglo-American propaganda wasn't subtle, but for once it didn't need to be.

By the end of June Cooke was in Chicago for the Republican con-vention, at which a subdued party chose Thomas E. Dewey as its can-didate. The occasion was memorable mainly because of the horrendous heat inside the auditorium – which, according to Cooke, reached 112 degrees. A newly arrived BBC reporter, Tony Wigan, had never experienced anything like it. 'He turned his streaming face to me,' Cooke wrote, 'and his eyes started to roll like a wicked doctor in a horror film. He gasped, "I'm not sure whether I'm going to faint or go mad." A delegate sitting nearby said, "You're going to faint sonny – you only go mad at Democratic Conventions".' Wigan had the chance to test that assertion three weeks later when he and Cooke returned to Chicago to witness the reselection of Roosevelt by an ecstatic crowd of 25,000.

For the journalists in general and Cooke in particular, there was a sting in the tail of this predictable coronation. Henry Wallace, FDR's Vice-President for the previous four years, had made a brave speech, raising the contentious issue of the poll tax – a tax which effectively disenfranchised the many black citizens who owned no property. 'Wallace had everything to lose', Cooke noted in his broadcast from a studio in the Convention hall, 'by bringing up the question. He needed all the support he could get, but he spurned it . . . The delegates, even those who hate Wallace, rose to their feet. They had seen the plain face of straightforward unpolitical courage and they knew it.' Before that steamy July day was over, Wallace had been unceremoniously dumped.

The next morning the delegates moved swiftly to confirm Roosevelt's alternative choice of a running mate – rather more swiftly than the candidate himself expected. Cooke was standing at a basement lunch-counter when the news came through:

> Next to me was a lobster in steel-rimmed glasses – a solid, square little man in a sky-blue double-breasted suit and polka-dot tie. In one hand he had a coke bottle and in the other a hot dog dripping mustard like butterscotch sauce. Way up there in the auditorium, a baritone voice was booming away, repeating something we couldn't quite catch. Then it came through loud and clear. 'Will the next Vice-President of the United States please come to the rostrum.' The organ started to play the Missouri Waltz and the sky-blue double-breasted jacket next to me jammed the bottle on the counter, took a final lick at the mustard, dumped the hot-dog in a trash basket and said, 'By golly, I guess that's me'.

Harry S. Truman was about to take his first big step towards the White House.

15

ONE DAY, MY BOY

During the summer of 1944, Cooke heard that the Air Transport Command was looking for newspaper and radio correspondents prepared to undertake lecture tours of army bases. Whether he felt it was time to 'do his bit', or whether he was trying to escape the angst generated by his divorce, the upshot was that he decided to volunteer. It was nearly his last trip. He was required to report for duty in Detroit, before setting off on a series of uncomfortable flights in military aircraft of the ATC's Ferrying Division – often flown by pilots in training. Would he mind signing an insurance waiver form, just in case anything went wrong? With some misgivings, he signed. The plan was for a long round trip – down to the Texas border with Mexico, then via Las Vegas to Montana in the far north of the country.

Although he disliked flying, his main preoccupation was the task he'd been set. Cooke had done very little public speaking and although he had a good voice for radio, he had grave doubts about projecting it in a large hall. There was also the alarming prospect of speaking in front of several hundred raw young servicemen. He had no idea at the time that he was launching a long and lucrative career as a performer on public platforms. When he published a collection of his favourite lectures forty years later, he described in the introduction his nervous anticipation on that first exposure to a large, live audience: 'I had a humbling baptism before pilots, navigators, mechanics and other grease monkeys crowded into gymnasiums or out on the tarmac . . . These "Show Me" sceptics were not there to be harangued about the beauty of Anglo-American friendship or the holy Christian mission of the Allies. They wanted as much entertaining sense as possible to be packed into the fewest words.' An audience preparing for active service over Tokyo or Berlin would not put up with platitudes. The solution he devised was a down-to-earth variation on his favourite themes – choosing six national stereotypes and deconstructing them to reveal the individuals within. There had to be jokes, too. One was about a British diplomat arriving in Yokohama and looking around for a reception committee: instead, a small boy nudges him and asks if he'd like a Chinese girl or a Japanese girl. When there's no response, the helpful child tries again. 'Perhaps you prefer Chinese boy? Japanese boy?' The irritated diplomat turns to him and says, 'I'm looking for the British Consul.' To which his new friend replies, 'Sorry, can only get Italian Consul . . . '

To his relief, all the venues were equipped with microphones and public-address systems. 'On these talkative safaris,' he wrote, 'I learned that the microphone enables a speaker to talk to an audience of two thousand with the same ease of emphasis and timing he would use before an audience of two.'

Things may have gone smoothly on the ground: the real crisis came in the air. Almost the last leg of the journey was across the Rockies to Great Falls, Montana in a C45 – a twin-engined executive plane, stripped down for military use. There were five people aboard – including Cooke and his minder, Major Tom Malone. Cooke was dozing when the co-pilot suddenly appeared in the cabin. 'I'm afraid we have a problem. We're losing a lot of oil from one engine.' Black liquid was indeed streaming past the port holes and the plane was descending fast towards the mountain side. Malone said, 'I don't want to worry you, but I don't think these things can land on one engine.' Cooke looked at the now motionless propeller beside him and assumed that his time had come.

Somehow the pilot kept the plane in the air long enough to reach Ogden, Utah where it made an ungainly landing and tilted over onto one wing. Nobody was hurt, but it was only as they extricated themselves from the wrecked plane that Cooke learned the truth: the pilot, who had collapsed in hysteria on the tarmac, was just eighteen and a half years old. He suddenly realised why he'd had to sign a disclaimer back in Detroit.

After this hiatus, the party finally reached Great Falls where Cooke was introduced to the servicemen, unhelpfully, as Mr Alice Cooke. Somehow he lurched through the final lecture of his tour, and as he was about to leave the platform he noticed Malone gesticulating in the wings, waving a piece of paper. It was a 'Greeting from the President' – or, less euphemistically, an invitation to attend basic military training. At thirty-five years old, Cooke was well inside the age range for military call-up and even though he was in a protected profession, he had to go through the formality of attending the Draft Board. On the appointed day he came with a letter from his immediate BBC superior, Bill Reid, a pipe-smoking veteran of the consular service in Singapore: this was to the effect that he had the formal status of a foreign correspondent, proved by his possession of a category 'C' petrol ration card.

The Draft Board lost interest and Cooke returned to the task of reporting the final stages of this first wartime election. Normal press credentials were no longer sufficient and he duly turned up at the White House to have his fingerprints taken and to fill in a special form. Since this demanded detailed information about names and dates, the secret service agents expected applicants to take the forms home. Cooke caused a bristling of suspicion by volunteering to complete the job on the spot – up to and including a list of the sailing times of the liners on which he'd travelled on his various transatlantic crossings. This bravura act of memory sent the officials scurrying for cover and it took a friendly presidential aide to vouch for him before the process could be completed. Grudgingly, they finalised their paperwork by asking his mother's maiden name and the make of his watch in order to establish the password to be used in all White House communications – 'Mary Elizabeth Byrne Lusserna'.

The campaign itself, as he remarked in his *Commentary* of 22 September, was another uphill struggle for the Republicans. Roosevelt, after all, was the Commander-in-Chief of the armies 'roaring to victory across the Rhine'. A month later Cooke and his new BBC colleague, Tony Wigan, were giving a two-handed account of an election night which saw Roosevelt's unique fourth-term victory and substantial gains for the Democrats in Congress, too.

Cooke was at last developing a strong and independent voice in his *American Commentaries* without any signs of discontent in London. In the weeks following the election he grappled – on the air – with various points of tension in Anglo-American relations, including such contentious issues as the future of Poland and the fate of the thousands of Japanese Americans who had been interned since Pearl Harbor. He was well aware that the programme had a wide and influential audience. During the winter the British Ambassador, Lord Halifax, had described it as 'the most important single link to the understanding of America in Britain'. Through sheer determination,

Cooke had barged his way to the apogee of transatlantic journalism and staked out his own territory.

There was incontestably a job to be done. Forty years later, Churchill's private secretary Jock Colville wrote Cooke a thank-you letter for a review of his war diaries, and – in passing – recalled that 'our irritation with American policy reached its zenith in the early months of 1945 when it did seem that the Administration considered the Russians to be fine, progressive democrats, and the British to be only interested in retaining their empire. Great men like Roosevelt, Eisenhower and even to some extent the greatest of them all, George Marshall, were so imbued with their own pride in being descended from successfully rebellious colonists that they equated colonialism with repression.' It was, Colville maintained, a simplistic view and he wondered what these notable Americans would have made of the way independence for colonial nations so often led to the suppression of freedom?

A BBC dispatch in the first week of 1945 carried Cooke's credo again, in case there remained any who'd still missed the point.

> Behind these talks is a simple and unchanging belief – it is the belief that, no matter how much we scream and kick at each other, we cannot break up the home. Not for any sentimental reason – not for any persuasive moonshine about our common origins – but because it simply isn't realistic any more to consider breaking up. We may dislike each other heartily, but we can no longer afford the luxury of acting on that dislike. Whether they like it or not, Britain and America are mixed together in a test-tube – the irreducible elements of a working peace on earth.

And in case anyone should forget, he added, 'May I remind you that I'm speaking to you as a native Briton, who years ago decided on a career that is still understaffed: the interpretation of the United States to the people of Britain.'

~

Did A.P. Wadsworth hear that broadcast? *American Commentary* was required listening for all serious-minded people and Wadsworth, new editor of the *Manchester Guardian*, was certainly that. He was sufficiently familiar with Cooke's attitudes and talents to react without hesitation to the cable he received on 4 March 1945 on the eve of the founding conference of the United Nations. 'Wondering what special arrangements you making about San Francisco. Shall be out there and should be delighted to do special or daily coverage for you, since now have no ties with other British press.'

Wadsworth replied by return. 'Yes. Should like daily coverage, say five articles weekly. Presume important speeches and proposals covered by agencies. Prefer explanatory comment, trends and progress. Shortish messages, not exceeding 500 words except critical occasions. Suggest five guineas per message.'

With that brief interchange was born an association which lasted well over a quarter of a century. Cooke turned out to be the answer to Wadsworth's prayers. The Yalta Conference in February had agreed that work on the construction of a new international body for peace should begin in April. The *Manchester Guardian* had an arrangement with an American journalist, Bruce Bliven, to provide some political coverage. But Bliven had a full-time job of his own as editor of the magazine *New Republic* and there was a limit to what he could do for the £500 the *Guardian* was prepared to pay him each year. Otherwise the paper relied on contributions from visiting writers, including Professor Denis Brogan. It suited everybody that Bliven should remain in Washington to deal with American politics and war stories, while Cooke took over full responsibility for the San Francisco conference.

Before it began, however, there was the shock of Roosevelt's death. Cooke was sitting in the BBC's Rockefeller Center office just before 6 p.m. on 12 April 'waiting for something to happen'. The window was open, allowing a clear view of the 'red sun flaring down over the Jersey flats'. Over the rumble of the Fifth Avenue traffic, he barely heard the urgent ringing of the bell on the news agency ticker-tape machine. He closed the window and began to pack up his typewriter. The door opened to reveal Tony Wigan, his Washington colleague. 'Alistair,' he said, 'you'd better get ready to do a quick Roosevelt obituary.' With that, he left. Cooke hurried down the corridor to see the ticker-tape 'chattering away like a drowning man'. He noticed that the news copy stopped in the middle of the previous story – about British Eighth Army advances in northern Italy: Allied forces had crossed the Santerno river ... except that the keys had paused at the 'r' of river. When they resumed, it was with the single sentence, 'Washt'n – Pres. Roosevelt died this afternoon.'

Cooke went down onto the streets to try to gather reactions, but found people lost for words. He walked for a while across town towards Broadway. Two girls were laughing and joking: they hadn't heard the news, and when he told them what had happened one of them screamed out, 'Oh my God!'. 'There has never been an evening like it in America,' he recalled a few years later, 'with people wandering aimlessly around; women sat down on the sidewalk and cried outright; music was turned off in factories; and when I got back up to the office, a rather rigid, unemotional man was sitting in his chair, crying.' Within ninety minutes he was broadcasting these raw impressions on a news circuit to London, although the transcript of the talk is full of gaps and question marks. Clearly the short-wave circuit that night, catching the mood of the moment, was stuttering and unreliable. Cooke was able to give a more considered view a few days later in his next *Commentary*: 'The curse of using big and splendid words on all occasions is that when a great man dies, you have used up your best, and there are no good and moving words to reach for. And if goodness and courage are so cheap they cannot continue to move anybody.'

Like most journalists, Cooke was no sentimentalist – but the passage also indicates a truth about the writer. It was not just that he disliked synthetic emotion: he found the real thing hard to deal with, too, both in his own life and in the wider world.

In the first few weeks after FDR's death, he did not feel ready, either, to make a final judgement about the man or his work. In any case, all observers were fully occupied distilling the idea that the man in the electric-blue suit, the hot-dog-toting Harry S. Truman, was now the President of the United States. Somehow, despite Roosevelt's evident frailty, the idea seemed scarcely credible. Cooke instinctively fell for his 'obvious humility'. 'It was as if everybody, including Mr Truman, agreed that he was a mouse in a great man's shoes; and there was a feeling that, so long as he stayed that way, everybody would like him and help him.' It didn't take long for Cooke and his colleagues to discover that the new President might not need their sympathy: 'When we went into his first press conference, even the no-nonsense reporters were saying, "Look, we ought to give him a break. He's a poor failed haberdasher who never wanted the job and he'll probably fumble it for a long time to come." Within ten minutes of that first conference, it was ourselves we felt sorry for.' Or, as he put it on another occasion, 'We staggered out after taking a drubbing from a rubbery sergeant-major. He always knew what he wanted. He might have failed as haberdasher, but he plainly had no intention of failing as a President.'

For Cooke, wedded as he was to notions of classlessness, the essence of Truman's charm was to be 'everything that the aristocratic Roosevelt was not: he had made it to the top in a way that reconfirmed the myth of the Land of Opportunity'.

~

Less than two weeks later on 24 April, Cooke cabled Wadsworth at the *Guardian* to confirm that he would be flying to San Francisco the next day. The UN conference was expected to last for seven weeks, and when he and Tony Wigan arrived, they found themselves plunged into a celebrity circus. Some 600 people had been deployed to cover the proceedings, and not all of them were conventional correspondents. Among those accredited were such experts on international affairs as Lana Turner, Orson Welles and Rita Hayworth, on the basis, presumably, that there was nowhere more chic for a Hollywood star to be than the creation of a New World Order. These tyro journalists did not stay long. Within a few days the novelty died off and the job was left to the professionals.

It would have been a gruelling business simply ensuring a proper service for the BBC. The time difference meant that talks had to be transmitted in the early morning, reflecting the previous day's – and night's – discussions. But by the time Cooke entered a studio, his daily quota of words for the *Manchester Guardian* had already been filed. Keeping track of developments during the day meant traipsing between the gatherings of the forty-six nations represented, and the simultaneous negotiations on different aspects of the UN's role – the Security Council, the General Assembly, the Economic and Social Council.

The working day was elaborately choreographed. 'The busiest time was the early evening. Tony and I tried to catch up with the chairmen of the various groups at 5 or 6pm. I would then write my piece for the *Guardian*, before meeting up with Tony again to divide up the BBC work and we were often broadcasting – mostly live – until 2 a.m. I got into the habit of going out for a meal when I'd finished. There was a chain of restaurants called Fosters, and I used to sit down to two eggs over easy, sausages, pancake and syrup before going to bed at about 4 o'clock.' Four hours later he was ready to start all over again.

There was one other vital component of each working day: telephoning or writing to Jane back in New York. 'We were hot and heavy in those days.'

The reporting cycle began within hours of his arrival in San Francisco: he sent over an *American Commentary* before dawn on Wednesday 25 April, previewing an opening session at which President Truman would make the address. He warned his British listeners that this was not to be a peace conference: the outstanding disagreement over the fate of Poland might not even be discussed. 'What this conference is about is to see if we can become good citizens of one world, before we become its victims.' Cooke was caught up in the general sense of hopefulness that this time, after the failures of the old League of Nations, there was a real chance of ending global conflict. On reflection, it was easy to identify the reasons for the temporary blindness which afflicted so many in the United States at the start – a deep innocence, as he put it in a 1958 *Letter from America*, about the Russians:

> We were not only prepared, then, to let bygones be bygones, we were touchingly eager to believe that the Russian – any Russian – was a new man, a new type in the world – subtle, courageous, a difficult bargainer, but one who believed in his Slavic (or was it Mongol?) way in the principles of justice, if not personal freedom, as they are understood in Brooklyn and Birmingham.

This touching faith was not immediately dispelled by such outward oddities as the arrival of Molotov, Stalin's Commissar for Foreign Affairs, for an early negotiating session at the San Francisco Opera House. A US Marine stepped forward to open the door, only to be bundled aside by two burly Russian secret-service men. Cooke witnessed the ensuing scuffle and registered this as the first sighting, for most Americans, of the identikit protectors of all Russian leaders – 'as solemn as pallbearers', and as well-drilled as rugby forwards.

It was only ten days into the conference that a horrible thought dawned on Cooke. The agreement that he had reached with Wadsworth – for 'five guineas per message' – had not been clarified by either side. Cooke had assumed that, like the BBC, the *Guardian* would translate 'five guineas' as $25, despite the fact that the pound's value had been slipping. What if the newspaper applied the rate on the day? He might only receive $22 for a 500-word piece. Tentatively, he suggested a flat rate of 5 cents a word, adding that if that was thought to be unjust, he would be quite prepared to accept the lower sum. 'I do not want you to feel,' he continued, 'that I have tricked you into an arrangement that might embarrass you. It is a great pleasure to write for a paper that allows the free play of the intelligence. The last English paper I wrote for (the rich and seemingly illiterate *Daily Sketch*) asked for "what the man in the street is thinking, provided it isn't politics or anything to do with the war, written for an audience that knows nothing about America." After some time, this became intolerable.'

The fact was that Cooke was relishing this return to daily newspaper writing. His letter to Wadsworth touches subtle pressure points. He was, he mentioned in passing, 'a native Mancunian', and he had heard that the *Manchester Guardian* might be looking to 'reshape its plans for American correspondence'. If so, Cooke thought he might be just the man for the job. And in case Wadsworth was wondering, Cooke reassured him that he was not on the BBC staff and that his 'first obligation would be to a newspaper with whom I was regularly employed'.

The language of this pitch for a permanent job is a perfect echo of all those BBC appeals: 'I want to report American politics, but always in an interpretative way, and to write colourful pieces on the social life of this country and its people.' This might include some longer pieces on 'some American place, institution, social custom, industry, or on some aspect of the language, the culture, the current literature of the United States': these could be sent by airmail, rather than clocking up huge cable costs. Cooke was also familiar with the desperate shortage of newsprint in Britain, which had reduced most papers to a few flimsy sheets each day. He was prepared to be patient. After all, he'd had some practice.

The good news was that Wadsworth had an insatiable appetite for Cooke's dispatches from San Francisco. After less than a year in the editor's chair, Wadsworth was already bringing his own style to the *Manchester Guardian*. His immediate predecessors had all received 'as good an education for an élite as any known in history'. That was the verdict of the paper's historian, David Ayerst. This had given them 'a profound sense of *noblesse oblige*', but it had 'cut them off from much of the common experience of most Englishmen'. Wadsworth, from the gritty mill town of Rochdale, represented the other side of 'the great divide'. His upbringing, according to Ayerst, had not isolated him, and his time as a labour correspondent had kept him in touch with the concerns of ordinary people: above all, he had recognised an economic and moral imperative to draw on the reservoir of young talent thrown up by the war.

With Wadsworth's active incitement, the cables from San Francisco came thick and fast – an average of one a day from 22 April to 27 June. For accounting purposes, Cooke kept a running tally: 22nd, 1023 words – 23rd, 477 – 25th, 567 – 26th, 423. The total, as the conference drew to a close, was 38,991 and his wordage had topped 40,000 by the time the bill was ready to be drawn up. To Cooke's relief (misplaced, as it turned out), Wadsworth accepted the BBC five-cent formula and authorised payment of $2025. More important, he liked Cooke's realistic, no-frills approach. At the end of May, for instance, with the great powers still haggling over how the right of veto should be exercised in the Security Council, Cooke gave this bleak assessment: 'Russia insisted on the veto – reputable and well-documented proof that of Europe's Big Three, Russia alone has launched a thorough policy of unilateral security that admits only a passing nod to the principles of collective security being established at San Francisco.' A month later, when the UN Charter was signed, Cooke reflected the dangerous doubts of the Russian ambassador, Andrei Gromyko. 'He pronounced with unambiguous firmness the words, "The Union of Soviet Socialist Republics can in no way agree to this." He walked doggedly from the rostrum through a silence that was heavy with embarrassment, fear and curiosity, a silence that spoke more honestly of the Conference feeling towards Russia than any conscious fear the delegates would be at pains to deny.' Gromyko signed, none the less.

Perhaps Wadsworth recognised in Cooke a kindred spirit – another Northerner who had come up the hard way. It was quite logical that Cooke should be asked to report the UN's work after its inaugural meeting on 24 October. It was an informal relationship at the start, but the *Guardian* soon came to rely on him for an increasing level of more general coverage. During October and November, for instance, he provided no fewer than sixty-three pieces, on such diverse topics as US relations with Argentina, a car-workers' strike and the New York local elections.

Only one cloud drifted over this burgeoning relationship: money. The *Guardian*'s accountants, presented with Cooke's suggested payscale, still managed to turn the system against him. They accepted the figure of $2,025 (40,000-odd words at 5 cents apiece), then recalculated the fee in pounds at the *old* rate of exchange ($5 = £1). This had the effect of reducing the final payment by ten per cent. Cooke was furious, yet unwilling to antagonise Wadsworth. The letter he wrote on 28 November lurches between the two sentiments. 'Twas sad that we seemed to have a misunderstanding over filthy lucre on the San Francisco assignment,' he wrote – and spent two long paragraphs trying (rather ineptly, in line with his self-confessed ignorance of economics) to explain what had happened. 'I hope this is clear,' (it wasn't). 'You must think me heartless. However, please believe I don't care at all about the $225 that got lost in Anglo-American misconceptions. I was delighted with the care and seriousness with which my stuff was handled. I'd just like to get clear about future assignments.'

The $225 must have mattered very much, for Cooke to risk alienating a potential new employer. He was trying to pay for two households, as well as supporting the sort of lifestyle which would keep Jane captivated. With the war against Japan still unresolved, life in the city could be expensive, as he explained in a news talk on 19 July: 'On Long Island a woman [Jane, presumably] who had left town for her summer cottage closed it up and came back to New York and the comforts of the black market, when she found that, living near a farm, it was impossible to get butter, cheese, eggs, bacon, sugar, syrup.'

BBC fees were never particularly generous either and as the war drew to a close so too did *American Commentary*. Cooke's last talk under this title went out in September 1945, but not before he'd had the chance to comment on two more great events. Labour's victory in the General Election at the end of July (and Churchill's defeat) was an incomprehensible phenomenon to most Americans, and a frightening one to a large number. Cooke reported that 'the Hearst newspapers had practically resigned themselves to world Communism, against which a brave but lonely Uncle Sam would batter out his brains and money.'

The other great events took place at Hiroshima and Nagasaki, driven by President Truman's desire to bring to an end the war of attrition with Japan. Cooke was one of a number of correspondents around the world to contribute a brief picture of the reaction to Japan's capitulation. 'Just before I came on air, office workers in some skyscrapers started to scatter ticker-tape and torn fragments of newspapers into the air and they're drifting down slowly, on this hot and sparkling day, into the streets. It's not yet anything remotely like the paper snowstorm that greeted the victorious Eisenhower, but just a starter.'

Cooke's next scheduled *Commentary*, ten days after the first atomic explosion, makes no specific reference to the arrival of the nuclear age. It's a strangely muted piece, playing down reports of manic enthusiasm about Japan's imminent surrender:

> Even in this country which has never been bombed or known the sight of the dead, it's remarkable to realise how tight and firm has been the discipline which most people have secretly imposed on themselves, even when they seem to be indifferent or far from world chaos. So Tuesday night in New York, and I'm told also in San Francisco, it was as if Barnum and Bailey's Circus had invaded Babylon. Wednesday morning was like a December Sunday in Woking.

There was no need for a valedictory tone in this *American Commentary* which turned out to be almost Cooke's last. The immediate post-war era would provide generous compensation.

～

Lindsay Wellington was the moving force behind Cooke's return to full BBC favour. After two years in the United States, Wellington had returned to London in October 1944 to take up the post of Controller of Programmes. From this lofty position, he advanced Cooke's cause with vigour and within weeks of the end of the war he fulfilled a long-standing promise – to invite his protégé to London at the BBC's expense. The purpose, as he wrote on 25 October 1945, would be to allow Cooke to re-acquaint himself with his old home and to discuss a range of future plans, including *Transatlantic Quiz* and an extension in some form of *American Commentary.*

'I remember we agreed in New York,' the letter said, 'that it would make all the difference to your work if you could get first-hand knowledge of present-day Britain, and I hope you still feel strongly enough to make this trip worthwhile to you, despite some of its obvious financial drawbacks.' Wellington was speaking no more than the honest truth. The BBC, along with other institutions, had entered a period of extreme austerity and was unable to lay its hands on foreign currency. Consequently, the whole exercise would have to be funded in sterling: Cooke would have to travel by British liner, and during his stay his travel and living expenses would be calculated on an 'actuality' basis. The memo warned that if he did any talks during his stay his fee would be subject to British income tax.

In case that seemed too formal, Wellington added a hand-written note explaining that actuality expenses, unlike a daily allowance, were at least free of income tax. Payments might not be lavish, but 'I hope we can assure you that your trip really is free – i.e., doesn't cost you pounds which you would be hard put to it to find'. Wellington sends his love 'to Ruth, when you see her' and invites Cooke to stay at his home for as long as he likes. The letter is signed 'As ever, Lindsay'.

At last Cooke had real friends in high places. His acceptance letter is almost indecently enthusiastic: 'my eagerness to see, taste, smell and feel Britain today is unabated . . . I have in mind several parts of the country very different in their work and landscape . . . the financial plan you outline is entirely acceptable to me . . . I have no wish to make money on a trip to Britain and I am very grateful indeed that you are making it possible for me to come.' Somewhat poignantly, Cooke says he must wait until after Christmas so that his ill-fated book about America at war can be prepared for publication.

The letter ends, 'I read this over and I, too, am appalled by its measured formality. Know then that I am tickled pink, rarin' to go, and hell-bent for Britain.'

The BBC's qualified generosity opened up other possibilities. Cooke told Wadsworth at the *Guardian* about his impending visit to 'hop around and smell and taste post-war Britain, though I know how meagre is the taste and non-succulent are the smells you have to be satisfied with these days. (By the way, if there is anything you particularly lack that you know is being freely sold in the United States, I should be very happy to bring it over for you.)' He then reminds Wadsworth about the idea that he might serve as a full-time American correspondent 'when controls on your newsprint are relaxed sufficiently'. In the meantime he would be grateful for the chance to meet the editor for the first time, as well as those handling his UN copy.

~

There was one more event of note before the end of this period of Cooke's life. His jazz contacts had led to an idea for a unique broadcast – a rehearsal session with Duke Ellington, which would lay bare some of the hard work and creativity behind a finished piece of polished 'improvisation'. First, the idea had to be sold to the Duke himself. Cooke's appointment was for early afternoon, at the great man's large, rambling apartment in what constituted the 'swagger side of Harlem'. The living-room, he noted, showed signs of some strenuous drinking the previous night and an unmade bed was visible through the open bedroom door. In circumstances rather different from the last time Cooke had been confronted with a half-naked luminary (Sir Arthur Quiller-Couch), Ellington emerged from the bathroom 'naked except for a pair of underdrawers and a towel woven round his head'.

Cooke was initially ignored in favour of a discussion with the butler as to what sort of breakfast would be most medicinally suitable after a hard night. Once this Wodehouse-like diversion had been dealt with, Ellington asked what Cooke's business might be 'at this unholy hour of the afternoon'. As he began to explain, Ellington watched him with suspicion, but gradually warmed to the idea which was for the listener 'to be, and feel, present at the act of creation'.

The sales pitch struck a chord and Cooke left with the Duke's agreement. The result was a long recording session in a hired studio on Fifth Avenue, including 'the roughest run-through with many pauses, trying this fusion of instruments and that, stopping and starting and transferring the obligato from one man to another, the Duke talking and shouting, "Now, Tricky, four bars", and "Barney, in there eight". And in the last hour, what had been a taste in the Duke's head came out as a harmonious, rich meal.' Eddie Wiltshire was an admiring spectator that day as Cooke paraded his skills as a jazz impresario. Much later, the BBC enjoyed a cut-down version of this ground-breaking event.

~

In mid-January, Cooke sailed on the *Queen Elizabeth* – still operating as a troop-carrier. Among the other passengers – a matter of months before his death – was John Maynard Keynes, who told him how much he'd enjoyed the *American Commentaries*. It was Cooke's first visit to Britain in almost eight years and it was an unmitigated success.

He met Wellington at Broadcasting House in the first week of February, and the two men instinctively understood each other: 'There was never a chance that we should beat the air, dictate important memoranda or go through any other of the strangulated motions that, I am told, are the signs of a "policy meeting" in action.' Instead, Wellington informed him that he was welcome to continue as one of three contributors to *American Commentary*. But he might like to consider something different: 'Lindsay began to talk about "vignettes" of American life – a book, a remembered incident out West, a favourite city...' Cooke interrupted him. 'How about doing in reverse the *London Letter* I used to broadcast to America?'

The foundation stones of a broadcasting monument were in place.

PART FOUR

THE
MARSHALL
PLAN

16

THE LONGEST LETTER

Wellington duly confirmed that Cooke should have a weekly Sunday evening slot to talk about anything that took his fancy. It was the brief he had always craved, in other words, 'no brief at all'. The concept would be based on the 'affectionate conviction that if a broadcasting executive had the sense to handle a story-teller in this vague but trustful way, he was entitled to get the best I had'. Each talk would be thirteen minutes long, and it was Cooke's understanding that the arrangement would continue 'indefinitely'. His Valentine's Day memo to Lindsay Wellington also dealt with a title for the series. 'Many ingenious and fanciful titles have occurred to me but the best still seems to be my first suggestion, namely "American Letter." ' The first talk was actually recorded in the archives as 'American News Letter', then became 'American Letter' and only adopted its familiar title, *Letter from America*, in 1950.

In the same memo, he put on the record his aspirations.

> As I understand it, it will be a weekly personal letter to a Briton by a fireside about American life and people and places in the American news. I shall try to give him a running commentary on topical aspects of American life, some of the intimate background to Washington policy, some pictorial excursions into regions and places, some profiles of important Americans who (because they work in the shadows of the limelight or are suddenly projected into it) are unknown to him as Personalities. The stress will always tend to be on the springs of American life, rather than on the bright headlines themselves.

In the event, more than half a century of *Letters from America* saw the basic format change hardly at all: thirteen or fourteen minutes of musings from wherever Cooke happened to be.

Wellington had a gap in his Home Service schedule for the programme. But Cooke's use of the word 'indefinite' provoked a hasty caveat, spelled out in nervous memos: 'indefinite' referred only to the general idea of such a broadcast. The initial commitment would be very narrowly defined indeed – to just thirteen weeks.

As soon as his business in London was concluded, Cooke headed north for a family gathering at the Ormond Avenue house. The only record of this reunion is a tiny cartoon on a scrap of paper, bearing his usual self-deprecating profile with its sharply pointed nose and prominent ear. 'With much love to Kathleen,' it says, 'from Uncle Alfred.' Followed by the signature, 'Alistair Cooke, Feb 10/'46.' The elder daughter of his brother Sam was twelve by now – old enough to remember the occasion vividly.

In Kathleen's recollection it was an alarming house, in which her grandmother still ruled with Victorian rigidity: 'Children were supposed to be seen and not heard, and preferably not even seen.' While her grandfather, Samuel, was a sweet little man, but 'rather henpecked, and under the thumb'. Cooke held court and hardly paused for breath until they left at ten in the evening. 'He talked right through tea,' according to Kathleen. 'My grandmother had always taught us that you shouldn't speak when you were eating and I kept thinking, "When's she going to tell him off? He's going to get a good rousting in a minute if he doesn't stop."' But there was no reproach, as he regaled his provincial audience with years of accumulated anecdotes and impressions. As they travelled home that night, Kathleen's mother remarked to Sam, 'My goodness, your Alfred can go on a bit, can't he!'

There is no record of how long Cooke stayed in Blackpool – not long, probably, since he had grown to despise its small-town atmosphere. He did not, it seems, spend much time listening to his older brother, either. Had he done so, he might perhaps have discovered that Sam's marriage was in serious trouble: five months later, he walked out on Elsie and his children, and moved to London with a woman called Mabel. This caused a permanent rupture between the Cookes and Kathleen's mother. It was, in any case, the sort of emotional complication from which Cooke would have found any excuse to distance himself.

~

If Blackpool was a disagreeable reminder of what he'd escaped, Manchester, fifty miles or so to the south, offered portents of a brighter future. Cooke's encounter with the editor of the *Manchester Guardian* is recorded in David Ayerst's *Biography of a Newspaper*: A.P. Wadsworth was inquisitive about the United States, and although he'd never visited the country, he'd been writing leaders on American affairs since the early days of the New Deal. He had reached the conclusion that New York would have to be put on the same footing as Paris in the paper's foreign coverage – and he suspected that Cooke, with his grammar school background and intimate knowledge of American affairs, was the right man for the job. Over a long lunch at the Midland Hotel, Wadsworth put his hunch to the test. According to Ayerst, Cooke's temperament fitted the bill: he was 'an observer rather than a campaigner, neither didactic nor interfering, but a man who gave his readers the sense of attending a "theatre in the round"'. In addition his work in the *Guardian* over the previous year showed that he had 'an eye, an ear, a mind that hustles into place the significant detail'.

At the end of the meal, Wadsworth scratched his nose contemplatively with the stem of his pipe and told Cooke that it was quite likely there would soon be a full-time *Guardian* man in New York. Not just yet, admittedly, but Cooke was left with the clear impression that if and when it happened, he would be that man. In the meantime, Wadsworth agreed that he would be paid 4 cents a word for all his UN coverage, and a flat rate of $50 for each middle-page feature – 'that is,' he hastened to clarify the point, 'whatever pounds will translate into fifty dollars.'

Cooke returned to London highly satisfied and, before heading back to New York, he made guest appearances on a number of BBC programmes (at 15 guineas a time), including the long-running discussion programme, *The Brains Trust*. From the transcript of the edition of Tuesday 19 February, Cooke seems to have been somewhat in awe of his forthright fellow panellists, despite the fact that his old sparring partner, Lionel Hale, was in the chair. Most of his interventions were brief, verging on the deferential. The other speakers were not so coy. George Woodcock, later General Secretary of the Trades Union Congress, when asked whether the war might have improved Anglo-American relations, reckoned there was a great deal of bad feeling between the two peoples, while the *Brains Trust* stalwart Professor C.E.M. Joad pushed the point further, maintaining that the war had made matters worse: 'There's never been so much communication, never so much reading of newspapers, never so much coming and going in the modern world and, as a result, never so much hating and grudging and envying and spiting.'

Then there was *Speaking Personally*, in which there were no competing brains. With fifteen minutes of live broadcasting to hold forth on any subject under the sun, Cooke chose to deliver a homily on austerity: was it really necessary? His point of view, as he acknowledged, was provocative. He argued that austerity – imposed by politicians who had little experience of standing in a ration queue in the hope of picking up a piece of fish – was 'a creeping paralysis of the spirit', and 'a vile thing, indeed the only infection that might sap the essential dignity of the [British] people'.

A few days later, Cooke boarded the *Queen Mary* – like her sister ship, still in unluxurious wartime order. The voyage was captured for posterity in the first *Letter*, establishing from the start the notion that Cooke's life would be a vital component of his broadcasting art. He had found himself in the company of some 2000 GI brides waving goodbye to their homeland as he himself had done: 'Along the entire main deck of the ship the handkerchiefs fluttered in an unbroken line, like washing day in Manchester and Leeds. And then a small coast-guard cutter came scuttering alongside the liner like a playful puppy. An American soldier stood at the cutter's bow, cupped his hands and yelled, "You don't want to go back, do you?" And the young mothers and wives, weeping like mad, yelled, "No!" ' Five days later the *Queen Mary* sailed into New York Harbour.

The talk is a gem of its kind. It has colour, compassion, information and humour. Of the cab that he took on his first night back in New York, for instance – 'The driver couldn't use his first gear, which had given up shortly before VE-Day, and he couldn't go in third which had been out of condition since the Battle of the Bulge. He also couldn't go in reverse. If he went too far past the address you wanted, he had to go right back round the block again to land just right. This is a useful money-making device which I offer without patent.'

Above all, Cooke makes a determined effort to persuade his British audience that life in New York is not all it's cracked up to be: long queues for meagre supplies of nylon stockings; no butter in restaurants; the desperate hunt for white bread; a thriving black market in all scarce goods. He seeks to dispel the notion of an American populace enjoying the good life while Britain yearned for a small piece of fish.

American Letter Number 1 was recorded on a 16-inch disc (at 33 rpm) and flown to London two weeks ahead of transmission. The talks producer in New York, Annette Ebsen, reported that she hoped soon to have a new supply of more appropriate 12-inch aluminium discs, following the end of an industrial dispute. The Broadcasting House hierarchy liked the result: the talks director, George Barnes, called it 'admirable', though he felt that some of the black-market descriptions might have been exaggerated.

The second *Letter* picked up many more of the themes which were to sustain the series over the years ahead: American social custom (living in apartments, rather than houses), history (the importance of the Indian tribes who preceded the European settlers), a dash of Cooke's own lifestyle (a train trip down Long Island), and a pinch of human interest (a demobilised sailor writing to a New York paper, alarmed at the prospect of another war when all he wanted was 'a new refrigerator, a dozen new shirts, an automobile and the stranger I was married to before the war'). Politics was one missing ingredient, and would remain rationed as long as the rival *American Commentary* was on the air.

As for the construction of the *Letters*, Cooke determined from the start that he would have no idea what he was going to say when he sat down to write. Like some journalistic beachcomber, he would wander down to the beach every seven days to see what ideas had been swept up by the tide. This eclectic technique might have sounded scrappy and disjointed, but Cooke had two more tricks up his sleeve.

The first he had picked up while eavesdropping on distinguished BBC speakers. Having listened from the control room to literary giants like André Gide, Aldous Huxley and W.H. Auden, it dawned on him that they had no idea how to speak on radio: 'They wrote lectures, or essays, or sermons. And they simply read them aloud.' The trick would be to find a way of writing words coherent in structure but conversational in presentation, complete with the syntax and quirkiness of spoken English.

The second principle stemmed from those countless sessions of analysis. Sigmund Freud had taught him to trust the unencumbered logic of his unconscious: if he allowed his thoughts to flow in a childlike fashion, they would have a directness which no carefully fashioned literary sentence could match. If the outpourings turned out to be too long, it was easy to trim them back afterwards, or 'to censor the more outrageous ideas in the interests of domestic tranquillity', as he put it to an audience of admirers just after his eighty-ninth birthday. Certainly, many of the original scripts have whole paragraphs excised by hand to fit the unrelenting demands of that thirteen-and-a-half-minute slot.

The Freudian requirement was that he should 'be himself', rather than some pale imitation of any other broadcaster, and addressing his remarks to 'two friends in a room, no more'.

~

Cooke's decision to marry Jane Hawkes on 30 April 1946 threw the BBC into turmoil. With only three of the thirteen *American Letters* under his belt, he announced to Annette Ebsen in the New York office that he was about to take a three-week honeymoon in San Francisco. Ebsen was understandably vexed and wrote rather plaintively to London that she would have to pre-record two programmes a week in order to cover the time Cooke was away. She assumed that he had written to Lindsay Wellington already, to inform him of the plan. He hadn't. Wellington's hand-written addendum to the memo is resigned in tone about the effect on the new series: 'It's a pity, but we did say that the *Letters* need not be immediately topical.'

George Barnes was less indulgent than Wellington about Cooke's departure. He thought it was unfortunate that, so early in its run, the series would have to be recorded even further in advance. For good measure, and perhaps stung by Cooke's somewhat cavalier approach, he added some minor criticisms of the first three programmes: '[They] have been very good, but I hope that you will watch Alistair's tendency to be glib, or at least to give us the impression that he is glib.' He and his colleagues thought Cooke might have been 'looking up old diaries for some of his material'. He advised Annette Ebsen in New York, 'You must watch statements – e.g. about when he was last in Arizona – to see that they are not only literally true, but actually true. Cooke is clever enough to fool the listener by careful phrasing but the listener won't go on being fooled if he detects any insincerity in Cooke's voice.'

There are signs in this critique of the old BBC misgivings resurfacing: Barnes, after all, had been an executive since well before the war. Yet what he called glibness may just have been the conversational style of a speaker who had rejected the more formal language, and sentence-structure, of other commentators. Cooke's reflection on his past experiences, as a way of illuminating subjects of current interest, came to be recognised as one of the strengths of the *Letters*. Ebsen probably didn't pass the comments on in any case, in the last few frantic days before the wedding.

~

Jane and Alistair were married on Tuesday 30 April 1946, with Justice John A. Byrnes officiating in a civil ceremony at the New York City Court building in Chambers Street. Jane wore a purple suit and hat. The only guests were her mother and the two Hawkes children, Holly and Stephen: a BBC colleague of Alistair's, Donovan Rowse, acted as best man. It was an informal occasion, made more so by the fact that during the service, conducted by the somewhat gruff New York judge, there were constant interruptions from a telephone ringing in the office.

The local paper in Jane's old home town in New Jersey, the *Montclair Times*, recorded that she was 'the daughter of Mrs William Penn White and widow of Major Albert Whitfield Hawkes, (son of US Senator Albert Hawkes of 166 Upper Mountain Avenue). Major Hawkes died in 1943 while with the 9th General Hospital Unit in the Pacific. Mrs Cooke, an artist, studied at the National Academy of Design, New York, and in Florence, Italy, on a Mooney Scholarship.' Mr Cooke was billed as 'Chief Correspondent on American Affairs for the BBC', which was stretching a point.

Afterwards the party decamped for an early lunch at a restaurant on Fifth Avenue, where Stephen, having been given a glass of champagne, turned to Cooke and experimented with a 'Hi, Daddy!'. Then the children were packed off home to be looked after by Jane's mother Nonie for the duration of the honeymoon. The much-loved family nanny, Emmy, had not been able to cope with the disruption in the Hawkeses household and had long since departed.

The following day the newly married couple flew to San Francisco. Jane had never been west of Chicago and Cooke was keen to show her his favourite state. The honeymoon began with an unexpected freelance commission from the *Manchester Guardian*: 'I started out on a sparkling day to see the wild lupins and the poppies pouring over the surrounding hills and to pluck a branch or two from the giant spruces and eucalyptus trees on the University's incomparable campus at Berkeley. Driving across the four and a half miles of the Bay Bridge, my enchanting but innocent companion looked across the Bay and asked which of the islands was "The Rock". '

He was able to point out Alcatraz to his 'charming and innocent companion' by the puff of white smoke emerging helpfully into the sky. This, although they didn't realise it for some time, was the start of a famous prison siege, in which a group of prisoners overpowered their guards, seized rifles and held the Marines at bay for three days. Cooke wrote a positively poetic piece for the *Guardian* of 6 May, describing the morbid curiosity of the citizens watching from the mainland: 'though the men bound on the rock are debased specimens of the tragic hero, yet the spectator could achieve a terrified identification with them in the knowledge that their end was from the start foreordained. There is no escape from the waters around Alcatraz.'

The holiday then resumed in a more – though not entirely – conventional fashion. How many people spend a honeymoon with a third party in almost constant attendance? For most of the three weeks the couple were accompanied on their travels by Cooke's old New York boss, Gerald Cock, now running the BBC's San Francisco office. He became an inseparable friend to both Alistair and Jane, and the touring threesome was thenceforward a regular feature of the Cookes' annual visits to California. From a base at the Fairmont Hotel, they travelled extensively. As Cooke explained in a note of apology to A.P. Wadsworth – 'I sincerely hope your professional conscience doesn't regard honeymoons as an unfaithful interference with putting the paper to bed' – he intended to cover the 'four hundred miles of the valleys' of southern California, but would be back on UN business by the end of May. From Muir Woods and Tilden Park, and the beauty spots around San Francisco Bay, to Los Angeles and Hollywood, they celebrated what was manifestly a match fuelled by passion. As Jane puts it, 'I married my first husband for my children, and my second husband for myself.'

Back in New York, Cooke finally moved into the East 71st Street apartment. Jane told him that she already had a big double bed and that all he needed to bring was his body. Instead, the long narrow 'railroad' apartment, with its central corridor, soon filled up with Cooke's accumulated journalistic baggage. Jane protested as even the corner of the living-room she'd set aside for her painting was gradually overwhelmed by files and paperwork. She was beginning to gain a reputation, particularly as a portrait painter: fortunately, she'd always maintained a studio outside the home to which she could retreat.

Like Ruth's, Jane's background was comparatively racy by the prim standards of East Coast convention. Having been brought up in New Jersey, she had spent a year studying art in Italy before marrying Whit Hawkes in London. His death had left her with a decent income, although the bulk of the money was held in trust for her children. In the precarious state of Cooke's finances this was an important consideration. He was perpetually struggling to meet his commitments, not least Ruth's alimony, and would have found it impossible to provide the fees to send Holly and Stephen to one of New York's expensive private schools. Jane was also entitled to claim a proportion of the rent and living expenses from the same fund. This comparative financial freedom enabled Cooke to launch out with Jane into a renewed round of jazz clubs, night-spots and movies. She remembers her new husband's constant irritation with the way films were projected, often ending in a direct complaint to the projectionist.

They soon slipped into a comfortable lifestyle whereby Jane rose early to see the children off to school before leaving for her studio: Alistair slept late – and the two would only meet after the children were ready for bed, at which point the evening's entertainment could begin. From the start, Cooke showed no more interest in the daily routine of parenthood than he had with Ruth and Johnny. He quite enjoyed reading stories however, and Holly recalls a period of illness when he sat by her bedside and recounted the tales of Peter Church Mouse, Alice and Winnie the Pooh. His relationship with Stephen was always more problematical. At five and a half years old, Jane's son was almost exactly the same age as Cooke's and that, perhaps, was at the root of the difficulty. Cooke was still seeing his analyst over the guilt which gnawed away at him and Stephen was a constant reminder of what he'd done: the antipathy was mutual.

Twenty blocks further north, at her modest apartment on East 92nd Street, Ruth was struggling with another unhappy child. Johnny refused to allow her to leave him at school and sometimes she had to sit at the reception desk all day so that he could find her. The two of them, she realised later, were clinging to each other in an unhealthy and unhelpful way. Inevitably, both were soon in therapy, but at least there was regular contact between father and son: on Saturdays Cooke would take Johnny and Stephen for a hamburger and a movie – Chaplin, Cagney, Bob Hope or the Marx Brothers. Johnny's favourites were the westerns, and his childhood viewing gave him an abiding interest in the history of the Old West on which he later wrote extensively.

Ruth's state of mind at the time emerges in a letter she sent to Blackpool in October of 1946. She'd just heard about her ex-brother-in-law, Sam Cooke, walking out on his wife and children in Blackpool. 'My dear Elsie,' she wrote, 'I wish there were anything I could do or say that would help. I send you my deep sympathy and I hope that making your adjustment won't be too long or too painful. It is certainly hard to rearrange your thoughts and feelings and your daily life. The girls will surely be a great comfort to you, as Johnny is to me.' Ruth had at least got herself a job as an infant-school teacher, though she was constrained by the fact that she had never completed her own college education. Money was a constant worry, and she went through a number of house moves to find somewhere acceptable and affordable.

～

American Letter was never seriously threatened with the axe at the end of its thirteen-week run. Programme Number 13 came and went, but Lindsay Wellington managed to lay his hands on the dollars to continue a series of talks which began to answer a genuine public curiosity in Britain about life in the United States. Throughout the rest of the year, the *Letter* operated in tandem with *Transatlantic Quiz*.

For many listeners in Britain, Cooke was beginning to build a reputation as the most authoritative voice on American affairs.

That voice was itself the subject of some tetchy correspondence. Many of the *Letters* were reprinted in the BBC magazine, the *Listener*, although its editors had to operate from a transcript taken from the recorded disc, rather than from Cooke's own script. Live broadcasts presented serious difficulties in comprehension; FM interference could eradicate words and leave the transcriber groping for meaning through a cloud of static. In the Roosevelt anniversary *Letter*, for instance, 'purple prose' appeared as 'purple prowess'. More revealing were the mishearings caused by unfamiliarity with Cooke's transatlantic accent – in particular the lengthened vowels. A Colorado landmark, 'the Garden of the Gods' became 'the Garden of the Guards'.

Another crisis arose over an attempt to give the *Letters* a (spurious) sense of immediacy to offset the length of time between recording and transmission. At the end of May, Cooke began his talk with a reference to an expected visit to Gettysburg by President Truman. The visit was never made and the talk had to be dropped. Annette Ebsen wrote apologetically that the experience 'brought home with a bang' the impossibility of risking topical references. 'Each time it has seemed as though the event referred to was absolutely inevitable and then something has always come up to interfere. We are therefore completely avoiding such references in future'.

More seriously – and mysteriously – the eighteenth *Letter*, scheduled for 14 July, was subjected to an apparently arbitrary cut on air: Cooke's words ended in mid-sentence, to be replaced by soft music. This caused a flurry of excitement in the British press and accusations of censorship. What was the BBC trying to hide?

Word soon leaked out. The final few paragraphs of an otherwise unexceptionable description of how tourism and leisure were regaining their pre-war vigour, were devoted to an unsavoury Southern Senator, Theodore Bilbo. 'He is 68,' Cooke had written. 'He looks like a wizened old bullfrog, with glasses. He has been to jail. . . . His policies, such as they are, are conceived in hate and illiteracy. He is hysterical against unions and against the Negro. He recently yelled at a country audience, "I call on every red-blooded white man to use any means to keep the niggers away from the polls." '

The BBC, on receiving the disc, took legal advice and were told that the remarks were actionable. Unfortunately, nobody told the engineers transmitting the programme. The result was an embarrassing hiatus: 'The first few sentences of the slanderous passage on Bilbo', Annette Ebsen was informed in a stiff note from London, 'were broadcast before the continuity announcer realised what was happening and cut off the studio from which the recording was going out. The result was a "hue and cry" in the Press.' The memo to Ebsen continues, 'We here cannot understand why Cooke should have been so short-sighted as to include such highly slanderous matter in his talk. In any case, this *American Letter* was certainly not up to his best standard.'

Perhaps because of these alarms, Cooke's reputation at

Broadcasting House remained ambivalent. While one Talks executive registered his 'very high opinion' of Cooke's contributions, George Barnes still sniffed glibness, though he accepted that the *Letters* were serving a useful purpose in removing misconceptions. But gradually, the *American Letter* settled into a comfortable routine. Friends made fleeting (and always anonymous) appearances. Cooke's own preoccupations were often aired, too: the search for materials to extend the Nassau Point house led to a diatribe against builders exploiting post-war shortages and a wider discussion on the continuing distortion in the market for all consumer goods. From Greyhound buses to the National Parks, from the history of the Gold Rush to atomic tests in the Pacific, from the stir caused by *Brief Encounter* to the street plan of New York and, of course, Cooke's pet scientific explanation for New England's incomparable autumn colours – the range of the *Letter*'s subjects was broad and its style became more confident by the week.

The settling of its tone and the soothing of its sponsors did not, however, mean that the *Letter* was immune to the vagaries of the BBC schedules. At the start of 1947 its slot was moved from 7.30 on Sunday ('when', as one producer put it, 'respectable people are in Church and cheerful souls in the pubs') to 9.15 on Friday, when the audience was far bigger. The disadvantage was that the *Letter* became fortnightly – and remained so until the summer of 1948.

~

The long apprenticeship to which the BBC subjected Alistair Cooke was not deemed necessary by the *Manchester Guardian*. Wadsworth wanted as much material as Cooke could conjure up, within the tiresome limits imposed by paper shortages in Britain. Cooke's letters, shifting subtly in tone, record the warming of their long-distance friendship, 'Dear Mr Wadsworth' giving way to 'Dear AP'.

The United Nations, by now operating from a temporary home in Connecticut, was the focus of Cooke's work, although the *Guardian*'s copy times provided him with constant problems. The main sessions began at 3 p.m. and often adjourned three hours later: important developments were quite likely to take place in the early evening, by which time the last editions were being put to bed in Manchester. To catch the main London edition, cables had to be sent as early as 4.30 in the afternoon from New York. Cooke also took to 'hoarding' his allocation of 500 words a day to concentrate on a smaller number of more substantial pieces.

In October, Wadsworth was telling Cooke how splendidly he'd been doing, and he singled out for special mention articles on Eugene O'Neill and the arrival of the *Queen Elizabeth* in New York bearing delegates to the United Nations. Soon Cooke found himself acting as liaison between Manchester and New York over a profile of the *Guardian* in *Time* magazine. This involved a careful decoding of Wadsworth's cabled interview with *Time*, in which he referred to his paper's 'Manchester liberal' tradition. Cooke was well aware that in America, the word 'liberal' was often taken as a polite synonym for 'Communist'. What the editor really meant, he explained, was 'progressive and independent'.

Yet despite the breadth of his contributions, the *Guardian* was still not able to give Cooke a permanent brief beyond the United Nations. Inevitably, perhaps, this led to further unseemly bickering over money. On 3 December, Cooke determined to confront the issue: 'I think we must get the financial difficulty straightened out before I start doing a regular feature piece.' The accountants in Manchester, he believed, must still be unaware of the terms agreed earlier in the year. Wadsworth was sympathetic, if puzzled, and promised that there would be no haggling if the *Guardian* had got its figures wrong. The accompanying statistics of Cooke's work from March to November of 1946 show his contributions building steadily, to a total of more than 83,000 words during the eight-month period, for which he received £836. The Alcatraz honeymoon report earned him £12.10s.0d. It was not an arrangement likely to solve his financial problems.

~

Cooke's first Christmas with his new family must have caused his overworked conscience further twinges. Doubtless he saw Johnny and maybe it was under the influence of his psychiatrist, as a way of exteriorising his feelings, that he mentioned the boy in his *American Letter* on 22 December. He was describing the comparatively lavish displays in New York toy-shops, while trying not to present the place to a ration-bound audience in Britain as an 'unthinking Babylon'. 'Perhaps it's too bad,' he said, 'that this isn't a talk for children, because for them the imagination holds luxuries that no money can buy, and it's a crazy comment on this city of great possessions that my own son, surrounded by all these enchantments, is most devoted to an old doll of mine that I rescued a year ago from my mother.' The Blackpool doll – a small, furless teddy-bear, was also, of course, one of Johnny's links to his absent father. Alistair Cooke was thirty-eight years old. He had two important and satisfying journalistic jobs, a new wife and family, and an enviable social life, which moved easily between distinct and different groups according to the preference he'd established in his student days. There were BBC colleagues in New York and political journalists like Scotty Reston in Washington – a place he visited frequently and where he stayed with one of the city's great hostesses, Kay Halle. He saw old friends from Harvard and Yale, and the leading exponents of the jazz world. He was on good terms with many leading figures in politics and the arts, and was able to provide an impressive list for the *Guardian* of men whom, he predicted, he could persuade to act as special correspondents, including the future Secretary of State Dean Acheson.

Money remained a nagging concern, though Cooke's knack of scrounging cigarettes from BBC engineers had more to do with habit than poverty. Herb Schaeffer joined the BBC in 1944 as a part-time assistant and in due course became a full-time employee.

'In the early days,' he recalled, 'there was a lot of editing to do on Cooke's *Letter*. I had to remove all the coughing and sneezing: it was a tricky operation, cutting from one 16-inch disc to another to get a clean copy. And there was a lot of coughing – he was a heavy smoker.' Schaeffer and his colleague, Chester Sikora, used to amuse themselves by guessing when Cooke would ask Chester for a cigarette and one day they decided to play a trick on him. 'When we cut the records, we were left with acetate shavings. It was a nice, smooth material, but if you heated it up it gave off a horrible smell. We took some of the tobacco out of a cigarette and replaced it with these shavings, and when Cooke made his usual request, Chet handed him the pack with the doctored cigarette sticking out. Cooke began to read, taking puffs in between sentences, and when the acetate was hot, he took a great gulp of this horrible smoke.' He went green, but in Schaeffer's memory was quite prepared to enjoy the joke afterwards; the two men worked together on the *Letter* until the 1970s.

Another young member of the BBC office staff in Rockefeller Plaza at the time, Lillian Lang, can still picture Cooke's tall, slim figure wandering in and out of the studios. 'He always carried a briefcase, and we used to tease him that it was full of ham sandwiches. He never seemed to have much money, and we reckoned he needed to fill himself up.'

Cooke was also consolidating his relationship with the *Manchester Guardian*. In April, Wadsworth finally decided that he could soon afford to establish a full-time correspondent's post in New York and wrote to Cooke to find out what the ground rules might be. Cooke replied at length on 8 June. He was unwilling to speculate about the salary he might require until the paper had decided how to handle the question of its Washington coverage. 'I could go along for a time covering everything, but I feel it's a bad principle as well as an appalling undertaking.'

The division of labour between New York and Washington was – and would remain – a matter of urgent concern to Cooke. He had enough experience to know that, however many friends he might have on Capitol Hill, he never wanted to be locked into day-to-day reporting of Washington politics. It was a chore which he managed to evade for the rest of his career, as he confined himself to the more colourful manifestations of political life, notably the Nominating Conventions.

The June letter to Wadsworth is characteristically forthright and self-confident. Cooke sounds like a man who knows what he wants, untroubled by anxiety that others might disagree. He proceeds to outline his travel plans for the summer and the articles he intends to write *en route*. 'From the surprising evidence of fan mail after a couple of travel talks I did last year, I begin to understand that people who have been stuck in their own town for most of eight years, hunger to share a travelogue, if only in imagination. So that is what I intend to do.' Almost as a throw-away at the end, he adds, 'One thing I had forgotten. I really think that if I am to become your chief correspondent here, I ought to make a short visit to England every two years. The unbroken expatriate is bound to be writing at attitudes and assumptions that are out of date.'

With that, he and Jane rented out the Long Island house, bought a second-hand car and departed for a two-month motoring tour.

~

For once, the couple travelled without company on their epic westward trip – the eighth of Cooke's American tours. He advised Wadsworth of some of the staging posts on the way in case a cable was needed – Kansas City, Colorado Springs, the Grand Canyon, Santa Barbara and finally the Fairmont Hotel in San Francisco. It turned out to be another scorching summer in which to spend three weeks on the road and its course was duly charted in the *Guardian* under the generic title 'A New Yorker Goes West'. Wadsworth evidently enjoyed the travelogues, because each stretched to a column and a half. The first, filed from Hamburg, Pennsylvania, was about the German communities who settled the area in the eighteenth century. Cooke admires the meticulously manicured farms and 'those majestic and exquisitely decorated barns that we can safely risk calling the most beautiful barns on earth'. In another episode ('Across the wide Missouri') he reflects the anger of a people left unprotected from the flooding of the entire Mississippi Valley – four times in the previous six years. 'The river is muddy and serene now, but there is a layer of dried scum on many a house and freight-car and barn. And on hot days the stench is rank. The farmers of Missouri want to know what the President is going to do about it.'

When the couple reached the Grand Canyon, Cooke took out his portable typewriter and wrote a two-page letter to Johnny to supplement the frequent postcards. It's a touching document, illustrated with line-drawings. 'Hey, man, how are you?' it begins. 'We started out from New York the day after the 4th of July and it was hot across New Jersey, but there were one or two places by the side of the road where you could get sodas – <u>real</u> sodas, not like that girl at Southold wanted to sell to you and me and Stephen. The real thing, like this [a cartoon of Cooke sucking foaming soda through a straw].'

After several more sketches, 'Tomorrow we shall start driving to the Coast, where the Pacific Ocean is. Maybe we can swim there, but I won't enjoy it as much as I would if you were there to throw away.' (The picture shows father larking with son at the water's edge). Finally, under a self-portrait in striped holiday shirt – and smoking cigarette in hand – he tells Johnny, 'I hope it isn't as hot in Southold as it is here. Yesterday it was 110 through the places we drove. Mighty hot, son, mighty hot.'

While Johnny was spending the holidays with the Emersons at Southold, Jane's children were discovering the joys of summer camp. Stephen, not yet seven, had disliked his first camp the previous year ('it was an "ethical culture" camp, and they were intensely interested in your bowel movements') and didn't find the 1947 version much more to his taste: 'It was called a music camp, and I thought I was going to learn the flute. But it turned out there was no one to teach me.' Stephen blamed Alistair's arrival for these unwanted excursions, just as he did when he was sent away to boarding-school in Connecticut at the age of eleven. He could have stayed at Dalton School in New York, with its progressive, liberal teaching methods, until he was thirteen, when it became girls only. Holly, by contrast, went on to complete her education there, just round the corner from her home. These perceived unfairnesses did not help the relationship between stepfather and stepson, though Stephen may not have realised that his mother had been fully involved in the decisions.

Life was easier at the end of Long Island where families and jealousies were blurred. It could be an idyllic place for children. The Cookes and their next-door neighbours, the reunited Bill and Marcella Burrows, lived permanently intertwined lives and the community extended to Marcella's mother's house on the adjoining lot. The Burrowses' daughter, Ann, was Holly's inseparable best friend and the three properties – with direct access to beaches and boats – were like a wild and extended playground. In the holidays or at weekends, the men would bring with them guests from the city. There was a complete absence of formality. Newer buildings, like Jane's redwood bungalow, had rapidly lost their sheen in the high winds and Atlantic storms. Furnishings were basic and unsophisticated, and the families took it in turns to feed the assembled company. Cooke's own leisure activities did not involve much physical exertion: apart from chess, a little light swimming was fine, though for a time he enjoyed fishing in the fruitful waters of Peconic Bay.

The atmosphere must have been rather different across the bay at Southold, under the beady eye of Dr Haven Emerson. Johnny found him a stern and scary figure, even if their contacts were usually benign: the boy also suffered from the fact that most of his Emerson cousins were of different ages. Sometimes – and more often as he grew older – he would spend time with the Cookes at Nassau Point, though he and Stephen occasionally came to blows. 'I suppose', reflects Stephen, 'he was the competition,' while Holly's friend Ann, in retrospect, saw Johnny's occasional misbehaviour as a classic piece of attention seeking. One brawl – involving a cap-pistol – ended with Cooke administering a clip to Stephen's ear, which helped to fuel his resentment. It was some years before the two boys learned to live together more peaceably on Long Island, when each had a small boat powered by outboard-motor, and they could meet on more or less equal terms.

Johnny's visits did give Cooke the chance to reassure himself that all was well in his relationship with his son. In a 1947 *Letter*, he related a conversation they'd had: 'What does summer mean to you?'

Johnny looked baffled: 'Just summer.'

'But what do you do in summer?'

'Oh.' And his face cleared. 'You go bare, go swimming, smash pennies on the railroad track, catch swell-bellies and have lots of fun.' The story was designed to show some of the particularities of American life: the laying of coins on the tracks so that the face of Lincoln was obliterated by a passing train. Or the 'swell-bellies', otherwise known as blow-fish, which inflate themselves into a ball when caught on a hook. Johnny himself was too young to take pleasure and comfort from his presence in the *Letters*, doing the matter-of-fact things that children do with their fathers.

17

TWO MASTERS

Before the summer of 1947 was over, Cooke began to fear that he might have been over-optimistic about his *Guardian* prospects. Sterling currency controls were making all overseas operations extremely problematical, and the Bank of England had banned any expansion of offices abroad. Wadsworth told Cooke that, none the less, they were intent on having him as the *Guardian*'s correspondent and were prepared to meet his terms: $12,000 a year, plus $4000 expenses, with special events like Conventions to be treated separately – all in the hope that 'inflation does not gallop too frantically in the months to come.'

Cooke was told that he could return home at least every two years, and possibly every year, at the paper's expense – to ensure that he didn't lose touch with his readers' experience of life. It's hard to imagine how the accountants in Manchester allowed the tradition to develop but it was duly established that Cooke and his wife would travel first class on the *Queen Mary*. Consequently, well ahead of each trip, they would book suite M53, one of the best on the ship. It had no fewer than five closets, as Jane quickly established from the deck plans they were sent. At the same time they made sure tables were reserved at the exclusive Verandah Grill, a French restaurant on the observation deck.

In the event, the Bank of England smiled on Cooke's appointment, regarding it as 'wholly admirable, not only from the point of view of Anglo-American relations, but in the general interests of British journalism' – quite an accolade from some beleaguered British banker.

~

If you are, by profession and conviction, a slayer of dragons, it's vital that dragons do not become extinct. Cooke's *American Letters* of this period seem partly designed to remind his listeners that they were alive and well, and stalking the territory where the new and the old worlds met. Thus on 15 May 1947: 'Well, here we go again. In spite of *Transatlantic Quizzes*, Anglo-American magazines, to say nothing of the simple honest souls who plug away at *American Commentary* and *American Letter*, it appears that those poor old relations of ours – Anglo-American relations, that is – have hardly ever been in worse shape.'

Cooke wasn't making it up, of course, and the distrust operated at various levels. In terms of pure gut feeling, where prejudice resides, all American soldiery and American post-war visitors were tarred in the British public mind with the same brush: they were, in the words of one opinion pollster, 'intellectually and emotionally immature or boastful, flamboyant and bad-mannered'. But at a different level the public mood was affected by real issues of politics and economics. In the late spring of 1947, work was being completed on the Marshall Plan for the reconstruction of Europe, whereby the United States would offer long-term financial help, provided it was used to purchase American goods. Britain, with its Empire, was the biggest beneficiary of all.

Many in Britain, however, resented the idea of a rich uncle offering largesse with strings attached – especially one who had grown prosperous in the very war which had impoverished them. That provoked accusations in the populist American press of rank ingratitude. Cooke quoted a report in the *New York Daily News* in May, a month before the Marshall Plan was agreed: 'It would seem just as well for the British that we are young, vigorous, optimistic, or as they put it – childish – people: if we were ageing, sour and pessimistic, like some other peoples we could name, we'd never have tried to rescue the British Empire in 1917–18 and 1941–45.'

The problem, in Cooke's comforting analysis, was no more serious than a family feud. 'Americans and Britons are rather like in-laws, and what is really humiliating in this relationship – just when you want to get very grand and announce you will shake off the dust of their house forever, is the maddening knowledge that they have a standing invitation for Christmas dinner.' In truth, the ancient family feud was the driving force behind his life's work: without it, the *Letter* would surely never have become a transatlantic institution.

∽

Cooke was due to take up his post as full-time correspondent for the *Manchester Guardian* at the start of 1948: his last freelance piece was commissioned for Christmas week, as part of an international round-up of seasonal sentiment. His writing stands out from the other rather mundane offerings and has a crispness quite different from the conversational style of the *Letters*. It has an edge, too, likely to appeal to the thoughtful, sceptical readership of a liberal newspaper with intellectual pretensions. Most interesting of all is the fact that Cooke does not feel the need to explain or justify the oddities of American life to this particular audience.

The piece is an entertaining account of Santa Claus coping with the pressures of post-war life, notably in the 'battle of Glen Cove', when a pack of Long Island children discovered that the gaily covered gifts on the civic Christmas tree were mere decorations, full of nothing. 'Spurred on by the piping cry of "Santa Claus is a fake", they attacked, bopped, pommelled and tore him apart,' Cooke wrote. 'The police arrived to rescue him, licking his cuts and crying for his reindeer. It used to be the most dependable slogan in the New Deal that "you can't shoot Santa Claus". The battle of Glen Cove is the final shred of proof that the New Deal is dead and that the counter-revolutionary generation is upon us. Peace on earth, goodwill to men.' A *Guardian* reader was expected to grasp the comic irony, where the broader BBC audience would presumably have been offered a word or two in mitigation of what could have sounded like a nasty manifestation of misbehaviour and greed.

Even as he wrote, snow had started to fall in New York, and it went on falling. He and Jane, having planned to take a Boxing Day outing to the Bergdorf-Goodman sale, were blocked in by deep drifts, and Cooke found himself adopting the mantle of 'Your Correspondent' a few days ahead of schedule. 'The New York Fire Commissioner cut in on all radio programmes,' he cabled to London,

> and announced the existence of 'the greatest emergency in the history of the New York Fire Department'. Mayor O'Dwyer, caught sheepishly sweating in a 100-degree temperature in El Centro, California, telephoned that he would fly at once to his beloved, beleaguered city. . . . Last night, if you felt like a pioneer, you could stagger up to the box office of any hit show on Broadway and buy a block of seats from clerks exuding a singular courtesy. At the Metropolitan Opera House ski costumes were literally *de*

rigueur, and a man with a coonskin cap appeared without comment in the dress circle.

It was a bright start to a new career which, like all Cooke's under-takings, would demonstrate exceptional longevity. His last *Guardian* report wasn't filed until August 1972. In this first winter, and doubtless anxious to impress, he took the trouble to arrange for CARE parcels to be delivered to the paper's editorial staff in Manchester. Geoffrey Taylor, who'd just joined the paper, remembers receiving a welcome consignment of tinned turkey, ham, butter, cheese and confectionery.

The biggest problem – in these early months of 1948 – was the BBC's declaration that an occasional contributor like Cooke could no longer expect an office of his own on the thirty-third floor of the Rockefeller Center. Cooke was reduced to the status of tenant, though he reassured the *Guardian* that it was still a cheap option. Any other office in Manhattan might cost four times as much. His letter of 16 January makes an urgent request for prompt payment of his salary on the 21st of each month: 'I find the expense of setting up the little outfit is depleting my balance badly, and there's almost nobody I'd rather hear from right now than your accountant.'

This letter also raises the question of Cooke's byline in the news-paper. It was still comparatively rare for correspondents to be named on a regular basis, but the *Guardian* had started to make exceptions for star performers like Cooke. This apparently caused him some embarrassment and he made the self-effacing suggestion that the compliment should be reserved for his longer pieces.

Wadsworth showed himself to be a patient admirer of his new man in New York, chiding him gently when necessary over the timing of his dispatches or his over-elaborate (and costly) cables. Although the editor was grateful for Cooke's story-ideas too, the notion of a report on Kinsey's survey of American sexual habits caused Manchester's alarm-bells to ring. 'I find it hard to think how you can put the really interesting facts in and yet preserve our reputation for decency! You know that discussion of these things is a good deal franker in New York than it is in England.' As for the money – well, he was sure it would all work itself out.

It did not. Cooke received $1329.92 on 20 January and waited for February's money in vain. By 18 March, he was desperate, having missed the deadline for income tax to be paid. 'I have many obligations which fall due on the first of every month, and you know that Americans have never had the gentlemanly tradition of stirring you in an apologetic way several months after bills are due.' He ventured the forceful view that it was 'extremely inconvenient to be paid six weeks or two months late'.

This tardiness never seems to have caused Cooke to waver in his new adherence to the *Guardian*, even when he was aggressively wooed by the *Observer* newspaper. 'They ogle and bow and spread "most attractive" propositions,' he confided to Wadsworth in May. 'Haven't bothered to reply yet, but I shall do next week, telling 'em please to lay off, I'm a married man and mean to stay so.' It was the first of many such blandishments from the *Guardian*'s competitors which he managed to resist, including one particularly pressing approach, a few years later, from Lord Beaverbrook. Providing they weren't talking about money or logistics, Cooke and the *Guardian* understood each other. By the end of 1948 his reputation would be fully established, thanks to a pulsating year for a political reporter, and the first scrawny flowerings of McCarthyism.

~

The prospect of the presidential election was absorbing on both sides of the Atlantic. There was a serious contest under way for the Republican nomination between Dewey and three challengers, while Democrats were confronted with a hard choice – whether to stick with President Truman, who was expected to stand no chance, or hope for some saving intervention from a popular figure like General Eisenhower who had, as yet, expressed no party allegiance. Cooke threw himself into the fray with gusto, seizing large quantities of scarce newsprint (the *Guardian* was allowed four pages on Mondays, Wednesdays and Fridays, and six on Tuesdays, Thursdays and Saturdays).

His profiles were vivid and entertaining, even if his predictions were finally as flawed as everyone else's. This was, after all, to be the election that broke the hearts of more psephologists than any other. Battle was joined when the Republicans rolled into Philadelphia on 21 June, convinced that they were going to nominate the next President for the first time in twenty years. The weather was steamy and most of the visitors rued the fact that the city had so comprehensively outbid San Francisco by offering its convention hall free of charge.

The Philadelphia experience was enlivened by the unexpected return to the press corps of H.L. Mencken. After a wartime in something approaching journalistic exile, the cantankerous 'Sage of Baltimore' had completed three volumes of his memoirs and – in the spring of 1948 – Supplement Two of *The American Language*. Mencken arrived in Philadelphia with his portable typewriter and pockets stuffed with 'enough cigars for a siege', and installed himself on the press benches: there he pecked out 'incomparably saucy sentences with that deliberate manual incompetence which is still one of the reporter's occupational vanities. Mencken carried it to the extreme of parody, hitting the keys only with his tiny forefingers and spacing with his right elbow, a routine that made him look like a bear cub imitating a drum majorette.' Cooke himself remained wedded to a small portable typewriter throughout his career, pounding away with two forefingers in unconscious tribute to his hero – though he did not go to the lengths of elbowing the space-bar.

The Turkish-bath atmosphere of the Convention hall, combined with the air-conditioning of his hotel room, gave Mencken a bad cold, and he left the city before the Republicans had nominated Governor Thomas Dewey to go through the formality of a one-sided election which would surely send President Truman into well-deserved obscurity. Wadsworth was delighted with Cooke's coverage of the event, which even received an unsolicited testimonial in the *New York Herald Tribune*. A review of foreign reporting of the Convention gave the *Guardian* its vote for 'erudition and intelligence' and Wadsworth purred his approval: 'How you can keep the sparkle up day after day, I don't know.'

Television was part of the explanation: Cooke had been struck by the fact that, while newspaper reporters were buried at the back of the set fifty feet behind the rostrum, television audiences had a perfect view of the proceedings. 'The NBC coverage was so devastatingly thorough, nosing all over the hall at the critical moments, leaping in a flash to each of the candidate's headquarters, playing over newsreel interviews taken a month or a year before . . . it made me feel like the old Tommies stuck in the trenches for months and writing home to know what the war was about.'

Cooke was one of the first to alert a British audience to the growing importance of the medium – a fact that was not lost on his masters back in London. There was still a debate about its potential, so that when Cooke opined in his *Letter* of 18 July that television was 'already as humble as a hot dog' in the States – in other words, food for the masses – he was widely quoted by the enthusiasts. The remark even found its way into Asa Briggs' *History of Broadcasting*: 'Most of the viewers would doubtless not have known what a hot dog was, but they would have corroborated (with remarkable speed) Alistair Cooke's prognosis that television was for the millions.'

More immediately, Cooke suggested to Wadsworth that he should cover most of the Democratic Convention, also due to be held in Philadelphia, from his TV screen. That proved to be an innovation too far and instead he managed to contrive himself a place in the press seats next to Mencken, who'd recovered from his fever but was still complaining about the air-conditioning as if it was some New Deal conspiracy.

As he watched Mencken type out his articles in triple space, 'on a ribbon that might well have been installed at the 1904 Convention', he particularly enjoyed the old man's description of a party organiser called Mrs Vredenburg, who lived up to the tradition that 'lady politicians shall resemble British tramp steamers dressed up for the King's birthday'. Mencken's was a style he admired – and imitated as far as he dared, though always within the bounds of north country respectability. For instance, on the Democrats' claims that the party would leave Philadelphia reinvigorated – 'It is a surface health and happiness that is applied by the artificial stimulation of the convention circus. It is an Elizabeth Arden treatment, a combination massage, Turkish bath and barber-shop tan. It tickles the muscles and capillaries, but leaves the dying tissue, the soul, untouched.'

The Convention nominated Truman after a final session lasting from 11.30 in the morning of 14 July until the small hours of the following day. 'What happened in these fifteen broiling hours was a tribute to the vitamin endowment of the American people,' Cooke wrote. The *Guardian* sub-editor enjoyed the joke and inserted a cross-heading into this serious political article: 'Value Of Vitamins'.

Unusually, 1948 brought a third Convention to attract the journalistic caravanserai. Henry Wallace's Progressive party occupied Philadelphia in their turn, intent on breaking the two-party mould. When confronted with the reality of the Progressives *en masse*, Cooke couldn't resist poking fun at the earnest oddities of these true believers in a third way: 'It is a slow-paced crowd, predominantly young, the men mostly with their shirt-collars open and folded back over their coat collars in the manner of an emancipated clerk setting out along Blackpool promenade, his sensitive head held high against the combined hazards of women and sarsaparilla. The women either have sandals and off-the-shoulder blouses, proclaiming a down-to-earth, no-nonsense approach, or have the piercing on-stage elegance of Greenwich Village *femmes fatales.*'

~

The Progressive party Convention was H.L. Mencken's last, as it turned out, before the crippling stroke which immobilised him later that year. Cooke spent a great deal of time with him in Philadelphia. The *Guardian* had reciprocal deals with the *Baltimore Sun*, which threw them together, and he sat back revelling in Mencken's expostulations against the lunacies on show – the plans to nationalise the banks, the railroads and the merchant marine, and the determination to scrap the Marshall Plan, abolish state taxes and end the colonial system.

Exactly four months later, Mencken's stroke seemed certain to have killed him at the age of sixty-eight. Cooke dashed off a lengthy obituary of his friend – some 4000 words in all – causing consternation at the *Guardian*: Wadsworth sent him a laconic cable: 'Many thanks. Hope he dies Tuesday, Thursday or Saturday.' Fortunately for all concerned, Mencken survived, after a fashion, until newsprint-rationing was a distant memory.

After the frenetic atmosphere of Philadelphia, Cooke pleaded time off to 'visit his stepchildren in camp in upstate New York'. Whether Stephen was especially glad to see him must be open to question, but Cooke was presumably doing his best within the limits of his inability to enjoy the company of small children. The man who ran the camp was the gym teacher from the Dalton School in New York (known as 'Muscle'): he once asked Stephen whether he spent much time with his father. 'Yeah,' Stephen told him, 'we often go to the movies.'

The teacher, clearly a believer in the principle of *mens sana in corpore sano*, had a suggestion: 'Gee, maybe you oughtta say sometimes, "Hey, pop, how about ten minutes catch and *then* a movie?" ' The idea of his stepfather with a baseball glove sent the boy into fits of laughter and Cooke, too, when he was told the story. But 'Muscle' had a point. He had correctly diagnosed Cooke's failure to relate to

Stephen – and the problem was magnified when it came to Johnny.

However much he knew – thanks to the psychoanalysis – that his own son was crying out for warmth and affection, he was temperamentally incapable of delivering it. He found outward displays of emotion as hard as speaking Chinese, and became more convinced than ever that this was a hangover from his own childhood. His experience in England – which he felt was echoed in Germany and to a certain extent in the United States, reaching its apogee in Vietnam – was that Northerners always resisted what he called the 'social floridity' of the South. 'Just consider the way those Silesian schoolteachers, in 1931, despised the behaviour of the Bavarians, and think of the fatal sentimentality of the South Vietnamese.' But he also knew that this was at best an explanation, not an excuse.

Was it in this summer of 1948 that he visited Johnny, too, who'd been packed off to a different camp in the west of Massachusetts? He remembers being taken one day for a picnic by a stream, an event so rare that it was never forgotten. However much Cooke hoped that psychoanalysis had given him the ability to rebuild fractured relationships, the seeds were still being sown for a lifetime of misunderstanding between father and son.

~

By coincidence, August saw the publication in London of a lengthy dissertation by Cooke on the subject of 'Psychiatry in the United States'. It appeared – with top billing – in Cyril Connolly's *Horizon* magazine (the 'Review of Literature and the Arts') and represents Cooke's tribute to the techniques of psychotherapy which had restored his own peace of mind. The article displays a decent academic gloss and is the fruit of some serious research: he interviewed a number of distinguished figures in the field, such as Edward Glover, the last man to be analysed by Freud himself. He even investigated the state of mental hospitals in Maryland.

Cooke traces the progress in the United States of the great – and often internecine – struggle between the neurologists (seeking medical prescriptions for mental illness) and the Freudians, offering treatment through analysis. Indeed, the burden of the piece is a plea for the proper understanding of the work of the analyst, which was still widely mistrusted in Europe: 'The intellectual in analysis . . . has usually to learn to shed a favourite conceit: that neurosis is a precious, and fertile, monopoly of the greatly endowed. Alas the past thirty years of American analytic practice have demonstrated beyond all vanity that neurotics are of all sorts, and that the same neuroses occur in the illiterate as the scholar, in the urban rich and the rural poor, in the failing and the successful, the talented and the dull.' In the Land of the Free, then, all psyches are equal on the couch.

Cooke is careful not to indulge himself with stories of his own experiences, except in the most oblique way. No stranger reading the piece will have guessed that it was anything more than a straightforward journalistic exercise. Even references to the cost of analysis are framed in terms of regret that such a valuable resource was available to so few sufferers, rather than as a complaint about the heavy financial burden of his own two years of treatment at a time when he could ill afford such fees.

Knowing what he went through, it is possible to read some of Cooke's conclusions as statements of personal gratitude. And he ends with a petition to the politicians that psychiatry should be brought into the mainstream of public health care. 'It is not the creative patience, the range of ability, or the psychiatric leadership that is waiting to make American psychiatry the best, perhaps the last, promise of liberty and the pursuit of happiness. It is the convinced support of Government, at a time when the United States is blessed with a Congress whose declared intention is to "balance the budget", whatever the imbalance of security and health this may entail.'

At a greater distance in time, Cooke came to take a much more detached view of psychoanalysis as 'the confessional of the agnostic' rather than the cure-all proclaimed in his *Horizon* article. He never lost his faith in the way Freud had enabled him to shed so much intellectual baggage, thus helping him to establish a writing and broadcasting style of striking directness; but his own relationships, especially with his children, were a testament to the limitations of his treatment.

~

In the same month as the appearance of the *Horizon* article, Cooke found himself reporting a volatile session of the House Committee on Un-American Activities. The Committee had been given a new lease of life with the injection of funds from the Republican majority in Congress – which doubtless hoped that a high-profile witch-hunt for communists within the old New Deal establishment might be very handy in an election year. At that moment Cooke had no idea how his own life and work would become so bound up in the fate of Alger Hiss, President of the respected Carnegie Endowment, who had just appeared before the Committee.

On 29 August, he reported on Hiss's attempts to defend himself against accusations that 'he used his high office during the war to infect the Administration with the political doctrine that is at present more dreaded than any other mortal plague, save only infantile paralysis'. Hiss was a supremely respectable figure – a protégé in the 1930s of such pillars of the community as Mr Justice Holmes and Dean Acheson, and the man chosen to be Secretary-General to the founding conference of the UN in San Francisco. Yet he stood accused, by a *Time* journalist, Whittaker Chambers, of being a committed member of the communist underground, known to his fellow travellers as 'Carl'. Cooke noted that the testimony of Hiss and Chambers was so strikingly at odds, that one of them – in the words of a Committee member – had to be 'the damnedest liar that has appeared on the American scene'.

Having learned the lesson of Philadelphia, Cooke watched the proceedings on television, admiring the intimate access granted to the observer. The cameras settled frequently on 'the intensely, darkly handsome Richard Nixon', one of the most tenacious of the Committee's questioners.

Even at this early stage of the affair, Cooke acknowledged that Hiss's answers to vital questions were often unconvincing or inconsistent – a fact which would cause Hiss huge problems as the case developed into a sensational spy scandal. For the time being, the Committee's findings were to be turned over to the Department of Justice for a decision on whether Hiss should face a Grand Jury and Cooke moved on to other assignments, still some months away from the day when he would have to put his judgement of Alger Hiss on the line.

～

Before the election campaign began, Cooke found himself subjected to his own small trial by media. Out of the blue, the American correspondent of London's *Sunday Pictorial* decided to pen a virulent attack on 'SEVEN FAMOUS MEN WHO TURNED THEIR BACKS ON BRITAIN'. One was Alistair Cooke, though he found himself in the elevated company of film stars such as Ray Milland and Cary Grant. The sub-heading left no doubt about the sentiment of the writer: 'They Could Not Have Reached Fame Without The Patronage Of The British Public, But They Have Sworn Allegiance To America'. 'It seems incredible,' the piece began, 'that any Briton should publicly renounce allegiance to his homeland, and then take an oath of loyalty to a foreign country.'

Cooke was torn between dismissing this as the maundering of an editor with an axe to grind filling space on a quiet news day, and bridling at the imputation of disloyalty. That the article touched a nerve seems clear from the fact that he used his *American Letter* of 12 September to answer the charges at some length. First item for the defence: what about all those great American figures ready to make the opposite choice – Henry James and T.S. Eliot, to name but two? None the less, he undertakes to proffer some possible explanations. 'I'd like to recall the various dilemmas of men I've known who've changed their citizenship and told me, as best they could, why. I say "as best they could" because a man who knows right off the bat why he does fundamental things seems to me to be a suspicious character, and one well worth watching.' There speaks the Freudian convert. Among the possible reasons for Americans becoming British: those seeking better business opportunities, careers as character actors, or an escape from the 'trade' which gave them their fortunes; scholars of English Literature needing to be close to their sources, or romantics yearning to be close to the objects of their affection.

And in the other direction? Any of the above motives might apply, and in any case, he reminds his audience, all Americans – apart from indigenous Indians – were immigrants of one sort or another. Any listeners waiting for Cooke's own motives to be revealed found their questions answered in the most roundabout way: 'In an anxious age, there is nothing quite so attractive and irresponsible,' he suggests,

> as the life of an expatriate, or a foreign correspondent, who can sit back far from home, complain about the weird customs and inconveniences and corruption of the country he lives in, and yet use his distant citizenship to excuse him from taking on any burdens of the people he lives with. In such people, the label 'citizenship', whether it is foreign or domestic, is a travesty of the word. They do the least they can for both countries.

Shortly before Cooke left for America, he and Hetty had a series of studio-portraits taken to ease the pain of parting: the pictures also appeared in the *Blackpool Gazette*, which boldly referred to Hetty Riddle as 'Mr Henry Ainley's Daughter'.

The Commonwealth Fellows sailed on the *Laconia* in September 1932. Two of Cooke's travelling companions, Sandy Honeyman (third from the right) and Charles Spencer (second left), were destined to accompany Cooke on his first motoring tour of America. Cooke himself is fourth from the left.

Above Justice Oliver Wendell Holmes, who attended the White House performance of the Hasty Pudding Club in 1934, became one of Cooke's greatest American heroes.

Left After a disappointing year at Yale, Harvard was much more to Cooke's taste. Francis D. Moore (Franny) is on his right.

Below Rehearsing the notorious production of *Cymbeline* by the Unnamed Players which proved fatal to a conservative critic.

This is probably the English coat which caused such hilarity amongst Cooke's peers at Harvard – reminding them of something likely to be worn by 'the foreman of a retired railroad gang in Siberia'.

One evening, in a break from work on a film script, Charlie Chaplin took Cooke and another friend for a meal in the Japantown district of Los Angeles. Chaplin was spotted, and pressganged into posing for this bizarre photo. The cause of the celebration is not recorded.

Above Andy (the skipper of the *Panacea*), Chaplin and Paulette Goddard. Cooke sent the picture as a postcard to his mother.

Right For a great director, Chaplin might have been expected to do better with this shot of Paulette and Cooke.

Above The postponed wedding party. Paulette's good cheer (right) was soon dispelled when a grumpy Chaplin, disenchanted with the floor-show, announced on the way home that 'one night a year was quite enough of that rubbish'.

Left Joan Charles, a source of more than merely dramatic interest for Cooke at Cambridge?

Ruth and Alistair spent a month with friends in Ibiza in the summer of 1935.

Norman Parkinson

Ruth's modelling career thrived until the
couple returned to live in America in 1937,
and she was much in demand for
magazines such as *Harper's* and *Vogue*.

Back in America, Cooke's early
months as a full-time resident
were dominated by his weekly
broadcast for NBC's Red
Network, just after the
Wednesday evening news.

At weekends Cooke would join
Ruth at the Emerson's family
home at Southold on Long
Island, often bringing a friend
for the weekend. This study, at
a soda fountain along the way,
was taken by his psychiatrist
friend from Yale, Gerry Hartz.

Sunday dinner at Southold, Summer 1941. The family tribe is supervised by
Dr Haven Emerson (with his back to camera). Alistair and Ruth are near the door,
with John – aged seven or eight months – between them.

Above Dr Haven Emerson,
Cooke's erstwhile father-in-law
and the man he described in an
obituary tribute as 'one of the
last of the great Puritans.'

Above Surf-fishing on a Long Island beach, and therefore on the Atlantic coast.
Cooke was vexed when this photo appeared in a magazine back to front:
an English audience, he reckoned, would assume that a man facing to the
left must be paddling in the Pacific.

One in the eye for the man from the *Sunday Pictorial*. But Cooke hasn't finished yet; what about the nagging question of the war? The next paragraph is definitely intended as a description of his own state of affairs:

> I knew Englishmen who were far gone with preparations for American citizenship, who had in fact already taken out their first papers, who renounced their intentions and offered their services to Britain. Whether those services were accepted in the straightforward way they were offered – I mean to fight in the armed services – depended a good deal on what sort of work they were already doing. Some were doing well here and gave up everything, and they need no praise from me. Some were doing badly, and leapt at the chance to be vigorously and dangerously useful. Many were told to stay where they were; many with a genuine romantic impulse were told to their sorrow that however fine and fit they felt, the best service they could do for Britain was to stay on in their job here.

That was Cooke's intellectual rationalisation for remaining in the United States when war broke out and, as the years wore on, he certainly came to believe it was true.

The *Letter* ends with the earnest hope that listeners will appreciate the complexity of his position and its possible value to the cause of transatlantic goodwill:

> In my case, since my own career is to try and explain this country to Britain, I have no sort of fame in this land. I'm simply 'Cooke of the *Guardian*' – a title I am as proud of as any that goes with citizenship. . . . So pardon me if I leave you now, thread my way through a picket line outside my office – the so-called Sons of Liberty boycotting British goods – and pitch in to the other half of my double life, and say a good word for Mr Attlee, and the British colonies, Mr Churchill, cricket and the women of England.

Alistair's and Jane's domestic routine was now well-established. Cooke had had a teletype machine installed at the house on Long Island, which meant that he could keep in constant touch with the news at weekends and file reports from the seaside when necessary. And there was a regular flow of guests through the apartment on East 71st Street, including Cooke's former Cambridge tutor, Basil Willey, who had taken over Q's chair of English Literature. He described in his memoirs having followed Cooke's 'meteoric rise to Anglo-

American fame' and his pleasure at being invited to dinner 'in a luxurious apartment' where the meal came 'complete with coloured maid service'. He also noted Cooke's refined American accent, 'adopted with such characteristic finesse so as to offend neither American nor British ears.'

Soon afterwards, the *American Letter* was pressed into service so that Cooke could offer a touching, if oblique, tribute to Jane's abilities as a hostess. 'I hope nobody will cry "Chauvinism!",' he remarked, 'if I say that American women, on the whole, have a flair for entertaining.' Indeed one of his abiding themes during that late summer and autumn was the way rampant inflation was making life hard for American families trying to maintain high housekeeping standards: if British listeners assumed that life in New York was a bed of roses, they'd be very much mistaken.

> What [the casual visitor] cannot see, which strikes me who am deep in this sort of life, is that the woman's pleasure, her standard of elegance and such leisure as she enjoys, is gained at the expense of her own slavery. 'Come back tomorrow morning', I feel like saying to these scrutinising visitors, or 'what a pity you didn't turn up an hour before supper, and see the labour, the drudgery, and the imagination that made your pleasant evening.'

Jane herself is allowed a brief personal appearance in this *Letter*, urging Cooke to mention that she had only bought beef twice in the previous year, and that some of the Americans who sent food parcels to Europe did so at a very real sacrifice to their budget and their family expenses. Cooke did indeed plan to send Christmas food parcels, once more, to the *Guardian* staff in Manchester who handled his copy, having asked Wadsworth's advice: 'Would it be thought condescending, too much the US Lady Bountiful? I could run up to about a dozen if you'd promptly send me their names and addresses.' More movingly, Ruth Cooke had not forgotten her abandoned sister-in-law, Elsie, in Blackpool. Elsie's daughter Kathleen still has a label stored in a box of family mementoes, describing the contents of the Christmas box they received. It was addressed to 'Mrs Sam Cooke, at 29 Bordman Avenue': nuts, rice, strawberry and apricot jam, raisins, chocolate, bacon, chicken, sugar, liver pâté and veal – total value $8.52.

In any other presidential year, September would have been too frantic for much socialising. 1948 was different. Rarely in the history of the western democracies has there been an election which so utterly confounded the experts as that between the incumbent Harry S. Truman and Governor Dewey of New York. Cooke was no exception to the general mood that this was one of the most predictable, and therefore most boring, campaigns imaginable. On 10 September, still more than seven weeks away from polling day, he wrote to Wadsworth, 'I'd like very much to know just how fully you'd like me to cover the campaign. There seems absolutely no doubt that the race is already won.' Consequently, Cooke thought he should stick close to the next President, the Republican Thomas Dewey, and felt it wouldn't be worthwhile traipsing across to the West Coast with his no-hope opponent. Wadsworth agreed.

Cooke was simply following the journalistic herd in assuming that the outcome was beyond doubt – especially when the trusted poll by Elmo Roper for *Fortune* magazine showed Dewey with a thirteen per cent lead, enough to secure him a landslide on the scale of Roosevelt's in 1936. Should Dewey even bother to go through with the ritual campaign train trip, Cooke wondered in the pages of the *Guardian*? By mid-October he was penning an *American Letter* about the mechanics of the voting system, in particular the unfamiliar (to the British) poll booth with its levers for each candidate. 'Mr Dewey will ask no more on Tuesday than that he shall become the mechanical man – the name that more millions of people will register on the voting machine than any other. From all reports, there's no doubt that he will be.'

Things were to get much worse still.

As the campaign reached its uninspiring end, Cooke reported for the *Guardian* on Dewey's final rally in New York's Madison Square Garden. So well-organised was the event (the headline read – 'DEWEY'S FINE STAGECRAFT'), that every second was accounted for in the build-up to the hero's arrival. Then the actor Robert Montgomery instructed the audience of 20,000 to strike a match on the count of three,

> and for a marvellous moment the Garden twinkled from the floor to the rafters, while an assistant local fire commissioner was treated for heart failure. . . . Suddenly the Governor glided on, chin high, teeth gleaming,

blue suit immaculate. To the split second he started his last campaign speech and ended precisely twenty-nine minutes and thirty seconds later, as the programme said he would. . . . Whatever else he is not, Mr Dewey is certainly the best one-man-band in America.

It was the unforgiving time difference that really rubbed salt in Cooke's wounds. The Dewey piece appeared in the paper of 1 November, the eve of the election. In the same edition there was a second contribution by the paper's American correspondent, entitled 'HARRY S. TRUMAN – A STUDY OF A FAILURE'. In two elegant columns (under a helpful paragraph explaining: 'the Presidential election takes place tomorrow. President Truman is expected to be heavily defeated'), Cooke gave his considered verdict on what had gone wrong. There were no weasel words – no 'ifs' or 'assuming that'. Truman, he reckoned, had been a man with decent instincts, wedded to the better principles of the New Deal, but with a fatal tendency to political misjudgement. And so it went on.

On the morning of the poll itself, Cooke's article noted that the Democrats were already packing up their Washington effects at the end of 'the brief, unhappy reign of Harry S. Truman'. A few hours later they were unpacking again. Truman had won by two million votes.

In his special election programme for the BBC, Cooke was contrite: 'The totally unexpected performance of the country boy, who everybody said was much too small for Roosevelt's shoes, has been called by the United Press "the political miracle of the century" and accordingly, everybody who writes and talks over the radio is at this minute the colour of a really fine English garden tomato.'

He wasn't the only one to wonder whether he should resign from sheer shame, but the communal embarrassment didn't ease the pain. 'Dewey and Truman', he wrote to Wadsworth, 'will haunt me till I die. Not that the result changes much in that profile of him. I fear greatly for the next four years.'

Ironically, historians later judged that one of the most significant elements of Truman's victory was that much-discounted campaign-train journey – the last great 'whistle-stop' tour before television finally took over the business of electioneering. It enabled him (according to Hugh Brogan's Penguin History) to get across in person 'his pugnacity, his good humour, and his partisan loyalty' as a counterbalance to the slickness of Dewey, who came to look like 'the little man on the wedding-cake'.

None of which was much comfort at the time, either for journalists or pollsters. 'Here we had come to accept Mr Roper's poll as a scientific discovery, as unquestionable as electricity or the force of gravity. . . . It is, in fact, as if word had gone out over the radio that there's been a slight slip-up in the fundamental theory of Sir Isaac Newton.' A week later he was still trying to puzzle it out and had lighted on the 'profound truth' that 'America was a middle-class nation which simply didn't like the well-oiled Dewey machine promoting a man who (in the words of the film star Tallulah Bankhead) never had a gravy-stain on his coat.'

Cooke's prediction of his own perpetual haunting was accurate and the story became one of the leitmotivs of his *Letters*, to be wheeled out every now and again like an original sin in the ear of a Father Confessor. The message was simple: he would treat any invitation to predict the outcome of a political contest with the same savour as the chance to cuddle a rattlesnake. In 1968, for instance, he toyed with advising listeners that Richard Nixon was bound to beat Lyndon Johnson, but was soon deterred: 'I should like to recall once more . . . the great crime of A. Cooke on the morning of the first Tuesday in November in 1948 . . . '; and again, four years later, resisting the temptation to regard Nixon's re-election as a *fait accompli*: 'Those who survived [1948] are loath to say that this year's election, with Nixon showing an overwhelming lead in the polls of 64–30 per cent, is a foregone thing.'

Although Cooke committed himself to a lifetime of abstinence from political prediction, he soon renewed his interest in opinion polls – especially as they began to offer a wealth of more or less trivial detail about American life. He himself had suggested to Dr George Gallup during 1948 that he conduct a survey of social attitudes – and he used some of the findings to contradict an aggressive English critic. In response to the allegation that 'New Yorkers are so restless in their nightly pursuit of diminishing pleasures, that the lonely heart of man cannot come here', Gallup discovered – and Cooke was glad to pass on the fact – that only one New Yorker in fifteen had ever been to a night-club, while ninety-two per cent were in bed by ten-thirty each night.

Alistair and Jane were, naturally, to be counted in the eight per cent of night-owls, though the pace of their lives slowed a little when Jane became pregnant.

~

The baby was born on 22 March, 1949. To everyone's relief (whether stated openly or not) it was a girl. Susan was a welcome addition to the family, a child with what amounted to four adoring parents, since her brother and sister were so much older. The pressure for space inside the apartment became so acute that the baby soon found herself carted round in Holly's doll's carriage or deposited in an Idaho potato box somewhere out of the way. There was still room for the piano, however. Indeed, on the night that Jane was rushed off to the maternity hospital, Cooke had been sent home for a while to await developments and idled the time away at the piano: on the disc of his finest musical moments ('An Evening with Alistair Cooke') he told the story of what happened. 'The doctor said, there's no point your going into labour if *she* isn't. So I slunk off home, the loneliest man in the world, and came up with a tune. It takes thirty seconds to play, and took about six hours to compose. We've since called it, "Janey in the Hospital".' It's a simple, melodious piece, with only the faintest hint of that ornamentation against which Jelly Roll Morton had so earnestly advised him.

Music was still a great relaxer for Cooke in the midst of the domestic turmoil. So, too, were the movies. During 1949 he was called out of the blue by the Paramount office in New York. In a panelled office high above Times Square, an executive asked whether Cooke would like to repeat the role he'd played before the war on *The March of Time*, this time for a feature film starring Bob Hope. *Sorrowful Jones* began with a long tracking shot up the Manhattan shore-line, over which a narrator introduced this story of a race-track tout. The narrator, the journalist Walter Winchell, had an instantly recognisable voice, but only – as Paramount had come to realise – within the United States. Cooke's tones were thought to be much more suitable for a British audience. He agreed immediately. How much would he charge for such a service? With nothing much to work on, he plucked the figure of $200 out of the air. The executive raised an eyebrow. He'd been looking into the *March of Time* arrangements, which were fifty-minute programmes. The narration would be just seven minutes in total. Perhaps $150? Cooke steeled himself and stuck stubbornly to the higher fee. With a corporate sigh it was settled and the contract, for all non-American distribution, was signed. Cooke gave himself a quiet pat on the back for the toughness of his negotiating stance.

Two years later, he happened to go to California on a trip with a BBC colleague who wanted to see Hollywood. Cooke arranged for a visit to a film set, a meeting with Chaplin, and a lunch with Paramount's press chief. Before they sat down to eat their host inquired whether Cooke would like to see the overall budget for *Sorrowful Jones*. He flicked through a thick file of papers until he found the outline budget: total, $2,020,200.

'What's this?' Cooke asked.

'Well the $20,000 is Winchell's fee . . . ' The press officer didn't need to complete the sentence. 'Sorry about that,' he said, clearly enjoying the joke. 'They'll never use you again, you know. Anyone who asks $200 – there must be something wrong with him.'

~

The trauma of the election may have taken Cooke's mind off two notable anniversaries at the end of 1948. The first was his own fortieth birthday. Then, on the following day, 21 November, the BBC broadcast '*American Letter* Number 100': the producer in London, incidentally, was a young man named Charles Curran – who went on to become the organisation's Director-General.

The centenary *Letter* caused Cooke to reflect on the purpose of what he was doing. He first claimed to have been taken aback at the way the landmark had been reached in a series which, he felt instinctively, was 'just getting into its stride'. 'It calls for some sort of celebration, I hope, and while I don't intend to go mock-modest on you and say what I've been trying to do in these *Letters* (because if you've heard some and don't know what they're about, then you never will – for I have failed), I think this is a good time to put in an appeal for some dramatist or film-writer – I think they'd be best – to make the effort of representing to the people of the United States the human experience of living in Britain in these days.' The thought had come to him after watching a new British play portraying a wealthy household replete with butlers, private secretaries and maids, in which the Labour government was the butt of cheap laughs for allowing these basic amenities of life to decline.

Cooke's thesis was that American play-goers might take unjustified comfort from these images. The country, he argued, was still plagued with nagging guilt over the way the war had left it comparatively unscathed – and would quickly latch on to any proof that things weren't quite so dismal in Europe after all. 'Such people go to this play, and they say, "Well, no lack of household help there – and champagne too! What's this about the Marshall Plan and austerity?"' It was the old dilemma of distance: austerity was 'a word in a newspaper three thousand miles away. They do not know what it smells like, what it looks or tastes like; what it does to human labour, to bringing up families, to love, health and humour. And I'm simply saying I think it's time somebody told them.'

While Americans had trouble dragging their ideas of Britain out of the Edwardian era, Cooke was sure that – even after a hundred of his *Letters* – the British had an equally false notion of the way Americans lived. Which was just as well, since there would otherwise be no point in carrying on with the *Letters*.

18

NEW GENERATION

The first trial of Alger Hiss, on two charges of perjury, began at 11.30 a.m. on Tuesday, 31 May 1949. The Statute of Limitations meant that he could not be charged with espionage, but in reality it was still a spy trial. The indictment stated that Hiss had lied to a Grand Jury the previous December, when he denied handing over secret documents to Whittaker Chambers before the war. In order to prove their case, prosecutors would have to demonstrate that Hiss had in fact been a Communist agent. Their strongest evidence was the batch of classified documents produced by Chambers, written on a typewriter which had once belonged to Hiss.

Cooke was fascinated by the case from the start. Having attended the District Court in New York on the first day, he wrote in the *Guardian* about another case taking place in a court across the square: eleven Communist leaders were facing charges which would determine whether membership of the party was, of itself, proof of a desire to overthrow the government of the United States. 'In the public mind the two trials set up a riptide in the ocean of fear and distrust that washes across all American discussion of Communism.' And, at an entirely different level, 'the degree of mystery that surrounds the personal relationship of two brilliant young men (Hiss and Chambers) has made this trial fascinating to people uninterested in the legal issue and made it read so far like an unwritten novel by Arthur Koestler.'

Much was already known about the protagonists, thanks to a series of preliminary court appearances – in particular, the Grand Jury hearings in December, when it had already begun to occur to Cooke that Hiss might represent something far beyond the confines of the charges against him. As a result, he dedicated himself to following the proceedings, even when they dragged on far beyond the fortnight originally set aside. For six long weeks he hardly missed an hour of evidence. And after the jury had failed to reach a verdict, Cooke was back in the press seats five months later for the second trial. Day after day, he sent off columns of copy to the *Guardian*, where Wadsworth was ready to indulge his obsession. No other British paper showed remotely the same interest. At the end of it all, most reporters would have been only too pleased to let the subject drop; instead, Cooke leaped at the offer to write a book about the Hiss case, which appeared in the spring of 1951 under the title *A Generation on Trial*. It is a remarkable work and unlike anything he attempted before or afterwards. It is both straightforward reportage – a clever distillation of the mountains of evidence – but also a psycho-drama, what in later times might have been called a docu-thriller.

Before getting down to the details of the trial, the book offers a lengthy preamble in which Cooke develops his thesis – that Hiss had become the symbol of a wider battle. The House Committee on Un-American Activities, in which Senator Joseph McCarthy was making his name, was eager to seize on any proof that the post-war Communist menace had its roots in those liberals who had created Roosevelt's New Deal in the 1930s. In this context, Committee members such as Richard Nixon sought to portray Hiss as a naïve intellectual, ripe for recruitment by the country's enemies.

'Hiss was almost unknown in the public eye,' Cooke wrote, 'although the subsequent craving for a full-blooded New-Dealer transmuted him in no time into the protector of great statesmen, and President Roosevelt's high-policy adviser at Yalta.' The Yalta Conference, according to many Republicans, was where Roosevelt had sold out to Stalin: what more likely than that Hiss had used his influence to speak up for his masters in Moscow? And had he not also played a decisive role in offering concessions to the Soviets at the founding conference of the United Nations?

It would have been very surprising if Cooke's instinctive sympathies had not lain with Alger Hiss, a man who represented the refined, intellectual 'liberalism' of his own background and that of the newspaper which employed him. While the House Committee, scrabbling around for sticks with which to beat political opponents, was a natural object of his derision and distrust. Yet Cooke set himself the task of laying aside his personal prejudice.

~

What makes the pages that follow so compelling is that Cooke manifestly does not know whether Hiss is guilty of espionage or not. His mood sways with the evidence, as it might in the mind of a juror. The tension is not just in the courtroom drama and suspense, but in the reporter's own transferred sense of uncertainty. As the trial itself proceeded, through June and July of 1949, with all thoughts of a book far in the future, he was utterly absorbed by the need to file his daily *Guardian* reports. The dramatic potential of the trial was heightened by the presence of several strong central characters – Hiss, Chambers and their respective wives; and the lawyers on either side, each with a propensity to impose his own personality on the proceedings.

The articles Cooke wrote for the *Guardian* were invaluable as source material, like an early draft of a novel. In the book he not only pulled the threads of the evidence together in narrative form, but was able to add the sort of colour which brought to life the courtroom scenes. Yet it was still avowedly an objective work. He informed the reader that he had no special insights into the inner lives of Hiss and Chambers since he had never met either of them. The closest he came to breaking this injunction was when he found himself in urgent need of a volume of the court transcript and in desperation phoned the home of Hiss's attorney Lloyd Stryker. He was told that he could come round and collect it. When he arrived – in a tropical rainstorm – Mrs Stryker greeted him at the door: 'Do come in,' she said, 'Alger and Priscilla Hiss are here.' Cooke apologised, explained his reluctance to meet the principals in the case and returned home in the rain.

When he started to construct *A Generation on Trial*, some of the key moments came raw from the pages of the paper, fleshed out with a few more lines of evidence here, or an added adjective there. But the effect is much more than anything that could have been achieved simply by stringing together a series of newspaper cuttings. One reason is that Cooke's fascination with the story – his anxiety to reach the denouement for his own satisfaction – draws the reader in.

～

The second trial began on 17 November, with a new judge and a new defence counsel. *A Generation on Trial* skims over those parts of the hearings where the old evidence is re-rehearsed; and Cooke himself was not such a religious attender, relying sometimes on the reports of other journalists. But he couldn't stay away for long and spent many more hours observing the unfolding drama, taking voluminous notes in an eccentric personal shorthand.

It became clear that important new evidence had been unearthed in the intervening months and on 21 January, the trial reached its climax. 'At twelve minutes to three this afternoon,' Cooke's *Guardian* report declared, 'the eighteen-month nightmare of Alger Hiss closed in on him and turned into reality.' Hiss was found guilty on both counts and was sentenced to five years in jail. Was it the outcome Cooke had privately come to expect? Did he think the jury had reached the right decision? As far as the reader can judge (because it is never stated) the evidence of the two trials wore away like a dripping tap at his natural sympathies for Hiss, leaving a permanent scar of doubt: but he certainly believed that, even if the charges were technically correct, they did not tell the whole story.

It was, as far as Cooke was concerned, a drama with a tragic ending, but the last few paragraphs of his book prove that his sympathy was not blind or unconditional. Even as he was writing *A Generation on Trial*, Klaus Fuchs was being sentenced in a British court for disclosing nuclear secrets to the Russians: this, he acknowledged, demonstrated that the Communist threat was real. The difficulty was to ensure that the innocent citizen did not get pinched between 'the reality of the threat and the epidemic fear of it'. As he correctly predicted, that fear would be brutally exploited by Senator McCarthy – his anti-Communist crusade galvanised by the convictions of Hiss and Fuchs.

The idea for a book on the case came from one of the leading figures in New York's publishing circles, Blanche Knopf: she contacted Cooke after reading an article he'd written in the magazine, *New Republic*, her eye having been caught by the title of the piece – *A Generation on Trial*. She told him that the family firm, Alfred Knopf, would be interested in pursuing and broadening that theme into a full-scale account of the Hiss story. The deal was struck after the second trial, with the stipulation that it be ready for publication in the autumn. Cooke sat down in the middle of March and began to write, hammering away until eleven each night before rewarding himself with an episode of *Perry Mason* and a nightcap. The job was completed, three hundred and thirty pages later, just ten days after the deadline of 1 May.

In relief and creative ecstasy he rang Jane, who was staying on Cape Cod, to tell her the good news. He intended, he said, to deliver the entire manuscript to Knopf the following day, then stretched back in his chair in the midst of the morass of papers, transcripts and reference books. Idly he leaned over to pick up and put away a large tome – and was stricken with an appalling back spasm which plagued him for the next eighteen months.

Listeners to the *American Letter*, naturally, had their own more homespun version of the Hiss story. They were invited to consider the contrast between the podgy, listless figure of Whittaker Chambers and the film-star looks of Alger Hiss – and then to cast it aside. They were given a dazzling pen portrait of six weeks of evidence from seventy witnesses, capturing what was most tangible and colourful: the fact that the stolen State Department papers were found hidden in an old pumpkin – and that the typewriter at the heart of the case had a give-away letter 'g', slightly distorted, which proved to be a crucial factor in the jury's decision.

~

Apart from that foray into hard news, the *Letter* continued to plough its own distinctive furrow. June 1949 saw the first full appearance of what became a familiar topic – the summer bachelor: it was a quirky theme which would vie for the honour of most-recycled *Letter*, second only, perhaps, to the wonders of the fall in New England. It embraced the threat posed to unprotected wardrobes by the all-consuming moth (as highlighted by the sponsors of Cooke's Commonwealth Fellowship). It went on to describe the fate of the working man abandoned by his family in the rancid heat of summer. 'Before they leave, they pack away the curtains, the bedspreads and his favourite chair and cover the rest of the furniture with old smelly slip-covers. . . . His wife leaves him with the warning that whenever he goes out he must see his garbage goes with him. He must draw the blinds and shut all the windows. The theory of all this is that the dust and sun will be kept out.'

In fact, according to Cooke, these defensive measures turned the apartment on East 71st Street into an uncongenial oven. 'In this lonely flat the telephone rings very seldom,' and when it does, invitations are made and promptly withdrawn when it's discovered that 'my wife doesn't live here any more'. He describes his ungainly efforts to make himself a sustaining breakfast of toast, coffee and diluted orange juice (though this is something of a distortion, since breakfast was the one meal on which Cooke particularly prided himself). Only on his outing to the office does this pathetic creature take on the semblance of a real man again, before returning to his lonely home where he reads 'parts of the newspaper he wouldn't think of reading in winter-time' – used-car offers and the results of trotting races. In truth this monastic lifestyle was rather to Cooke's taste: no disturbance for the late riser, no children's clutter and the chance to cultivate off-beat acquaintances with whom Jane would have no truck.

The *Letters* also keep up their plangent commentary on the state of Anglo-American relations. August brought another dollar crisis in Britain and another 'epidemic of ill-will'. American senators snarled about the idiocy of spoon-feeding Britain with hard-earned currency, while the British press bemoaned the hardening of attitudes in Washington towards the Labour government. And still holding the ring between the old sparring partners, Cooke found himself in February picking his way cautiously through a live broadcast on American reaction to the British election result – stressing that what Washington wanted was a strong government in London. He did not want to feed the suspicion that the return of another Labour administration would look to some Americans like Communism rampant.

That election broadcast, transmitted on 24 February 1950, had another claim to fame. For reasons that nobody can remember, it was billed not as *American Letter*, but *Letter from America*, the title which was to sustain the series for the rest of its life.

~

As Cooke grappled with the final chapters of *A Generation on Trial*, the editor of the *Manchester Guardian* arrived in New York on his first transatlantic visit. The timing was helpful. Cooke had just failed to meet his formal deadline, and Wadsworth told him he could abandon his daily reporting until the task was complete. It wasn't only Wadsworth who had to wait patiently for the completion of the Hiss book. During the previous year, Cooke had made contact with an old acquaintance from almost twenty years earlier – Rupert Hart-Davis, ex-actor and ex-husband of Peggy Ashcroft, who was now the proprietor of his own publishing house in London. He had suggested to Cooke that he should put together a collection of his *Letters* in book form – but the grinding process of compiling between three and five thousands words a day on Hiss had relegated the project to the pending file.

Even when *A Generation on Trial* was finished, further inter-ruptions intervened. What was supposed to be a quiet month in June was suddenly disrupted by the unexpected outbreak of hostilities in Korea which (as he wrote to Hart-Davis) 'threw me into a stew at the worst possible time'.

~

The start of the Korean War did not delay his first trip home under the auspices of the *Guardian*. He and Jane sailed on board the *Queen Mary* on 8 July 1950: in Southampton they rented a car for a scenic tour of the Wye Valley and the Cotswolds, before a rendezvous with Hart-Davis at a pub by the Thames a few days later. The rest of their four weeks' stay took in a flip to Paris and what Cooke called in one of his letters to Hart-Davis 'an accursed ten days in the north of England'. It was Jane's first visit to Blackpool, where her new parents-in-law – both now in their seventies – were still living in the same Ormond Avenue house. Cooke's brother, Sam, attended the reunion, too. One reason for the visitors' disenchantment was the Northern timetable of meals through the day – 'five or six', in Cooke's bloated recollection, 'what with "elevenses" and "tea" and "how about a cup of tea?"'

Once this chore had been completed, Alistair and Jane returned to the more congenial surroundings of what was to be (for many years) their favourite London hotel: the Dorchester. Here they entertained some of their British friends, including Hart-Davis and Wadsworth, who travelled down from Manchester for the occasion. Cooke hired a dining-room and terrace overlooking the park for the princely sum of fifteen guineas: one proviso was that, with rationing still in force, customers were required to provide their own wine. 'It was a great success,' Cooke recalls. 'A.P. became rather squiffy and started won-dering aloud what he was doing there, so far from his roots and the high-thinking, plain-living traditions of the *Manchester Guardian*. And then he decided he loved it.'

This encounter sealed the two men's mutual respect and affection and until Wadsworth's death in 1956, Cooke – as the *Guardian*'s man in New York – could do no wrong. One anecdote, quoted in the *Guardian* history by David Ayerst, encapsulates the respect in which

Cooke was held. When Stafford Cripps, the British Chancellor, devalued the pound in 1949, Cooke attended a Washington press conference on the subject alongside the paper's City Editor, R.H. Fry. Cooke's version of the story drew attention to the suffering that might be caused in some agricultural areas of the US if the British drive to win dollar exports was successful. A Minister at the British Embassy, Roger Makins, was furious and made a formal complaint to Fry that Cooke had 'let the side down'. The next day Wadsworth cabled his City Editor: 'Tell Makins, Cooke's job is to let the side down.'

~

Not long afterwards *A Generation on Trial* was published in the United States, and Hart-Davis followed this up with a British edition in November. In between these two events, Cooke was free with his advice about how the book should best be publicised. 'I hope and <u>pray</u> that you will do me the honour of letting my name stand naked and alone on the dust-cover,' he wrote to his publisher at the end of September, 'without any "*Manchester Guardian*" or "famous broadcaster" tags on it.'

A few days later he was proposing that Hart-Davis solicit 'encomiums' from such luminaries as 'Harold Nicolson; J.B. Priestley; Bertrand Russell? [Somerset] Maugham is over here and we have rushed a copy to him and hope he can stay awake long enough to read it and maybe say a good word.' He also gave an insight into his own sense of the book he'd created: despite its journalistic genesis, he told Knopf's salesmen that they shouldn't ignore the potential of fiction readers.

(a) This is a book for anyone interested in the tragedy of two husbands and two wives.

(b) This is a book which will challenge all whodunit addicts to bring in their own verdict.

An interviewer in the *New York Times* quoted Cooke as saying, 'I was trying to write a novel about a trial . . . but a true novel.' It seems a fair description of an unusual piece of work, but Cooke went further, suggesting that this was what foreign correspondents always did – 'write fiction that can be checked against the fact.' This was a highly unconventional description of the reporter's task, and the interviewer asked him to elaborate. 'What I wanted to do most in the book was to put the reader as a non-political animal in a courtroom and have him watch what happens to human beings when they judge each other. There is nothing more dramatic.' Had he really remained objective throughout? 'I suppose you can't help but hope that mercy comes in the nick of time. But it had nothing to do with Hiss. Nothing could be further from the truth than that I think charity ought to be brought to traitors.'

The Hart-Davis edition of *A Generation on Trial* appeared on 20 November, Cooke's forty-second birthday, in a bold green and red dust-cover with a picture of the author on the back, reading a BBC script. The blurb straggles curiously from the front cover to the inside flaps: there are no celebrity encomiums. Despite the author's helpful advice, the book struggled to make an impression in Britain. J.B. Priestley's failure to provide an encouraging review, Cooke feared, might have something to do with 'the razzing I gave him in a broadcast three years ago'. He still had hopes of Somerset Maugham, who (after 'an agreeable hour' of chat) had promised to read the book on the boat back to England.

The reviewers on both sides of the Atlantic found it an intriguing book, but couldn't agree on its value. Was it history or not? Could serious analysis of such a political trial be presented as a thriller? It was the preamble, rather than the story itself, that caused the trouble, especially in the United States. The young historian Arthur M. Schlesinger (later special assistant to President Kennedy) wrote in the *Saturday Review*: 'Mr Cooke runs wild in his endeavour to demonstrate that the New Deal was a kind of pro-Soviet *front populaire*, in which Alger Hiss was just a bit more activist than the rest. His facts are inaccurate, his logic is faulty and even his prose, ordinarily crisp and incisive, becomes in his opening chapter diffuse and garrulous.'

By dramatic contrast, the *New Yorker* called it 'not only the finest report of the case, but one of the best descriptions of an American political event that has ever been written'. Harold Nicolson, venerable critic and biographer, was similarly bowled over. 'No man could handle this fascinating and important story with greater balance and discrimination than Mr Alistair Cooke. He was present throughout both trials and, in that he is one of the most gifted of living descriptive writers, he enables us to take part in the drama and share his distress. . . . His account is vibrant with life. Behind it all one is conscious of an anguished common-sense. I congratulate him on a most intelligent and moving book.' The criminologist Edgar Lustgarten loved it and the future Labour Party guru, Dick Crossman, offered a lengthy tribute in the *New Statesman*. There is no evidence that Somerset Maugham made good his promise to cast his vote in either direction.

~

In the midst of the excitement of the book launch the Cookes were made an offer of a new apartment. 114 East 71st Street was becoming increasingly impractical for a family which included a ten-year-old boy, an older sister and a crawling toddler. Cooke described the scene in a *Letter from America*:

> It was a place of bends and twists, and crazy and endearing in other ways. Every bedroom had a wash-basin and cupboards built in. . . .what with the cracking plaster, a whole sagging rhomboid in our bedroom ceiling so that you never knew if you'd wake up successfully or not . . . it was so broken down when I first saw it – when my wife was living there as a war widow – that in a rush of pity and chivalry I said to her, 'Marry me and let me take you away from all this.'

Susie was the last straw. For a while she slept in the same room as Stephen, but she kept him awake and was shifted into the dining-room. The solution was to move to a familiar building twenty-five blocks further north: 1150 Fifth Avenue, the very place where Cooke had once lived with Ruth. That original apartment was now occupied by their Long Island friends the Burrowses, and it was probably they who alerted Alistair and Jane to the availability of another apartment – this time on the top floor, overlooking Central Park. The symmetry of this arrangement was completed when, some time later, Ruth and Johnny moved into 114 East 71st Street, which Alistair and Jane had just vacated.

Moving day was fixed for 1 December on the understanding that Alistair would take time off work, but the plan fell foul of events. It had been reported in Britain that President Truman was considering the use of nuclear weapons in Korea. This caused consternation amongst MPs in London and before long Prime Minister Attlee announced that he was flying to Washington to reason with the President. The panic, in Cooke's eyes, was completely unjustified – an almost wilful over-reaction to an innocent remark at a Washington press conference. But that didn't alter the fact that Cooke would have to station himself in the capital for the duration of the Attlee visit.

Cooke was rapidly becoming a profound pessimist about the chances of avoiding a nuclear war. In a letter to Hart-Davis on 3 January 1951 he wrote (apparently from the heart), 'Is there any hope, or point, in publishing the *Letters* with the oncoming war? I guess we must live as if it were 1919 and our lives were ahead of us.' This sense of resignation never really left him and resurfaced whenever international tension was greatest – most notably during the Cuban missile crisis. It may well have lain at the root of his gradual conversion to a more complex political standpoint: distinctly hawkish on foreign policy, yet with an abiding sense of his liberal roots in many areas of social policy.

As Cooke pursued his story in Washington through the first week of December, it was left to Jane to supervise the move to Fifth Avenue, which would be their home for the rest of their lives. Thankfully, he told BBC listeners, she was 'a veteran work-horse': only the day before she had 'walked into this shambly place – big as Grand Central Station – cleaned it out, swept and washed it, plastered odd holes in the living-room walls, sized it, mixed the paint and painted it.' She had also helped her husband pack his disparate and disorganised belongings, unearthing such treasures as a much dry-cleaned cheque, drawn five years earlier on a London bank, and moulded to the pocket of an old shirt. Jane, he said, 'resented Mr Attlee who took me off to Washington just when I might have been some use as a stevedore and plumber's mate.' (Though not *much* use, with his bad back and lack of interest in household practicalities.) When he returned four days later, the job was done anyway.

Apart from a terrific view, west and south-west across the Central Park reservoir, the new apartment's main joy was its light and space – two master bedrooms and a pair of maids' rooms for Susie and Stephen, the latter also laying claim to what was supposed to be the dining-room for his toys and train set. There remained plenty of room to eat in the kitchen or on a drop-leaf table in the long hallway. Jane set about decorating the place with the zeal of an artist presented with a blank canvas.

Cooke was never shy of singing his wife's praises across the air-waves, nor of drawing wider lessons from his domestic experience.

'I'd rather scrape by in England on ten pounds a week,' he claimed, 'than starve in New York on thirty dollars [the US equivalent].' His usual working lunch of hamburger and a glass of milk cost 5 shillings – and as for a haircut, that could set a man back 10 shillings. 'It's one reason why I have not been near a barber's shop for – well, it happens to be about six or seven years: they don't do it as well as the private place I go. Haircutting, you see, happens to be another incidental accomplishment of that trim, chic, lazy ne'er-do-well, the woman I married.'

~

The family's lifestyle at the start of 1951 is laid out in the popular British magazine, *Picture Post*, which devoted a five-page feature to Alistair Cooke in its edition of 3 February. The lengthy interview – 'The Way I Live' – is accompanied by a series of photographs by Leonard McCombe who spent several days getting to know the Cookes at home and beyond. A separate photo for each child shows Holly in a sulk ('Holly has her problems. They're insoluble, of course, as with all teenagers. Having her around the house cures omniscience'); Jane is seen holding the baby ('Mrs Cooke and Susie, who wakes her father by climbing into bed, sticking her fingers into his ear-drums, and announcing another day'); and Stephen is there, too, playing the flute. The sequence is completed by a delightful picture of Alistair and Johnny laughing together in the back of a car. It bears, however, a horribly misprinted caption – 'It's Cooke's one holiday. He takes his son Jimmy to Western movies. Jimmy loves Westerns. Cooke hates them, but loves Jimmy.' The journalist's three-fold repetition of the wrong name seems to symbolise the distance between father and son.

The remaining pictures illustrate Cooke's daily routine: in dressing-gown and slippers he sits at the kitchen table after midnight reading the next day's papers, after which he eats an omelette and 'reads some good writer to take the journalism out of his mouth'. This he describes as 'a bedtime ritual as necessary as cleaning my teeth'.

And the way he lived? 'When I was a boy, my father used to moan that I had "no system". I still haven't and, of course, it's very deplorable. I do know foreign correspondents who put down their impressions in notebooks and transfer them to cards, four inches by six, which they then arrange in filing cabinets. Any notebook I ever had is still stuck in the lining of my raincoat; and the articles in magazines and newspapers that I spot like a hawk and conscientiously clip are locked up in a big file that is never consulted except when I move offices.' Instead of a system, however, he could rely on a memory which was then (and remained) dauntingly impressive, full of unexpected and intricate interconnections. This, he reckoned, enabled him to take the sort of intellectual short cuts which so suited the trade of journalism.

He summarised his daily routine for the magazine –

MIDNIGHT: to the news-stand round the corner for the *New York Times*, the *New York Herald Tribune*, the *Daily News* and the *Daily Mirror* – more than three hundred pages in all, but filleted for their relevant news in a matter of ninety minutes. Then the omelette and a glass of milk over a good, mind-cleansing book. [Sterne, Mencken, Somerset Maugham, Cyril Connolly, Mark Twain, Voltaire or E.B.White.] To sleep after 2 a.m.

9.30 A.M.: surrender to the noise of children departing for school (dealt with by Jane) and the arrival of Susie in the bed, announcing another day. Breakfast over the last edition of the *Herald Tribune*, the *Washington Post* and the *Christian Science Monitor* and the latest magazines. [From the *Bulletin of the Atomic Scientists* to *Popular Photography*.]

LATE MORNING: to the office to inspect the news ticker-tape and make phone-calls to contacts.

MIDDAY: Typing stories, to be collected by a copy-boy for delivery to the cable-company – if necessary in several takes.

At this point Cooke's account takes in an important digression. Because his *Guardian* contributions had to be filed so early – usually before the first Congressional session of the day – he felt no compulsion to change his view about spending time in Washington. 'I go there about once a month and pick up all the gossip that will take time to simmer into news. By writing ahead of time for special interviews, I see the people in government that I want to see. . . . I have not found it hard to talk – by pre-arrangement – with the highest people in Government and get them to talk frankly on the strict understanding that they will not be quoted.'

The diary resumes:

3 P.M.: a bite of lunch, followed by a mooch round the town to 'pick up stories from the simple spectacle of the streets'.

4 P.M.: back to the office to catch up with the mail.

5.30 P.M.: a short nap. ('Especially if a party is planned, I stretch out on the office floor. This may sound very affected, but I got the habit when I had no office sofa. I go into total coma for an hour, more or less, and wake up in raging good spirits.')

6.30 P.M.: Return home for an hour with the children, 'playing records to them, prodding Stephen to perform on his flute, or suggesting solutions for Holly to those ghastly problems of childhood which suppose that two trains are approaching at different speeds.'

Finally, with the children dispatched to bed, it was time for relaxation. The first drink of the evening ('a fruit punch, of course . . .') and only one rule: no politics, the day being for work and the evening for relaxation. 'We rarely eat before 8.15. We have friends in, or go out to them, three or four times a week. Once in a while we go dancing. Twice a week, we fool around till 10 p.m. and discover a movie we long to see is showing some place across town. We get in at midnight, my wife goes to bed, and I retire with the papers to the world's woes. Which is where we came in.'

The remainder of the article offers an explanation for restricting his travel around the country, whenever possible, to trips with Jane ('unpleasant things tend to happen to the marriages of newspapermen who are always on the road') and a résumé of his hobbies: 'On Saturdays I take Steve and my son Johnny out to lunch and either to the wonderful Museum of Natural History, or to football, but more often to a movie, a Western, always a Western.'

This, then, was a pattern for living and working which was to remain substantially unaltered for the next twenty years. It involved a strong element of routine and predictability; it was dictated largely by Cooke's own disciplines and pleasures, which (among other things) required children to be kept in their place; it turned his inclinations (not living in Washington, for instance) into a professional creed; and it helped – above all – to build up the mystique of a correspondent not quite like any other.

Further evidence for Cooke's growing popularity in Britain comes in another early 1951 profile: a fellow *Guardian* man, John Beavan (later Baron Ardwick) – the paper's London editor – colours in the flesh and bone behind the 'dark silk voice' listened to by millions of Home Service listeners each Friday night. The English, says Beavan in *Everybody's* magazine, assume that Cooke is American – while every American, listening to the distinctive timbre of his voice, assumes that he is English. Beavan sets out the facts: 'Cooke is English by birth, but he has an Atlantic Pact accent. He is a natural mimic. When he goes to the deep South for a few days he comes back with a drawl. Give him a year in England and he would slide back into the accent he soaked up at Cambridge twenty years ago.'

In passing, Beavan remarks on Cooke's readiness to tackle an unlikely range of subjects outside the ambit of most correspondents' interests: 'I suspect,' Beavan speculates, 'that Cooke is not much more interested in boxing *as boxing* than is his paper. But he is a great admirer of the writer Ernest Hemingway who, he thinks, "has done something no one has done since Dryden – transformed the English sentence into a most fluent and resilient thing". Hemingway has, of course, written magnificently of bull-fighting and since there are no deaths in the afternoon to report in the United States, Cooke perhaps thinks the best way to emulate his literary hero is to write in fluent and resilient sentences about knock-outs at night.'

Cooke himself marked the 200th *Letter from America* with an auto-biographical article for the *Radio Times*, including his own view of the *Letters'* stylistic development: the least successful, he reckoned were those over which he had brooded, researching and crafting his material. 'The odd and tremendous discovery I began to make on hearing the talks back (I always hear them back twice) was that the planned talks, the conscientious, good-boy talks sounded like lectures. . . . But there was one talk I wrote in fifty minutes that tumbled out like water over a broken dam. It had pace, it was vivid, it was *talk*.'

From this he had deduced that preparation would be fatal: thus, starting with a clean sheet of paper and a clear mind, he would sit down on the day of the recording (usually Thursday) and spend ninety enjoyable minutes crouching over his typewriter, communing with a friend – a blind friend, for whom every sentence had to count.

'To write a dull sentence, a sentence without suspense, a sentence that doesn't make you want to know what is coming next – that is the only gross incompetence in broadcasting.'

The applied artlessness of the *Letters* had by now given them an established place in the BBC schedules, though Cooke's sponsors still had to fend off sporadic carping: Lindsay Wellington, at the end of 1950, wrote to one dubious manager, 'I feel that Alistair's good points still outweigh the others. But I am the first to agree that we should not blind ourselves to signs of deterioration in his output, if such signs appear.'

One person who did have cause for some complaint was Rupert Hart-Davis who had been waiting for almost a year to receive a set of revised *Letters* for his anthology. The truth was that Cooke was finding it far more difficult than he'd expected to convert his spoken words into a cogent written text. He missed another deadline at the end of March, because it had proved unacceptable to 'toss the originals into an envelope and call it a book.' He also made a startling confession to his publisher: 'All my books are now by my side, so it has been possible to check everything I wrote in a hurry and straighten out some of the facts and quotations. The percentage error is never less than about twenty-five per cent.' So much for the stream-of-consciousness approach to the *Letters*: errors, he accepted, were 'endemic to the process'.

It was nearly three months before he was able to inform Hart-Davis on 14 June that the end was in sight, by dint of long weekends in the city ('Jane will divorce me if I don't go to the country this weekend'). 'I have stayed and sweated for you and smoked too much and missed meals and sleep. . . . As soon as I have put the next and last batch in the mail, I shall send you a cable with the two words, "Bombs Away". You will then know you can go off and get drunk. I shall toast you in Pimms No. 1 and wish you were here.'

At last, eighteen months behind schedule, he applied the finishing touches and enclosed a brief introduction, explaining the philosophy behind the *Letters*:

Even the prospect of early annihilation should not keep us from making the best of our days on this unhappy planet. And it would be a crime against Nature for any generation to take the world crisis so solemnly that

it put off enjoying those things for which we were presumably designed in
the first place, and which the gravest statesmen and the hoarsest politicians
hope to make available to all men in the end: I mean the opportunity to
do good work, to fall in love, to enjoy friends, to sit under trees, to read,
to hit a ball and bounce the baby.

He had set out, at Lindsay Wellington's prompting, to write about
everything that interested him for a 'large and very mixed audience,
ranging from shrewd bishops to honest carpenters.' The resulting
collection, therefore, belonged to 'the people who sponsored it: the
brave, tolerant and courteous people of Britain, who after ten years
of austerity and four of being poor relations could yet choose to sit
down on Friday evenings and want to understand the foibles of the
rich uncle across the seas. A.C.'

Cooke suggested that a proof copy be dispatched to Bertrand
Russell, who – the previous year – had told Cooke that 'he liked my
stuff better than that of any journalist now writing'. He also stressed
the importance of recommending the book to Blanche Knopf, on the
basis that her husband, Alfred, had promised to publish anything he
cared to write.

In this euphoric post-completion period, Cooke underwent
another of those sporadic spurts of interest in a different sort of
writing. On 28 September, he told Hart-Davis, he had started 'a short
and intriguing novel which is impossible to explain, as a technical
novelty, in a letter. I shall see how this comes along. I'd like to put out
what you snobs call "a real book" – i.e., one solemn theme strangled
to death in three hundred pages – before I do another book of pieces.'
He signed off his letter to 'the Good Provider and Fount from whom
all sterling flows' with a rather plaintive query about the final sales
figures for the British version of *Generation*.

~

Letters from America was published in November with twenty-nine
pieces, some being composites of a number of original talks, on
subjects as varied as the cowboy-philosopher Will Rogers to the heart-
warming story of a stolen baby; from the history of the Spanish in
California to an early Harvard computer. The differences between the
spoken and written word are telling. The text of his talk on the family's
move to Fifth Avenue includes this paragraph:

And I felt suddenly sad and lonely. And not only because of the war news.
I discovered for the first time something about New York that endears me
forever to it, though I have done in all, I think, about a dozen talks on
New York and beaten, all these years, ineffectively about the bush. We
were suddenly displaced persons who knew nobody. Why? Because we
had left our neighbourhood. Our neighbourhood, like all New York
neighbourhoods, was just two blocks. Everything you would ever want
was round one corner or the other.

By the time this appeared in the book, it had changed in many ways,
both subtle and substantial:

Then I felt sad and suddenly lonely. Not lonely in the privileged ways that
great cities let you be. But out of it, an outcast from a community I had
hardly been aware of. It was the community bound by 72nd Street and
68th Street on Lexington Avenue. Suddenly we were displaced persons,
who knew nobody. Why? Because we had left our neighbourhood. Like all
New York neighbourhoods, it was three blocks [sic] long... There is
nothing known or defined about this fact. It is not a system, like the even-
numbering of eastbound and odd-numbering of westbound streets. But
it just happens that almost anywhere you live in New York, everything
you ever want is around one corner or the other.

The volume was hardly a critical triumph. Cooke's old *Transatlantic
Quiz* sparring partner, Denis Brogan, wrote a friendly review in the
Spectator, but he also picked up the difficulties inherent in the project.
'It takes a great deal of skill to compose talks that are first-class because
they are first-class as talks, and equally effective in print. Not quite
equally effective, although they are as readable as they are hearable,
for we miss the "tone" of "Good evening", the air of controlled speed,
that makes Mr Cooke so easy to listen to. But readable these talks
certainly are.'

It wasn't enough to seize the imagination of the target audience.
Instead of the 50,000 copies he had hoped for, Hart-Davis printed
15,000. Cooke was disappointed, but the publisher was right. 'I
imagined that the explanation [for the smaller print-run] had to do
with rising costs,' Cooke wrote. 'In view of the mad apathy of the
buying public, perhaps God had a hand in it, too. If it would help to
have Jane do a tour of the provincial book stores, signing copies, of
course I'll have her sent by air-freight at once. PS. Can't you bribe

Harold Nicolson to proclaim in a double-column *Observer* piece the deceptive importance of our book?!'

He was clearly unhappy about the way the book was being marketed: in frustration, he even put forward some ideas of his own, trying all the while not to sound as if he had lost confidence in his friend.

> By the way, I see the *New Yorker* 25th anniversary album of drawings has a slogan which you might like to snatch or amend. It is, 'everybody's first choice for Christmas.' I almost bought a copy because the ad told me to do so. How about an ad saying simply, '*Letters from America*, everybody's first choice of Xmas present'? Or does this make you groan? It's impossible to know at this end – we are so used to advertisements that say, 'towering, epic, sublime' or 'not since Homer has any writer had such mastery of chichi'. Then we open an English newspaper and see, about the same work, 'Quite interesting, really' – Harold Nicolson. Or 'A book . . . ' – *Daily Mail*.

As the truth started to dawn, Cooke was left to analyse what had gone wrong:

> Wadsworth remarked to me once that he thought my best BBC stuff was harder to do than the *Guardian*. He's right. The *Guardian* stuff . . . is a matter of falling back on purely literary habits – the sentence composed on the reliable architectural principles of the right noun, a couple of odd or 'sensitive' adjectives, the clauses disposed and balanced according to a foot rule. Writing for talking is no less than abandoning architecture altogether and trying to imitate the movement of a bird or a river.

19

LEANING BACK

Cooke's complaint was rooted in the complexity of the task he had set himself. Later volumes of *Letters* were much more successful, as he himself came to terms with the subtleties of translating the spoken word to the printed page. For now, the two creative strands were developing separately and his *Guardian* work – what he self-deprecatingly called 'piling stuff up from the ground' – was attracting considerable acclaim in its own right. Nothing made a greater impression than his coverage of the middleweight boxing bout between the British fighter Randolph Turpin and the American Sugar Ray Robinson, desperate to regain the title he'd lost to Turpin a few months earlier.

In the run-up to this spectacular sporting event, Cooke was in California covering the San Francisco talks which ended in the belated signing of a peace treaty with the Japanese. He knew the paper wanted him to return to New York to cover the fight, but his instinct, as always, was to seek an excuse to cling to his beloved West Coast at somebody else's expense. He cabled the *Guardian* that he intended to travel inland to investigate the greatest hydro-electric scheme the country had ever seen – the California Central Valley Project. Wadsworth's response was immediate: 'Go New York soonest. Blood thicker than water in this country.' Cooke obeyed and found himself thrust into the middle of the most vivid possible manifestation of Anglo-American relations.

As he packed up to leave San Francisco, the prospect seemed not only unattractive but pointless. But even as he travelled back across the country by train, he became aware of the growing expectations generated by the contest. 'In Pittsburgh this morning, at three o'clock, an engine-driver offered to swap his job for mine, but since your correspondent has never operated diesels the deal fell through,' he wrote in his fight preview on 12 September. By the time Turpin and

Robinson squared up to each other later that night, he found himself swept along by the mood of anticipation.

It was an epic struggle. No fewer than four million British listeners switched on their radios in the small hours to listen to the commentary, to the despair of the electricity generators: their power stations burned an extra seventy tons of precious coal. Cooke's report inevitably had to wait until the following day, 14 September, but what it lacked in immediacy, it made up in passion and flair with a gracious nod to Hemingway's bullfights for good measure.

> No myth dies harder, and none is more regularly debunked by the facts, than the one about international friendship. . . . Last night Sugar Ray Robinson, tiring to the point of panic before the concrete insensibility of Turpin's massive flesh, wrung everything he had from a brave heart, fought from his finger-tips, and at last had Turpin helpless by the ropes, his arms by his thighs, his stubborn body reeling back and forth like a beaten bull when the flags go in. I have never seen a human being receive so much punishment with such dumb bravery. For almost a whole minute Robinson crashed and shot and pounded at him until his head sagged from one side to the other with the flopping rhythm of a broken pendulum.

Turpin had lost in the tenth round, counted out on his feet. Yet, to the amazement of the baying throng, he recovered with improbable speed. 'Three minutes after the fight was over, [he] was standing in mid-ring with his arm round the smiling Robinson, hugging his homely face with all the charm of a baby learning to wink. He stood up straight and he was breathing at a normal rate.'

Cooke was so enthralled by the experience that he even tried to score the fight himself – though he ended up in bewilderment at the difficulty of judging 'two men who might have learned their fighting on different planets. How do you compare rare roast beef and crêpes suzettes?' – Robinson the elegant boxer and Turpin the purveyor of brute strength. 'Time and again Turpin came on last night, with that modest homely face, and those wide glassy eyes, as untouched by the impossibility of human interference as Marley's Ghost, clanking up from the cellar, or Boris Karloff wheeling into the petrified drawing-room. "He's not a man," an admiring youngster cried, "He's The Thing!" '

Among those who took the trouble to express their appreciation was the *Guardian*'s revered cricket and music writer Neville Cardus, who told Cooke that he carried the Turpin piece around with him to show to young journalists. The two men had never met, but Cooke wrote back to say that he'd been an admirer ever since the 1920s when Cardus used to cover the cricket festival in Blackpool for the *Guardian*, and – at the age of fourteen – had once asked him for his autograph. Cardus replied that he was delighted to hear it: 'You had my autograph and now I have yours.' They made a vague promise to meet in London, but failed to do so until shortly before Cardus's death in 1975. Cooke was invited to a tiny London flat, one of whose two rooms struggled to contain a baby grand piano; he was surprised to be taken out to a glorified café for dinner, with fluorescent lighting and none of the fine wine which he'd expected from a noted bon viveur. 'Afterwards, we sat and talked about the *Guardian* and its ability to let people live by C.P. Scott's high-thinking and plain-living principle,' in the habitual absence of a decent salary. And to his surprise, Cooke discovered that the *Guardian* had been no more generous to Cardus than it had been to him.

~

One way and another, 1951 was a further year in which Cooke had little time to spare for his family. After four weeks touring the Southern states and much longer immured in his study on the anthology of *Letters*, it was time for the children to be packed off to camp again: Stephen to Maine and Holly out West, to Steamboat Springs, Colorado. At least there was Christmas: Stephen remembers that 'Alistair owned Christmas. He always participated and we felt it was a very English thing. I loved it. He would read to us from "A Christmas Carol" and we always had a tree and the *Messiah*.' And in a light-heartedly seasonal item for the *Guardian*, Cooke actually listed the children's present list for 1951: 'One twelve-inch velocipede with siren and adjustable seat. One long-playing record of ditties assembled under the title *Love me tonight*. One pair of railroad switches – 'O' gauge. One set of military miniatures, cavalry, Army of Northern Virginia.' The preferences, presumably, of Susie, Holly, Stephen and Johnny.

Christmas also allowed Cooke a small flight of creative fancy – and something very different from his normal line of work. In 1951, for the third year running, he wrote a special Christmas story for the BBC – a tradition which had become popular enough for him to be allotted an extra half-hour slot on 25 December. With the prospect of such a large captive audience, he told Hart-Davis a month before-hand, 'I don't know what it will be about, but this is something I can't afford to flop on.' What emerged from his labours was a fairy-cum-morality tale explaining the tradition of Santa Claus delivering presents on Christmas Eve.

Rupert Hart-Davis evidently liked this piece of whimsy, because a few months later he published a slim volume containing the story as well as the broadcasts from the previous two years: the tale of Zebby Adams – who graduates from Santa Claus school but ends up in court after commandeering a New York taxi in an excess of Christmas zeal – and the travails of Larry, a snow-starved Connecticut boy who deserts his post on a Hollywood film set to reach home before the Christmas clock strikes twelve. The book was illustrated by one of the Cookes' friends, Marc Simont, who had recently been working with James Thurber. Despite that pedigree, Simont nearly brought cultural shame on the enterprise, as Cooke explained to his publisher when he saw the proofs: 'The dope spelled Dickens' famous – but not famous enough, evidently – work, *Christmas Carols*. Is it possible to delete the "s"? I mention it merely to protect the fabulously literate reputation of the house of Hart-Davis.' The error was duly corrected. Cooke was also at pains to make sure that the language kept its distinctive American timbre: 'I beg you only to indulge me in the matter of a "stein of beer", "scaring up", "a well-meaning bum" and other localisms, all of which I think keep the American flavour and will not really baffle anyone's understanding of the plots. The BBC is quite used to "bum" from me, and I have never had a rude letter from the North of England.'

The finished work was published in the autumn of 1952, with the title *Christmas Eve*. Along with the *Guardian* short stories twenty years earlier, this was Cooke's only excursion into the world of fiction.

～

In the first week of 1952 Winston Churchill – recently re-elected Prime Minister – arrived in the United States to meet Harry Truman. It seemed to Cooke – as a long-time Churchill admirer – like a fine symbol of a cheerful new year. Which was not to say, of course, that a scribe for the *Manchester Guardian* could openly celebrate the return of a Conservative government in Britain. But his 250th *Letter from America*, which appeared on 4 January, drops the broadest of hints that he might find the world a more amenable place if there were to be a change of administration on the other side of the Atlantic too and General Eisenhower's chance of taking the White House for the Republicans looked increasingly realistic.

The *Letter* looks back to the end of the previous New Year, 1951: it was a depressing time, overlaid with 'the thought of the hopeless turn in Korea, the sudden and very real prospect, as it then seemed, of a war carried into the vast plains of China. Mr Attlee had come running to Washington and gone again and some of us wondered aloud if it were possible that a year from then we'd still be sitting in our warm house with our children and our friends.'

One friend had even made contingency plans to invite the Cookes to hole up in their country retreat for the duration, 'if the thing we all dreaded, happened'. Sunk in gloom and contemplating camp-beds in a stone cellar as a refuge from nuclear fall-out, the party had speculated whether the Russians might choose to strike on the stroke of midnight, so that the air-raid sirens would be mistaken for a piece of New Year revelry. (Cooke was for a while the designated deputy chief air-raid warden of his apartment block, required to report to the building's Superintendent, Captain Brown, when the sirens sounded – and to hurry residents of higher floors to what was supposed to be the safest spot: at the dead centre of the building.)

Cooke conceded that, as things turned out, Europeans might regard this pessimism as a ludicrous piece of American exaggeration. They should remember, he said, 'that Americans were convinced two years ago that unless Europe re-armed with a will and all together, the invitation of an undefended Europe would prove too much for the Russians to resist'. And who had heeded those fears, determined to display resolution in case they should be well-placed? None other than the Supreme Commander of NATO Land Forces, General Dwight D. Eisenhower. 'Who shall say,' Cooke wondered, 'now that we care to think the tide is turning, how much we owe to him and the example of his leadership?' Eisenhower had not yet declared his willingness to stand for President, but Cooke's anticipation at the start of 1952 is evident. 'The general mood is far lighter than it has been for several New Years now. I don't want you to think I'm being mystical in attributing this lift of heart to one man. But I would simply be muffing my job as reporter if I didn't tell you that the "year of decision" has lost its original meaning of "the year of the Russian decision" and has come to mean "the year of Ike's decision". '

It was in this atmosphere that Cooke spent the first week of 1952 in Washington, watching Churchill's address to Congress and then following him to New York. His coverage of the visit for the *Guardian* brought a high compliment from the *Financial Times* in London, who believed that he'd surpassed himself.

> Few correspondents have shown more liveliness and skill in describing the doings of the denizens of Washington. With equal verve and knowledge, Mr Cooke comments on the activities of the churches, Hollywood, university presidents, baseball players, gangsters and scientists. People who want to know what really goes on in America cannot dispense with Mr Cooke.

It was a tribute marking the start of another golden period in Cooke's career. In February he and Jane took a three-week holiday in Florida and Jamaica, knowing that a summer of Conventions would be hopelessly congested. The trip gave rise to a series of *Guardian* articles, both political and frivolous. They were in Kingston on the day that King George VI died and watched the ceremony of the Jamaican legislature swearing allegiance to the Queen: 'A solemn Negro came in bearing the Mace. He was followed by another Negro taking small important steps, a man in a puffing black gown and a large cream-coloured wig. This was Mr Speaker.' Once the ceremony was over, they returned to the beach and, as Cooke wrote later to Rupert Hart-Davis, Jane soaked up the sun until she looked like 'a particularly gorgeous fugitive from Bali. At nights,' he went on, 'we could go anywhere because in native night-clubs she looked like a native dancer – obviously half-caste, anyway. This satisfies some ancient retrogression in me and is very agreeable.'

On the way back, Cooke took advantage of an offer to buy a fin-winged Cadillac belonging to a rich Florida friend. Cooke's own jalopy had done well over 100,000 miles and he expected to cover many thousands more in the course of an election year. Even when he finally became a wealthy man, he never shook off a reluctance to waste money on new cars. The vehicle he'd been offered was a comfortable five years old, but had only done 25,000 miles – and he decided to drive it back across the Southern states for an early taste of the country's election mood. Yet what struck him first was the proliferation of advertising billboards as he drove north from Miami. This was to become one of the abiding irritations of his life – the ribbon developments subsuming every main road. 'Eat at Joe's Lagoon, super-duper malteds, jumbo burgers, build a paradise in Palm Grove, Guard Your Tyres, Change that Oil, Bozo's Beer is Best, Only Fifty Miles to Snookey's Pecan Peanut Brittle.'

He took with him for company one of the latest generation of Commonwealth Fellows from England – Alec Sturrock, who later wrote about the trip in the *Guardian*: 'It was a journey more varied and exciting than any that I (who had seen, at Army expense, Srinagar and the Pyramids) have ever made, rendered so by infection from the gaiety and darting interest of my travelling companion.' Cooke was supposed to be thinking about politics, of course, and the next few days demonstrated his ability to tackle tough subjects at different levels for different audiences.

Four substantial pieces of analysis appeared in the *Guardian* during March: Cooke did not much like the way the Democrats maintained their iron grip on the South. As he travelled from Florida, through Georgia to North Carolina and Virginia, he reflected on the survival of such tendentious political creatures as Governor Herman Talmadge, whose adherence to segregation was unwavering – so much so that he had introduced a special grant for bright black children, to pay for them to take a train to another state for their college education. Yet Cooke was no enthusiast, either, for the careless imposition of equality laws: the liberal Southerners he met clearly persuaded him that there was another way. These 'good Southerners', Cooke wrote in his final article, 'have worked, very many of them, with sincere zeal and patience, to transform in fifteen years the schooling, housing, the employment rights of the Negro in most states of the South. Many Southerners popularly tagged as "nigger-haters" and reactionaries have done more in any year for the coloured poor of their states than the sworn liberals of London, Manchester and the Clydeside have done in a lifetime for their slum people, or for that matter than Liverpool has done for its Negroes.' Cooke's consistent view was that a sudden, sharp end to segregation could cause as many problems as it solved: benevolent, gradual and pragmatic change might achieve far more. It was not a view shared by all his readers.

While his newspaper dispatches plumbed these dangerous depths, the *Letter from America* tended to stay nearer the surface of any argument. BBC listeners were regaled, for instance, with the story of a torrential downpour as Cooke and Sturrock were leaving Florida – a story considered too trivial for *Guardian* readers. The rain forced them to take shelter in a traditional country store which sold 'everything from flour to hairpins'. Inside Cooke discovered an old man, an archetype of the wiseacres so beloved of journalists and usually found at the wheel of taxi-cabs. As the rain tipped down outside, he sat on an upturned packing case and absorbed the old man's homespun opinions of the political scene. He was a Democrat, of course, and he had no time for one of the leading challengers, Senator Estes Kefauver, whom he described as 'crooked as a barrel of snakes'. The only certain thing was that the Republicans could never win: 'No sir,' he told Cooke, 'you cain't come in on sixty-four million folks with money in their pockets and tell 'em you're pining to take care of 'em. Truman got there first and you cain't beat money in the pocket. No sir, that money game's sure gonna be hard to beat.'

Which only goes to show that even homespun wisdom can get things wrong. Cooke, with 1948 still engraved on his heart, wasn't saying that he agreed – but he was moved none the less. 'In these simple sentences was as good a political analysis as I've heard from any pundit or windbag in Washington. I sat for an hour with this old man and I wish I could tell you everything he said. He was old, prejudiced, fairly illiterate, kindly, offhand and an indestructible Democrat, convinced that the United States was made for him and not he for it. I felt at home again. I knew I was going to enjoy the summer's work and the election and the intensely human and proud people who will decide it.'

~

In the same spring of 1952, Cooke wrote to Rupert Hart-Davis about the American edition of his *Letters* anthology – to which Knopf had given a new title, *One Man's America*. Cooke joked about his appearance as the guest of honour at the *Herald Tribune*'s 'Book and Author' Luncheon on 22 April ('5,000 large matrons in white hats gave me a gurgling send-off'). And in a typical aside – a mixture of self-deprecation and self-promotion – he added, 'I hear I have been awarded the annual Peabody Award for "modest contributor to international relations through radio" or some such. Radio awards are twenty to the dozen, but this is the only one that has a Pulitzer flavour.'

He hoped his friend could come over for the ceremony and stay at Nassau Point, where 'the willows are lemony, the elms are struggling back to life again in the Park, the girls are hitching their uplifts and all in life is coming awake again'. Hart-Davis didn't come, but Alfred Knopf was there, delighted to have such a fanfare of free publicity for his book.

The School of Journalism at Georgia University, which promoted the Peabody awards, nominated Cooke's *Letter from America* as 'Radio's Outstanding Contribution to International Understanding during 1951' – a rare honour for a broadcaster whose work was predominantly heard overseas. The lunch-time ceremony took place at the Waldorf-Astoria Hotel in New York on 1 May and the other winners included Ed Murrow, now fronting the weekly CBS documentary programme, *See It Now*.

For many of those present, Cooke was a relatively unknown figure: they had come expecting to be entertained by such stars as Bob Hope and Jack Benny, yet even in this company, Cooke more than held his own. His old BBC colleague, Leonard Miall, now one of the Corporation's news correspondents, remembers Cooke's speech as a show-stealer. 'It just seemed that, in comparison, the comedians' gag-writers weren't on very good form.' Not that Cooke told jokes: but in front of these ranks of radio executives and associated media folk, Cooke did risk a little gentle teasing, drawing a comparison between American and British radio: the first, he said, was a sort of 'audible wallpaper, against which the so-called listener slaps down his children, plays poker, eats and goes to bed'. In Britain, on the other hand, 'people warn their children to be quiet before the radio comes on, father lights his pipe and the family then gathers round the one piece of coal which the British victory in the late Holy War entitled them to.' There was another difference: 'Whereas the American listener, hot for news and excitement, leans forward, the British listener leans back.' For this reason, he prayed for the early exodus of American forces from Europe: 'The day the British get too Americanised, the day they learn to lean forward, I am through.'

The audience was intrigued. Who was this witty, elegant figure with the gentle, undemonstrative voice and ironic sense of humour ('I always assumed international understanding was promoted by people who don't know their own country and will never understand any other. International *mis*understanding is the field I like to wallow in')? A senior executive of RCA, NBC's parent company, offered him a job on the spot with the promise that he could name his own salary. Cooke replied, 'And what would the hours be?' The reply was – any hours that anything was happening. 'I'm sorry, then. At six o'clock I turn off my telephone.' But that wasn't the only media interest inspired by the speech. One man listening to a radio relay of the lunch – Robert Saudek – suddenly realised that he knew the answer to a problem that had been vexing him for months.

Saudek was an established figure in ABC radio, who had recently been head-hunted by the Ford Foundation to investigate how television could be exploited for serious programming. He had looked the medium over and, as Cooke put it many years later, found that it was 'a refuge for old vaudevillians – which was just as well, since vaudeville was about to expire': and that apart from that, it was pushing out nothing much more than headline news and a little drama. He believed fiercely that television was capable of much more. Saudek had met Cooke fleetingly at dinners with a mutual friend – the latest BBC representative Norman Luker– but until this moment he had never given much thought to the possibility of using his professional services. As he listened to Cooke's speech it dawned on him that this might be the man he'd been seeking to present a new kind of television programme, which had a name – *Omnibus* – but no host.

It was not so much what Cooke said as the way that he said it. 'His acceptance speech was very eloquent,' Saudek recalled shortly before his death in 1997. 'I remembered from our earlier meetings that he was a very elegant-looking man, but it was his distinctive manner of speech that struck me. I felt it would be different enough so that, almost any time you heard that voice – British, mid-Atlantic, or however it seemed to you – you'd think of *Omnibus*, in much the same way that you recognise immediately the banner on the front page of the *New York Times*.' He called Cooke and they met for dinner. 'Alistair didn't know what it was about, but he didn't need much convincing.'

This putative programme was a high-risk, high-budget leap into the unknown. The Ford Foundation had given Saudek $1.2 million to put on a series of ninety-minute programmes: there were no restrictions on what he could do except for the absolute inexperience of all those involved. Saudek's inspiration came from a visit he made to the

New York Zoological Society, where he was shown a slow-motion film of a jack-rabbit running across a field. He'd never seen anything like it – the lithe body in tight close-up swaying from side to side. The film lasted less than a minute, but it produced a spontaneous round of applause from the Society's members. Yet there was no outlet on the television schedules for such an oddity: how many more aspects of life might there be which had never benefited from the magic of television?

Having won the Ford contract, there remained the small problem of translating the inspiration of a few seconds into hours of television programming. With the money burning a hole in his pocket, Saudek consulted the journalist Walter Lippmann – and it was he who suggested that *Omnibus* should become the *Life* magazine of the air. Saudek's cultural background spiced with Lippmann's journalistic instinct set the process of planning in motion. *Omnibus* would take as its themes not just art, theatre, music and literature, but science, technology and sport, education and history. It would be the ultimate polymath programme, pitched at a broad non-specialist audience.

The problem of a host had vexed Saudek sorely. The obvious solution was a celebrity, preferably one with a good stage presence. An approach to Laurence Olivier, who was in a New York production of *Antony and Cleopatra*, was swiftly rebuffed. Choosing a journalist might create a different, more inquiring, sort of programme. When the idea was put to him Cooke hardly paused for thought: a man who loved jazz; had been an opera commentator, film and theatre critic; was an author in his own right as well as being a voracious reader; nourished an insatiable appetite for medical and scientific novelties: it seemed tailor-made for him. And if he had done next to no television, then that only put him in the same boat as almost everybody else.

Saudek's budget was $65,000 per programme. The first series had been bought by CBS and was due to be broadcast at 4.30 on a Sunday afternoon, starting in the autumn. Work began almost immediately on selling the idea to sponsors. A glossy pamphlet was prepared, placing Cooke at the forefront of the sales drive: 'Alistair Cooke . . . has become perhaps the century's foremost interpreter of America', it proclaimed with the modesty of the ad-man. The hype was forgivable and necessary, perhaps, for such a little-known figure. The blurb went on to explain that Cooke's role would be 'more than that of a conventional Master of Ceremonies.'

> He will pace and unify and set the character of the whole show.
>
> He will be the Good Companion, always welcome in your home for his fresh and witty slant on the doings of the human race;
>
> . . . in short, the kind of fellow you will be glad to have drop in every Sunday afternoon, because he leaves you with a new story to tell, a new subject to talk about, a new sense of expanded horizons.

Potential backers were told that *Omnibus* would have a minimum of five features each week, filmed or live, 'depending on their nature, immediacy or scope'. The segments would be separated by commercial messages from up to five sponsors. This opportunity would be offered to five 'non-competitive advertisers of appropriate character': five-minute institutional commercials for $13,000 per programme including agency fee. It was, in sum, 'ONE OF THE HISTORIC OPPORTUNITIES IN TELEVISION.'

One of the first to accept was Willys Overland Motors and the inaugural programme was timed for the second week in November, immediately after the presidential election.

~

The BBC, as was its right, claimed a share of the reflected glory from the Peabody prize. That week's *Letter from America* was preceded by a description of the Waldorf scene from Leonard Miall and a tribute from the journalist William Clark: 'I turn like a thirsty soul to Alistair Cooke. He tells us something about the trivialities that make up life, the ambitions of little men and women which lie at the bottom of politics, he keeps me informed about the difficulties that face an American mother, or a high-school kid, or an author, or a broadcaster. And he makes all of this sound somehow normal and natural.'

Cooke used the *Letter* itself to describe how commercial pressures were turning authors into impromptu salesmen of their own work. He had been required, for instance, to appear on an American oddity called 'breakfast television'. These programmes were 'usually conducted by a man and his wife – I mean that's their status in real life – sitting over the breakfast table and chatting adoringly to each other. . . . The coffee is poured, the sugar is dropped in, tinkle! tinkle!' Then, as if in their own home, the husband opens the paper and notices that A. Cooke has brought out a book. Why not invite him along to say what he thinks of Americans? 'You come in at that point and are interviewed about your life, how you came to do this sort of thing and you are urged – without too much arm-twisting – to read from your book.'

The peripatetic book salesman was back in New York by mid-May to take part in a curious exercise, yet a rather appropriate one, considering his forthcoming career as a television personality. The actress Celia Johnson, whom Cooke had known since before the war (she was married to Peter Fleming, who had helped him find his job at *The Times*) arrived in New York to do a television play and came to visit Alistair and Jane at their apartment. Out of the blue, this visit was followed by a telephone call from the director of the play: there had been a casting crisis – would Cooke like to come down to the studios to read through one of the parts? He was being asked, as he confided in his listeners the following week, 'to rub off the dust of nineteen years and reveal to a gasping world the shining talent that I once chose as a career and abandoned'.

Nobody ever explained what had happened to the actor who was supposed to play the part of a young, dapper man who was in love with the second-lead lady. Cooke simply reported for rehearsals in the unlikely setting of a gymnasium. It wasn't ideal, but television was expanding so rapidly that there was no way of accommodating every production in a custom-made studio. The gruelling schedule of the play in which he'd been asked to perform allowed the director forty-eight hours to mark up a shooting script; rehearsals were scheduled to last five days, from one until six in the afternoon; actors saw the studio sets for the first time only on day six, with just two run-throughs before the broadcast – live – to an audience of twenty million.

Cooke was grateful to Celia Johnson (he presumed) for mentioning his name, but he approached the performance with understandable trepidation. His big scene involved a lover's tiff across a table and he had learned his lines with the assiduity of the very anxious. When his moment came, all went smoothly until he realised with horror that the actress sitting opposite him had dried. He ad-libbed desperately until she found her place and then it happened again. 'The whole thing was a mess,' he reflected, 'although perhaps it didn't look quite so bad to the audience.' That was the end of Cooke's acting career, though *Omnibus* would give him plenty of chance to exploit his thespian skills in unforeseen ways.

~

The children were packed off to camp at the end of June as usual and Jane retired to the cool of the coast, leaving the summer bachelor once more to fend for himself: with the apartment sealed down against the heat, Cooke was confined to the use of two chipped kitchen plates, one damaged saucer, a coronation mug (Edward VIII) and a spoon given to one of the children by Jane's mother. It bore the legend 'A present from Jacksonville, Florida' and was shaped like a petrified alligator.

The Conventions, back in Chicago after a gap of eight years, saw television seize control as never before, though fortunately the sweltering stadium of 1944 was now fully air-conditioned. First came the Republicans who, despite President Truman's unpopularity, had managed to manufacture a steaming internal dispute of their own between Eisenhower and Senator Robert Taft. When the proceedings opened, Cooke luxuriated in the space now available in an expanding *Manchester Guardian*. On the rapidly fading prospects of one candidate, Harold Stassen, he wrote: 'His headquarters are as empty and forlorn of camp-followers as a Foreign Legion outpost deserted by Marlene Dietrich. Stassen's ambition has a shameless tenacity. Like a deep-sea fisherman who has no luck luring swordfish with mackerel, he will then go after mackerel with sprats. If he cannot be President, he would settle for Postmaster-General in an Eisenhower Cabinet.' (In fact, he became the General's Administrator of Foreign Aid.)

Eisenhower's victory at the Convention gave Cooke some barely concealed satisfaction, although he highlighted how hard it would be for the General to reconcile the party. He was even well enough disposed to the Republicans to cast a benign eye over the choice of Richard Nixon as the vice-presidential candidate: he accepted Eisenhower's opinion that the ambitious young lawyer who had helped expose Hiss was just the man to draft a new code which might control McCarthy's witch-hunting enthusiasm.

Alec Sturrock, the Commonwealth Fellow who'd travelled through the South with Cooke earlier in the year, watched him working the Conventions, recording the highlights for British readers 'clad in beach shirt, shorts and slippers in a hot Chicago hotel room at an impossibly early hour (to meet the *Guardian* deadlines) – which done, he taxied desperately between odoriferous Convention hall and hired television set' to gather material for the BBC's evening broadcasts.

A week later the Democrats trooped into town to find a replacement for Harry Truman, who had announced his retirement. Although Adlai Stevenson, the Governor of Illinois, was thought to be most in the Truman mould, Senator Estes Kefauver had tried to seize the successor's mantle – 'a lean, suburban-schoolmaster type, forty-eight years old, a veteran New Dealer, a diligent prosecutor of monopolies and now a great bore to the party'. Cooke did not presume to repeat the phrase he'd heard from the old man in a country store – 'crooked as a barrel of snakes'. In any case, it was Stevenson whose complex character captured his attention.

The *Guardian* of 18 July printed his preliminary assessment, which smacks of one of the private briefings on which he relied so heavily. Stevenson – it appeared to Cooke – had so much respect for Eisenhower that he believed his opponent might do a better job in the White House than he could ever do. This sense of inferiority, Cooke concluded, was certain to hinder his campaign prospects. In retrospect, that assessment looks highly perspicacious. In due course, many would join Cooke in seeing Stevenson as a flawed presidential candidate because of a fundamental failure of self-belief and a sometimes self-destructive integrity. Few saw the issue so clearly, so soon and on so brief an acquaintanceship.

There were other names in the Chicago hat. Cooke listed no fewer than eighteen possible nominees jostling for position as the Convention began, while Stevenson stayed coyly in the wings, wrestling with his conscience. But after five days of tortured negotiation, both on the floor of the hall and behind the scenes, Truman directed the Illinois delegation to cast its vote for Stevenson and the tide turned decisively in favour of the reluctant Governor. It still took another day and 'three of the most laborious and exhibitionist votes in Convention history', before the final choice was made. STEVENSON NOMINATED, the *Guardian* duly declared. He was, Cooke observed, his own man: in Stevenson and Eisenhower the country now had 'two finely-wrought Americans' to choose from.

For the correspondent, the 1952 Democratic Convention was an arduous affair. The final session lasted fourteen hours, finishing at two in the morning. There followed the acceptance speeches and even then Cooke couldn't rest: he had to stay up to write up his *Guardian* article and at eleven the next morning he was recording a *Letter from America* – one of those which had to be recorded before, but transmitted after, a crucial decision. He avoided embarrassing predictions by the simple procedure of not making any. It was only two weeks later that he was able to reflect at leisure, for his BBC listeners, on Stevenson's credentials and to paint a picture of this little-known political figure: 'He is fifty-two years of age, just above medium height, has a halo of black hair around a high, bald dome, pop eyes of a mischievous and intelligent blue, an erect little figure that bounces on its toes, the shoulders back, rather like Chaplin's take-off of Hitler. He looks to be always on the verge of a smile or a witticism and is very ready with both of them. . . . The great question is whether he can match in decisiveness and judgement his quite remarkable gifts of intellect and personal charm.'

Cooke was smitten. For him, Stevenson would never be just another politician.

~

The summer of 1952 saw another pictorial representation of the Cookes' family life – this time in the hallowed pages of *Life* magazine itself, trailing his appearance in *Omnibus* later in the year. He can be seen having his hair cut by Jane ('he has not been to a professional barber since he was married') and chatting to a newspaper seller to get 'a man-on-the-street view'. The only child to feature in this sequence – shot, once again, by Leonard McCombe – is Susie, now four years old. She hoots with delight as her father reads her a book and, in an elaborately choreographed shot, stares up at him in adoration as he works at the teletype machine installed in the Nassau Point house. Cooke wears only striped shorts and tennis shoes and Susie is holding a long strip of paper from the machine. The caption quotes Cooke as saying that 'of all the seasons, summer is the one that drains away the energies of Americans and makes them a little more limp and a lot more lovable'. The other children were absent, naturally, at camp: indeed Stephen was about to be sent away to school, much against his own eleven-year-old judgement.

McCombe's final picture shows Cooke on a lilo, with the weekend papers perched precariously in front of him. 'What a horselaugh this'll give the boys at the National Press Club,' he quips. Behind him, steep wooden steps stretch up the sandy bluff to the house. The brief text of the article observes that, apart from his bi-monthly visit to Washington and an annual tour of the country, he works out of New York and Long Island, 'gathering his information in a most informal way by interviewing his grocer, his maid or the cabbie in the park'. The magazine also gives him the chance to register some Menckenesque aphorisms. 'ON BECOMING MIDDLE-AGED: The first time a pretty girl calls you "sir" is of course a catastrophe. When I met Ginger Rogers, she called me "Sir". I've never thought much of her as an actress since.' And 'ON GROWING UP: Maturity is a fighting word with the Americans. Being one of the boys is more of a compliment.'

~

The 1952 presidential election was the last in which a campaign train played a significant part. Cooke found a way of assigning himself for a spell to Stevenson's entourage, which – after covering the South, the mid-West and the length of the Pacific Coast – set off into New England in the fall. It was a heady combination of people and place: 'Entire mountain ranges in New England seen as buckled carpets of scarlet maples, valleys pouring floods of gold from the peaks and in between all the fire and glory, tough little forests of evergreens.' That description, typical of many more, appeared in a 1972 *Letter from America.*

The campaign was not going well for Stevenson. He was behind in the polls, though not nearly so far behind as Truman had been four years earlier. But in Cooke's mind the apprehension was growing that, for all Stevenson's qualities, he was doomed to come second. He continued to feel affection for both men. In the more down-to-earth words of the *Letter,* Eisenhower oozed 'the directness and simplicity of manner of a Kansas farm boy,' with 'dollops of charm in the form of an almost desperate candour when he talked to you – "you" being the corner grocer, a cowboy, banker or the Queen of England.' Stevenson, meanwhile, displayed 'a deferential concern' for all and sundry; 'he always noticed sick and poor people and was visibly uncomfortable passing through slummy neighbourhoods.'

As the Stevenson train trundled through Rhode Island, Cooke was finishing breakfast in the dining-car. 'It was in the days when they had white tablecloths and platoons of knives and forks,' he wrote in 1972, 'and courteous, cheerful waiters: black – not necessarily Uncle Toms – trying to sell you on the shirred eggs or the corned beef hash and saying, "the little dollar-sized pancakes are specially fine this morning, sir." ' A thin, swarthy-skinned man with mocking brown eyes sat down beside him and asked, 'How's tricks? What happened overnight? Did we pick up Massachusetts? Where are we now?'

Cooke's tale continues: 'I tell him that we're going through Rhode Island and there's no good news about Massachusetts or any other state.'

' "You want to double the odds?" the other man asks. The night before we'd had rather a long night and I'd taken a bet with him that Stevenson was going to lose and lose badly. This seemed preposterous to the swarthy skeleton – whose name was Bogart.'

Humphrey Bogart and his wife, Lauren Bacall, were Stevenson groupies. 'Up there on the screen Bogart might be professionally cynical about many things, but he was a ten-year-old about the magic – the inevitable about-to-be conquering magic – of Adlai Stevenson.' Shortly afterwards the whistle-stop journey stopped at some rural outpost far too early for any sort of crowd. A bleary-eyed governor went through the motions of a speech to the handful of farmers and their wives, and the crew of a fire-engine. Then he told them he'd like to introduce one or two friends: the actor Robert Ryan came out and waved, followed by Lauren Bacall, 'who gave the boys a wink and said, "Hi!" '

And then there was Bogart. 'The tiny crowd, which had been listening to Stevenson in a slightly puzzled way as if he'd been selling a new kind of insurance policy, exploded and clapped and the little boys wrapped round the trees crowed and released one hand to finger an imaginary machine-gun. Bogart made a quick, nervous bow and was gone.'

Later on the same trip, Cooke was flattered to be invited to drinks with Bogart and Bacall, but they were disturbed by a commotion in the corridor. News had just reached Stevenson's aides of a stroke of genius from the Eisenhower camp, which had declared that – if elected – the General would travel without delay to Korea. The unspoken implication was that he intended to end the war. 'Why didn't we think of it first?' muttered Stevenson, with the air of a man reading his own obituary. Cooke returned to the Bogarts' compartment to relay the depressing news, which reinforced his sense that Stevenson's campaign was doomed. Bacall looked at him with what he hoped was 'a temporary mixture of a little affection and a lot of contempt. "You're a helluva friend, betting against your friend," she said.'

Cooke replied, 'I'm a reporter.'

If it was contempt, it didn't last long: the Cookes were destined to become friends of the two stars and remained close to Lauren Bacall long after Bogart's death in 1957. Cooke warmed to them immediately and later chose Bogart as one of the *Six Men* featured in his chronicle of famous acquaintanceship. He found Bacall irresistible, too, with her 'honey-coloured eyes and baby-leopard slouch . . . so that to the curious animal magnetism of Bogart, as of an attractive armadillo, was now added the pleasure of beauty mated with the beast'. He also noted the courage of those celebrities prepared to risk allying themselves to Stevenson. So fierce was the burning heat of the McCarthy crusade that a well-meaning liberal, or even an anarchistic free spirit like Bogart, risked upsetting nervous studio bosses by making any political statement which could be interpreted as left-leaning. Could that explain why Bogart seemed unnaturally diffident, a tough guy out of his element? 'I would learn later', he wrote in *Six Men*, 'that Bogart's correctness and modesty aboard the train – appearing when he was told to, bowing briefly and seeing that the limelight never veered from the candidate – had nothing to do with fear or timidity. He was simply doing his bit in a strange milieu and minding his manners.'

As for Lauren Bacall, she was sufficiently impressed by Cooke to name him as one of her six favourite men in a magazine called *Look*, along with Adlai Stevenson and the film director John Huston. The article was headed 'I HATE YOUNG MEN' and Bacall explained first why she had excluded all film actors: 'Not that I don't find many of them extremely appealing – I do. But the ones I'd like to mention have been on too many lists. They know who they are, so I thought I'd look the other way, away from my natural habitat and see what I could see. Besides, this will keep peace in my house and keep Bogart from turning into Bogart.' What did she see in Cooke? 'I have always found Englishmen most attractive. He is articulate, very bright and an easy man. He has become fond of America and knows a darn sight more about it than I do. He has been able to remain highly thought of in England as well as America, which is not easy. Quick to smile, he leaves nothing for you to do but to do the same.' The picture shows Cooke smiling – and with ever-present cigarette in hand.

～

By the last day of October, Cooke's report for the *Guardian* was comparing Eisenhower's slick and well-managed campaign with 'Stevenson's mishaps'. 'At New London, the Volunteers for Stevenson had whipped up a huge crowd, but the public address system broke down several times and before the Governor started to speak, the frail platform collapsed. This happily caused no human damage except a slight bruise on the left knee of the adorable Lauren Bacall.' Despite these setbacks, Cooke was not in any circumstances ready to risk a reprise of 1948 except in the most circumspect way. 'Many correspondents', he ventured cautiously, 'believe that the election comes about a month too soon for Stevenson.'

This tentative assessment was correct and Eisenhower won at a canter. But while Jane, the ardent Democrat, nursed her disappointment, Cooke himself was not unduly dismayed. Indeed, although he didn't confess the fact to his wife, his own finger quivered over the lever marked 'Eisenhower' in the voting booth for more than a moment – deflected only by the thought of her terrible revenge if she ever found out. 'I thought she'd probably throw me out of the house,' he admitted. In any case, he had some powerful distractions on election night: not just the old lament for the fate of the political reporter in the television age ('when, with hardly a second's pause, you can move up to the elbow and look in the confident but glistening eyes of Governor Stevenson, reading out his telegram of congratulation and the next second be in front of General Eisenhower, 1,200 miles away, beaming and incredulous, as he unfolds the Governor's telegram and reads it to a howling audience'). No, the real excitement of that Tuesday night was Univac: the first election computer.

Cooke's fascination with opinion polls had at last found its consummate expression in this large, lumbering piece of gadgetry – 'the silent, unseen, all-wise automaton who will preside henceforth over elections', housed in a laboratory in Philadelphia. Cooke was approaching his forty-fifth birthday, this child of the Edwardian age. And he would never really come to terms with the advanced technology of the late twentieth century. Instead, he was filled with wonder at a machine which, forty minutes after the polls had closed – and from a mere two million votes around the country – had calculated the final outcome to within four electoral college votes.

So comprehensive was Eisenhower's victory that Cooke revised his assessment of the importance of the General's Korean initiative. Nothing, it seemed, could have stopped his advance on the White

House, the first Republican inmate for twenty years. That made it easier for Cooke to offer some comfort to Adlai Stevenson when he was invited to meet him soon afterwards at the Governor's mansion in Springfield, Illinois: they soon fell to discussing the reasons for the November drubbing. 'The inevitable tendency of all such post-mortems is to weave a self-justifying cloak of rationalisations, hind-sight discoveries of false techniques. It was one of the heartening, and always startling, things about Stevenson that he could pierce this sort of fustian with a single touch of candour. He leaned back and grinned and said, "Who did I think I was, running against George Wash-ington?" '

PART FIVE

THE
GOLDEN
YEARS

20

STAR BILLING

The first of 166 episodes of *Omnibus* was broadcast on CBS at 4.30 on Sunday, 9 November 1952. It would continue more or less uninterrupted – in winter runs of up to twenty-six programmes – until 1961, changing networks twice in the process, before it was finally swept away by the tide of commercialism.

Viewers of that first show had no idea what to expect: there had certainly been nothing like it before. The Ford Foundation brief was 'to conserve and increase knowledge and enrich our culture through the more effective use of mass media . . . for better utilisation of leisure time for all age groups'. The most important task, in the first instance, was to offer a hint of the breadth of the *Omnibus* agenda. To that end Bob Saudek and his team devised 'The Maze' – a spectacular piece of studio presentation which made stern demands on the presenter.

A series of screens had been set up across the floor of the CBS studio in the Grand Central Station complex in New York: there were doorways, openings, alcoves and an assortment of props, and Cooke was to wander at a leisurely pace through the maze of scenery, picking up an object here, pointing out an actor or musician at work there. He would stroll, cigarette in hand, from one item to the next, without benefit of helpful devices like an auto-prompt on the front of the camera – a continuous, live, multi-camera shot cueing a series of potentially unpredictable bits of live action *en route.*

When the moment comes, Cooke is discovered with his back to camera, before he turns and gestures with his head for the camera to follow him into the Maze. 'The Television and Radio Workshop of the Ford Foundation', proclaims the caption. He moves past a series of busts, before picking up *Webster's Dictionary* and reading the definition of *Omnibus* – 'a large number of subjects all at once, something for everybody'. 'My name is Cooke, Alistair Cooke,' he goes on. *Omnibus* will be 'a vaudeville show', covering the arts and skills of many countries and many centuries. He comes upon Rex Harrison and his wife Lili Palmer, miming some unnamed drama; and around another corner a lugubrious modern painter called de Diego. The programme, Cooke says, may take in the fairy-tales of Charles Perrault or (picking up a human skull) the excitement of medical research. There is then a pause for the promotion of Willys Overland Motors, before Cooke resumes his walk, opening doors on musicians and singers: a model railway is revealed to be a foretaste of a film about the train taking Lincoln's body to its resting place in 1865. Cooke finishes by exchanging a few words with Martyn Green, the Gilbert and Sullivan veteran, about an eight-minute distillation of the entire plot of *The Mikado*.

It was a more polished performance than could have been expected of a novice television host, who had been working full-time on covering the election until four days earlier. Cooke's lines were not flawless, but they had a directness and immediacy that dealt bravely with that promise that he would act as 'the Good Companion', welcome in the viewer's home. The first week's show, he revealed, would include a short play by William Saroyan, specially written for *Omnibus*, the mini-*Mikado* and a film about two Haitian witch-doctors. If his own performance was confident to the point of nonchalance, so too was Saudek's direction, which had taken unprecedented risks and carried them off with some style.

Most of the reviewers loved it. One New York columnist gave it his top rating of four exclamation marks followed by three further dots. And, crucially, the advertisers liked it, too – Willys Overland Motors were soon followed by other sponsors, including Greyhound Buses. The range of stories covered, even in the first year, was truly eclectic – from Gilbert and Sullivan to a full-scale performance of *Die Fledermaus* – Benny Goodman, ballet and G.B. Shaw; films on aerial torpedoes, telephones, tugboats and young foxes; the first moving X-ray film showing a girl swallowing a soft drink; and even an adaptation of scenes from *Pickwick Papers* written by Cooke himself, in which he made a cameo costume appearance and which also featured the gratefully ennobled Sir Cedric Hardwicke.

At the heart of everything was Bob Saudek's imagination. Cooke delivered a tribute at his memorial service in 1997: 'You'd never have guessed it from this modest, earnest rather scholarly man. The great thing was his inventiveness. It wasn't enough to say, "Let's have a ballet." He'd say, "I tell you what we do. We bring in Sam Snead and have him show the most beautiful golf swing – we get a tennis player to demonstrate an elegant backhand . . . " ' The result, in this case, was a unique balletic experience, with a series of sporting super stars choreographed live by Gene Kelly and Cooke playing the bemused bystander.

Timing was the key and, because so many of the items were of variable length, there had always to be a measure of flexibility at the end of each programme. Ideally, about a minute would be left for Cooke to trail the following week's show: but conditions were not always ideal. An unfortunate excision of twenty-two pages from a live drama produced an impromptu discussion between Cooke and the trial lawyer Joseph Welch (who'd come to talk about the American constitution) on his most famous jury trials. And one actor who was perfectly sober during the run-through of a short play by Jean Giraudoux took some refreshment before the performance itself and became somewhat less predictable: so much so that, instead of being thirty-seven minutes long, the piece lasted little more than half an hour, as the hero flitted desperately through the script, alighting on vaguely remembered parts of the text. If the viewers were bewildered, Cooke was left with a seven-minute gap to fill.

An elderly carpenter named Albert, who was in sole and protective charge of moving Cooke's chair around the set, was heard to say, 'That Allison McCooke – and his you-ologies.' Thenceforward, the producer Bill Spier used to parrot the phrase at any production meeting where there was an awkward gap to fill: 'we'll just get Allison to do one of his you-ologies'.

Various awkward customers conspired to make life difficult, but Groucho Marx was one of the few who steadfastly refused to appear:

To Alistair Cooke: I was a little disappointed on receiving your rather lengthy letter to find no mention of money. I am, of course, an artist with my head in the clouds. And I was very happy to be invited to appear gratis, or thereabouts, on 'Meet the Press', 'The Last Word', the City Centre Theatre in New York, two all-night telethons, etc. But my business manager, Mr Gummo Marx, has a passion for money that is virtually a sickness. I am constantly being embarrassed by it. Still, he is my brother and rather than upset him, I have to bow to his wishes. I hope you and

your charming wife are happy and gay as the weather permits and that
this note will not end our fragile friendship.

Cooke's most cherished *Omnibus* story concerned a priceless art treasure from the Metropolitan Museum – an ornate cup attributed to the
sixteenth-century Italian Benvenuto Cellini. This was brought to the
studio after weeks of negotiation and under conditions of exceptional
security: it arrived by armoured car with two permanent guards who
were under instruction not to let it out of their sight. As it revolved
very slowly on an electronic pedestal, exquisitely lit, Cooke interviewed the curator about its provenance. The only problem was that
Cooke didn't like it. It was February, he had a bad cold and was
generally out of sorts and as he turned away from the camera to stifle
a sneeze, he said quite audibly that the piece was 'too rich for my
blood'. It was the only time Bob Saudek had occasion to scold him
and Cooke acknowledged that he deserved it for his unprofessional
outburst. He, however, had the last laugh. Ten years later the Cellini
cup was revealed to be a Victorian fake.

~

Throughout its life, *Omnibus* generated a strong team spirit. Apart
from Saudek, the director Bob Spier and Cooke himself, there were
half a dozen others, including the set-decorator Gene Callaghan, who
became one of the Cookes' closest friends and Mary Ahern, who
arrived as a programme consultant but ended up as one of its moving
spirits. A post-programme tradition developed that team members
and any guests who were interested should repair to the Cookes'
apartment for supper, prepared by Jane. It was always the same –
chilli con carne and tamales, avocado salad and ample supplies of
German beer. Among the celebrities who called were Leonard
Bernstein (frequently) and, on one dramatic evening, Roald Dahl and
the recently discovered Eartha Kitt – who had a stand-up row when
the singer decided she had been insulted.

Another visitor was Peter Ustinov, who made two appearances on
Omnibus, including a portrayal of Dr Johnson which gave rise to a
fund of stories for later post-programme parties: Ustinov says that he
was terrified at the prospect of such a long, live show and he told
Kenneth Haigh (playing Boswell) that if he got his lines wrong he
would simply cry out, 'Oh Bozzy, why did you always misquote me?!'

In the event, there were worse problems to overcome than the odd lost line. A scene in which Johnson watched a hanging went awry and the actor on the gallows began to choke: Ustinov improvised a move which would lead the camera away and allow the unfortunate man to be rescued. Then, in his own death scene, Ustinov remembers, 'I had to get out of bed and walk across the floor barefoot to make my last entry in the dictionary. At that moment, a lamp exploded, covering the floor with broken glass. I tiptoed across like a long-distance skier, but still suffered fearful lacerations.' He was already labouring under other dramatic disabilities: '*Omnibus* came in the middle of a run of my play *Romanoff and Juliet*, for which I wore a full beard. Johnson was clean-shaven. Luckily there was a marvellous make-up man who built Johnson's copious chin *over* the beard. It was an extraordinary achievement. Afterwards the critics praised the great restraint of my performance, but they didn't realise that I was simply trying to stop my make-up disintegrating.'

~

Omnibus was successful enough to survive the withdrawal of funds by the Ford Foundation after five years: it carried on under its own steam until 1961, although it failed to find an outlet for its penultimate season. At its peak, it pulled in an audience of fifteen million and it made Cooke famous in his adopted country for the first time, winning him an 'Emmy' award in 1958. Not expecting to be a winner, he watched the ceremony on television – and heard the master of cere-monies, Jimmy 'Schnozzle' Durante, read out the nominees until he came to 'Alistair Cook-ie'.

An official leaned over and corrected him: 'It's Cooke, Mr Durante, Cooke.'

'But it says 'Cookie here,' Durante protested.

After only a few months as a television personality Cooke felt the need to take a privately listed phone number to avoid the constant pestering of a fascinated public: 'With the exception of Hemingway and a handful of others, there is probably no living American author whose face is so familiar to the population at large,' according to one magazine. Cooke himself conceded that, especially in the early days, he attracted criticism for 'a certain uppitiness in his manner and delivery'. 'I guess that if you have a nose like mine, it's impossible *not* to look snooty.' It took him a considerable time – and Jane's frequent prompting – to learn to be more himself. Fame even earned him the attention of the celebrity columnist Don Iddon, who mentioned the rumour that Cooke was earning a thousand dollars a week. 'If he isn't, he is being underpaid,' he wrote. He was and the money certainly helped: the Cookes were almost immediately in a position to pay off the mortgage on the plot of land they'd bought next to the Long Island house as protection against unwelcome development.

Cooke's tenure was not without its high-level detractors, too. At the end of the first season, CBS's Vice-President of Programmes took Bob Saudek out to dinner to review the series. 'I have a suggestion for a host for you next year,' he announced. 'Alistair Cooke is fine, of course. But he's kinda remote and a little special. I have someone in mind who'd be just right, somebody very acceptable to Americans. What's more,' the executive went on, 'he's very experienced on TV and I reckon he's got a long way to go.' Saudek waited patiently for the name. It was Ronald Reagan. Saudek told him he intended to stick with Cooke.

~

On 12 December, 1952, the local paper in Blackpool reported that Cooke's father, Sam, had been knocked down by a car in Church Street, suffering head injuries and lacerations. He was said by the hospital to be in a satisfactory condition. This story of an accident in a depressed northern corner of Britain, on a grey December day, was a sharp reminder to Cooke of the distance he'd travelled. He was, by now, in more regular contact with his parents by letter, but he wasn't due to return to the town for another eighteen months.

His new home, thanks to Jane's attentions, was developing its own stylish character. The feature in *Life* magazine had spawned a series of further articles and one English writer, Lesley Blanch, had the opportunity to spend time with the family at Nassau Point and in New York: 'The big living room is discreet, softly grey-green. Some good pieces of eighteenth-century furniture, a grand piano, books, porcelain, old silver, flowers and pictures – most of them by his wife, Jane. She has decorated the entrance hall with a large mural, a *grisaille*, of old Regent Street.' In his study, Cooke had already begun to organise his books across one wall in the shape of a map of the United States: Maine and New England on a 'north-eastern' shelf and Arizona down at the bottom left-hand corner.

Lesley Blanch, writing for a family magazine, was keen to get to know Jane and the children better. 'Jane Cooke is a pretty, dark, graceful creature of French and Texan ancestry, whose interests are lively; dawdling in and out of the antique shops of Third Avenue, inventing lordly dishes, redesigning the house and above all creating and keeping that atmosphere of home which their sprawling family needs.' And the children? 'Stephen is musical and plays the flute; Johnny is scientifically inclined. Both of them, like all the American young, are absorbed in space-fiction, and what Cooke calls the mysteries of machinery. Holly, rising sixteen, is typical of her generation: is at college, has a crush on actor Mel Ferrer, writes essays in the Hemingway style, is a gay and pretty extrovert and has spent her last two vacations working as a farm and house help on a ranch out west. Susie, the baby, is four and a half and passionately interested in everything.' Whether Blanch was right to conclude that Cooke was the 'king-pin or pivot-point' of the household must be questionable.

Another unnamed profile-writer pointed to 'Mrs Cooke's passion for the baroque style of decoration and her husband's equal passion for the simplicity of modern and Queen Anne furniture', and reckoned that compromise was the keynote of the marriage. Jane liked to be surrounded by people 'free-flowing' through the house. Her husband had not lost his British respect for privacy: 'I believe in friendship and the symbol of friendship which is a closed door,' he told the interviewer. The meeting point between the two cultures was – and remained – the hour before dinner, when 'the most beautiful sound in America' was to be heard, to quote one of Cooke's most admired writers – the essayist and humorist, E.B. White: the tinkle of ice in the whisky glass.

~

All who met Cooke in this period were struck by his energy and range of interests. His professional output was certainly prodigious, even when help arrived on the *Guardian* front in the shape of a new Washington correspondent, Max Freedman. The paper was undergoing one of its periodic bouts of domestic turmoil, grappling with the problems of being a regionally based paper with ambitions to achieve a more balanced national distribution. Foreign coverage was important and Cooke's preference for New York made it sensible, in 1952, for Wadsworth to consider creating a staff post in Washington.

Freedman was a very different character from his New York counterpart. Bookish, earnest and meticulous, he had been a journalist in
his home town of Winnipeg before and after the war, as well as serving
a brief spell as a civil servant. He was famed for his erudition, having
read – it was said – every book in the Parliamentary Library in Ottawa.
Abandoning his degree out of boredom and shortage of funds, 'he
read what his contemporaries at University were required to read, but
much more besides', in the words of an obituarist (in 1980). 'Soon the
librarian and various faculty members became aware of the interests
of this dedicated young man. The result was that four years later,
when his colleagues were graduating, Max – albeit without a degree –
was a country mile ahead of them.'

Freedman was five years younger than Cooke and, at first,
approached the senior man with extreme deference: indeed, he paid
court to the whole family in a way which they found embarrassing to
the point of distaste. 'Whenever he came to dinner,' Cooke remembered, 'he would bring not just one present, but several – not just one
gramophone record, but a whole set; Susie might get three or four
gifts in a single visit.' Jane was acutely aware that Freedman was trying
too hard. It was she who dubbed him 'Uriah Heap', following his
remark, *sotto voce*, that it was 'an enormous privilege and honour to
be working with the master'. Unaware that he was coming to be
regarded as a latter-day Dickensian hypocrite, he continued to ply
Cooke, directly and indirectly, with outrageous flattery.

One particular letter in the *Guardian* archive exposes the nature of
the problem: 'It's a joy having Alistair back,' Freedman wrote in
August 1954, 'and the *Guardian* readers will rejoice to have his copy
once more.' He didn't really deserve his own byline, he went on –
though Cooke should write under his own name because 'every dispatch is signed with the signature of his genius.' Such unctuousness
laid the foundation for an uneasy relationship, which was destined to
implode in spectacular fashion a few years later.

In his celebrated assessment of the newspaper business *The Sugar
Pill*, T.S. Matthews saw the Cooke-Freedman rivalry as an indicator
of the essence of the *Manchester Guardian*. Indeed Matthews claimed,
some years later, that he had pestered the Nobel Committee to award
Cooke its Literature Prize. 'If it were possible,' he wrote in 1959,

to name the most generally popular feature in the *Guardian*, a likely choice would be Alistair Cooke's dispatches. And yet this laughing cavalier does not quite seem to fit the generally Roundhead tradition of the *Guardian*; he remains something of an anomaly, a significant oddity.

Max Freedman ... fits more nearly the orthodox likeness of a *Guardian* writer. Sometimes, indeed, the fit is almost uncomfortably tight. Freedman comes from Canada but gives the impression of even more distant origins – say the late eighteenth, or early nineteenth century ... he is never light, either of mind or heart. In fact, he is sometimes pretty heavy.

In the short term, however, Freedman's arrival meant that the 'cavalier' Cooke was spared any nagging sense of guilt at his lack of commitment to the minutiae of life on Capitol Hill. And during the same period, he met another *Guardian* figure who was to play an influential part in his professional life. Alastair Hetherington had been awarded a Harkness scholarship to Princeton University as a mature student – having spent the war in the army, followed by five years on the *Glasgow Herald*. This had given him plenty of insight into Cooke's talents, since the *Herald* took much of the *Guardian*'s overseas coverage on a cost-sharing basis. (The Scottish paper was reputed to have two spikes for rejected articles, one bearing the legend FL which stood for F*** ing Literature, where some of Cooke's more flowery offerings ended up.) Hetherington himself moved to the *Guardian* as a leader-writer in 1950 and, when he sailed for America in September 1952, he knew he would be returning to take up the post of Foreign Editor and, as such, would be Cooke's immediate superior.

Their early meetings were cordial enough. At Wadsworth's suggestion, Alistair and Jane entertained Hetherington in New York and Long Island and helped him through the logistics of his first few days in the country, including the compulsory driving-test for foreigners. The two men also shared a BBC studio, since Hetherington had been invited to give some fifteen-minute talks of his own while he was in New York, transmitted on the same circuit to London as *Letter from America*. Hetherington was forcibly struck by the contrast between his own nervous, much-rehearsed performance and Cooke's nonchalant, apparently off-the-cuff approach. Neither man, however, felt any great warmth for the other and Hetherington was rather more impressed by his first contact with Max Freedman in Washington. Something about the Canadian's style appealed to a Calvinist streak in Hetherington, who found him 'a splendid journalist' with 'an

encyclopaedic knowledge of British history and foreign policy ...
Max lived and breathed journalism and politics, knew everything and
everyone in Washington – if a cat killed a mouse there, Max would
be the first (after the mouse) to be informed of it.' Did this tribute
implicitly point to a doubt about Cooke's 'knowledge of British
foreign policy' – and his readiness to adjust his US coverage accordingly? Hetherington's first impressions of his transatlantic team were
to exercise an important influence on his dealings with each when –
on Wadsworth's death in 1956 – he took over the editorship of the
Manchester Guardian.

~

In the summer of 1953, with the children safely packed away at camp,
Alistair and Jane were able to take their annual trip to the West Coast.
Cooke did not continue to provide a *Letter from America* while on his
travels. At this stage, even after 323 editions, nobody thought it odd
that he should miss a few weeks for his summer break. It was only
some years later that the *Letter* became an unmissable weekly date,
earning a mythical reputation as the 'show that never closed', with
the gaps in the earlier years conveniently overlooked. The couple's
1953 tour – peppered with articles *en route* – was by way of Dallas,
Hollywood and the Central Valley Hydro-Electric scheme at Tracey
in California, which Cooke had been prevented from visiting two
years earlier by the more urgent demands of the Robinson-Turpin
bout.

On the way up to the town, they stopped at a gas station and, as
the young attendant filled the tank, he looked inside the car and said,
'It's Mr Cooke, isn't it?' He started to explain how much he loved
Omnibus. 'It's a great show,' he said. 'And you know one thing I like
about you? You never do those TV commercials.' Cooke agreed that
he'd never been tempted. 'Not like Bing Crosby,' the young man went
on. 'I was a great fan of his and then he went and did those Birdseye
ads.' He shook his head sadly and the Cookes went on their way. The
encounter hardened Cooke's resolve to avoid exploiting his fame in
such crass ways. He consistently refused offers to take part in product
advertising and promotion, even when – years later – a highly respectable American bank made him an enticing offer: 'Their letter came
on very grand, embossed paper and began, "Congratulations ... you
have been chosen as the image to represent our business." They

wanted me to make one commercial – which amounted to one day's work – a year. Over ten years they were proposing to pay me a million bucks.' He rejected the offer.

~

By now Cooke's new, elevated profile had begun to attract wider attention far beyond Tracey and not always in desirable quarters. No public figure could stand aside from the invasive attentions of the McCarthyites, whose anti-Communist campaign was now in its full, final flowering: the Senator's Permanent Sub-Committee on Investigations – with its televised hearings and remorseless questioning of witnesses – was taking few prisoners. Reputations lay littered in McCarthy's wake and Bob Saudek and his *Omnibus* team confronted the consequences: the regular 'Red Channel' lists of suspected Communists and fellow travellers could skew the casting of a play at short notice.

One day, Cooke suddenly found his own name quoted in unflattering terms by a McCarthy apologist, George Sokolsky, whose newspaper columns often gave early warning of the Committee's targets. After the event, Cooke devised a theory to explain this unwelcome interest – that he had (mistakenly) been identified as the moving spirit behind a new and sympathetic book about Alger Hiss. In fact, Cooke had reviewed the book quite dispassionately but Sokolsky didn't know that. Recognising the risks, Cooke threatened to sue, pointing out that he'd never met the author of the book, nor, for that matter, Hiss. Sokolsky backed off, but in the following weeks Cooke received a suspiciously inquisitive note from a Senator who wanted to know more about his writing: he sent the man a copy of the collected *Letters*, *One Man's America*, (complete with such subversive topics as 'Will Rogers, The Cowboy-Philosopher') and heard no more about it, though for a while there were strange knocking noises on his phone.

There was never any doubt that a *Guardian* correspondent would regard Senator Joe McCarthy as a figure to be reviled, but Cooke never engaged in ritual bashing of the Communist hunters. His approach was always more balanced, as it had been throughout the Hiss trial. Even the Permanent Sub-Committee was entitled to a proper journalistic examination, however damning the journalist's conclusions might be.

He himself had by now become convinced of Hiss's guilt and even told an interviewer in San Francisco that Hiss was 'the true father of McCarthyism'. The writer of the article was impressed by this unconventional assessment. Cooke, he reckoned, displayed a healthy distaste for clichés and stereotypes and was quite prepared to challenge conventional liberal thinking: 'Liberals,' Cooke is quoted as saying, 'have made McCarthy into a rather boring myth – a myth which has little relation to reality. They don't come to grips with him at all. They just do battle with these stereotypes they have of him. While he seems to have thrown them into a panic, perhaps for good private reasons of their own.'

There follows a striking section, in which Cooke recalls rereading a famous speech in which McCarthy claimed to have files on eighty-one Communists working in the State Department. 'He did everything to describe these people short of naming them,' Cooke told the reporter. 'My God, he had them all. I recognised one after another. And a lot of those people aren't around any more. He must have worked like a slave getting that speech together. This isn't intended as a defence of McCarthy but rather to point out that you can't fight McCarthy if you try to avoid reality.' The sound advice to liberals – that they should know their enemy – is tinged with more than a hint of Cooke's suspicion that there might be a grain of truth in the Senator's notorious lists.

The episode says much about Cooke's refusal to take people at their face value, or to judge them by their labels, even where he risked the obloquy of his peers. His was a complex reaction, motivated in part by his abiding pessimism over the fate of the world and the near-certainty that it would end in nuclear disaster. The first test-explosion of a hydrogen bomb on Bikini Island on 1 March filled him with renewed trepidation: 'This is obviously a turning-point in history', he told his listeners, 'that cannot be shrugged off or pacified with appeals to decent feeling.' The best hope was that it 'may have proved to the most ruthless Governments that the new law of peace is safety first'.

However Cooke's hunch – about the presence of fellow-travellers at the heart of government – did not cause him to desert the liberal cause. When McCarthy's star began to go into rapid decline throughout 1954, Cooke tracked its progress across the American sky for a jubilant *Guardian* readership. He singled out for particular praise the television broadcast by Ed Murrow, the reporter who in some ways had once been his mirror-image – enlightening Americans about Britain and Europe through his reports from London. Murrow's programme used a series of clips of McCarthy himself, linked with a sparse commentary, to expose the Senator's shortcomings. The effect was devastating, as were Murrow's closing comments – that the nation should look into its own soul to discover the reasons for the McCarthy phenomenon.

For a British audience there had been no hint in Cooke's writing of his personal – and easily misunderstood – sense of what had been happening. His *Letter from America* on the same subject, on 18 March 1954, is an even more intimate paean of praise for Murrow's achievement – verging on an apology that he had not been so forthright himself. Cooke admitted that much of the time it had been safer, more tactful and more comfortable for those in the public eye to look the other way as McCarthy passed by. And in the end it was not the politicians who had broken the spell, but a fellow-journalist. Soon afterwards McCarthy was censured by the Senate for the first time and when the Democrats seized control of Congress in November his power began to drain away.

A postscript to this uneasy time came with Cooke's public recognition – some time later – of the damage it had done to Anglo-American relations, as reflected in his own postbag. The cue for this soul-searching was the 1964 film *Point of Order* based on the Army hearings a decade earlier. He used a *Letter from America* to recall that, before McCarthy, the vast majority of his British correspondents – as many as eighty to ninety per cent – expressed their support for what he was doing:

> By the time McCarthy was dominating Congress, defying the President and Eisenhower was looking the other way in disgust and wishing McCarthy would go away, the mail on the *Letters* was frightening. Approval of America – and also of me – had dropped to about one letter in four. ... Being a writer who thought McCarthy was a scoundrel and being a foreign correspondent, especially, who went on expressing opinions during that ghastly time and getting my fill of accusations and tapped telephones, it may be that this movie brushed the scars of that forgotten time; or it may be that most of us who lived through the McCarthy era will never get over a paranoid tendency to see things under the bed.

～

At forty-five, Alistair Cooke was a rising celebrity on both sides of the Atlantic, but one who – despite all the personal anecdotes – gave little away about himself to viewers, listeners or readers. The *Spectator* magazine in London was intrigued. 'I have never met Mr Cooke and do not feel that I know him. I am an admirer of his articles in the *Manchester Guardian* and I regard him as the most competent broadcaster of three continents. But his personality remains an enigma to me, being strangely compounded of salt and sugar, of acerbity and sentiment. . . . I picture him as a youngish man, lean and handsome, derisive of fraudulence, yet capable of soft affection for outworn conventions and lost causes. I see him standing there by his refrigerator, thinking out his next broadcast, with a cocktail shaker in one hand and in the other, a child's milk-bottle. A smile of loving irony moulds his virile lips.'

In June 1954, this evidently enigmatic figure – in whom the *Spectator* reviewer detected (without identifying its make-up) an amalgam of Methodist morality and journalistic scepticism – delivered a 'Commencement Address' to the graduating students at Smith College in Massachusetts. Alfred Knopf published the text in a celebratory booklet. The invitation marked a sentimental return to the scene of his youthful outings with Edna Rostow, though there was no mention in the address of avant-garde nude film-making. Indeed, he took his responsibilities as a mentor of these ranks of young women extremely seriously.

His main theme was the difficulty of being 'a self-respecting American in a world that half distrusts and half hates us'. It was a rare chance to spread the word directly to those who might have it in their power to mitigate or magnify the ill repute in which the American abroad was held. 'You will need to do something that no previous Americans have had to do. Instead of looking on Europe as a picturesque breeding-ground of the first Americans, and a continent well lost, you will have to learn to make new ties with that continent and to live with Europeans as equals.' It wasn't 'the Roman sheen of our biceps' that would make America admirable in the eyes of others, but tolerance and an understanding that 'liberty is not the monopoly of Protestant whites with a paid-up subscription to the country club'. He pleaded for this quorum of gilded youth to accept that real friendship sprang from the awareness of the differences between nations and an acceptance that others might have something to teach Americans. The

British Parliament, he reminded them, had recently passed a law banning billboards in the open countryside. 'You are going to know a generation of Britons who will soon look on billboard advertising outside towns as a routine obscenity, like spitting in church.'

The *Spectator*'s puzzlement about the nature of the man was understandable. Superficially, at least, he was something of a conundrum – at home in so many different spheres and wedded to none of them. Those who knew him well marvelled at the way he perpetually created his own diverse circles of friends and contacts: he travelled to Smith College, for instance, with one of Jane's best friends, who afterwards took him to meet the novelist Jerome Weidman. This encounter led to an unlikely lifetime's comradeship between Weidman, a chronicler of Jewish life on the Lower East Side whose books were rooted in his own history, and Cooke, who'd managed to shake off his lower-middle-class background so effectively.

A year or so earlier Cooke had been taken up by another of the great Manhattan characters of the moment, Benjamin Sonnenberg, one of the begetters of the art of public relations. His skill, as Cooke teasingly put it, was to build 'large pediments for small statues'. Sonnenberg habitually collected people who might be useful in weaving the web of influence and contacts on which his art depended and, according to Brendan Gill, doyen of the *New Yorker* and a close friend of both men, Cooke was a very early protégé. 'Ben had a way of looking out for likely people and fostering them . . . Alistair was perfection. Sonnenberg, as a deracinated Russian Jew, adored the British, and Alistair had everything; he had looks, he had charm, he dressed exactly the way Ben wanted to dress.'

Even though invitations to Sonnenberg's house at number 19 Gramercy Park were among the most cherished in New York, Cooke treated his initial approach with disdain. Sonnenberg made the mistake of wondering whether Cooke might care to introduce *Omnibus* seated at the wheel of a cross-country coach. It so happened that the Greyhound Bus Company, one of the sponsors of the programme, was on his client-list. Cooke recoiled at the very idea. He was just as dismissive of an approach from the mighty tsar of CBS, William Paley, channelled through Sonnenberg. Paley wanted to buy Cooke as a roving correspondent; he could 'write his own ticket', was Paley's message. When Sonnenberg passed on this offer Cooke told him he was perfectly happy with the *Guardian* as his main employer, since he decided for himself which stories to cover and where to go. He had no wish to become a creature of any media tycoon. Paley was furious at being thwarted, but Cooke begged Sonnenberg, just for once, to suppress his natural inclination to fix and manipulate everyone: 'Ben,' he said, 'I don't owe you anything, and you don't owe me anything: we're friends.' The message struck home, and Alistair and Jane soon became relaxed regulars at Gramercy Park.

Number 19 was itself a monument to Sonnenberg's search for an expression of his own character and aspirations – a building so perfect, so exquisitely presented, that nobody could question its place in society, however unlikely its provenance might be. It had been built in the grandiose Empire style in 1845, with some forty rooms spread across five floors. Never having managed to save much of what he described to Brendan Gill as his 'torrential income', Sonnenberg suddenly found himself a millionaire after the sale of a successful farm business. Number 19 was the result.

Englishness was an abiding theme. When Sonnenberg entertained – and he entertained tirelessly – the idea of having a quondam Englishman among the guests was highly appealing. Cooke was soon in demand, even though he had spurned all professional services. As a host, Sonnenberg took delight in drawing together unlikely combinations of people – actors, bankers, musicians, journalists and business people – to see what would happen. Those who did seek his advice could expect to pay thousands of dollars for a few minutes of his time. As Cooke put it: 'By the time clients had got up to the ballroom at the top of the house, they were ready to pay any fee. He was utterly open about the degree to which the house could be used as a means of achieving the income needed to keep the house itself going.'

In that ballroom, with its views across the private park at the centre of the square, friends could enjoy sneak previews of the latest movies. It was here that Cooke watched the first showing of *Limelight*, Chaplin's melancholy re-creation of the London of his childhood, the last film before his exile to Europe. As the guests were ushered into their seats, Cooke found himself in one half of a love-seat: in the other sat a woman whom he'd never met but who had inspired his first book – Greta Garbo. She was no longer making movies; indeed, she had become something of a recluse, imitating in life the air of mystery once so assiduously cultivated by the studio publicists. She still left an impression on Cooke: 'We sat there watching and every time I lit her cigarette, I could see this wonderful profile. Sadly, she had very little to say for herself.' He didn't like the film either, finding it maudlin, self-indulgent and over-long.

In Brendan Gill's view, Sonnenberg's house came to represent an important element in Cooke's own life. 'Ben's house became Alistair's house, in a sense. It was a place where people felt fortunate to see him and he was the trump that Ben played.' Both Gill and Cooke became founder members of the Number Nineteen Club, along with other Sonnenberg protégés. Gill's assessment was that 'it was important – an "in" thing – to be a friend of Alistair Cooke. Predictably, Cooke would always be late for dinner but – according to Brendan Gill – 'because he was the most important figure there, we all waited. Ben had iron nerves. He never showed any displeasure or fretfulness. We all waited in the study till the great man appeared, without apology or explanation.' Nothing was asked of Cooke in return, except that he remain Sonnenberg's friend, to eat and travel with him, and to be part of the elegant accoutrements of number 19. Gill – who pictured himself in the second tier of the hierarchy – had no doubt Cooke and Sonnenberg were genuinely good friends, a friendship unbroken until the latter's death in 1978. 'Others might have been shaped and moulded by Ben, but not Cooke. If anything it was the other way around – Ben wanted to be more like Alistair, as well as adoring Jane.'

Sonnenberg's death left a great gap in the Cookes' lives: 'He had a circle – a very small inner circle – of close friends, of several conditions and talents,' Cooke's obituary tribute explained. 'And to them, he was father confessor, helper, companion, kidder, incomparable host.' Cooke was also the natural choice to present the television eulogy which tried to fix the man and his house for posterity. He and Jane watched the film go out with Sonnenberg's widow and children – sitting in the pine-panelled library which was soon to be dismantled. The Sotheby's auction of number 19's effects lasted three days.

~

The constant exposure to New York's cultural élite – through Sonnenberg and at the *Omnibus* studios – had another unpredictable consequence for Cooke. A well-known radio and television producer, Lou Cowan, listened to him one evening tapping out some favourite jazz pieces on the piano in his living-room. Cooke still played by ear and startled one admiring interviewer with his preference for 'the tough key of B, which is all sharps and excites the professionals to wonder'. Cowan conceived the idea of a long-playing record, which became *An Evening with Alistair Cooke at the Piano*, to incorporate all his favourite pieces, linked with a conversational commentary. It was on this disc – issued in 1954 – that Cooke re-created the music of his younger days, from 'Cupid is a Lovesick Maid' (written for the Mummers' performance of *Tom Thumb the Great*) to the tune he wrote while waiting for the birth of Susie – 'Janey in the Hospital'. The driving force behind the record was Cooke's love-affair with jazz.

How had it come about? 'People sometimes ask how an Englishman came to take such an interest in such things, or could even keep up with them,' according to one of the conversational links between the tracks. 'It's true, it was quite a trick in the Twenties. Half the best jazz records weren't issued in England and we had to guess who was the new man on clarinet. But the English have to go after things which are out of reach. Tell 'em about a flower that grows only at the South Pole and some Englishman is going to save up for an expedition. If it blooms only once every ten years, so much the harder and so much the better.'

The cover, emphasising Cooke's versatility, featured one of his own caricatures of himself at the piano. The sixteen pieces inside, with whistling and singing interludes, did not make him a fortune: in fact, he had to chase CBS to get any royalties at all. It did attract a certain amount of critical attention and was reissued in Britain a year later, with the same blurb provided by George Avakian, one of America's leading producers of jazz and popular music. The text is extravagant in its promotion of the novice performer and draws together all the most enthusiastic endorsements Cooke had ever received in his day jobs: 'The most competent broadcaster on four continents and one of the most gifted of living descriptive writers' (Harold Nicolson); *'l'excellent Alistair Cooke, que je considère par le talent le meilleur journaliste du monde' (Le Monde);* and 'the best ambassador we ever had' (an American diplomat in London).

Avakian also drew upon the judgement of the critic Kenneth Tynan, who had just produced (with Cecil Beaton) a slim, self-indulgent volume called *Persona Grata*. They described it as 'an alphabetical anthology of one hundred unique human beings', in which '. . . we sought, as we made our choice, certain qualities; chief among them –

craftsmanship, energy, elegance, wit and a dash of the unpredictable'. Cooke appeared in the company of such celebrities as Peggy Ashcroft, John Betjeman and Benjamin Britten, as 'one of the great reporters. Nobody can reproduce events, giving the feel as well as the facts, the pith as well as the husk, with greater clarity or gentler wit. It is hard for a journalist to read his dispatches without dismay. Using a fluent, hands-in-pocket style, appallingly slack on the surface, he always contrives to say more in less space than any of his rivals. He has dignified journalism by the odd expedient of not taking it too seriously.'

An Evening with Alistair Cooke also attracted the rather less welcome attention of Local 802, the New York branch of the Musicians' Union. Cooke had already had a minor run-in with the union the year before after an impromptu performance on the set of *Omnibus*. The script then had him sitting at a baby grand and rehearsing a few chords of blues music before moving on to the next location. It wasn't much, but it was enough. When he returned to the dressing-room, two bulky figures were waiting to invite him to visit the Union offices, so that he could sign up as a professional musician. Cooke protested, 'Look, this is a one-off. I won't touch a piano on camera again.' The visitors needed some convincing, but finally agreed that he should be allowed that one television performance for free.

Then came the CBS recording contract. The studios were highly unionised and Cooke's sessions were never likely to remain a secret. Within days, Avakian received a call from the head of the Musicians' Union, James 'Caesar' Petrillo, inquiring when Mr Cooke would be calling by to pick up his membership card. There was no choice in the matter. Petrillo's grip on the studios was unshakeable and the following Monday Cooke reported to the Union offices on Madison Square Gardens. He came into a huge cacophonous hall, full of musicians signing up and paying their dues – biding their time with a tune on the trombone or a crooner's lament. He waited in line, was issued with his card and became perhaps the only man in history to hold, at the same time, a White House press pass and membership of Local 802. And even if there was a competitor for this dual honour, surely the claimant could not also boast of having been appointed an Honorary Colonel in the Household Guard of the Governor of Kentucky – a distinction bestowed on Cooke at a surprise party and one he shared with (among others) Bing Crosby and Marilyn Monroe.

21

THE CHEMISTRY OF HUMAN AFFECTION

At the time of Cooke's recording debut his son, Johnny, was thirteen years old. He had spent the last two years at a coeducational boarding-school near Lake Placid in upstate New York. It was the sort of place at which pupils called teachers by their first names and the informality appealed to the boy. In the autumn of 1954, however, he was due to move on to a prep school. Ruth, by now a teacher at Dalton in New York (where Holly was still a pupil) favoured Putney School in Vermont – and Johnny liked it too, since it operated on the same liberal progressive principles to which he'd grown accustomed. Cooke was not so sure. When he heard about the choice he wrote to his son: certainly, Putney had a decent academic reputation – but wouldn't it be a good idea to consider one of the more traditional schools, like Andover or Choate (and perhaps, at the back of his mind, like the better sort of English public school)? Johnny disagreed profoundly. He had no intention of going to a single-sex establishment where collar and tie were required. He and Ruth stuck to their original decision.

Cooke was doing his best to keep his lines of communication open to Johnny. He was constrained both by time and his own awkwardness, but in May 1954 he did take his son with him on a working trip to Canada. It turned out to be a bad time to be away from his desk. On the evening of 17 May, he sent Johnny down from their Montreal hotel room to collect an evening paper. Five minutes later he was back, brandishing the paper and yelling, 'They've done it!'

'It' was the Supreme Court decision in the landmark case of 'Brown versus the Board of Education of Topeka, Kansas' – in which Justice Earl Warren and his colleagues ruled that racial segregation in the provision of publicly funded schooling was unconstitutional. This was the start of the great tide of change on which the Civil Rights movement was launched and Cooke knew that he was in the wrong place. He ended up writing a *Guardian* piece with the rather oblique headline, 'SALUTE FROM AFAR FOR US NEGROES – MONTREAL WELCOMES END OF SEGREGATION'. His own instincts about the risks and dangers of change had never been dispelled and were on display even at this moment of liberal triumph: 'The new decision of the Court undertakes to enforce by law the Negroes' graduation from second- to first-class citizenship. There will be a price for this . . . In the fine tough weave of Southern life, black and white are warp and woof. Their differences, their subtle and peculiar friction and interdependence go back to the first land leases and the earliest songs and stories of childhood.' The sentiment was clear – and the imagery evidently designed to appeal to a reader in the industrial North of England, home of the textile industry.

The muted nature of this welcome will not have escaped the more assiduous readers of the paper and probably lodged, too, in the minds of some at the newspaper's offices in Manchester, reinforcing those inclined to be suspicious of his liberal credentials. In an essentially emotional debate no application of a cold douche of logic was likely to be well received.

~

As Cooke was preparing for the latest of his transatlantic visits at the *Guardian*'s expense, he devoted his parting *Letter from America* in June 1954 to a review of relations between the two countries. It was inspired by the fact that Winston Churchill and his Foreign Secretary Anthony Eden were about to arrive for a summit meeting with President Eisenhower and the Secretary of State, John Foster Dulles. Cooke warned the British audience that they shouldn't expect much solid information to emerge at the end of the affair. In a strangely self-denying observation (for a newspaperman) he maintained that an absence of news might even be highly desirable. After a previous summit in Bermuda, the participants hadn't even troubled to issue a communiqué, so that 'correspondents were reduced to writing little essays about the vegetation of the island, or finding out what the principals had for breakfast. It may be the same this time for – as it always seems to me – the excellent reason that the more honest the talks and the more serious the decisions made, the less safety there is in advertising to the world a common strategy. The absence of juicy copy for correspondents is no sign of an unsuccessful meeting.'

If anyone doubted the need for a common strategy, Cooke catalogued the outstanding post-war policy differences between the two
countries: from the recognition of Communist China – through India
and Pakistan – to the Suez Canal and the Gulf and – most ominous
of all – the Cold War. The rhetoric of the Republican administration
had shifted from containing the menace of Moscow to 'liberating
satellite states', but Europe should not believe that the United States
was ready to drop hydrogen bombs on the Red Army to drive them
out of Poland and Czechoslovakia. He pleaded with his audience not
to pay heed to the odd hot-headed Senator whose fulminations might
be quoted in the British press. 'I am constantly amazed at the intelligent Europeans who, somewhere along the road of our prickly
friendship, believe Mr Dulles or the President has seriously advocated
using one of the monster bombs to break up the Cold War.' The
problem, he argued, was too grave to be derailed by such nonsense.

There was no mention by name of Vietnam, Laos or Cambodia,
but Cooke ended his piece, 'I had not meant, in this last talk before
the holidays, to talk about politics. But the four men in the White
House will not be talking about politics, they will be talking about
survival.'

On that note, he and Jane headed for England, revelling once again
in the luxury afforded by the *Queen Mary*. The ship's photographer
frequently captured the elegant couple at ease in their sumptuous
surroundings, supping cocktails or posing on an ornamental stairway.
Cooke is almost always smoking a cigarette. His adherence to the
habit was not interrupted by what he'd discovered in his own writing
for the *Guardian*. He was one of the first correspondents to take
seriously new research linking smoking and cancer, revealing as early
as February 1954 that 'the long golden age' of the cigarette manu-
facturers – twenty years of continuously soaring sales – had 'exploded
in a bombshell'. He gave prominence to one report demonstrating
that mice painted with tobacco tar were contracting skin cancer in
alarming numbers and another that heavy smokers were twenty times
more likely than non-smokers to contract lung cancer. A year of this
sort of publicity had had its effects: the week before he sailed, one of
Cooke's dispatches indicated that one and a half million Americans
had given up smoking in the previous eighteen months. He himself
was not among them.

The *Guardian* might not have been the most generous of employers

(Cooke had enjoyed no real increase in pay since joining the paper in 1947), but the free trip remained a perk to be savoured. A few days later he and Jane were translated to the rather more mundane surroundings of Ormond Avenue in Blackpool. 'Mr Cooke', the local paper reported, 'spent the weekend at his parents' home before going to Manchester. He paid another short visit yesterday.' The impression is irresistible that these visitations were as brief as humanly (and humanely) possible. Blackpool Grammar School, having got wind of his arrival, tried to inveigle him into presenting the end-of-term prizes in July – or alternatively, giving a Speech Day address in September. Neither could be fitted into his diary.

Within days, the restless son was on his way. Among the Cookes' ports of call was the home of Alistair's publisher Rupert Hart-Davis and the two men discussed a further collection of *Letters*. This project, true to form, took a further fourteen years to come to fruition. Back in London, Cooke's passion for Georgian furniture – Hepplewhite and Sheraton – was fuelled by the chance to call on two favoured antique dealers who, along with the auction rooms of Parke-Bernet, became his main sources of supply. At last, the income from *Omnibus* was enabling him to become the collector he'd been in spirit – ever since his dim but engaging room-mate Hugh Munro-Fraser had opened his eyes to the wonders of fine furniture in Cambridge, twenty-five years earlier. Cooke even found himself back at Colston's antique shop – this time as a customer, not merely a gawping bystander. There were treasures to be had on the still depressed British market, especially for a buyer with dollars in his pocket. It was during this period that Cooke accumulated some of his proudest possessions, including a Queen Anne chest he found at a shop in Kensington High Street: this was a rarity, made of padauk – a rich, honey-coloured Burmese wood used only for a few years in the early 1700s when English craftsmen found their supplies of mahogany cut off because of the war with France. A Parke-Bernet auction threw up six 'Medallion' place settings which came (with apparently reliable provenance) from the collection of Tsar Nicholas II. And the couple also began to build up an eclectic array of art, including a Renoir engraving bought at auction in London and a painting by Raoul Dufy. Hart-Davis presented them with a landscape by John Piper and they'd also been given a set of Piper's costume designs for *Gloriana*, Britten's coronation tribute. If such items had been acquired as investments – and not simply for pleasure – the Cookes could have been well pleased with the long-term commercial potential of their purchases. In the 1980s a dealer offered nearly $30,000 for the Renoir, which had cost $600, and the padauk chest showed a similar appreciation. As it was, nothing was ever sold.

At the end of July they left London for a week in the Mediterranean – leaving behind a certain amount of dismay at the BBC. A bright spark at the West London television headquarters in Lime Grove had persuaded Cooke to appear on the programme *Speaking Personally*, just as he'd done in 1938 and 1946. Arrangements, as so often with Cooke, were hazy. While he sunned himself in Italy the producers had no advance script, no clear plan about visual aids and no idea whether Jane would be making a contribution. Worse, his masters at BBC radio felt they'd been bamboozled. In a hasty exchange of memos, they considered ways either of using a sound version of the television broadcast, or persuading Cooke to do something specifically for radio: 'Cooke told us that he was coming for a holiday,' one executive scrawled plaintively. 'We played fair and left him alone. Now we are in the position of looking foolish – partly his fault, partly TV's disregard of his express wish.'

In the event, Jane did not join her husband on the set of *Speaking Personally*, nor were any props brought into play. After a light-hearted overture, it was rather a serious affair – dedicated to the beating of a familiar drum. 'Now this evening I would like to tell a few amusing stories and have just a quiet family time with you. But I have been in Europe for six weeks and it would be foolish of me to pretend that I'm not impressed by something that impresses everybody; namely, that the present state of Anglo-American relations is about as bad as it's ever been.' He confessed himself disturbed by this miasma of mutual misunderstanding and spoke up for the Anglo-American alliance which, he judged, had never been more necessary, however irksome it might seem. He put in a good word for the Marshall Plan, which he believed had proved its value despite all the carping communist propaganda. His tour of Britain had shown him people in good spirits, goods in the shops, life back to normal. 'I think it would be natural for you to say that the dose of tonic, the Marshall Plan, was not really necessary in the first place. I have a friend who has a tremendous and very amusing contempt for doctors, but always when the stitches are out and the crutches have been thrown away and he's beginning to navigate on his own. It's very easy to feel that way.'

It was part lecture, part sermon, part exhortation – delivered extempore, with uncharacteristic stumbles and corrections and a glaring verbal tic: almost every sentence began with the word 'now', the classic sign of a speaker playing for time. Yet his ease of manner, charm and personality sugared the pill. The *Guardian* commented that his talk 'rippled along with such ease that ten minutes seemed gone all too soon'.

∽

Beyond the terms of his mission to explain, Cooke's own interests were never narrowly defined and frequently flew in the face of the prevailing fashion. He was, for instance, a keen promoter of a minor literary figure, William March, for whose collected works he contributed an introduction – worked up from a lengthy obituary in the *Guardian*. What he liked about March's novels and short stories was something he believed critics tended to undervalue: a crisp, uncluttered writing style and a preparedness to quarry into the murkier byways of the spirit – 'the dark underside of human nature.'

It wasn't the only instance of an admiration for writers widely regarded as being, in one way or another, beyond the pale. March, like H.L. Mencken, spoke his mind and didn't care if he trampled on the niceties of literary society. Each uttered truths which Cooke, still influenced by his deep immersion in analysis, felt must be lurking beneath even the most urbane exterior – like his own, for instance. If his duty was to smooth over the rough surfaces of American life for a British audience which might otherwise misinterpret what it saw, (and since he found the expression of his own feelings so fiendishly difficult), he was happy to commend those prepared to portray life in the raw.

That was one explanation for Cooke's ardent enthusiasm for the work of Ernest Hemingway, though he was drawn as much by the books' style as by their content: 'To a degree impossible, perhaps, for Europeans to gauge,' he wrote in the *Guardian*, 'Hemingway took the daily speech of the non-literary American and turned it into literature.' Cooke pursued the point in a *Letter from America*: 'Hemingway started to knife away all the fat he could find in the language; he leaves only the heart and muscle and nerves – the verbs and the nouns and the adverbs. And all their living movement, their circulatory system, is in the prepositions – the "ons" and "fors" and "withs" and "bys" and "froms".'

If Hemingway, still carousing in Cuba, was an outsider, so too was the cartoonist and humorist, James Thurber, whom Cooke had met through a mutual friend, Marc Simont, the illustrator of his Christmas stories. Thurber's separateness was a function of his deteriorating sight, which had left him almost completely blind by the time Cooke interviewed him for *Omnibus* in March 1956. He introduced their filmed discussion with a memorable turn of phrase: 'Wordsworth defined poetry as emotion recollected in tranquillity. If that's so, then we might say that Thurber is chaos recollected in tranquillity.' Later he and Jane visited the Thurbers at their home in Connecticut and entertained them in New York and Cooke was enthralled by the way Thurber 'spoke exactly as he wrote'. 'We would be sitting at dinner, with Thurber in mid-story and he would announce that he needed to go to the bathroom. He had to be lifted and guided and to have the seat lifted for him. And all the time the story continued. Occasionally he'd get carried away and when he stood up at the table to illustrate what he was saying with actions, he was quite likely to fall over the furniture.' Even when Thurber became conspicuously cantankerous the Cookes kept in contact – and remained so until his death in 1961.

In fact Cooke was a lifelong fan of that acerbic and world-weary American humour represented by Twain, Thurber and S.J. Perelman and later, Woody Allen. When he was invited in old age to choose his fifteen favourite books, he added English writers like the critic James Agate (whose autobiographical series *Ego* he collected) and Max Beerbohm – revered for the parodies which had inspired him as a schoolboy writer. 'As a steady diet,' he explained, 'I must say I prefer writers of the second class who seem to me to have perfectly realised their talent, rather than the giants who dig deep and, while striking gold, also come on slag and muddy streams.' Given the chance, he added, he would have included William March, as well as the journalist Bill Buckley – a close friend of his later life. Journalism provides a useful link between these disparate characters – and with Cooke himself. It's almost as if, in honouring members of his own much-maligned profession, he was unconsciously trying to convey a subliminal message about the way in which the peddling of daily news might be elevated to a higher plane in the hands of a true artist.

In Cooke's mind, the most complete expression of this vision of the journalist as enduring creative talent remained H.L. Mencken. After Mencken's stroke – and Cooke's premature obituary – in 1948, he had seen little of the Sage of Baltimore, but on Good Friday 1955 he visited him at his home – the same house in which he'd been born in 1880. 'He was clearly embarrassed by his physical decline, but not for long.' As they talked, Cooke was relieved to notice that 'whatever parts of the brain had been switched off, the one that coined his inimitable way of talk was still active'.

Nine months later, though, Mencken finally expired and Cooke's tribute, dusted off and updated from the day he had his first stroke, finally appeared in the *Guardian*, covering most of the obituary page: 'H.L. Mencken – Newspaperman and Philologist', it began and recorded the fact that, since his illness, Mencken had been unable to focus on the written word. 'He bemused [could this have been a *Guardian* misprint?] himself during these pitiful years with a form of amusement he had scorned throughout his life; he went to the movies. But this form of moonshine could not succour his enforced idleness and at a lunch given by the *Baltimore Sun* on his seventieth birthday, he confessed that he was "ready for the angels". '

There was nothing forced or fragile about Cooke's respect for the Sage of Baltimore, even though he represented, in many ways, a very different journalistic tradition – that of the polemical writer without inhibition and with a full set of prejudices. (Cooke had plenty of the former and tried to keep the latter under wraps.) But the prejudices never diminished Cooke's respect and in 1955 he collaborated with Alfred Knopf in the publication of *The Vintage Mencken*, a collection which appeared a few months before the old man's death and for which he penned a lengthy introduction.

In the years that followed he helped to officiate at the opening of the 'H.L. Mencken room' in a Baltimore library, lectured on Mencken at Cambridge, tried to sell a television programme about him to the BBC, quoted him extensively in *Letters from America* and attended the Baltimore celebrations of the centenary of his birth in 1980. Their friendship, he told the gathering, had been a typical Mencken absurdity, violating five rules: 'I am English and he despised the English, sharing the deep American belief that the English are born speaking American and then put on the dog; I am Methodist and he abominated Methodists; I am in broadcasting and he hated radio and

television; he hated liberals and, shaking his head in mock wonderment, said he did not know how God had managed without
the *New Republic* and the *Manchester Guardian*; and I am a golfer.
Mencken said that "if I had my way, any man guilty of golf would be
ineligible for an office of trust in the United States". ' Then, rhet-
orically, Cooke asked, 'Why am I here? Because even Henry Mencken
could not solve the chemistry of human attraction and the chemistry
triumphed over his principles.'

~

The chemistry of human attraction: it was a phrase which said much
about Cooke's proclivity for forming friendships with unlikely people
and for sustaining those friendships over long periods without the
need for external stimulation or support. There was no logic to these
liaisons: with the breadth and depth of his contacts, from politics
through art and science, how was it that so many of his most enduring
relationships fell outside the orbit of his professional life? What was
it that bound him to the arch-conservative McCarthyite banker Paul
Mannheim? Or the navy commander turned submarine salesman
Alan Russell? Each became, during the 1950s, part of a small separate
circle of devoted friends, very much on the model Cooke had established as a student at Cambridge – each circle quite likely to last until
broken by death.

On the same basis, it surely wasn't obvious that the Cookes should
establish such a warm intimacy with Bogart and Bacall: yet they did
and Cooke was one of the few close friends to see Bogart in the
months before he died of cancer in 1957. He described in *Six Men* how
he arrived just after Bogart had finished making his will. 'Whether his
wife knew about this, I am unsure, but he spoke of it to me and of his
illness and the sudden uselessness of money, with an entirely unforced
humour and an equally unforced seriousness; neither with complaint
nor with a brave absence of complaint.' Cooke ended his essay with a
tribute to 'a much more intelligent man than most of his trade, or
several others, a touchy man who found the world more corrupt than
he had hoped; a man with a tough shell hiding a fine core,' who 'lived
in a town crowded with malign flatterers, hypocrites and poseurs,
fake ascetics, studio panders and the pimps of the press.' From all of
these second-rate people, Bogart had been determined to keep 'the
rather shameful secret in the realistic world we inhabit, of being an

incurable puritan, gentle at bottom and afraid to seem so.' Or as Cooke phrased his tribute in his *Guardian* obituary, 'a gallant man and an idealist.'

~

Not all the chemistry of human attraction was under Cooke's control. From the summer of 1956 onwards, he and Jane found that their relationship came increasingly under strain. The fact that he was so busy didn't help: juggling three jobs meant that his home life was bound to suffer and Jane had friends, interests and a career of her own. Under her maiden name, Jane White, she was in demand as a portrait painter, though she resisted taking formal commissions – not liking to take money from sitters if they didn't approve of the result: she was renowned for painting what she saw and not what her subjects wanted to see. She once accepted a mink coat in exchange for one of her works, but often she was happier painting friends and members of her family, singly and in groups.

In general, Jane rented a studio away from the apartment. But she also began to discover the attraction of travelling without Alistair, especially to Italy or France. As time went on, both suffered considerably from this alienation – Cooke, in particular, found it hard to cope with Jane's independent life. But somehow the marriage survived, to emerge – after more than a decade of troubles – as something with an innate strength which belied the pressures to which it had been subjected. Thirty years later, neither could bear to talk about the emotional traumas of that period.

Yet those traumas certainly defined how Alistair and Jane related to each other thereafter even if, on the surface, nothing changed. As far as their acquaintances were concerned they were two strong-willed people who – for much of each day – ploughed their own individual furrows, but who retained a strong and (as it turned out) indissoluble bond. This was expressed in the rituals by which they ran their lives, sometimes, it seemed, in parallel, but never diverging too far and with a perennial tradition of the early evening reunion – for drinks, supper or a night out; and in later years, for an evening in front of the television. Cooke's analyst might well have acknowledged the role of ritual as a guard against insecurity. Nearly all who knew them, especially new friends, wondered at the strength and solidity of their marriage and the sense of slightly sardonic mutual respect – each

being more than ready to deride the other's foibles, but in an affectionate and entertaining way. Most assumed that Jane was the rock
on which he built his life – for he certainly had no other deep conviction on which to fall back. He was, he once confessed, a true sceptic
in all matters of the spirit, for whom organised religion was essentially
illogical. He liked to quote Mencken on the subject who, when asked
what he would say if he found himself in heaven, replied: 'If I do fetch
up with the twelve apostles, I shall say, "Gentlemen, I was wrong". '

~

Cooke's lack of interest in taking consolation from the Church
inspired – in March 1955 – one of the most powerful pieces of his
years as a *Guardian* correspondent – covering the performance of
the evangelist Billy Graham in New York's Madison Square Garden.
Cooke's first-hand experience of the evangelist at work in his own
backyard was soul-searing – but not in the way Graham would have
hoped. The sceptical correspondent surveyed the crowd and drew his
own corrosive picture of the penitents: 'The great bulk of them, it
seemed to one sinner, were joyless matrons and their lumpish daughters. Not a smitch or smear of lipstick violated their well-pursed lips.
Not a pretty girl or a roguish buck in the lot. But neither were
they drab. There is something in the full-time practice of virtue that
inclines the female of the species to hydrangea blue. It would take a
complexion as blooded as Santa Claus and a skin-tone as flashing as
a Hawaiian to rescue the human face from such an ocean of ghastly
blue. Ava Gardner herself would drown incognito in it.'

Graham stood at a lectern kindly provided by International Business Machines and launched into his spiel, seeking donations so that
he could save souls on a mission to Scotland. 'There was a rustle and
clinking as many bodies leaned over to reach in their pockets, to dig
deep for the unshriven souls of Glasgow.'

It was, in Cooke's eyes, a brilliant piece of showmanship and a
despicable use of the psychology of the masses – and all in the name
of a nasty, mean-minded deity. When the preacher spoke of Jesus – it
was not the 'black-browed, bearded Old Testament avenger,' but
neither was it the 'frail, effeminate hero of the calendars'. Graham's
Jesus was 'a snooping, darting detective, spotting you in your mirror,
riding in the Underground, watching at the foot of your bed, antici-
pating the waking excuse, posted at every exit of the Garden if you

Jane White, at the age of about twenty-one, some ten years before she met Cooke – Texas belle with a hint of Mediterranean glamour.

On one of their first trips to England after the war, Alistair took Jane to Blackpool, where she was introduced to Cooke's parents and his older brother Sam – still plying the butcher's trade.

In the BBC's *Transatlantic Quiz*, Cooke was the US question-master
– but his team had to answer questions posed in London.

Only rarely did the two question-masters meet: this shot, in 1946, shows
Cooke with his UK opposite number, Lionel Hale – who, by chance, became
the biographer's godfather soon afterwards.

Jane and Alistair on honeymoon in San Francisco, May 1946.
The shot was taken in the Tonga Room of the Fairmont Hotel.
Later he recommended the place to a friend for its 'Hawaiian hors
d'oeuvres and drinks with camellias in'.

" GO IN AND BRAND 'EM, COWBOY "

Cooke was a great fan of David Low, and the feeling was mutual. Low presented him with the original of this cartoon of the McCarthy witch-hunt, which was based on a phrase in one of Cooke's report.

A.P. Wadsworth, editor of the *Manchester Guardian*, as viewed by Low
– one of many cartoons which found their way into Cooke's den
at Nassau Point, Long Island.

The *Omnibus* years, through the eyes of the show's official photographer, Roy Stevens. The shot of Cooke, cigarette in hand, speaking to the camera, comes from the first season – 1952–3. He can also be seen in conversation with the short, balding figure of the programme's founding father, Bob Saudek. Smoking on air was thought quite normal until the late 1950s.

Letter from America, c 1953, with props: coffee, ashtray and makeshift lectern. Cooke had finally found his niche, and he would prove a hard man to dislodge.

should dare to bolt for it'. And so they stayed and shuffled up to receive their benediction, 'the halt and the lame in spirit, surely, but also the pasty-faced, the careworn, a hangdog sailor, "teenagers" in desperation, a mountainous mother and her huge, sullen daughter, regiments of the awkward and the unloved'.

The correspondent was only too glad to walk out into 'the comparative wholesomeness of Eighth Avenue, with its movie houses and pawnshops, drugstores and bars, and cops on clanking horses'. This article caused a journalistic uproar, appearing as it did just before Graham left on a mission to Britain. In the eyes of some outraged souls who bombarded the paper with their complaints, Cooke was represented as nothing less than 'the devil incarnate'. A few weeks later the paper had nominated him for a very different assignment – as a guest reporter for the British General Election of May 1955.

∼

There was just time for another of his great continental perambulations with Jane – to New Orleans, across the Gulf of Mexico to Texas, up into the Rockies and eventually, inevitably, to California. They arranged to take lunch with Groucho Marx in Hollywood, as Cooke told his *Letter from America* listeners a few weeks later:

> He wasn't in sight when we came to the country club, but my wife spotted him and before I saw him I heard a voice over my left shoulder say, 'Mr C.? This is Mrs C., I presume. If it isn't Mrs C., Mrs C. is going to hear about this.' That was the beginning. And the end was at the end of lunch when a big, rather boring man had stood at our table first on one foot, then on the other, dropping pearls of unwisdom, till Groucho said, 'Listen, don't you think you'd better be on your way?' The big man looked at his watch and said, 'That's right, I'm going to San Francisco, I've gotta be pushing.'
>
> 'Well,' said Groucho, 'Take it easy, drive slow.'
>
> 'I'm not driving,' said the man, 'I'm flying.'
>
> Groucho took a deep breath and said, 'Okay, fusspot, then fly slow.'

From Los Angeles the Cookes themselves followed the country club bore to San Francisco, where they made another of those chance connections which led to a lengthy friendship. Usually, when advised to 'look up so-and-so' in a far-away city, they declined to do so; this time, they did call Carroll Lynch and his wife Virginia and were invited over to their rented home on the Belvedere Peninsula, just north of the city. It was an enchanted location, surrounded by eucalyptus and cypress and looking out over the bright white expanse of the city across the water. The two couples struck up an immediate and lasting rapport. Cooke remembers seeing Lynch emerge from his bedroom in a dressing-gown: 'My first thought was that they'd recreated Charlie Chaplin, a familiar dapper figure, with wistful eyes and the same graceful movements.' Lynch was one of the country's top industrial arbitrators, in demand for the resolution of disputes between management and unions and there was certainly nothing reverential in his attitude to the host of *Omnibus*. He spoke his mind with that laconic sense of humour, verging on cynicism, which Cooke so admired. Another regular watering hole had been established in his favourite city.

Cooke knew the place and all the sights of California better than most of the natives. So frequently had he criss-crossed the state, that his friends used him as an informal information service. Mary Ahern, from the *Omnibus* team, was issued with a detailed briefing document – 'Cooke's miniature Tours'. It advises her to take a warm topcoat and a tweed suit, which might sound 'silly in the East, but can be a godsend "out there", where the nights are damp with mist and chilly.' Among the recommended San Francisco attractions he includes Tilden Park, where he had taken Jane on their honeymoon on the day of the Alcatraz riot; and the redwood groves of Muir Park, across the Golden Gate Bridge.

Cooke also has plenty of views on the possibilities for gracious living: he identifies San Francisco's two most expensive restaurants, Amelio's and Alexis Tangier, while Skipper Kent's has 'very rohmantic surroundings'. In addition, 'the Fairmont Hotel has an amusing bar – The Tonga Room – where you get Hawaiian hors-d'oeuvres and drinks with camellias floating in them (all drinks in SF after the fifth have camellias floating in them)'. And in the same hotel, 'The Papagayo Room, with Mexican food that's genuine. Its main usefulness is that it stays open till four a.m. If you don't want to go far from home after a rowdy night, that's the ticket.' Both locations, he might have added, also boasted in-house photographers who, more than once, captured the Cookes in party mood.

∼

It was while Cooke was enjoying these delights that the message came through from A.P. Wadsworth, summoning him to the hustings in Britain. There was little time to spare. A train journey back across the country left him just one night in New York before his departure. For once he flew, rather than sailed, across the Atlantic and the speed of his transition from the Papagayo Room to Brixton and the Rhondda Valley perhaps explains why, when he began his tour, he was far less capable than usual of concealing the Anglo-American culture shock. It started from the moment he travelled into London from the airport: 'To an American, there is something hopeless about the very solidity, the air of permanence, of an English slum. Mostly, American slums look like theatre-sets and circus tents pitched on a bare field on a windy night and left to rot and sprout garbage and stray newspapers and brassy children. They look as if they could be cleared in a couple of hours.' Whereas in London, 'scores of the streets our bus swerved into might have been there in Cobbett's time and will surely outlast [Sir Anthony] Eden.'

It was the trains which really got under his skin. Abandoning his usual reluctance to crow about the superiority of America (on the grounds that it might feed prejudice among the poor British relations) he laid into British Railways with a will. 'Ten days ago,' he wrote in an article purportedly about an election meeting in Shropshire, 'I rode the 2,400 miles of track from San Francisco to Chicago in the scheduled 48 hours. That is an average of 52 miles an hour, through much skimming desert to be sure, but also for one night we climbed up to 7,000 feet in the Sierras and the next long afternoon to 9,000 feet in the Rockies and down again through two of the world's highest mountain ranges.' This feat was a function of competition, he proclaimed, with capitalist enterprises trying to tempt customers with 'newer rolling-stock, more ingenious gadgets, better food, more ample lounges, stacks of reading-matter, writing rooms, second-storey vistadomes, loads of time-tables, pretty hostesses, a choice of radio or taped music at an elbow, switch telephones and fresh trout brought aboard from the bounteous Colorado streams'. British Railways couldn't quite match all those facilities. In fact, it couldn't match any of them. A week later, as Cooke spent five hours covering the fifty-five miles between Newport and Leominster, he had plenty of opportunity to dwell on the fact that his train did not appear 'to have attracted an hour's attention from industrial designers, the light metals interests, interior decorators, sanitary plumbers or even from a conscientious carpenter in the forty years I have known them. The trains are still clattering assembly jobs of brown wood and glass, the third-class lavatories suggest we should be grateful to have emerged from the caves; and the parsimony with which the time-tables are hidden from the traveller on the train imply that an invasion is imminent.' This indictment is only the most extreme of a number which appear in the course of his coverage of the campaign.

It was, admittedly, the first time he'd reported on British affairs for nearly twenty years. (He'd turned down the chance to cover the coronation because he didn't want to muscle in on the journalists in the home office, as he put it, 'like some third act hero' and steal their thunder.) His odyssey also bypassed the more appealing rural corners of the country and took him largely to the great industrial cities of Wales, Scotland and the North of England. But Cooke's sense of a nation trapped in the past, still bereft of most of the benefits of progress, is manifest throughout: 'the heavy-lidded audience in rain-coats and mufflers'; or 'I set off across the wild Saddleworth Moor, so blinded with grey mist and black with millstone grit that a lost dino-saur would have been no surprise'; and 'the pudgy children leap and frolic on playing-fields planted on levelled-out slag-heaps'. He felt no need to spin a yarn, nor to put the best possible gloss on the state of things – not when he was writing for the well-versed, politically aware readers of the *Manchester Guardian.*

As for the politics themselves and in the absence of a serious Liberal challenge to warm the hearts of his readers (the Liberals won only six seats) Cooke clearly developed a sneaking respect for the Conservative leader Sir Anthony Eden. He followed Eden on a tour of Lancashire mill towns and was surprised at how well the patrician premier (who had just succeeded Churchill) coped with his working-class audi-ences. At one point Cooke lapsed into a rather lyrical account of these unlikely meetings, which were taking place just a few miles from his birthplace in Salford. Each, or so it seemed to him, was attended by the same people, an indistinguishable mass of humanity: 'Whether the bodies are stocky or spindly and however bent the backs, they have firm mouths and sceptical pale eyes. There is no clairvoyance by which one could guess how these people will vote. But most, I would think, had a grave respect for the big and engaging man who waved at them.' He was right. Eden won the election comfortably.

When it came to summing up his impressions for the *Letter from America* audience, he remembered himself sufficiently to seek out the bright side of the affair: 'I think the Americans are, in general, a more civilised people (perhaps I mean sophisticated) while the British are emotionally the more mature nation.' The evidence for his generalisation was that Britain – 'where you barely knew an election was going on' – enjoyed a seventy-six per cent election turn-out, while in America – 'where an election rings and shatters the country for eight months until we are all deaf from the hullabaloo of it' – only half the people bother to vote.

~

Towards the end of 1955, A.P. Wadsworth fell ill and went into a steady decline. He didn't immediately surrender control of the paper, but editorial meetings often had to be held at his home; he did, however, have the strength to steer the paper through one last crisis. Nasser's annexation of the Suez Canal in July 1956 put the paper on its mettle. Although Eden's bellicose response to the snub was cheerfully accepted by most of the press, the *Guardian* was among the minority which refused to accept that there was a need or justification for the use of force. This stance was first developed during a forty-minute conference of leader writers at Wadsworth's bedside at which it was agreed that Nasser had not broken any international convention. Any attempt to seize the canal back by military action would, they decided, risk wrecking the United Nations and leave Britain facing international opprobrium.

It was an unpopular line to adopt. Some readers, they knew, would find their position defeatist and unpatriotic. They took strength, however, from a stream of inside information provided by their Washington correspondent, Max Freedman. In one of many private memos he advised his head office that the Eisenhower administration had expressed horror at the prospect of war in Egypt. This flew in the face of conventional British thinking – that a soldier-President would automatically favour a military solution. Freedman's account of the alarm in Washington persuaded the *Guardian* that there must be something to be alarmed about – in other words, that Britain and France, despite their protestations, really were planning military action. Alastair Hetherington, by now foreign editor, wrote the *Guardian*'s leader that day, and later paid tribute to Freedman and his 'excellent contacts in the US State Department,' which formed a solid basis for the paper's crusade against the Suez adventure.

In this emotionally-charged period and only a few days after it was announced that he would be retiring to an honorary post, Wadsworth died – on 4 November 1956. Alastair Hetherington, at the age of thirty-six, having emerged as his successor almost by osmosis, spent his first few days in the job covering the dramatic conclusion to this foreign policy débâcle. Small wonder that he should feel so warmly thereafter towards Max Freedman, whose Washington sources had helped to establish his reputation as an upholder of a noble newspaper tradition.

There was no immediate impact on Cooke from the change of editor. He claimed that Wadsworth had told him, in one of their last conversations, that he was 'afraid' that Hetherington would succeed him because none of the other possible candidates was suitable. Thus prepared, he simply got on with his job. His own reporting on Suez was limited, though he did feel compelled to confront the consequent breakdown in Anglo-American relations in a *Letter from America* penned from the depths of the crisis. Despite the policy chasm between the two countries, he wished to convey the 'extraordinary restraint' of Americans towards their wayward ally, causing them to act, talk and write with 'astonishing bewilderment or gentleness because they have been poleaxed by the event itself and are still reeling in a daze of shock and disbelief'. He warned that this restraint might not last: 'There may be a recoil into bitter recrimination. The tremendous fact cannot be blinked at that on Thursday sixty-four nations of the world, very few of them lackeys of the United States, stood together in moral condemnation of Britain and France.'

Throughout the Suez crisis Cooke was in any case preoccupied with American politics – though, as so often, he found himself the butt of anti-British feeling: the *ex officio* ambassador received 'sackloads of angry mail' for 'his' actions in invading Egypt. It was only a passing distraction from the nominating Conventions – the Democrats in Chicago, followed by the Republicans in San Francisco – and then the election campaign. He prepared for this task by taking a few days' holiday at Nassau Point, where Jane had just ordered an entire cactus garden to brighten up the sandy expanse between their house and the edge of the cliff. He described (in a *Letter* that summer) the guilty pleasure he'd taken in spending an entire day examining this horti-cultural acquisition and neglecting the daily newspapers. This, in the unwritten rule book of his daily life, was a mortal sin, but it was a sin in which he began to luxuriate – 'the life of a vegetable, which I had always scorned as a witless, drooling existence, seemed to be a noble and calming experience'.

August found him back in harness as the Democrats began their search for a man to beat Eisenhower – something they were confident of doing, especially because of the President's heart attack the previous year. At the time it had seemed to many people (including the ultra-cautious, once-bitten, Cooke) that Eisenhower was unlikely to be strong enough to run for a second term. In a *Letter from America* of November 1955 he had even ventured a prediction, in a roundabout way: 'After the President's illness and Stevenson's declaration [that he was prepared to stand] the Republicans are now asking, "Who can beat Stevenson?" ' The view of former President Harry Truman, as expressed to Cooke, was that Eisenhower would be easy meat for anyone – 'even with an accent like yours'. Cooke himself may even have played an innocent part in persuading Stevenson to take the plunge again, since it was he who passed on the opinion of a leading surgeon that Eisenhower might be lucky to live another year. In the following weeks Cooke began to notice 'a new, if tactful, gleam' in Stevenson's eye.

The increasing dominance of television had reinforced the *Guard-ian*'s view that there was no point in trying to compete on contemporaneous coverage of the Conventions: distinctive, thought-ful, reflective writing could be just as effective even if it was more than twenty-four hours old. Consequently, Cooke's 1956 Convention reports do not have the frantic air of earlier years. Stevenson was the party favourite and Cooke had already spent time with him during the primary elections, witnessing his friend's victory in the California primary – a victory which involved a measure of personal humiliation. Stevenson's advisers unwisely suggested that when he attended the Merced County Spring Fair, in the peach-growing capital of the state, he should demonstrate the common touch by 'dressing in blue jeans, a denim coat with lampshade tassels flapping from the shoulder pads and a red string tie.' Nor was it a good idea to arrange for the candidate to ride a high-stepping strawberry roan – trailing behind Miss Merced County 1956 and a float bearing 'a group of local beauties, all frills and teeth and grins pinned from ear to ear, sedately erect in giant papier-mâché ice-cream cones'.

Despite Merced County, California fell to Stevenson. Yet when news of his success came through, Cooke and other reporters, who'd arranged to meet him in a Los Angeles hotel, were surprised to find how down-trodden the Governor seemed. 'There was no quippery, no laughter and incidentally no champagne, no beer, nothing to wet a whistle. After a rather awkward interlude, more like a confessional, in which he said something about gratitude and humility, he got up briskly, apologised for his tiredness and showed us out.' Stevenson had done nothing to dispel Cooke's nagging sense that he was a presidential loser. Yet – like most observers – he was still shocked by what happened at the start of the Convention, when Harry Truman let it be known that he would be throwing his weight behind a rival candidate.

Why? Was it personal? Were the rumours true, that Truman simply couldn't stand Stevenson and wanted to stop him at all costs? Cooke had a unique chance to test out this theory during a private end-of-Convention session with the ex-President – an interview secured by the simple expedient of calling him in his hotel room. 'No, there's nothin' personal in this, I like the man,' Truman assured him. Cooke did not believe this. On the Freudian principle that 'where the patient denies is the place to dig,' he probed away until the truth began to bubble to the surface. Truman did indeed despise Stevenson and the type of American he represented – 'a country-club tweedy snob, mixed up with a bunch of defeatists and reactionaries.'

Cooke listened dumbly to this astonishing character-assassination of his own party's likely presidential candidate. Yet he decided to suppress the story – on the grounds that it would have been 'too cruel to put into print'. It only came to light when he published *Six Men* twenty years later – and when all the principals were dead. The *Sunday Telegraph* critic judged that his sensitivity had been unwarranted: 'I should imagine the readers of the *Manchester Guardian*, for which Mr Cooke then worked, would have found it interesting.'

~

The Convention press corps had almost no time for reflection on Stevenson's victory before heading west to San Francisco, where the

Republicans – unless something went seriously awry – were due to re-nominate Eisenhower and his Vice-President, Richard Milhous Nixon. Cooke spent the first few days in a city-centre hotel, but was then invited to camp out with the Lynches on the Belvedere Peninsula. There, thanks to his arrangement with the *Guardian*, he could write his copy in the evening and rise at 6 a.m. to dictate it to London for the following day's paper.

In the absence of political drama, he fell back on such staples as the weather and the barbed blessings of television. Cooke might bemoan the loss of spontaneity and naturalness, but it suited the lazy streak in his character – facts and images presented on a plate which he could re-package for a distant audience which hadn't seen the real thing. The final moments of the Convention touched new heights of televisual awareness – as far removed from the earthy realism of a British election campaign as Saddleworth Moor from San Francisco. On the platform were idealised ordinary Americans: 'a young and handsome Texas housewife, mother of six, with a disarming *Saturday Evening Post* smile and a superb figure; a twenty-seven-year-old dirt farmer from North Dakota; a Rhode Island steel-worker waving his union card; a history teacher in the brave shape of a Negress.' There was a famous football coach who happend to be a Catholic, a volunteer nurse and a Senator who had 'left his legs on the fields of France.' They had all been 'recruited with infinite care by a committee whose casting office called this production "Cross Section USA".' It might be artificial, but, for Cooke at least, it had something real at its core: a vision of the breadth of Eisenhower's appeal at a time of unequalled prosperity.

～

The campaign that followed saw Cooke and Max Freedman working in comparative harmony – though the first straws of discord between the two correspondents could be detected in the wind. Freedman, without consultation, had broken a cardinal rule by inviting an outsider to participate in the *Guardian*'s coverage of the Conventions. The outsider was a man Cooke much admired, Denis Brogan, American historian, journalist and erstwhile star of *Transatlantic Quiz*: but Cooke regarded the Conventions as his fiefdom. Freedman could pay court to whomsoever he pleased on Capitol Hill, but the Conventions were not for sharing and the idea was apparently dropped. Alastair

Hetherington was still only foreign editor and Wadsworth still notion-ally in charge at head office.

On 12 September, Cooke penned what he described at the time as a piece which said 'everything I'm likely to say about this and every other election campaign'. The campaign train had finally been shunted into retirement. Stevenson intended to fly by two-engine plane to fifteen or twenty airport meetings each day. 'He calls it his "flying porch",' Cooke reflected, 'which is a meaningful dig at the one issue every Democrat wants to bring up and doesn't dare to mention: the President's health and his prudent immobilisation on the front porch of the White House.' Eisenhower was not taking to the stump at all. Yet 'when all the cross-country campaigning is done and the "issues" are inflated to the bursting-point, nothing could help the Democrats so much as (in the words of one faceless and greatly daring Democrat) "a harmless bout of five-day pneumonia".'

There was to be no such medical miracle to save Adlai Stevenson. Eisenhower enjoyed a bigger victory than in 1952 – a landslide – leaving Cooke to write up the obsequies of the man he came to call 'the failed saint', Governor Adlai Stevenson.

22

FAMILIES AND FRIENDS

It was after Alastair Hetherington's occupation of the *Guardian* editor's chair that opinions of Cooke's unreliability on the subject of race started to proliferate. In his autobiography, Hetherington is quite frank about this perceived shortcoming: Cooke 'had a slight blind spot about Civil Rights in the South, which contributed to the friction with Max Freedman'. His private view was more uncompromising – that 'Cooke did not *seem* to us to be sufficiently concerned at that time with reporting the injustices suffered by black people in the South and it caused us some anxiety in London'. However this view developed (and whether Freedman played any direct part in spreading the unkind word), it certainly had nothing to do with the amount of space Cooke devoted to the subject. A seven-part series, appearing in the summer of 1956 under the title 'Ordeal of the South', added up to a fair-sized thesis on the subject which was published by the *Guardian* in booklet form.

The problem, as in the past, was not the level of his interest but the direction of his analysis. Cooke continued to worry away at his belief that well-meaning Northerners were imposing rules on a Southern society whose complexity they simply didn't understand – risking the gravest of social consequences. ' "Integration" [Cooke's quotation marks] is not a Southern problem exclusively, but a challenge to all of the United States to transform the Negro from a traditional servant, a cheap labour pawn, a licensed clown and entertainer, into a citizen with equal rights and opportunities before the law.'

As he trekked from Cincinnati in the North across to Baltimore and on into North Carolina, Alabama and Louisiana, he traced the effect of the new laws on the communities through which he passed, but with an eye for examples that would support his thesis. There were still single-race schools in Baltimore, for instance, simply because of the make-up of the local population – 'for the same simple reason there are no Salford schools that have cockneys'. (It was natural, in other words.) This article ended with an observation to send a shiver down any liberal spine: if, *de facto*, blacks and whites were working together in factories and offices, 'why should a mixed school be such a symbolic fright? Because the school-house is the club-house, dance-hall, civics class: the heart of social life among the young. And the deep, unspoken fear is that sanctioned familiarity will breed inter-marriage. Thus we come down to the old question, which only the intellectual, the superficial and the foreigner far from the dilemma can afford to pooh-pooh: "Would you want your daughter to marry a Negro?" ' Cooke's use of the word 'unspoken' was directed towards his English readers, since the fear was openly discussed in the states he was visiting.

Cooke moved on to take a sympathetic look at Montgomery, Alabama, where the city fathers were prosecuting the leaders of a long-standing bus boycott and trying to deal with the well-organised campaign of the NAACP (the National Association for the Advance-ment of Colored People). The atmosphere of the place brought back memories of his first visits to the South two decades earlier, when all he cared about was the music: he wrote about himself as a disembodied third person, an unnamed innocent abroad: 'On any blinding summer afternoon he could come on a fat coloured wench pausing from the chore of cotton-picking to throw her head high at the sun and whine, "Go down, ol'Hannah, don't you rise no mo".' In the scruffy parts of towns, he would sit deeply satisfied in dark corners of saloons while 'bent-over pianists beat out immortal twelve-bar blues.' In that romantic half-light, the overt signs of segregation, Cooke said, had been invisible to him. Now they were the focus of all visiting eyes. He made his way to the Mount Zion African Episcopal Methodist Church to witness a service at which thirty-five 'coloured pastors' officiated, including a young black leader whom he'd never before seen in the flesh – the Reverend Martin Luther King Junior.

The taxi-driver dropped him off two blocks away so that he'd be less conspicuous and, as he walked, the blues seeped from juke-boxes behind the sprung screen-doors of small saloons. At the church, too, where there were 500 or 600 people 'blacker than the night around them', he heard the same rhythms – the minor chords and heaving melancholy. This was not a Methodist service like those of his childhood: 'a sister was "testifying", standing and improvising a prayer in many a King James sentence chanted through the uvula in strangulated quarter-tones.'

The arrival of Martin Luther King was met with a salvo of applause from the faithful and he started to deliver what he described as a new constitution for the cause of emancipation and for 'the dignity of the individual with respect to transportation'. What struck Cooke was not King's message but the words he used: 'This great movement had started, he said, "without the external and internal attachments in terms of organisational structure." They listened in awe. If they or their children came to be "integrated" they too could get to write like this. The Rev. King was indeed a master of Pentagon, or Federal, prose and the constitution was written almost wholly in it. It was "implemented" with eight committees, staffed by the leaders and was heady with executive boards, trustees, public relations committees, provisions for tenure of office, just like General Motors. . . . This appalling document was heard in a marvelling silence.'

The piece produced a howl of outrage from the NAACP as being flagrantly 'anti-Negro'.

On his return to New York – and before the articles appeared in the *Guardian* – Cooke distilled his thinking for the BBC listeners to *Letter from America* and attempted to relate the issues to domestic British concerns:

> Before we judge the South too hastily, we must put ourselves in their place. Suppose that half the population of Birmingham (England, not Alabama), or Sheffield, or Brighton or London was coloured. And suppose it had been so for two or three hundred years. With the coloured people going to their schools and you going to yours. Would you at once accede to a law going through Parliament that next autumn your children must go to school with coloured people? It is a crude question and no doubt some people will be irritated by it. But it is the first question to put. Because what a parent thinks of is that his children will mingle equally, as scholars and playmates, then, later on, as friends and sweethearts, with coloured people.

The races co-existed in the South, Cooke told his audience, because of – not in spite of – the well-understood taboos, up to and including an unbreakable injunction against intermarriage. 'The Supreme Court's order not only imposes the quite harmless custom of working and playing with children of another race. It threatens to destroy the taboo which allowed them safe familiarity. I will not beat about the bush. It brings to all Southern parents the spectre of intermarriage and eventual wholesale miscegenation.' Cooke went on to say that he thought the process was inevitable anyway, in a matter of three, four or five generations. This was strong stuff – not ritual apologia for his adopted nation, but something deeply felt.

~

These musings were a good deal closer to the bone than his normal *Letter from America* fare, where members of the family continued to make sporadic appearances. In March that year he recorded the departure of Holly, aged seventeen, to visit London – the city which would eventually become her home. A little later she was back on stage, appearing as an incomprehensible (to Cooke) teenager, whose friends provoked in him utter cultural bewilderment. Would anyone in Britain really credit it? A girl stayed the night, 'staggered awake one morning and drifted like a Zombie to the kitchen to renew her link with life; to get her orange juice? No! Coffee? No. Cereal, eggs, toast – water, even? No. She grabbed the thing in a daze and staggered back to bed, loping along the hall with her head tilted back and her elbow up and her lips rounded against the mouth of – a bottle of pop! I presume she is recognisably human in some ways, but . . . so far as I am concerned she might be a woman from Mars.' He was only partly joking.

Holly's best friend, Anne Burrows, found herself playing a much more dramatic role in Cooke's professional life. In August 1956 she was returning home alone from a year's study in Paris on board the Italian liner *Andrea Doria*, when it collided with another ship in fog and sank fifty miles off Nantucket Island. Cooke was on the dockside as the rescue ships brought the survivors into New York and he battled his way through the chaotic crowds of relatives, medical staff and officials. With his press credentials he was able to bypass the authorities and to reach the dockside. His *Guardian* report captured the moment of relief for Ann's parents, Bill and Marcella: 'A swarm of coatless families pressed against the police cordons and put their faces up to hear a monotone coming from loudspeakers on top of a police car: "George Annino, US; Lucio Barba, Italy; Angelo Belardo, US; Bernardo Bartolo, Italy; Anne Burrows, US . . ." '

Anne had been picked up by a fruit freighter, the *Cape Ann,* and Cooke made his way to the appropriate part of the docks. At last the squat little vessel edged its way to its mooring and Cooke caught sight of Anne, a moment he captured for his readers without revealing her identity: 'There was a tall young girl with a shock of blonde hair up somewhere near the bridge. It was a happy, pretty American face and she was waving gently with her left arm. This was the way it would look, the way it ought to look, in the newsreels.' The story the survivors told was shocking: ninety of those on the *Cape Ann* had signed a protest letter, condemning the behaviour of the Italian crew of the *Andrea Doria,* who left them clinging to the high side of the ship with 'no stewards in sight, no instructions, no leadership'. Cooke's normal journalistic detachment was tested to the limit, as he proffered an 'expert' view that the radar seemed to have been working on both ships and that man, not machine, had been the likely villain of the piece.

In Cooke's broadcasts, Susie was the most frequently quoted family member and the only one to be referred to directly by name, partly because of her youth, perhaps, and partly because she was more securely in Cooke's orbit than the other children. A Florida trip to cover the visit of an English politician, for instance, was combined with a short holiday allowing Susie to take her first flight: 'She was under the delusion, as seven-year-olds tend to be, that the plane had been specially made, or at least chartered, for her.' Her father did nothing to dispel this notion. 'I go on the theory as a parent that modern psychiatry is a very fine thing and has thrown some healthy light into some murky corners of human ignorance and prejudice; but anybody who wants to abolish Santa Claus, or tell Susie the airplane wasn't her own property – well, stranger, you'd better watch out, that's all.'

Then, in 1959, he took her on a long-promised outing to watch the Kentucky Derby. Susie was horse mad, but horses were among the rare subjects about which her father knew next to nothing – less, he quipped, than he knew about horse-flies. But he wallowed in the vicarious pleasure of her excitement, of 'lunch, lying on the grass, of chicken hash and potato pancakes and the best succotash I have ever eaten', and of a breathlessly close race in which Willie Shoemaker, on the English-bred Tommy Lee, won by a nose. The account is a rarity for its unashamed display of emotion.

I truly wince at sounding folksy and I don't mean to bring Susie into this story more than I must, but I fear that to tell about taking a horse-crazy ten year old to the Kentucky Derby and then to leave her out, would be like rewriting *Tom Sawyer* and forgetting Huck Finn. I had the beautiful and complete impression that I'd lived for three days in another land, in another century; Susie had the impression and mentioned it, that she had died and gone to heaven. It was a perfect weekend, spent among the drollest and most agreeable people in eighteenth-century America.

He ended with the note of caution he'd felt to compelled to introduce, as Susie 'rattled on in ecstasy' on the flight home:

I jumped in to remind her that, though it was wonderful, life was not like this.

'How d'you mean?' she said.

'Well,' I preached, 'we might have had bad seats at the Derby, or keeled over from the heat, or there'd be no horses for you to ride. Everything *was* perfect, but just look out. It isn't always so.'

'I don't get it,' she said and fell asleep.

The death of Dr Haven Emerson did not feature in the *Letters*, but it did prompt a warmly worded obituary in the *Guardian*. Cooke listed the public health developments at home and abroad attributable to his former father-in-law, from fluoridation to the epidemiology of polio, TB and heart disease. Cooke did not reveal his own special interest in the subject of his eulogy, though observant readers might have wondered how he came to have such insights into Emerson's personal habits – like the use of soap to clean his teeth.

Emerson's death was one of those events which must have caused Cooke to reflect on the past: his ex-wife, Ruth, a school administrator at Dalton, but still spending her holidays at Southold; and Johnny, finding his adolescent feet as a sixteen-year-old at Putney school in Vermont. The boy at least had discovered a real interest in life – the folk music which was sweeping through the trendier sections of American youth. By the time he left Putney, Johnny was an enthusiastic performer on the guitar, sowing the seeds of a career in the music business which was far removed from what his father had expected and, perhaps, hoped for. With Holly in London and Stephen still sulking at his own boarding-school, Alistair and Jane were able to plan their usual springtime saunter through the Southern states to

San Francisco, taking in such favourite locations as the Yosemite National Park. But Cooke left New York, on reporting duty, two weeks before his wife and she returned home a week early, leaving him to drive up to Oregon alone. This was to be the pattern of their gradual estrangement, a pattern of separate holidays and disconnected diaries. The unpredictable chemistry of human affection had begun its unwelcome work.

~

On 8 September 1957, Cooke recorded his 500th *Letter from America* – now with a transmission time at 9.15 on a Saturday evening and a repeat the following afternoon. As he celebrated the notable happenings of the previous eleven years, he can hardly have guessed that he was less than twenty per cent of the way through one of the greatest broadcasting marathons of all time. He sat on his terrace overlooking Peconic Bay and the sun caught the windows of a house across the water, causing them to 'glisten like flies preserved in amber', while the cat flapped a lazy paw at his paper. In this soothing environment, he mused on the task he'd been set by Lindsay Wellington on that dark January day back in 1946 and admitted to a sense of pride that the project had survived so long. 'It does occur to me as a chastening afterthought that pride is a swollen form of self-respect and I recall with a twinge the definition of self-respect given by my favourite American author. "Self-respect," said H.L. Mencken, "is the secure feeling that no one, as yet, is suspicious." So I had better stop preening my feathers. After all, the BBC giveth abundantly, but the BBC also taketh away. Not yet awhile, I hope!' A friendly reviewer in the *Radio Times* compared Cooke's discursive style with that of Bernard Shaw, 'taking us to unexpected places, proceeding in kangaroo hops, sometimes affecting garrulity, never for a moment losing his mastery of *broadcast* conversation. Thank goodness, he has not yet got even to his fiftieth birthday.'

Cooke had little enough cause for professional concern, whatever was happening in his private life. Apart from the BBC, the *Guardian* and *Omnibus*, he had just become a part-time Hollywood film star, in the wake of a letter from a man he'd never met. Nunnally Johnson was a successful film producer and director and a man who wrote much of his own material, having spent many years as a reporter and short-story writer on the *Saturday Evening Post*. His latest project was a psychological study of a woman with a split personality, *The Three Faces of Eve*, starring Joanne Woodward. Because it was based on a true story, Johnson conceived the idea of having his film presented as if it were a television documentary – complete with a reporter speaking to camera before the unfolding of the action. He picked on Cooke, having watched him week after week on *Omnibus*, and wondered whether he'd care to fly across to Hollywood.

Cooke was flattered and mentioned the offer to the author Jerome Weidman who told him that he should not, in any circumstances, proceed without taking advice from an expert. Cooke had been ready to accept on the basis of a free flight to his beloved West Coast, but was persuaded to allow Weidman's agent, Carol, to do the negotiations. 'They offered me $1,200,' Cooke recalls, 'which seemed fine to me. But Carol wrote back saying, "Mr Cooke wouldn't go to Hoboken, New Jersey, for $1,200."' As a man with no instinct for the accumulation of money, Cooke shuddered at her effrontery – but managed to quell his doubts when she struck a deal for a fee of $10,000, plus full VIP treatment for him and Jane while they were in Hollywood.

On the first evening, they were invited by the producer to watch some footage of the woman who'd inspired the film, as she switched overnight from a dowdy and repressed creature into an uninhibited extrovert. The next morning, Cooke appeared at the studios at ten o'clock and was met by Nunnally Johnson, to whom he'd been briefly introduced the previous night: would Johnson like to see the script Cooke had prepared? According to Cooke, the director showed no interest in reading it through beforehand and simply led the way into the small theatre which had been prepared for the shooting of the sequence. Cooke was asked to stand in front of the screen as if the movie was about to begin and to read out the words he'd memorised. Johnson was quite satisfied and told him he'd have to do it again so it could be shot from a different angle. 'The important thing', he said, 'is that the beginning and end of the script be exactly the same as the first take.' Cooke promised that there'd be no changes. Twenty minutes later, the whole thing was over. 'That's just fine,' Johnson reassured him. 'Vintage Cooke. And now it's time for lunch.'

As they walked away from the theatre, Cooke said, 'Look, Nunnally, I feel terrible about this. All that money – I thought at least it would take all day.'

'So did I,' Johnson replied. 'But you're something special: we call it "flesh".'

'What's flesh?'

'People who can write their own stuff and deliver it. Robert Bench-ley could do it, but there aren't very many of you.' Cooke protested that the fee was still out of all proportion to the work involved. Johnson explained the logic of the business: 'Do you realise what the alternatives were? First we hire a script-writer, maybe two. Then we call up James Mason, or some other actor, who has to be auditioned. Then the whole thing goes on to the teleprompter and we do it over and over again until it sounds natural. With you, the whole thing took twenty minutes.'

It was the start of another long and fruitful association, which became close enough for the Cookes to take holidays in Europe with Johnson and his wife Doris. Nunnally Johnson was more obviously engaging than some of the others in Cooke's concentric circles of friends – a tall, drooping man with a sad face and a sardonic Southern sense of humour which Cooke found irresistible.

The Three Faces of Eve was a success and won an Oscar for Joanne Woodward. Cooke attended the ceremony, over which he cast a jaun-diced eye – 'a sadly amateur affair, giving the impression of a ship-load of stars marooned with their floating scenery on a desert island who discovered too late that they had failed to carry a quota of writers.' But Woodward, in his biased estimation, duly wept what he thought might have been genuine tears. The triumph was celebrated with particular enthusiasm in Augusta, Georgia, home not just of Johnson, but of the two doctors whose dramatised account of the case inspired the film. 'AUGUSTA HONORS NATIVE SONS AT BRILLIANT WORLD PREMIERE,' blared the *Augusta Chronicle* of 19 September 1957. 'Handsome British-born Alistair Cooke, noted columnist, actor and narrator of the film' was at the top table alongside Johnson, Wood-ward and the two Georgia doctors. Among the guests in the Bel Air Hotel was 'the beauteous Jody Elizabeth Shattuck of Atlanta, wearing a white lace gown and her title of "Miss Georgia" with a queenly air'.

The Hollywood experience did bring some curious spin-offs in its wake. In October 1960, Cooke received a telegram from Roger Stevens, a New York impresario: 'Most interested to know if you would con-sider playing a fascinating part in a Broadway production I am plan-ning for this winter. Could you please contact my office Monday as to whether or not the project might appeal to you. If it does, we can send you a script immediately.' The whiff of greasepaint did not lure Cooke from his routine. Then, two years later, Nunnally Johnson, by then living in London, took him to see a film preview at a small private cinema in London. Afterwards he was approached by a stranger, who introduced himself as the director of a new version of *Cleopatra* – Rouben Mamoulian. He'd been watching Cooke in profile, he said, and wondered if he'd be prepared to do a screen test for the part of Caesar? With the memory of his lucrative morning's work on *The Three Faces* still vivid in his mind, Cooke asked how much time it would take. When he heard that filming, on location in Italy, might last three months, reality swiftly exploded into his day-dream. 'I couldn't possibly do that,' he told the producer. 'I'm committed to the *Guardian*.'

'Are you sure? Perhaps I could call you in the morning . . . ' With a rising sense of panic, Cooke tried to explain that it was out of the question.

Johnson watched with amusement. 'Your trouble is that you're too law-abiding,' he said. Cooke protested that – even if he earned in a month four times the *Guardian*'s annual salary – there was no way he could face Alastair Hetherington with such a proposition. The part went instead to a certain Rex Harrison, who managed to win an Oscar as Best Supporting Actor.

~

There could hardly have been a greater contrast between Nunnally Johnson and another of those with whom Cooke formed long-term relationships during the 1950s. Alan Russell had been a US Navy Commander during the war. His father had been in the business of selling uniforms and medals and it evidently ran in the blood, because when Russell left the Navy he set about building up his own career as a merchant of military equipment. Other acquaintances couldn't see what Cooke had in common with Russell: they found him vulgar and dull and one commented that he didn't seem ever to have read a book in his life. 'Look,' Cooke retorted, 'I read the books. I don't have to have friends who read them, too. You have friends for different reasons.' They would eat together and play chess in New York during the 'summer bachelor' months and on one occasion Russell accompanied Cooke on a motoring tour of south-west England – while Jane was away in Italy on her own again.

Russell's greatest feat was to have himself appointed as a leading sup-
plier of armaments to one of Venezuela's more brutal dictators, though
a deal to supply the country with two surplus US Navy submarines fell
foul of a sudden military coup. Despite this setback, he continued to
pursue his unlikely trade and to remain one of Cooke's closest con-
fidants. Russell, a playboy salesman to offset all the highbrows in
Cooke's life, never mixed with any of the rest of the couple's Man-
hattan-Long Island circles. It was always just the two of them: Russell
once travelled with Cooke on a lecture trip to Seattle, from where they
drove south so that he could have his first glimpse of Hollywood and
experience a genuine showbiz party. Cooke also offered to introduce
his friend to Groucho Marx, who, improbably, was taking part in a
television version of *The Mikado*. When he rang, he was put through
to Groucho in make-up: 'Get the hell over here, Cooke' came a voice
squeezed between teeth clenching a cigarette holder, 'and see the positive demise of G and S.'

'Just a moment, let me check with my room-mate.'

'What is this? You got a dame up there? You'd be mad, mad, to leave
her for me. Better still, bring her over and you can go.'

'No, he's a navy commander, a submarine salesman to be exact.'

'Do I salute or submerge? Remember, I'm only a civilian.'

'The question is, do I bring him along?'

He and Russell watched as Groucho flounced his way through the
recording. 'How the Japs ever attacked Pearl Harbor in these outfits is
something I'll never know,' he mumbled.

'Groucho is crowding seventy [Cooke wrote in the *Guardian*], though not
very hard, but his energy belies and makes more touching the extreme frailty
of his body.

'You're going good, Groucho,' a young man would whisper.

'Yes, after the show, I'm going good – to Canada or any place they
can't extradite me. By the way, (indicating Alan Russell), meet Captain
Bradford.'

Cooke knew better than to correct him.

Public speaking represented a further string to Cooke's bow during
this fruitful period. After his first hesitant appearance in front of an
ungainly horde of young soldiers during the war, he had built this up
into a useful sideline. Television was still enough of an oddity to make
him a decent draw for a provincial audience and he had a repertoire

of stories with which to regale them, speaking smoothly and with a minimum of notes: 'an extremely informal and humorous talk', as a writer for the *Repository* newspaper in Canton, Ohio, described his performance in 1956. He discoursed on the subject of foreign corresponding and interlarded his talks with observations about Anglo-American relations: Americans should realise, he told one audience, that people throughout the world did not, on awakening in the morning, ask, 'What is America doing today?'

While *Omnibus* was still on the air, Cooke was often in demand for other television appearances, too: one saw him brought in as moderator of a discussion between Frank Lloyd Wright and the poet Carl Sandburg on a Chicago television network and – the following day – with a panel of local dignitaries. The eighty-nine-year-old Wright – who, half a century earlier, had inspired much of the dramatic cityscape alongside the lake – was in skittish mood, as Cooke revealed in the *Guardian* in an obituary tribute later the same year. 'The panel consisted of real estate men, a housing commissioner, a young professor of architecture and Wright. It was sponsored by a steel company that legitimately hoped to popularise the "steel curtain" which is now the first constituent of most of the skyscrapers going up. Wright outraged his sponsors and almost broke up the forum, first by professing boredom over the arguments of the builders and real estate men and consequently walking out to take a nap.' Afterwards, Cooke drove him back along the lake front into Chicago and heard him ridicule the glinting skyscrapers and the cars ('rectangles on wheels') – but felt that the rage against the city he adored was somewhat synthetic. 'His only genuine sigh was for the universal misuse of steel, "this beautiful material that spins like a spider and produces a tension so perfect that you can balance a monolith on a pin-point". '

As the 1950s drew to a close Cooke also became a much-consulted expert on the vexed subject of television itself – a role thrust on him by the problems of keeping *Omnibus* on the air. Bereft of its Ford Foundation sponsorship, the series had been fending for itself in a hostile commercial environment. The last programme went out in April 1961. In the view of Cooke, the producer Bob Saudek and the rest of the team, it died not of natural causes but of strangulation by the advertising industry. Cooke expounded his gloomy prognosis whenever he was offered the opportunity – when, for instance, local newspapers interviewed him in the course of lecture tours. 'Television', he told the *Chat-*

tanooga Times in April 1960, 'is a gorgeous girl led astray early in life by a travelling salesman. She is taken round the country as a come-on for his detergent.'

Cooke's fury seems genuine, despite what was inevitably a self-serving element. He wrote lengthy articles in American magazines about the woes of the industry – 'American Television: The Bartered Bride' was one. Television might have reached nearly fifty million homes, created a hundred thousand jobs and revived the careers of countless actors and artists. But 'for every shining hour, there are days and weeks of dross.' It wasn't reasonable to expect first-class entertainment for nearly twenty-four hours a day, but 'the homes of America receive a daily tidal wave of perfumes, cigarettes, beers, detergents, toilet tissues, patent medicines, automobiles, headache powders, cake mixes, refrigerators, breakfast cereals and laxatives.' This disaster had come about, Cooke said, because of the unwise mating of the artist and the salesman, in which the sponsor was allowed to call the shots. Unlike the advertiser in a newspaper – or on commercial television in Britain – it was open to the sponsor, or his advertising agency, to dictate what appeared on the screen.

At the time, it was both radical and risky (for a performer) to state aloud that television networks trimmed their output according to 'Moron's Law: that what is most popular is also best' and that 'bad taste and complacency sell goods.'

~

Just a year after Cooke's fiftieth birthday his father Samuel died in Blackpool at the age of eighty-four. Cooke was in the middle of an *Omnibus* season, which made it difficult to contemplate returning to England for the funeral. Or rather, as he came to admit in later life, it gave him an excuse for staying away. 'I don't like funerals,' he said. 'At the time I wouldn't have put it that way, but maybe my work provided an unconscious contrivance.' Bob Saudek was trying desperately to keep *Omnibus* on the air and couldn't hide from Cooke his panic at the idea of losing his presenter in mid-series. It must have been easy enough to justify the decision to himself. Subconsciously, he may have found the prospect of dealing with his bereaved mother simply too awful to contemplate – something for which his North Country background had left him dangerously ill-equipped: his was a family with no emotional vocabulary to deal with the crises of life and death. But inevitably, Cooke's absence meant that there was unfinished business between father and son.

Over the years he developed an idealised way of describing the quiet, gentle man of principle – without a malicious or unkind thought in his head, but with an iron readiness to stand up for his beliefs, Christ-like in his patience and forbearance. He regretted more and more the disappearance of a sculpted wooden hand his father had carved for him as a child and, in 1994, greeted enthusiastically an approach from the civic authorities in Blackpool. They told him of a plan to have an antique metal weather-vane returned to the roof of the town hall from which it had been removed years earlier during building work; it had emerged, in the course of research, that the *Golden Hind* design was his father's handiwork. There was even a legend in the town that Cooke senior had used materials from Nelson's former flagship, the *Foud-royant*, which sank off Blackpool in 1897. Cooke said he would be delighted to attend a ceremonial re-installation of the weather-vane. It would have been a neat way of celebrating a life he hadn't properly appreciated at the time and expiating the nagging sense of guilt about his lack of attention to the demands of his family, but the ceremony never took place.

He had continued to call in at the Ormond Avenue house whenever he was in England, a task made less irksome because of Blackpool's proximity to the *Guardian* headquarters in Manchester. And he also kept in touch with his brother, ensconced in North London with his partner Mabel, travelling out to see them by Tube to an anonymous suburb whose name did not remain lodged in his memory. Cooke found Mabel much easier to get on with than Sam's first wife and felt that the two were well-suited, though in the absence of a divorce from Elsie they had never married. Not surprisingly, Cooke accepted the version of this story presented by his own side of the family: that Sam's first wife had been no good for him and he was much better without her.

Cooke's mother adopted a remorselessly unforgiving attitude to Sam's abandoned family, refusing to have anything to do with Elsie (who still lived in Blackpool) or her two children – her own grand-children. One of them, Kathleen, by then in her mid-twenties, decided to attend her grandfather's funeral because she remembered him with great fondness – and because she knew her own father, whom she hadn't seen for nearly fifteen years, would be present. So great was the rift between the two sides of the family that her mother had refused to let her go to work in London, for fear that she would re-establish relations with him. Kathleen also hoped to see her Uncle Alfred, to whose broadcasts she listened every week. Instead, her uncle was inexplicably absent, her father had nothing much to say about why he'd left home and her grandmother cold-shouldered her. Perhaps, in the circumstances, Cooke's instincts served him in good stead. It must have been an excruciating afternoon. Yet he and Sam were always on friendly terms and Cooke grew more and more admiring of his brother's lack of bitterness or jealousy at the way fate had treated each of them.

His mother survived until 1965. She was eighty-six when she died, but Cooke couldn't make it back for that funeral, either – nor did he return to England after his brother's death four years later. He was left, as the years went on, with the haunting knowledge that he had never been able to make amends for the distance he'd travelled from his family. In fact, he never returned to Blackpool.

COLD WARS

There was one area in which Cooke was unable to conceal his own instinct for an uncomfortable truth – even from the cosseted listeners to *Letter from America*. Nothing had happened to relieve his gloom about the prospects of avoiding a nuclear holocaust – quite the contrary. He regarded the successful launching of the first Russian Sputnik, in October 1957, as a matter for serious alarm. Nobody, he told the BBC, had been much comforted by President Eisenhower's reassurance that the Sputnik had not added to the nation's insecurity 'by one iota'. He gently chided the Administration's response: 'the usual American reaction to the threat, as we call it, of a new Russian bomb, or a cheap foreign car', which was to institute a ' "crash programme" to develop a bigger and better satellite, or a cheaper car, in double-quick time.' In Cooke's view, the reality was no joking matter. Until then, the electronic front line of defence against incoming Russian planes had been the so-called Dew Line up beyond the Arctic Circle: 'Before last autumn,' he explained in the *Letter* of 20 April 1958, 'this signal gave the boys in Omaha anything from three to six hours to get briefed, to get equipped, to load bombs on their planes and take off – theoretically to divert or destroy an enemy plane. Since the Soviet Union successfully fired its first Sputnik, the mighty Dew Line can promise the boys two thousand miles to the south no more than a fifteen-minute alert.'

Cooke soon had the opportunity to delve further into the realities of US relations with the Soviet Union, with no punches pulled, when the Soviet premier, Nikita Khrushchev, embarked on an official visit in September 1959. Cooke was to accompany him for the *Guardian* and, by way of a preview, he reported on the travails of the State Department in drawing up a suitable schedule, which would strike a balance between 'the Premier's known inclination to farms and factories and the irresistible tendency of American cities to throw distinguished visitors a municipal banquet'. He noted that frantic efforts were being made to overcome the blunder of fixing a tour of Hollywood on a Saturday when the studios were deserted. Crews were being bribed with triple pay so that Khrushchev would have something to see other than bare lots.

The humorous side of this deadly earnest affair did not dissipate, even when Khrushchev finally arrived: each day seemed to be dogged by black comedy, in which an underlying sense of menace was never far away. For many observers this was the first chance to watch at first hand the antics of a man on whom their lives might depend. Khrushchev in Hollywood, in Cooke's imagination, became 'the Script that got away'. In a city where every word, camera angle and beam of light was subject to the most diligent attention, the Russian premier's progress was haphazard and unpredictable and soon deteriorated into bad-tempered farce. He was placed at a banquet table with Gary Cooper, Eddie Fisher, Marilyn Monroe and James Mason, while 'the supreme accolade was reserved for his wife: she was seated next to Frank Sinatra. American hospitality can go no further.' "And yet and yet . . ." as the old silent movie captions used to say, the production blew up in the faces of hundreds of skilled politicos, directors and protocol experts who had written it.'

First, Khrushchev was infuriated by a decision (on security grounds) not to let him go to Disneyland. Then a tactless remark by the Mayor of Los Angeles – 'If challenged, we shall fight to the death to preserve our way of life' – soured the atmosphere further so that bellicose phrases began to trip from Khrushchev's lips: 'It is a question of war and peace . . . I have not come here to beg. . . . Our rockets are on the assembly lines and on our launching pads.' Finally, he announced that he might simply cut his losses and go home.

The entourage moved on, none the less, to San Francisco. The State Department officials were on tenterhooks and admitted to reporters their fear that one more outspoken mayor might cause Khrushchev to fulfil his threat to curtail the visit. Cooke's impression was that the Americans were being manipulated. The atmosphere lightened for a time when people in Santa Barbara and San Luis Obispo clapped and cheered the visitor (who appeared to be 'drunk on this furtive nip of popularity'), but later that night gloom descended once more. American Labour leaders spent three hours berating Khrushchev on such topics as disarmament and the right to strike, only to be told that their fears and their questions were stupid.

What Cooke was looking for was any indication of the underlying Soviet strategy: 'Had he come to America to bring an olive branch or an ultimatum?' Nobody seemed quite sure. A day or so later he groped for an assessment: 'Nikita Khrushchev is a madly spontaneous and highly unstable man who will chuckle over friendly generalities, but a man who will not allow, except on his own terms, the discussion let alone the settlement of the accumulating issues that leave us ripe for Armageddon.' The instability haunted the Secretary of State, Henry Cabot Lodge, as he tried to keep a tenuous hold on the diplomatic initiative: mostly, this rested with the Russian leader, who at one point

> decided not to go to a typical suburban supermarket but six hours later dashed into one unscreened and, to the squeaks of teenagers and house-wives in flabbergasted shorts, he was goggling over cuts of meat in plastic wrappers, a choice of twenty pre-cooked 'television dinners', several hundred varieties of canned and frozen foods, ice-cream cakes in fifteen flavours and other vital baubles clearly not available in the Soviet Union . . . . Too often in these vignettes, too often for the Government's peace of mind, there is an element of shrewd contrivance, as if Mr Khrushchev knew exactly what scenes of American life could be pieced together later by some cunning Eisenstein and edited to convey the adoration of the plain people for Nikita and the solidarity with the Soviet workers of the captive drones far away.

The cavalcade moved eastwards to Des Moines, Iowa, where Khrush-chev (Cooke suspected) teased his hosts by having his interpreter read out an interminable after-dinner speech in English replete with statistics of Soviet tractor production, until Henry Cabot Lodge was snoozing, Mrs Khrushchev nodding and weaving and the Foreign Minister Andrei Gromyko 'had his eyes open, but his soul was as blank as a window-pane.'

For the reporters themselves the spectacle helped to alleviate their own weariness: another piece of State Department bungling had seen them arrive after a sleepless night to find their hotel beds occupied by snoring and unmovable Rotarians. The following day the Russian delegation flew home, leaving its hosts puzzled, unnerved and more than a little exhausted: 'Your faithful reporter is squeezing drops into his flaming eyeballs, repacking for the eighth time a suitcase of smelly linen and, stripped for ever of the pomp of his blue press card, queuing up with the common people for the first available plane to New York, home and beauty.'

~

If relations with the *Guardian* in the Hetherington era were entering an uncomfortable phase, Cooke's contacts with the BBC were far more straightforward. *Letter from America* was becoming an institution with which managers tampered at their peril. It arrived from New York and was broadcast in London a day or so later. That was that. Cooke's gradual realisation that he had in his hands a professional resource to be cherished and defended can be dated from the early 1950s when he was due to take one of his spells of UK leave, and intending to let the *Letter* lapse until his return more than two months later. A well-known BBC figure came to hear of this proposed hiatus and wondered whether he might be able to fill it. Frank Gillard, Britain's best-known war reporter, was by now a BBC executive – he had just relaunched the BBC's West Region operations in Bristol and felt in need of a rest before taking up an even more important post in London. 'It occurred to me', Gillard recalled, 'that I might spend three months in the United States and keep the *Letter* going on a Saturday evening with my own impressions as a first-time visitor.' The plan was at first well-received but, according to Gillard, it never left the drawing-board. 'I was told that when Cooke got wind of the idea, he informed the BBC that he had no intention of letting it happen – and that it might prejudice his whole relationship with the Corporation.' Gillard's protestation – that he couldn't be a threat to Cooke because he already had a job waiting in London – cut no ice. The whole project was quietly shelved.

The memory of this close shave may have lodged in Cooke's mind and by 1958 he had dreamed up the idea of perpetuating the series even when he was away from home. In June of that year, he produced what he called a *Letter from England* – typed in fact on board the *Queen Mary* as he returned from a European tour – a tour which allowed for Jane to spend 'a week or ten days in her beloved Florence' while he remained in Britain. This *Letter*, which is numbered as if it were a 'genuine' *Letter from America*, extols the virtues of British liners. It is in itself an interesting social document, praising elements of life in the country of his birth which were becoming unfashionable – and casting gentle aspersions at the modernity (and sense of superiority) of his adopted home. What Cooke liked about the *Queen Mary* and her sister ships was a 'combination of seamanship and service'.

British stewards, in Cooke's experience, still took an unusual pride in their jobs. He offered an anecdote about a man who looked up from serving his soup and pointed out another ship across Southampton Water on which his son had just been promoted to full steward. 'He said it with pride,' Cooke said, 'as a man might see his son take his first staggering step across a room. It seemed to me that this pride became him and that no class struggle, no involuntary servitude was entailed in his son's choosing to follow the same trade and be good at it. I've mentioned this small story to Americans from time to time and they look pityingly, as at a man who is warped and poisoned by blood ties to feudalism.' Consequently, it was becoming rare to find an American-born waiter, since everyone was compelled to strive towards an ever higher social status: 'Ours is a land – said an American in *Martin Chuzzlewit* – where any man can look another man in the eye. The only trouble is that, once you've looked each other over, somebody has to stoke the furnace, cook the meals, weigh the anchor and drive the cab.'

It was perhaps because he couldn't trust anyone else to draw such subtle distinctions, that he began to cling so tenaciously to the ownership of the *Letter*. He did so from a strong position, basking in sustained public approval of his role as 'ambassador without portfolio to the United States', as he was dubbed in one American newspaper. An audience survey of this particular *Letter* from England scored well above the average on the BBC's 'appreciation index' and the researchers found that an overwhelming majority of listeners approved of his 'attractive style' and 'warm personality'. A number of quotations were adduced to prove the point: 'In the art of broadcasting Alistair Cooke is a genius. Through radio, he now belongs to our lives and we feel it when he is absent' (Listener in Retirement). Only a very small group 'did not care for his accent, or considered the talk too slow and not forceful enough.'

In the following year, 1959, Europe beckoned again and once again the travel arrangements allowed Jane to make a solo visit to Italy before rejoining Cooke in Austria. This time it was agreed with the BBC that there would be no gaps in the *Letter*s: Cooke would pen epistles from his holiday locations and sent dispatches over the next five weeks from Vienna, Morocco, Spain, Cornwall and London. The pattern was the same in 1960, when Cooke combined the holiday with a BBC commission to provide the narration for a film called *The Blitz of Britain*. 'This agreeable chore fits in snugly with our plans and desire to see you, as usual, in the spring,' he wrote to Rupert Hart-Davis. 'Take note, however, that while Jane will be in Italy the latter part of April, she will meet up with me at the Dorchester on the 3rd of May.'

When they stayed in Britain, Cooke invariably used the Dorchester Hotel as a base for his social activities. He might dine with friends, complain about the iniquities of taxi charges, or bemoan the decision to turn Park Lane into a 'divided highway' to ease the congestion at either end. 'I am sorry to see this old-fashioned, and fatal, solution being attempted in Hyde Park,' he sighed in his London *Letter*. 'You will soon have less park, more noise, more carbon-monoxide – and what is much worse – more traffic.'

Cooke did not, on any of his visits, spend much time on keeping contacts warm inside the BBC. Most of the managers were now strangers to him and his instinct was to duck out of all well-meaning invitations to take part in extra programmes, or to meet the new top brass. 'To the Director of News and Current Affairs – Alistair Cooke thanks you very much for your kind invitation to lunch during his forthcoming visit to London . . . he has a large number of personal friends and relations to meet in a very short time.'

His complete lack of interest in BBC politics is perhaps the only way to explain the scandalous way he was treated when it came to payment for the *Letter from America*. In the course of 1959 it dawned on Cooke that, despite significant inflation over many years, he had never received a pay rise. 'I assumed,' he wrote, 'that this was the standard high fee. It never occurred to me that anybody received "residuals" in the form of fees for repeat broadcasts, for reproduction in the *Listener*, etc.' For thirteen years he had been paid the same flat-rate fee of $100 to cover all uses of his weekly talk: he raised the matter with a newly arrived North American representative, who immediately passed Cooke's query on to London, along with his own observation that other commentators in New York were likely to earn twice as much. There was some shamefaced scurrying for the ledgers at Broadcasting House. The Talks Booking Manager let it be known that, if the contract were starting from scratch, Cooke would probably be offered 31/6d per minute: that, with a repeat fee, would amount to 55 guineas a talk, or $175 at the existing rate of exchange. In the event, they offered him $150, probably guessing correctly that a man who had allowed matters to drift for so long was unlikely to object to such a large percentage raise when it came – however long overdue.

For a time, Cooke kept the bit between his teeth. Two years later he bumped into a friend in England who'd been doing some BBC talks: 'He mentioned what appeared to me a rather lavish fee for an initial broadcast, plus a repeat,' he wrote in his official letter of complaint, 'plus the printing of the script in the *Listener*. Without any guile the friend commented, "Of course, I imagine this sounds rather modest by your standards." I loyally failed to disabuse him.' In addition, he had discovered that the talk appeared four times each week on the overseas services, as well as being reprinted in the BBC magazine. 'I can't remember any time in the last twenty-seven years that I have had a penny from the *Listener*. My retroactive bill would, I imagine, amount to an inheritance now.'

His complaint was addressed to the Head of Talks, George Camacho, with whom he had had some dealings and thus felt able to give vent to his feelings: 'All this is put as simply as possible,' Cooke told him, 'and I hope it does not carry on paper a suggestion of baldness or rudeness. I am temperamentally allergic to business dealings, though I find they can be hashed over fairly and amiably in conversation.' He continued, 'Since there is nothing I enjoy quite so much as this broadcast and since I have long had a hankering to put an end to the chore of a daily piece, I have come to hope that one day I might be able to keep myself by broadcasting alone. I am not even hinting that I should be subsidised towards this worthy end; but there are some things that radio and radio alone, can do better than any other medium.' In the event, he was not to be relieved of the 'chore' for another decade and was surely exaggerating his disenchantment for the purposes of strengthening his case to Camacho.

The pressure paid off – and Camacho, for a while, ensured that there were regular increases: by November 1964, the fee reached $250 a week. Yet Cooke's allergy to salary negotiations soon returned. In 1989 a newly appointed producer to the New York office, given responsibility for the *Letter*, learned that Cooke's fee had remained unaltered – at $400 a week – for some twenty years and set about persuading him, once again, to ask for more.

If public esteem for the *Letter* was unquenchable, professionals sometimes remained leery, perhaps finding it hard to categorise its mixture of information, sentiment and propaganda. It was based in the news, but not constrained by the news; it claimed to give insights behind the headlines, but didn't bother with the tiresome business of sources; it gave the impression of intimacy, but maintained an emotional distance between the writer and his subject. An edition of a BBC programme called *The Critics*, in the first week of 1962, exposes the perplexity this formula could induce in those who sought to unpick it. The humorist Stephen Potter introduced the debate with a friendly summary of the previous week's *Letter* – which was not the most weighty Cooke had ever delivered. It had a little gentle fun with some new year astrological predictions, floated effortlessly into a trip Cooke had taken to the Kennedys' seaside retreat in Palm Beach, touched on the comparative golfing abilities of the new President and his predecessor and ended with some pious hopes for 1962, using words placed in the mouth of the President. Potter, who had met Cooke and was in the process of becoming more closely acquainted, was biased – and admitted it. He recalled his own pleasure at listening to the broadcasts over the years, especially during the war: 'We all began to look forward to the caustic friendliness of his voice,' he said and applauded the fact that 'his description of the American attitude seemed refreshingly free of the poisonous desire to say the right thing'. He claimed to have identified Cooke's theory: 'that the "human story" should not be the exclusive property of tabloid and pulp'.

The assembled critics, a serious-minded bunch with a duty to display their intellectual rigour, were not so sure. All agreed that the *Letters* sounded good, but what about the content? One complained of 'a certain broadness and coarseness of emotion' and demanded that Cooke be more 'astringent' in future. Another, a young man named Bamber Gascoigne, thought the *Letter* in question 'rather empty' and not up to the usual standard. 'Anybody can be funny about astrologers,' he opined. 'It was interesting to hear President Kennedy's golfing score, but there wasn't very much in the quarter of an hour, was there?'

A third member of the 1962 critics suggested that Cooke sounded less a political commentator and more an 'observer of the human scene and the human comedy, above all.' The chairman chipped in with his view that it was hard to tell whether Cooke was a reporter or 'some kind of public relations officer . . . generally for the United States of America.' It was left to Stephen Potter to mount a defence, which he did with gusto: just because they'd been reviewing a light, rather whimsical piece, shouldn't blind them to 'all the other things he has done', like his coverage of elections or the tough line he'd taken on McCarthy.

Potter was right, but the critics had a point, too – especially since they were confining their remarks to the *Letter*. Cooke was an unusual sort of political reporter – attracted largely by the big events and the personalities. He was no dilettante: it was not that he ignored the daily business of politics, the subtly shifting sand on which the great edifice stood – all that was part of the 'chore' inherent in his commitment to the *Guardian*. Cooke's coverage of such matters in the *Letters* was different: it assumed that listeners would have only a passing interest in the grinding detail – and that, in any case, radio was not the best medium for disseminating such information. Hence, perhaps, the critical puzzlement.

~

The 1960 presidential election campaign was one of those momentous events that brought together Cooke's knowledge, experience, familiarity with the players and personal prejudice – all this to be deployed directly in the pages of the *Guardian* and indirectly (whimsically, according to *The Critics*) across the airwaves of the BBC.

For Cooke, the election was the story of the conflicting fortunes of three men, each arousing in him strong and contradictory emotions: he loved Adlai Stevenson for his hopeless and misguided ambition; he respected Richard Nixon's capabilities, but found it hard to shed the general dislike for the man himself; and he could not quite suppress the suspicion that there might be less (or rather, less to be admired) to John F. Kennedy than met the eye.

Like all correspondents, Cooke had charted Kennedy's progress carefully, noting particularly his good fortune in not being selected as Stevenson's running mate in 1956 – and the assiduous efforts of his Boston backers to prepare for the 1960 election. As early as October 1957, Cooke was writing appreciatively about Kennedy's political skills, pointing up as one example his decision to make a public stand on the brutal war in Algeria. This served to raise his profile in Washington, but carried no collateral risks at home in Massachusetts – Algeria being one of the few countries not represented in the State's rich ethnic mix. Any intervention on Italy, or Poland, or Ireland would have been risky. But Algeria 'nicely suggested to his newspaper supporters that the Senator is a statesman, something like Stevenson, of majestic disinterestedness.' Cooke saw this as an astute piece of pre-election planning and a sign that Kennedy might be cleverer than his enemies had suspected.

A year later, after the Congressional elections of 1958, he compiled a three-part series on the party machinations which would lead eventually to the White House. At the end of the third piece, he clearly felt he should make some sort of prediction – if possible, one that would not return to haunt him. He was right to be cautious. The Republicans, he believed, were blessed with two 'towering candidates' in Nixon and Nelson Rockefeller. By contrast, 'the Democrats have at least ten egos, including six senators, each of whom means to prove that he and he alone, is the "available" man.' The chances, he concluded, favoured a Republican President with another Democrat Congress.

To give Cooke his due, a *Letter from America* at the same period latches on to Kennedy as the most successful practitioner of the politician's art in sight – the man who knows how to 'talk idealism, stay loyal to his friends and watch his own career with a calculating eye'. 'He is,' in Cooke's assessment, 'a man to follow. The examination not of his eloquent speeches, but of the way he really goes after the Presidency in 1960 – that will be quite a sight to watch.'

Another sight to watch was that of Cooke and Freedman trying to find a working accommodation to deal with the campaign. Freedman's eccentricities – Cooke claimed that after one lengthy absence he reappeared without explanation in Belgium – had not reduced Hetherington's respect for his capabilities. After growing signs of discord between his two star correspondents on the East Coast, the editor decided to impose a rule: Cooke could have free rein to cover anything he pleased, provided that he never wrote directly about Washington. He would, however, be allowed to 'keep' the Conventions. Cooke, at first, was furious. 'I told Alastair [Hetherington] that, after all these years, I couldn't do that. Not end up just writing about Macy's, or personality pieces and obituaries.' Would he not be 'the only foreign correspondent in the world banned from his own capital city'. He was on weak ground. His long-time reluctance to immerse himself in what he felt was the cramping and claustrophobic atmosphere of Washington made it hard for him to argue with Hetherington's decision. 'At one point,' in Cooke's recollection, 'things got so bad that I went to have it out with Alastair in Manchester. We went for a long walk and he tried to convince me. The problem was that although he was a fine journalist and terribly conscientious, I found him sometimes tactless and uncommunicative.' Despite such difficulties, he remained on civil terms with his editor and used to stay with him and his wife Miranda in Manchester, and returned the hospitality when the Hetheringtons were in New York.

Yet Cooke came to believe that, if he'd been offered another job during this strained period, he would have accepted it. There had been approaches from time to time, notably from Lord Beaverbrook, who had taken him aside at a dinner and offered him a substantial pay-rise to move to the *Express* group. Cooke declined, because of Beaverbrook's reputation for behaving as if he owned the journalists he'd paid for. The *Sunday Times* had also once expressed a strong interest. But now, with no alternative available, he returned, seething, to New York. Since he and Freedman found it hard to speak directly to each other, a system was devised whereby they communicated through head office in Manchester. A new young foreign editor, Geoffrey Taylor, found himself at the centre of this bizarre arrangement. 'In the middle of our afternoon – at the start of their working day – each of them would ring up to discuss his plans. It rather depended who rang first, but often they would both decide to cover the same thing and it was up to me to arbitrate. My usual preference was for Cooke, since Freedman was supposed to confine himself to the White House and Congress.' In the dispute between the two, Taylor was bound to be even-handed, but instinctively he was in the Cooke camp – even though he'd acted as a sub-editor on both men's work. 'Cooke wrote with a special elegance and grace which made it difficult to cut. He wrote like G.K. Chesterton – the whole thing was a unit and cutting it was like trying to reduce a sonnet to twelve lines. If you decided to remove something in the first take of copy, you'd find it was cross-referenced in the third. With Freedman, every sentence was a bald statement of fact and you could simply choose which to take out.'

It was going to be an interesting campaign.

~

Could 1960 ever have been the year of Adlai Stevenson's apotheosis? In his heart, Cooke knew how unlikely it was, yet he had a sneaking feeling that his old friend's frailty would force him to the hustings again. As he put it in *Six Men*, 'Once a man is X-rayed for the Presidency, he is radioactive to his paltering old age.' All the evidence, however, was that Stevenson would suffer another crushing disappointment.

Cooke had several good contacts at a high level in the Democratic party. One was Abe Ribicoff, the Governor of Connecticut, who told Cooke with great confidence, at a dinner soon after the 1956 election disaster, that Kennedy would be the next President. Being himself a politician with absolutely no national appeal, Ribicoff began to plot on Kennedy's behalf. Another of Cooke's sources was Paul Ziffern, California's representative on the Democratic National Committee. In December of 1959 Ziffern was one of a horde of party figures attending a glamorous banquet in New York, whose ostensible purpose was to celebrate the birthday of Eleanor Roosevelt. In fact, it was a beauty contest for the Democratic contenders, preceded by a number of preliminary parties designed to increase a candidate's chances of winning New York's 114 votes at the Convention. The banquet itself was a rowdy affair, with Harry Truman in the chair, calling the hopefuls in geographical order, west to east, and sometimes wielding a gavel to silence speakers in mid-peroration. The diners listened to Kennedy and a string of others. But it was Stevenson who 'stampeded the ballroom' of the Waldorf-Astoria and the ecstatic reception persuaded him that maybe he should have one last shot at the Presidency. Flushed with pleasure, he 'retired to his tent' – in Cooke's words – vowing that he would make no further direct appeal for the nomination. He would simply wait for the offer to be made.

Cooke's 1200-word dispatch to the *Guardian* described the scene and added some intriguing details about the secret manoeuvring later that night: his account was based on information provided by Paul Ziffern, who told him that Jack Kennedy had gone round to Stevenson's hotel room and warned him, in unequivocal terms, that having 'worked his tail off' for the Governor in the two previous elections, he now expected a pay-back. There was no way he would tolerate the nomination being handed to Stevenson 'on a platter' if the Convention turned against the Kennedy camp.

What Cooke didn't know was that Max Freedman had also turned up at this gathering and had filed his own report. This must have presented a nice dilemma for the duty editor in Manchester – two rival pieces from the same function. For some reason, the choice fell upon Freedman, even though he was operating well outside his patch. The article duly appeared two days later, under the headline 'Democrats Await A Messiah'. Freedman paid tribute to the success of the former Governor of Illinois, though there was no mention of any late-night contact between Stevenson and the Kennedys. When he heard what had happened, Cooke was apoplectic. There were further transatlantic ructions and Hetherington was compelled to elucidate even more precisely who should do what for the campaign year.

The story of Kennedy's late-night call may not have appeared in the paper, but it had its own sequel a few months later. Ziffern arranged for Cooke to attend a Kennedy campaign party in Washington. Cooke watched as a delegation from Ohio arrived at the narrow, elegant Georgetown house to listen to the Senator's pitch and soon found himself at the side of the room with Jackie Kennedy. 'We were like orphans in the storm,' Cooke says. 'She couldn't stand the Ohio crew and since I was looking at pictures on the wall, we got to talking about art. We both liked the impressionist painter, de Segonzac, and I told her about two engravings of his that I'd bought at auction.' Suddenly Kennedy himself appeared beside them and shook Cooke's hand: 'How are you? Great to see you,' he said. And then without a pause, 'By the way, that meeting in New York – it never took place. See you in Los Angeles!' Cooke was shocked. How had Kennedy heard about his story? It's hard not to conclude that Freedman had been made aware of what Cooke had written and had mentioned it to Kennedy – with whom he was developing (in Cooke's jaundiced eyes) an unhealthily close relationship.

Cooke never got to know Kennedy well, though he had occasion later to admire again the information systems on which the President relied. He had attended a number of Democrat parties and functions in Washington, where Kennedy's 'Irish mafia' treated him like an expatriate English toff. He told the story in an interview with Michael

Parkinson on BBC television many years afterwards: 'It got very boring. They would say, "Well, old chap," and "Jolly good, what?" One night, everybody got a little liquefied and at about two in the morning I said, "Look, if you don't stop this, I shall call on my grandmother in County Wicklow and she will slice your throats." This evidence of Irish blood caused an abrupt change of attitude, but Cooke pushed their proffered hands aside with a histrionic cry, 'take your filthy papist hands off me!', explaining in mitigation that his grandmother's family were Irish protestants forced out of Ireland by the Kennedys and their like. Some time later, when Cooke was covering a Presidential event at a university in Miami, Kennedy left the ranks of gowned academics and approached him. 'He shook my hand,' Cooke told Parkinson, 'and said, "I hope you don't mind my filthy Papist hand." '

24

HIGH HOPES

With the *Guardian* pecking order re-established (the paper dropped the 'Manchester' in the title during 1959), Cooke set to work on the campaign trail, 'trying to get close to people who are buddies of the candidates and the people who will run the Convention.' His predictive powers took some time to become finely honed. On 29 December 1959 his byline appears on an American newspaper article headlined: 'Bowles for President'. This was based on the theory that Congressman Chester Bowles, sometime Ambassador to India, had caught the imagination of a number of party leaders who feared that Kennedy might falter. Cooke repeated this opinion several times: 'There is a well disguised strategy working now for Chester Bowles,' he told the *St Louis Post Despatch*.

Cooke was wrong about Bowles, but before long it ceased to matter. Kennedy began to look unstoppable and by the time he entered the New Hampshire primary, he had gained a public recognition factor of eighty-three per cent. In mock amazement, Cooke wondered who the seventeen ignoramuses in a hundred might be who 'could not identify at once the slim, Ivy League figure with the tow-rope hair'? – especially when he was 'accompanied everywhere by his aide-de-camp who surely does him no harm, since she is a wife and exquisite brunette whose fragile and terrified air is belied and boosted by her scarlet coat'.

Other candidates, including Lyndon B. Johnson, occasionally threatened a serious challenge, but Kennedy was rampant – as was Richard Nixon for the Republicans, who began to defy popular mythology. Cooke watched his appearance in San Francisco, which was 'gay, brief and unsullied by any of the smells and smears that a decade ago used to linger after a Nixon election rally. It presages bad news for the Democrats, for this was the kind of man they had not planned to fight.' By June, the 'egg-heads in the button-down collars' – Cooke's description of Stevenson's backers – had, at long last, given up any hope of persuading their hero to re-enter the lists.

Yet Stevenson continued to tease and infuriate his supporters. The crowd which greeted him on his way to the Convention in Los Angeles, on a steaming afternoon in July 1960, was half as big again as Kennedy's. As he looked out over the adoring masses, some of the women in tears, he repeated in Cooke's hearing the sentence he'd uttered after his first defeat by Eisenhower – 'I am too old to cry, but it hurts too much to laugh.' 'It is a decent epitaph,' Cooke wrote, 'because the mania of the Stevenson fans has a piercing, John the Baptist quality; and it is easy to confuse the touching loyalty of these lay preachers with the unspoken determination of the actual delegates not to vote again for a two-time loser.' Stevenson wouldn't shift from his lofty perch above the fray, no matter how fervently those fans might implore him to do so. For his pains he won 82 delegate votes, against 785 for Kennedy and 409 for the man chosen as his running-mate, LBJ.

The following week, Cooke was invited once more to Stevenson's home in Libertyville, Illinois and found him apparently in relaxed mood, wearing an open shirt festooned with donkeys, a pair of sandals and shorts as tight as a bikini-bottom. Yet Cooke and his fellow guest, a Washington columnist, soon realised that something was amiss. Stevenson was twitchy and distracted and started to ramble on like a man 'free-associating without thought of an audience'. Gradually it emerged that Stevenson was waiting for the phone to ring – and the voice of the successful candidate offering him one of the great offices of Government. The call never came. Much later he was appointed Ambassador to the United Nations, a position which, as it transpired, ensured that his humiliation at the hands of the Kennedys would be prolonged for several more years.

The Republicans, a few days later, provided thin gruel for the political reporters who descended upon Chicago. Cooke did his best to play up the minimalist drama over the party platform and the choice of Nixon's running mate, but his reports lacked passion. The eventual nomination provided the weary onlooker with a smidgen of wry amusement: 'Nixon was denied the tribute of a vote of acclamation by ten stubborn and fumbling Louisianans, who gave their share of the state's 26 votes to Senator Barry Goldwater of Arizona, the last conservative. From Alabama to the Virgin Islands, the roll call was sounded by a large lady with the endearing name of Mrs Heppelfinger; and all except Louisiana cast their votes for Nixon, as automatically as Etonians checking in for the glorious Fourth. At the end of the first ballot, Nixon had 1321 and Goldwater 10.'

Cooke had never been one to pander to his *Guardian* readers' prejudices, but his own instinctive distaste for Nixon could not be disguised. As the Louisiana delegation tried to extricate itself from its embarrassment, he wrote that 'Nixon, the 47-year-old Quaker boy from Whittier, California, sat in his hotel suite and was "humble" and "greatly moved". He was subsequently moved to a 16-minute ad-lib monologue about the feelings of a poor boy who had never expected any such glory and who prayed he might even come to bear comparison with "the dignity, the grace, the decency, the wisdom and judgement" of his beloved chief, Dwight D. Eisenhower.'

∼

After the Conventions, Cooke took a Long Island break. Jane's two children were well beyond family holidays: Holly was already in Europe, while Stephen was ensconced at Berkeley, far away on the West Coast. As for John, he had just finished his second year at Harvard. Cooke had been encouraged by (but slightly nervous of?) his son's academic choices: 'I am frankly delighted with the run-down of the courses you are taking,' he wrote in October 1959. 'Don't decide on your English major until you are quite sure that you have the time and the temperament to do a vast amount of reading in the great stretch of literature that reaches from Chaucer to Kerouac. (On second thoughts, I think you can skip Kerouac.)' A few months later, he responded to what had evidently been an awkward Christmas confrontation over his exam results: 'I am completely satisfied with your explanation of last term's marks. The English thing brought you down and the Spanish débâcle was too absurd to go into. Keep up with your reading and answer all the questions, however foolishly – as you say. The main thing is not to fight the system but to join it!'

Cooke was far less satisfied with Johnny's decision to take a year off college, starting in that summer of 1960, to tour Europe by motor cycle. This expedition perplexed Cooke: where was his son going to find the money? He had thought vaguely about offering a free trip as a post-graduation inducement: he sketched out the scene in a *Letter* a few years later:

I said to him, 'You've worked pretty hard and well and if you keep it up for the next eighteen months and you come out with a half-way decent degree, I'll give you a fare for a trip to Europe.' It was the first time I ever heard myself sounding like the fathers I knew in my time, all of them (I then believed) professional fathers born into middle age.

Of course I thought my son would fall on his face with gratitude. Instead, he looked at me with the peculiar tenderness that twenty year olds reserve for their well-meaning but dotty parents. 'Dad,' he said, 'I'm going to Europe a month from now.'

'Really?' I said. 'And where do you expect to travel?'

'Oh,' he said, 'a little time in Rome and Florence, a month or so in Paris, maybe a stretch in Tangier.'

Cooke was nonplussed and Johnny explained about special cheap charter flights for students. 'My son is a cagey mathematician where rent, food and expenses are concerned and he had done a calculation on which I could not fault him. Even including the cost of the trans-atlantic air trip, he could live noticeably cheaper for three months in Europe than he could by staying in his rooms in Cambridge, Mass and living in America.' Cooke used a parochial story, as so often, to generalise – this time about students.

Most of them live cheerfully like cave-dwellers, anyway. A room as we knew it is not the same as a 'pad'. We were ludicrously fastidious in my day, requiring such things as beds raised above the floor, curtains on windows, chairs for sitting on. These things are now looked on as Estab-lishment fetishes: American college boys are throwbacks to the wandering minstrels of the Middle Ages. They live from hand to mouth. They have a common uniform – one pair of pants, one shirt, a jacket (maybe), a toothbrush (sometimes) and a guitar.

By the time he wrote those words, Cooke was nearly sixty and there's a strong and familiar sense of self-mockery in his descriptions of his own innocence – or ignorance – of the ways of the young. There is an undertone of his habitual intolerance of them, too. The passage ends, 'I've discovered that the motto of my school was "*Ubi Bene, Ibi Patria*". [Actually, it was *Meliora Sequamur*, but it made a nice point.] It's the motto of the American young, and roughly translated, it means – "Wherever there's a handout, that's for me, man." ' Cooke knew that the country's youth were gaining something of a reputation on their travels. Normally, his instinct in speaking to the faithful BBC audience would have been to ask their indulgence for this innocent American roguishness. This time, his judgement was less kind: 'It is the reason why all the countries of Europe and some of Africa, see these identical types rustling around the continents like cockroaches.'

Did he also reflect, as he wrote, on why John was such a practised economiser? Cooke had remained vague about money and, over the years, sometimes had to be reminded to make alimony payments to Ruth. (He had never repaid the loan she had made him in 1940: this omission, he confessed, lurked in his subconscious until, at long last, he settled the debt – and cleansed his conscience – using the proceeds of the life insurance policy he'd taken out when he started work.) It was generally assumed to be less a question of meanness, than a lack of interest in the humdrum aspects of budgeting. He had, after all, supported his son through Harvard with an allowance of $200 a month: much to John's surprise (and gratitude), he arranged to continue the payments during the unscheduled European vacation.

Cooke was certainly never a hoarder of money and he found it particularly hard to resist a fine piece of furniture. He continued to collect eighteenth-century pieces, though he was foiled in his search for a Hepplewhite desk sturdy enough to act as a work surface: instead he had one made by two craftsmen in Virginia. This passion for excellence was matched by his taste in hotels, travel and expensive clothes for Jane. Yet his stepdaughter Holly noticed that he rarely spent large sums on jewellery. 'I think it was something to do with the Methodist in him: the idea of baubles offended his puritan spirit.' Her brother Stephen remarked on another example of Cooke's financial blind spots: he had acquired a stock of rare wine from a friend who had run into financial trouble. At first, he was offered the whole cellar at a few dollars a bottle and Stephen – with the retrospective expertise of a wine-producer in California – believes it would have been an astonishing bargain. Cooke declined, on the grounds that it was too expensive. He did agree to come round and choose a few bits and pieces as keepsakes, ending up with six bottles of Romanée-Contee '34, an eighteenth-century sherry, some 1859 Château Lafite-Rothschild and a magnum of white Bordeaux from Château Climens. This treasure-trove sat undrunk and deteriorating in the Manhattan apartment. Every now and again, Cooke would do as he'd once been advised and drip candle wax on the tops of the bottles to preserve the corks. Looking back, Stephen can hardly bear to think about the dereliction of the duty of care which – he felt – was incumbent on the owner of such treasures. By the time he was able to taste them, the Climens might as well have had 'mice swimming in it' and the sherry had converted to vinegar.

Out of all four children of the family, the relationship with John remained the most troubling on both sides. The young man felt aggrieved at how little interest his father had shown in what he was doing. He had started to play folk songs on the guitar at high school and at Harvard he discovered the folk music revival in the coffee-houses of Cambridge. In due course he joined up with a group of students calling themselves 'The Charles River Valley Boys' – the CRVB – who specialised in bluegrass music: they went on to enjoy a professional career, spanning a decade, appearing on television, producing three albums and performing across the north-eastern states. At the height of their popularity, in 1963, the group featured in a show at Carnegie Hall in New York, in aid of four children killed by a bomb blast in Alabama. So absorbed was John in his new life and the burgeoning counter-culture of the early Sixties, that he isn't even sure if he told his father of his appearance in New York's most pres-tigious concert hall. John's determination to make a living from music and his adoption of a lifestyle so different from anything that could sensibly be explained to his parents helped to ensure that the distance between father and son remained as great as ever.

In that summer of 1960, then, Susie was the only child with the Cookes at Nassau Point. Cooke took the opportunity to go fishing with her and – at the age of eleven – she expected results. He hoped out aloud (in an August *Letter*) that she would be the one to land a cherished bluefish, while he was left with the consolation prize of a dog- or blow-fish: 'This feeling is not quite so Christian as it sounds. Another couple of blank days and I suspected she might be through with fishing for ever.' It was indeed Susie's day and her success was capped by the catching of a large kingfish. 'I knew it was something special, but when we got back to Captain Jim's,' Cooke reported, 'we looked at the 1960 east coast chart of standards for the national competition. The best catch to date is one and a half pounds. She had come within four ounces of the record and I guess I can bet on a steady partner for another year or so at least.'

The fresh air must have done him good. For a man smoking twenty or thirty cigarettes a day, he remained remarkably fit – though more by luck in his constitution than by judgement. 'I have declined', he wrote at the time, 'into a very recognisable sort of New Yorker, the sort that is as tanned as an Apache in summer, madly healthy from swimming, dancing, fishing, even running and diving, but who, in winter, rides between one chair and another, whose only exercise, aside from spanning tenths in the left hand, is to rise and shake a hand and sit again.' In an attempt to offset this potential problem, he had made a New Year's resolution which left his family open-mouthed with astonishment. 'On the first of January, at ten o'clock in the morning, I threw a panic into my children – who are about twice my size – by telling them I was going for a walk.' Walking, he explained to his BBC audience, was something no American did without a purpose. The idea that it might be an activity valid in its own right was bewildering. Despite these good intentions, it's doubtful whether Central Park saw much of Cooke striding purposelessly through the snow. Nor, at this stage, was he attracted by Eisenhower's remedy – a round or two of golf. 'Thirty-six holes of golf would, I'm convinced, put me in bed.'

In the week following his fishing excursion, after promising that his *Letter* would return to matters of more moment, Cooke was once again distracted on the home front. Hurricane Donna suddenly slewed from its normal course and headed for Long Island, where he had left Jane in residence. He had a special feeling for hurricanes, a mixture of objective interest in meteorological phenomena and personal memories of the great winds of his time: the 1938 storm that had devastated the Emerson property and Hurricane Carol in September 1954, which had impinged more directly on his own life. 'I was in our house on its high bluff a hundred feet over Peconic Bay that morning and I shall never forget seeing one side of the house move, hearing a big picture window explode and seeing the other windows bounce as much as four or five inches at a time. There was a dismal howling – no, howling is wrong – a pounding, booming, fifteen minutes, when I thought we were airborne.'

The story had a happy ending: in the course of repairing the damage the Cookes extended the front of the house into a covered terrace. But each time the winds roared across the Caribbean, the storm shutters would go up and, even if there was no damage to the house, they would find great heaps of sand deposited across their cliff-top garden in the morning. In 1960, Hurricane Donna veered north and east from its expected track and up towards the eastern seaboard. It was a weekday and when he heard the news, Cooke was playing chess in Manhattan, late at night, with Burrows or Russell. His first instinct was to race back down the island 'to rescue his wife and children', but there was a catch in this plan. Jane, he told his listeners, 'takes as dim a view of being rescued as a mule in the Grand Canyon that has spotted a dandelion just over the edge of a three-thousand-foot precipice'.

Cooke's description of his wife's relationship with the grey wooden structure is touching. It was her creation. She had defended it against all that the weather – or sneering architectural cynics – could throw at it. She was not about to panic at Donna's approach. 'She is absolutely convinced, on principle, that no hurricane brewed by an all-seeing Providence could possibly destroy it,' Cooke said, with weary resignation. This time, the storms left Nassau Point comparatively unscathed.

~

After Donna's demise, there was no excuse for not buckling down to the campaign. Apart from a few excursions, Cooke intended to cover most of the Nixon-Kennedy battle from his comfortable base in New York. The candidates simply moved too fast, by now, for the correspondent to stay on their heels. Cooke was content to let television do the job he'd predicted for it, though he did spend one week on a press plane in pursuit of Kennedy, which took its physical toll on the reporters:

> Whistles blow from an epiglottis, gargles trip over an uvula, baritone groans come rumbling up from an oesophagus. One man snores, I swear, from his stomach. It would be a horrible scene if it were not for its overwhelming pathos. . . . The abominable tow-head from Massachusetts [Kennedy] is probably looking over a file of telegrams in the intervals of reading Cicero. Last night – or was it the night before? – he had four hours of rich, refreshing sleep. He is good for thirty pounding hours on the stump. The men in the press planes that drone behind him are good for nothing, unless it is a convalescent home. He may not lick Nixon, but he has reduced the reporters to pulp.

It turned out to be the most closely fought duel he'd covered and it was television that helped to seal the outcome. The first of four live debates between 'Foxy Jack and Tricky Dick' entered American political folklore. Even before the broadcast, Cooke was one of those expressing bemusement that Nixon, with 'a beard bluer than one of Castro's boys,' should decide to face the cameras without benefit of make-up. 'Perhaps he is going to bare himself, on the Cromwellian principle of "moles and all",' he wrote. When it came to it, then, no one could fail to be struck by the contrast between the suave, clean-cut Senator and a Vice-President who looked, frankly, unshaven and, in Cooke's words, 'drained and rheumy'. The Republicans learned their lesson. The next time he appeared in public, 'there rose up a smart and handsome smiler, a well-dressed, broad-shouldered giant with a copper tan'.

Cooke spent the last week of the campaign on the road – with Nixon in Illinois and Ohio and with Kennedy in California. His valedictory election-eve article ended with a suitably gnomic comment for an unpredictable outcome: 'The campaign has ended as it always does. Both men are puffy with exhaustion. They mask their fatigue with a melodramatic cloak of resolution and honest indignation. The suspicion is rampant, however, that under their cloaks Nixon has a rage to win and Kennedy is resigned to the Presidency.' The next day he had to file in advance a report to be published as the polls were about to open. 'Although both sides say the die is cast, they are not overlooking the possibility that the election could turn on a handshake from a New Hampshire farmer or a telephone call to a lumberjack in the redwood country of Humboldt County, California.' Two columns later, he subsided into a joke at the expense of his own professional limitations: 'To sum up, Kennedy is a sure winner unless Nixon ends up with more electoral votes.'

All through the evening the outcome was in doubt. Cooke, in what became a firm tradition, invited a few friends to watch the television coverage and this time the party included Lauren Bacall and her new husband, Jason Robards. They left in deep depression, some time before midnight, when it looked as though Nixon was going to win. Kennedy's tiny victory – by a handful of electoral votes and 'a few thousands of farmers and lumberjacks out of 66 million taking part in the popular vote' – took a number of days to confirm beyond all statistical and legal doubt.

Some weeks later, the *Guardian* printed a plaudit from the playwright, Arthur Miller: 'When Alistair Cooke reports on American politics, I am charmed into the feeling that the subject may still be written about with wit and yet with serious concern, that one does not have to assume a cynicism or an alarm as though in the Last Days in order to show that an election of a President is both important and ephemeral. Mr Cooke, an Englishman, makes one feel that there is something steady underneath us.'

~

And where, throughout these long weeks of endeavour on behalf of the *Guardian*, was Max Freedman? For much of the time, taking his editor's instructions quite literally, he was absent without leave. The latter stages of the campaign did not take place in Washington, ergo they had no need of his attention. He simply dropped from view until a day or two before polling, when he finally cabled an article to Manchester. Alastair Hetherington replied on 7 November, 'I've been much bothered about your position. I know you hate writing letters, but I wonder if you could tell me how things stand? I hope I'm not being unreasonable when I say that a silence of three weeks by one of our two staff correspondents in the United States at the height of a presidential election – and without any explanation – is a bit troubling.'

Freedman's response, written by hand on the wide-ruled paper of an exercise book, was peevish in tone. He found Hetherington's statements 'unexpected and perplexing'. 'Unless I am morbidly sensitive or strangely stupid, it remains my clear and painful memory that I was placed under special instructions to regard everything related to the primaries, the nominating conventions and the Presidential campaign as forming no interest of mine.'

~

Cooke spent the few weeks after the election, like all professional observers, weighing up the new President. To begin with, little was given away: Kennedy was slower than most to appoint the members of his cabinet and Cooke described in his first post-election *Letter from America* the routine of the White House press corps in waiting, as it tried to get close to the new administration. Were there some sly digs at Max Freedman? 'Senator Kennedy listens to everybody's opinion and recommendation and is infatuated with no one. He goes off to bed and he wakes up and he says, "It will be so and so." It's rather a poor basis for news stories. The reporters have to pretend to be closer to the man than they are; they have to appease their editors by seeming to have very confidential tips; and they have to be bold in proclaiming them – but not too bold, or the actual news next day might make them look silly.' Freedman would surely have taken umbrage if he'd heard those lines.

Somehow, it fell to Cooke to spend the New Year at Kennedy's Palm Beach retreat – what was to become the 'Florida White House'. It was a curious excursion. The President-elect, while maintaining his fearsome work schedule, conducted as many meetings as possible on the golf course on the basis that it was the last chance he'd get to indulge in such frivolities. The new Press Secretary, Pierre Salinger, gave briefings to correspondents who were dressed in beachwear and, in many cases, turning various shades of puce in the unaccustomed sunshine. The first full press conference in the courtyard of Kennedy's Mediterranean-style villa left some of the older journalists marvelling at the new man's grasp of detail and introduced them to the picture potential of the dashing Senator and his young family. 'Suddenly, this enchanting moppet, Caroline – the President's three-year-old – trotted up to her father and held up some huge black shoes.' Cooke described how Kennedy bent down and placed Caroline's feet in her mother's shoes and 'the press photographers who'd been making occasional routine shots suddenly went into hysteria'. Then, still blushing slightly, the doting father continued to describe his plan for a new breed of ambassador drawn from outside the ranks of the very rich. 'These notes may not have contributed anything at all,' Cooke said apologetically at the end of the broadcast, 'but they may, I hope, contribute to your sense of the working habits of the new President, of his curious, calm character and the fascinating self-possession of John Kennedy.' This was not to be taken as a considered judgement on the man: merely a quick pen-sketch, dashed off by a beach artist.

In the *Guardian*, where he reported on some of the appointments agreed in Palm Beach, he wrote: 'There have been moments, in the Nirvana of the past two weeks, when [reporters] have yearned for a thunder shower, a sniff of passion, the sound of a monkey-wrench in the flawless machinery of John Kennedy's flawless routine, his systematic planning, his alabaster-smooth temper.' With such conflicting thoughts in their collective mind, the reporters reluctantly headed back for the inauguration in Washington – where Cooke's job was to focus on the human interest of the occasion, Freedman, naturally, being in charge of the political spin. Cooke gave his piece the sub-title 'What the People Saw', which – in the circumstances – was very little indeed if they happened to be on the streets of Washington. In Cooke's eyes, this was almost television's total victory. He himself certainly monitored the entire occasion from the small screen. At the end of the ceremony the cameras recorded the solemnity of the moment and he thought he saw 'Mrs Kennedy's smooth throat twitch for a second as the "unbearable office" passed over from a national hero to her young husband'.

Then, of course, it was back to normal. One surviving memo a few weeks later has Cooke informing Geoffrey Taylor in Manchester, 'Nothing today. Would like to know which of the following Max has *not* covered. . . .'

~

Seen from his Manhattan eyrie, the Kennedy presidency looked to Cooke, almost from the start, as if it might turn out to be a disappointment – that there might be a distinct gap between aspiration and performance. On 12 March 1961 he described in the *Guardian* the torrent of legislative ideas tumbling out of the White House, which seemed to take little account of the realities of Capitol Hill, where deeply entrenched interest groups were ready to repel every clause. 'On his [the President's] Super Highway Bill, it is the billboard lobby. On medical care for the aged, it is the American Medical Association. On low cost housing it is the real estate lobby.' The accusation was of a lack of realism and political nous – the very skills which, in Cooke's assessment, would soon be exemplified by Lyndon Baines Johnson.

At the end of March, Harold Macmillan flew to the United States to meet Kennedy for the first time. Cooke was invited to a reception at the British Embassy in Washington and at one point was drawn out of the crowd by the Prime Minister. Macmillan told him that every Monday morning, as he stepped into his car to go to work in London, the chauffeur would switch on to the Home Service for the repeat of *Letter from America*: 'And there you are!' Macmillan smiled in delight. He asked Cooke one or two questions and, before moving on, mentioned how much he enjoyed the ambience of the Kennedy White House. 'There's something very eighteenth-century about this young man,' he mused. 'So elegant, lovely wife, lots of pretty women around . . . '

Cooke did not share Macmillan's enthusiasm for the emergence of the Camelot tendency. Instead, he concentrated on the business side of the Kennedy-Macmillan relationship, which formed the subject of his next *Letter*. The question was, how could anybody really analyse the personal chemistry between two world leaders – on the basis of such brief appearances viewed from afar? Cooke called in aid his longest-standing journalistic friend, Scotty Reston of the *New York Times*, whom he dubbed in his broadcast as 'quite possibly the best political reporter now extant'. It was with Reston that he had made his heartfelt vow in the 1940s to 'resist consorting with politicians beyond the bounds of acquaintanceship'.

If anyone knew how the two leaders were getting on during that anxious springtime, it would be Scotty Reston and Cooke's respect for him was absolute. The two men were almost exact contemporaries and Reston, too, had been born in Britain. One crucial difference was that his parents emigrated in 1920 and took out naturalisation papers immediately: as an American citizen (in the words of his *Times* obituary), he was 'spared the sort of embarrassment that was to affect his great friend Alistair Cooke, when he changed his nationality at just about the grimmest point of the war'. He started work as a sports reporter and spent the war in Britain – first covering the blitz, then as an important figure in the (US) Office of War Information. This background confirmed him as the insider that Cooke could never be. Thereafter he rose rapidly to become what *Newsweek* called 'the perfect information broker for the Cold War' and the magazine remarked that 'it was impossible to exaggerate how important Reston was in his prime'. Cooke liked to tell another story, from the early 1960s, of a particularly uninformative Anglo-American summit: Reston emerged from nowhere at 11 p.m. with the glow of satisfaction given off by a reporter with a scoop. On the understanding that Cooke would write nothing till the next day, 'he told me who said what to whom, what the communiqué would say. Better – something communiqués are designed to hide – what the communiqué *meant*. Unlike most journalists proud of a coup, his story was exactly right, letter perfect. "Where did you get all this from?" Cooke asked. "I was under the carpet," Reston replied.'

The scoops never convinced Cooke that his friend had infringed their golden rule about consorting with politicians. Yet there were some who believed that Reston's brilliance and authority drew very deeply – too deeply – from the wellspring of his personal contacts with the Democrats. When he died in 1995, the *Guardian* obituary (which Cooke was distressed not to have provided) spoke of the critics who 'objected to Reston's cosiness with the high and mighty.' The obituarist claimed that Reston had, more than once, given way to White House pressure, by witholding what would have been exclusive reports on developments in Cuba.

What nobody questioned was Reston's integrity. If he did mince his words over the Bay of Pigs, it was because he believed he was protecting the country's vital national interest at a critical moment. As Kennedy's decision to support the abortive coup against Fidel Castro went horribly wrong, all friends of the United States were tested to the limit. Cooke delivered a *Letter from America* in the immediate aftermath of the invasion by anti-Castro forces, in which he described the welter of misinformation on all sides. There was no gainsaying the underlying fact of American involvement, even if the details were hazy: but there were other matters to be borne in mind. Cooke suggested that 'any fair-minded American or Briton' should take into account the reality of Soviet involvement in developing and training a Cuban air-force on America's doorstep as a partial justification of American actions.

Cooke's concluding thought on this subject was an almost perfect example of the spirit of the *Letters*: the truth about a nation is never monochrome. It has shades and shadows which the careless observer might miss and Cooke's task was to provide that subtle coloration:

> The President took the risk of embarrassing the legal and moral position of the United States [he said] by backing a small rebellion in order to warn the Soviet Union that any big excursion out of Cuba into Latin America, when the Cubans become powerfully armed and trained, will be met by American arms. This I believe to be the gist of American policy. Unhappily, the United States was the nearest place the refugees could flee to and so the Kennedy doctrine was applied to a rebellion encouraged in the United States and to an adventure so puny that, when it fell, it brought down with it the prestige of the United States as a keeper of international law and her reputation as a powerful defender of the weak.

Kennedy's reputation was hurt, but no man suffered greater collateral

damage than Adlai Stevenson. In the build-up to the invasion and in
the face of detailed press speculation about American involvement in
fomenting an invasion of Cuba by anti-Castro troops, Stevenson was
required to appear at the United Nations to support the Kennedy
line – that there would not be, under any conditions, 'an intervention
in Cuba by the United States armed forces'. These carefully selected
words left open a large semantic loophole: no intervention by US
forces, perhaps, but by Cubans trained, aided and armed by US forces
in Florida. This was something Stevenson had not been told: indeed
he was given falsified photographs of planes with Cuban markings to
back up the half-truths he was broadcasting to the world.

A few hours later, according to Cooke, Kennedy's representative
arrived at the UN to congratulate Stevenson on the speech, adding
almost as an aside, 'The President thinks you ought to know, it *was*
our show.' When Stevenson spluttered something about the photographs, he was told that they'd been faked by the CIA. Cooke became
aware of this horrible truth a day or two after the speech when
Stevenson called round to his apartment. It started as an occasion of
some jollity. Cooke was fixing drinks in the pantry, when the twelve-
year-old Susie let slip in a stage whisper something she'd heard her
father say – that the visitor really did have a 'bosun's roll', the hobbling
gait of a man prone to corpulence. Stevenson heard the remark too
as Cooke recalled. 'From the living room there rang out a merry
tenor, "You can say that again, Susie." She gave a voiceless scream and
vanished, never – I think – to come near him again.' And then came
the revelation.

'I handed him his drink and congratulated him on his splendid
speech. I remember now the deliberate way he put down his glass,
adjusted his tie, put the tips of his chubby fingers together and looked
away from me into the far corner of the room with an expression
half-way between shame and despair.' He told Cooke the story of how
he'd been duped. 'It was his bitterest disillusion,' Cooke felt, 'the
supreme humiliation of his public career.' Stevenson said he was
trying to decide what to do and Cooke assumed he was simply
working out the terms of his resignation. Gradually he realised that
his friend intended to hang on to his place, however compromised
and uncomfortable, in the corridors of power. He had nowhere else
to go.

Cooke's incipient doubts about Kennedy were certainly nurtured on that evening. Stevenson, he wrote, 'repaid Kennedy's treachery with tedious hard work, obedient loyalty to the White House, unfailing courtesy and good humour.' Khrushchev drew his own conclusions from the affair. The erection of the Berlin Wall in August and the Cuban missile crisis of October, demonstrated (to the nervous) a Soviet willingness to exploit weakness, division and inexperience in Washington. By chance, Cooke included Berlin in his European tour that summer, arriving in June, just as Khrushchev's latest threats were starting to sink in. He experienced for himself the Brandenburg Gate crossing point, through which thousands of East Berliners passed each day to work in the West and thousands more crossed in the evening for entertainment or family visits. He read the literature to which the citizens of the German Democratic Republic were exposed and marvelled, in his *Letter from Berlin*, at what was supposed to be the policy of the American imperialists, egged on by the German generals in Bonn. 'First, you will be surprised to hear, we and they are planning, as the first stage, a "liberation" of the GDR by a "small atomic blitzkrieg". ' In a related *Guardian* article, he added the grim reflection that at first no one had believed Castro's claims of American involvement in the Bay of Pigs affair: could anybody be sure that the far-fetched Soviet conspiracy theory might not turn out to contain a modicum of truth?

He left the city more convinced than ever that the holocaust was at hand: 'After this brainwashing in East Berlin, you find yourself sitting down and taking stock and wondering why a new crisis has arisen, who provoked it and what in fact are the Western military plans for a showdown.'

~

At the end of his European wanderings Cooke wrote a touching *Letter from America* on the benefits to a relationship of taking separate holidays. The issue arose from a familiar discussion of the melting pot of cultures within the mass of continental America: 'My own family has, on the female side, strong ties of blood with France and Italy through New Orleans and Texas. Somehow this subtle poison has flowed through two generations and marrying an Englishman is no antidote.'

From these musings he drew the conclusion that it was very sensible for an American couple to savour separate parts of Europe. In his case there were logistical reasons, too: he explained that he couldn't leave America before the middle of May and Jane had to be back in early June when Susie finished school, so 'my wife goes on ahead and spends a couple of weeks in her spiritual home – Italy (imagine?!) – and I come on later and we meet in London.' The punctuation marks are in Cooke's original typescript. 'Having had her fill of Italians, she is prepared to roll with the punches in my native land.' There was a moral to be drawn from this – an extra advantage, because it meant that a wife

> has enjoyed the privilege, so she says, which in our society men enjoy every day at their work, of being greeted and treated as a person in their own right, not as the appendage or chattel of the male, tethered by his brood. She discovers again that she is a woman and an individual. And the husband, fending for himself in an isolation ward of self-pity, rediscovers again a fact he had forgotten: he is a poor fish . . . I am the last man to say that husbands and wives (who can benefit) should not be together. But I am saying it is an excellent thing for them, once or twice a year, to be apart. So at the risk of upsetting the Society for the Maintenance of Conjugal Boredom, I am passing on the lesson of my last four annual vacations and strongly recommending separate holidays for husbands and wives.

Was this a case of post facto rationalisation of an unwelcome reality? On the world scene there was nothing to relieve Cooke's pessimism. 'I had a sweet letter the other day from a lady in England,' he began *Letter* Number 685. 'I am still suffering from the acid indigestion caused by its first sentence. "I wonder", it began, "if it would be possible for you to talk about something other than gloom and doom." The simple answer is, well, yes madame, it would and once we seal off Berlin on our side of the curtain, or pasteurise it, or find a tranquilliser for Mr Khrushchev, then I see no reason why some Sunday evening soon, we shouldn't have a rollicking time."' This came just twelve days after work on the Berlin wall had begun.

And there was even less cause for rollicking when, in mid-September, the UN Secretary-General Dag Hammarskjold died in a plane crash in Africa as he tried to negotiate an end to the Congo crisis. Cooke had come to know the Swedish diplomat in the course of a lengthy interview undertaken for the UN archives six years earlier. This was a rare event, secured on the basis that it would be 'a conversation between equals' between a Secretary-General who shunned publicity and the calm, cultured host of *Omnibus*. The opening shot of the film had the two men relaxing into armchairs in Hammarsjkold's private apartment on the thirty-eighth floor of the United Nations building: each took a cigar from the box on the table and puffed away contentedly throughout the proceedings. Yet the Secretary-General, despite Cooke's best efforts, remained aloof and careful, weighing every word. The habit of diplomatic caution was deeply ingrained, as it had been from the moment he was pitch-forked, without warning, into the most sensitive job in the world.

The interview was replayed on the United Nations' own television service as part of a series called *International Zone* – which was briefly scheduled by the commercial networks at Sunday lunch-time or in the small hours of the morning, watched by almost nobody. Its producer, George Movshon, was a friend of Cooke's who persuaded him to present the programme for the next two or three years. Despite its tiny audience it impressed the *New York Times*: because such a pro-gramme had to 'report the facts' but not 'precipitate a quarrel', it required somebody with Cooke's 'diplomatic phraseology' to walk the narrow chalk line with 'unerring skill'.

Partly because of these personal contacts and partly because of his own attendance during the birthpangs of the UN, Cooke regarded the organisation in general, and Hammarskjold in particular, as prob-ably the best chance of avoiding an East-West conflict. On this issue of national security, Cooke the sceptic – the non-believer – was moved to express a sort of faith in a distant ideal.

Hammarskjold, Cooke concluded, was the UN's first martyr.

PART SIX

THE
UNLOVED
SIXTIES

25

LIBERAL DISCORD

There was no let-up in world tension, but Cooke had many distractions. In these non-election years he felt at liberty to cover for the *Guardian* the stories that interested him. A hand-written schedule for the spring of 1962 shows him taking reporting trips to San Diego, to Hot Springs and to Seattle for the new World's Fair. He was also enthused by John Glenn's space flight on Tuesday, 20 February, which finally stilled the American sense of grievance at the Russian victory in getting a man into space ten months earlier. From Cape Canaveral, Cooke described the last few seconds before the Atlas rocket lifted off: 'Twenty seconds from the word, the umbilical cord dropped away and Mercury Control intoned the countdown in seconds. There was the deep, low-frequency rumble modulating to an enormous whoosh of sound and a vicious tongue of flame; and soon the Atlas was a fiery keyhole and then an acorn and then a snowflake.'

The technology exercised a strange attraction over Cooke – such events turned him once again into the schoolboy at the feet of his Blackpool schoolmasters, or the young man enthralled by Haven Emerson's tales of medical detective work. He liked to show off his layman's grasp of a complex subject and his *Guardian* description is spattered with scientific buzz-words – Glenn would orbit 'between a perigee of 100 miles and an apogee of 160 miles'; or 'it took only one pound of thrust, delivered by a hydrogen peroxide exhaust, to keep the capsule yawing and rolling according to a plan'.

The following Thursday Cooke penned the *Guardian* article which seemed to him the most memorable he wrote for the paper: John Glenn's triumphant return to New York coincided with the crash of an American Airlines 707 'Astrojet' into Jamaica Bay, just beyond La Guardia Airport. Eighty-seven passengers and eight crew died instantly, as the first scheduled non-stop flight from New York to Los Angeles ended in catastrophe. For Cooke, the concurrence of these two events – with television viewers receiving intercut images of the search for bodies and the joyful procession a few miles away – had a cinematic quality reminiscent of Fellini. And that was how he wrote his report:

> Within twenty minutes, the tension of Glenn's arrival and impending tour was suspended while we went out to the Bay and watched policemen wading into shallow waters, firemen and the coastguards fishing bodies into rowboats, priests and nurses stacking gruesome packages under blankets. From then on, for the three hours it took for the Colonel to crawl through the cowpath the vast crowds had left for him, we were always going back to the dishevelled scene by the bay.

It was rare for Cooke to employ such high-flown imagery without a hint of self-mockery.

> Neither scene had any connection with the other, except by way of hammering home a crude irony, a gross and gratuitous contrast between the man who circled the globe three times and was plucked safe and sound from alien space and eighty-seven non-aviators who flew two minutes in the tried and tested Astrojet and were snuffed out in a wink.

His piece ended solemnly, 'the sweet smell of success will always be soured by the acrid odour from Jamaica Bay and the tasteless mistiming of whatever Gods preside over the art of science and human flight.'

Among the other events which set his journalistic juices running was the arrival, on Independence Day – 4 July – of Francis Chichester, who had just broken the record for a single-handed transatlantic crossing for the second time. There was the time, too, to indulge his growing passion for tennis – and to pass on his sense of disenchantment with the blistering high-powered speed of the men's game. He reported on the final stages of the 1961 American championship for the *Guardian* and was carried away to flights of creative fancy reminiscent of his writing on boxing in earlier times. The men's finalists, Roy Emerson and Rod Laver and the eventual women's champion, the American Darlene Hard, were – in Cooke's eyes – no better than tennis automata. Into this machine age had stumbled a British contender, Ann Haydon, 'a forest nymph who appeared as astonished as the rest of us to discover herself being dragged out like a wispy Christian martyr into the blinding light of the arena'. As for the men – 'it all comes down to this melancholy lesson: The mania for the service produces shoulders like cannon balls and the thighs of a stallion. It improves the tennis, but inhibits social movement off the court. Chuck McKinley, as the best contemporary example, can bound around like Superman – but seen on the way to or from the pavilion, he can barely walk, substituting a barrelling motion produced from the axles of his enormous thighs.'

In between his eclectic assignments, he joined Jane and Susie in Bermuda for a long weekend in the middle of their two-week holiday in the Caribbean. This came about through Cooke's membership of the Advisory Board for an annual almanac of world events: the *World Book Year-Book* was sponsored by Field Enterprises Education Corporation and board members were required to attend an annual meeting to discuss its editorial content. The board included experts in various aspects of human endeavour and the Corporation eased the onerous nature of their labours by sending them to relaxing locations to carry them out. So it was that Cooke, who was responsible for the arts, and Scotty Reston, in charge of 'National Affairs', could spend a few reviving days in the sunshine at somebody else's expense. Other luminaries tempted by these delights included the Belgian statesman Paul-Henri Spaak and the soon-to-be Canadian Prime Minister Lester Pearson. Jane was properly grateful for the reflected pleasures provided by these luxurious Field trips, but in 1962 at least, she was off almost immediately afterwards to her beloved Italy, leaving her husband, yet again, to follow her across the Atlantic a few days behind.

When Cooke arrived in London, he was the guest on *Desert Island Discs*. The eight records he chose were predominantly jazz – Fats Waller, Duke Ellington, Jack Teagarden and Earl 'Fatha' Hines. About the latter he had good stories to tell. Some time earlier he had met the great pianist by chance in San Francisco, discovering him playing an out-of-tune upright in the Hangover Bar. 'It was the nadir of Hines' career – working in this saloon with the reek of sour air and spilled alcohol and the lights turned down to a maintenance bulb or two. It was like Handel or Haydn appearing in the local pub.' From then on, until the revival in Hines's fortunes carried him to more salubrious venues, Cooke would call at the club whenever he was in San Francisco to hear his hero play.

Cooke also had something to say about Teagarden's 'Basin Street Blues': 'there's an interesting period flavour to this recording,' he said, 'because it's the only one I know where the original lyric is sung. You're not allowed to sing it any more. Teagarden says, "Basin Street – where all the dark and the light folks meet". Now, because of our absurd touchiness on this subject, we have to say "Where a-all the folks meet," or "Where the élite meet". '

Roy Plomley seems to be taken aback and stutters, 'That seems carrying things a little—' and Cooke interrupts, 'Well, I think all men are created equal but I don't think they're all created the same.'

'True enough,' says Plomley and moves swiftly on.

The other record choices were classical pieces and, as usual, the final stages of the conversation turned to the subject's personal tastes and habits. Plomley inquired about Cooke's hobbies. 'I'm interested in climatology,' Cooke replies. 'I have barographs and call up the Weather Bureau and bawl them out from time to time and I would, I think, know about cirrus and stratus and cumulus and what sort of weather was coming up.' After a skimpy review of Cooke's practical capabilities – including an unlikely claim that he might be able to build his own hut – they conclude that Cooke might be happy to spend years alone on the island, another dubious assertion for a man so dedicated to the business of friendship. Plomley comments on his 'charming light American accent' and asks, naturally, about the state of Anglo-American relations. Were they better than when Cooke had started work? 'It would be nice to think so, wouldn't it? No, I think this is as complicated as relationships between individuals – they are never frozen, they can never be static, you have to put in under-standing and tolerance and patience all the time, so that nobody will ever complete this work.' With that message for his BBC bosses, he ended by choosing an H.L. Mencken anthology – *Chrestomathy* – as his permitted book and a tape-recorder as his luxury, with a good supply of batteries: 'I feel I would go mad if I couldn't comment on what was happening and make notes and write via the tape-recorder. Also, if the rescue-boat arrived, I'd have a whole series of *Letters from a Desert Island.*'

~

Month by month, Cooke's relations with the *Guardian* were growing cooler. The dissatisfaction continued to grumble away until it burst out into the open in October of 1962, when Cooke travelled to England in an effort to clear the air.

Hetherington told his Chief American Correspondent that the duplication with Freedman's reports was still a serious problem, though he felt the working arrangement they'd agreed was bearing fruit. He had three other concerns to pass on: the shortage of first-hand reporting by Cooke outside New York, the lack of assurance that what was promised would be delivered and the nagging sense (in Manchester) that Cooke's other interests might be taking a higher priority than writing for the *Guardian*. The criticism was pointed. Hetherington bemoaned the fact that none of his team had, at the critical moment, been at Oxford, Mississippi – where 300 Federal Marshals had used force to allow a black student to gain access to a white university, inspiring widespread riots. 'As it was, we were getting the *New York Times* beautifully rewritten by Alistair Cooke, but that wasn't enough.' There was simply no meeting of minds, but there was no virtue for either of them in bringing matters to a head. The *Guardian* couldn't afford to lose Cooke and he probably had no desire to spend the time and energy ingratiating himself with a new employer. The official memo records that Cooke would try to do more at first hand and 'give a better account to our interests', while Hetherington promised to watch the incoming copy more carefully.

A new young *Guardian* reporter, Hella Pick, found herself in the no man's land between the Cooke and Freedman trenches. She had originally been sent to spend three months on attachment as the *Guardian*'s United Nations reporter and remembers floating through her first meeting with Cooke in the Delegates' Lounge on a sea of daiquiri. When she returned to New York to take up the job on a permanent basis she naturally found herself – for geographical, if for no other reasons – in the Cooke camp.

Her sympathy was reinforced by the encouragement he offered her. As her Bureau Chief, he not only helped her to exploit the journalistic potential of the UN, but also to travel further afield. She judged him to be a generous and thoughtful boss, though a keen young reporter was obviously an asset for Cooke when there were inconvenient assignments to be dealt with. Before long, when communications with Manchester were problematical, Pick would act as liaison (or buffer) – ringing the Foreign Desk with details of the stories Cooke would be covering, as well as her own plans. She became well aware of Hetherington's frustration and began to think he would be grateful if Cooke were to retire gracefully: 'Alastair [Hetherington] wanted news stories – he was not really interested in good writing,' she believed. 'He never fully understood that Max Freedman was writing the kind of thing that was being fed straight out of the White House. I don't think he ever appreciated either Cooke's style or his popularity.'

It was in this fraught and fragile working atmosphere that the news broke of a new Soviet military build-up in Cuba in the autumn of 1962. As the Kennedy White House weighed up its options, it was clearly Max Freedman's story. It was also, as it turned out, both his finest hour – and his swan-song.

The first the outside world knew about the crisis was on Monday 22 October, when the United States issued an ultimatum to Khrushchev: all Soviet missile sites on the island of Cuba had to be dismantled. The clear threat was that refusal to comply would have dreadful consequences. For the next six days, as the super powers squared up to each other, Freedman was on the inside track of American strategic thinking. His closeness to LBJ, the Vice-President, meant that he knew, in Hetherington's words, 'much more than he had put in the paper'. In his autobiography Hetherington pays tribute to the way Freedman steered the paper's coverage and emboldened it to take a tough and contentious editorial line. At the beginning of that terrifying week, for instance, the *Guardian* questioned the right of the United States to blockade Cuba and drew comparisons with America's insistence on keeping bases close to Soviet territory – in Berlin and Turkey. This looked suspiciously to many like sympathising with Moscow. Then, when Freedman had revealed the existence of a plan to launch a nuclear attack on the missile bases, the *Guardian* demanded that the British government break ranks in the face of such madness.

As the week wore on, Cooke was left playing second fiddle to Freedman, whose dispatches carried that irresistible White House imprimatur. The contrast was at its most pointed on the Wednesday when Cooke was writing at length on how the American nation 'had fallen in behind the President', while Freedman filled the leader page with three columns of analysis based precisely, as Hetherington recalled with glee, on 'the papers and thoughts of the President's Executive Committee'.

The only area in which Cooke held his own was in coverage of the United Nations, where he watched Adlai Stevenson challenging his Russian opposite number. It was a brave display, though in due course it emerged that – once again – Stevenson had not been kept fully informed: all the real decisions were being taken behind closed doors in Washington. Less than three years later, Stevenson was dead, leaving Cooke to mourn 'a courtly, twinkling, roly-poly comical man of that estimable order of Americans . . . who left a lasting impression by the energy of their idealism but who were never quite strong or ruthless enough, in the pit of the political jungle and the critical relations of life, to turn goodness and mercy into law or policy'. His epitaph for his friend was that he remained 'the liveliest reminder of our time that there are admirable reasons for failing to be President'.

~

As for Freedman, he capped his Cuba performance by arranging a ceremonial post-crisis visit to Washington for his editor: how could Hetherington fail to be impressed, as his White House correspondent introduced him first to influential officials like Walt Rostow in the State Department, then to LBJ – and finally led him into the presence of President Kennedy himself? JFK sat in his rocking-chair and brushed aside Hetherington's apology for the way his paper had covered the crisis: the *Guardian*'s editorial line, he said, had not been so very far wide of the mark, except that it underestimated the ferocity of Russian expansionism. Hetherington must have glowed with pleasure to know that his words had reached the most powerful man in the world, and he had Freedman to thank for it. He was bowled over and left, giving thanks for 'the presence of Jack Kennedy in the White House in October 1962'.

All of which made Freedman's next decision even more baffling. A few weeks after the crisis, he announced that he was quitting his full-time *Guardian* job to concentrate on writing books and a column for a Chicago newspaper. On 12 December, Hetherington wrote to Cooke confirming the rumours and keeping any dismay he may have felt under wraps. Max, he wrote, would – for the sake of continuity – be doing three columns a week for the *Guardian*. 'One incidental benefit of the new arrangement,' he suggested innocently, might be 'a diminution in the demarcation disputes between Washington and New York. I know those have been a great trial to you.' Richard Scott was appointed to replace him, but couldn't take up the post immediately.

Hella Pick was sent to Washington at short notice, only to find that Freedman had removed the entire contents of the office – reference

books, cuttings, contacts. The bookshelves were bare. When she confronted him, Freedman replied that he had collected the material and
it belonged to him. He even had the office mail redirected to his home
so that Pick didn't receive standard Capitol Hill hand-outs. She rang
Cooke in despair and within a few days he had organised a large
party at the Mayflower Hotel: it was packed with influential figures,
including Kennedy's Press Secretary, Pierre Salinger, who became one
of her close friends. 'After Alistair had pounced,' she says, 'I never
looked back.'

The two *Guardian* rivals didn't meet much thereafter. Freedman's
career took him back to Canada for a time, where he became a policy
adviser to the Prime Minister, Lester Pearson. He died in 1980 at the
age of sixty-three – in the words of Geoffrey Taylor's *Guardian*
history – 'a greatly talented, but evidently not very happy, man.' Cooke
never experienced similar professional problems again, either with
Hella Pick or with Freedman's successor, Richard Scott. As for Cuba
and the world's flirtation with catastrophe, Cooke's relief was profound and he shared it with BBC listeners on the day of Khrushchev's
climb-down:

> An hour ago, a neighbour of mine who is a hi-fi buff and mighty proud of
> an amplifier that practically fills his living-room, telephoned me and asked
> me to listen to the clanging sound of his gramophone. He was playing
> 'Oh, What a Beautiful Morning!'. It was corny, but it was spontaneous and
> good and I looked out over the riffling waves of the reservoir in Central
> Park; a bird back-lashed to the water and was airborne and soared off to
> the land and a high elm. I should like to say it was a dove. It was, however,
> a seagull and its clean, swinging flight is also, I imagine, a tiny thing I shall
> remember until the day I die.

In the period of calm after Cuba – and with Max Freedman suddenly
out of the picture – Cooke was able to return to *Letters* of a more
jocular and discursive kind. In February he reported on Kennedy's
sudden interest in the physical fitness of the Marine in the modern
age: Cooke was struck by the unlikely claim from Pierre Salinger that
he intended to start a regime of walking to improve his health. 'This
was sheer bluster,' according to Cooke, 'according to reliable
enemies – I mean sources – in the White House. Mr Salinger had no
intention of walking more than two blocks and then only if he was
out of cigars.' In due course Salinger withdrew his offer, quoting

eminent physicians on the risks to the unfit of sudden and prolonged exercise. But by then Cooke himself, fearing that he might be sent to report on Salinger's excursion, had set out on a training walk in the Connecticut countryside: 'There was a slap of ice and for a short second I saw my feet and legs against the sky. Next thing, a doctor was holding up three fingers. That is why I am talking to you this week from my bed and that is why I have just mailed to Pierre Salinger, care of the White House, Washington DC, a bill for three broken ribs.'

While he was recovering, Jane travelled to London to help Holly prepare for her wedding to a magazine journalist. Holly, by her own description, had become something of a King's Road 'Dolly Bird' and was living in a flat in the scrupulously fashionable Cheyne Walk. Cooke wrote to Rupert Hart-Davis that Jane's task was 'to prepare the love-nest', which meant helping the young with 'such rudimentary skills as the fastening of windows, the plugging in of electric wires and the mixing of a bearable Martini.' In the event, the preparations were in vain. Holly called the engagement off, but only after Alistair and Jane had arrived in London for the big day in June. It took her a considerable time to pluck up the courage to tell her mother. Jane was not surprised and Cooke was left with more time to compile his *Letters from Abroad*.

Within a month, he was travelling again, this time on a world tour to make films for the UN's *International Zone*, taking in Fiji, Australia, Thailand and India. As he boasted afterwards, this required him and his producer, George Movshon, to take eighty-two flights in two months. They were old friends and it was a congenial exercise: the Indian leg of the trip was especially memorable. In the first instance, they came to film the Asian weather centre in Delhi, recording its work in monitoring monsoons throughout the region. They discovered that there wasn't much to see – two or three civil servants and a weather map – although that didn't prevent the attendance of a Sikh general and a staff of twelve to 'help'. A diversion to Calcutta to record sequences for another film, about poverty, had a traumatic effect on Cooke: he found the squalor of the street scenes almost impossible to cope with. But it was while they were in Delhi that he was offered the chance to meet Nehru. The Indian Prime Minister was not on the list of interviewees, but as they finished their work, their UN minder picked up the phone: 'Sharma, Banarjee here. Does

the PM know that Mr Alistair Cooke is in town? No? I think it would
be rewarding on both sides . . .'

Cooke was told that Nehru would see him at 7.00 p.m. and he was
issued with a set of guidelines: at 7.25, he would be offered a glass of
lemonade which he was to accept gratefully and drink. Ten minutes
later the cigarette box would be produced and Cooke was told to
decline politely, make his excuses and leave.

At five to seven, he took his place in the guest-room. The second-
hand on the huge wall-clock ticked loudly and precisely at the
appointed hour, Nehru entered, sat down and placed his finger-tips
together. There was a pause, apparently for thought, before Nehru
said in his clipped Harrow tones, 'Where are you coming from?'

The syntax threw Cooke and he stumbled over his reply: 'I am
coming . . . I mean, I came. . .' It broke the ice and they started to talk
about the ominous developments in Laos and Vietnam. 'I told him I
feared that the US "technicians" would soon turn into soldiers and
then there would be more technicians and so on. Nehru asked if there
was the possibility of a truce or a peace conference. No, I told him:
it's a question of the pride of a President.' Whether or not Cooke's
prescience was as impressive as it appears in his memory, Nehru was
certainly absorbed by the conversation. At 7.25 the lemonade appeared
on cue and at 7.35 the guest, as soon as he was offered a cigarette,
made to leave.

Nehru brushed his apology aside. 'No, no, no,' he said, 'this is not
form.' Cooke didn't leave until 10.15.

The discussion ranged over war, peace – and the business of politics.
Cooke said that he had never contemplated the life of a politician,
because 'I was brought up to believe that there is always much to be
said on both sides,' and in any matter of serious import, there might
be three, four or five sides to be taken into account.

Nehru said, 'You have discovered the Hindu view of death.'

~

It was, in part, because of the amount of travelling he'd done through
the autumn of 1963 that Cooke turned down an offer to join Kennedy
on a routine presidential outing to Dallas in November.

There was another reason, too, why Cooke wasn't in Dallas on 22
November, as he recalled in a *Letter* some years later. He was bored
with Democratic politics, so that when the invitation arrived – despite

the best efforts of a friend in the Kennedy camp – it didn't sound sufficiently enticing.

'A two-day flight, a couple of dinners, a night in Fort Worth, a stop-over at Dallas, a first-rate political row . . . all this and Jackie, too. It should be fun.' Not even the attraction of Jackie Kennedy's first appearance on a purely political trip, nor the vicious feuding among Texas Democrats – which her husband was supposed to sort out – could change his mind.

So Cooke stayed in New York, planning to cover the Texas jaunt from his desk overlooking Central Park. Astute readers of the *Guardian* could have caught him out: how was it that he was apparently filing copy from San Antonio, Texas, on 21 November only to be reporting from New York the following day? Cooke's main concern when the President set out was to highlight the blurred boundaries between a 'non-political' tour (funded by the taxpayer) and a partisan rally. Under his spurious 'San Antonio' dateline, he wrote about the dinner Kennedy was giving in honour of a Democratic Congressman to which 'Mr Salinger, the President's press secretary, says that Republicans are welcome!' The exclamation mark, a piece of punctuation he rarely deployed in print, was a mark of Cooke's disapproval.

26

THE APOLOGIST'S ULTIMATE TEST

When the dread news broke Cooke was compelled to resort to the television screen. This was how he described his *modus operandi* to Alastair Hetherington in a letter the following month: 'Three networks had somehow sent crews off to the Repository Building, the freeway, the hospital, the police station, the homicide bureau and had anchor men in New York. Susie Cooke, by the way, happened to be here and she was a splendid leg man (leg girl?), watching two networks in another room while I tried to stab out the piece. She kept tearing in correcting times, identifying the judge who swore in Johnson and in other ways saving me from errors and the wrong continuity. I could have made it infinitely more detailed even in the first take, but I simply had no idea how much space there'd be.'

His report was simple and chilling.

President John Fitzgerald Kennedy, the thirty-fifth President of the United States, was shot during a motorcade drive through downtown Dallas this afternoon. He died in the emergency room of the Parkway Memorial Hospital 32 minutes after the attack. He was 46 years old and is the third president to be assassinated in office since Abraham Lincoln and the first since President McKinley in 1901.

After laying out the bare details of the arrest of Lee Harvey Oswald, he continued:

This is being written in the numbed interval between the first shock and the harried attempt to reconstruct a sequence of fact from an hour of tumult. However, this is the first assassination of a world figure that took place in the age of television; and every network and station in the country abandoned its daily grind and took up the plotting of the appalling story. At this hour, it begins to form a grisly pattern, contradicted by a grisly preface: the projection on television screens of happy crowds and a grinning President only a few seconds before the gunshots.

There followed the details of the shooting and the first fruits of the police investigation.

His coverage demonstrated that his old reporting skills were as lively as ever and he was called upon to repeat the exercise two days later when Oswald was murdered by Jack Ruby.

Looking back on these events in his 12 December letter to Hetherington, he reflected on the implications of the fact that he'd been so far away from the action. It was obviously in his interests to put the best possible gloss on his detachment and this he did with some vigour. 'It was a stroke of luck that I wasn't along [on the Dallas trip] except – and this is always the snag – for the dateline. The White House press corps was thirteen cars behind the President and by the time they swung round the bend and through the tunnel, the main cars were on their way to the hospital. Not one member of the press bus guessed the truth, though they were puzzled by people lying on the ground. They turned off the freeway and went to the Trade Mart, where he was to make the speech.' One journalist from Hearst newspapers telephoned her New York Office to warn of a possible delay in filing her copy. 'Her dumbfounded news editor was incredulous, told her the truth and she rushed out of the booth and told the corps. They were then a couple of miles from the hospital and as stranded as the men in the trenches in the First World War. Some took off for the hospital and most retreated to bars (they had no hotel reservations in Dallas, since they were winding up that night in Austin) and made fast notes from the TV.'

As, indeed, Cooke himself had done a couple of thousand miles away. But beyond the *post facto* rationalisation, Dallas was (in his mind) yet another mile-post on the road to damnation for the old-fashioned peripatetic newspaperman. Ironically, he had been writing on the same topic only days before, predicting the arrival of 'transatlantic television ships or floating transmitters or whatever', which would allow simultaneous coverage of – say – the Conventions. 'When that happens,' he said, 'I intend to cover the Conventions from a hotel-room in London. There are no distractions and the weather is about 30 degrees cooler. And anyway, I can watch and ponder while eating breakfast, all day long. I have a passion for English bacon.'

With a request to Hetherington for a note acknowledging Susie's help on the day of Kennedy's death, he ended by announcing his plan to travel with the new President to Austin, Texas, immediately after Christmas. It was typical of the punctilious Hetherington that he obliged, by return, with a letter for Susan Byrne Cooke: 'Our very excellent chief correspondent in the United States tells me that you were of the greatest help to him on the night of the tragedy in Dallas. It's very good of you to have helped him in this way.'

The assassination left Cooke with the feeling that much of the good work of recent years, his included, had been undone during those two bloody days. 'I don't recall ever being so depressed,' he told Hetherington, 'by the reading of English and American papers: the foul deed released something very ugly among even very intelligent people in Europe.' Even the best, he felt, could get it dangerously wrong. 'I just saw a piece by James Cameron about the coming Civil War, America rent by "vicious hate", the population rushing round scrawling swastikas on Jewish shop windows . . . . this is the very essence of the thing he affects to despise . . . . so violently against violence, so hateful against "hate"! I had meant to say on my account that the editorial side [of the *Guardian*] stayed wonderfully sane and balanced through all the worst days.'

There was much for the disciple of Anglo-Americanism to do and Cooke set to work in a special edition of the *Letter* broadcast on the Sunday evening, just two days after Kennedy's death. He chose an oblique approach, not yet addressing the more rabid outbursts of European reaction head-on, but pointing up the civilised and genuine pain of a nation on whom the horror had been visited. The hurt was intensified, he maintained, because of the way television had familiarised Kennedy, making him, in some measure, part of the family: 'This charming, complicated, subtle and greatly intelligent man, whom the Western world was proud to call its leader, appeared for a split second in the telescopic sight of a maniac's rifle and he was snuffed out. In that moment, all the decent grief of a nation was taunted and outraged, so that along with the sorrow there is a desperate and howling note across the land.' He ended with Dylan Thomas's 'Do not go gentle into that good night. Rage, rage against the dying of the light.'

Apart from this poetic epitaph, this *Letter* was notable for its utter lack of sentimentality. Cooke was never a sentimentalist, always the rational observer. Any personal pain he felt remained well below the surface of his work. Consequently, even though Dallas was still so raw in people's lives, he did not draw back from an early sketch of how history might deal with their lost President – not least by indicating the gulf between the inspiring rhetoric of Kennedy's inaugural speech ('Let the word go forth from this time and place to friend and foe alike, that the torch has been passed to a new generation of Americans. . . .') and the reality of legislative sclerosis which hobbled his administration. 'If we pause and run over the record of the very slow translation of these ideals into law – the hair's-breadth defeat of the medical care for the aged plan; the shelving, after a year of strenuous labour, of the tax bill; the perilous reluctance of Congress to tame the Negro revolution with the civil rights law – we have to admit that the clear trumpet sound of the inaugural has been sadly soured in three short years.' It was strong and honestly felt and written about a man dead just forty-eight hours.

~

Cooke's judgement on JFK did not grow more mellow with the years and was not helped by the immediate and instinctive respect which LBJ inspired in him. Six days after he had taken office, Cooke was writing in the *Guardian*, '. . . though the high style of the Kennedy regime is gone forever, as the White House reverts to the folksier manner of the county courthouse square, it will not surprise the friends of Lyndon Johnson if he emerges as a second Harry Truman, who arrived blinking in the White House one day, a failed haberdasher needing all our prayers and the next sprang fully armed as an irascible all-American legionnaire and, more astonishing still, a twentieth-century statesman.' Three weeks on and Cooke was waxing even more enthusiastic. 'In the inner sanctum sits the man himself, his massive torso usually bent over towards a telephone (he makes about a hundred personal calls a day). To all his visitors it is clear, from the old ease of the Texas vernacular and the new authority with which he uses it, that he is in command.'

On a more personal level he discovered – when he travelled with the President to Texas after Christmas – how different things would be in a Johnson presidency. As he strolled round Austin, he saw a policeman step out into the road to halt the traffic: then, 'suddenly, a six-foot-three man came lumbering across the street with a little cluster of people around him, old and young, garage mechanics and small children. It was the President on his way to get his hair cut and incidentally to call on a jeweller, a lunch-counter owner and a couple of other shop-keepers he'd known since boyhood. It was quite shocking, one month after the assassination to see this carefree stroll.'

This was a President very much to Cooke's taste. Freedman might still be acting as an occasional conduit for inside information about the Johnson White House to an insatiable Hetherington, but Cooke felt that a weight had slipped from his shoulders. In fact, nothing much had changed back at head office. On the Texas trip, for instance, Cooke delivered a lengthy piece from the town of Stonewall, where the new President met the German Chancellor. When the article was cut from the top and bottom, he complained and Hetherington felt it necessary to point out that the elaborate preamble, detailing the ceremonial and catering arrangements, had simply been too long-winded. 'We didn't really get going with the essence of the story until about the eighth or ninth paragraph,' he wrote. He accepted that the loss of the last few paragraphs was a shame, but added, 'Readers won't ever be induced to get to the essentials – and, indeed, to the best of the writing – if the preliminary catalogue was too long.'

Cooke's reply is only mildly peevish, though he did miss 'Mrs John-son's grocery list ("800 lbs of beef, 200 lbs of German potato salad, 1800 sourdough biscuits, 600 fried fruit pies") which gives the scale and tang of Texan hospitality'. It was no good: Hetherington just didn't like the frippery. He wanted facts.

~

Cooke's connections with the rest of the Kennedy clan were limited, with one important exception. About a year after the assassination he was approached by Columbia Records: would he be interested in com-piling an oral history of the Kennedy years on disc? 'The idea', as it was put to Cooke, 'was very appealing. I was to talk to all kinds of people who knew him – friends, colleagues, sponsors and school-teachers – but also to his favourite bartender or senate pageboy.' Unfortunately, he soon realised that he would have minimal editorial control of who was interviewed and what was said. It emerged that Jackie and Bobby Kennedy were to do some of the interviews themselves and the result was an in-built censorship of most critical (and interesting) opinions. The Cookes were away for several months in 1965 and when they returned all the extracts had been cut and compiled, leaving him to act merely as a linkman. 'I soon discovered that what they'd done was to have John Kennedy tied up in pink ribbons, four long-playing records of pure, nauseating sentimentality.' Cooke insists that he wasn't proposing an unexpurgated account, complete with a Mafia godfather explaining how he provided a regular supply of delectable young women for the President's pleasure; but the paean of praise composed in his absence was worse than his worst fears and he was committed to providing the commentary. 'I remember going to see Jackie after the material was assembled, having a drink and telling her that I wished I'd been able to do more interviewing myself.'

Her reply took him aback. 'We decided that you wouldn't be the right person,' she told him, 'because you're rather formidable.'

Cooke couldn't believe it: hadn't he spent his life interviewing every type and condition of man and woman – 'cowboys, guys who manufacture shoes, burlesque strippers'? How could she, the ultimate figure of authority and power, be calling him 'formidable'? He says it reminded him of a story he'd once heard about Lewis Carroll, who was asked why he preferred girls to boys. 'Because boys are so rough and brutal and cruel,' he said, 'and girls are like pussy-cats.' Jackie Kennedy did not fit the Carroll mould. 'She was so gentle', Cooke says, 'that you could barely hear her talk. But unlike a kitten, she was always ready to show her claws.' And when she finally married Aristotle Onassis Cooke penned some memorable lines in his *Letter from America*: 'She was and is always most at home with the chic, busy, wealthy, Atlantic-hopping jet-set. In marrying its presiding monarch, who shares her loathing of public jostling and has several sanctuaries fortified against it, you might say that Jacqueline Kennedy is simply the prodigal hot-footing it home.'

~

There was never any shortage of offers of work, though Cooke was nearly always immune to the blandishments of BBC producers trying to lure him onto their programmes: one memo from his New York amanuensis, Lillian Lang, has him turning down the chance to do an eight-minute talk on 'Old People in the United States' for an outlet called *Home This Afternoon*. Mr Cooke, she wrote, was extremely interested in the subject, on which he had been collecting notes for several years, but sadly was busy with politics.

In any case, Cooke spent much of 1964 either travelling or planning future expeditions – all of which had to be fitted around the last election campaign in which he played a full role for the *Guardian*.

Yet he did find time to write extensively about the phenomenon of LBJ. Two lengthy magazine articles in the summer celebrated the flowering of Cooke's first favourable impressions and recorded further his disenchantment with Kennedy. One, entitled 'LBJ vs. JFK', acknowledged the spell Kennedy had cast over the young of all nations and characterised him as an American statesman perfectly tailored to the European taste. 'That his most admirable qualities were not invested in his handling either of politics or power hardly occurs to those admirable elegists who now bemoan the death of a hero, the replacement of the White House intellectuals with energetic fixers (what Johnson calls "valuable hunks of humanity") and the premature passing of the Kennedy "style".'

Cooke then proceeded to cut a swathe through the Kennedy myth:

> Like other reporters who covered him as a Senator and as President, from the White House to the black homes of the South, from the Philadelphia slums to Palm Beach, I have many delightful, funny and admiring memories of him. They make it all the more unpleasant to look at the political record and admit the poverty of it and consider the near-despair with which, in the last month or two, he wondered how and when he could persuade the powerful House Committee men, the Senate's great elders, to give him a tax cut and a civil rights bill.

Why was Johnson likely to make a better pitch at the job? Cooke thought he had spotted something in LBJ's philosophy which chimed in with his own reflections on the state of the nation – and which had much to do with the jaundiced condition of modern journalism. America, he felt, was a much more complex creature than tabloid editors were prepared to acknowledge. So obsessed had the media become with the superficial glitter that the richness of the rest went largely unreported. It was this less glamorous substratum in which the earthy figure of Johnson had his roots. 'A great deal of a nation's life,' Cooke wrote, 'still falls between scandal and hard news.' Johnson, he maintained, lived in this real world (which Cooke himself sought to portray in the *Letter from America*) – a world far removed from the rarefied retreats of the Kennedy clan. Journalists found this disconcerting and had fallen back on a characterisation of Johnson as an amiable curiosity. The differences could be summed up neatly: 'the Kennedys entertaining Pablo Casals, Johnson lifting a beagle by its ears'. Thus the new man's special talents, he believed, lay outside the interests of the intelligentsia and possibly beyond their grasp. Yet Cooke predicted that this unlikely and anti-intellectual figure might yet surprise the intellectuals. '[Johnson's] is at worst a talent, at best a genius, for political action, for the reconciliation of opposites, for the subtle exploitation in friends and enemies (in enemies especially) of the vanity, the needs, the self-interest and the self-righteous or genuine desire to do good, that lie in all of us. The skill with which Johnson practises this ancient but rare art is so fiendishly difficult to articulate on paper because it is as fluid in movement as the nervous system.'

For once, there was no mincing of Cooke's words: 'On the evidence of his first six months in the White House, I would go out on a limb and say that Johnson may well turn out to be the most mature practitioner of Presidential power since Abraham Lincoln, with whom, incidentally, he has much in common. . . . Though cosmopolitan sophisticates may now look with a bilious eye on the supplanting of the graceful, brooding Kennedy by the folksy Texan, they may yet live to discern in Foxy Grandpa the possibilities, at least, not of a good President but a great one.'

~

Throughout 1964 Cooke was juggling his professional life in an increasingly familiar way. The *Guardian* was expecting him to cover the British general election (as he had done in 1955), but when it became clear that it was likely to be delayed until the autumn Cooke went off the idea. 'After much prayer and fasting,' he told Alastair Hetherington in August, 'I have come to the conclusion that it would be a mistake for me to barge in on your election and try to write any sense about it in a week or so.' Hetherington noted laconically that Cooke's decision probably had more to do with the requirements of his non-*Guardian* diary.

None the less, Cooke was still ready to throw himself into the preparations for the 1964 presidential elections. As Convention time approached, it was evident that race would play an important part in the outcome, not least because of Johnson's determination to succeed – where Kennedy had failed – in driving the civil rights legislation through Congress. Cooke's views hadn't changed. He remained deeply dubious about laws which tried to redesign the shape of society, however well-meaning the lawmakers might be. He could certainly never be accused of ignoring the issue: the *Guardian* files carry more than two dozen pieces by him on race-related subjects in 1963 alone. He had covered in daily detail the dismal events in Alabama, when Governor George Wallace resisted to the last the enrolment of black students at the University of Alabama: indeed, when a Presidential proclamation was delivered to the embattled Governor by the US Deputy Attorney-General, Cooke was present in the 'huddle of reporters and television cameramen, most of them disguised with cockades improvised from newspapers or handkerchiefs and other useless protections against the steaming 100 deg. heat'.

His doubts crystallised around some of the (to him) profoundly unattractive characters leading the civil rights campaign. 'The Rev. Adam Clayton Powell, the Democratic Party's permanent Gauleiter in Harlem,' he wrote in the *Guardian* in October 1963, 'put in one of his rare appearances yesterday as a preacher in a clerical dog collar.' He did so, to Cooke's unconcealed derision, in order to recommend a black boycott of Santa Claus as a 'white invention'. But there was no gainsaying the threat of social breakdown as black frustration grew and Cooke reported in sombre tones the ultimatum of radical figures such as Malcolm X who, in March, 'urged a roaring audience of Negroes in Harlem to "let the Government know it's bullets or ballots",' demanding an end to the property requirements which prevented many blacks from voting.

Finally, in July 1964, Johnson succeeded in placing on the statute book a far-reaching piece of race legislation, banning segregation in employment, education and accommodation. Cooke's *Guardian* report on 4 July explained: 'Throughout most of the States, but in the South especially, Negroes will now be appearing, in the presence of lawyers or witnesses, at public beaches, restaurants, theatre box offices, hotel desks, golf courses and every sort of social facility which the new law defines as "a public accommodation".' The leading Republican candidate for the Presidency, Senator Barry Goldwater, had done his damnedest to block the bill, carrying out the longest filibuster in the Senate since 1917. When it ended he voted against the legislation, thus attracting to himself the odium of liberals everywhere and uncomfortably rabid support from pro-segregationists.

Goldwater presented Cooke with a problem. He had little obvious sympathy with a man of such deeply reactionary views, but recoiled at the idea of condemning him out of hand or even taking him at face value. 'I hope you will contain your shock awhile if I say he is one of the most attractive human beings I have ever met. . . . It is that legendary figure immortalised by Gary Cooper: a man who looks like a whipcord and acts like a penitent: the rangy, athletic, gentle sheriff of total integrity.'

It was a poetic fantasy, he admitted – Goldwater as a character who had strayed off the set of *High Noon*, a throwback to a legendary (imaginary) race of heroes. Not for Goldwater the complexity of the modern world, Cooke suggested, but rather the simplicity of gun-slingers facing each other on an empty street, while townsfolk cowered behind the creaking saloon doors. 'And here coming straight ahead, with measured stride, Mr Khruschev – Two-Gun Nick – coming towards the moment when the Arizona kid will challenge him and the guns will flash and Nick will keel over and that will be the end of the Russian menace and high taxes.' Was this to be taken in full seriousness? 'I have gone on in this not wilfully facetious way,' he conceded, 'because I believe these are considerable virtues. Unfortunately, they apply to an America and a world, that went over the Western horizon about eighty or a hundred years ago.'

None the less, Cooke's fixation on the need for objectivity led him to communicate his concerns to Hetherington when Goldwater grabbed the Republican nomination: 'I have tried to impress on [Hella Pick] the need to be as fair as possible to Goldwater. The automatic hand-wringing of the European correspondents is foolish and inhibits good reporting.'

Goldwater's campaign never came close to threatening LBJ and the Senator's chances were not helped by a chance remark about 'defoli-ating the supply lines of the Viet Cong in North Vietnam,' which was taken to be a threat to launch a nuclear attack. As the Johnson landslide was confirmed, Cooke told BBC listeners, 'I can't remember a more even-tempered, more inevitable, predictable election night – and from the point of view of the Republicans, more hopeless.' There had, after all, been no white backlash among 'the Slavs, Italians, Czechs, Poles, Germans, Russians – first- and second-generation Americans, manual workers mostly, in seething cities of the East and Midwest – who fear that their ten thousand dollar house is going to drop in value to five thousand when the Negroes move into the neighbourhood; and who fear a Negro foreman. It seems to me to be an understandable, even an intelligent fear.' He might have added – but didn't – that he himself had expected the worst.

Johnson's inauguration, the following January, reinforced in Cooke's mind the President's folksy image. Since Washington was the territory of the *Guardian*'s White House correspondent, Richard Scott, he could ignore the formal proceedings and enjoy the linguistic luxury of a colour piece – unworried by Hetherington's lurking disapproval. No observer could fail to notice the security precautions: the podium protected by bullet-proof glass and the snipers on every roof. Cooke's report ended, 'It was a bright, white festival afternoon on Lyndon Johnson's day. But the pale sun was always having to filter through a couple of invisible clouds, one blowing up from Texas and the other drifting in from the Atlantic. The memories of a dead Kennedy and a dying Churchill.'

~

Churchill died a few days later. He was one of the men Cooke most admired and among his prized possessions in later life was a copy of the *Collected Works*, inscribed by Churchill's wife, Clemmie. It read, 'Presented to Alistair Cooke, whose broadcasts gave such pleasure to the author.'

~

In September of 1964, Susie – at the age of fifteen – was sent away to school for the first time. She was thrilled to be going to Putney, in Vermont, where her brother Johnny had been several years earlier. She didn't like living in the city and the apartment must sometimes have been a lonely place. Holly and Stephen were occasional visitors and Johnny was practically a stranger. 'It sometimes felt that I saw him for five minutes, twice a year,' she says. 'I can remember how he would come to the apartment on Christmas afternoon and be sequestered with Daddy in his study.' The family had not grown closer with the years and Susie's independence would soon have unexpected and alarming results. The immediate effect was to give her parents a new-found sense of freedom. As Cooke wrote to Alastair Hetherington, 'This will be the first time in twenty years that Jane and I have been on our own at home.' What he proposed, however, was not to stay at home at all, but to take a lengthy break from the *Guardian*: 'Nineteen years of the daily piece, more or less, is a long stretch to go without an extended break. We think this is a fine time to go around the world.' The trip, he suggested, might last through February, March and April of 1965.

Not content with this request, he also applied for a month's leave beforehand during November and December of 1964. This was partly to allow him to be the guest of honour at the annual London dinner of the Pilgrims' Association (an organisation dedicated to the furtherance of Anglo-American relations) and partly so that he could travel to Stockholm: he'd been invited to present a one-hour television documentary to coincide with the 1964 Nobel Prize ceremony. It was the year in which Jean-Paul Sartre became the first man to turn down an honour offered by the Nobel Committee and Martin Luther King won the Peace Prize. Overall, Cooke was impressed by the way the system operated: 'Though an occasional exhibitionist does slip through, there is in the world no comparable body of expert and disinterested men, fitter to salute the intellectual pioneers of our age.' In addition Cooke intended to visit his mother in Blackpool. For this he scheduled a stay of a single day.

Alastair Hetherington seems to have had no stomach for a fight with Cooke over these lengthy absences. He wrote back that he agreed to the plans in principle, though the *Guardian* files express his real feelings: in a sarcastic memo to the foreign editor, Geoffrey Taylor, he said that – after London and Stockholm – Cooke would 'start working for us again about 12 December. He will "taper off", however, about mid-January, or soon after that, "so as to unwind before we start on our strenuous world trip." In February and March he will be on unpaid leave. I wouldn't like to take any bets on what date in April he'll actually come back to work.' Hetherington did agree to make the introductory speech at the Pilgrims' dinner and he did so with typical good grace, keeping his frustrations to himself: 'It is a cliché of the English view of the United States that everything there is uniform – clean, neat, hygienic, cellophane-wrapped, pre-packaged, dehydrated and a bit lacking in flavour; everything from food to women. But it was Cooke who produced Cooke's law, that the strength and richness of an ice-cream sundae rise the further west you go. He did the basic research, I believe, by sampling "double chocolate malteds" all the way from Massachusetts to California.'

Cooke, Hetherington said, was 'more than a journalist', he was a historian as well. 'Years hence, when academics come to write of American life in the mid-twentieth-century, it is to the writings of Alistair Cooke that they will turn and they will not have to do much rewriting; the record will be there, perfectly observed, perfectly reported and perfectly presented.'

Cooke's own speech was made in front of an all-male audience of awesome quality – ambassadors past and present, a strong spattering of British nobility, soldiers, bishops, editors, politicians and business leaders: a gathering, as Cooke portrayed it, 'so frighteningly restrained about its own importance, so knowledgeable about my only speciality, so bristling with distinction, so blinding in its medals and decorations that the light of them bangs my eyes and almost causes me to sneeze. I stand before you as a naked, undecorated journalist – save for the noble red rose of Lancaster.' The only honour to which he was entitled, he told them, was that of honorary Kentucky Colonel: he hoped he wouldn't be called away to defend the state before the dinner was over. There were old friends in the audience, including Nunnally Johnson. The BBC contingent boasted Sir Lindsay Wellington, Gerald Cock, Frank Gillard and Leonard Miall. But for the most part, these were strangers – for whom Cooke laid out his definitive view of the Anglo-American relationship as he perceived it in 1964. It was part history, part political commentary, part traditional after-dinner knock-about. The English influence on American political life, he said, had been in decline ever since the Mayor of New York had started to choose as his European holiday destinations, 'Rome, Dublin and Tel Aviv'. What was left of the English heritage? 'A very lively prejudice in favour of shaggy young English university cynics (considered as comedians) and in favour of even shaggier females (considered as *femmes fatales)* who have turtles at their necks and dragons on their legs; for you have successfully managed to export, I am sorry to say, what is known as the "Chelsea look".' There was malt whisky, of course and English motor bikes were still in vogue. 'But what, in the long inheritance from Chaucer to Churchill, are the examples of British genius universally applauded by every generation of Americans? The answer is very plain: Shakespeare, Richard Burton, Terry-Thomas . . . and the Beatles. In other words, the natives of this sceptr'd isle are credited with one divine poet, with (periodically) a romantic devil and the rest of the race are enjoyed as Merseyside minstrels or amusing half-wits.' This led him to his main theme – the need for the togetherness of nations in the face of forces seeking to wrench them apart.

The dinner was the highlight of the European trip, though the

Blackpool Gazette drew attention to the fusty atmosphere of the occasion. 'A pity that so influential an organisation as the Pilgrims,' he wrote,

> should have left unheeded the recent official announcement that decorations may now be worn with a dinner jacket. Even the cautious City now gives guests the option of wearing a black tie on formal occasions. But at the Savoy, for the dinner in honour of Mr Alistair Cooke, I saw only one guest in a dinner jacket and he did not wear any decorations. I can understand men preferring to go to the extra trouble of wearing tails as a compliment to their wives' toilettes, but at an all-male gathering, surely all that dressing up is hardly necessary.
>
> At those Blackpool social functions where once upon a time 'tails' were the rule, they are now very much the exception. The dinner jacket has firmly established itself.

Back in the States, Cooke confirmed Hetherington's suspicions when he announced that his last piece would be on 29 January and that he and Jane would be gone 'about three and a half months'. 'I am hoping to break the habit of a lifetime,' he added, 'and not feel haunted by the daily piece. But I must admit that sometimes I feel beckoned by it. So I don't promise absolutely not to write anything. You may get occasional airmail screed from God knows where. Of course, if I ran into a first-class revolution, five-alarm fire, or the assassination of Sukarno, I'd be on the job.'

His trip was revolution- and assassination-free.

Despite Hetherington's carping, there were other *Guardian* figures more kindly disposed towards their senior man in America. L.P. Scott, chairman and managing director and grandson of the group's founder, had been asked to sanction two months' paid leave for Cooke and took the opportunity to find out about the current salary levels for American staff. He discovered that – taking salary and expenses into account – Cooke was still earning just $19,000 a year, a paltry $5,000 more than what he'd been offered by A.P. Wadsworth in 1946. By comparison, Richard Scott, in Washington, was on nearly $25,000. It was an indefensible disparity. The chairman advised Hetherington that a raise for Cooke would be in order – and that he should have his paid holiday to boot.

The world tour also presented the BBC with a poser. The Corporation, too, had just increased Cooke's fee – to $250 a week. This was to cover all outlets for the *Letter* and Cooke further won an agreement that it would not be rebroadcast on the General Overseas Service of the BBC (renamed the World Service later in 1965) without a seven-day delay: this was to ensure that local stations in America didn't recycle the programme for their own use without making any financial contribution to the writer.

However, when Cooke proposed that – as in the past – he should provide *Letters* from the countries he was visiting, the General Overseas Service cried foul. 'Alistair Cooke's style and manner is ideal for coverage of American affairs but, to judge by his previous short tours, is not so satisfactory when we have to broadcast back to a sensitive area sentiments about it which Cooke intended for UK ears. Since a lengthy period of *Letters* from elsewhere might diminish Cooke's general acceptability to our audience, I would, to preserve him, prefer to drop his *Letter* during his tour.' There were even rumblings from managers like George Camacho, who felt that, whereas a gap of three weeks might be acceptable, thirteen weeks would mean finding a replacement. Blissfully unaware of these caveats, Lillian Lang in the New York office was providing an itinerary for the tour and the cities from which Cooke was hoping to broadcast.

By this time, London was distinctly uneasy. Camacho wrote a firm, but polite, note to Cooke, asking for more details of the trip. While to Lillian Lang, in rather more peevish terms, he gave vent to his feelings: 'I must say, with due respect, that Alistair should have been a little more explicit and rather earlier with giving us information about this project. . . .You will know that we view with some alarm the absence from our schedules, for so long a period, of this special coverage of the American scene.'

What is striking about the whole row is Cooke's unconcern. He felt no need to soothe the BBC managers, to attend their meetings, to sympathise with their difficulties. He was, by now, confident in his own position – remarkably so, for a man still prone to (particularly financial) insecurity. Since nobody at the BBC had ever bothered to establish a warm transatlantic relationship, none developed. New men would arrive to take over the office of the US Representative and some would be utterly won over by Cooke. But he himself lacked the patience to work on his London contacts and the corridors of Broadcasting House remained alien territory, even though he was already one of the Corporation's longest-serving contributors. This particular disagreement became unusually vitriolic. Cooke did not offer an apology for keeping his plans to himself. 'I assumed you would be eager to do as you did last time,' he wrote to Camacho, 'namely, keep the *Letters* going as "*Letter* from Geneva", "*Letter* from Cairo", "*Letter* from Addis Ababa", etc. I ought to throw in the interesting fact that my mail from that last world tour was about three times as heavy as the regular mail for *Letter from America*. All in all, he reckoned, there would only be eight '*Letters* from the World': surely no one could object? 'I think it all boils down to the question of whether most people want a "*Letter* from Cooke" or a *Letter from America*. We all assumed, I think, last time that the BBC's excellent Washington and New York Services would amply take care of any political crisis. As for the rest, it's a little tough to ask somebody to imitate another man's whimsy.' For which read – nobody can do it but me. Ironically, the man ultimately responsible for resolving the matter was none other than Frank Gillard, now Director of Sound Broadcasting, who had – long before – had personal experience of Cooke's jealous protection of the *Letter* when his attempt to volunteer as a replacement was summarily squashed.

Reluctantly, the BBC acceded to the strong-arm tactics. Camacho's document of surrender has almost a cloying tone: 'There can be little doubt that the listener is more interested in Alistair Cooke than in America. . . . .' and 'an interruption of eight weeks in the *Letter from America* is a great deal less than thirteen!' Only the Overseas Service held out against the '*Letters* from the World', and the head of Overseas Talks, Gerard Mansell, declared that he would make his own arrangements. This meant that Cooke's fee was docked accordingly (by $45), but more painfully, Mansell decided to do what had never been done before – and was never done thereafter: he allowed other speakers to broadcast under the title *Letter from America*. Amongst those chosen – Gerald Priestland, just starting a long and distinguished career as a BBC Correspondent, Anthony Wigan – Cooke's one-time colleague at the UN – and the future ITN newsreader, Leonard Parkin. In his note of explanation, Mansell was brutally frank: 'Alistair Cooke's main expertise lies in the field of US internal and external affairs and we cannot afford to run the risk of one of his *Letters* from a country other than the US being either inaccurate or possibly offensive to listeners in that country. In our view, this might well happen, in the light of our previous experience of Cooke's *Letters* from foreign parts.'

's displeasure at the hijacking of his title could not be dis-
In March, while he was in Nairobi, he sent a stern note to
the Director-General himself, complaining about his alter egos. The
functionary who took in the message faithfully recorded Cooke's
words:

> people are saying to him – what odd scripts you're writing for someone
> else to read. He says that it's causing him some dismay. It's being broadcast
> from New York normally, but read by someone, purporting to be read for
> him. Could you please consider changing the name of this substitute
> programme? Saying that it's an 'American Round-up' or something of that
> kind, read by Joe Snooks or Joe Stokes, or whoever it may be. He feels very
> strongly about this, but he doesn't want anybody to get him wrong. He's
> only saying that for the good of the programme and for his own public
> relations. He would be delighted if someone could think of a new name
> and announce it's nothing to do with him.

It was no coincidence that – as soon as he returned from his tour (he
was, in fact, away from base for twelve weeks, despite his reassurances
to Camacho) – he made a private vow never to let the *Letter* out of
his hands again. From 16 May 1965-*Letter* Number 859 – he never
missed another week, an unmatched and unmatchable consistency
which turned him into a broadcasting legend.

27

THE SCOTTISH TORTURE

The Cookes' World Tour ranged across Europe to Kenya, Ethiopia, Egypt and Israel, then on to India, Thailand and Japan. It was by no means pure holiday. Cooke agreed to mark his travels with a limited-edition book, celebrating the fiftieth anniversary of the Field Educational Corporation, publishers of the *World Book Year-Book*. The company asked him to assess half a century of change in each of the countries he visited for a tome to be entitled *Around the World in Fifty Years*.

Even before Cooke left the country, the trip caused a small diplomatic tremor. When the White House heard about his plans, LBJ's press secretary, Jack Valenti, rang to ask whether he would care to use US embassies as a base in the countries he visited. Cooke thanked him, but said that the British Foreign Office had already made the same offer – and he had accepted it. Shortly afterwards, the phone rang again: 'We are innerested in your plans,' the voice announced. There was no mistaking the President's drawl. 'I've called the Head of Protocol,' he went on, 'and I've told 'em: any place you come by and you need to know anything, you don't hesitate. They'll be waiting for your call.' Cooke understood that if he was going to write about sensitive corners of the globe, America did not wish its point of view to go by default. 'I wanna hear all about this when you get back,' LBJ concluded. 'Yes, Mr President.' The Cookes left, ready to take full advantage of these competitive offers of diplomatic hospitality – a shopping trip for Jane here, a game of golf on the rocky cliffs overlooking the Bosporus there.

The conceit of the book's title required Cooke to produce two sections for each country – 1915 and 1965 – the two epochs properly compared and contrasted. In fact, the latter section of each chapter drew heavily on the *Letters from the World*, while the 1915 descriptions relied on some rapid historical revision when he returned to New

York. In the Britain of 1965, for instance, he painted a picture of a people gravitating from the countryside into the cities and trying to reconcile a long-term policy of emigration with the need to rebuild an industrial workforce decimated by two world wars. In these shifts of people he detected the influence of the great issue of the age: race. 'The opposition of the countryman to the planting of big new towns in his neighbouring valley', he wrote, 'contained an element of fear that was rarely mentioned by town councils, but it was very vocal in the pubs and shops. It was the fear of the "dark million", a threat to the social stability of Britain undreamed of fifty, or even twenty, years ago. Namely the million coloured people, some from India and Pakistan, most from the British Islands of the Caribbean, who had made the most of their British citizenship by emigrating to the so-called Mother Country.' Cooke found London 'brash, plutocratic, confident and carefree', with 'better theatre and more scandalous amusements than any other capital'. Yet the Swinging City failed to dispel his sense that Britain was still prey to post-imperial insecurity.

In East Germany he pondered, once again, that the Government were in preparation for a nuclear attack sponsored by the Americans. In Italy he reflected Jane's deep affection for the place: 'Few countries of the world attract foreigners under such favourable auspices as Italy. Europeans go to the United States to see how raincoats or tyres are made in Akron, Ohio, or to perform their scientific speciality in Berkeley or Ann Arbor. Journalists descend on Spain or India to clock the miseries of their people hour by hour. But everybody goes to Italy prejudiced in favour of the great beauty of the country and the amiability of the people.'

When the couple reached the Middle East they were particularly taken by Beirut, still touting itself as the Paris of the region. They contacted a young couple working for the British Council: out of the blue David Curnow, the one-time Blackpool refugee, received the phone-call from his wartime protector. 'They were staying at the St George Hotel – *the* Beirut hotel,' he remembers. 'One of the first things Alistair did was to seek out a noted jazz pianist, playing at a new hotel called the Phoenicia, where we all had dinner.'

The biggest shock of the entire tour came in India. Even though Cooke had been to the country before and seen for himself the squalor of Calcutta, he became deeply depressed by the wretchedness of the street-people – so much so that Jane decided to cancel a number of planned excursions, including one to Nepal. Cooke took refuge in hotels and embassy compounds until it was time to leave for Thailand. The journey home took them via Hong Kong and Japan. Jane recalls how the news from Vietnam became more and more disheartening as they travelled. The first air-raids by American planes in February were followed by an horrific explosion outside the US Embassy in Saigon on 30 March, which killed two Americans and twenty Vietnamese. President Johnson dispatched the first Army combat units and the 3rd Marine Division to the country, bringing the number of troops to 75,000 – news which filled Jane with gloom. She and Alistair argued about the wisdom of the move and the row was unusual and intense enough to be remembered thirty years later: in her recollection, 'He was the hawk and I was the dove. In the end, I blew my stack and he spoke to me as he'd never done before.'

Cooke's views were consistent with his general approach to the communist advance. The previous December, in a *Letter from America*, he had discussed the unpopularity of the United States, 'or let's say the very dangerous and widespread boredom with the United States, [which] comes mainly from Europe, from America's own allies'. Its cause, he thought, was that Europe was not feeling threatened by Communism. 'If you want to find a country that is rousingly pro-American at the moment, that is getting aid and is grateful for it and looks across a vast ocean to America as its main protector, you have to go to Australia.' The Far East might be a long way from London or Paris, but to an Australian it was the Near North. 'The prospect that Asia and the Malay Peninsula could go Communist in a year or two is quite visible and a nightmare to the Australians who would then be in the front line, as Britain was in the summer of 1940. Bluntly, I am saying that Australia appreciates American policy because it knows the stakes and it is threatened.' Three weeks later he made a further plea for understanding: 'If Vietnam goes, there is no question that we shall suffer a Munich that will instantly turn Cambodia, Burma, Thailand and Lord knows who else to the Communist side. It will look as if we jibbed and betrayed every non-Communist nation in Asia.'

∼

It's doubtful whether Cooke's *Letters from the World* – if they had been broadcast on the Overseas Service of the BBC – would have led to a deterioration of relations with a string of foreign governments. Most were gentle and inoffensive, treating even the most serious topics with a light touch. But there were excitements along the way. In Tokyo, the Cookes were first greeted by hordes of screaming teenagers and discovered they'd been travelling with the Rolling Stones. Then, while their bags were being put in the boot of an American Embassy car, a student approached and asked if he was 'Mister Wostow'. Cooke knew that Walt Rostow, by then the National Security Adviser, was on his way to Japan to speak about the war and that he was a deeply unpopular figure – a symbol of American imperialism in Asia. He told the young man that he was not Mr Rostow, he was Mr Cooke. 'That was odd,' he said casually to the diplomat assigned to greet him. 'Worse than odd, it might have been a close call,' came the reply. Cooke was told that the Ambassador himself had been attacked some time earlier by a student wielding a sword after a similarly polite greeting. Cooke felt that he had risked paying a heavy price for accepting American hospitality.

~

Before he'd been back on American soil for more than a few days, Cooke had a much more painful brush with mortality. He and Jane were dining with Carroll and Virginia Lynch at a restaurant on Nob Hill in San Francisco. Cooke felt ill and retired to the lavatories: when he failed to return, a search party was dispatched to find him and Virginia Lynch summoned a doctor-friend, Robert Woods Brown. Within the hour, the patient was in the nearby Franklin hospital. Brown had swiftly and correctly diagnosed the onset of a violent and painful diarrhoea as a condition of the bowel – diverticulitis – excruciatingly painful, though not life-threatening. Cooke was so impressed that he formed a deep affection for the doctor, which was reinforced by a shared love of golf and sealed when Brown – many years later – really did help to save Jane's life after she was stricken with a severe intestinal disorder.

Cooke's sojourn in the Franklin Hospital was the first of many occasions on which the *Letter* had to be recorded at the invalid's bedside – usually without the BBC in London realising that anything was amiss. Indeed after the immediate inconvenience and anxiety had been dealt with, his diverticulitis, like his pseudo-gout and his uncommon skin-complaint, became a source of endless fascination.

He took an intense interest in the mechanics of each and a comparative stranger might well find himself regaled with the unappealing details of the symptoms over a gin and tonic. He loved talking about medicine and by chance, one of his first public-speaking engagements after the tour was to be at the world-famous Mayo Clinic in Minnesota on 28 May – where Bob Brown's brother was on the staff. It was a notable occasion. Most years, the Annual Convocation of the Mayo's Graduate School was addressed by someone with a medical background. Cooke chose to challenge the medics – as a layman – on their home ground. It was the job of a journalist, he suggested, to be the social link between the expert and the public: he intended, therefore, to speak up for the patient. He spoke on the subject of medical jargon, issuing a plea to the young clinicians to avoid the self-serving obfuscation of their profession and to treat with the deepest suspicion each passing medical fashion. These were themes that gave him the chance to vent his own scepticism and he told them a story he'd once recounted to an audience of American heart surgeons. If cholesterol were as dangerous as it was cracked up to be, why was there any adult still living in Britain? 'Of all civilised communities the British are the connoisseurs of animal fats, with their morning toast and eggs bubbling in bacon fat, their biscuits at eleven o'clock, their lunch of meat and potatoes and (worse) suet, then tea and more biscuits and cake and dinner with meat and bread again and potatoes and pudding – and perhaps an emergency snack of cheese and biscuits to guarantee coming safely through the night.'

This menu was straight from his memories of the North of England – authentic Blackpool fare. The heart surgeons were suitably shocked. And when he'd answered his own question by pointing out that the British, unlike the Americans, were still accustomed to walking – both for business and pleasure – they reacted with grateful surprise: 'keep moving', they agreed, should be adopted as a slogan for healthy living. This experience had emboldened him to offer advice to a new generation of doctors and only partly in jest: should not every medical student undergo a parallel course in basic English? In that way, phalanges might once again become finger-bones, 'lumbar' would revert to 'loin', 'clavicle' to 'collar-bone' and 'oedema' to 'swelling'.

'Ladies and Gentlemen,' he pleaded, 'do not equip yourselves with appropriate cathartics. Get some starters. Do not contrast living humanoids with deceased subjects. Study rather the quick and the dead. Do not implement a directive, ever. Carry on.'

He was in his element. The teacher *manqué*, the amateur expert, the honest broker – with the chance for a little bit of acting thrown in and all in front of a receptive audience. The Mayo lecture became the basis of a collection entitled *The Patient Has the Floor*, published in 1986 and featuring Cooke in a number of other lions' dens – talking about American history to the State Department or about the role of the soldier to the West Point Military Academy. The book was dedicated to Robert Woods Brown, to whom he'd already paid an oblique compliment in the text of the Mayo address. It came in the section on cholesterol, during which Cooke referred to the countless dietary fads into which the American consumer was lured – the latest being an attack on carbohydrates. 'There is a national retreat from pastries,' he said, 'and a grateful stampede back to beef and lately, a learned pamphlet advises me, back to alcohol.'

The 'learned pamphlet' in question was *The Drinking Man's Diet*, which purported to be a foolproof means of losing weight without reducing the intake of alcohol ('also recommended for ladies and teetotallers'). Among its progenitors was Carroll Lynch, boasting all the medical background of an industrial arbitrator and Robert Cameron – and another San Franciscan who was to play an important part in Cooke's life. The book started as a joke, the product of idle banter at the golf club. By the time Cameron published it – at a dollar a copy – its detailed daily menus and helpful quasi-scientific charts turned it into a national bestseller. As part of the joke it carried a dedication to (a very embarrassed) Robert Woods Brown MD, who feared it might utterly wreck his professional credibility. In the event, nobody seemed to rumble the joke and Brown even found his brother at the Mayo demanding to know where more copies could be acquired. He decided to stop worrying and accept his token share of the royalties.

Bob Brown, Bob Cameron and Carroll Lynch became part of a charmed West Coast circle for Cooke and at the root of their friendship lay the game of golf.

~

Until the fateful day in June 1964 when Cooke was bitten by the golf bug, he had – as he liked to recall somewhat ruefully – shared Mencken's attitude to people who played the game: that all golfers should be disqualified from public office. At the age of fifty-five, he was taken by Pat Ward-Thomas, the *Guardian*'s long-serving golf correspondent, onto the Van Cortlandt Park course in New York. He claims to have taken 168 strokes to get round – about as bad as it's possible to get – and the experience ought to have been enough to put him off for ever. But, as he wrote in *Golf* magazine four years afterwards, 'The narcotics experts define a true narcotic as one that produces a recurring cycle of desire. Well, sir, it took only a trembling week or two for the Van Cortlandt itch to seize me again.' Aided and abetted by the same friend, he went to Macy's and purchased 'a driver, a brassie, a 3-wood, 5-, 7- and 9-irons, a putter, two balls and a glove,' the whole ensemble neatly stored in 'a hideous little bag' – total cost, $77.

At the back of Cooke's mind was a warning from Jane that he needed to take more exercise, or risk becoming a 'typewriter arthritic': with this encouragement, he rang the golf course nearest to their Long Island home and inquired about the possibility of lessons. When he arrived at Island's End, he was directed to the practice ground, where 'a small, blond barrel of a man' was finishing a lesson with 'a dour character, wearing a white cap'. As the pupil mooched away, he claims to have heard the instructor say, 'I hope that will help, Ben.' It was, naturally, Ben Hogan, one of the world's greatest golfers, straightening out some technical problem before a tournament nearby. Cooke, then, was to learn the game at the feet of a master – George Heron – a celebrated Scottish professional with a long list of high-powered clients.

'What's your problem, Mr Cooke?' Heron asked, recognising his new student from his *Omnibus* days.

'No problem,' Cooke replied, 'except that I'd like to know which end you hit with.'

Heron gave him a short, sharp look, then realised that Cooke was newly hooked and deadly serious. 'All right, then. Take out a seven iron and let's see what happens.' In his 1968 article, Cooke wrote, 'Under his patient care I have become in the space of three years as fine an example as I have seen of the fairway spastic, that is to say a man who in practice hits effortless shots of heartbreaking beauty, which then evade him from the first tee to the nineteenth, where mysteriously the beauty and skill reappear.' He added that he'd just sneaked back to Van Cortlandt and managed to halve his previous score. If so, it was a remarkable learning curve for a middle-aged man who'd come to the game so late.

There was certainly no question of the earnestness of his desire:

friends remember him buying books and manuals in profusion, always searching for that elusive piece of advice that would transform his performance. He became a member and share-holder at Island's End and often played in Cutchogue – the nearest town to his home – where George Heron had created his own par-three nine-hole course, the Cedars. Cooke maintains that he held the course record there for a while – an impressive score of 25 – and once scored a hole-in-one, while on the West Coast he made the San Francisco golf course his second sporting home. The passion was never to leave him, but opinions are divided about how good he became. Cooke himself points to a round of 79 at Island's End as the pinnacle of his career, while 82 was his best score at the San Francisco club. But his playing partners, some of them of near-championship standard, were always moved by the gap between the effort that went into his reading and research and the results on the ground.

However hard he tried and however many books he read, mastery of the game eluded him. He wasn't used to it. The age at which he started didn't help. One of his closest friends, commenting with affection on Cooke's performance in later life, said, 'you assume that if a guy is playing into his eighties, he must have been quite a player in his fifties. That's not true of Alistair. He's probably the most enthusiastic guy about golf and knowledgeable about its history, who is as poor a player as he is.' Yet he never lost his appetite. In San Francisco, he played for years with Brown, Carroll Lynch and a few other regulars and later in an informal competition known as The Joust: this perennial foursome brought together another medical man, Carl Borders – an orthopaedic surgeon – and two senior members of the city's golfing establishment, Sandy Tatum and Grant Spaeth, who became President of the United States Golf Association in 1993 at a ceremony in which Cooke gave the welcoming speech. The Jousts were occasions so eagerly awaited that Cooke couldn't bear to miss them, even when he was injured. Tatum remembers one Joust when Cooke insisted on taking part, even though a painful back made it impossible for him to lift a club. Instead, he stood on the tee, nominated his score for that and each subsequent hole and won the match with unaccustomed ease.

Cooke's devotion to the game never wavered. He continued to potter around San Francisco in a mechanised buggy even when he was ninety and, with the help of Carl Borders and a generous handicap, often ended up on the winning side. In some ways golf came to define Cooke's

The *Guardian*'s uncharacteristic largesse turned luxury liners into homes away from home. The *Queen Mary* was always the Cookes' favourite.

Leonard McCombe, one of the great feature photographers of the age, spent several days with Cooke and his family in 1950, when they were still living in the cramped conditions of East 71st Street. The pictures appeared in *Life* and then in the British counterpart, *Picture Post.*

The McCombe street scene captures Alistair and Jane, Stephen holding a dubious Susie, and Holly in the background, distinctly disenchanted with the proceedings.

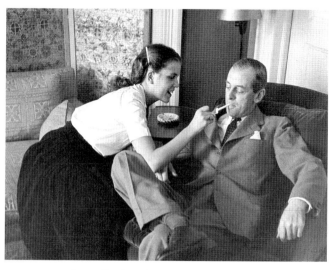

Generally, though, Holly got on well with her stepfather.

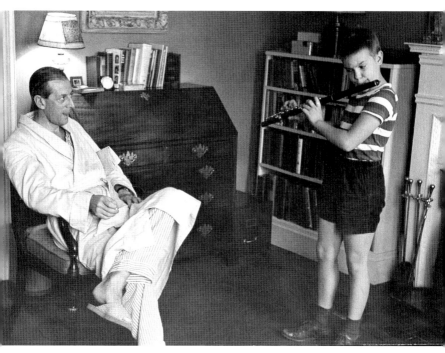

It was always more difficult for Stephen. Note Cooke's pursed lip – and his scarcely concealed wish to be somewhere else.

A touching moment of intimacy with Johnny. The resemblance between father and son is striking, and it's a shame that one magazine captioned the boy as 'Jimmy'.

Jane's beauty was much admired. Cooke is unlikely to have bought the necklace himself

Once Susie had learned to walk, a change of apartment became inevitable. Soon afterwards, the family moved to the spacious surroundings of Fifth Avenue.

Bill Burrows was one of a number of chess-partners in New York and on Long Island. This – and a little fishing – were Cooke's most strenuous leisure activities until he took up golf.

John Cooke took this picture of his father in the study at 1150 Fifth Avenue, sometime in the late 1950s. The bookcase was already plotted out like a map of the US – books about California on the left, across to New York on the right.

Ben Sonnenberg, the 'man who invented public relations', was perhaps the Cookes' favourite companion.

Jane was never happier than at her beloved Nassau Point. The steps lead down to the beach below the house. In later years, she would spend the whole summer here.

Cooke habitually travelled to Nassau Point at weekends, often bringing friends. During the week in New York he learned to cope with the life of what he called 'a summer bachelor'.

attitudes as he grew older – a game relying on assiduous preparation and an impeccable respect for etiquette, marked by good manners and unshakeable traditions, and comparatively unsullied by the gross commercialism which had wrecked his enjoyment of tennis. He took every opportunity to write about golf for the *Guardian* or anyone else who would pay him to do so. In 1965, just as the fever began to grip, he was drafted in by the temporarily absent Pat Ward-Thomas to cover the closing stages of the US Open at the Creve Coeur course in Missouri. The tournament was won by the South African, Gary Player: 'a very worthy champion', in Cooke's view, 'a throwback to the Bobby Jones era; and like the immortal one himself, it is not his carefulness, the painful putting together of his strokes, or his mastery of memory; nor even his undoubted nuttiness about yoga, health foods, pillows and the like; but the simple and refreshing fact that, in a game which more and more is engulfed by publicity, advertising and lavish stakes, he is a gent.'

This produced an acknowledgement from Bobby Jones, a golf champion from an earlier era who – it transpired – had been an avid fan of *Omnibus*. Then, in 1967, Cooke contributed a review of a book distilling Jones' golfing wisdom. In the white heat of his own recent golfing conversion, the reviewer confessed to having read almost every expert manual on the market: yet somehow the Jones book was different. 'What we have is a unique manual. One of the handful of very great golfers is also revealed as a literate and intensely thoughtful man who modestly shares the agony of Flaubert: to re-experience a feeling and transmit it with exactness to another person. In other words, unlike the vast majority of golfers, he knows precisely what he is doing. Unlike any other before him, he can *say* what he is doing.' The piece was entitled, 'THE MISSING ARISTOTLE PAPERS ON GOLF.'

Bobby Jones was so moved by this tribute that he dropped Cooke another note: 'Offhand, I can't think of another contemporary author who has been compared, in one piece, to Aristotle, Flaubert, John Donne and Walter Lippmann.' At the next US Masters at Augusta, Georgia, the two men were properly introduced by Pat Ward-Thomas and continued their annual contacts at the Masters until Jones's death in December 1971. By the time of the first encounter, Jones was already in the final stages of a crippling disability – syringomyelia, a progressive degenerative disease of the spinal cord. Cooke's first impression was the shock of seeing 'the fine strong hands, twisted like the branches of a cypress, gamely clutching a tumbler or one of his perpetual cigarettes in a holder'.

After Jones's death, Cooke contributed a foreword to a book about his hero. He ended his encomium, 'What we are left with in the end is a forever young, good-looking Southerner, an impeccably courteous and decent man with a private ironical view of life who, to the great good fortune of people who saw him, happened to play the great game with more magic and more grace than anyone before or since.' Long after Jones had gone, Cooke continued to travel to Augusta for the Masters each spring, attending a Saturday night party for the British press and re-connecting with another circle of friends. And then, back home to the more mundane surroundings of Island 's End, playing with Heron's successor – and former ballroom-dancing teacher – Johnny Piccoze, a gnarled, bronzed figure almost as old as Cooke himself; or with Richard Somerset-Ward, a one-time BBC executive who had settled in New York.

Yet despite the intensity of Cooke's own feelings about the great game, he did become an unlikely contributor to one of the funniest books about golf ever written. When Cooke launched himself as a writer on the subject, Stephen Potter contacted him and the two men corresponded for a while before they were introduced in London. Cooke took to Potter, author of *One-Upmanship* and many other humorous bestsellers – as he had once taken to the cartoonist, James Thurber, charmed and amused by his egocentric eccentricities. Potter would smoke endlessly, even when he was suffering from cancer and tried to persuade the Cookes that cigarillos didn't count as smoking: whatever weed he was burning, ash constantly dropped on his clothes with considerable collateral damage to all surrounding furniture.

It was Stephen Potter who persuaded Cooke, against his better judgement, to join the Savile Club in Mayfair, thus contravening his strict (self-imposed) injunction against joining any English gentleman's club. Such institutions, Cooke insisted, were invariably seedy and their food was disappointing: he only remained a member of the Savile until Potter died in 1969, in order not to hurt his feelings. One of Stephen Potter's last books, *The Complete Golf Gamesmanship*, has two contributions from Cooke, including what Potter christened 'The Doug Sanders Ploy', referring to an American golfer with a raffish dress sense. This was the information allegedly provided by Cooke 'by cablegram' to help readers seeking a psychological advantage on the course: 'in America, since the blooming of Doug Sanders into puce shoes and magnolia trousers, any small eccentricity of colour in the opponent's dress can be chucklingly and incessantly referred to along the way as "a touch of Sanders".'

Cooke repaid the compliment with a charming, and obviously completely unbiased, review of the book: 'To say that this book is a landmark study in human sensibility comparable to the Old Testament or Freud's *Interpretation of Dreams* is, of course, obvious.' And later, 'It will be fussily argued by some readers that Potter is writing about golf. Nothing could be further from the truth. You might as well say that in *Othello* Shakespeare was writing about a handkerchief ... [Potter] makes clear that his prime concern is with life, for as he says, in brilliantly demolishing the oldest cliché, "it is not golf that is a microcosm of life, but rather that life is golf in miniature." ' The review, in *Life* magazine in 1968, showed, at least, that Cooke's obsession had not completely obliterated his sense of humour and the two characteristics continued to co-exist (more or less) as his scores first fell and then – inevitably – started to rise again. He became friendly with Jack Nicklaus and corresponded with Bing Crosby on the subject of their shared pleasures and frustrations. Crosby's last letter arrived from Europe two days after he'd dropped dead on a golf course in Spain in 1977. He'd been on a golfing holiday with his son, later an amateur champion and in the letter told Cooke, 'My golf is woeful, but I will never surrender.' It emerged that he had expired immediately after playing one of the best rounds of his life. This story Cooke found very cheering. His own writing continued unabated and, when Michael Parkinson invited him to compile a retrospective selection of pieces on sport and leisure (*Fun and Games*, published in 1994), almost a third were about golf.

~

For all Cooke's ability to make, keep and cherish friendships across a broad – if compartmentalised – social spectrum, he was finding it no easier to deal with relationships closer to home. One of the lowest points was reached in the summer of 1965. Holly, still living in London, had grown listless and unsure of herself and was attracted to a small, obscure group known as The Process, run by a pair of self-promoting amateur psychotherapists. Robert and Mary Ann de Grimston had met through the Church of Scientology and set up their own headquarters in London, soon gravitating to Mayfair. To begin with, they offered radical sessions of what they called 'Compulsions Analysis' in return for fees. But in due course, their 'patients' were sucked into a complete commitment to the group, sometimes handing over large sums of money, and giving up friends and family. Many years later, The Process would gain international notoriety as the Grimstons gathered an ever larger group of disciples who were taught that Lucifer, Jehovah and Satan had been reunited: there were reports of orgies, blood sacrifices and other occult rituals. The cult, known also as the Church of the Final Judgement, was even alleged to have had connections with Charles Manson, the sect-leader who murdered Sharon Tate, wife of the film director, Roman Polanski. At one point, leading members of The Process sued a British publisher over an investigative book that linked their name with Manson. The court found in their favour, but refused to impose a single penny in damages.

When Holly first became part of the Grimston's inner circle, however, The Process was still comparatively unknown and comparatively benign. To begin with, she found comfort in the therapy sessions but soon became seriously hooked. Three hundred sessions later it was impossible to extricate herself. It took many months – and a visit home to the United States – before she was able to break free, as she explained in a *Sunday Telegraph* interview given to Duff Hart-Davis, Rupert's son, in 1966. Gradually, she said, she had become nauseated by the group's nihilistic and self-centred attitude. 'The central theme of the questions became one's problems in relation to The Process, not in relation to oneself. It was so inbred. It lost all touch with reality. I lived in an atmosphere of tremendous guilt. If I ever slacked off and missed some sessions,' she went on, 'I was made to feel so evil it wasn't true. Always someone was being attacked and reviled – the retribution was terrible.' She was bitterly disappointed at the way her original enthusiasm had been dashed. She lost two stone in weight, reducing her already slim figure to skeletal proportions. 'I could see what was happening to me, but I was completely paralysed.' It was, she realised afterwards, a sort of brainwashing. Unfortunately, while she was still deeply involved, Susie arrived in London on her way to spend the summer with friends in Paris.

Susie was sixteen years old and had just finished her first year at boarding-school. Her first ever trip to Europe on her own would have been an intensely exciting experience in any case: but she found herself staying with a much-admired elder sister at the heart of 'Swinging London' and was full of teenage curiosity about The Process. With real reservations, Holly took her to meet the Grimstons who welcomed her with open arms. The first the Cookes knew about the crisis was a telephone call announcing that Susie would not, after all, be going to France. She intended to remain in London, where – Holly had established – there would be no problem finding her a good school. Cooke was devastated. Susie, after all, was his baby – the one child with whom he felt he had strong emotional bonds. Suddenly she'd been stolen from him. The story that began to emerge was alarming. Susie, having run through all the money that was supposed to see her through her trip to France, was spending most of her time cleaning the house occupied by The Process. The Grimstons, it seemed, had adopted her as a kind of mascot. Jane decided that decisive action was required and commandeered Stephen, who was expecting a week's holiday in New York, to accompany her to London. It was a tense and uncomfortable experience. When they arrived, the Chelsea flat was empty: a note informed them baldly that Susie and Holly were at a Process session. They waited. Eventually, the door opened and the two young women came in, greeted them peremptorily and refused to discuss the idea that Susie should leave.

Jane decided that Holly was in no state to take part in a rational discussion: instead, she announced that she and Stephen would like to experience a session for themselves and it confirmed their deepest apprehensions. Jane remembers going through the ritual incantations and 'testifying' in front of the group. She emerged with a greater sense of certainty that Susie had to be detached from Mary Ann de Grimston, whom she dubbed 'Cruella deVil', after the character in Dodie Smith's *101 Dalmatians*. Cooke himself, fretting in New York and lacking Jane's black sense of humour, had in his own mind a picture of Lady Macbeth. He also, however, had friends in high places, among them the American Ambassador in London, David Bruce, who had been present at the Pilgrims' dinner the year before. The Ambassador informed him that, since Susie was still only sixteen, her parents had the inalienable legal right to take her home. Armed with this reassurance, Jane confronted the Process leaders after the session and had a long and uncomfortable discussion during which they told her that, if Susie was uprooted, it would take her at least two years to recover. Jane and Stephen ridiculed that threat and prepared to take her home.

Cooke met them at the airport in New York and found Susie a different person from the one to whom he'd waved goodbye a few months earlier. 'She had been gay and merry and twinkling. Now she was just sulky and angry.'

Mary Ann de Grimston's warning proved to be accurate. For more than two years, Susie found it hard to settle down. She went back to Putney School, but continually broke down or fell sick, not helped by the regular siren calls from The Process, rubbing salt into her emotional wounds. Frequently she had to be brought back to New York, where Jane tried to restore a sense of normality: she painted a number of portraits of her daughter during this period. Holly, meanwhile, came home for Christmas, having finally managed to disentangle herself. In time she felt strong enough to appear on a television debate in London with representatives of The Process. Susie completed her schooling in 1967, but – having been given a job as a proof-reader for the summer – turned down the opportunity to go to New York University. By the age of nineteen, at the end of 1968, she was married, just a month after Holly. Neither relationship lasted. Stephen was the only one whose first marriage – at almost the same time – survived and thrived.

All those involved in these traumatic events recovered in due course: Holly in London and Susie in Vermont, both remarried – happily: Holly had two children and Susie five. Stephen and his wife, with three children, set up a vineyard in California on the Russian River. All three children soon re-established a strong relationship with their mother and all, with the exception of Stephen, a good adult understanding with Cooke. Yet The Process left its mark. Cooke, despite his experience of analysis at times of stress, never found it easy to talk about what had happened. It filled him, he said much later, with horror and revulsion and helplessness. It was not until 1974 that he found a way of crystallising his feelings. Pattie Hearst, kidnapped by the self-styled 'Symbionese Liberation Army', had been identified as one of those taking part in a bank robbery with her erstwhile jailers. She had then delivered a series of chilling messages proclaiming that she was no longer a prisoner, but an active and enthusiastic member of the group. Middle-class America was appalled and comforted itself that she had been 'brainwashed'. That sent a chill down Cooke's spine, as he explained in a *Letter from America* in April:

> The blanket word that covers a lot of doubt is 'brainwashed' by which a lot of people seem to mean that she has been either drugged or tortured into an insensibility in which she'll say anything that's spoon-fed to her. Or that she is acting out the tough guerrilla recruit under threat of having her sister kidnapped, or her family murdered. There is, however, one other definition of the word 'brainwashed' and I incline to it. Maybe because of an old painful experience with a group not political but pseudo-religious, skilled at recruiting impressionable young people, able to tap the dynamite of their unconscious, but not to guide it, so that a daughter, say, that you knew deeply, could explode into an unrecognisable monster giving her all – money, devotion, total belief – to the movement. And incidentally, renounce and despise the parents in a language and a voice that had its own alien and brutal and unfamiliar tone. In such cases of what you might call maligned conversion it is a dreadful experience to be an onlooking parent, for the loved child has been brainwashed into a genuine conversion and is for the time being lost. At worst, is lost forever.

This bleak passage is a very rare example of Cooke allowing his feelings to be exposed in public. The old reluctance to indulge in any open display of emotion, inherited from his parents, had never been properly shaken off. But he felt he understood something about the abusive psychological techniques of the SLA that he should, as a reporter, pass on; this enabled him to tell his personal story with a protective, journalistic gloss. Two months later, as the Hearst saga continued to unfold, he returned to the subject.

> It's as if these people walked down into a cellar with a torch and said, 'But don't you understand there's dynamite down here?' and then set it off. It was the whole mission of Sigmund Freud, on the contrary, to make the patient aware of what is damaging and explosive in his or her unconscious, so that the doctor could then show precisely how the most destructive forces in one's nature could be controlled. Freud once said, 'The psychiatrist's couch is the field of purgation, the place where the unconscious may explode under control, so that the patient doesn't let it explode in life'; or, as he added another time, 'to release inhibitions under controlled conditions and then guide the patient into seeing what inhibitions it's necessary to put back, so as to cope better with the life ahead.'

The SLA – and The Process – had exploited and betrayed those honourable aims, he believed, for their own pernicious purposes.

~

As for John, he was pursuing a career quite different from anything Cooke might have imagined for him. There had been some discussion of a job in the State Department, but John's appetite for government service evaporated after Kennedy's assassination. Instead, he stuck with the Charles River Valley Boys, products of the Harvard folk scene, and managed to earn a living from his music. Among the influential figures with whom he came in contact was Albert Grossman, manager of such stars as Bob Dylan and Peter, Paul and Mary. Before long, John was to lay down his guitar, but only to become the road manager for one of Grossman's biggest attractions, Janis Joplin. Yet, despite the gulf between father and son, each was undoubtedly on the other's mind, even if neither knew how to bridge the gap. In May 1965, John spotted a fleeting reference to Cooke in *Newsweek* in a column which described him as 'a British newsman'. Cooke Junior immediately took up his pen and wrote to the magazine to set the record straight: 'Although he has written for the *Manchester Guardian* for thirty years, he has lived and worked in this country during that time. He has come to know the United States better than most of the natives and has explained and commented on the American political scene and our role in international affairs for the benefit of England and the rest of the world, often with more insight and clarity than we could offer.' He concludes, touchingly, 'At no time in the past thirty years has he hidden behind the shield which protects "foreign" observers from criticism about the country in which they write – my father became a US citizen before I was born (in New York City) in 1940.' Even though the dates were wrong – Cooke's citizenship came in 1941 – the sentiment was clear enough.

28

PAY ANY PRICE

Two weeks later the 'British newsman' was making the news again. He and Scotty Reston were given a lengthy, exclusive interview with President Johnson to discuss Vietnam. A stir was caused when it emerged that the two journalists had spent longer in private with LBJ than the newly arrived British Ambassador, Sir Patrick Dean. One Washington diarist noted that Sir Patrick had been greeted in the most peremptory fashion, compelled to share his audience with his Danish and Chilean counterparts. 'Diplomatic eyebrows were raised', wrote Drew Pearson, 'when it leaked out that the correspondent of the *Manchester Guardian* [sic], Alistair Cooke, had seen the President for three hours, whereas the British Ambassador had not been able to see him alone for five minutes.'

The meeting, though long, was not altogether comfortable. Cooke and Reston were first subjected to the President's manifest disapproval of the way they were covering Vietnam. 'We were pained to read this,' LBJ declared, slipping disconcertingly into the royal pronoun and launching into an hour-long diatribe on the realities as seen from the White House. And then, without warning, they found themselves pitched into the unaccustomed position of sitting on LBJ's side of the table. Johnson handed over all the day's papers and demanded to know how President Cooke, or President Reston, would deal with them: what, for instance, would he tell the families of sixty-five marines, killed in a grenade attack by South Vietnamese soldiers who had – without warning – changed sides and joined the Vietcong?

Having arrived with an instinctive sympathy for Johnson and a genuine sense of alarm about the Communist build-up in South-East Asia, Cooke took the point. In a newspaper interview years later he was asked whether 'President' Cooke had dared to suggest that America pull out of Vietnam forthwith: 'No,' he replied. 'I was completely overwhelmed by the data and the complexities and by the overwhelming sense of tragic mess.'

He still risked the most vexing question of all: 'Mr President, are you likely to commit to Vietnam the 400,000 troops committed, finally, to Korea?'

Johnson was on his feet, 'a great elephant of a man', from Cooke's – seated – viewpoint. 'My dear boy, I'm going to tell you – aren't going to be 400,000, aren't going to be 300,000, not 200,000, not 100,000 men going to Vietnam: you have my word.'

But the numbers had already begun their inexorable rise to more than half a million before the dismal end finally came. Even in those early days, a sympathetic observer like Cooke was sceptical about the official optimism that this was a war which could be 'won' in any conventional sense of the word. And it presented him with one of the most difficult tasks of his journalistic career – the telling of the Vietnam story in such a way that a British audience would not be either repelled, or bored, or both, with the consequent risk that much of his good work on Anglo-American understanding would be undone. An additional complication, no doubt, came when he returned home each night to Jane's immutable, and often repeated, view that the whole Vietnam enterprise was morally indefensible.

In the first two years of the conflict Cooke – by his own reckoning in July 1966 – did 'about twenty talks' on Vietnam. They track his growing sense of disenchantment, a sense checked only by his respect for the extremity of the position in which President Johnson found himself. Cooke's message, increasingly, was that listeners could condemn what they saw and heard of the war, but they should understand that there was no easy escape from the crisis: and above all, that there was an inner core of justice in the American cause. He underlined the humanity of the President whenever he had the chance: 'His most dependable reflex in the last year and a half', he said on 19 June 1966, 'has been to reach into his left hand pocket and pull out a poll – a bit of paper testifying to his popularity. He even has one in his pyjama pocket, for the world, with its woes, is never tucked away for LBJ.' This account was based partly on his own conversation with the President.

Cooke was well aware, however, that the British were seeing the same television pictures as those which were fuelling the peace movement in the US and he ended the 19 June *Letter* with an unusually ferocious condemnation of American tactics:

> Night after night, we see on the most popular television news show in America, evidence of American torture schools on the Vietcong model; the jelly-bombing of villages; and now the poker-faced contention that a special band of South Vietnamese criminals, recruited as American spies and parachuted into Vietcong territory, constitute a valuable weapon in the war for freedom and democracy. Millions of Americans see these obscenities every evening, they are dazed at the mockery, the Dr Strangelove distortion of our values, that these things imply. This, as much as anything else, I believe, makes more and more people feel hollow and shamed about the war.

However uncomfortable Cooke might feel about the conduct of the war, he would not go so far as to condemn the enterprise outright – not even when Scotty Reston finally gave up the unequal struggle for balance. A new series of American bombing raids on targets outside Hanoi and Haiphong provoked Reston to a scathing attack on the President. In his *New York Times* column, syndicated around the country, he listed the promises broken by the White House in the escalation of the war – ending with these chill words of condemnation: 'There seems to be no guiding principle to what the President is doing. There is certainly little faith here in the official spoken word.' Cooke mulled over his friend's conclusions and found that, for once, he begged to differ. 'It has been easy and comfortable from the start to deplore the war in Vietnam as a cruel assault on human life. It has been just as easy – but nothing like so comfortable – for other people, including President Johnson, to say that it is a tough but necessary crusade to save Asia from Communism, just as American power and American resolution saved Europe from Communism in the late 1940s.' Cooke had not lost his belief in Johnson's integrity. There were no caveats in his final statement on that June day. 'The President honestly, bravely, passionately believes ... that the Chinese mean, in the fullness of time, to conquer their neighbours and the whole of Asia and subdue the capitalist world. He looks on South Vietnam as the Rheinland – the place where the Second World War ought to have been stopped.'

In the year of his sixtieth birthday, Cooke's innate conservatism is understandable. He wrote in the comfortable knowledge that neither his son, John, nor his stepson, Stephen, was in danger of being dispatched to the war zone. Stephen had been undergoing a lengthy period of psychoanalysis (following in the family tradition) while John's draft was first deferred thanks to his student status: then, after graduation, he was declared medically unfit because of a history of bronchial asthma and migraine.

The mounting gloom about Vietnam was universal and was reflected in the *Letters* whenever Cooke felt that the subject could be ignored no longer – notably on the occasion of the 1000th *Letter from America*. The date, by coincidence, was 24 March – twenty-two years to the day after the penning of the first talk in the series. (If the old myth had been true, of course, and Cooke had 'never missed a week', the milestone would have been reached almost two years earlier.) He was under no absolute compulsion to deal with the most important news stories, any more than he had ever been, but in the event he didn't feel there was any choice: 'I wish that this thousandth *Letter* could be about the spring, or American children, or any one of the many amiable things we have talked about down the years. But it must be about the thing that bewilders the American people like nothing else in all those thousand weeks.'

Cooke sketched the pathway from the certainty that America had both justice and invincibility on its side, to the dread realisation that 'an elephant can trumpet and shake the earth, but not the self-possession of the ants who hold it'. He reviewed the domino theory which was supposed to make sense of it all and the self-imposed obligation of the United States to resist aggression against free nations. And finally he gave his verdict on the 'Pax Americana', whereby Washington made treaty commitments to forty-three nations around the globe – but was prevented from exercising its real power by the injunction against the use of its nuclear weapons. The 'early glow' of America's aspiration to be a world power reached its defining moment in the Kennedy Inaugural and his promise to 'pay any price, bear any burden, meet any hardship' to help a friend or oppose a foe. 'This, I suggest, is fine to read but fatal to act on. It may be the wish of a strong nation to do this, but in reality it will not support any friend, or fight any foe, or bear any hardship, or support the burden of a civil war in its own land, in order to rush to the aid of forty-three friends and fight forty-three foes. Vietnam, I fear, is the price of the Kennedy Inaugural.'

The 1000th *Letter* was not allowed to slip by uncelebrated. A grand BBC dinner was arranged at the Charterhouse Suttons Hospital in London, the last such occasion to which Cooke willingly subjected himself. Thenceforward he became increasingly cantankerous in his relations with the upper echelons of the BBC, as a succession of functionaries came to discover to their cost. But in 1968, there was none of the later angst. The proposed guest list included friends of the Cookes as well as a phalanx of senior BBC personnel from the Director-General, Sir Hugh Greene, and the Chairman of the Governors, Lord Hill, downwards. Among those whose absence Cooke most regretted were his first university friend – the actor Erik Chitty – and Rupert Hart-Davis; he also wondered, beforehand, if an invitation had been sent to Lord and Lady Reith. 'I don't, of course, know what the relations are between him and Sir Hugh and the Corporation,' he wrote to the BBC Secretary, 'but if at all possible, he should be asked. You will be astonished to hear that he is a devout fan of *Letter from America* and writes to me with warmth and enthusiasm. He would be bound to hear about the dinner and might possibly descend in His wrath on the Charterhouse with His wondrous great sword.' The BBC's founding father did not, in fact, put in an appearance. Nor did Harold Macmillan, the ex-Prime Minister, though he was invited.

Lord Hill gave the main speech, an event preceded by a predictable scratching around for material, since the two men didn't know each other. Leonard Miall, by now the Corporation's US representative, was drafted in to help. As part of a comprehensive review of Cooke's achievements, he reported to London that he had consulted Nunnally Johnson, 'a very amusing man and a very old friend of Alistair's'. Were there any good anecdotes he could pass on? Johnson had replied, 'Alistair is a smart fellow and smart fellows don't yield anecdotes.' Miall added, 'This is my own experience. I have known him well for twenty-five years but cannot produce any very good examples for the chairman.' It was a revealing observation: 'anecdotes', after all, relate to remarks or incidents in which the subject's mask has slipped, allowing glimpses of the inner man – his humour or humanity. Cooke always disliked anything which implied loss of control of himself or his circumstances.

Lord Hill had to make do with a more formal tribute in which he maintained that Cooke had 'managed a virtuosity not far removed from genius to talk about America in human terms', leading listeners away from the stereotype towards the real world of America and Americana. Among the eighty guests were Jane and Holly, the faithful Lillian Lang from the New York Office and Charles Chilton, Cooke's pre-war sound engineer – the man he'd once advised to emigrate to the United States; Ben Sonnenberg, Gerald Cock and Lindsay Wellington – it was a comfortably familiar, though typically varied, group. Cooke had made a special point of adding the Independent Television supremo Sidney Bernstein and his wife, who had become firm friends on the London circuit – and Stephen Hearst, a BBC television executive who had worked with Cooke first on some UN films in the early 1960s and then, in 1966, on a fifty-minute documentary about H.L. Mencken. This was an acquaintance which would help to shape the latter stages of Cooke's career.

The 1968 anniversary also gave rise to a second book of collected *Letters*. This had required Cooke, the previous summer, to undergo lengthy reading sessions at Broadcasting House in London where he ploughed his way through 263 hours of talks. The selections, instinctively or by design, did little to advance his status as a political analyst. Quite the contrary. Apart from a section on race relations and a Vietnam epilogue, the book was devoted almost entirely to the quirks and charms of American life. It was, in the round, the testament of a social commentator – which was exactly how Cooke liked to characterise himself, when he forgot for a moment that he didn't like such labels. When he'd finished the job he listed joyfully the fads and trends which had come and gone in the intervening years: 'I've been amused at the breathless naïveté of the broadcaster – that's me – in telling you, long ago, about parking meters, self-service laundries, off-the-rack dresses, comparison shoppers, how a discount house works, what a supermarket looks like, what it feels like to put up the windows of your car and drive into – brace yourself – a "washomat" and having your car flooded and cleaned in two minutes flat.'

Having put off the compilation for so long, Cooke discovered to his dismay that Rupert Hart-Davis was no longer available to publish the volume: his company had been absorbed by Sidney Bernstein's Granada group, whose commercial television business repelled Cooke – however well he liked its boss. After much havering, he plumped for Bodley Head, where Max Reinhardt soon became a publishing ally as Hart-Davis had been, or Alfred Knopf continued to be in the United States.

Knopf was happy to turn out a US edition of the book, *Talk About America,* and the blurb was unstinting in its promotion of the sixty-year-old writer though it did contain the familiar exaggerated reference to his 'First Class Honors in English at Cambridge University'.

The fact of the 1968 anniversary caused the BBC to have a close look at the way the *Letter* was working. It had been accepted all along that, although it drew its material from current events, it was not to be regarded as an extension of the corporation's news coverage. The Watts riots in Los Angeles, during August 1965, provided a classic example. On the Sunday after the trouble broke out, Cooke's broadcast was preceded by a curiously old-fashioned preamble, read by an announcer in London: 'Before *Letter from America,* here's a message we have received from Alistair Cooke. He says, "The Los Angeles riots are too sudden and too serious and the cause of them too uncertain, to warrant an immediate commentary." Mr Cooke hopes to talk on this subject next week.' There followed a gentle piece about the oddities of politics in New York. Only a week later did he turn to the appalling scenes of violence and destruction in a black suburb. By then he felt more confident in expounding his theory that the trouble had nothing much to do with civil rights and a great deal to do with envy – what he called 'a twisted form of ambition'. He inveighed against 'the pimping role of television with its tantalising exposure of the white man's dainties for sale at your nearest grocer's or department store'; and he warned against simply pumping more federal funds into the area – the immediate response of distraught politicians. Instead, he believed, Watts needed a 'full-time birth-control programme, the return of parolees to jail, a couple of churches, a public works project, six playing fields and an army of coloured men in the police force'. Cooke, practical to the core as always and untroubled by traditional liberal remedies.

He was always aware of the risks he took by recording a talk forty-eight hours or so before it was due to be broadcast. He reflected ruefully in a 1967 *Letter* about the time the first Russian space-flight – on a Sunday afternoon – had made his harmless musings on 'summer in Long Island' sound feeble and out of place. 'The following week,' he groaned, 'a critic in the *Listener* wrote a piece suggesting that you could always trust Cooke to fiddle while Rome was burning.' If this irritated Cooke himself, it infuriated the BBC. The worst kind of mismatch occurred when the *Letter* was more straightforwardly over-taken by events, as it was on the day in 1968 that President Johnson announced that he would not be running for re-election. Unfor-tunately he chose to drop this political bombshell while Cooke was incommunicado – flying back from the anniversary dinner in London. *Letter* Number 1001, recorded before he left, had been devoted to the developing party battles for presidential nomination, ending with the speculative thought that the election might turn out to be a fight between the familiar figures of Nixon and LBJ. That sounded fine on its first outing on Sunday morning. But within hours, LBJ's decision made a nonsense of the prediction.

The BBC was faced with an unpalatable choice between running the outdated *Letter* and filling the gap with a bland alternative: reluc-tantly they stuck with the *Letter*, but executives vowed to redouble their efforts to prevent a repetition. One possible solution was to draft in a US correspondent in London to do a replacement piece covering unforeseen weekend developments. This was not mentioned to Cooke, who would have been outraged at the very suggestion.

Meanwhile, Frank Gillard – by now in the elevated position of Director of Radio – was asked to use his diplomatic wiles in an approach to Cooke for a standby tape, an idea that Cooke had always rejected out of hand. Even allowing for Cooke's status, the language used by those preparing the missive was delicate, almost grovelling. 'Rightly, in my view, your *Letters from America* are as topical as circumstances permit; but as you know only too well, developments can overtake the best possible dispatch from the most far-seeing correspondent and this has happened twice in recent weeks.' And further on: 'To meet the situation that may arise when an entirely new *Letter* is clearly desirable,' one draft drooled, 'but impossible to organise, may we please have from you a standby talk, not topical, which we could put out in place of the topical one you have sent us?' As an added carrot, this talk would naturally attract an extra fee. Cooke's airy reply, when it came, may have produced a mildly apo-plectic reaction from his managers in London. 'I was on the verge of sending you one or two Talks to hold in reserve. In fact, I have been saying to Lillian for several weeks that we have flirted with fate far too long . . . Your gentle request shall be heeded and very soon.' There's no evidence that the standby tape was ever made.

Even at this stage, Cooke did not like to take instruction from London. The *Letter* was his baby and he knew best how it should be nurtured. The tradition had been established – and it was never to be abandoned – that he was in total control of its editorial content. Until 1977, Lillian Lang acted as his producer in New York, but she did not regard it as her job to question what topics he chose or how he decided to deal with them. He might call her on a Thursday morning to check what the news correspondents were talking about – but often that was simply to avoid following their well-trodden path. Thereafter, she made sure that all the arrangements were in hand for his arrival at the studio and generally acted as a buffer between Cooke and the outside world. That included fending off unwanted approaches from people within the BBC, as well as those from outside agencies. 'Many times, he was asked to do commercials,' Lang remembers. 'I always told them, Mr Cooke doesn't do commercials. One man wouldn't accept it and said, "Look, everybody has his price. What's Cooke's?" I simply repeated, "He hasn't got one." '

The Thursday ritual became unshakeable. He would settle himself in the studio, leaving strict instructions that no one should stare in through the glass at the back of the control room. One long-serving sound engineer, Ken Pursley, who took over from Herb Schaeffer in the late 1970s, remembers drawing the blinds to deter the curious: he also had to provide a small lectern for the studio table, placed very precisely, eighteen inches from the edge, as well as a special microphone preserved, despite its obsolescence, at Cooke's particular request: 'It was the only time this microphone was used – a boom-operated Neumann – and it had to be positioned at exactly the right distance above the lectern.'

When Cooke was settled, Lang and the engineer would retire to the control room and wait for the *Letter* to be delivered. It was an intimate experience. Lang kept a note of the time, discounting the pauses for coughs or splutters and from time to time Cooke would look up and see what reaction he was getting. 'We were his listeners,' according to Pursley, 'and he was testing out his stories and anecdotes on us through the glass. If we smiled or laughed in the right places, it reassured him.' Pursley came to appreciate the subtleties of Cooke's technique. Pauses were part of the package. A sound engineer might be tempted to tighten the script by excising the gaps between sentences, but Cooke wanted them left where they were. They helped to create the sense of a conversation rather than a lecture and he would ring up and complain if the editing was too sharp. 'I did that for a reason,' he insisted. 'It was imperative to keep those two thoughts apart.' Pursley felt it had much to do with Cooke's musical background, in which the flow of the words was more important than perfect neatness.

When Lillian Lang retired a new tradition began, whereby ambitious young producers were posted to New York for six months at a time. Pursley had to tutor them in the niceties of the task, not least in the need to overcome their natural desire for perfect editing. Cooke would stumble slightly on a word and Pursley would suggest leaving it in; if Cooke was consulted he tended to say, 'Yes, leave it. It's natural. People don't talk perfectly, they make mistakes.' For a newly trained producer, this went against the grain. In fact, 'producing' the *Letter from America* was something of a misnomer: none tried very often (or very determinedly) to impose their own ideas on Cooke's output. It was permissible to proffer a polite correction in the case of factual error, but even this wasn't easy since the producer's first exposure to the talk was when Cooke began to record it. One of the six-monthers, Tony Hall, who eventually rose to become the BBC's Managing Director, admitted, 'This grand job of producing Alistair Cooke actually meant nothing. You just didn't interfere with him.' Such extraordinary editorial indulgence was evidently sanctioned at the highest level in London. Or rather, even those at the highest level did not think it was worthwhile confronting Cooke over a weekly column which began to take on the sanctity of Holy Writ. Mistakes were sometimes made, but that was a price which the BBC was prepared to pay for its artistry and – just as importantly – its enduring popularity. It would have been like cross-questioning St Paul about the strict and literal truth of his Epistles to communities far away. The invulnerability of the *Letter* grew in direct proportion to its longevity: the 1500th talk in November 1977, the 2000th in June 1987, the 2500th in January 1997. There might be occasional mutterings at Broadcasting House, but Cooke remained impervious to criticism or doubt.

Only on rare (and ill-documented) occasions did any senior manager seriously try to impose new thinking on the *Letter*. The most public occasion concerned Ian McIntyre, who took over as Controller of Radio Four in 1976. He first decided that it might be worth shifting the repeat of the *Letter* from its familiar time at 9.15 on Sunday morning to 12.40 on the same day. Cooke was not amused. 'A hell of a time for anyone to listen,' he muttered to a newspaper interviewer who was supposed to be celebrating the 1500th *Letter*. 'I'll be competing with the lunch-time cutlery.' Before long McIntyre found himself summoned to see the Managing Director of Radio, later Director-General, Sir Ian Trethowan: 'I think you'd better move Alistair back,' he was told. McIntyre was convinced that Cooke had been busy behind the scenes, whipping up opposition to the change, but Cooke denied it and the charge was never proved. The *Letter*, none the less, was moved back to its original place in the schedule less than three months after the start of the experiment. Tampering with the *Letter* was never easy. In the same newspaper conversation (with the *Sunday Times*) Cooke was still complaining about the loss of his weekday morning slot which he'd occupied in the late 1960s: 'When I used to broadcast in the mornings I had a captive audience of guys trapped in their automobiles and wives starting the day at home. I'd get a blizzard of mail.' The interviewer, Philip Oakes, seemed to agree that changing the *Letter*'s location was 'as mindless as shifting Nelson's Column to Stoke Poges'.

McIntyre is also the man widely regarded as having come closest to scrapping the *Letter* altogether. In retirement, he confessed that he had raised the question because he felt that Cooke had started to 'coast'. 'The talks were very mellifluous,' he recalled. 'But the funny thing was, if you asked someone afterwards what had been said they could never remember. "He had such a lovely voice," they used to say.' McIntyre moved on, Cooke stayed put. But although he was the most outspoken, he was certainly not the only Controller of the network to ask awkward questions. Richard Somerset-Ward, who settled in New York after years as a BBC executive, remembers McIntyre's successor suggesting that the *Letter* might take a Christmas break. Cooke was deeply affronted and there was no Christmas break.

Then, at the end of the 1980s, another manager, Alistair Osborne, found himself promoted to head the department whose programme stable included the *Letter*. This coincided with renewed managerial muttering about whether Cooke's performance was losing its edge. Was Osborne, as the press reported, sent to New York to give Cooke his cards? Osborne denies the charge strenuously, claiming that his mission was simply to test out, as tactfully as possible, whether – at the age of almost eighty and perhaps on the occasion of the 2000th

Letter – Cooke might himself decide to pack up his portable typewriter for good. It was a fruitless mission. 'I think he guessed,' said Osborne ruefully. 'He behaved distinctly puckishly. I think he knew what was going on and was deliberately ambiguous.' Michael Green, who had just taken over as Radio Four Controller, insists that he never did any more than 'look under all the stones' in the rambling property he'd inherited. He summed up the, not altogether unpleasant, predicament in which he and his kind found themselves in graphic fashion: 'Radio Four is a national monument and Alistair Cooke is one of its best-known gargoyles. He's part of the fabric of the network. I can't imagine a controller giving some poor person a farewell letter to deliver to Alistair. There'd be public outrage. The plane would be shot down over the Atlantic.'

From Cooke's point of view, especially as he started to reach the more rarefied air of old age, matters didn't look quite so cut and dried. He had never had a formal contract with the BBC. Somerset-Ward thought that the possibility of losing the *Letter* preyed on his mind – hence the insistence on never missing a single week, on the grounds that the slightest sign of weakness or a gap in the schedules might bring the whole enterprise to an untimely end.

Yet the *Letter* did not owe its survival to the fact that nobody knew how to end it. It was a chronicle with the most faithful band of followers, including world statesmen, leading literary figures and members of the royal family. Both the Queen and the Queen Mother were said to be faithful followers and Cooke was one of those asked to record a special short tribute to the latter on her eighty-fifth birthday.

Transmissions of the *Letter* on the World Service ensured that he became just as important a figure in fifty English-speaking countries as he was in Britain: F.W. de Klerk, while still President of South Africa, was a regular listener; so was Arthur C. Clarke at his home in Sri Lanka. Raymond Seitz, when he was American Ambassador in London, regarded the *Letter* as an important contribution to Anglo-American relations. 'He's provided insight,' according to Seitz, 'but also comfort that things which appeared to the British eye bizarre or impetuous or ramshackle – all of which we are – he could put it all in context, in a wonderful, conversational, matter-of-fact way. He could say, "Don't get so excited about this. That's the way we do things over here". ' Or as the *New York Times* put it, 'He loves America as a shrewd child loves a stepfather or stepmother, without the blinding passion of a blood relation.' Ironically, the only area of the world where the *Letter* remained virtually unknown was the United States itself, thanks in part to Cooke's continuing concern that he might be constrained in what he wrote by the sense of a local audience, unable to appreciate the subtleties of his message. This stricture was only lifted in the last few years of his career.

If public respect rarely wavered, neither did Cooke's method of working and each of the 'six-monthers' had to get used to it. Only a few broke through his natural suspicion of the stranger: most felt they were tolerated, rather than accepted as partners in the enterprise and fitted the *Letter* in alongside many other duties. One exception was Marifi Chicote, who arrived with the fixed idea that she would exploit the chance to work with Cooke. She pampered him and he responded with invitations to visit the apartment and even the final accolade of dinner at his favourite restaurant in the Carlyle Hotel.

Otherwise, the routine of the *Letter* helped protect him from the vagaries of visiting producers. He always denied plotting out his piece during the week: 'We do not go out to dinner', he once wrote, 'with a little agenda in our pockets of what the evening's conversation is to be about.' Inspiration came only when he sat down in front of his typewriter and inserted the first sheet of yellow paper. Two or three hours later the finished script emerged – five or six pages, scarred by excisions and splattered with handwritten insertions – lasting close to the required thirteen and a half minutes. A brief flirtation with a computer keyboard lasted only for a matter of days, after he discovered that it was destroying the flow of thoughts and feelings. The only way was to 'bang away and let it all come out uncorrected, then, at the end, slash it down to listenable length.' The ritual was important and not just because it imbued what was a fairly unremarkable journalistic process with an almost mystical quality – the teacher communing with his unseen audience through the medium of those yellow sheets of paper. It was also more than a little misleading. Like most writing that is based on principles of simplicity and directness, the polished article was as much technique as instinct – the interlocking threads of thought spun into an unexpected design: such things do not generally happen by accident.

The trick was based not just on a lucid writing style, free of the tiresome Latinisms which he abhorred: but also on a remarkable breadth of knowledge stored in a fine memory bank, combined with a story-teller's ability to build up suspense and artistic tension. When the finished talk was delivered in those 'mellifluous' tones, listeners were drawn in, seduced and finally satisfied by the way the pattern of the piece emerged, sonata-like, from the apparently disparate elements out of which it was constructed. What was remarkable was the way he succeeded in perpetuating a broadcast form – the straight, unvarnished talk – which had been the staple diet of the early BBC days and which might otherwise have become obsolete: he was still there when the idea came back into fashion towards the end of the millennium.

~

And then, from time to time, the *Letter from America* leaped out of its normal bounds, with no way of avoiding the worst and with nothing to laugh about. 1968 was such a time. Cooke was, anyway, deeply gloomy about the state of the nation: he sensed in his bones that society was on the slide. 'I felt that wherever I went, the blacks were on the edge of erupting,' he told Abe Ribicoff one day. Ribicoff was moved by this uncharacteristic sense of doom and asked Cooke if he'd be prepared to share his thoughts with a few senior Democrats. Over dinner at the Cosmos Hotel some days later, he found himself in a group of sixteen Senators and Congressmen, including Robert Kennedy and even Vice-President Hubert Humphrey, expatiating on his theories of social meltdown. His audience was very attentive: 'I told them, "If you're going to avoid a second American Revolution, it's going to need such an outlay of money . . . Thirteen years after the first integration judgement, most blacks believe it's just not happened. Utopia has not arrived. The cities are in danger of exploding." '

In retrospect, even Cooke himself was impressed by the self-confidence this must have required.

Cooke was visiting the New York home of Nunnally Johnson cloaked in the pseudonym 'Donnelly' for the purposes of the *Letter* when he heard about the assassination of Martin Luther King in Memphis. Just one more city, he reflected, whose reputation would be permanently scarred by a moment of violence. He had heard the commentators describe Beale Street as 'the dangerous core' of Memphis and allowed his mind to drift back to his first experience of the place in the 1930s, ' . . . a very young white man strolling on a hot August morning, safe as the wind, along a street that to me was as magical as the Acropolis to a classical scholar. Two Negroes were bent over a tyre they were fixing,' he told his audience and 'one of them was tapping the rim and setting the beat for the blues they were singing together in low harmony. It was the Beale Street Blues.' He paused. 'Well, on Thursday night, it was paved with blood. And it will be, from now on, like the Dallas Blues, one song that no party will care to play or sing with any taste or tact.'

How would Cooke deal with this disaster? Where would he find Ambassador Seitz's sense of comfort in the impetuous and bizarre scenes of that night? The answer was not what listeners might have expected, unless they'd paid close attention to Cooke's writing over the years:

> It's odd that we never guessed this in the early and rousing stages of the Negro revolution. As the Negro got the vote, and went onto juries, and sat in lunchrooms and trains among white men, and mixed in theatres, and as increasingly Negroes moved up – and they are moving up, from field labour and unskilled factory jobs into offices and telephone switchboards and white collar management – as this has happened, and even more if a Negro has found a decent low-rent house, he is not – to our amazement – overcome with gratitude. He is furious. He sees what he's been denied all these generations.

This Pandora's Box theory of race relations brought him to his conclusion: that the nation had only itself to blame for 'dinning into them the gorgeous promises of the Declaration of Independence and the Constitution and the mumble jumble of the American way of life. We talk too much. And promise too much. We are victims of our own advertising.'

Cooke's report for the *Guardian* on King's funeral, by contrast, reverted to the vivid, unfussy style which had become his newspaper trademark:

> Today, on a flaming spring day, with the magnolias blooming and the white dogwood and the red sprinkling the land, they brought a farm wagon and its mules to stand outside the church on the street where Martin Luther King was born and, after the funeral service, to carry the body four miles to his college and lay it to rest. The mule train is the oldest and still most dependable form of transport of the rural poor in the Southland. And somebody had the graceful idea that a mule train would be the aptest cortège for the man who was the apostle of the poor.

29

BEING THERE

King's death was covered by a man writing from the distant calm of New York. The second political assassination of that murderous year did not allow Cooke the luxury of calm or distance. Although he was expecting to attend the nominating Conventions, he was not playing as full a part as usual in the *Guardian*'s coverage of the presidential campaign. So when an eager young sports correspondent, David Gray, volunteered to take on the California primaries – and with the distinguished figure of Peter Jenkins handling profiles of the two main candidates – Cooke found himself in the unfamiliar position of enjoying the spectacle as a spectator.

He was staying with an old Hollywood friend – an actress named Inge Stevenson – and hadn't even bothered to bring his typewriter. On the night of the primary, they were sitting at her home high up in the hills above the city, watching the results come in. The computer said that the California battle between Bobby Kennedy and Senator Eugene McCarthy was likely to be close and they decided it might be fun to wander down to the campaign hotels for the climax of the evening. By the time they reached the Beverly Hilton, the McCarthy supporters were downhearted.

They moved on to the Ambassador, a few miles away on Wilshire Boulevard and here the atmosphere was frenetic. There were hundreds of people swarming around the public spaces, hoping for a glimpse of Kennedy but, as for all Kennedy functions, special credentials were required to get beyond the barriers. Cooke was carrying only his normal press card. Having been shoved and jostled towards the heaving ballroom, the two were on the point of abandoning the enterprise when one of the campaign team spotted Cooke in the throng and ushered him into the press room – waiving his lack of the appropriate papers. Here the quiet was disturbed only by 'a booming television set, switching between the rumblings of defeat at the

McCarthy hotel and the clamour of victory in the adjacent ballroom'.

The press tables had been set up in a private dining-room, separated from the ballroom by the hotel kitchen. Cooke chatted to friends and colleagues and heard Kennedy's parting platform words: 'My thanks to all of you – now it's on to Chicago and let's win there.' They watched the television pictures:

> A delirium of cheers and lights and tears and a rising throb of 'We want Bobby! We want Bobby! We want Bobby!' He tumbled down from the rostrum with his aides and body guards about him. He would be with us in twenty seconds, half a minute at most. We watched the swinging doors of the kitchen. Over the babble of the television there was suddenly from the direction of the kitchen a crackle of sharp sounds. Like a balloon popping.

Bobby Kennedy was dying a few feet away from where Cooke stood. Cooke was – just for once in his life – not the detached reporter in control of his circumstances, but a man caught up in a moment of history. And he froze. It never occurred to him to take up his pen, or call his office, or do the things that reporters are supposed to do. 'The doors of the pantry swung back and forth and we would peek into this obscene disorder and reel back again to sit down, then to glare in a stupefied way at the nearest friend, to steady one boozy woman with black-rimmed eyes who was pounding a table and screaming, "Goddam stinking country!"' Through the mêlée he caught sight of Kennedy, bathed in the blueish light of the fluorescent tubes and 'looking up like a stunned choirboy from an open shirt and a limp huddle of limbs'.

For some time and even after Kennedy had been removed to hospital, he and Inge Stevenson remained in the press-room, before seeking out the security man who'd let them in. He guided them to the street. Back in Stevenson's Monica Hills home, they watched television, where 'pandemonium is rebroadcast in tranquillity and where a little unshaven guy amok in a pantry is slowly brought into focus as a bleak and shoddy villain of history.' Cooke's words describing the scene were written at four in the morning after a desperate phone call from the *Guardian* office in London. Alastair Hetherington himself was on the line, simply making contact, not even knowing that Cooke had been almost an eyewitness to the assassination. Would he write something now? Cooke told his editor to ring back in an hour, found a few pages of rough paper and drafted out the piece that ended ' . . . a shoddy villain of history.'

Two days later, with equanimity still not totally restored, he had to relive the experience for the *Letter from America*. He recalled the great movie-versions of the correspondent's role, always at the heart of the action:

> In life it's not like that; only by the wildest freak is a reporter, after many years on the hop, actually present at a single accidental convulsion of history. Mostly we write the coroner's inquest, the account of the funeral, the trial of the spy, not the hatching of the plot. Last Tuesday night, for the first time in thirty years, I found myself by one casual chance in a thousand, on hand in a small, narrow serving-pantry of the Ambassador Hotel in Los Angeles, a place that I suppose will never be wiped out of my memory as a sinister alley, a Roman circus run amok, and a charnel house.

With his respect for psychoanalysis, he felt the need to delve into his own response: 'It would be quite false to say, as I should truly like to say, that I'm sorry I was there. It's more complicated than that. Nothing so simple as a conflict between professional pride and human revulsion, between having the feelings and then having to sit down and write them.' It was Cooke at his most introspective, for once abandoning the carapace protecting his emotions from public view.

What were those feelings? As with JFK's assassination, Cooke was appalled at the rush to judgement on the sickness of American society. 'I for one do not feel like an accessory to a crime and I reject almost as a frivolous obscenity the sophistry of collective guilt, the idea that I, or the American people, killed John Fitzgerald Kennedy and Martin Luther King and Robert Francis Kennedy. I don't believe either that you conceived Hitler and that in some deep, unfathomable sense all Europe was responsible for the extermination of some six million Jews. With Edmund Burke, I do not know how you can indict a whole nation.'

~

The 1968 celebrations of Cooke's BBC endeavours were widely – and sometimes wryly – noted, not least by the *Guardian*. In a leader headlined 'OUR MAN OF *LETTERS FROM AMERICA*', the foreign editor Geoffrey Taylor wrote, '[Cooke] is a nuisance. He telephones his copy at the last moment. He says that he will be in Chicago and turns up in Los Angeles. He discards the agreed subject to write about something that has taken his fancy. If all his colleagues were like him, production of this paper would cease. But we think he's worth it.' This was picked up and recycled by a number of commentators, including *Time* magazine, which based a short profile on what was described as this 'praising with faint damns'. Taylor's words were apposite. They described accurately the relationship between the paper and its admired but wayward son on a foreign shore.

When the paper was relaunching itself, yet again, in the early months of 1969, Cooke was one of those dragooned into a contribution to the publicity campaign. The man who had so vilified the advertising business over so many years found himself appearing – for the only time in his life – in a thirty-second television commercial, shown on almost all the independent stations in Britain. Cooke's beautifully groomed figure was seen reading a copy of the revamped paper with its new, stronger, typeface: the message of the campaign was: 'the *Guardian* has changed – could it be your paper now?' (When the magazine *Campaign* covered the story, it paid the *Guardian*, with its reputation for spectacular misprints, an oblique compliment by quoting the paper's 'Criculation Manager'.)

Cooke also provided a column for the paper itself entitled 'AMERICA: ONCE OVER LIGHTLY.' It began, 'Anyone who is sufficiently shrewd, intelligent and on the ball to be buying the new and shining *Guardian* is not going to settle any more for the old, square-type newspaper that lines up the news in long, grey columns, as dreary as Napoleon's men on their way to Moscow.' With tongue well-rooted in cheek, he invited readers to cast aside the dictionaries and almanacs they might have needed in the past to plumb the depths of the paper's erudition. 'The new paper, I understand, is going to tell it short and fast and like it is.' New readers, he deduced, wouldn't have time for lengthy articles on arcane subjects. 'A special Cooke poll, conducted so late as noon this very day, discloses the astounding fact that most Americans, like most Britons or Tibetans, are interested first in sex, then the weather, then in what money will buy, then in what women will be wearing next summer, then in sport, then in such lively disasters as earthquakes and diseases and afterwards in a steadily descending curve of such other topics as politics, sex, crime, marijuana, sex and good works.'

The article was a pleasant piece of journalistic froth, but the head-line remained to haunt him long afterwards. 'Once Over Lightly' was picked up and reused by critics, suggesting a superficiality which he felt was grossly unfair.

Behind the jokiness, Cooke was in any case wearying of his *Guardian* duties. The drudgery of his 'daily pieces' on such matters as economics, health care and industrial disputes made him ponder other possible ways of exercising his art. As early as 1965 he was proposing to Alastair Hetherington a series in which he would travel the globe interviewing world leaders: 'I think it would be terrific if we could line up everybody from Wilson (Heath?) to de Gaulle to Sukarno and Pig-Iron Bob to LBJ. By then, even Mao Tse Tung may be possible.' (Pig-Iron Bob was Sir Robert Menzies, the Australian premier.) Apart from the LBJ interview in 1966, the idea lapsed. Another underlying point of contention was that the *Guardian* never had the resources to fund its overseas offices properly. When 1967 came, Cooke was pleading for help in covering the UN Security Council: 'It has not been possible in the past fortnight to cover the United States at all and in the last week to write a *Letter* or pay an insurance premium.'

Cooke had also been fending off a long-cherished *Guardian* scheme for a newspaper version of the *Letter from America*. On 17 February 1968, he told Geoffrey Taylor that – having reconsidered the proposal – he was still inclined against it. 'A column must have a shape and a theme and I feel it would nag at me over weekends and probably immobilise Sunday and Monday morning for anything else.' This letter caused no surprise at head office. Hetherington appended a typewritten comment, reeking with resignation. 'Cooke and his column: I'm not surprised that he has said "no" after at first saying "yes". I don't think there's much point in trying to press him. We would probably get late copy and poor results.'

Yet the idea refused to expire completely. Hetherington was trying again in June, citing one of the young reporters who had been working with Cooke – John Cole, later doyen among political correspondents for the *Guardian* and the BBC. Cole had heard and admired a recent *Letter*, 'a brilliant piece about your experience with the students at Berkeley.' Hetherington remarked that Cole had said, 'not for the first time, that it's a pity we don't have some of your thoughtful and discursive comments for the *Guardian*'. Unmoved by the flagrant flattery, Cooke replied that he still believed such a project would be 'fraught with perils.'

After a while, temptation must have started to seep into his consciousness: could he really resist the further chance to pound away at his favourite themes and get paid for it? Finally and without fanfare, the edition of 24 March 1969 appeared with a new feature – 'Cooke's Column' (in modest lower-case type), consisting of an obituary of Ambassador David Bruce, a preview of an elaborate Department of Defense mission to study world weather and a jokey piece about the Mafia moving into labour relations. Four weeks later and again with no effusive preamble, the column was re-named 'Alistair Cooke's America', complete with photographic inset. By June, the typeface was bold and the pattern was set for the rest of Cooke's sojourn at the *Guardian*.

Comparisons between the *Guardian*'s letter and its senior partner on the BBC prove that Cooke was aware of the dangers of overlapping themes. Except in cases of extreme newsworthiness, different topics were covered in each: and where a story couldn't be avoided it was tackled in a different way. On 27 July, for instance, the audio version of the *Letter* was devoted to a detailed account of the aftermath of the drowning of Teddy Kennedy's companion, Mary Jo Kopeckne, at Chappaquiddick and the prediction that he, unlike the unfortunate Mary Jo, would live to fight another day. Cooke's *Guardian* column the following day mentioned the story, but mainly in order to demonstrate its possible impact on American party politics. But it left space for anecdotes on popular music, Chairman Mao and the possibility of an expedition to Mars.

There was also a fundamental stylistic difference between the two outlets. The *Letter from America* continued to be a monolithic construction, while 'Alistair Cooke's America' was unashamedly episodic – its elements disparate and unrelated – essentially 'dashed off', more seaside postcard than *Letter*. It continued until he left the paper at the end of 1970.

～

One last great political event marked the final period of Cooke's *Guardian* service: the election campaign which brought Richard Nixon to the White House. He was, he reassured Hetherington, intent on covering the 1968 Conventions himself: 'You needn't fear that I will cover the conventions as a pundit – you know from experience that they are high or comic drama and the trick is to weave the information, the colour and the analysis together, as in a page by Balzac – or perhaps by Thurber!' As it turned out, the Democratic Convention in Chicago was more Balzac than Thurber.

Inside the Hilton Hotel, Hubert Humphrey was chosen as the party's presidential candidate. Outside, it was – in Cooke's words – bedlam, as police moved in to clear away peace protesters and disperse demonstrations. On the express orders of Mayor Richard Daley, the last of the great city bosses, no prisoners were taken. In the words of Hugh Brogan's *History of the United States*, the young had gone to Chicago in droves 'hoping by some miracle they could win the nomination for Senator Eugene McCarthy (no relation to the communist-hunting Joseph McCarthy), and there were brought to battle by Mayor Daley's police, who loathed them because they were dirty and anti-war and sexually uninhibited and politically radical and didn't belong to Chicago'.

The natural caution of the respectable media led some commentators to treat the violence as something regrettable, but perhaps necessary. Cooke was not among them: 'In thirty years of attending presidential Conventions, I have seen nothing to match the fury and despair of the delegations inside this Chicago amphitheatre, or on the outside, anything like the jumping-jack ferocity of the police corps around the Hilton Hotel. They began by clubbing and taming peace demonstrators and jeering hippies and ended by roaming the hotel lobby like SS men and roughing up astonished guests, marooned families and other innocents sitting or walking through the hotel lounges.' Inside, where many delegates remained oblivious to what was happening in the name of public order, Cooke's old friend Abe Ribicoff – nominating George McGovern – abandoned his prepared script, stared coolly at Mayor Daley and the Illinois delegation and cried, 'With George McGovern as President we would not have Gestapo tactics in the streets of Chicago.' Daley's men booed and shook their fists at Ribicoff and Daley himself yelled inaudible abuse at the platform.

Cooke spared a moment to consider the oddities of the moment – not least the fact that the only people in full possession of the facts were not the political activists in the hall, but those sitting at home in front of their television sets – a terrifying demonstration of Mc-

Luhanism, he called it, after the author of *The Medium and The Message*: in this case, both medium and message were available to viewers, but obscured to people in the 'real world'. He also had no doubt what effect the brutality would have. He quoted a Chicago police official as saying, 'At least no one was killed.' Really? 'No one, that is, except the Democratic Party. Now that the smoke and clatter and weeping have died down, there is only a faint rhythmical sound ruffling the horizon on this beautiful day. It is the sound, North, South, East and West, of the Republicans counting votes.'

The *Letter from America* inspired by the Chicago violence makes the same points. But in the process, remarkably, it sows the occasional seed of doubt in the mind of the listener about the moral of the tale. Daley's behaviour was intolerable – but, faced with real assassination plots against the candidates, 'no mayor of a city could sit back and trust to the folksy protection of musical comedy cops'; many innocent people were beaten and abused – but there was at least a measure of vile provocation from the 'derelict and calculating young' woven in with the good and naïve, who 'invited what they got'; the Democratic party would pay the price – but mainly just for being there and thus smelling of 'blood and tear gas and general helplessness'. The *Letter* was no apologia, but it was a brave effort by a dedicated man to defend the cross he had chosen to bear, regardless of the flying brickbats.

And for once the election result was predictable: Richard Nixon's time had come. Cooke had watched Nixon's career from the start and never found much to arouse affection. It was not so much to do with memories of Hiss and the Senate committees. He simply found Nixon charmless, a political time server who owed his success largely to forces outside his control: these included the Chicago riots and the debilitating effect of the Vietnam War – which Nixon claimed (spuriously) he could bring to a swift conclusion. He was many voters' choice, Cooke opined, only by default: in other words, he might be a party hack, but at least he was the hack of a different party from the incumbent. He might be a conservative, but at least he wasn't a rabid conservative like Governor George Wallace of Alabama.

Cooke's BBC broadcasts had no unkind things to say about Nixon. He was, after all, the new President and that entitled him to a period of respect. So Cooke threw in some of the folksy details which the news coverage might have missed: for instance, the information that Nixon had an old crony in Florida named Rebozo, one of the few people with whom he felt he could really relax. 'He is a simple pal, he goes fishing with Mr Nixon, he knows many things, but best of all he knows how to keep his trap shut. He is the essential private balm against the slings and arrows of the Presidency.' The court jester, Cooke felt, was an important, unsung role.

~

Cooke's work on the elections ensured that, in September 1968, he still qualified for the title of the *Guardian*'s 'Chief US Correspondent'. It was clear to everyone concerned, however, that this era was drawing to a close. Through 1969 and the first half of 1970, Cooke's most striking contributions were the offbeat and personal insights of his columns. One, in particular, stands out.

In July 1969 he wrote about his favourite city, San Francisco. Under the title, 'San Francisco Myth' it began, 'Among the unwritten books that I have often wished somebody else to write is one that would sketch the rise of myths of certain cities and the tenacity with which the myths are maintained when they have lost all reality.' He might have added that this was one of the books that he had, at one time or another, thought about writing himself. Cooke had spotted an anonymous article in the *Guardian* describing San Francisco as a gourmet's paradise and this set his journalistic juices running. He decried the general standard of cuisine available and rued what had happened to some of his favourite places: 'India House, which was once the best curry-house restaurant in America, has pathetically declined.' Jack's was 'a shabby parody of its old self', while the best that could be said about the pasta-house, Vanessi's, was that it retained 'the appeal of an all-night kitchen run by the Marx brothers'.

Cooke's tendency was to be faithful to a few restaurants, where the fare was reliable and predictable. Rather like his choice of friends, his favoured eating-places were a mixed bunch – from the priciest joints in town to brass counters serving hamburgers and milk shakes. His (life-saving) doctor friend Bob Brown and his wife Vera describe the way he would take control of an evening – demanding high standards and fine service, ordering the wine, even though he was invariably drinking whisky or beer himself and objecting strongly to sudden changes in menus he'd grown to like.

These minor dietary obsessions became part of the folklore of the Nob Hill area of the city. When the Cookes finally settled on the

Huntington as their favoured hotel, local shops were put on notice: running out of Dewar's White Label was serious, but nothing like as bad as having no Campbell's Scotch Broth on the shelves. VJ Groceries, run by Spiro and his extended Greek immigrant family, established a regular order of Cooke's favourite soup which was not generally available in San Francisco. Indeed, the hotel itself would sometimes be persuaded to ship large quantities of the stuff to New York when supplies ran short. Other friends were drawn into feeding the obsession. Jason de Montmorency, honorary treasurer of the National Arts Club in New York, remembers the day the soup first dried up: Cooke complained to Campbell's and was sent a voucher for tomato soup in compensation.

De Montmorency scoured the city to find alternative sources and eventually managed to arrange regular shipments, which he helped to unload at the Cookes' apartment. Jane, a notable cook herself, refused to help on the grounds that it showed such poor taste.

The end of Cooke's tenure at the *Guardian* came sooner than either he or his employers expected. Kenneth Clark had just completed the epic television series *Civilisation*. So dazzling had been its critical success that the BBC was urgently casting around for ways of capitalising on the public appetite for history that Clark's series had unearthed. Its producer, Michael Gill, was toying with the possibility that the history of the United States might be the perfect subject.

~

'I am not,' Cooke said repeatedly, 'a "whither America?" man.' Yet in the course of three decades, Cooke had accumulated more knowledge, and remembered more of what he'd accumulated, than almost anyone alive. It was the secret of his *Letter*s – the ability to make connections and to detect the patterns of life across the years. This talent had always been applied in the comparatively frivolous field of journalism, but somewhere at the back of his mind there may have lurked a sense that the resources of his memory bank were being wasted. He had not written the books he might have written. He had made no serious original contribution to academic study. Suddenly, out of the blue, came the chance to demonstrate that he was more than a mere scribbler.

A number of people, not surprisingly considering the success of the enterprise, are convinced that they thought of the idea first.

Michael Gill, the producer of *Civilisation*, says that it was he who came up with Cooke's name (in April 1969) as a possible presenter of a series on American history – an idea which had first occurred to him on a filming trip to Virginia with Kenneth Clark. He'd been casting about in the academic world and had briefly considered Norman Mailer, when he happened to read a transcript of a *Letter from America* in the *Listener*, on the subject of Eisenhower's funeral. Gill contacted the BBC's head of arts and features, Stephen Hearst, who pointed out that he'd mentioned Cooke's name a month earlier. Gill maintained that, in that case, it was only as one name among many and, what's more, it hadn't sunk in. Hearst remembers matters differently, claiming that Gill came up with another choice altogether and that he had to be dissuaded from taking on a young man recently arrived in the department – named Melvyn Bragg. It's a friendly dispute, but the upshot was the same in any case.

The problem was whether Cooke, with all his other commitments, could be persuaded to take part in a project which would take at least a year and probably longer. Gill had his doubts, but Hearst heard that Cooke happened to be staying in London and contacted him – in May 1970 – at the Dorchester. Hearst, after working with Cooke on a number of projects, felt he knew him well enough to apply some pressure: he rang Cooke and told him, 'Alistair, I think you've wasted your life.'

'How come?' came the reply.

'All that knowledge in those weekly instalments – what you need to do is a thirteen-part television series. I think there could be a wonderful book in it, too.'

Cooke's perspective emerged in an interview long afterwards for a publication called *Living Philosophies*: 'Stephen Hearst challenged me with his conviction that any writer just turned sixty was at the stage when he should be required to make a testament of his beliefs. If this idea carries a nudge of compulsion,' Cooke continued,

it is because Hearst is an idealist with the temperament of a headmaster and cannot bear the thought that anyone he intellectually respects should quit this life without turning in a final examination paper and committing himself to what Maugham, at just that age, called 'The Summing Up' of his philosophy and his beliefs about everything. 'Make a statement,' was Hearst's favourite command: 'you have lived in the United States for well over thirty years and it is high time you made a statement about it.'

To ideologues, mystics, parsons, party politicians, joiners and other *philosophes manqués*, this command no doubt sounds right and proper, almost an obligation of citizenship. But I am not an ideologue. I am not religious. I belong to no political party, not by any means from an indifference to politics: indeed, most of my life has been much engaged with politics and the societies of two countries. But, at an early age, I found that I was temperamentally more suited to the profession of a journalist, that is to say of a curious onlooker, than to any other.

For such reasons Cooke was initially non-committal and Hearst didn't want to risk using his friendship to extract a professional advantage, but a meeting with Michael Gill was agreed for the Thursday. It was a success. Cooke's diary note for that day read, 'Michael Gill of BBC to drinks . . . TV proposal,' and on the next line, in red ink, a later annotation: 'Ended in *America*!!!!!' There was a more formal gathering the next morning – 9 May – with a senior BBC executive and the idea was approved in outline. The following day, Cooke met Gill again and presented him with a copy of his *Letters* anthology, *Talk About America*. It was inscribed: 'With high hopes and trepidation.'

Cooke's first encounter with Gill is clearly engraved on his memory, as he told a previewer of the *America* series: 'There was a tentative knock at my door followed by a tall, handsome man with greying Byronic looks and an air of what I was later to learn was very deceptive gentleness. Gill arrived, puffed away on his pipe and generally acted like a priest about to handle Al Capone seeking his first instruction.' Well briefed by Hearst (whom Cooke described as 'a beguiling Viennese with the moral muscle of John Calvin'), Gill trotted out the dictum that a man of substance owed it to himself to distil his experience for a wider audience. Faced with 'a duty that would be scandalous to ignore, like refusing to take in your crippled old Mom,' he gave in. 'The trouble with Gill is that he can charm the birds out of the trees before they know that their flight pattern has already been determined for them,' he told the *Guardian* later.

On 23 June, a further diary item records 'Begin BBC *America* draft', though the first serious negotiations took place in July, when Gill travelled to New York to stay with the Cookes at Fifth Avenue and on Long Island. Gill remembers it as a fruitful period, during which Cooke discoursed about the subject vividly and enthusiastically and was instrumental in taking many of the core decisions which established the shape of the series. 'We had talked about doing the programmes thematically – the Dutch in America, the fate of the Indians and so on,' Gill recalls. 'Cooke insisted that the programmes should be chronological. That way, he said, you could hold the audience's attention from week to week. In fact he turned out to be brilliant at providing a trailer for what was coming in the following programme.' Cooke had strong feelings, too, about dramatisations: 'no actors, no wigs, no quill pens, no casting-bureau Jeffersons, Robert E. Lees, Eisenhowers.' Instead, 'We see lots of living Americans doing their thing – selling a cow in Illinois, selling bloomers on New York's Lower East Side, rehearsing the war alert on a submarine, bidding on the floor of the commodity exchange . . . ' Gill feels that Cooke was determined to stamp his thinking on *America*, partly to make up for the fact that somebody else had had the idea. A BBC document dated 24 September, with Cooke's brief digest of the thirteen programmes, demonstrates that most of his first-draft titles made it all the way through to the final programmes – 'Inventing a Nation', 'Gone West', 'The Firebell in the Night', 'The Huddled Masses'. By Cooke's own account, 'if you get the right title, everything will come into focus.'

The question remained – how would Cooke find time to work on *America*, with its lengthy filming trips and more or less open-ended commitment to writing and editing – and still fulfil his daily quota for the *Guardian*? And how much more problematical would the equation become when he became embroiled in writing a companion volume?

Alastair Hetherington knew immediately how the wind was likely to blow. As soon as he heard about the project at the end of the year, he wrote a graceful note to Cooke, predicting that 'American Civilisation' would have them all glued to their televisions on Sunday evenings. 'We might even get a colour set this time,' he added. He wondered, as unaggressively as possible, if – during filming – he might have time for an occasional article, just 'to show that you're still in some degree a *Guardian* man.' Writing to his colleagues at the same time, Hetherington was more realistic: the project would mean writing Cooke off for the autumn of 1970 and 'most of 1971'. However, 'if the series is a success, of course, we shall want to keep some link with him. Probably the series will be a great success. It's right up his street. Hence my enquiry about occasional articles in 1971.' Hetherington will not have been unduly shocked that it took Cooke six months to reply. The answer was that, given good notice, there was no reason why the *Guardian* link might not be preserved by occasional contributions filed on location.

The truth was that he felt unable to risk walking away from the newspaper which provided the bulk of his monthly salary. He hoped to be able to cling to his post by invoking all the leave he could muster and capitalising on a hint by Michael Gill that the first programmes might be finished more quickly than originally planned: 'Let's wait awhile, if you don't mind,' he wrote, 'before suggesting an adjustment of this year's salary. God knows, the way things are going in this country, we need every hundred penny piece.'

Thus Cooke managed to spin out his *Guardian* salary until the end of 1970. He signed off with his last 'Alistair Cooke's America' column on 28 December and shared the occasion with readers. 'When I joined the *Guardian* I was given to feel that I had been inducted into an order hardly less austere than the Franciscans: facts are sacred, comments free; think high, live plain; fight for the right (or left), keep the holiday short. Yet, as it must to all journalists, even the soul-savers, comes at last the sabbatical. It has come to me. From this day forth, for one year exactly, I shall be absent from these pages though you may be sure that some historic American happening (the death of a hero, the invention of a better mouse-trap) will bring me running back to base.' It probably made him feel better – that little phrase 'one year exactly': the comfort blanket would still be there when he'd finished. Cooke's pleadings even succeeded in extracting from the notoriously parsimonious *Guardian* accounts department the promise of a retainer. He would receive the equivalent of one and a half months' salary, for intermittent pieces during 1971.

'Intermittent' turned out to be an overstatement. There was a lyrical piece in March about the defeat of Muhammad Ali at the hands of Joe Frazier and very little else. In July, Hetherington was moved to complain to Cooke, 'It is rather sad to see you so little in the paper.' But Hetherington was already bowing to the inevitable. He told Cooke in July that Richard Scott was moving to Paris and that his place in Washington would be taken by Peter Jenkins. 'Inevitably,' he warned, 'Peter will want to be active on the major political stories, including the conventions . . . during the election and afterwards, he will want to move into areas that have traditionally been yours.' Tentatively he fingered the nettle. 'It would, in truth, be invaluable to have a forecast or foretaste of your own plans for next year. I suppose, however, that it would be realistic – especially after your year away on making the film – to assume that you won't be coming back to quite the same scale of activity as we once had. Do you in fact want to return to daily writing and reporting, or are you thinking more in terms of occasional commentaries and those special pieces on topics that attract your eye.'

Cooke's reply was typical. The letter, he told his editor, had touched on 'matters which I have been thinking about,' and he was 'eager to sit down and have a long talk with you'. If rupture was looming, let it be rupture on Cooke's terms. Three weeks later he was in London, speculating about the possibility of restarting his column in January 1972. Hetherington's record of the meeting comments wearily that it had been impossible to pin Cooke down on what could and couldn't be managed in between his filming commitments, though he thought that the message might have got through about how little the *Guardian* had to show for its retainer. If so, it was getting through slowly. A letter from Cooke in December remarked that he had checked the payments made: 'I think I'm right in saying that it comes to $2370, which is too much for the little I've been able to do.' Perhaps if he delivered a dozen or so pieces running into the New Year, they could call it quits? Thereafter, regretfully, it was clear that he wouldn't have time for anything before the end of June (1972). By Good Friday, he was writing that he hadn't forgotten the dozen promised pieces. 'I have now broken the back of all thirteen [*America*] scripts and in the light which is now blazing from the end of the tunnel, I hope to sit down and get some sage pieces off to you.' As an afterthought, he confided that he would not be available for the Conventions, either. The pieces never came: there was to be no return to the *Guardian* fold.

PART SEVEN

YEARS
OF
CONTENT

30

LIBERTY

Cooke could be blasé about the *Guardian* for one simple reason: much to his own surprise, he had begun to appreciate that *America* might finally make him rich. Left to his own devices, he could easily have let the opportunity slip, driven by diffidence to accept gratefully a flat-rate fee for each programme. But his lawyer had other ideas.

Irving Cohen described himself as a theatrical lawyer and, over the years, he had represented film stars, actors, writers, producers and directors, from Rodgers and Hammerstein to Ingrid Bergman. He had first advised Cooke informally over the contract for *Around the World in Fifty Years*, but this was a project of a very different order. Cooke explained the background. He told Cohen that Kenneth Clark had received no great financial benefit from the series *Civilisation* and its accompanying book. Could Cohen do better for him? The lawyer couldn't believe the deal Cooke was being offered. 'It was a joke,' he said, the memory still raising a smile twenty-five years later. 'Alistair alerted me to the fact the BBC was always short of funds and that I should realise that it was not a commercial organisation. I told him, "I'll bear that in mind." Cooke was demonstrating such charitable loyalty that I didn't like to argue with him.'

Nothing happened quickly. The BBC were busy arranging for Time-Life to co-finance the series in the United States and Cohen – with little direct experience of public-service broadcasting – decided to feel his way into the discussions. He learned that Time-Life were claiming certain rights as their part of the deal and, after some initial jostling for position, there was a contract 'summit meeting' in New York in the winter of 1971. The BBC sent over a large team: Cohen remembers travelling to the location in a snowstorm and finding himself confronted by a dozen or so people, including Time-Life's representative Peter Roebeck. 'They seated me at the end of the table and every other seat was taken. It felt like a peace conference and I remember thinking – surely nothing can be accomplished here, with so many people.' Before he had opened his mouth, one of the BBC group began to lecture him: 'You have to understand that we are not one of your American television networks and therefore we have a completely different payment structure.' Since the series had no commercial sponsorship, the spokesman went on, it would be like the arrangements – say – for the American PBS, the Public Broadcasting System.

'What if you do get a sponsor?' Cohen inquired. 'Don't you think we should consider the possibility and set a rate for that?'

Instead of quibbling, as he'd anticipated, the BBC lawyers said they were quite happy in principle to have a separate pay structure which would be triggered if *America* won any commercial backing. What figures did Cohen have in mind? He began to realise that this was no ordinary negotiation. 'We can talk about figures,' he suggested, 'but let me tell you what my philosophy is in cases like this. There should be a guarantee – and an overage.' That meant that if the programme was sponsored Cooke would receive, on top of his basic fee, a percentage of the profits *over* a predetermined level. Again, there was no demur from around the table. Having established the ground rules, Cohen had it in mind to start the bidding reasonably low, in deference to Cooke's warnings about the BBC's financial state. Once again, he was taken aback by the generosity of the Corporation's offer. He suggested that Cooke would get a basic $5000 for each programme, far more than Clark had received for *Civilisation*. This guaranteed sum would cover only Britain and the United States. Every other country to which the series was sold would attract a further payment – perhaps $500 or $750. That was impressive enough. What elevated the deal into a different sphere was the 'overage': if sponsors were found, Cooke would be able to claim ten per cent of all the subsequent gross profits, once the BBC had recouped its production costs.

Evidently, the BBC did not believe that sponsorship was likely and in any case had insufficient experience to work out what its consequences might be. Such percentage deals were relatively common in Hollywood, but only after the moviemakers had reclaimed not just their production costs, but a whole range of other charges, including distribution and advertising. Then a star or a producer might be able to claim a share of the residual profits, but even then, never as much as ten per cent. It depended, of course, on there being a commercial sponsor: and before long, Time-Life announced that they'd found one. The Xerox Corporation decided to invest $4 million in *America* and the overage pay-scale was triggered. The BBC preferred not to use the word 'sponsorship', but Cooke didn't care what it was called: in the acknowledgements section of the book of the series he singled out the company for special thanks – 'Xerox, the only sponsor I know willing to let a fifty-minute programme run fifty minutes, without wrenching intervals for the contemplation of the transverse colon or a fluid with the cleaning properties of sulphuric acid.' Thus he praised the company's respect for artistic integrity, though he might have added a few words on the peripheral benefits which their involvement brought him. Irving Cohen put the matter colourfully: 'The films made serious money. They were sold everywhere you can think of. Once Xerox picked up the costs, everything else was gravy – and Alistair was in on it.'

If the film contracts were easy for Cohen, the book of *America* was a very different story. Cohen had enjoyed Cooke's satisfaction with the film deal, but he knew that it wouldn't provide a big enough windfall to satisfy his client's underlying ambition: 'What Alistair was really dreaming about was resigning from the *Guardian* and never having to meet that deadline again. He kept asking me when I thought he could afford to do it. I told him, "Alistair, it's a judgement you'll have to make." ' In the initial negotiations there had been no detailed discussion of any ancillary sources of revenue. Cohen had simply included in the contract a standard clause – 'all rights not granted are reserved to the author'. The word 'book' was not specifically mentioned. In due course, however, the BBC approached Cooke and told him that a Time-Life subsidiary (Little, Brown) intended to publish the scripts. When Cohen heard about the approach, he insisted on knowing what precisely was planned. If it were literally a question of the film scripts being transcribed, either in the *Listener* magazine or in book form, there could be no objection: anything beyond that would entail new payments under that catch-all section in the contract. It soon became clear that what was being proposed would mean substantial extra work for Cooke and Cohen was adamant that the BBC had surrendered those rights.

The natural place to turn was to Cooke's long-time publisher, Alfred Knopf. Cohen made contact with one of the senior editors, Tony Schulte, and proposed a simple – but audacious – deal. If Knopf were prepared to guarantee Cooke half a million dollars over ten years, they could publish the book. Cohen told them, 'You won't have to do any marketing: the television series will sell the book for you.'

To begin with, Schulte was incredulous: an advance of half a million dollars? It was completely unheard of. 'What if it's a failure?' he inquired.

Cohen replied, 'How can it fail? Look at Kenneth Clark: nothing sells a book like TV.' He estimated that sales of half a million were a perfectly reasonable prospect, which would make the offer realistic rather than spectacular. It was, none the less, a gamble.

Although Cohen had convinced himself that he was right, no one had much experience of the interrelation between books and television series. The idea that a publisher would commit himself to such hefty royalty payments required a leap of faith. However, Knopf knew Cooke well: his previous books had done decent business without a major advertising effort and Cooke had been a well-known public figure since the *Omnibus* days. Eventually, Schulte and Cohen struck a deal for a minimum $400,000 over eight years.

That's when the trouble started. When the BBC, Time-Life and Little, Brown heard about the arrangement they were furious, fuming that Cooke had no right to sell his book elsewhere: they had assumed that they would be able to repeat the publishing success of *Civilisation* at their leisure. Cohen recollects talk of action through the courts to block the deal. An emissary from the BBC was sent round to the lawyer's office to press the case and the meeting was decidedly confrontational: Cohen says he told them, quite simply, that the rights belonged to Cooke and that was that. A nasty transatlantic impasse developed, in which both sides became more deeply entrenched. Eventually, after several months of argument and in the depths of the winter of 1972, when the filming had already begun, a crisis meeting was called in London: Cooke, Cohen and Schulte flew over from New York to fight their corner and found the city immersed in the gloom of a power shortage caused by the miners' strike. The mood inside was no brighter.

It took a Cohen brainwave to break the logjam. He suggested that a proportion of Cooke's fifteen per cent royalty on each copy – two and a half per cent, as it turned out – would simply be handed over to Time-Life to make up for their concession of the publishing rights. Cooke readily agreed, since the overall figures were potentially so huge that he could scarcely contemplate them and relinquishing a small chunk of this mythical money seemed the least he could do. Schulte chipped in an extra per cent or two – quite happy that the new arrangement would cost Alfred Knopf little more than the old one. And Time-Life probably recognised that it was perhaps better to get something from the deal, rather than prolong a costly negotiation which might leave them with nothing.

The most interesting position was that of the BBC, whose representatives executed a subtle volte-face as it became clear which way the financial and legal winds were blowing. Having started in the opposition camp, they gradually edged round to the Cooke/Cohen axis. Cohen explained, 'They were anxious to publish the book themselves in Britain and if it turned out that we did indeed have the rights, they needed us on their side.' Honour, up to a point, was satisfied and Cooke had a deal. Knopf would publish in the Americas and certain other specified locations. The BBC would have the British market, though they, too, would pay Cooke fifteen per cent of the proceeds. Cohen was elated. 'If this thing works out,' he told Cooke, 'there'll be no talking to you. You'll be like a rock star.' Cooke brushed the remark aside. None of those present on that dank winter's day could have guessed how well Alistair Cooke's *America* would do.

There was a great deal of work to turn the scripts into the finished book. As Cooke explained in its introduction, 'Film has to be direct and immediate, at the expense of reservations and intellectual subtlety. Film as history is therefore inevitably oversimple. In all, the book is about four times the length of the spoken television scripts.' The programme content was not only expanded, but also reorganised, so that the finished volume had a character all of its own – oral history, couched in accessible, popular language and with none of the feel of a quick television rewrite. But it had to be done in haste. Chuck Elliott, who had just arrived at Knopf from Life's own publishing department, found Cooke a fast and fluent writer. His only reservation was that he felt the prose on the page didn't look, sometimes, as good as it sounded. As they raced to get the book out in time for Christmas there were some fraught moments: Elliott's re-working of Cooke's first draft was delivered to the Huntington Hotel and – according to Elliott – caused a minor eruption of authorial rage. It took a series of meetings in New York to restore the equilibrium between the two. Elliott adjusted himself to Cooke's tendency to 'cut corners with the history'; Cooke's knack, he felt, was to 'make a good story out of something without distorting the facts, but pushing them a little further than they'd normally go in the hands of someone more scholarly'. He summed it up as 'extremely skilful historical story-telling'. Space was even found for eight of Cooke's own photographs – all landscapes – to illustrate the introduction.

From the start, the book of *America* was a publishing phenomenon: reprints tumbled over each other into shops desperate for copies and sales soared way above any of the figures mentioned in the contracts. The first printing (120,000 in the United States and 50,000 in Britain) disappeared so quickly that the shops were bare by 1 December – a potential disaster for the 1973 Christmas market. An advertisement in April of the following year was headed, in huge type, 'Back in stock at last!' It included a tabulation of sales to date – '1st printing: 120,000 copies – sold out! 2nd printing: 50,000 copies – sold out! . . . ' A total of 335,000 copies were already on the market within six months of publication. On book-signing tours, minions were dispatched from big stores to gather up all the copies they could find, so urgent was public demand, and the money poured in. The $400,000 guarantee over eight years turned into $2 million well before the eight years were up. At the agreed rate of $50,000 a year, Cooke would have had to wait forty years to collect all his royalties. Cohen arranged for Knopf to release the money more quickly in return for a specially reduced royalty on Cooke's next book.

America remained in the top ten of hardback bestsellers for two full years (dislodging *The Joy of Sex* in the process) and, with con-sistent sales over the next two decades, it became one of the most enduring successes in publishing history. Irving Cohen, when asked to check the US figures in January 1996, discovered that the total had reached 1,900,000, with the book still in print. It sold well in Britain, too, where the BBC's publishing arm had been on the sidelines of the earlier contractual shenanigans: once Time-Life had reached agree-ment with Knopf, their contract was straightforward and those involved remember it as being settled with a single exchange of letters. Peter Campbell was assigned to help in the book's design and the choice of photographs. He concedes that the concept of making money from spin-off books was new and uncharted territory within the BBC – a way of off-setting production costs, rather than as a commercial exercise in itself. In that respect, there had been no real sense of grievance at the deal which was finally struck. For once, the BBC was happy, too.

~

With one deal, Alistair Cooke was free. Cohen sat back, content in the knowledge that he had turned his client from being 'easy pickings for anybody' into someone aware of his own worth. There was no immediate torrent of money, but *America* was the end of the road for the *Guardian*. Alastair Hetherington informed his colleagues in July 1972 that, because of the book, any idea that they might squeeze some work out of Cooke that winter could be abandoned. On 31 August, with the Cohen film contract safely in the bank and the book contract already on the table, Cooke wrote to his editor, 'I have come to a decision: which is that at my age, when the swishing of the Old Man with the scythe can so often be mistaken for the east wind, it is high time I stopped doing daily journalism. Twenty-seven years is enough. It has been a wonderful fling and I'm quite sure that I would never have kept it up with any other paper than the *Guardian*.' He and Jane wanted to spend more time at Nassau Point, in San Francisco and in London. 'Anyway, here I go resigning. I shall do some pieces for you through the rest of the year. And when some hero of mine kicks the bucket, I may well offer to write his epitaph.' As he wrote to his son, Johnny, immediately afterwards, retirement would not affect his BBC talks 'which I love doing and which, considered as a journalistic chore, are about as strenuous as falling out of bed.'

The *Guardian* was left to prepare a proper farewell party, though inevitably even this corporate gesture of goodwill caused trouble. Hetherington sent Cooke a list of guests for a putative lunch in London, including some of the paper's Board of Directors, foreign editors past and present and a group of friends – the golf correspondent, Pat Ward-Thomas and A.P. Wadsworth's widow Janet. Parts of the list rankled with the guest of honour. He didn't fancy dining with people he didn't know, 'those whose *Guardian* is demonstrably not my *Guardian*'.

Cooke's list comprised mainly men and women with whom he'd worked – Ward-Thomas, John Cole, David Gray, Hella Pick, Richard Scott. He had no desire to spend 'a nervous evening with many anonymous faces'. He apologised, 'If it's all too difficult, please skip it. One other thing – a private room at a *gemütlich* restaurant would be fun, don't you think – I have suggestions.' And in case Hetherington was toying with the possibility of fixing a meal at the club to which Cooke had recently been elected as a life member (for 'services in literature or science'), he counselled against it: 'Very shyly I pass on the universal belief, which I share, that the Athenaeum food still immortalises English club food between the wars.' Above all, he would prefer 'a merry evening with congenial, not to say beloved friends.'

Hetherington, with the tact he had nurtured so meticulously in years of dealing with his troublesome star, wrote back that 'of course, the proper place to hold it would be the Friends' Meeting House in Euston Road, with soft drinks served. That would be in keeping with the frugal and non-conformist spirit which hovers over us.' After much correspondence, a compromise panel of guests was agreed and Cooke even managed to enjoy the evening at L'Escargot restaurant – having successfully argued that a lunch-time function was not ideal for a man who never ate lunch.

Like many large organisations, the *Guardian* neglected to remove Cooke's name from the staff list for some time. One of the last items in his personnel file is a memo from Alastair Hetherington in December 1973, after he had been asked whether the file should be closed. 'I have regularly asked [Cooke] to resume writing and he has regularly said that he will do so. In practice nothing comes and I do not think we shall ever seriously have him on our books again.' The parting was not altogether sweet on Cooke's side, either. In 1982, Harry Jackson, working for the *Guardian* in Manchester, suggested that Cooke might jump at the chance of writing a piece on the fiftieth anniversary of Roosevelt's first election victory. He refused. Rather puzzled, Jackson persisted. 'Is it that you don't want to write about FDR, or that you don't want to write about yourself?' he asked. 'No,' Cooke replied. 'I don't want to write for the *Guardian*.'

Why such bitterness? He always told anyone who asked that he never received a penny by way of pension from the *Guardian* and that if it hadn't been for *America* – his annuity – 'he would have been begging PBS for an announcer's job'.

~

There is no question that Cooke's thirteen-part television series,

America – a Personal History, is the highest and most visible landmark in a career with many peaks. It absorbed much of his time for the two and a half years between the start of work on the film scripts to the completion of the book. Only the *Letter from America* survived unscathed among his other commitments. The basic shape of the enterprise – thirteen one-hour programmes – was established early on: and so too were its radical pretensions. Instead of starting American history with the arrival of the *Mayflower* in 1620, he was determined to pay proper respect to those who had preceded the Pilgrim Fathers – the native American Indians, the French and the Spanish. The *Mayflower* doesn't appear until page seventy-six of the book. When he previewed the series for the American 'TV Guide', he warned that some viewers might be shocked by this historical blasphemy: 'The series begins in New Mexico, with a tribe of the original Americans who live there today, much as they did a thousand years ago. And it ends with the two lonely guys who descend to one of our Minutemen silos and have on hand two keys that would trigger all the missiles around the world. If they ever used them, it would, naturally, be the end of American history and much else besides.'

The underlying philosophy was ambitious, too. In the introduction to the accompanying book, he described his frequent journeys backwards and forwards across the continent, armed with the excellent guidebooks written 'by penurious writers and local historians' enlisted by FDR's Works Projects Administration (WPA) during the Depression. This had given him what Theodore Roosevelt said every President should have, namely, 'a sense of continent'. Drawing on recollections of his travels and a wide reading in American history, he had then jotted down a list of places associated with memorable (if sometimes unfamiliar) events – 'Catherine, Kansas (the first planting of Turkey Red wheat); the Humboldt Sink (the cruellest ordeal of the Gold Rush); Newfane, Vermont (the epitome of native New England architecture)' and so on and on. No wonder Michael Gill was so excited by what Cooke wished to bring to the project – not just a story, but also the locations whereby it might be illustrated, all rolled into one.

Cooke did not set out to compete with the 'rafts of formidable and brilliant historians', nor with the Cassandras whose dire prognostications filled the columns of newspapers and magazines. It would be an honest chronology: 'Whether it was to succeed or fail, it seemed to me a good, though tortuous, thing to attempt: to try to say what is moving about the American experience over four hundred years at a time when that experience is either forgotten, badly taught, or shamelessly sentimentalised; and to recall what is tough and good about the American system of Government at a time when that system is poorly understood and, in some high and low places, perilously close to corruption and betrayal.' Those words were written at the end of the project, after the Watergate scandal had broken. But his disenchantment was deeply embedded much earlier. Cooke started work on *America* with his esteem for his adopted home at a low point. He hated the 1960s. One of his last articles for the *Guardian* had inveighed against a decade which had brought assassinations, hopeless foreign wars, racial polarisation and social disorder. 'Other nations have their hippies and their rock culture, their drugged youth and their "alienated" students, the Babylonian heritage of the sixties, plunging its unhandleable populations into headier and headier materialism. Only America has suffered the traumatic disillusion, in ten short years, of losing its status as the beneficent leader of the world and turning into a giant, writhing in its own coils, suspect, frightened and leaderless.'

The programmes would be made by four different film directors: Gill himself took responsibility for five episodes, with the rest divided between Ann Turner, Tim Slessor and David Heycock. With military precision, film-crews would work their way across the country, following the logic of a particular programme and trying to make best use of their presenter's time. Filming started on 5 October 1970. It happened to be John Byrne Cooke's thirtieth birthday.

~

John had found himself a satisfying niche. Thanks to his association with the music producer Albert Grossman, he had become the road manager for a group called Big Brother and the Holding Company, fresh from a sensational appearance at the Monterey Pop Festival. The sensation had been created by the lead singer, a young performer of blues and soul, Janis Joplin. Nobody had ever heard a white girl sing with such raw emotion and she was in huge demand for rock concerts, especially on the West Coast. Hence the need for somebody capable of keeping a grip on an ill-disciplined collection of musicians with a weakness for drink and drugs. John Cooke, according to Laura

Joplin in her account of her sister's life, became indispensable.

Over the next two years, as Janis Joplin became a superstar, she began to live her life increasingly close to the edge. She left Big Brother and set up a new band in her own image. She took to appearing on-stage with a whisky bottle in her hand – a symbol of her off-stage existence. The gulf between the glamorous and sexy public figure and the tortured artistic soul made life almost impossible for those she worked with. In the autumn of 1969, John Cooke had had enough. With two months of a tour still to run, he announced that he was retiring because 'it just isn't fun any more'. Then, in April 1970, the singer's state of mind and health seemed to be improving. She had found a new group of musicians with whom she felt comfortable and was suddenly stricken by the need to have her old road manager back. After much heart searching, John Cooke gave in, convinced that she had genuinely cleaned up her act. There was a successful summer performing across North America, before the entourage reached Los Angeles to record a new album.

On the other side of the country, the *America* team was assembling for the first day's work: Cooke, Michael Gill, the cameraman Ken MacMillan, his assistant Colin Deehan and the sound recordist Malcolm Webberley – the nucleus of a shifting team, which would live together most intimately for more than a year. 'The first day,' Cooke recalled in a later *Letter from America*, 'we were very courteous with each other; and wary, in the way of boxers hearing the first bell and stalking each other at a respectful distance till they discover, or think they discover, loopholes in the other feller's defences.' They were to film at the Old South Meeting House, cradle of the American Revolution in Cooke's eyes, where the local populace retreated in 1770 after what became known as the Boston Massacre: Cooke was due to explain the circumstances of the assault by British soldiers in a sequence which would form part of the fourth programme. Geography and logistics took precedence over strict chronology.

They buckled down to their first pieces-to-camera. Cooke had advised Gill that he would not need a teleprompter, confident that the techniques he had learned during ten years of *Omnibus* would not fail him. Gill had his doubts, but Cooke's confidence was well placed. Even the lengthiest speech of that first day – lasting one minute and thirty-five seconds – was executed with the immaculate, yet conversational, delivery which characterised the weekly *Letter*. He stood in front of one of the building's clean white pillars with the hint of a dark gold-framed picture to one side, his silver hair unfeasibly smooth, perfectly turned out in dark-blue blazer, understated striped tie and neat pocket handkerchief: Cooke the history teacher, in the guise of story-teller, performing faultlessly. It was not a simple piece: it ranged from the competing British and American stories about how the massacre was provoked and wound its serpentine way to a conclusion embracing more modern events. The British version of the old story, he said, was that a young redcoat was clubbed to the ground, slipped on the ice as he rose and accidentally fired his musket: in American eyes, it was nothing short of murder. 'What happened next has been decided ever since by the passion and the prejudice of whichever side you were on when you first heard about it. I'm afraid that part is true, because that's history. Not what happened, but what people convinced themselves must have happened.'

It was an impressive technical achievement and, in the process, it also expounded much of Cooke's philosophy of history – the notion that there were no absolute truths and that, since every party to a historical event was likely to interpret it differently, his series was of necessity a *personal* history. Gill was impressed. Not only could Cooke learn and recite long passages quickly, he could also change them at will. If the director, having heard the statement, decided that a section could be removed or that a particular thought needed to be developed, Cooke would simply reformulate his words and deliver the new version with equal composure. They finished their work that day with some satisfaction. Cooke went back to his hotel, with the vague idea that he should make a birthday phone call to his son. For the second time in his life, he was stopped in his tracks by a billboard on a Boston Street: 'JANIS JOPLIN DEAD'. The singer's body, he read, had been discovered by her road manager, John Cooke.

Frantically Cooke telephoned Los Angeles, but in the chaos created by Joplin's demise, messages failed to get through. John himself was caught up in the aftermath of what he had seen at the Landmark Hotel. Janis Joplin had retreated to her room the day before and injected herself with heroin, which turned out to be ten times stronger than she'd expected. Shortly afterwards she fell, struck her head on the bedside table and collapsed. She lay beside the bed, undiscovered, until late the following afternoon. Only when she failed to turn up for a recording session was John alerted. Laura Joplin took up the story. 'When John saw Janis lying on the floor, he approached her, holding out a hand as if to shake her awake. One touch of her cold, firm flesh was all he needed to realise that he would not need to call her name again.' It was a traumatic experience, compounded in the next few hours by a fantastic explosion of media interest. A stash of heroin first disappeared, then was found in the room – there was talk of suicide, or even some ill-defined conspiracy. The gaudy and scurrilous coverage ensured that, by the time Cooke finally got through to his son, he was in a state of some distress. 'I was very touched by the phone call,' John remembers.

～

Throughout the filming for *America*, Cooke was the local expert – the source of many of the ideas and much of the planning: it was an onerous responsibility and a quick way of dispelling any notions of his infallibility. At the end of the first week, the plan was to record New England in its full fall glory and, as a fervent amateur meteorologist he chose the time with care. 'The next few days – the only days we could spare from a very tight shooting schedule – they had warm, humid fog in the mornings so dense you couldn't have photographed an elephant at twenty paces. When the fog burned off there was a hot haze and the temperature went up to 84 degrees – a seventy-five year record. The maples were already burning up and turning russet before they'd gone their usual scarlet.' They abandoned the exercise and headed for the next location. The following year, 1971, the crew was back, but the result was still disappointing. Only in 1972, with the last frame shot and the films in the cutting room, did nature in Vermont resume its habitual pattern – 'as far as you could see a circle of scarlet and gold, with cool inky clumps of evergreens here and there'. By then, it was too late.

From the spring of 1970 onwards sporadically, and from the autumn of that year in earnest, Michael Gill and his team leap-frogged each other, filming sequences or carrying out recces for subsequent films. Ann Turner, who began as Gill's assistant producer and ended by directing two films herself, kept a diary of her travels and the progress of the wider enterprise:

28/7/71   AC in London
2/8/71   AC reviews rough-cut Progs 5 and 7

12/8/71	Commentary recording Prog 3
13/8/71	Commentary recording Prog 6
19/8/71	AC 10 a.m. in cutting room(!) [The exclamation mark is Turner's]
23/8/71	AC shooting with David Heycock in UK
30/8/71	Prog final mix
4/9/71	Prog 3 final mix
6/9/71	AT [Turner herself] to Boston for camera recce
10/9/71	Meeting with AC chez lui re Prog 1
11/9/71	AT travels to New Orleans
13–14/9/71	New Orleans filming (Prog 1)
15/9/71	AC filmed in bar New Orleans
16/9/71	Travel to Washington, drive to Baltimore
17/9/71	AC sequences on Mencken.

And so on. It required discipline and flexibility from all concerned, not to mention a great deal of hard work. Cooke covered 100,000 miles and stayed in eighty-seven motels, enduring in the process 'innumerable days of standing around waiting, waiting, waiting – for the rain to stop, for the light to clear, for the jets to pass over, for emergency generators to arrive, for the tourists to stop strolling, for the truck on a hill across the river to change gear, for house historians with a corner on their specialty to get lost.' Or, as he wrote in a letter to Johnny on 30 April 1971, apologising for the long gap since his last missive, 'In the last month, I have filmed in places whose immense importance to even the sketchiest narrative of US history you will instantly recognise: Oil Creek, Pennsylvania; the Morgan Library; Bluffton, Georgia; Crump, Tennessee (the Battle of Shiloh); John D. Rockefeller's bedroom; Lincoln's bedroom in the White House; the Hancock Building in Chicago, also the freightyards, the stockyards, the grain market, the river; Valley Forge, Massachusetts . . . .' The list was interminable. 'You name it, we shot it,' Cooke told his son. He was looking forward to finishing Programme Eight – 'Money on the Land'. 'Of course, you will guess that the eighth programme is only the fourth we have finished. Nothing in this business is done in sequence.'

He also thanked John for providing some details on native Indian history (a subject in which the latter had been taking a keen academic interest for three years) but felt compelled to add, 'I'll let you know in a couple of months or so how much of my distillation of your notes ever got into the script. Every day I see my pearls flung before swine – an inevitable accompaniment of making a film, it seems.' A little later, in September, after John had spent two days on location in the California gold country, he upgraded the warning: 'I certainly hope you have a carbon of that vast and enlightening screed you wrote me, but you may be sure I shall keep it. I'm especially grateful for your exposition of Indian leadership, a point that had puzzled me when you first brought it up. . . . My gratitude for your helpful research is unbounded. Don't feel cheated when you find that this whole TV form requires me to say in ninety seconds of synch what generations of scholars have said in twelve volumes.' He evidently wanted to let his son down lightly and did so with some grace. 'The merciless requirements (a visual location, a clear argument) act very much the way a sentence of death struck Dr Johnson: "it wonderfully concentrates the mind." I manage to do fairly well with the simplest of words in the shortest time, mainly because of my long practice at the bench of the radio talk.'

He needn't have worried. The very business of establishing this professional relationship with his father was certainly a matter of profound satisfaction to John, who was still trying to recover from his Los Angeles experiences. Nor was the research effort wasted. In 1985 John Byrne Cooke published the first of a series of minutely observed novels of life in the Wild West – *The Snowblind Moon* – a 700 page epic rich in historical detail.

~

Those who worked with Cooke during the making of *America* were pleasantly surprised by how adaptable he was. Other 'stars' they had worked with caused far more trouble: the tensions which might have arisen from a sixty-four-year-old presenter and a team whose average age was thirty rarely materialised. Cooke was prepared to rough it in low-grade motels if necessary: one Hollywood establishment called the Saharan provided some unplanned entertainment by way of a police raid on the prostitutes operating at the other end of the corridor. Cooke was perfectly happy provided that nobody tried to shake him from his basic routine: not too many early starts, no formal lunch, (which sometimes led to complaints from the recordist, Malcolm Webberley, about rumbling stomachs on the sound-track) and a good long evening of food, whisky and chat. Ken MacMillan recalls Cooke's motto – 'Never accept a drink before 6 p.m., nor refuse one after.'

One other stricture involved the old maxim about working with animals. While Cooke was trying to do a shot walking through a woodland glade near Susie's home in Vermont, her dog – called Thurber – tagged along behind him. The crew thought it would enhance the sequence if the dog was allowed to feature in the shot. Cooke would have none of it and the dog was banished. On location, he kept charge of the airline timetable, too, partly to ensure that he could slip away once a week for the recording of a *Letter from America*. Diane Sullivan remembers discussing with her colleagues a sudden change of plan and wondering how they could best get to New Orleans in a hurry. 'Without looking up from his typewriter, he would say – "Delta flight xxx, change at Atlanta" and carry on with his work.' Michael Gill, who spent as much time on the road with Cooke as anyone, had few complaints. 'We travelled tourist class and had a deal with a motel chain to keep costs down.' Privately, as the man responsible for the budget, he was said to suspect that costs tended to rise whenever he turned his back. The highest-voltage working relationship was between Cooke and Ann Turner. He regarded her as academically accomplished – but stubborn. They would argue over points of historical exactitude – whether it was right, for instance, to film a recreated palisade at Williamsburg, Virginia without admitting it was a fake – and Cooke was once moved to invite her to come round to his side of the camera if she was so sure of her facts.

Such sparring was the exception. The main hazard for them all was that Alistair would suddenly remember a restaurant in a strange town where he had once eaten twenty years before. Once the place had been tracked down, there would be a lateish meal, followed by a review of the day's proceedings and the prospects for the next day. Then Cooke would suggest strolling back to the hotel to help the digestion, oblivious of the need for an early start in the morning. There was no question about who did most of the talking: one cameraman is reputed to have warned a director newly arrived on the team, 'You'd better be a very articulate listener.' The only serious exception to his unquestioning acceptance of cheap and cheerful accommodation came in San Francisco. There Cooke stayed in the Huntington Hotel, one of the 'big four' establishments on Nob Hill, where he was treated like visiting royalty.

So faithful was he to the Huntington and it to him, that he started to enjoy special privileges. One day he arrived to find that his usual quarters had been re-decorated in exotic pink silk. He was displeased and showed it. 'But Mr Cooke', the concierge protested, 'you're only the second person to experience the new décor. The first was Richard Nixon and he loved it.' That settled matters and the Cookes' bags were removed to a suite on the top floor. They never tried another room and in due course Number 1204, with fabulous views across the city, was renamed 'The Alistair Cooke Suite'.

Otherwise, there was no class distinction to break up the *America* team spirit – indeed the series led directly to the marriage of the cameraman Ken MacMillan and the production assistant Diane Sullivan. Typically, as well as Cooke and the director and his PA, the cameraman and his number two, there might be a grip, a sound recordist, a fixer and an electrician – who would bring in extra help when required.

On one occasion, the *North Shore* newspaper in Massachusetts wrote a glowing account of the filming at the Nurse House, an historic building in Danvers, Massachusetts, home of one of the victims of the Salem witch-hunt. It records the BBC's first approach. The curators, Mr and Mrs Raymond Swinnerton, told how 'out of the blue one day, two young ladies came to the door asking in delightful English accents if they could see the house. They signed the guest-book as Ann Turner and Sally Evans, British Broadcasting System [sic].'

Some time later the crew rolled up in a caravan of cars, including 'a nice quiet man in a white shirt and grey slacks' looking for somewhere to change. 'Of course it was the famous Alistair Cooke,' sighed the smitten Mrs Swinnerton. She found the visitors a 'close-knit group working hard and well together, knowing precisely what they wanted and enjoying the doing of it', and marvelled at the fact that Cooke was made to repeat seven times his walk from the field towards the house. As the BBC invasion came to an end, the Swinnertons noted that the 'English girls were looking forward to doing their washing at the nearest laundromat' before moving on to the next location.

The report also gives a hint of Cooke's working methods. 'Alistair Cooke came out wearing an informal kind of English-y sweater for the camera,' it quotes Mrs Swinnerton as saying. She watched the brief discussion between Cooke and Ann Turner at her kitchen table: then, 'Alistair sat down right there and typed for about twenty minutes and that was his script. A few minutes more of talk and bingo, they were ready to shoot.' This relaxed attitude to the final script was in marked contrast to the way Kenneth Clark had operated. Michael Gill described how Clark would write a 6,000-word essay which formed the basis of an episode of *Civilisation*. Then, on location, he would be required to adapt his words to fit the circumstances on the ground, which he did meticulously – and although he sometimes had to repeat the exercise in the cutting rooms the result was always recognisably in line with his original thesis.

Cooke's approach was far more relaxed. He provided a series of ideas – vignettes, Gill calls them – which formed the bones of a programme but not its final shape. Gill described the relationship in a *Guardian* feature: 'If the narrator is off the screen too long, it turns into a different kind of programme, a conventional travelogue. Cooke has to keep coming in to emphasise that it's America seen by him, not his view of it. The result, in a way, is a lot of mini-films within each film.'

Gill remembers being offered anecdotes by Cooke: for example, 'I once knew a man whose entry in *Who's Who in America* began, "Born March 8th, 1841, Boston. Captain 20th Massachusetts volunteers, wounded in the breast at Balls Bluff, in the heel at Fredericksburg, in the neck at Antietam." He survived to become the most distinguished jurist in the English-speaking world. He was Justice Oliver Wendell Holmes.' It was up to Gill to find a way of introducing this story into the Civil War film – and to check the precise details of place names and dates, which were sometimes at variance with Cooke's confident memory.

The final details were often left until the eve of shooting a sequence, or even (in the case of the Nurse House) to the day itself. Every programme, therefore, was different. There were parallels with the way Cooke constructed the *Letter from America*: the script was not imposed on the place and people, it adapted itself with considerable flexibility to what turned up. Ann Turner and the researcher Sally Evans would sometimes fix new locations for a particular sequence while they were on the road, because the need only emerged once shooting had begun. One of Turner's strongest memories is of Cooke sitting at some kitchen table, pounding away at his Olivetti typewriter, reorganising a story because the cameraman wanted his shot to pan from left to right, not right to left. Gill's assessment is that Cooke was simply a fantastic story-teller: 'He had the best sense of timing of anybody I worked with. He might play a piece on the piano eight times, but at the moment he paused, picked up a glass and looked at the camera, it was always the correct moment for maximum impact. He was a great performer, where Clark was a great writer who had to make himself perform.'

This did not mean that there were never disagreements. Because each programme was more fluid, much more was left to the director in the cutting room and, in February 1972, Michael Gill sat down late one night to confess his doubts about the structure of the programme on early American history. 'I'm sorry to tell you', he wrote to Cooke, 'that despite some felicitous moments from you and some very striking visual material, it doesn't work. Our worst yet. It just won't do as an opening film as it stands at the moment.' Among Gill's anxieties were that there were 'lots of interesting small observations' which didn't quite add up and that the commentary was 'too slight for the scale of the material' and failing to 'live up to the grandeur of the theme' of what Cooke had decided to call the 'New Found Land'.

Such setbacks were perhaps a natural function of a series growing organically from those enticing historical vignettes: the solution, in this case, was for Cooke to provide a new opening, making use of his own study overlooking Central Park: 'You know, when I told an old Southerner, a friend of mine, that I was going to try and tell my version of American history in thirteen hours, he said: "Better talk fast, boy." So we ought to begin with the simple, colossal question, who was the first white man to discover America, which incidentally was named after a Florentine businessman and promoter, who promoted himself so well as to get his name attached to a continent. He was Amerigo Vespucci.' And they were on their way.

Generally, despite occasional rumours to the contrary, Cooke and Gill got on well enough, considering the intensity of their working relationship over such a long period. Sir John Drummond, later director of the Edinburgh Festival and the Proms, knew both men well as one of the BBC arts executives in charge of *America*. Gill, in Drummond's judgement, had moved so swiftly from *Civilisation* to *America* that he found it hard to adjust to a very different sort of presenter. Cooke was 'a working journalist who looked at things and spotted the detail from which he could generalise. Clark, on the other hand, came with his mind made up, as if he'd been considering the matter for about forty years and was ready to make the quintessential statement about, say, Botticelli. Drummond detected some frustration in Gill at Cooke's intellectual openness: 'Michael wanted the great statements that a historian might make and as a result they didn't get very close.'

All the directors who worked on the series found Cooke a good man to have in a cutting room, with an easy ability to bend and twist a script to fit an awkward shot. Only one major change was introduced from the basic shape suggested by Cooke in the first place. Gill conceived the idea of coaxing the viewer with an introductory programme, before launching into heavy history. 'I thought that Cooke needed to be better known and that we could use his essays – about the fall in New England, or jazz in the South – to establish what he liked about America.' 'The First Impact' was given to Ann Turner, who took Cooke back to Cambridge University to describe his early misconceptions as a Blackpool schoolboy, to his beloved San Francisco, to Vermont (in spite of the weather), to the Mayo Clinic in Minnesota and to Baltimore, where he told of his affection for the old rogue, H.L. Mencken. One of the highlights was Cooke in New Orleans, seated at a piano playing the twelve-bar blues and recounting his first memory of 'a very raddled, bent-over Negro' playing the same chords, in the same bar, forty years earlier. The electrician was so taken by the Southern hospitality that he allowed one of his lights to set fire to the curtains. In the final shot you can still see the – very atmospheric – smoke.

In retrospect, Michael Gill wasn't sure that 'The First Impact' worked: he now feels it would have been better to give the space to an extra programme set in the modern era. In any case, it was placed at the end of the series when it appeared in the United States, while for the book (in twelve chapters) it was folded down into an extended introduction. Gill's own favourite programmes were those made by David Heycock – 'Money on the Land', about the great tycoons and the story of mass immigration, 'The Huddled Masses'. Cooke, too, felt that Heycock was 'in some ways the best'. 'He has a fine sense of timing and of mischief and of the ironical possibilities of music,' he wrote to Johnny. 'He has done a honey on "The Huddled Masses".'

In Britain, however, 'The First Impact' was launched upon an expectant public as Part I of *America – A Personal History* on Sunday 12 November 1972 at 7.25 p.m., repeated the following evening at 10.10 p.m.

31

THE CHIROPRACTOR'S REWARD

From the start, *America* was a critical success. It had a freshness and vigour which had rarely been seen in a documentary. It was simple, friendly and approachable, and soon began to register audiences twice those achieved by *Civilisation*: five million was a huge total for the supposedly minority channel, BBC2. The official audience report after the first broadcast was glowing: 'a superb start to the series'; 'if the whole series is as good as the first episode, it should be really memorable'. Listeners enthused about the transfer to television of Cooke's musings in the *Letter*. Those finding 'The First Impact' 'gripping', 'informative' and 'clear' outnumbered the sceptics by more than nine to one. By May the following year the series had already won ten awards, including no fewer than four 'Emmys' (television Oscars) for Cooke and Michael Gill (Cooke's were for narration and writing – he submitted in particular the Civil War script, 'A Firebell in the Night') and recognition by the Writers' Guild of Great Britain among many others.

The critics were mostly appreciative, both in Britain and subsequently in America, where the series was screened (and shown on alternate Tuesday nights). The *Christian Science Monitor* wrote, 'The first good television documentary on American history . . . has been produced not by the major American television networks, but by Britain's BBC!' It believed the BBC had developed 'perhaps the largest single reservoir of talent in the broadcasting world'. *Newsweek* summed up the view of the converted: 'the series is the first and perhaps the finest, gift to the nation for its 200th birthday,' while the *New York Magazine* took the prize for sheer adjectival diversity – 'civilised, literate, rational, graceful, humane, nobly-intended'.

Reviewers were often making judgements without having seen the whole series: in 1972 there were no neat boxes of advance tapes for preview purposes. Richard Schickel, for instance, *Time*'s television critic, was initially ready to 'write off the whole enterprise as that most dismal of phenomena – television that is *merely* educational'. Yet gradually he found himself won over and produced this rounded appreciation: 'The more you see, the more it becomes clear that Cooke is not out to make a quick killing, that he conceived the series as, perhaps, a kind of concluding unscientific summary of a long career as a popular, but incorruptible, interpreter of the United States not only to the folks back home but to us as well.'

Cooke must have enjoyed most of the coverage apart from the (to him) pestilential repetition of the adjective 'urbane' to describe the narrator, his script, or both – and the tiresome laziness of sub-editors parroting the headline 'COOKE'S TOURS' or some variation on that theme. There were dissenting voices, too. The *Times Literary Supplement* took exception to 'random explanations that would leave the reader almost certainly hopelessly confused' and a biographer of George Washington thought the work 'full of historical errors'. Others nit-picked over detail or – in the case of the 'Pan American Council' – protested that *America* was a region stretching from Alaska to Argentina and that the title of the series was therefore an insulting misnomer. A few mainstream critics challenged Cooke's readiness to confront the most awkward social issues of the moment, or quibbled over the extent to which *America* could be regarded as serious history.

The most trenchant attack, however, came from an unlikely quarter – the pages of the *Guardian* newspaper. In the interests of balance, no doubt, the paper invited two knowledgeable figures to cast a jaundiced eye over *America*. One was Martin Walker, a young reporter with first-hand knowledge of the country: he felt that the old correspondent was so insulated by the comfortable lifestyle of the white middle class that he had failed to spot what was happening in the black ghettos and college campuses. 'As his ear became more privileged,' he wrote, 'the sharpness of his eye was dimmed. This series is called "A Personal History". I barely recognise it.'

Almost equally damning was a companion piece by Bernard Nossiter, London correspondent of the *Washington Post* and it was perhaps more hurtful because it targeted his academic aspirations: 'Cooke himself calls the first episode ("The First Impact") an "anthology of admiration" and that is certainly its informing spirit. But what can one make of the second mish-mash about New Spain and New France? On film Cooke tries to pull it together by concluding that they left "an indelible mark" on American culture. But this is invention rather than history. It is astonishing how few traces of Spanish and French culture survive in America in spite of the presence of both empires in the country for nearly three centuries.' Nossiter compared the series with 'those big, glossy volumes bought at Christmas, looked at once then left lying on the coffee table'.

The irony was not lost on unsympathetic observers of the liberal press. John Crosby, in the *Observer*, commented, 'Of course, Cooke's view of America is not the currently fashionable one of the cocktail party Left. The *Guardian* . . . assigned two – not one, but *two* of these fashionable leftist thinkers to torpedo Cooke, an incredibly ungracious thing to do to a man who has been the *Guardian*'s distinguished American correspondent for forty years.' (Give or take a decade.) Crosby waxed sarcastic: 'Why, asked Walker, no mention of the child death-rate in Chicago? A good point. This same omission always spoils the Mona Lisa for me. The child death-rate in Florence at the time was appalling and you'd think a great painter like Leonardo could have found space on the painting for it somewhere, wouldn't you?'

Cooke unfortunately missed the main London launch of the book at a Mayfair Hotel: one of the BBC publication managers, John Hore, recalls the panic when the message came through – Cooke was unwell and was sending his wife and 'a friend'. There was nothing to be done, however and the BBC team turned up gloomily, regretting in advance the lost publicity. There were compensations. The 'friend' turned out to be Lauren Bacall, who had not lost contact with the Cookes after Bogart's death. Indeed her admiration for the man she had once named among her 'six favourites' never wavered. In the 1970s, she would use the *Letter from America* as a lifeline when exiled on theatre tours to Britain and expressed her 'awe' of someone who could be 'so entertaining and such an egghead' at the same time.

The roots of this friendship lay in the shared affection for Adlai Stevenson, whose failure to win the presidency seemed to Bacall to have been a huge loss to the nation. 'Alistair and I don't always agree politically', she admits; she does not find in Cooke all the same liberal instincts which are so important to her, 'and if he doesn't agree with you, you're in trouble. You may as well not be there'. But the mutual affection was strong enough to survive such differences and both Alistair and Jane found themselves supporting Bacall when her second marriage to Jason Robards was going through 'lousy times'. It was Cooke's respect for 'Bogey' that sealed the matter, culminating in the chapter devoted to him in *Six Men* which Bacall never forgot.

Cooke also celebrated Bacall herself in one of his last pieces for the *Guardian*. It purports to be a review of a Broadway musical called *Applause*, but is in fact a hymn of praise to Lauren Bacall. He decries the dimness of producers who had for so long cast her as a romantic and fragile figure – either siren or helpless fawn: 'How often did we watch strong males, from John Wayne to Kenneth More, attempt to be tender with Miss B., who is as susceptible of protection as a tornado and as easy to embrace as a swordfish.' At last, the truth had dawned and with stunning results: 'Miss Bacall defuses and obliterates every other talent on the stage . . . she sings with a blissful élan which implies that Ella Fitzgerald is a pedant for singing on pitch . . . The theatre is Bacall's private heaven.' This eulogy concludes, 'At the end, the lovely rascal threw her head up and her arms high and the Palace Theatre resounded with a tumult unlike anything heard in this town since Laurence Olivier wiped the paint from his eyes and bowed himself out as Oedipus. Quite simply, Lauren Bacall has achieved her reincarnation.' When, in later years, Lauren Bacall felt that she was drifting apart from her old friends across Central Park, it was a cause of real and puzzled regret to her.

But of all the comments from all the reviewers of book or film around the globe, none gave Cooke more intense satisfaction than the verdict of the man known as the 'dean' of American historians, Samuel Eliot Morison. Cooke had consulted, directly and indirectly, a number of leading academics, including Denis – now Sir Denis – Brogan, erstwhile competitor in *Transatlantic Quiz*. He chose to pay particular tribute to Morison for throwing him a lifeline when he was 'floundering in whirlpools of competing "facts" and theories'. It's clear that he waited in considerable apprehension for the great man's imprimatur on his finished work, as he had once waited upon Q with his Cambridge essay. This time, the outcome was much more enjoyable. Morison found the book 'magnificent' and added a phrase which Cooke would have emblazoned on the cover for all future editions if he'd had the chance. 'I should have been proud to have written it myself.' And for good measure, 'It warms my heart.' After that, all the rest was candyfloss.

〜

Back at Jesus College in Cambridge, they saw the programmes and read the book too, and drew their own conclusions. The college could have seized this moment to celebrate the triumph of a former pupil, but – despite the passing of the years – there were still those who remembered Cooke and were inclined to regard anything he wrote as *de facto* lacking in academic rigour. When his name was put forward for an Honorary Fellowship in 1974, the idea was discussed – and then mysteriously shelved. What had gone wrong? A rumour began to circulate that he had been blackballed – on the grounds that his work contained 'inaccuracies'. Old professors have long memories. This academic insult remained a cloistered secret which was never revealed to its victim.

By then Cooke had succeeded in suppressing his natural inclination to regard honorary degrees as Mencken had done – as a 'form of certifying a pompous ass, fit only for realtors, chiropractors and Presidents of the United States.' Cooke had given in first to Edinburgh (in 1969) then – in the wake of *America* – to St Andrews (because of its golfing credentials) and to Manchester, which might otherwise have taken 'a dim view of a local boy who had demonstrably got too big for his breeches.' And then, in idle moments, the gnawing doubt had begun to trouble him: it was not that he was in the business of collecting degrees, but if he was good enough for such illustrious institutions as St Andrews and Manchester, why had there been nothing from Cambridge and nothing from Yale? Recognition from the latter finally arrived in 1977, when he was presented with the university's Howland Memorial Prize (previous recipients – Indira Gandhi, Ralph Vaughan Williams and Rupert Brooke). But it was another decade before Jesus College reconsidered his case. Fifty-six years after leaving Cambridge, Cooke was finally made a Fellow of the College but only after the university decided to offer him an Honorary Degree. The Duke of Edinburgh officiated at the degree, which enabled Cooke to begin his acceptance speech – with a chuckle – 'I must say what an honour it is, for the first time in my life, to respond to a Philippic.' Cooke, inevitably, quoted Mencken's admonishment, which had caused him, he said, to turn down several more university honours in the intervening years. 'But all this time I've been aware of a subconscious, sneaky yearning – a hope flickering but never extinguished – that one day I might hear from my own *alma mater*. When I did, I instantly cabled the Vice-Chancellor, "Yes! Mencken or no Mencken." '

The only other serious hiatus in this stream of academic plaudits came when the President of Harvard University wrote to Cooke in the early 1980s to offer him another Honorary Degree. This was at the prompting of Dr Francis Moore, once a fellow thespian with Harvard's Hasty Pudding Club and by now – still based at the university – one of the country's best-known surgeons. Cooke accepted, after a little ritual grumbling, but just before the appointed day he was stricken by a recurrence of the bowel condition, diverticulitis: it was so painful that he couldn't contemplate travelling to the ceremony and rang to apologise. Soon afterwards, instead of a letter of sympathy, he was informed that, having failed to appear, he had not qualified for the Honorary Doctorate of Letters.

Cooke took umbrage at what he perceived as a severe slight. Francis Moore, who expected the offer to be renewed automatically the following year, was told by the governing 'Harvard Corporation' that the next recipient would be the President of Germany. And that was that. When Harvard issued a new invitation some years later, Cooke turned it down with dignified disdain.

The *America* series conjured up a further distinction even longer delayed. Cooke was finally made an honorary Knight Commander, Order of the British Empire. A quarter of a century earlier – in 1948 – he had, briefly, been considered for a knighthood, only to see the offer hastily withdrawn when it was realised that he had become an American citizen. Now he was named in the section reserved for foreigners and the ceremony was carried out the following year by the new British Ambassador (Sir Peter Ramsbottom) in Washington, since Cooke couldn't make it to London for the investiture. As with all overseas knights, the title was not to be used, but – in Cooke's case – kept in his closet: he was not a man to flaunt his trophies in a glass-fronted cabinet.

As an honorary knight he was invited later to a luncheon at Buckingham Palace. Around the oval table, with corgis in attendance, were other newly ennobled guests, including the soprano Heather Harper and the author V.S. Naipaul. Cooke risked a story about Edward VII's lack of cultural pretensions: at a similar function, the King had asked loudly the identity of a man towards the end of the table. 'That, sir, is the greatest living authority on Lamb.' 'On lamb?' the King expostulated. The story went down well. He was slightly less bold when the Queen expressed her amazement that he could sit down on a Sunday morning and just 'talk for fifteen minutes off the top of your head.' Cooke was tempted to reply with the truth, 'Ma'am, they're written to a fare-thee-well.' Instead, he lied gracefully: 'Ma'am, I don't know either.'

There should have been a second visit to the Palace later that year, to receive from the Duke of Edinburgh the Franklin Medal awarded by the Royal Society of Arts. The citation was for the 'notable contribution which he has made through his outstanding services to promoting Anglo-American understanding.' It also spoke of his 'record of sympathetic and balanced observation and interpretation.' Cooke, however, was unwell and sent Jane instead, who dressed for the occasion in a dramatic Chanel suit of geometric design, a black bow-tie, fur hat and knee-length boots. She was directed to a modest drawing-room and was introduced to a small, crumpled man who turned out to be Sir John Betjeman. 'He looked so terrified,' she remembers, 'that I told him he should do what I'd done and order a Bloody Mary.'

~

Throughout this rewarding period, there was one other dramatic new development in Cooke's life – one more new post to fill for a twenty-year stretch. Rather like *America*, *Masterpiece Theatre* was an idea so simple and so successful that the moment of its conception has become a matter of further mild dispute. The most detailed version comes from Frank Gillard, who had retired from the BBC in 1970, but left almost immediately to take up a newly created post as 'Distinguished Fellow' of the embryonic Corporation for Public Broadcasting in Washington. One of his first tasks was to attend a concert being transmitted live on the Boston PBS network – WGBH – by the city's Symphony Orchestra: an influential Congressman would be in attendance and needed to be cosseted. The programme featured the usual Boston Pops menu of Strauss waltzes and marches by Sousa, but despite the noise the Congressman – after a hard week in Washington – slipped into a deep and impenetrable slumber. Gillard found himself chatting to the WGBH President, Sandford (Stan) Calderwood, across the recumbent body. He congratulated his new colleague on the success of their latest enterprise, the full twenty-six episodes of the BBC's *Forsyte Saga*, which were in their final few weeks. 'What are you going to follow it with?' he asked.

'Follow it?' Calderwood replied. 'I'm afraid that, once it's finished, it's finished.'

'Not necessarily. The BBC has got stacks of serials filed away in London. Why don't you take some more of them?'

As the Congressman slumbered on, the two men agreed to meet the following day and the plot was hatched. Gillard's theme was that hundreds of thousands of people had come to associate 10.15 on Sunday night with classic television drama. Why not capitalise on the habit? WGBH were enthusiastic, but it soon occurred to them that the historical dramatisations in particular might throw up social habits and traditions of which the audience knew little. Could Gillard think of anyone who could introduce the programmes and set them in context? Gillard's recollection was that he immediately came up with the name of Cooke (bearing him no grudge, evidently, for being slighted over his ambition to take over the *Letter from America* in the 1950s).

Gillard wasn't the only one. Christopher Sarson, a leading producer at WGBH and another English-born expatriate, had also decided that it would be a mistake not to build on the popularity of *The Forsyte Saga* – the first serialised drama on an American commercial network, which Sarson remembered arriving 'like soft rain in the desert'. The official history of *Masterpiece Theatre* maintained that, by 1970, 'the quality of American commercial television entertainment was deteriorating . . . . Viewers who weren't interested in bimbos in peril, or teenagers in heat, were forced to join the lost audience, doomed to wander the television wasteland looking in vain for entertainment that didn't upset their intelligence, their tastes, or their stomach.'

Sarson's long-term plan was to encourage domestic production of serious television drama and thought that a spell of sustained transatlantic pressure would be a force for good. 'I suggested that we should continue buying UK products until we could produce them ourselves,' he explains. 'Stan Calderwood immediately put me in touch with Mobil.' To his delight and surprise, the oil giant leaped at the opportunity to involve itself in such a worthwhile – and politically worthy – project and promised to underwrite the long-term purchase of BBC material. Mobil's Herb Schmertz was so keen that he pressed for a new series to be ready as soon as *The Forsyte Saga* finished in January 1971, which left little time to work out the details.

And who chose Cooke? 'Cooke was my immediate choice for

Masterpiece Theatre,' by Sarson's account, 'because I had listened to the *Letters from America* when I was growing up in England and I knew how well he could portray a different culture. Then, in America, I'd seen on *Omnibus* how good he was at introducing people to things with which they weren't familiar, like the arts. I knew he was the right person.'

Thinking of Cooke was one thing. Persuading him to do the job was another. He was on the point of starting to film *America* and had it in his mind that the public would be distracted from this major journalistic exercise if he were to dabble in presenting somebody else's programmes. Sarson discovered that his quarry was due to film in Boston with a WGBH crew and arranged to meet him for a drink – tempting him with the chance to reminisce about Blackpool, where his own grandfather had been a headmaster. 'I tried to persuade him that the audiences for Public Television were very different and tended not to watch commercial channels. I was as persuasive,' he says, 'as a charming Englishman can be.' Cooke smiled and declined and Sarson went back to his office to resume the search.

There was, however, a third party to this encounter – Cooke's daughter Susie – and she took a very different view of the project. She thought it would be 'right up his alley'. 'It sounded wonderful,' she explained. 'He was so familiar with literature and he loved telling people what he thought. You only had to listen to him at the cocktail hour.' She decided to try to woo him. Her approach was that viewers of *Masterpiece* were likely to watch *America* anyway, while people who tuned in to *America* wouldn't necessarily know about *Masterpiece*. In other words, the combination was more likely to help than hinder.

Sarson was still struggling for a solution. The sense that Cooke was the perfect choice, the 'Mr Bridge-Water' between America and Britain, haunted him and robbed other candidates of their charm. With a self-imposed deadline of 1 December drawing close (the first series was due to be transmitted in January 1971) he was growing desperate. He tried a string of English actors, actresses and historians, on the basis that an American would lack credibility, but none of the final shortlist of four fitted the bill. The deadline arrived and Sarson decided, reluctantly, to fall back on a purely visual introduction. On the afternoon of 1 December he sat down with his assistant to start working on the scripts for these illustrated essays when the phone rang. It was Cooke. He had, he announced, spent Thanksgiving with

Susie and thought that, on balance, Sarson had been right after all. He assumed that someone else had been given the job, but he just wanted to put the record straight. Within seconds, the offer was renewed.

This was not what Cooke expected and it put him in a quandary. He rang Irving Cohen, seeking a way to extricate himself and the lawyer turned to one of the oldest show-business tricks: frighten the proposer away with a prohibitively large fee. He plucked a sum from the air – 'say $30,000 for a series of programmes . . .' Sarson initially gulped and retired for consultations. But soon afterwards he was back, with the news that WGBH had decided to accept Cohen's terms. 'We laughed about it,' Cohen reflected, 'and I told Alistair that this was the first principle of negotiation. First convince yourself you don't care – then ask for what you know you can't get. Just be aware that you might get it after all.' There was no escape, though Cooke insisted that the contract be for one year only. Against his better judgement, he was about to become the purveyor of all things English to an American audience, just as he had been for so long in reverse.

The opening series was *The First Churchills*, thirteen episodes of potted television history, set in the late seventeenth and early eighteenth centuries. It was an object lesson in what Cooke would be asked to provide – historical and social background to a complex plot. In retrospect, Cooke was surprised it didn't strangle *Masterpiece Theatre* at birth: 'The story of religious, political and military turbulence was one of tortuous complexity that defied dramatisation.' The confusion was compounded by 'a curious decision by the producers to put most of the men in black wigs and sometimes have them pronounce their lines with their backs to the audience. You never knew if you were in Holland unless they had a tulip on the table.'

Whatever the length of the original programmes, Mobil's agreement to forsake commercial breaks meant that WGBH always had a full hour to fill. Cooke's introduction and closing remarks (the 'extro' as it became known – Cooke claimed to have contributed the word to the American language) would serve the dual purpose of explanation and filling the missing minutes. The format was to be as unfussy as possible, in line with Sarson's minimalist principles – a simple set at the studios in Boston, with a chair for the presenter in front of an appropriate background, perhaps a carefully lit Dickensian drawing-room, a laboratory or the backyard of a miner's cottage. Cooke would speak to camera for three or four minutes, either sketching in the context in which the play should be viewed, or attempting a résumé of the 'story so far'. Beside him on a table would be an object relating to the story-line, a prop to which he could refer. Then, at the end, he reappeared with a few further thoughts and a nod towards the following week – the extro.

What Sarson had not fully realised when he hired Cooke was the remarkable expertise he got for his money – not just the broad range of cultural references, but the speed of writing, the accuracy of delivery and the uncanny knack of speaking directly to an unseen audience. No one before had ever insisted on performing without benefit of prompter or make-up, but it all helped to create the natural – unstaged – feel that Sarson had envisaged. Cooke explained his preference for memory more baldly: 'Until I am conspicuously overwhelmed by Alzheimer's,' he wrote in 1986, 'I intend to stay with it and with the implied conviction that an MC ought to be at all times a person thinking aloud about something which, at the moment, interests or absorbs him.'

Naturally, a routine soon developed. In the early years Sarson sent details about the programmes, and in due course the programmes themselves on tape, to New York where Cooke would construct preliminary scripts, before flying to Boston to finalise the details over dinner and Scotch. Cooke relished the research required, especially for historical works like *Elizabeth R* and *The Six Wives of Henry VIII*. These, as he told the *New York Times*, 'allowed me to rouse the sleeping-dog days of my university history studies' (skating over the fact that he hadn't read history at university) 'and to discover such fascinating oddities as Henry's appalling medical history and the formula for Elizabeth's cosmetic mask – white of egg, powdered eggshell, alum, borax and poppy-seeds mixed with water.' The pattern was set: Cooke flying up to Boston every few weeks with his draft scripts for the next set of programmes, usually typed on sheets of yellow paper (the same ones he used for *Letter from America*) – checking them with the producer – rehearsing them to himself to the side of the set while the technicians were at work, in what came to be called 'the learning corner' – and delivering them to camera with the (in Sarson's eyes) phenomenal ability to trim or expand a piece to fit the allotted slot. Lapses were rare. On one occasion, all thirteen episodes of *I, Claudius* were to be filmed on a single day. There were so many characters in such intricate relationships that Cooke's script – in the gap between programmes six and seven – sank into the Roman mire. 'I'm not sure you've made clear who's doing what . . . ' the producer tentatively interrupted. 'Sometimes,' Cooke replied icily, 'I just want to say – "Screw the plot. Watch the show." '

The routine involved booking into the same room (1201) at the same hotel, the Ritz-Carlton, with the furniture specially redistributed to suit his working requirements. The furniture stayed the same even when the producers changed over. Sarson gave up the job in 1974, to be succeeded by Joan Wilson and eventually – for *Masterpiece*'s last six years – Rebecca Eaton, whose biggest challenge was to learn the art of concentrating on scripts while being plied with Scotch. The studio set also developed into a battleground between the directors' instincts and Cooke's prejudices – over the lighting, in particular. The presenter argued for several seasons against stage-style overhead lighting which, he felt, emphasised his rather prominent eyes and decidedly prominent nose. 'You have to have a helluva face with small features to withstand it,' was his justification in the *Masterpiece* history for this peevishness. 'The switch to a second camera during the commentary was something I also resisted. When the director jumped from a medium shot to a long shot, a friend of ours said it looked like a stranger had come into the room and he would scream, "Who's that guy on the sofa?" But they thought it gave the pieces variety, so they did it. Otherwise, I left everything to them, although I did say, "Please don't bring the camera in through 16 pepper trees and then eventually come to me". '

His director for many years, David Atwood, became attuned to the great man's moods and moans. In his recollection, 'It didn't always go smoothly.' There would be irksome technical faults requiring retakes after Cooke had delivered what he regarded as a definitive version of the script. New crew members would intrude on the routine, or noise levels would build up in the studio while Cooke was in his learning corner. 'Suddenly he would snap,' Atwood recalls. 'He would say something which would shut everyone up for a week and a half.' The *Masterpiece* team tolerated these idiosyncrasies with the sort of wry affection reserved for old stars, because – in return – they got more than most old stars could hope to offer. Atwood's favourite anecdote was of a 1987 show, when Cooke arrived in Boston to discover that he'd left his scripts in New York. 'At the age of nearly eighty, he told us he intended to go back to the airport, catch the 10.30 New York shuttle, pick up the scripts and be back to start recording after lunch.' Brushing protests aside, that was exactly what he did. They still finished recording on time.

Before long, Cooke's brief interventions were becoming as popular and familiar as the pieces they introduced. *The First Churchills* notwithstanding, he was scrupulous about avoiding overt criticism of the programmes, even when they left him cold. The Cornish adventure *Poldark* was a particular bugbear because it lacked any basis in historical fact and consisted simply, in Cooke's view, of cardboard figures indulging in a bit of harmless – but to him tedious – swashbuckling. *Poldark*'s other crime was that it followed immediately after the latest run of one of his all-time favourites, *Upstairs, Downstairs* – which, from first sight, appealed to him at a highly personal level. It covers, after all, the period (1903–29) of Cooke's own formative years and he clearly relished the chance to experience vicariously both sides of the class divide which he had left behind.

Perhaps the most controversial choice, though, was *Portrait of a Marriage*, the story of Harold Nicolson and Vita Sackville-West told by their son Nigel. Cooke's first instinct was to refuse to have anything to do with it. Dealing as it did with the homosexual affairs of both partners, he found it shocking and inappropriate. He debated his doubts with Rebecca Eaton and she persuaded him to read the original book. She also pointed out that if he failed to appear on the *Masterpiece Theatre* set for the first time in twenty years, his absence itself would bloat the affair into a major media news story. Did he really want to fuel the controversy? He gave in, but delivered an unusually personal peroration. 'I'd been brought up on the Old Testament,' he told viewers.

> I knew that the sin of Ham was seeing the nakedness of his parents. How about *staging* the nakedness of your parents? And the Commandment, 'Thou shalt honour thy father and thy mother.' But if you can't do that, the decent least you can do is not rat on them when they're dead. So I felt that I could not conscientiously introduce the dramatisation of such a book. Then last Christmas I came on the book again and read it over and I must have been blind with distaste the first time because my scruples crumbled under the weight of the discovery that Vita Sackville-West makes it clear as hell that she wants her autobiography and her diary – and it's

the substance of the book, its agonised candid account of the whole affair – published to the world. And so she did and here it is.

Very occasionally, *Masterpiece* leaped into the news pages, too. In 1986, Cooke was compelled to apologise to the actor Nicol Williamson over an unguarded remark to an interviewer. Thinking the formal part of the discussion was over (and doubtless relying on the scrupulousness of his own journalistic ethics) he let slip what he thought of Williamson's performance as Lord Mountbatten in *The Last Viceroy*. As the *Daily Mail* crowed delightedly, Cooke described the actor as a 'lug' – American slang for a boring, untalented fool – and said that he looked like 'an LSE professor who had never worn a suit'.

By then, *Masterpiece Theatre* had embedded itself not just in the Public Broadcasting schedules, but deep in the consciousness of the American public. Its fifteenth birthday party – at the St Regis Hotel in New York, where Cooke had stayed on 'the day the money ran out', fifty-three years earlier – attracted a glossy crew of celebrities whose shows had been featured: Diana Rigg, Ian Richardson, Tim Pigott-Smith, Janet Suzman and even Nicol Williamson. *Masterpiece* had not, to Sarson's regret, caused a flowering of classic American TV drama, but it had become a cult in its own right, with its unlikely catch-phrase, 'Good Evening, I'm Alistair Cooke'. The comedian Jackie Gleason had included a character called 'Aristotle Cookie' into his act in the *Omnibus* years (Lauren Bacall used to address Cooke as Aristotle), but now *Sesame Street* introduced the 'Alistair Cookie' (a creature much given to stuffing its face with biscuits in a most un-Cooke-like fashion) the host of 'Monsterpiece Theatre'. There was the supreme accolade of an appearance in a 'Peanuts' cartoon – 'Good Evening, I'm Alistair Beagle,' says Snoopy – and an invitation (not finally taken up) to appear on the *Muppet Show*. Even the chair on which Cooke perched took on the distinction of a national monument, though, strictly speaking, there was no single chair – but a succession of seats appropriate to the period. (The *Economist*, Cooke's favourite magazine, incurred his disapproval for mentioning his regular appearances in a 'book-lined study'. He had never, he insisted, introduced anything from a book-lined study.) Somehow, the image became distorted by familiarity. As John O'Connor of the *New York Times* put it, 'The truly remarkable phenomenon for *Masterpiece Theatre* fans is how the memory of each production is so firmly stamped with the personality of a single person: the soft-spoken fellow sitting with a book in his lap, looking up just long enough to tell us what it's about.' Cooke's own assessment was that he was sometimes able to give the pieces more depth than they would have had on their original (British) transmission.

> I like to believe that the interweaving of fact with the fictional life of the players gave body and verisimilitude to the characters and plot they were enacting. That [was] the main, the cunning, pleasure of commenting on so many great authors, so much social history – the attempt to convince the viewing audience, subliminally, that the characters they were watching were, indeed, the real inhabitants of Tolstoy's Russia, Thomas Hardy's Dorset, the First World War, the suffragette movement and so on. Played cold (as in England) with no commentary, they appear less as slices of history than as fictions at one remove from the life of the time.

32

THE REST YOU KNOW

The biggest *Masterpiece* news story of all came in June 1992 when – out of the blue, as far as most viewers were concerned – Alistair Cooke decided that he would quit that mythical chair, in that mythical book-lined study. 'Genteel icon for upscale TV programming to retire,' as the *New York Times* put it.

Because the announcement was made so far in advance, interest was intensified in his last show – an adaptation of Conrad's *The Secret Agent*. The intros and extros were recorded in September and WGBH laid on a surprise party, with production staff and members of his family including Jane, Johnny and Susan. Cooke was presented with a portrait of himself by the cartoonist Al Hirschfeld and twenty-two bottles of Dewar's whisky – one for each *Masterpiece* season. Then came the emotional last Sunday in November, when those who tuned in saw the MC turn to the camera and deliver a formal farewell:

> I was hired for two years and they turned into twenty-one, but also – forty years ago exactly this month – I first became a regular television performer as what one of my old directors called 'our writer-narrator-host'. Forty years is enough. I don't have many more miles to go, but I do have promises to keep before I sleep and one or two ambitions, among them an insane desire to shave a stroke or two off my golf handicap. So that I can say with King Lear, ' . . . it is our vast intent to shake all tears and business from our age, conferring them on younger strengths while we unburdened crawl towards the practice tee.' And so I just want to say to all those men and women and tots who, down the decades, either in the mail or in the flesh, have told us what they liked and why: a very grateful thank-you, so good night and goodbye.

It was a major media event and it set in train a man/woman-hunt of epic proportions to find a replacement. Rebecca Eaton would not be rushed: she told reporters there were no plans to try to 'replicate' or 'duplicate' Cooke: 'He has defined the role, so we want to take great care to maintain our standards but to move on. We felt we wanted to do this with some deliberate speed. Our priority has not been how quickly we can do it, but how well.' Cooke himself added to the general air of mystery by refusing to give any interviews on the subject.

By the day of Cooke's last broadcast Eaton had studied the tapes, books and speeches of more than 150 candidates, including 'academics, actors, broadcasters, directors, historians, journalists, producers and writers'. Everybody had their own opinion. The celebrity television writer Marvin Kittman conducted a tongue-in-cheek straw poll which put the Anglo-American actor Simon Jones (one of the stars of *Brideshead Revisited* and *The Hitch-Hiker's Guide to the Galaxy*) at the top of the ballot, ahead of Kenneth Branagh, Emma Thompson, Derek Jacobi and many others. One genuine candidate was his old friend Brendan Gill of the *New Yorker*, who suspected that Cooke would be a very hard act to follow. 'He was so absolutely self-confident in what he was going to say,' he observed. 'Everybody else has the adrenalin flowing in the wrong direction because they fear they're going to break down in the middle of it. Alistair's suavity and casualness was the authentic article – not just make-believe. Nobody could touch him in that.'

Another aspirant, whose name did not feature in any public speculation, was a man with a very particular reason for wanting the job. John Byrne Cooke was entranced by his day at the WGBH studios celebrating his father's retirement. It set him thinking. Did he himself not have some of the right credentials to be a *Masterpiece* presenter – novelist, film writer, musician, lover of American history? The idea took root and finally, with some diffidence, he wrote to Rebecca Eaton with a formal application. 'This', he confessed to her, 'is an exercise in hubris.' He expressed the view that it would be a mistake to try to generate an Alistair Cooke clone. Surely the replacement would need to be somebody capable of developing his own style? A new face? He wondered whether viewers might not be intrigued by the idea of keeping the job in the family. . . . At his home in Jackson Hole, Wyoming, John wrote test pieces and rehearsed himself – pacing up and down, memorising a few paragraphs at a time. It was a scheme of considerable bravado from a son who had spent so long in his father's long shadow and it was probably doomed to failure from the start. *Masterpiece* needed a star. Although Eaton was sympathetic, she couldn't quite bring herself to invite Cooke junior all the way to Boston for a screen-test with so little prospect of a successful outcome. She explained, gently, that there were simply too many applicants and John was left to comfort himself with the thought that it might, in any case, have looked like nepotism.

He never told his father.

WGBH lighted, at last, upon someone to fill Cooke's shoes – another journalist, Russell Baker, though the columnist and commentator resisted Rebecca Eaton's overtures for many months. The two men had never met and when Baker wrote to Cooke, he was invited to the Fifth Avenue apartment. 'My first thought when he opened the door was, "My God! He looks just like Alistair Cooke!" Our conversation was genial and not very grave. Just chat, really. It was a bit awesome to be talking to Alistair Cooke man-to-man, as it were. I probably didn't make much sense.' Scotch flowed freely. 'It was the sort of civilised meeting one arranges, I suppose, when the sceptre is passed from one hand to another.'

To mark Cooke's parting, WGBH broadcast an hour-long tribute, introduced by Christopher Sarson, the original *Masterpiece* producer. It was a piece of unashamed TV emotion, but it did no more than reflect the feelings of thousands of people who wrote in to wish him farewell. The best of these letters were assembled in a presentation album which looked, for all the world, like a book of condolence. Norman and Carol Clary of Cleveland: 'You, who inform Europe about America . . . Many come to criticise and to compare Europe's best with our worst. But you came to analyse and remained to praise, to become part of our best and part of us.' Rosalie Davidson: 'When was it on *Omnibus* you spoke Dylan Thomas's "Do not go gentle into that good night"? That day opened my mind to poetry and literature. You touched my soul. I was torn apart. I wept that entire day.' Or, in a child's scrawl, Jamie: 'You don't have to leave, take two years off and we will watch your tapes. Or doesn't England know how to tape? Can't you get paid for your reruns? That's what you call programs played the second time. It's hard to write small with no lines. My mom prays for you every day.'

Among the televised celebrity contributions was one from Lauren Bacall and despite the soft lighting and elegant coiffure, there's nothing stagy about her words: 'I have seen you in every programme you've ever made and you've enriched my life,' she says, looking straight into the camera. 'I suppose I've been somewhat enamoured of you from day one. And it's only because of your charm, intelligence, wit, way with words – the fact that you continually surprise me with what you know and how much you know . . . So, as you are a dazzling gent with an active mind, I know that we haven't heard the last of you.'

~

One footnote to the *Masterpiece* years: it was understood from the start that WGBH would pick up all Cooke's hotel and travelling expenses, yet the company's business manager rarely received any receipts. When she pointed this out first to Joan Wilson, then to Rebecca Eaton, each tried to persuade her presenter to catch up on his paperwork. It made no difference. The full extent of the shortfall only emerged after Cooke's retirement, when it transpired that he was owed thousands of dollars in unclaimed expenses. Jane found out and insisted that he sit down and work his way through his diaries – most of the receipts having been lost beyond recall. Eventually, she was compelled to apply a touch of familial blackmail by refusing to cut her husband's hair until the job was done. Cooke had never lost his peculiar ambivalence towards his financial situation – on the one hand, a love of luxury linked with a pseudo-aristocratic carelessness (he had a habit of keeping huge sums of money in a non-interest-bearing bank account, to the despair of Irving Cohen); and on the other, a keenly developed sense of the value of things: he habitually complained, for instance, about the mark-up on a bottle of wine in a restaurant compared with his local liquor store and stuck to whisky instead. In Cohen's view, wealth did not change him: he remained, throughout, naïve and careless about money.

~

America – the series and the book – and the formative years of *Masterpiece Theatre* coincided with the biggest White House ructions of Cooke's journalistic career. He was not, therefore, best placed to follow the story of Nixon's downfall at source. He still had good contacts in Washington, but this was the first big political story he had attempted to cover outside the hothouse of daily newspaper reporting.

Some of those who watched him at work felt that he was slow to seize the nettle of Watergate. Charles Wheeler, the BBC's long-serving Washington correspondent, found it frustrating that *Letter from America* often received more attention in Britain than news broadcasts – and that consequently the BBC, along with most American television networks, trailed in the wake of the *Washington Post* and the *New York Times* in the early stages of the story.

The initial report of the burglary at the Democratic Party offices in Washington's Watergate Building appeared in the *Washington Post* on 18 June 1972: the first full-scale fruits of the Woodward and Bernstein investigation came six weeks later when the five burglars and two White House aides were indicted and the pressure continued to build through October. Yet the public was resoundingly unmoved. Voters swept Nixon to a second term as President at the start of November and the *Post* found itself caught up in a welter of legal challenges in the weeks that followed, which hindered its pursuit of the story.

In that light, Cooke's early reticence is perhaps more understandable: on 16 September, his first shot at Watergate was blithe to the point of light-heartedness. He outlined some of the legal complexities arising from the break-in and the claims of unexplained campaign funds: 'Is this already confusing?' he inquired. 'Do I sense the first polite suppression of a yawn? If so, your instinct is a healthy one and may soon be shared by the American people. The elephantine progress of all suits and countersuits through the long and winding corridors of the American courts will, I should guess, guarantee that nothing at all will be proved or settled before the election.' That at least was on the mark.

Cooke had never been a Nixon fan, but the early Watergate whisperings did not seem to him likely to touch the President himself. Cooke was more concerned with the general souring of the political atmosphere, which made the Nixon inauguration a uniquely acerbic affair. There was no way of skating over these matters for his British audience, however badly they might reflect on the American body politic: Nixon, he reported, had been 'reviled like no President before him. He's been assailed in print, in caricatures in all the mass media, as a willing agent of the devil and he's confessed to an intimate that he's been worn down by this ceaseless criticism, that he feels himself to be surrounded by "enemies and spies" who "pervert every word which falls from my lips" and who "invent the facts" whenever they fail to find them. Nobody can say it is a joyous inaugural, but it has to be done.'

It was not in Cooke's character to associate himself directly with the detractors. He did not see it as part of the correspondent's role, especially not a correspondent with his self-imposed task. There was a more subtle point, too. Cooke's lively perception of the Communist menace remained undimmed by the signing of the final Vietnam cease-fire in Paris at the end of January: Communists were inherently untrustworthy and it would be a foolish commentator who helped to weaken the main bulwark against such treachery – namely the President of the United States.

None the less, in the *Letter* of 21 April, a mere fortnight before Woodward and Bernstein were awarded a Pulitzer Prize for their investigations, Cooke re-introduced his listeners to what he thought might be turning into 'a very big scandal indeed'. He gave a brief summary of the break-in, the resulting court case and the decisive action of Senator Sam Ervin in demanding that White House aides should testify before his committee. A week later, Watergate finally reached the top of Cooke's agenda, though only by discursive way of that natural Watergate (his pun) – the Mississippi River – which was rising alarmingly. The evidence against the Nixon administration, Cooke admitted, was piling up, but he had no intention of galloping to judgement: 'I think it's still too early to moralise about the top command at the White House,' he opined. 'What is and will remain truly alarming is the quality of the men the President chose as his advisers, the shabby gang around him.'

By 5 May, after Nixon's stumbling television address appealing for the trust of his people, Cooke was finally in full flight. Once again he focussed on the 'team of crafty public relations men' in the White House, determined to sell Nixon by fair means or foul. They came – and he drew on his own blacklist of least-loved professions – 'from the worlds of advertising and public relations and real estate and cosmetics'. In the eyes of such degraded men, the constitution was little more than an airy abstraction. And Nixon himself? This was his surprising conclusion. 'I think we must, for the time being, give the President the benefit of the doubt, for to believe that he knew all about it is to say something worse than that Mr Nixon is a disastrously gullible judge of character. It is to imply that a vast majority of voters are morally numb. And if that was so, then the days of the Republic would be numbered.'

Not many commentators, by 26 May 1973, were ready to be so understanding. Yet another seven days and Cooke was reminding his audience about some of the greatest oddities of the whole affair. Why had so many senior figures taken such hair-raising risks to ensure the election of a President whose election was already a racing certainty? And what had happened to the standards in public life which once compelled an Eisenhower aide to resign over the gift of a refrigerator?

On 9 June Cooke made the unfashionable point that Nixon was right to protest against 'the flood of allegations that masqueraded in the public mind as facts. . . . The *Washington Post* and the *New York Times* in particular have not been queasy about reporting masses of hearsay and then covering themselves with the end phrase "he alleged" '. Back home at their apartment on Fifth Avenue, Jane was undoubtedly content to accept the version laid out day after day in the *Washington Post* or the *New York Times*. But Cooke continued to cavil at the conduct of the affair, even as the scandal spread exponentially, dragging in more and more top-level administration figures and as newspapers celebrated the triumphant vindication of their campaign.

Taken in the round, Cooke's coverage of Watergate in the *Letter* was balanced, thoughtful and no doubt infuriating for those who saw matters in black and white. Mostly, he resisted the temptation to predict the outcome – mostly, but not entirely. After Nixon's defiant State of the Union address in January 1974, the *Letter from America* speculated about the possibility of impeachment: 'There are only about fifteen Senators disposed to vote for impeachment and there would have to be sixty-seven to vote for conviction. It may be that the President, after all, has felt the public pulse better than anybody.

'Probably, I should guess now, he will survive.'

Yet there is no doubt that the old Methodist in Cooke was deeply shocked by the details of the White House tapes when they were finally made public that summer. Richard Nixon, he believed, had grown so accustomed to the microphones around him that he forgot they were there – rather like the unknown actresses chosen by Chaplin precisely in the hope that, with the cameras left running, they would display the natural innocence he had first noticed in them. By this account, Nixon simply reverted to type – expletive deleted. Cooke, who rarely swore at all, found the President's day-to-day language deeply distasteful.

The end, when it came, gave rise to one of the most memorable of all the *Letters*, but not for the obvious reasons. Cooke was in San Francisco, as usual for the beginning of August. This meant that the BBC recording had to be completed a day early, for shipment first to New York, then London. There would be two days between his laying down the piece and its first appearance at 9.15 on the Friday evening. As he prepared his script, the latest developments – televised in full – suggested that Nixon's career was in its death throes, not least thanks to the grudgingly released tape proving that he had heard about Watergate a mere six days after the break-in and had actually ordered his chief of staff, H.R. Haldeman, to get the FBI investigation stopped.

Cooke sat before the microphone, not knowing what Nixon would do next, but guessing that the decision would be taken before the scheduled broadcast of the *Letter*. He listed the possibilities – resignation, impeachment and conviction by the Senate, bargaining for immunity, a sudden change of heart in the Senate. . . . 'These were the alternatives he faced, as three or four of the leading conservatives in the Senate were meeting to decide whether to tell him he had to go.' That much was safe. But how to end the piece? He fell back on a piece of journalistic sleight of hand.

He intoned four portentous words: 'The rest you know.' The breath-taking simplicity was duly noted and admired. Because, twenty-four hours after the recording was made, Nixon appeared on television to announce his resignation – and the following day – the day of the broadcast itself – he left the White House. How lean and spare Cooke's comment seemed, how restrained his emotions on such an emotional day. . . .

~

Six weeks later, on 25 September 1974, Alistair Cooke was paid a signal honour. He was invited to address a special gathering of the United States Congress – only the third non-American to do so, the others being the French revolutionary leader, Lafayette and Winston Churchill. The invitation caused him a momentary tremor of conscience. He had already agreed to speak to another much-revered body – the Royal and Ancient Golf Club at St Andrews. But there was no real choice to be made.

The invitation, from the Speaker of the House, Carl Albert, was to help in the celebration of the 200th Anniversary of the 'Continental' Congress in Philadelphia – the first joint gathering of all the rebel colonies in September 1774. A full ceremonial programme of events included the 'Old Guard Colonial Fife and Drum Corps', a trooping of the Flag, two speeches by American professors, a performance of the 'Liberty Song' and 'Free America' – and Cooke's speech. The programme notes identified the *America* series as the main reason for the choice: 'The series has won 18 awards around the world, including five Emmy awards, the Peabody, the Annual Gavel Award of the American Bar association and the Wrangler Award of the National Cowboy Hall of Fame.' It had also, the writer pointed out, been sold to 'the United States Information Service for showing to government officials, scholars and the diplomatic corps in seventy-three cities'.

Cooke confessed, on the day, to a rare outbreak of nerves: 'Standing here now, I feel as if I were just coming awake from a nightmare in which I saw myself before you unprepared and naked (as one often is in dreams) looking around this awesome assembly and blurting out, "I accept your nomination for the Presidency of the United States." ' This was greeted with a roar of approving laughter.

The main theme of his address was more serious, as befitted such a hazardous time in the nation's affairs. He recalled some of the heroes of the Revolution – but heroes on both sides of the Atlantic, like Edmund Burke who dared to support the American claim for democratic representation: there was always a danger, he maintained, in sentimentalising history, or teaching it as 'a continual clash between the good guys and the bad guys, between America and Britain, the white man and the Indian, industry and labour – between us and them'. If the forthcoming bicentennial celebrations were to be conducted on such a simplistic basis, they could turn into 'an orgy of self-righteousness', in which 'every man who signed the Declaration of Independence is at this moment being measured for a halo, or at worst a T-shirt.' History – all history – was more complex than that and, if taught in all its variety, young people might learn that 'courage and cowardice know no national or racial frontiers and that when we say a man or woman is a credit to the race, we should mean no more or less than the human race'.

He saved for his peroration a plea for the country not to spend the bicentennial year 'proclaiming that we are unique and holier than anybody'. The pessimistic preacher – and teacher – in him conjured up the three great evils facing society, a 'triple threat to representative government', which could only be overcome in a spirit of international co-operation. 'For the first time since the fifteenth century our cities are threatened by the success of violence; for the first time since the 1920s our countries are threatened by unstoppable inflation; and for the first time in human history our planet is threatened by an unstopped nuclear arms race.' It was no time for declarations of national sovereignty.

Cooke finished with a direct reference to the Watergate crisis and the spawning of that domestic 'politburo' which he believed had come close to perverting the balance of power in Washington. And he praised the way in which elected members of the Congress had, finally, restored that balance by 'debating with sense and dignity and seriousness the most dire threat to the Constitutional system since 1860'. It seemed to him a happy coincidence that, '200 years after the first Congress met as a team of watchdogs eager to corner a tyrannical executive, this House should have made it possible for us to say without complacency and with some legitimate pride, "I have seen the past – and it works!" '

Just four years later there was further evidence of the respect in which Cooke was held in Washington's Establishment circles – though admittedly it came through the good offices of his friend James 'Scotty' Reston. Reston used a *New York Times* column to offer some advice to the newly installed Jimmy Carter: why not abandon the tarnished tradition of using government posts to pay back fat-cat benefactors? Perhaps the President would consider creating the post of Minister of Culture for the opera singer Beverley Sills – or better still, appoint the best-informed man on Anglo-American affairs to the Court of St James's: Alistair Cooke for Ambassador. This would have seemed like a harmless piece of journalistic whimsy, if it hadn't been for Reston's huge reputation and influence. Sure enough, there soon followed a telephone-call from an aide to President-elect Carter: would Mr Cooke stand ready to take a call from the President later that week? Naturally, he would. But cold reality swept over him as he put down the phone. He remembered what ambassadors of his acquaintance had told him: David Bruce, during his London posting, remarked that it required just two qualities – a perpetual grin and a lead stomach. Cooke fired off a letter to the Carter team, advising them that – if asked – he would have to decline the honour.

Jane's view was more practical. With half an eye on the residence in London, just round the corner from her daughter Holly, she said: 'You should have told them we'd try it for a month.' They had once flirted with the idea of leaving New York, if only to escape the punitive tax regime when the *America* money started to come in. Cooke's advisers told him he'd be better off in Florida or Connecticut: the only drawback was that he didn't want to live in either place. Cooke's own choice would have been San Francisco, but that wouldn't have helped on the tax front. London was the only other possibility and he and Jane did have a short meeting with a firm of lawyers, recommended by Lauren Bacall. In this case there turned out to be an even bigger drawback: 'Just remember, Mr Cooke, that if you come to London, you must never touch your typewriter while you're here. A single article for, say, the *Evening Standard* would mean you'd end up paying tax in both countries.'

~

Alistair Cooke, in his mid-sixties, had achieved more than most: he had even been declared one of the twelve best-dressed men in the world by an American newspaper ('the TV commentator who dresses like a dream'). But he was never tempted to stop work. There were many factors to drive him forward, apart from the fact that he was still in demand to write, broadcast and speak in public.

At home, Cooke and his wife had gradually overcome their painful differences of the Fifties and Sixties, moving imperceptibly into a solid and comfortable relationship of mutual affection. This depended to a considerable extent on the way they had come to live their lives in parallel. Jane was still a busy professional painter with a wide circle of friends of her own and she had no more sense of preparing for a quiet retirement than he had – it would have driven them both to distraction. She was wedded to the Long Island house for as much of the summer as she could manage. The place, after all, was her refuge. She had a studio, an improbable beach-buggy to drive to the shops, a precarious single scull which she rowed around the bay in all weathers (to the alarm of her family) and the trees and plants lovingly nourished, though frequently laid waste by the storms and the sandy soil.

It was Cooke's second home, too, of course, but Jane was in charge –

except in the bunker, which she built alongside the house, created in 1983 so that she wouldn't be pestered by his obsession with sport on television. The bunker was fitted out by Cooke himself and cartoons festooned the walls. One was sent to him by David Low after he'd been inspired by a Cooke metaphor in the *Guardian*: it shows McCarthy, at the height of his investigations, with a branding iron bearing the hammer and sickle. Another consists of an elaborate sequence of sketches by the great *New Yorker* cartoonist Whitney Darrow, who was a frequent visitor to Long Island, recalling 'An Afternoon with Alistair Cooke'. Other pictures from the same magazine included a dog with a briefcase: 'Does Voice-Over for Dog Commercials', reads the caption. There are drawings by George Price (also of the *New Yorker*), Al Hirschfeld and Thurber. One photograph recalls the first edition of *Omnibus*, complete with smoking MC. (Cooke only gave up smoking, under duress, while recovering from a prostate operation in 1990 – after more than sixty years of devotion to the weed.)

In all the years of their Long Island occupation, the Cookes never became part of the local social scene, beyond the cluster of houses on Nassau Point occupied variously by family and friends. The North Fork of the island remained sequestered, quiet and comparatively unfashionable – a world away from the Hamptons along the south shore. No fast cars or flashy restaurants, no society balls or grand house parties: in 1992, Cooke spoke at a fund-raising function for the North Fork Environmental Council and pleaded for planners to 'beware of hectic, unplanned, greedy development' which might turn the place into 'Staten Island with sand'. He conjured up the horrors in store for an unwary rural community – 'typical all-American drek; second-hand auto lots, tacky motels and fast food chains'. The Cookes liked it the way it was, a simple agricultural corner first developed by immigrant Polish potato farmers – some of whose families were still working the land. Visitors were given the same detailed instructions about the water supply and the television and alerted to the benefits of the place: hiring an outboard from Captain Jim, buying fruit and vegetables from roadside stands with names like Farmer Mike's and Thunderbird, watching the racoons which came to scavenge for scraps and not worrying about security: 'We lock the doors only if we are going away for several days. Otherwise and unless it's raining, we leave all the doors and windows wide open, day and night. We also leave the keys overnight in the cars – there is no compulsion to do this.'

The couple had more than enough money (though none of it was spent on cars: Cooke's Long Island conveyance, parked next to the buggy, was an ancient red Datsun of alarming decrepitude). One further factor in their continued independence was that both enjoyed good health – with those occasional dramatic exceptions for which Dr Robert Woods Brown in California was so often on hand. Cooke's attitude to his own health was always inquisitive rather than morbid: his friends dubbed him a valetudinarian, not a hypochondriac. He started to subscribe to *Journal Watch* – a fortnightly review of all the newly issued medical literature – to keep himself up to date and he continued to pester Brown for information, either for his own self-diagnosis or for use in lectures and writing. What could Brown tell him about syringomyelia, the wasting disease which killed Bobby Jones? Was it true that descending, rather than ascending, syringomyelia was less pernicious?

This hunger for medical knowledge and fascination with the pathology of his own body led him to collect doctors. In London, after another medical lecture, he established a British circle of physicians and psychiatrists to match the San Francisco group. One favoured figure was the city's most flamboyant varicose vein surgeon Stanley Rivlin, who operated on Cooke and promised him beforehand that there would be no pain. Cooke wrote back that he'd heard that sort of thing before and didn't believe a word of it. Afterwards Rivlin was rewarded for his skill by an invitation to Nassau Point.

Cooke had no hesitation in sharing his thoughts on his own afflictions with his BBC listeners, from a sniffle-inducing sinus to the intermittent back-problems with which he was plagued. The crippling pain he suffered at the end of the writing of *Generation on Trial* had left its mark and it struck again in 1973 in Britain in a week's break from editing *America*. After long days and nights crouched over editing machines, he made the mistake of trying to do too much, summoning Alan Russell for as many rounds of golf as could be achieved in seven days, first at the Royal Norfolk at Brancaster – twenty-seven tough holes – and then immediately afterwards in Scotland where he was immobilised, in agony, on the first tee. He used the same broadcast to recall his scepticism about the wider medical profession, describing the eighteen months it had taken to recover from that first seizure, during which three specialists had recommended by turn surgery, exercise and neglect. 'When you choose the doctor, you choose the diagnosis,' he concluded wearily.

This (mostly) healthy scepticism was fine as long as Cooke continued to be spared more serious complaints. Not until much later life did he finally agree to hand himself over to the mercies of the surgeon – and only then after lengthy procrastination. Throughout the late 1980s and early 1990s, he became progressively less mobile – and suffered considerable pain – from a deteriorating knee. By 1991 it was so sore that when he was handed a BAFTA lifetime award for his contribution to television – by the Patron, Princess Anne – he felt his knee giving way under the weight.

Family and friends, and Jane in particular, tried to persuade him that he would benefit from surgery, and that something in any case had to be done to restore his energy and enthusiasm for life. A cheerful Cooke, however single-minded and opinionated, was usually charming, courteous and thoughtful. A morose, tetchy Cooke was a different proposition. By the autumn of 1992 the pain had become excruciating. It was certainly a factor in persuading him to give up *Masterpiece Theatre* and it had wrecked his enjoyment of golf, producing in him – for the first time – an old man's stoop. Sometimes he even needed a walking-frame. Aficionados noticed a change in his broadcasts, even if they weren't sure why. The idea of a 'total knee' operation, more complex than a hip-replacement, was daunting, but especially so for a man of eighty-three. Out of medical curiosity he had already asked Carl Borders in San Francisco, golfing partner and orthopaedic surgeon, to show him a video-tape of what was involved. Eventually, on his next visit to San Francisco, he told Borders that he'd been given the name of two possible surgeons and Borders had no hesitation in recommending an Indian called Chitranjan Ranawat – a 'total knee' pioneer.

Cooke booked an appointment with Ranawat at the Hospital for Special Surgery in New York. 'An hour before I was due to see him,' he recalls, 'I had a series of X-rays. He wasn't remotely interested in the beautiful MRI scan I'd had earlier, he just had the X-rays. I walked into his office in my little white shift and he said "walk towards me".' He walked and sat down opposite the surgeon. 'Ranawat said, "Degenerative arthritis. On a scale of one to ten, your left knee is a two – that's very good at your age. Your right knee is a ten. I think you will have a date with me."' Cooke was still absorbing this information, when Ranawat went on, 'I also notice that you have arthritis of your thumbs.'

'That's true,' Cooke replied.

'Please make a span for me.' Cooke stretched open his hands. 'Your left is much better than your right. You play the piano, I think.' The bemused patient agreed that he did.

'Jazz piano?'

'Yes.'

'That would account for it,' Ranawat continued. 'The left hand has to span tenths on the piano. The right has not had so much exercise.' Cooke was flabbergasted. It was a piece of detective work which probably overcame any remaining doubts and a date in November was set for the operation. But it couldn't be allowed to interrupt the continuity of the *Letter from America*. The BBC would certainly have been prepared to tolerate a couple of missed talks in the circumstances, but Cooke was both superstitious and mildly paranoid. His trusted producer, Heather Maclean, believes that he feared the *Letter* would be dropped if he ever demonstrated a sign of weakness.

With Cooke's own children far from home, Maclean had become almost part of the family. She was extremely worried at the prospect of the 'total knee': could such an old man really withstand so a long a spell in the operating theatre? Cooke's main concern was to ensure that there would be no hiatus in the *Letters*. Maclean hunted around the hospital for a suitable site: the private bedroom he'd been allocated was too noisy and the best temporary studio she could find was a conference room in the basement, which had some curtains and couches to deaden the echo – as well as some cushions to stifle the air-conditioning hiss. Unfortunately, when she returned the following day with the engineer Ken Pursley they discovered that the room was just below the hospital's heli-pad. The whole procession – including nurses and PR people – traipsed around in search of a quieter corner. One promising spot was ruled out because of the clanging of the MRI machine. At last, Pursley found somewhere tolerable, but only by keeping the microphone as close as possible to the speaker's mouth. At no stage, in any of the hospital broadcasts, was any reference made to the peculiar recording conditions. It was up to Pursley to conceal the truth. Cooke got away with it just as he had in all his previous unscheduled hospital broadcasts, starting in San Francisco twenty-five years earlier when diverticulitis struck. There was never a hint in the themes he chose – Presidents, women in politics, European immigrants – and no one in London was any the wiser.

The operation was a success, but not before Cooke's family had suffered a number of scares. To the surprise of his daughter Susie, he was sent home within days and without any special nursing plan. That was what happened to patients who suffered no post-operative complications and who had good family support. 'There were no arrangements for therapeutic care,' Susie says. 'He was told what exercises to do, but that was it. He started to become dehydrated and got sicker and sicker.' Cooke contacted Carl Borders who told him brutally that, at the age of eighty-three he should not be at home: he should demand readmission to hospital. After a few days, Jane arranged for him to be taken to the Rusk Rehabilitation Centre, where he rapidly regained his strength, won a reputation as the star knee patient and – inevitably – became one of the world's great amateur experts on this entire branch of surgery. His son John came to see him towards the end of his rehabilitation and his father – not content with walking up and down the corridor with his newly straightened gait – opened the fire door and mounted the outside staircase to prove his point. 'He was so proud,' John realised. 'The combination of the knee and giving up smoking revitalised him.'

Cooke emerged, just in time for Christmas, a new man. 'He seemed ten years younger,' according to Susie. Everybody noticed and if they didn't they were soon given chapter and verse. It took a long time for the novelty to wear off. The first return trip to San Francisco, early the next year, meant a whole new series of demonstrations to his friends. Jimmy, the doorman at the Huntington, saw his car draw up and moved in ready to help Mr Cooke negotiate the steps. Cooke brushed him aside, and proceeded to dance a jig up and down the hotel steps. His favourite concierge, Cynthia Reid, was summoned from her desk to witness the transformation. Every friend in turn was regaled with the story of Ranawat's brilliance. Cooke was back in business.

More medical crises lay ahead. In 1996 a routine check-up revealed an irregular heartbeat and Cooke was fitted with a pacemaker. As usual, it caused no interruption to his output of *Letters*: 'Within a day or two, I was back at my loyal Royal [typewriter],' he told the *Sunday Times*, though another hapless BBC executive – when asked whether this might affect his future as a broadcaster – was forced to confess, rather despairingly, that nobody had told her about the operation. And in 1999, further mild heart attacks and heart surgery required yet more ingenuity from producers and engineers to maintain the illusion that all was well in the transatlantic firmament.

PART EIGHT

CONCLUSIONS

33

STAYING ON

Throughout the post-*America* period, there were further publishing enterprises. But already, in 1969, Cooke had conducted a television interview with ex-President Eisenhower which gave rise to a limited-edition book in a presentation case – *General Eisenhower on the Military Churchill*. The introduction explained that the interviewer had been helicoptered in to Eisenhower's farm at Gettysburg and spent three days in conversation with the old man shortly before his death. For the cameras they spoke about Churchill. When the filming was over, they simply chatted 'about everything from politics to golf, from the code of a soldier to the temptations of a newspaperman, from the private trials of the Presidency to the public life of a small Kansas town in the early 1900s'.

Cooke paints a somewhat mournful picture of the occasion. He noticed a makeshift putting green, with a flag bearing the insignia of a five-star general, which was so overgrown that the hole had practically disappeared. Eisenhower explained that he was following the edict of the Governor of Pennsylvania by saving water and he revealed his growing anxiety that his arthritic hands might never wield a club again. Like Cooke, he was a late convert to the game and he confessed that in the 1950s, during briefing sessions on the disposition of Russian forces, his mind would drift guiltily to the problem of the hook which was wrecking his swing.

1971 saw a re-printing of Cooke's collection of 1930s film-criticisms, *Garbo and the Nightwatchmen*, but the most important enterprise, without doubt, was *Six Men* which appeared in 1977 – pen portraits of Chaplin, Edward VIII, Bogart, Stevenson, Mencken and Bertrand Russell. This involved much original work, although some of the essays were worked up from 1950s magazine articles. He explained the logic behind his cast of characters in an introduction entitled 'A Note on Fame and Friendship', stressing that the book was not just an extended piece of name-dropping, nor should readers expect to find sensational revelations. 'In our day,' he wrote, 'the marketing of confidences "spoken in the candour of private conversation" has become a big and frequently disreputable business,' and it was not a business in which he was going to participate.

Having thus laid out his own ground rules, he explained his choices: '. . . of all the eminent people I have had occasion to run into, these six were the ones who most demonstrably took to me!' The rare use, by Cooke, of the exclamation mark in print gave the sentence an abnormally coy character. What else linked his six men – apart from the neatness of the selection of three Americans and three Britons?

> What is involved in such relationships is a form of emotional chemistry, so far unexplained by any school of chemistry I am aware of, that conditions nothing so simple as a choice between opposite poles of attraction and repulsion. You can meet some people thirty, forty times down the years and they remain amiable bystanders, like the shore lights of towns that a sailor passes at stated times, but never calls at on the regular run. Conversely, all considerations of sex aside, you can meet some other people once or twice and they remain permanent influences on your life.

Cooke seemed to feel that he needed this gloss to justify – in particular – the inclusion of Edward VIII. He had, after all, only met him a handful of times and always in formal settings. 'It would be absurd for me to pretend I was ever more than a nodding acquaintance,' he admits. 'But he is a special case: a schoolboy's idol who left a lifelong impression (though mine on him, I am sure, left barely a trace); and a journalist's once-in-a-lifetime assignment to follow, at close quarters, the downfall of a King-Emperor.'

A further consideration had been to avoid those who were both alive and active, since they were always being written about for the purposes of immediate canonisation or debunking. Of his *Six Men* only Chaplin was still alive (though he died soon afterwards) and all were 'comfortably removed from the heat of idolatry or belittlement'. He detected other common factors, too: 'They all seem to me to be deeply conservative men who, for various psychological reasons, yearned to be recognised as . . . brave progressives. Perhaps that is the real link with this writer.'

Six Men was published by Knopf and dedicated to Nunnally Johnson, who had just died. Cooke wrote to a friend, 'The publishers are vastly pleased and my so-called editor – a laconic type who thought *America* "sound and competent" (so it bloody well was) thinks *Six Men* is "wonderful." ' It sold swiftly – 180,000 copies in the first six weeks and occupied a place close to the top of the *New York Times* bestseller list. Cooke did a number of book signings and became known in the press as the fastest autographer in town. *The Times*, having wondered at Edward Heath's ability to sign 300 copies of his new book, *Music*, in an hour, conceded that 'Cooke, with his head down, can do 500.' But he had a most excruciating lapse of memory when drawing up a list of a hundred people to whom complimentary copies should be sent: too late, he realised that he had failed to include the name of his son John.

Six Men was generally well received by the critics and the *Economist*'s unnamed reviewer looked beyond the text to the writer himself: 'Serendipity is Alistair Cooke's second name. Ever since he was given a Commonwealth fellowship to study, of all things, "American theatre direction" at Yale, happy days have been here for him.' The book, therefore, consisted of 'scenes from Mr Cooke's serendipity.' It seems a useful image. Apart from his twin ambitions – to work for the *Guardian* and the BBC – things did keep turning up. The success of *Six Men* led Cooke to dream of a companion volume of sketches which finally came to fruition when he was well into his ninety-first year: most of the portraits were lifted from previously published work, but there were new pieces on Roosevelt and George Bernard Shaw.

In 1979, many years after it was first proposed, a third volume of *Letters* appeared under the title *The Americans*. Sitting at his desk in Nassau Point, he penned a brief introductory 'Note to the Reader': 'The word reader', it began, 'ought to be in strong italics. For these are talks meant to be listened to. . . . Radio is literature, so to speak, for the blind.' This was a distinction which intrigued the jazz musician, broadcaster and sometime *Spectator* book critic, Benny Green: in his view, the act of speaking for radio replaced the application of style in the written word. Cooke, he pointed out, had admitted to straightening out the syntax to avoid conversational idiosyncrasies and introducing more precise, literary words designed to put book readers at their ease. Green's assessment was that most broadcasters who attempted this remodelling exercise failed abjectly, which made Cooke's success unique. 'He is one of the most gifted and urbane essayists of the century, a supreme master of that form of literary work which seems to simulate the effect of physical personality hovering just behind the reader's shoulder.'

Two further collections of talks, transmogrified from the spoken word, followed. *The Patient has the Floor* appeared in 1986. The sources were the many lectures and speeches Cooke had given – starting with the Mayo College address which had caused such a stir in May 1965, with its layman's view of medicine. Five of the fourteen pieces were medical. The others included the speech to Congress and one given at the Howland Medal ceremony at Yale.

The link was always Cooke, the honest broker, casting his unjaundiced eye over other people's specialities. He enjoyed bearding experts in their own dens. He had agonised over the title, uncertain whether it would immediately convey the intended message. He tried it out on friends and casual acquaintances, and even stopped people in the street. He delved into its derivation and consulted William Safire, the *New York Times* writer on language: 'Some friends say the idiom is not American. Is Zat So?' When no confirmation was forthcoming, he told Safire, 'I imagine I'll call it – so nobody will be baffled – "A series of Lectures Given Before Medical Societies by a Layman Who Has Frequently Been a Patient". It's got rhythm, you have to admit.' His editor, Chuck Elliott, tried to persuade him to choose something less abstruse, but in the end Cooke convinced himself that readers would understand: it was time for the doctor to shut up and leave the talking to the patient.

In 1994 Cooke agreed to co-operate with Michael Parkinson – whom he'd got to know and like in the course of two chat-show appearances – in another specialist volume, this one called *Fun and Games*. It traced – through articles and talks – his love of sport (and by neat extension, his love of music, theatre, film and television: the section was called 'Night People' and included a sketch about a burlesque club in Manhattan, which had been rejected by the *New Yorker* in 1940 as being too raunchy). Golf was the dominant theme, but the book did reprint one quirky piece called 'My Life with Gabriela Sabatini', based on a speech he'd given at Wimbledon in 1994.

Cooke had been a fan of tennis – especially women's tennis – for many years. Each summer he would repair to Wimbledon, hoping to watch the final stages of the women's competition, before heading off to the Open Golf Championship. His host was often John Barrett, journalist turned administrator, who – as a thank-you for an unpaid speech to The All England Club – arranged for the Cookes that year to sit in the Royal Box. No player thrilled Cooke more than Sabatini, the Argentinian with flashing eyes, raven hair – and a tendency to lose out to opponents with more of a killer instinct. He would follow 'Gaby' as assiduously at the US Open, too, and it was there that John Barrett contrived an unlikely meeting. Cooke was moping, because he'd discovered that he'd come on the wrong day to watch Sabatini, but it was a blessing in disguise. Barrett led him to the players' lounge, promising that – at last – he would come face to face with his idol. Cooke was highly dubious, suspecting an elaborate joke, especially when the appointed hour slipped past. 'He was convinced he'd been stood up,' Barrett remembers. At last – fresh from the massage-table and radiant in tennis kit and track-suit – she appeared: 'It was a marvellous moment: he was like a schoolboy on his first date.'

That was the story Cooke told in *Fun and Games*, in the intro-duction to which he attempted to rationalise his passion for sport. 'For more than fifty years, I can truly say that scarcely a day has gone by when I didn't think about government, its plethora of ailments and its depressing range of failed panaceas. In politics, nothing is ever settled for keeps, nobody wins. In games, the problems are solved: somebody wins. Hence the "isle of joy" offered by sport in an ocean of anxieties.'

～

A completely different literary exercise brought Cooke into part-nership with one of his San Francisco golfing cronies, Robert (Bob) Cameron, co-author of *The Drinking Man's Diet*. Cameron had built up an international reputation for his aerial studies of cities and landscapes – *Above San Francisco, Above Los Angeles*, as well as volumes on Hawaii and Washington DC – and he had it in mind to tackle some European subjects. With the enthusiastic encouragement of Max Reinhardt at publishers Bodley Head, he arranged to col-laborate with Cooke on a volume to be called *Above London*. As in his previous projects, Cameron's technique was to spend long hours dangling from a helicopter, photographing landmarks and distinctive scenery below: these pictures were then laid out in a large, glossy coffee-table book, with text either by Cameron himself or by another writer. The shooting took place in the summer of 1978 and the book was published, with a handsome study of the Royal Naval College, Greenwich on the cover, in 1980.

Reinhardt was delighted with it and reckoned it was the most successful of the series, while the captions allowed Cooke to pander to his twin fascinations for history and architecture, indulging his own prejudices along the way. Modern buildings were given a particularly rough ride: 'Nobody, except some of the people who live there, has a good word to say for The Barbican,' or, 'The destruction of Nash's Regent Steet in the mid-1920s was properly regarded as an artistic crime.' There had to be a photograph of a golf course, naturally, as well as all the palaces, stately homes, bridges and parks. The collection was an immediate success – and it was still selling well nearly twenty years later.

Above London had another, quite unexpected, result – the abrupt severing of a friendship which Cooke had cultivated. Soon after the end of the project, Cameron suddenly announced that he wanted nothing more to do with his old friend. Such a thing had never happened to Cooke before and he was hurt and perplexed. As time went on, various possible explanations emerged. There had been a disagreement over one of Cooke's book tours: Cameron wanted him to stay away from large retailers (with whom he himself was in dispute) but Cooke's publishers insisted that he complete the tour as planned. Cameron was said to believe that Max Reinhardt hadn't tried hard enough to sell the book in London. A dispute over royalties, involving a stiff note to Cameron from Irving Cohen, may have been a contributory factor. There was even a suggestion that Cooke had slighted one of Cameron's daughters at a big literary function. Whatever the underlying cause, it brought to an end a long-standing association, to the extent that they had to contrive to avoid each other at the San Francisco Golf Club, which both had patronised for so many years. Just once their friends persuaded them to try a round together, but it was a silent and miserable affair – never to be repeated. Two decades later Cameron, by then in his eighties and still hanging from helicopters in pursuit of his art, was too upset to discuss the affair.

~

For all the successes of Cooke's later years there were a few disappointments, too. The most painful, by some distance, was the

failure of two cherished film-projects conceived in the wake of
America. Xerox was so pleased with the result of its investment in
America that Cooke was asked if he would like to make another film
with the same backers. He had, indeed, been harbouring an idea – a
study of genius, inspired by a picture he'd seen on television of the
eight-year-old Mozart playing the spinet. It would be called *The Best
in the World*. He visualised shots of youngsters mixed through to the
great men they became in later life: Mozart, for instance, or a little
boy climbing on a stool to reach a blackboard, dissolving into the
figure of a man with tousled hair writing out a formula, $e = mc^2$. Or
possibly another child, golden-haired this time, being transformed
into the revered shape of the golfer Jack Nicklaus. He even went to
see Nicklaus in the days leading up to the 1974 US Open Golf at
Winged Foot, New York State, not far from Nassau Point. He accompanied him on a practice round, reduced for once to the role of
acolyte in the footsteps of the master, picking up every scrap of
conversation – observations about the type of grass seed the course
makers had used, or the comparative importance of different species
of tree in planning a shot. 'It wasn't showing off,' Cooke was sure, 'it
was just what he did naturally.' Then he watched as Nicklaus started
firing balls into the driving range, before pausing, without warning,
and turning to Cooke: 'I can tell you one guy who isn't going to win
this tournament.'

'Why, what's happened?' It all looked immaculate to Cooke.

'Didn't you notice? I'm hitting the ball absolutely straight.'

Something had gone wrong with the great man's grip – a minute
and unnoticed alteration which had robbed him of his fade, the
ability to drift a ball from left to right. It was enough to wreck his
preparations and the competition was, as he'd predicted, a lost cause.
It was won by his great rival Gary Player. Cooke was riveted by these
revelations. He began to visualise the film which would lay bare the
soul of the greatest golfer alive and demonstrate to a wider public the
complexity of his talent. With all the images and insights which he
would be able to impart bubbling through his mind, he went to see
his sponsors. They turned him down. The public didn't want to see
how somebody had become the best, they wanted to see stars *at* their
best – Nicklaus winning tournaments, not plotting his tactics. Cooke
was disappointed but not dismayed and gradually a different plan
emerged – a light-hearted personal history of golf and, in addition, a

documentary about Mark Twain, whom he had always revered both as a writer and an iconoclast.

The BBC was offered the chance to co-sponsor the films, but bowed out because of fears that the project would be too heavily dominated by Xerox. However, through Michael Gill, Cooke had already met Kenneth Clark's son Colin, who was running an independent television production company. At the end of 1974, Clark wrote to Cooke pointing out that by using his company he could maintain much greater control over the projects than he could have hoped for from the BBC. Xerox had no objection to the arrangement and each film was given a budget of $200,000 with a similar amount promised to Cooke. The plan was for Cooke to make his directorial debut (with the help of one of the *America* directors, Tim Slessor) as well as writing and presenting both films.

The programmes were to be shot in tandem through the spring of 1976 and edited in London during the next two months. *Mark Twain* drew on many of the techniques that had been so successful in *America* – old photographs and prints, historic sites and readings by an actor of Twain's words, all linked by Cooke: Slessor was in overall charge. *The Marvellous Mania: A History of the Scottish Torture* was much more ambitious and Cooke was to be the lead director. Work started in April 1976 and the shooting schedule required the crew to travel through England and Scotland, via Greece, the South of France and on to various locations on both sides of the United States.

Among the zanier filmic ideas was a plan to show the presenter standing in a barrel with a weight around his head, to demonstrate the difficulty for a golfer of learning to keep the body still when hitting the ball: 'Now, the masters have told us you must imagine you are standing in a barrel. If you sway, your hips will touch the right edge. To get the feeling of a straight left arm, you are *not* hitting anything, but pulling down on a bell-rope. And to keep your right elbow pointing to the ground, imagine you're carrying a tray. Finally to maintain a true tempo, you must imagine you are swinging back to the first two bars of "The Blue Danube". '

The script was generally agreed to be witty and persuasive and Cooke even managed to prevail upon Bing Crosby to take part, talking about the California Tournament to which he had given his name. As he explained to Crosby in a deferential letter, he intended to put himself – 'the goon' – through the agony of playing one of the world's great golf-holes – say the eighteenth at Palm Beach – intercut with Jack Nicklaus playing the same hole in competition: 'It would add immeasurably to the pleasure and freshness of the sequence if you would quietly appear – without blare of trumpets – and tee up beside me and play the hole along with me. Just to show the varieties of luck, skill (?) and trouble two old gentlemen can have, mimicking their idol. . . . It's hard to describe except face to face. But I hope it will be entertaining, funny and beautiful. . . . I'd be tickled pink if you'd say "yes". ' Crosby did.

The celebrity contributions could not save the day: Slessor did not find it easy to accommodate Cooke's dabbling in the direction of the film and Xerox decided without much hesitation that it could not be broadcast. But how was Cooke to be told that his pet project was a 'turkey'? A crisis meeting was convened at the apartment, attended by Alistair and Jane, his lawyer Irving Cohen, representatives of Xerox and Colin Clark. It was an awkward occasion and in the gathering silence Clark plucked up the courage to break the news. 'Alistair, I'm afraid what no one has cared to tell you is that the film is simply no good. They're not going to screen it. It happens to us all – it's just dead.'

'I see. Fine,' Cooke replied, teeth well-gritted. 'I don't know why they couldn't tell me straight out.'

Clark believes his effrontery was rewarded by an invitation, later the same day, to spend the weekend at Nassau Point. 'We had a marvellous time, we played golf and we never mentioned the film.' All involved, however, concur on one point: Cooke's careless dismissal of the rebuff was an act of bravado. In fact, the news was a cruel and unexpected blow to his pride, the more painful because he was a stranger to such setbacks in his professional life. He was not accustomed to hearing people tell him that something he'd done was 'no good'.

The fate of *Mark Twain* was even more disheartening. This film reached its final, polished version before suffering the same ignominy as *The Scottish Torture* – and for a time, Cooke simply couldn't work out why. Its adherence to the *America* formula, its knowledgeable and thought-provoking script and the obvious passion of the presenter combined to make it entertaining enough. He quoted many of his favourite *bon mots* from the Twain canon. On the British, for instance: 'Dear England! In all this grave and gentle country, I discovered one genuinely humorous idea – the Albert Memorial.' But Cooke also focused sharply upon Twain, the brutally honest social critic of the era of the robber-barons: *Huckleberry Finn*, in Cooke's judgement, not only demolished the wall between the American language as written and spoken by the people, it 'blew aside the whole structure of genteel morality' in the country. Twain's catalogue of vitriolic (and not very satirical) abuse ended with the deadly phrase from 'The Gilded Age', 'It is an era of incredible rottenness.'

Cooke was delighted with the finished piece. It seemed to him to encapsulate perfectly the story of how a provincial man from the banks of the Mississippi became an internationally acclaimed humorist and satirical scourge of American high society. 'I'm proud of it, because it's moving,' he said years later. 'It gets the character of him, in all his queerness and marvellous gift of phrase and tough character.'

Then, while the glow of satisfaction was still upon him, came the bitter blow. The US television networks turned *Mark Twain* down flat. Cooke sniffed a conspiracy: there were still plenty of Vanderbilts, Goulds, Rockefellers and Harrimans in town, whose forefathers were the very same robber-barons so vilified by Twain. The networks, he deduced, were simply too scared to broadcast such propaganda for fear of incurring the wrath of the Establishment. The only known copy lay, gathering dust, in one of Colin Clark's cupboards.

Two decades later, Cooke was still describing *Mark Twain* as 'the best thing I ever did. Better than *America*, better than anything.' And on another occasion, he said in all seriousness to one of his closest friends, 'Play it when I die.' The double disappointment left him permanently disenchanted with the documentary medium. When Slessor invited him to make some films several years later – on music, journalism, Mencken, his life in America – Cooke replied, 'No more fillums. Finished with all that.' Thinking this reluctance might be from a fear of the travelling and physical effort, Slessor promised that most of his contributions could be shot in his own study. 'No more fillums.'

~

The association with Colin Clark did produce one project which saw the light of day more or less as planned and which gave Cooke another opportunity to hob-nob with royalty. The theme of *A Much-Maligned Monarch* was the reputation of George III, which Cooke was to debate with the Prince of Wales at Windsor. The excuse was the 200th anniversary of the American War of Independence in 1976: did George 'lose' the colonies as the history books usually maintained? Or could a case be made for a little royal revisionism?

A preliminary meeting, face to face, was held in Charles's office at Greenwich Naval College and the filming date was fixed for November. Things were not quite as the visitors expected. Somewhat taken aback by the signal lack of formality, they found a buffet laid out on a sideboard and were told to help themselves to chunks of bread and ham and bottles of beer. There were no members of staff in evidence. The absence of ceremony probably helped establish a measure of rapport between interviewer and interviewee, as they settled into high-backed gilt chairs before a vast portrait (by Gainsborough) of George III. Cooke treated his subject rather like a bright nephew, while Charles, as so often, seemed to find it easy to relate to an older companion. Clark's recollection, none the less, is that Cooke had to work hard to coax the shy young man to be sufficiently forthcoming: 'If he hadn't been able to weave his magic, I don't think we'd have been able get a film out of it,' was his considered judgement. It was certainly more like discussion than interview and another interpretation was that Charles had trouble getting a word in edgeways. Some of Cooke's questions were nearly a minute long (in a thirty-minute programme). Both men, however, were at one in wishing to dispel the widely held view that George was the villain of the 1776 rebellion, certainly mad and probably bad, too. Charles explained his motive as being a desire 'to clear the name' of his great-great-great-great-great-grandfather. For Cooke, it was a chance to pursue his lifelong theme – that relations between Britain and America should not be defined in the simplistic terms of most history books.

A Much-Maligned Monarch went out on the BBC, but failed to recoup its investment in America. According to Clark, it was simply given to PBS without charge. Cooke's only other contact with the Prince came five years later, when he wrote and performed the commentary for a film compilation of marriage to Diana. And then, in 1981 (and presumably on the strength of his exposure to the wedding pictures) he felt emboldened to write an article for the human interest magazine Parade. It had the title 'Why Prince Charles can Marry for Love'. His first instinct, when invited to venture into this hazardous area of public life, was to run for cover. Then the magazine told him it would pay $7.50 a word for 2000 words. At $15,000, Cooke's pride was promptly swallowed:

> Prince Charles emerges as the first British heir to the throne to be born into a welfare state and into a Europe where every other powerful nation is a republic. There is no need for him to seek – as his great-grandfather, George V sought – a princess from the House of Württemberg. . . . No need to change his name to something more recognisably British, as his father had done. The long tradition of mating English royals with other royals is broken. And Prince Charles has found that happy rarity – in the memorable words of a former member of the royal household – 'a charming girl, of sufficiently noble lineage, who is English and untampered with.'

Cooke did not name his sources.

34

NO GOLD WATCH

Another grave – and long-running – source of irritation was the BBC's failure to produce a video version of *America*. If arrangements had been made at the time (in 1972), it might have been possible to sort out the relevant copyright problems. But it was only some years after the series first went out that the growth in the market for home video made the enterprise commercially viable. By then, it was a much more complex task to secure the necessary rights, particularly for the music. Cooke knew it wouldn't be easy, but never believed that the BBC had tried hard enough to make it happen. It became such a contentious issue that he put off for years his co-operation on an audio cassette of *Letters from America* that the BBC was desperate to release. Even when the Corporation suggested putting it out to coincide with his eightieth birthday in November 1988, Cooke simply declined to help – a point that was picked up by the media. The *Sunday Times* said baldly that Cooke had issued an ultimatum: no videos, no audio cassette: 'Cooke is not known for his false modesty,' the article continued, 'is aware of his worth and keen on monetary rewards and has every right to make this demand. But there are those in the BBC who regard it as being held to ransom and so it looks unlikely that the cassette will appear for a while yet.'

Cooke took exception to the reference to his fondness for financial rewards. 'This is news to me,' he fumed in a letter to the paper. 'I have never had any interest in "monetary rewards" as a bargaining chip or as a spur to anything I wrote.' But Cooke also wanted to correct the *Sunday Times* about the real *casus belli*. His latest complaint was that the BBC had been dilatory in producing a recorded version of another of his favourite programmes – a five-part series on the life and music of George Gershwin. They were the best music programmes he'd ever made, he reckoned, and the BBC had promised, more than once, to put them on cassette. 'My stipulation stands: the moment the

Gershwin cassette is positively in the works, I shall be delighted to record any number of *Letters* if – by that time – breath is still in me.'

In private, Cooke's correspondence with the BBC was stern: in August he had written to London, listing the exact sequence of events and the undertakings he'd been given both on *America* and Gershwin, starting in May 1988 when he'd been told: 'A man who was supposed to do it apparently didn't do it. But he is going to do it and is getting cracking now.'

> JULY 1988: I wrote to you about how cracking is 'cracking' and had no reply.

> 30 JULY 1988: I have received a letter saying 'it will be some time before all the records in the Gershwin are cleared' (!) Somebody called 'Business Affairs' 'say about two months'!!!!! [He added a PS] As for the 'clearing of the rights for *America*' – how come the Macarthur Foundation has cleared them and made the video-cassettes and distributed them to every public library in the USA??!! My own local village library on Long Island has just sent me a proud public notice that *America* is now available for borrowing – thirteen one-hour cassettes.

Cooke was very cross indeed, but to no very great effect. Neither *America* nor Gershwin ever reappeared, even though he had an ally in Sue Anstruther, who had just become the Radio Marketing Manager in London. She felt that it was a classic case of bosses promising what couldn't, in fact, be delivered and she soon learned that there was no appetite for the Gershwin among the people who would actually have to do the work.

Her problem was that she was still charged with producing the *Letters* cassette and in 1990 she had a stroke of luck. Through the good offices of the *Daily Telegraph*'s radio critic, Gillian Reynolds, she was assigned to shepherd Cooke through a brief visit to Glasgow where he was due to speak on 'The Future of Radio Broadcasting' at the Radio Academy Festival. She met him at Heathrow, flew with him to Scotland and made the right noises of indignation when she found that his hotel room wasn't ready. Then, when he discovered he had left his cufflinks at home, she went out to Tie Rack and bought him a replacement pair. This small act of service consolidated Cooke's friendly feelings towards her: 'This might get you your tapes, my dear,' he told her. The lecture was safely delivered and Cooke returned home. Nothing transpired immediately and over the months that followed a desultory exchange of messages within the BBC demonstrated a sharply declining belief that anything would ever come of the cassettes.

5/10/90: Are we going to pursue Cooke, or are we giving up?

11/10/91: Are we still trying to do anything with Alistair Cooke?

It was more than four years after the original proposal and only after Cooke's 'total knee' that Anstruther had a postcard – a picture of Paulette Goddard with a brief message on the reverse: 'Dear Sue, now I'm back on my feet – literally – and all the pretence has been dropped that the BBC will ever do the Gershwin, yes, I think I am ready to think about putting together a collection, mainly because you're the one that wants it.'

Sixteen *Letters* were to be re-recorded in the spring, since Cooke was unhappy about what might have been the uneven quality of the original pieces. He needn't have worried. Most of the tapes of his talks had long since been lost or wiped: only ninety-four survived in the archives and only three pre-dated the 1960s. This gloomy statistic made the idea of the cassettes even more attractive. The chosen pieces began in 1947 and finished with the assassination of Bobby Kennedy twenty years later, taking in the Watts riots, John Glenn's space-walk and more homely matters like 'The Summer Bachelor', 'My First Indian' and 'Beizbol' – an entertaining spoof on Russian claims to have invented America's favourite game. The *Letters* turned out to be one of the bestsellers in the BBC's 'Radio Collection': 15,000 were sold by Christmas 1993 and they remained a popular item thereafter. The title – *The Early Years* – suggested (intentionally) more to follow, but inevitably a second edition was not immediately forthcoming. Volume two finally appeared in 1996.

Still Cooke would not let go of his hopes for *America* and Gershwin and his vexation increased when Kenneth Clark's *Civilisation* was issued on video in 1993. Cooke knew that the game was up when one of his ex-BBC friends rang an executive in BBC Worldwide to inquire how the Macarthur Foundation had succeeded in getting the clearances which the BBC had found so elusive.

'Which series?' the woman asked.

'*Alistair Cooke's History of the United States.*'

'Oh, does he do television? I thought he only did radio.'

Cooke immediately sent a stiff note to the Director-General, John Birt.

Such experiences coloured all Cooke's relations with the BBC as a corporate body. He felt increasingly detached from the headquarters in London, developing a sense that 'they' were not like the BBC management in the old days of Lindsay Wellington or Gerald Cock. The truth was that he didn't know any of the Corporation's top brass. His information came solely from press reports and occasional contacts with other old-timers.

There was no single event which could be blamed for the coldness, but the twin anniversaries of the 2000th Letter (1987) and Cooke's eightieth birthday (1988) didn't help. The *Letter* landmark was supposed to be observed with a formal dinner, but shortly beforehand Jane was taken ill in San Francisco – the intestinal trouble which saw Doc Brown called into service again. She underwent surgery and began her slow recovery, but – according to Cooke – nobody from the BBC bothered to contact him to find out how she was. For that reason, as he wrote to a friend in London, he couldn't tell when he would next be travelling to England: 'When disaster struck in San Francisco, it was assumed that a later date would be fixed. I am inclined now to skip it, since I never had a note from Hussey [the Chairman], Checkland [Director-General] or Green [the Controller of Radio Four], hoping for Jane's recovery and hinting at an autumn substitute. My friends were astonished at this lapse and – as one Anglophile puts it – "The English are not very good at this". I don't feel it's up to me to say "all seems well" and "when are you going to give me my dinner?"'

Such oversights are a feature of large organisations, but it reinforced Cooke's belief that nobody in London really cared – and that he was taken for granted. Instead, he enjoyed the event vicariously and through a number of lengthy newspaper tributes which he called 'obits'. The *Daily Telegraph* sent the distinguished writer John Mortimer to New York for the sole purpose of an interview. Both men seem to have enjoyed themselves, dining expansively at Cooke's favourite restaurant – a 'snob eating-place' in Mortimer's words. 'We sat in his regular cushioned corner of the dining-room in the Carlyle Hotel ... The conversation moved gently but dazzlingly on, diving down the backwaters of his long and charmed existence, fishing up the names of his friends' – Chaplin,

Stevenson, Duke Ellington, Bobby Jones. Cooke also greeted the news that the newspaper would be footing the dinner bill with the remark, 'That's wonderful! Do you hear that?' He smiled at the waiter. 'Our dinner is being paid for by the apostles of monetarism.'

The 2000th *Letter* made the briefest of nods to the significance of the day, after a conventional spin (language, health, environment, AIDS) through the issues of the week. He had been urged, he said, to deliver some missionary message: 'Missions are for bishops, I'm a reporter.' He ended instead with an anecdote about the ninety-nine-year-old man from California who offered as his recipe for a seventy-eight-year marriage – 'frequent separations and a growing loss of hearing'.

Cooke's only other broadcast contribution to the proceedings was a special edition of the international phone-in programme *It's Your World*. It didn't go very well. Conscious, perhaps, of his responsibility as an unjaundiced observer and aware of the possibility of causing offence with an audience spanning the globe (via the World Service), he said nothing very interesting at all. 'Repeatedly, he refused to be drawn on the rights and wrongs of US politics,' one critic observed, 'preferring to scan his vast mental data base for extracts from *Letters* that would serve as answers – a process of recall so automatic that you could almost hear the disc-drives humming.' A score-card of presidential achievement had to be dragged out of him (Truman 7, Eisenhower 5, Kennedy 4, Johnson 7 for domestic performance and Carter 5 for intelligence). The programme was hosted by Charles Wheeler in London, who was surprised to be asked since he didn't know Cooke well. He, too, was left with a sense of frustration that Cooke gave so little away: 'He couldn't even be persuaded to name his favourite jazz musician,' Wheeler remembered. (He offered three options – Beiderbecke, Teagarden and Hines). 'I could tell the caller was disappointed and he tried again – without success – in a supplementary.' The same horror of controversy, Wheeler felt, was a characteristic of other presenters of Cooke's generation, like Richard Dimbleby. 'Maybe they don't have the kind of minds that come to conclusions. Nowadays, I don't think we pay quite the same obeisance to objectivity for its own sake.'

The general scratchiness of their transatlantic star can't have endeared him to the BBC. The abortive attempt to find out whether he might be ready to retire – the row over the party – the failure to reissue his favourite programmes made the atmosphere distinctly cool. But, as he approached his eightieth birthday ('the dreaded Eight Oh!'), one more attempt was made to bridge the gap. Cooke had decided to stay away from Britain to avoid being fêted either by the BBC, or by his publishers, or indeed by anyone else – restricting himself to small celebratory dinners, organised by Knopf and the British Embassy in Washington. The BBC felt that the best hope of mending bridges was to fix something in New York and the local office drafted in Freddie Hancock, widow of Tony, who acted as a part-time consultant for them on PR matters. The location was easy: it had to be the Carlyle. She established that the BBC chairman, Marmaduke Hussey, was ready to fly to the States for the occasion with his wife Lady Susan, along with a small group of executives, but Cooke was given the chance to vet the rest of the guest list. He wanted some of his friends on hand as well as more official representatives.

Hancock's plan was to play to Cooke's two great enthusiasms (or so she thought). Golf was obviously one and she organised a telegram of congratulation from Jack Nicklaus. She was less successful on the music front. After *Omnibus*, she assumed that Cooke would be a rabid fan of Leonard Bernstein, who had just returned from an exhausting tour of Europe and – for old times' sake – agreed to attend with his sister. Hancock made sure there was a piano available at the Carlyle, out of sight, so that Bernstein could provide a high-toned rendering of 'Happy Birthday'. Her next brainwave came when she noticed that the flautist James Galway was also due to be in town on that November evening. What better? A classical duet of impossible distinction to serenade the guest of honour. The plan nearly imploded. Messages became scrambled in the run-up to the dinner and Galway arrived bearing no musical instrument of any kind. A panic-stricken Hancock commandeered the chairman's car and swept round to Galway's hotel, remembering the instruction 'not to touch anything'. She returned with a bag of assorted flutes and managed to smuggle them into the building without attracting Cooke's attention.

The performance was unusual, to say the least. After a 'Happy Birthday' duet, Galway broke into an impromptu rendering of 'Danny Boy' complete with variations: for all its eccentricity, it worked as a post-prandial entertainment. But the biggest surprise was still to come. Hancock had reserved the starring role for a video-recorder wheeled into the room at the end of the proceedings. The lights were dimmed and the Presidential seal appeared on the screen. 'Ladies and Gentlemen, the President of the United States,' intoned an unseen voice. Through contacts in the White House, she had secured a vote of thanks from Ronald Reagan himself, filmed in – what else ? – a book-lined study.

'Alistair, we have both seen many changes in this country and around the world,' Reagan said. 'War, peace and matters in between, and as I think about it, it seems to me that your life is a symbol of one of the few things that hasn't changed: the great good fellowship between the people of the United Kingdom and the people of the United States.' After this endorsement of Cooke's life work, Reagan paid tribute to *Masterpiece Theatre* and more particularly Cooke's own masterpiece, *America*. 'The episode I remember best is about the poor and huddled masses who came to our country yearning for freedom and found it. It was a matter of great pride that Nancy was able to present a Soviet school with a copy of that film when we were in Moscow.' Russians, he thought, would do well to heed its message. 'I'm sorry that I can't be with you and Jane in person, but you have Nancy's and my affection and respect.' And with an actor's grin, he ended – in the fashion of *Masterpiece Theatre* – 'For Alistair Cooke, this is Ronald Reagan. Good Night.'

After that exotic occasion, the birthday itself was celebrated with extreme simplicity. Cooke wrote to a friend about the family's plans: 'Jane is off every day painting a family portrait from a palazzo atop the Marin mountains that command a dazzling view of the Bay on one side, the ocean on the other. Tomorrow we have son Johnny here, along with Carl Borders and Abby; the Bob Browns. That's all. We shall raise a glass to you.'

Cooke's pleasure at the BBC event helped establish unusually warm feelings towards Duke Hussey, considering his senior position at the BBC. The warmth did not radiate to any Director-General, then or later. Cooke was suspicious of John Birt from the start of his tenure in 1992, a suspicion fuelled by press reports of wholesale change at the Corporation and exacerbated every time disenchanted BBC stalwarts registered their disapproval. Economy measures began to impinge on his own working life: his trusty engineer, Ken Pursley, was told that he was surplus to requirements – though he continued to work on the *Letter* from time to time on a freelance basis. The *Listener* magazine, in which so many of Cooke's talks had been published, had ceased publication in 1991. Gradually, however tenuous his direct connection with any of these decisions, Birt became the figure in whom all Cooke's frustrations and irritations were vested. All doubt was banished when it was announced in 1994 that the BBC was to leave its Rockefeller Plaza headquarters on Fifth Avenue, in favour of poky offices many blocks to the north, beyond the Lincoln Center and above a branch of the Jamaica Bank.

Naturally, when Birt contacted Cooke that year about the possibility of another party – to mark the sixtieth anniversary of his first BBC job – he turned the idea down flat and wrote what he admitted afterwards was an ungracious reply pleading for 'no more state funerals!'. Why not wait until the 2500th *Letter* and do the job properly? He did relent to the extent of agreeing to come to London to receive instead a Media Society award (the first it had offered for 'outstanding achievement') at a dinner at the Savoy. Duke Hussey gave a speech. John Birt was invited – but did not attend.

∼

The BBC never really found a way back into Cooke's affections. Which did not mean that he ever thought of severing his umbilical cord to an organisation that had sustained him for so long. There was the *Letter*, of course, but there was also a long succession of music programmes, all made with a single producer, Alan Owen. It was an extraordinarily fruitful association which, between 1974 and 1987, generated no fewer than seventy-four broadcasts in eleven separate series. The two men covered almost every aspect of American popular music from 1920 to 1950, creating in the process a vivid testament to Cooke's musical tastes, and culminating in the *pièce de résistance* – *The Life and Times of George Gershwin.*

From a position of comparative subordination, Owen established a comradeship of depth and complexity with Cooke. (He was one of a select band of friends who ended up on canvas: Jane was discriminating in her choice of domestic subjects.) In many ways it was the perfect example of how Cooke latched on to somebody whom fate had thrown in his path and drew him (there were few women involved) into an ever deeper intimacy – while maintaining a proprietorial interest in the conduct of the relationship. Their first contact was at the prompting of Stephen Hearst in London, who recommended Cooke as the possible presenter of a short series of programmes for

Radio Three on Gershwin, Richard Rodgers and Cole Porter.

> OWEN TO COOKE, 2 APRIL 1974: Dear Mr Cooke. . . . I would not presume to suggest a style of presentation and cannot improve on leaving this to you, but, simply for your interest, I enclose a rough draft script of the sort of thing I envisaged before I knew Alistair Cooke would be part of the programme.

> COOKE TO OWEN, 2 APRIL 1974: Dear Mr Owen, I had not known that this was to be a program of relatively 'unknown' songs. It has been my experience that they are usually unknown for the best possible reason: they are lous-ay.

> AO TO AC, 11 APRIL: Dear Mr Cooke, Has there been some misunderstanding do you think? Please do not worry! It depends what is meant by 'relatively'. In any case, I solemnly promise you no lous-ay songs at all!

By June, they were on first name terms and Owen was informing Cooke that he had bought a television set specifically to watch *America*. 'I'm hooked! It and you were absolutely marvellous and I'm looking forward immensely to the rest. The use of the Copland at the opening, so calm and unexpected, was a knockout.' In July he was recommending books Cooke might read to help his scripting and they met for the first time on 19 August – the day that the invitation to speak to Congress arrived. The first series went out at the end of October.

> AO TO AC, 17 OCTOBER 1974: I have not yet heard any official comment on the programmes. I do hope Stephen is pleased with the result, as I would dearly love to do some more on the same lines with you. [He soon had his wish.]

> AO TO AC, 24 FEBRUARY 1975: I have today received permission from my lords and masters to travel to New York, in spite of the economic axe which threatens to throttle the BBC. (How's that for fine writing!)

That visit sealed the friendship. Owen stayed at Nassau Point and when Cooke was in England they indulged in joint outings with spouses. Programme ideas bubbled backwards and forwards across the Atlantic, as Cooke revelled in reliving his musical past and Owen proved a tireless, sympathetic and patient collaborator. The latter quality was specially useful.

> AO TO AC, 10 OCTOBER 1975: I face the rejection of my ideas with fortitude. I'll sound out the powers that be about the piano series. I don't see how we can get thirteen half hours of sufficient variety, but no doubt you have some clever wheeze.

When the Cookes came to London, they no longer stayed in hotels, preferring an apartment in a Mayfair block owned by Sidney Bernstein, which gave them a better social base: a dinner with the Owens was a regular sortie. Even after they'd known each other for some time, Owen remained somewhat star-struck and the mutual affection went well beyond the professional:

> AC TO AO, CHRISTMAS EVE 1976: Our family sends you the warmest greetings and fervent hopes that your Yule encounter with Mamma was an occasion for the appropriate tenderness and jollity. How was *your* venison? Jane sends mad love to you both.

It was up to Owen to refine the flow of ideas and draw from it projects which might make it onto the air. They prepared obituaries together for Ethel Merman, Benny Goodman, Stephane Grappelli and Ella Fitzgerald. They battled with Controllers for the time they felt they needed. And – as a constant refrain – they exchanged information about the weather, a source of endless fascination to Cooke and acquired fascination to all his correspondents.

> AC TO AO, 27 APRIL 1983: After eight straight weeks of tumbling rain and not only the wettest April in history, but the wettest *month* since 1882, suddenly the Park burst into bloom.

> AC TO AO, 23 MAY 1983: Last Thursday, suddenly it was 89 degrees, followed by 92 on Friday. But 'dry as a bone,' to coin a racy phrase, since the city was having one of its very rare off-shore winds, straight from the desert.

> AC TO AO, 16 OCTOBER 1984: Outside my window, the park is an Impressionist fantasy of gold and orange and lemon and copper, with blobs of intervening green.

The shared pleasure of a trusted (and unthreatening) confidant and the revisiting of Cooke's musical past helped establish and maintain the mellow atmosphere – notably in the construction of the chronological series *The First Fifty Years*, whose subtitle was 'A personal view of social life in Britain and the USA from 1900–1950, reflected in the popular music of the time'.

> AC TO AO, 5 JULY 1983: Odd that I didn't think, when we were thrashing over these first two programs ('The End of the Victorians' and 'The Edwardians') of simply throwing a tap root back into my childhood (I am, you recall, an Edwardian). The whole charming, bouncing, lachrymose, cocky, maudlin era came alive again.

The correspondence became ever more intimate. Cooke took to providing pen-pictures of his life, like his New Year's Eve celebrations at the start of 1984, typically free of crowds and strangers – just the cartoonist Whitney Darrow and his wife; Paul and Simone Mannheim; the novelist, Jerome Weidman and his wife Peggy.

> AC TO AO, 2 JANUARY 1984: Our 'jollification' was mainly an eight-way conversation stopped just before midnight. The cork popped. Jane and Middy Darrow drank a toast. Simone sipped a teaspoonful. Whitney dipped his lips in the stuff. Jerome, a non-drinker, quaffed tonic. Paul and I faked it with champagne glasses bubbling mit Scotch and spritzer. Peggy Weidman looked at her glass.

He wrote often of his family – stories of grandchildren ('In haste. Have to take the two girls – Eliza, aged 5 and Phoebe, 3 – to tea at the Plaza') and about Jane:

> AC TO AO, 17 JANUARY 1984: The old lady – Frances Jane White Hawkes Cooke – recently had her seventy-first, but nobody believes for a minute – in or out of her smashing new Fortuny dress – that she's a day over fifty-five.

When Owen's marriage ran into difficulty, there was a constant stream of messages of comfort and support – and even some free advice, gleaned from Irving Cohen.

> AC TO AO, 16 JANUARY 1987: How do things go? If Jane were not an atheist and I were not an agnostic, we'd be praying for you every night . . . . Divorce, even under the most amicable circumstances (which mine was) is still defeat in a most important life decision and the humiliation rankles for some time. But I've noticed that once the decision is firmly

made, a little light begins to filter in, if only because you've decided to drop the emotional baggage of the past – all the good and the bad of it – and are forced to look ahead. I hope you'll find this so.

Cooke noted with growing gloom the sickness and death which had begun to decimate his circle of friends and acquaintances: Joan Wilson, his *Masterpiece Theatre* producer, who died of cancer, Nunnally Johnson, George Movshon, one-time director on his United Nations films and many more – among them a casual golfing partner.

> AC TO AO, 23 APRIL 1985: I was due to play golf on Sunday with Bob Nelson. . . . Nelson didn't show up – he'd played tennis the day before and dropped dead on court! I tell you! – some year. Keep your fingers crossed and lay off the French fried potatoes.

In that same year, Cooke had the simple but elegant idea of delving into his own store of records and tapes for inspiration, the basis of a new series – *Alistair Cooke's American Collection*. One was to be called 'Classic Blues', a subject on which Cooke had already corresponded with a devoted British follower of his programmes, the poet Philip Larkin. Luckily these radio cassettes had not been damaged when – two years beforehand – a scorching summer and the breakdown of the air-conditioning in his apartment wiped out much of his treasured store of video tapes.

> AC TO AO, 20 JUNE 1985: Philip Larkin wrote to me and said he'd like to have one or two cassettes from our vast repertory. He mentioned the 12-bar blues [the opening edition of 'Alistair Cooke's Jazzmen' – 1977] and I told him that I must have been in a stupor when we did that program – masses too much early, scratchy, primitive stuff. I believe this could be a knockout program. I have been going through my Closet and found some treasure trove.

The Larkin correspondence had been sporadic, but typically wide-ranging. In his first letter, Cooke had written to say how much he'd enjoyed Larkin's *Required Reading*, with its boost for unfashionable poets like Masefield and Hardy. 'Masefield, whom I heard as a boy, was very good – plaintive, modest, regretful – and quietly moving. I can do it to this day ["Sea Fever"], being a sometime – and to my friends' distress a continuing – mimic.'

Then, in November of 1985, he wrote to Larkin, 'The long gap in our sometime correspondence has not, I hope, been caused on your side by a lengthy convalescence.' By the time the letter arrived, Larkin was dead. He never heard the transmission of 'Classic Blues'. At Cooke's suggestion the programme included a formal dedication 'to the memory of Philip Larkin, for whom Alistair Cooke put it together'.

There is no doubt, however, about the climax of the Cooke-Owen association: the six Gershwin programmes, which Cooke hoped might begin in January 1987 – the fiftieth anniversary of Gershwin's death. They missed the date but the series was accepted. None of their previous work had undergone such close and self-critical preparation in New York and London. So dear were the programmes to Cooke's heart, that he deferred reviewing the final tapes for several weeks:

AC TO AO, 14 APRIL 1987: My big anxiety is about the first programme. Critics review only the first of a series and the serious sagging part comes on page 2, with the bit about GG's influences. The Berlin recording is not good. . . . I feel that the 'Alexander's Ragtime Band' is too brass bandy and not raggy enough. . . . Programme Two seems to me to fall away at the end.

After many weeks of labour, most of the wrinkles were ironed out and Cooke sent his final comments on the five programmes. The last, in particular, he found to be 'without fault or flaw. A splendid end. I think, all things considered, it's our best program. Ingrid [Cooke's secretary] wept. As my headmaster used to say, "Gratters, Owen. Well done! If you go on in this fashion, boy, one day you'll be working for the BBC!" '

He himself wrote a preview piece for the *Radio Times*, in which he argued that Gershwin was much more important than he might seem from the popular tunes by which he is remembered. 'Over the thirteen years that Alan Owen, my producer and I have been working on American popular music, the conviction has dawned slowly but surely on both of us that of all the very gifted men and women who made the 1920s and 1930s a golden age of American song, Gershwin more and more looks like the truest original.'

And finally, medical advice of all kinds continued to be dispensed, liberally, from Cooke's pharmacopoeia.

AC TO AO, 22 JUNE 1991: I assume that – like 85 per cent of ageing (!) males – you are getting the first twinges of osteo-arthritis. *Mine* started in the right thumb and joint. Let me cheer you at once by saying the pain will go! It's always painful at the start when the calcium is mooching around. Once it settles, your thumb, wrist or whatever, may be slightly mis-shapen but will no longer hurt.

He himself had undergone 'traction, deep heat, electrolysis and massage' when the condition affected his upper back, before Carl Borders told him to 'screw the treatment' and take four to six aspirins a day, which he had done in the form of Ascriptin, ever since. 'So – what else? Oh, copper bangle!!!!!!!! Rubbish! Discredited ages ago as a mere talisman. The people who swore by it were all found to have lost the pain *while* wearing the bracelet – bangle!! – for God's sake. You could wear a crucifix, or walk round with no clothes on and – once the pain subsided – you could put it down to the holy cross or going naked. An elementary case of *post hoc, propter hoc*.'

In March 1994, Alan Owen raked through his own 'Closet', sorted through two decades of paper and – reflecting on a turbulent period in his personal life – wrote to Cooke:

AO TO AC, 4 MARCH 1994: In the five inch deep wedge of old cheque stubs, press cuttings, sunglasses etc were fifty-seven letters and seven post-cards from you. I appreciated them at the time, of course, but now in retrospect I see more clearly what trouble you took and care you expended on my welfare. . . . It's not only the letters that counted, but also the knowledge that you and Jane were rooting for me all along.

35

KEEPING IN TOUCH

Alan Owen wasn't Cooke's only regular correspondent in these later years. He kept in touch – sporadically – with the declining band of school- and college-friends in England, mulling over the demise of mutual acquaintances and recalling the old days. Eddie Done, for instance, the Blackpool boy with whom he had shared a house in Cambridge: (30 November, 1990: 'I am, of course, deeply impressed to hear that you are in good health. I have never forgotten how my mother used to brood and shake her head after you'd spent an evening at 55 Ormond Avenue, and vent the fear that "he sometimes looks as if he'd not be long for this world. I wish he'd put on some more weight." ') Or J.N.G. (Norrie) Davidson in Dublin: (30, December, 1990: 'I see you stay with a manual typewriter. I complained over the air about the "phasing out" of decent ribbons. Within the month I had packages of ribbons from Dorset, France, Malaysia, Australia and India.')

Other long associations built up around different sorts of relationships and one of the most striking grew from Cooke's unquenchable interest in language and linguistics. It began in 1980 with a fan letter from Cooke to William Safire, whose language column in the *New York Times Magazine* he read with the faithfulness of a disciple. Safire was familiar with Cooke's work: he had quoted two of his *Guardian* pieces in his definitive *Political Dictionary* which had just been reprinted. But Cooke's 1980 letter set the tone for a long-term – epistolary – relationship, light-hearted but based on a serious shared interest in the protection of the language. Cooke would let off steam about some horror perpetrated by politician or journalist, and Safire would feel free to use these expostulations in his own writing.

4 APRIL 1982: Yeah, Ronnie! (or, the Split Infinitive of the Year, possibly the Century) – On being asked if the *New York Times* report was true that

the 1983 deficit will be $124 billion, rather than the $91.5 billion in the Reagan budget... A: 'I couldn't answer until we have to, by law, shortly, in a couple of weeks, present an updated project.'

Cooke's approach was sometimes pitched at the technical level you might expect of somebody who had studied English Language under Q and Linguistics at Harvard: 'Watch out for the ellipse in "as if" and amend the tense accordingly: e.g., "He looks as if he <u>had</u> suffered a stroke' NOT "he looks as if he has suffered a stroke." That is, "he looks as (he would look) if he had suffered a stroke" ' If he caught Safire out in some transgression in the *New York Times*, he could scarcely contain himself:

> 17 MAY 1982: Hot Damn! If the teacher himself doesn't commit it this very morning. I pray that an illiterate copy editor changed your stuff. Brace yourself: '... the evangelist of today who obviously identifies with the first evangelist who is trying to ingratiate himself <u>to</u> (!!!) the leaders of the Soviet Union.' Webster gives 'ingratiate himself with ...' So does the Oxford. So does every dictionary I have.

The two men didn't meet for many years after the start of their correspondence, yet the linguistic freemasonry to which both belonged created a stronger bond than many conventional friend-ships.

> AC TO WS, 22 SEPTEMBER 1985: The revelation that in your college days you 'scored' is a shocking admission of your extreme youth. In my years (1932–34) at an American school, 'making out' was the operative announcement... A brief note on the then going sexual lingo at Cambridge might amuse. We had only two words for scoring: poking and grinding. There was a lock at one point on the River Cam. It must have been named when there was a ferry to take horses across the river. Its formal name was The Horse Grind. We thought this coincidence extremely funny.

He added that 'off on a grind with a tapestry bitch' was the charming description used by undergraduates to denote dalliance in a punt with a mill-girl. Safire published these reminiscences, along with many other extracts from their etymological duels.

Cooke religiously jotted down items for Safire on the yellow pads he kept by his desk as he watched the television news or read the newspaper – to be collected, collated and handed over in due course:

AC TO WS, 24 FEBRUARY 1986: The winner of the 1986 Quadruple Tautology Award: Larry Speakes, finally announcing President Reagan's bold, no-nonsense stand on Marcos: 'The President is watching the current situation, which is ongoing at this moment.'

Safire was one of several contributors to the 'Alistair Cooke Salute' tape produced by WGBH to mark the end of *Masterpiece Theatre* and, eventually, Cooke devised a special acronym for Safire's older contributors: OGPU – Octogenarians Guarding Proper Usage. Cooke's correspondence, according to Safire, 'has enlivened and enriched my work'.

~

At about the same time, Cooke launched into another, more complex, correspondence with (Sir) Isaiah Berlin. He was already an adherent of Berlin's, notably of the philosopher's most celebrated maxim, dividing humanity into foxes and hedgehogs – between the fox 'seizing upon a vast variety of experiences and objects for what they are in themselves, without seeking to fit them into a unitary vision', and the hedgehog 'who relates everything to a single central vision'. For Cooke, Berlin's fox was a kind of journalist's charter, the intellectual validation of a career in which only the immediate really mattered, and in which objectivity and openness to ideas were the most important qualities. By definition, the fox was agnostic, too, and never sought to compare what he saw with some template drawn by others.

Berlin was one of the most influential philosophers of a liberal tradition of which Cooke – instinctively – felt himself to be a part. Hence, when in the late 1970s Cooke had time to read more widely and came across a new collection of Berlin's essays – *Against the Current* – he decided to pay his respects in a congratulatory letter. Berlin was delighted. He brushed aside Cooke's concern that a mere journalist should be seeking to bandy words with a philosopher. His own favourite radical thinker was a Russian journalist – and if Cooke were to write about 'the transforming events which changed or at least deeply affected' his life, it would certainly stand the test of time.

This touched a chord. Like so many journalists, especially those with passable academic qualifications, Cooke was aware of the lack of permanence in what he did. That was why *America* had meant so much.

AC TO IB, 30 JANUARY 1981: Only in private, among a few friends, and in reading, have I been much occupied with the life of the mind. This genuine itch to know how people tick, whether he's a rancher, a Mafia under-lord or a golf pro – is enjoyed at the expense of any steady, deep concern with a political or philosophical <u>idea.</u>

The proof of his pudding, he suggested, lay in the diaries of his favourite critic of the 1930s and 40s, James Agate.

I have just finished the nine volumes of Agate's *Ego* and wish there were nine more. He was cocksure, vain, reactionary, depressingly bigoted, selfish – and he has no shame in letting all this out – but he is enormously alive to everything going on about him and rejoices over a new performance of *Lear* or the passing remark of a London cab driver.

Berlin still wasn't sure that Agate's reputation would survive. But the two men did agree that no one with an ounce of humanity could remain immune to criticism, bad reviews and public disapproval. They flattered each other shamelessly. Berlin congratulated Cooke on a lecture at Cambridge, while Cooke, in turn, quoted Berlin in his review for the *New Yorker*, of a new book on Churchill – 'the largest human being of our time'. Berlin was impressed. 'Your piece – I do beg you to take my sincere word for it – seems to me both brilliant (you know <u>that</u> – one always knows when one has brought something off, and when not) and absolutely true.'

They mused on the afflictions of age, which in Berlin's case caused throat problems and the loss of 'one or two vocal chords', thereby producing a guttural sound, 'a kind of croak, which distresses and disgusts me'.

IB TO AC, 19 SEPTEMBER 1983: Otherwise, I am not too bad for my years – and, my God, nor are you. You are wonderfully productive: I moderately: but I wish we could meet, it would make me very happy.

As with William Safire, meetings did eventually take place: towards the end of 1985, Berlin invited Cooke to lunch at his club in St James's – the first time, Cooke said, that he had been tempted to eat at a London club. Berlin was one of the few people to whom he sometimes deferred: the philosopher, looking back, said that he never felt he had trouble making himself heard.

That first lunch led to the most profound exchange of letters between the two. Cooke had been rereading Berlin's essay on Chaim Weizmann, Israel's first president, and been struck by what he felt was a failure to recognise the anti-Semitism of the Englishmen who had worked towards the foundation of the Jewish state.

AC TO IB, 25 NOVEMBER 1985: There surely must have been in Weizmann a streak of saintly naïveté that blinded him to a prejudice that was quietly, but firmly, rooted in those tolerant, fair-minded, decorous English of all classes: namely, anti-Semitism. Perhaps 'all classes' goes a little far. Among the middle- and working-class people I knew as a young boy and man in Manchester, the oddity up the street or round the corner was confidentially described: 'he is also a son of Abraham.'

Then, when Cooke reached Cambridge, he had been 'shocked at the blithe, offhand use of the phrase "Jew boy" by young men who in all other manners and matters appeared to express the essence of kindness, sensitivity, gentle manners and the rest of it'.

This adduced a closely argued five-page reply from Berlin, discoursing widely on the root-causes of anti-Semitism (in the tenets of Christianity and its Gospels, he believed) and on the Weizmann he himself came to know in later life. He apologised for the length of his 'sermon' and warned that he might, given the opportunity, carry on in the same vein for hours when they next met.

Cooke expressed cheerful unconcern at the prospect.

AC TO IB, 14 JANUARY 1986: Need I say? – I will say – that your enormous sermon was deeply absorbed and greatly enjoyed. As the winter crawls along and slows the operating lobes, I may provoke you with some other burning, or ashen, topic in the hope of releasing another outburst.

At eighty, Cooke repeated his view to Berlin (who had just reached the same landmark) that at such an age, 'a man has nothing to contribute to the young and the middle-aged who are running affairs'. He didn't really believe it – certainly not in respect of his correspondent. And age decidedly did not remove their pleasure in sharing an unkind word or two about unloved public figures like the Soviet spy Kim Philby.

AC TO IB, 1 MAY 1989: I was considerably bucked this week to read – in Knightley's exchange of letters with the bounder – that two things chronically drove Philby up the wall during his long stay in Moscow: he could not get his favourite vegetable, and he was infuriated every Sunday by the 'preposterous' talks from America of 'The BBC's Cooke smartie – Alistair of that Ilk.' (His grasp of American idiom must always have been shaky – 'Smart Cookie' would have been correct and good).

And when Berlin asked if he had known Philby, he replied:

AC TO IB, 16 MAY 1989: No, I never knew Philby, Burgess or any of them. They arrived at Cambridge a year or two after me just when the avant-garde moved into politics. Throughout my time, the double-domes were all literary: Bronowski and James Reeves (both at my college, both friends), and Empson (whom I knew – if it was possible to know a man with a brain in ferment and an icicle for a heart).

And so it continued, two men whose brains remained resolutely unsoftened while all around them drifted and declined.

IB TO AC, 11 JUNE 1990: You ask me if I flourish. I do. And so, I am sure, do you. Arm in arm, we march into the future.

The affection of the old *Guardian* man for the apostle of liberal philosophy seems, superficially, a natural enough thing. But Cooke's own politics, let alone his philosophy, did not allow the affixing of simple labels. His friendship with the journalist Bill Buckley, doughty defender of right-wing values, as with the equally conservative William Safire, points to something more complex in Cooke's make-up and helps to explain why he was so reluctant to come out with formulaic judgements on his adopted country. Such judgements can only be made from solid political or sociological ground, and Cooke never found that reassuring place from which sweeping statements can be safely peddled.

William F. Buckley came to prominence, during the 1950s and 1960s, as a man unflinchingly ready to challenge the liberal consensus. Through his magazine *National Review*, founded in 1955, and his television show *Firing Line* he became a leading figure of the intellectual right: in the words of Harold Evans (in *American Century*), Buckley, 'despite his defence of McCarthy and other youthful indiscretions, helped to make Conservatism respectable'.

In September 1970, before they had met for the first time, Cooke reviewed Buckley's latest book, and to Buckley's surprise, it was a friendly, thoughtful review. Cooke, he learned, regarded him as the true inheritor of Mencken's mantle – a sceptic with attitude, prepared to fight for the principle that a democracy could not allow the ceding of too much ground to a single ideology. 'If there is no case to make for conservatism in the United States today then the country, certainly the Constitution, is in a very bad way indeed. Buckley's value, it seems to me, is as a sensible lance to the emotional fat that weighs down so many middle-aged liberals.'

Buckley was enchanted by this praise from a relatively unexpected quarter and dropped Cooke a note of thanks, suggesting lunch. The meeting took place at the Carlyle, and thereafter – for the next twenty-five years – the two men lunched every six weeks, enjoying conversation unfettered by political prejudice, and with no other motive but the pleasure of argument. 'It's a friendship', according to Buckley, 'which hasn't been disturbed at all by any positions I take which are eccentric, or his that are unorthodox. It's the best kind of friendship you can have.' Buckley felt, in any case, that Cooke had never been a dyed-in-the-wool liberal. Indeed, he had detected in some of the *Six Men* essays – on Edward VIII, for instance – what he called 'Alistair the stern'. It was a view shared by many of his friends.

Gene and Edna Rostow had remained extremely close to the Cookes since the 1930s, Edna becoming as fond of Jane as she had been of Ruth. Although Rostow's most senior administration post was LBJ's Under-Secretary for Political Affairs, he remained an influential and well-informed figure, with a reputation for being a hawk on military matters. When Jimmy Carter won the 1976 election, Rostow and the arms negotiator, Paul Nitze, set up the Committee on the Present Danger to lobby for the maintenance of the defence budget. Summoned to a meeting with the new President, they found him chillingly naïve about the Russian threat: Carter was torn, he said, between those advising him that war was inevitable, and those who said it was all a terrible misunderstanding, and it only needed a decent man to straighten Moscow out. That encounter strengthened their resolve, and the Committee set about raising money and recruiting high-profile supporters, among them Ronald Reagan. Even after Reagan reached the White House, Nitze and Rostow pursued their campaign – which continued until the collapse of the Soviet system.

Gene Rostow discovered by chance from one of the Committee's staff that Alistair Cooke had been making regular contributions to the cause. He was surprised, but only because Cooke had never mentioned it. It seemed perfectly consistent to him that Democrat-leaning figures who had lived through the inter-war years (like himself and Cooke) should believe in firm leadership and strong defence. Yet, even afterwards, Cooke was shy of admitting his support for the Committee. 'Oh no, no, no,' he protested. 'That was Gene's obsession. I was aware of it, of course, but only as any reporter might be.' He conceded that he sympathised with Rostow's views, especially during the Carter years, and sometimes looked over the Committee's literature – which paid unrelenting attention to Soviet nuclear developments. He was forcibly struck by the revelation that the Russians had their own version of Reagan's 'Star Wars' programme and he used the information to inform his own writing. ('You'll remember that the Reykjavik Summit collapsed the moment that Mr Reagan refused to shelve the Star Wars project,' he remarked in a *Letter from America* in December 1987. 'Strangely – I've puzzled over this before – Mr Reagan did not say then, "Look who's talking – they've been busy for years with their own Star Wars." ') In the circumstances, a private donation to the Committee on the Present Danger would have been quite logical – but still not quite 'right' for the journalist. Hence, possibly, Cooke's denial, though a denial with a rider: 'Perhaps', he said, 'my objectivity in this was a little blurred by my affection for Gene.'

Whatever the truth of the matter, the story seems informative. A drift over the years from left to right, liberal to conservative, is a familiar political pattern: but Cooke never really drifted far. His background and upbringing gave him a strong sense of social order, which made the excesses of the 1960s unattractive: he was liberal in a more intellectual sense – because it seemed right and proper that any sensible social order should treat people fairly – but he was no automatic Democrat. He rarely spoke about his own voting record, but Jane occasionally felt the need to implore him not to cancel out her own vote. 'I have never voted Republican,' is her proud boast. And, with marginally less assurance, 'I don't think Alistair has, either.'

Perhaps the biggest question mark is over Carter's second term. Like many Americans, Cooke never really found a way of fathoming what Carter was made of. In the end he concluded that he was probably a good and decent man, but lacked the requisite political skills for the job of President. The first alarm bells rang when Carter told *Playboy* magazine, two months before the election in 1976, that he had 'looked on a lot of women with lust' and 'committed adultery in my heart many times'. It was not the sort of talk Cooke expected of a putative President. After Carter's victory there followed a brief honeymoon, which led Cooke (in April 1977) to speak of the President having acquired 'a poise and confidence he never had when he was campaigning'.

This generosity didn't last long. After a mere nine months of the Presidency, Cooke was writing, 'It's now quite common to run into intelligent and well-informed people who say, "I still don't know what he's about." ' He had started disappointing the liberals, without being a credible conservative, Cooke felt, and the last television debate with Reagan in 1980 settled the matter, as Carter tried – but failed – to depict Reagan as a dangerously rabid right-winger.

> The last thing Reagan appeared was dangerous. He appeared engaging, good-humoured, his brow wrinkled sorrowfully at Mr Carter's mis-interpretations, he recited in the idiom of ordinary American speech his devotion to peace, to the workers, to the families of America, he longed for the old days of decent folks and lots of jobs. And he clinched this simple appeal to half the population with the sunny but deadly question: 'Are you better off than you were four years ago? Do you think America is stronger than it was four years ago?'

On election night itself the Cookes, as usual, invited their friends to share the occasion. One regular was his banker friend Paul Mann-heim, with whom he'd been discussing politics for decades but who, unlike the majority of Cooke's circle, had 'never voted Democrat in his life'. That night, Mannheim was delayed and missed the first solid computer prediction for Reagan. As he came up in the lift, Cooke inserted into the video machine a tape of Carter's 1976 victory. During the pouring of drinks he set the tape running – and Mannheim's jaw dropped. 'Why, what do you know?' he intoned in disbelief at the idea that Carter might have won. It took some time for reality to dawn.

~

Even at the start of the Reagan era, Cooke's coverage of politics was quite a distant affair. He was seventy-two years old, and was extremely busy – writing, broadcasting and travelling. Consequently, his per-ception of Reagan and subsequent Presidents was gleaned mostly

from newspapers and television, which he perused with more fanatical attention to detail than ever: the yellow pad for random jottings
and impressions was never far from his elbow. He was by no means
as perplexed by the oddity of the actor-turned-President as those
involved in day-to-day political coverage. Indeed, for an admirer
of political skills (by whomsoever they might be exercised) Ronald
Reagan was a phenomenon. 'He surprised everybody by coming to
Washington at once, not with the demeanour of a new Commanding
Officer but with the modest air of the new boy, eager to learn the
ropes.'

Reagan, then, looked like an operator, with the bonus that he
seemed ready to take the nuclear issue seriously. His decision to
draft into the administration members of the Committee on the
Present Danger including Paul Nitze – and Gene Rostow – was noted
approvingly in a *Letter from America*. 'By giving the Committee that
title,' Cooke explained, 'they wanted to dramatise what they took
to be a situation of neglect and sleepiness in this country and the
West, similar to the inertia or indifference of Western Europe in
the face of German rearmament during the 1930s.' Rostow's elevation
was especially pleasing. Cooke confided to listeners that the new
head of the Arms Control and Disarmament Agency had been his
first friend in America – 'a twinkling, brown-eyed, genial nineteen-
year-old of athletic build' – who had heard about the lonely
Englishman in his college and had come to welcome him. But
Cooke also remarked that the former Yale water-polo captain would
need all his dexterity to juggle the competing demands of an end
to the arms race, and the dangers of giving ground to the Russians.
A year later, Rostow was out – after he had encouraged Nitze's
famous 'walk in the park' with his Soviet opposite number in July
1982: the discussions were judged to have strayed too far down the
arms reduction line.

Only towards the end of the Reagan era did Cooke relax sufficiently
to accept that the Soviet Union might have found in Mikhail Gor-
bachev a leader who really understood the futility of mutually assured
destruction. And it was, he suggested to Isaiah Berlin, those early
contacts – by men like Rostow and Nitze – which formed the basis of
the successful arms limitation agreements which followed.

As Reagan struggled with the recession of the early 1980s and the
monumental budget deficit, Cooke was usually prepared to give him

the benefit of the economic doubt, too. He would sometimes lean on Paul Mannheim for enlightenment, a man with no sentimentality about politicians. Mannheim's view was that Reagan would end up printing money and stoking up inflation, but somehow (and Cooke was not the man to explain how it happened) the American economy pulled through. He wrote to Isaiah Berlin six years later, 'While Thatcher satisfies Labour prejudices by having low inflation at the price of high unemployment – Reagan infuriates and bewilders the Democrats by having – against all the rules – very low inflation, unprecedentedly low unemployment, and the longest steady increase in the number of employed.'

On a more personal note, his own Social Security cheque (to which he had been contributing since 1937) started to shoot up in value. When it rose from $1200 to $1700 a month he almost wrote an official letter querying the figure. Jane told him not to get involved, and the sum grew bigger and bigger. The Cookes dubbed it 'the Reagan cheque'.

In the *Telegraph* interview for his 2000th programme John Mortimer asked him about Reagan, who had, by then, been mired for some time in the Iran-Contra affair and other troubles, and Cooke took up his theme: 'You know,' Cooke told him, 'this administration is the most corrupt since Harding. One hundred and ten officials have left under a cloud or been indicted. And yet nothing upsets Reagan, he's always smiling. I call him the "Most Happy Fella". He'd make a wonderful head of state, a sovereign, because he's great at kissing babies and the bereaved. That's why sixty per cent think he's lying about Irangate, and sixty per cent think he's a good guy.'

'He should be King and not Prime Minister?'

'That's it. You know the first thing he does every morning? He puts on his bullet-proof vest as soon as he gets up. That's why he walks around in that funny rolling fashion. But he's always so damned cheerful!'

'How would Mrs Thatcher do as an American politician?'

'The Americans are allergic to headmistresses. I find it inconceivable that Mrs Thatcher would have got on here as a politician. I can't see her being elected as a small-town mayor.'

Cooke then forgot his own golden rule, as Mortimer asked, 'Who'll succeed Reagan? Not Bush?'

'No. That's inconceivable. I guess it'll be a Democrat. Sam Nunn's

very good, very cool, a liberal conservative. And Cuomo is an inter-
esting man, if he could be drafted. He's a great speaker, no fake at all.
He has his own cadence. A great theatrical performer.' The rest, as
Cooke himself might have said, you know.

When Raymond Seitz ended his ambassadorial stint in London in
1994, Cooke gave the valedictory toast. Cooke admired Seitz because
he was the first career diplomat to be given such a coveted post, which
was so often handed out as the sort of sinecure against which Mark
Twain had thundered: Seitz was a prime example, in other words,
of a functioning meritocracy, in which neither background – nor
campaign contributions – played a part. In turn, Seitz admired Cooke,
because he felt he had genuinely contributed to an understanding of
the United States during a time of rapid change: 'Cooke is a rather
shrewd observer,' according to Seitz, 'and being so old and acute, he
has become a tremendous resource.'

36

SETTLING ACCOUNTS

It was no surprise that after so much journalistic enterprise, in so many forms, over so many years, somebody should seek to draw the threads together – and to attempt an assessment of Cooke's contribution to Anglo-American understanding. He had already turned down a number of requests by biographers, when he was approached by an American academic from Grand Falls, Michigan. Ronald Wells had carved out a specialist area of study – the interconnections between British and American history and current affairs. The proposal – to which Cooke agreed – was for a collection of articles from the *Guardian* which would demonstrate that, behind the superficial coverage of daily events, there lay a profound and important record of more than forty momentous years.

The initial contacts between the two were warm and fruitful. Wells spent time in New York and at Nassau Point, and talked to Cooke at length. As the project developed, however, it became clear that there was a mismatch between Wells' aspirations and Cooke's idea of what the book would be like. Both he and his publishers were alarmed when Wells delivered a long, dense and carefully argued analysis of the material he'd collected. 'The original version', Cooke wrote to Chuck Elliott at Alfred Knopf, 'was a model, or stereotype PhD thesis. He had it in sections: Portraits; The Black Rebellion; Politics; Attitudes, etc etc etc – with numbered references and a preliminary essay for each section. I told him this looked like a compilation by Professor Dry-As-Dust (a more acceptable euphemism, of course). I pointed out that since it constituted a running commentary on a changing nation, the only possible way to run it was chronologically.' He added the (to him) startling information that Wells had thirty-five graduate students signed up for a course on 'The America of Alistair Cooke'.

Wells was understandably irritated that the publishers had become involved even before he had had a chance to clarify matters with

Cooke himself. 'I realise that the book is large,' he wrote, 'but I thought this was the point, i.e., that this was to be a "monument" to your long and distinguished career in journalism.' That was the nub. Knopf regretted that, however good the individual elements might be, they were not – as commercial publishers – in the business of publishing 'monuments'. They felt it would simply be too unwieldy and unreadable for a trade house, as opposed to a university press. Elliott was implacable: 'A large assemblage of old newspaper pieces, even by someone as fluent and interesting as Alistair (or perhaps *especially* by someone of Alistair's lightness of touch, since the bulk is usually at odds with the tone) is never going to make a viable book.'

It was an awkward dilemma, since Cooke liked Wells and realised how much work had already been done: 'He has worked his tail off on this opus,' he told Elliott, and he took to calling him his 'Boswell'. He himself wrote to Wells as the months went on, anxious to find a compromise involving fewer pieces and less academic erudition. In time, that compromise emerged in the form of *America Observed (The Newspaper Years of Alistair Cooke)*. To all intents and purposes it looked just like the three earlier volumes of *Letters*. The main difference was an extended introduction – the residue of the Wells commentaries condensed into a few pages, with two contributions from Cooke himself. The first was mostly historical and descriptive, with an elegant (if sanitised) portrayal of the book's genesis.

> When Ronald Wells began his safari through the jungle of the *Guardian*'s files, he had no preconceived idea about the specimens he was going to collect. But early on, during his heroic trudge through several million words, he found that the principle of selection – or rather, of rejection – pretty much announced itself, [!] if only by the proliferation of hundreds of pieces of 'straight' reportage that, however apt or informative they might have seemed at the time, now read as elaborate glosses on the sort of event, great and small, you look up in an almanac.

A few extra pieces had been added from the 1980s, to show that Cooke had avoided declining into 'the brooding silence of senility' – a quip with a hard edge, in the light of the way so many of his friends had slumped into terminal decline.

Ronald Wells then laid out what remained of his thesis: to examine whether Cooke might properly be recognised as an Alexis de Tocqueville for our times. The French author of *Democracy in America* had experienced the country in the 1830s, when the concept of democracy was in its infancy in Europe. Wells pointed out that it was this study of a potentially (universal) political system that gave de Tocqueville's work such lasting relevance. Could something similar be argued for Cooke? Or was the much-quoted comparison simply making the trite point that both men were Europeans interpreting America for a transatlantic audience? Was it enough that Cooke should have been such an accurate and assiduous observer of 'the threads and textures' of American life?

Wells approaches the answer to his own questions by way of a vexatious matter of fact: Cooke's own refusal to play, in any overt way, the part Wells wishes to ascribe to him. 'Cooke typically eschews the grand theme in favour of the particular event or person,' he admits, but 'he has much to say, in his own way, about the "meaning" of America'. In Wells's interpretation, even when no effort is made (and no effort *is* made) by Cooke to draw wider lessons for other nations, those characteristics 'reflect universal human traits.'

It is hard to disagree that 'while Cooke is not unaware of the more untoward aspects of American culture, he generally sees more hope than fear in it, both for America and for the world...' and that this hope is 'tempered by realism'. But what is notable about Cooke – indeed it often seems to be his defining motive – is that he views American experience for what it is, not for what lessons it might have for anybody else. Apart from a soft spot for hamburgers and the American Constitution, that is, and an implacable loathing for cranberry sauce, peanut butter and drum majorettes – and apart from a belief that the richness of American television outweighs the crassness of many individual programmes, he is unusually – perhaps uniquely – non-judgemental. It is America, therefore he has reported it.

Ronald Wells did, however, tempt Cooke into one lapse from his steadfast vow never to answer the question 'Whither America?' He quoted the closing section of Cooke's television history, 'In this country – a land of the most persistent idealism and the blandest cynicism – the race is on between its decadence and its vitality'; and he asked Cooke, in February 1988, how that race was going. The resulting conversation covered six pages.

After a lengthy preamble about his lifelong abstention from dogma and ideology, Cooke finally proffered a few entries on either side of the decadence/vitality ledger. First, decadence: the money mania, which had been a feature of American life since Mark Twain's 'era of incredible rottenness', but which he felt was 'as bad now as any time since then' (the evidence – too many business schools churning out too many investment bankers and not enough people to make things); the collapse of public education; the overcommercialisation of sport; the lure, in the arts (quoting Gibbon), of 'freakishness, pretending to originality, enthusiasm masquerading as vitality'. Then there were the bigger, moral issues: Cooke spoke out against 'the widespread persistence of a phoney counter-culture (the replacement of thrift, work, minimum social duties by what Philip Larkin called the new hippie syllabus – sex, not working, drugs). I suppose, not to beat about the bush, that much of what I take to be the social sickness of the time – beginning in the Sixties and exacerbated in the Eighties – could be attributed by a moralist to a clutch of certain deadly sins, namely greed, envy, lust, covetousness.'

The most serious indictment was of successive governments: an ambitious (and insanely expensive) foreign policy, whose most damaging manifestation, the Kennedy Inaugural, led to the Vietnam War and thence to the debilitating budget deficit. Cooke saw this as a severe case of 'imperial overstretch', when once-great nations attempt 'to maintain their power far beyond the borders they were able to discipline or contain'. It was a depressing catalogue.

In case anyone felt that this amounted to a jeremiad, he was happy to affirm that America's vital signs were still detectable – 'vivacity, humour, courage, serenity. In general, there doesn't seem to be any decline in curiosity, inquisitiveness, enlisted in the dogged belief that things can be made better, that tomorrow ought to be better than today. The stoic and the fatalist are not yet familiar American types.' He offered three encouraging examples: 'the unflagging energy of the media in digging out and facing all the nastiest problems of the country'; the number of rich Americans making fortunes in order to give a good deal of them away to worthy causes; and 'third, among the people at large, an unsleeping passion for liberty, even when it slops over into forms of licence absurdly defended by the First Amendment'.

And what did he conclude from this balance sheet? For a man who had devoted so much energy to looking for the silver lining around every American cloud, he sounded surprisingly gloomy. 'If I were filing daily pieces today, instead of in the Forties, Fifties, Sixties and

Seventies, I don't think I could be – shall we say? – so sprightly without guilt.'

As a postscript to that judgement there is at least some anecdotal evidence that, with the passing years, this gradual disenchantment made Cooke *feel* less American. He would tell interviewers that, as a younger man, he felt '110% American' (or even more). By the 1980s, he was occasionally caught referring to his fellow-citizens, in private, as 'they' rather than 'we'. This entailed not so much a nostalgia for Britain, but rather a sense of detachment from the America of Carter, Reagan or Clinton. By 1994 he was quoted as saying, 'I'm still an Englishman in America. An Irish Lancastrian, really, that's what I am. I don't kid myself that I'm from Arkansas.'

Perhaps any old man, with an aching knee and too many funerals on his mind, might have reached the judgement which emerges from the introduction to *America Observed*. It was still quite an indictment. Nor did his opinions soften as the years went on. In the updated *America* introduction of 1992, he struck an even more melancholy chord than in the original, or in his Congressional address. An absence of domestic wars since 1865, he believed, had caused America to grow complacent and self-satisfied. 'The question remains, in looking towards any American future, whether a century and a quarter of surcease from war has not engendered a deep love of comfort, which will have to be outgrown if there is to be a general revival of American industriousness, morale, and justifiable optimism in the traditional belief that each generation is bound to do better than the last one: what we call the American Dream.'

～

In 1986, Cooke was awarded the Ellis Island Medal of Honour. It was an idea dreamed up by Mayor Ed Koch to mark the centenary of the Statue of Liberty's dedication. From 15,000 nominations, just eighty names were chosen to represent the immigrants who had made special contributions to 'the culture and ethnic mix of New York'. Like so many other pieces of congratulatory hardware, the 'Mayor's Liberty Award', as it was also known, was large, bronze and ugly. And it would surely have ended up in the darker reaches of Cooke's closet, or acting as a paperweight in the corner of the kitchen, if it hadn't been for the citation: he had been selected as 'A Social Historian'. It was the first time the title had been used officially and at last he felt comfortable with the idea of having a label stuck to his lapel. It was certainly the way his friend Bill Buckley came to see him: 'He was never a very political creature – he's a man of letters, an intense student of human behaviour. He'd have made a wonderful sociologist except that he's too literate to qualify.'

It seemed to Cooke that this was a description which made sense of his life's work. Who else had charted so faithfully the shifts in the American way of life, the large and the small, the significant and the subtle? He had done so in many media, and before many audiences, though the *Letter from America* was probably its most successful manifestation. But, as Ron Wells commented, 'His life has been his work.' In the early years, almost every titbit of information was new to his British audience – such as his celebration of the latest household gadgets in November 1946:

> I'm thinking of such things as bean-slicers, the toasters that pop the toast up when it's done; and peelers with a rotating blade that simply bear down on a potato or carrot and peel it; electric mixers into which you throw, say, milk, butter, flour and raw vegetables and which in a few seconds produce a fine purée; and the more recent godsend of mops made of cellulose sponge, which clean a floor, the dishes or a table, without you ever having to touch a mop end or worry over how damp it is, since it's fitted with a steel cradle that graduates the moisture.

The physical changes in society were only a tiny part of it (though housework and the cost of maintaining a maid seemed an early obsession). A glance through the stories Cooke covered in the late 1940s in the *Letter* included such items as the excellence of New York's public transport, bringing up teenagers, the American male's preference for blondes, farming techniques, the arrival of colour television, the celebration of Christmas in different states, national parks, New York's ethnic complexity and baseball; all intermingled with the perennial themes – the weather, the state of Anglo-American relations, the beauty of New England in the fall (and of California at any time of the year). These observations were sharpened and extended in scope by his annual trips around the country, which provided mountains of material new to the British listener.

However, as the novelty of the United States began to wear off (and when Cooke's working life on the *Guardian* kept him constantly attuned to Washington life) the *Letters* were more often overtly political, with frequent calls for 'the class' (the listeners) to pay attention to the workings of American institutions. Later in life he refined the technique of drawing together all these elements – bringing in the historical background, updated by his reading for *America* – into the elegant and complex essays which his fans so enjoyed. The glue which held the whole construct together – and enabled him to produce *Masterpiece Theatre* intros to order, for that matter – was his memory. Cooke rarely boasted about it, but in one 1957 *Letter* he described this undeserved talent: 'It's not that I take pride in remembering dates, you understand. It's just that I can't ever forget them and am undoubtedly more cluttered in the upper storey with useless knowledge than a quiz-winner.'

The only drawback was that it made Cooke's confidence in his account of things past unassailable. Whenever he made mistakes – and several of those deputed to produce the *Letter* during their six-month stints in New York spotted them – it was hard to convince him that his memory might have let him down.

The *Letter from America* has been like a personal diary, too, though with most names and precise dates withheld. For many years of Cooke's life, indeed, it is the only record of his week-to-week activities. His long-serving, and doubtless long-suffering, German secretary, Ingridluce, was given the task one summer of making some space in the morass of papers accumulated in the Closet. When the Cookes returned from holiday, all his appointment books from 1949 to 1967 had been junked. Ingridluce was forgiven for this lapse and stayed with Cooke until her death from cancer. Just three secretaries – Ingrid, along with Linda Wichtel and the most recent incumbent, Patti Yasek – have provided yet another aspect of the continuity and routine on which Cooke has increasingly depended.

Age inevitably made it harder to keep in touch with the social changes, the tiny tremors which he had picked up so astutely in his younger days. Nothing demonstrated this more clearly than his attitude to matters of political correctness. In truth, he was never very PC. In March 1973 he apologised for the tone of his *Letter*: 'There will be those who are disgusted at my seeming crass indifference to the rocketing issues of the world – though I might say that I have thought for years that women maintain their serenity, their sanity, in fact, not because they are superior creatures but because they pay very little heed to the crashing issues of world politics and concern themselves instead with really important things – like the composition of the next meal, the comfort of the baby, and the flattery of their ridiculously vain husbands.'

It was only partly a joke. It echoed precisely a *Letter* written sixteen years earlier, when Cooke was still in his forties: women, according to Cooke, had their news priorities straight. 'I mean such things as fashion news, hints on new lipsticks, the latest trends in plastic floors, or of white and gold draperies in the living-room, or advice to the lovelorn, or whatever it is ... No survey I've ever seen of women's reading habits ever hints that they jump at once for the political news.' It was a theme of the *Letters*, and it reflected Cooke's Edwardian instincts. He knew that the women's liberation movement took offence at what – for him – were statements of fact. But fixations that, in the Fifties and Sixties, had seemed charmingly old-fashioned, became a serious bone of contention in his later life.

One piece, in particular, led to a public outcry. In November 1996 Cooke decided to chew over a new report on sexual harassment in the armed forces. In his mind the scope of what should be judged 'harassment' had become absurdly broad and he thought the report highlighted some of the absurdities: 'twenty-three per cent [of women in uniform] complained of being whistled at; forty-four per cent of being the object of teasing; thirty-seven per cent, of interpreting dubious looks or gestures. In all, it comes out that about eighty-five per cent accuse their brothers in arms of whistling, or teasing, or giving suggestive looks. Of the prime, near-criminal, category which is called "actual or attempted rape or assault" – four per cent.'

And then came the killer sentence. 'I'm sure I'm alone in thinking that this reveals an armed force where ninety-six per cent of the men show remarkable restraint.' It may have been intended to shock, but it was seriously ill-judged. *The Times* published an article entitled SEXIST COOKE FACES CHECKS ON HIS US FREEDOM: the writer Bel Mooney declared that 'He is a man of a certain generation, and perhaps that sort of remark was acceptable when he was young. Today it is not.' As the BBC conducted an internal inquiry, the row (with media assistance) surfaced in a San Francisco newspaper (ALISTAIR COOKE IN HOT WATER OVER RAPE REMARK) and on Capitol Hill. A Congress stalwart and Cooke admirer, Pat Schroeder, condemned his 'breezy banter about rape. We're not talking about office flirting, we're talking about a serious felony – rape. The victims have been scarred for life. Cooke owes them, and his listeners, an apology.'

What they got was a bravura (and not very apologetic) performance by Cooke on the Radio Four programme *Feedback*: he believed that he had been wilfully misunderstood and his answers – for once – abandoned his usual diplomacy. 'Look, I discovered from these *Letters* that in talking about relationships between men and women who worked together, you must not introduce one tinge of humour,' he told the interviewer, Chris Dunkley. 'If you do, it's racist, sexist, élitist and homophobic – none of which I am. I was just saying that I thought four per cent (in a huge armed force) attempted or actual rape is a rather remarkably low figure. All armies rape and loot. Especially when they're at war.' It was the nature of the survey which had irked him, and continued to do so. 'When they say that over sixty per cent – I think it worked out on average – reported sexual harassment, you think "Good God! That's frightful!" and so it would be, but it includes teasing and joking and whistling and looking at a woman – I maintain that is scientifically ridiculous.' Later, warming to his theme, he hit back at the minority of the feminist movement that 'sits with gritted teeth, and they don't respond to your talk, they respond to what they think they hear.' For good measure he lobbed in a defiant statement of personal principle: 'I don't think it would do to campaign for equal treatment. I think women in the military should have special treatment – I'm quite serious about this – a special kind of courtesy. And this may be news to these – er – campaigners [the word was invested with a special scorn] because women *are* different from men, as Aristotle noticed, physically and emotionally. I can't help it if I was brought up on a tradition, a practice, which was called gallantry. I'm too old to change.'

He spoke no more than the honest truth. He regarded himself, in a strange way, as a non-religious Puritan, still subconsciously exhaling the dogma of the Methodist chapel in Blackpool. In his parents' terms, Puritanism had been a critique not just of loose morals and bad behaviour, but of the decadence, corruption and laxity of the established church. He never found it easy, for instance, to discuss gay rights: the very word 'homosexuality' conjured up lurid phrases from Leviticus. To avoid offence, he simply skated round the subject whenever possible, but the prejudices lodged in his psyche coloured a much wider area of life: he couldn't accept, for example, that it was right to spend so much on research into AIDS when cancer remained incurable. Despite his best endeavours, these atavistic streaks in his character kept reappearing.

When there were complaints, the BBC did not usually pursue the matter too vigorously. Cooke's position as a monument of British broadcasting, and the certainty that his career was (despite appearances) finite, meant that there was little virtue in a hue and cry. The *Letter*, after all, had not lost its faithful audience, even if it was an audience of a certain age. One survey suggested that, towards the end, forty per cent of Cooke's regular listeners were over sixty-five. It seemed appropriate, somehow, that his followers should include the Queen Mother and John Major with his propensity for nostalgia. His Prime Ministerial letter of apology for declining an invitation to the Media Society dinner in 1994 said,

> Generations of British listeners – among whom I number myself – have delighted in his deep knowledge and acute observation of the United States. To this he has brought a subtle sense of humour and an abiding, if clear-eyed, sympathy for America. It is a rare compliment to Alistair that he is equally appreciated by many Americans. Edmund Burke, in talking of relations between America and Britain, once wrote of 'ties which, though light as air, are as strong as links of iron'. These are precisely the ties which Alistair Cooke has helped to forge over more than half a century of broadcasting.

John Major's applause caught the eye of Cristina Odone, deputy editor of the *New Statesman*. In one of a number of celebrity opinions canvassed by the *Guardian* for Cooke's ninetieth birthday, she told the paper, 'Cooke is an old bore. I don't know how he's managed to make a society which is so vibrant and exciting sound so flaccid. It's a real perversion of this brash, young, energetic country. Having a letter read out by a nonagenarian, who sounds limp-wristed and past it, is a real contrast ... He looks like John Major sounded, this nostalgic, dreamy view of Britain.' Odone's was the only dissenting opinion in a welter of kind words, and – in one sense – her comments were obviously accurate. The *Letter from America* had long ago ceased to be a picture of day-to-day life on the streets of New York, San Francisco or Chadron, South Dakota. But what it had lost in immediacy, it often gained in richness and depth. Besides, Cooke always argued with some justice that his reading of the *New York Times* for ninety minutes each morning, close scrutiny of magazines like the

In August 1965 President Johnson spent three hours trying to persuade Cooke that there was no alternative to a build up of American forces in Vietnam. The meeting had a profound influence on Cooke's coverage of the war.

Filming of *America* began in 1970. In this publicity picture, Cooke is 'exchanging a joke' with the director, Michael Gill, in Cambridge. The first episode began with Cooke standing on the bridge, recalling his early misconceptions about the United States.

The filming required Cooke to enter into the spirit of the story – in this case, by sporting a beaver hat to illustrate the fur trade wars of the early nineteenth century.

The making of *America* encouraged Cooke to use his own familiarity with the country, gathered on countless coast-to-coast journeys over the previous forty years, as the bedrock of the commentary. Not for nothing was it called a personal history. Tapping out the blues on a piano once used by Jelly Roll Morton was, for the presenter, one of the most evocative moments.

Cooke caught the golf bug in the summer of 1964 and never shook it off. John captured this sneaky practice session in the corridor of the New York apartment soon afterwards. His father was still at it thirty years later, beyond his ninetieth birthday.

Above At the height of his golfing powers (never quite the height he dreamed of) Cooke had this shot taken to demonstrate his prowess. His playing partner, a Long Island local, looks on with something just short of unbridled admiration.

Above right Another good day. Cooke is pictured with Frank, his favourite caddy, and two much-loved playing partners: Carrol Lynch (the industrial arbitrator who reminded him of Chaplin) and Dr Robert Woods Brown.

A never-to-be-repeated musical moment at the Carlyle Hotel. Leonard Bernstein and James Galway in a rendering of 'Danny Boy', for Cooke's eightieth birthday.

The producer of *A Much Maligned Monarch*, Colin Clark, looks mildly perplexed at the prospect of editing a rather one-sided conversation about Prince Charles's ancestor, George III.

Despite their professional differences, Cooke and his *Guardian* editor, Alastair Hetherington, always remained on friendly personal terms.

The 'surprise' party to mark the end of *Masterpiece Theatre* in 1992. Cooke, at the age of eighty-three, has John on his right, with Susie and her husband Charlie on his left. Jane, if anything, looks relieved that the gruelling trips to Boston are coming to an end.

John Byrne Cooke, in 1995. The paternal nose is unmistakable.

Ruth Emerson Cooke outside the Bungalow, a guest-house in the grounds of the Southold estate once owned by her family. In old age, she returned to take holidays here – in the very building where she and Cooke had spent the summer months more than half a century earlier.

Alistair and Jane in front of the Nassau Point house. Their Long Island routine never really varied. In later years, Cooke often made the weekend trip from New York City by bus.

Right Jane in her Nassau Point studio. She went on painting until, at the age of eighty, she decided overnight that she could no longer meet her own demanding standards. Cooke tried in vain to persuade her to collect the pictures scattered around friends and family for an exhibition.

The Nassau Point house viewed from the edge of the bluff. The basic shape – pre-war Bauhaus – never changed, though the veranda was a post-hurricane addition. The existence of this rural retreat was one of the rocks on which the relationship between Alistair and Jane was built.

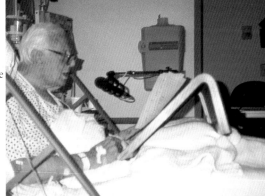

On 4 June 1999, after a mild heart attack, Cooke broadcast *Letter from America* No 2625 from his hospital bed. It was, he estimated, the sixteenth time that such emergency measures had been called for. Usually, nobody knew apart from the producer and sound engineer.

Jane's portrait of Alistair, which hangs in the Alistair Cooke suite
in the Huntington Hotel, San Francisco.

Economist and *Newsweek*, voracious consumption of history and biography, often late into the night, and an easy familiarity with thirty cable networks, from the Discovery and the Biography channels, to news and sport in profusion, not to mention stations specialising in science, medicine and natural history – all this made him better informed than most working journalists could ever be.

Another young critic, Mark Lawson – a contemporary of Odone's – tended towards this kindlier interpretation in the same *Guardian* feature. 'Alistair Cooke is the master of the past tense: a living archive of American and British history. Such experience, wisdom and education are unlikely ever again to combine in one journalist. He is not a broadcaster who could obviously be copied – no one starting now would ever be allowed to talk that slowly and quietly – but he is radio's history man and, when he is finally silenced, journalism will seem even more amnesiac.'

37

SURVIVING

Cooke never expected that he and Jane would stay alive and alert so long – and so much longer than their contemporaries. When the Royal Television Society formed a North America branch, and invited Cooke to deliver its inaugural lecture, he declined – although he was genuinely honoured at the idea that the event might be named after him. 'I probably won't be around for the next one,' he told the organiser, Peter Marshall, in May 1989, 'but why not?' And he replied more formally to the Society's President in London, Paul Fox:

> I have lately become a compulsive decliner of invitations to
>
> 1. accept Honorary Degrees
> 2. write introductions to books
> 3. address any club, association, society, devoted to any cause whatsoever
> 4. associate my name with Anglo-American anything
>
> [In this case, however] since no burden falls on me, and you think that the memory of this and that I have done over the microphone and through the tube 'personifies that theme succinctly', I don't see how I can decently turn you down. I just hope your Inaugural Lecturer is not some professional do-gooder, chronic Anglophile, earnest Ph.D., or other pompous ass.

Cooke then proceeded to do what he always did when confronted with offers that were hard to refuse. He hid his head in the sand. The invitation became mysteriously buried in a heap of unanswered correspondence (a perennial Cooke problem). He found it six weeks before the event, and might still have avoided it if it hadn't been for the choice of lecturer – one of the broadcasters he most admired, Robert McNeill, co-presenter of the current affairs programme, the *McNeill-Lehrer Report*. For once, he tendered a gracious apology and was there on St George's Day 1990 to launch the first 'Alistair Cooke Lecture'. He made a decently modest reference to the honour being paid to him: it was as embarrassing, he claimed, as a tycoon donating his art collection to a museum, with the proviso that it should bear his name in perpetuity. 'However, the more I get used to the idea, I'm enjoying the flattery more than the embarrassment.'

Despite his gloomy prognosis, Cooke was around for the second Lecture in 1991, and the RTS discovered that they might have got more than they'd bargained for. He wasn't very good at being a figurehead: once you had him on board, you'd better be ready to allow him to take the wheel. When he was told the identity of the second speaker he objected: he had known Jack Valenti long before he became President of the Motion Picture Association of America and his memories were far from warm. For him, Valenti was the 'slick Swiss-suited press man for LBJ'. Privately he told the RTS that he was not prepared to travel to Washington to introduce him and embarrassment was only avoided by a diplomatic flaring of Cooke's knee.

In fact, Cooke repeatedly broke his own four golden rules. He contributed introductions to a quantity of books and pamphlets: from an anthology of obituaries and a sleeve note for Bing Crosby to a book on longitude – from a Bobby Jones tribute to the brochure for New York's Museum of Broadcasting. Introductions – provided he was interested in the subject – were too good an opportunity to pass up – Cooke opining on a favourite theme, as he might from his study with glass in hand.

Through such connections, there was never any likelihood of running out of work and interesting things to do – as he passed eighty, eighty-five and even ninety. Plenty of organisations were ready to offer him up to $10,000 to speak at functions of varying degrees of desirability. He accepted increasingly few, though he did happily re-cycle one talk – *The History of American Humour* – whenever the chance arose. It was invariably popular and when he appeared at the Bath Festival in 1988 an extra matinée performance had to be arranged for the following day. The *Western Daily Press* described it as 'an evening of pure pleasure' featuring Twain, Thurber, Benchley – and, of course, Mencken. The style was like that of the *Letter*, only even more discursive: 'There he stands,' wrote another critic, 'slightly stooping, with hands thrust deep in pockets, relaxed, fluent, always ready with a quick anecdote that spins off at a tangent and brings him back – oh so artlessly – exactly where he wanted to be.'

Knowing that this was likely to remain one of his staple lectures, Cooke went to some trouble to prevent any recording being made. He wrote to the Bath Festivals Trust, 'NOTA BENE! – by no means must you allow the BBC or anyone else to tape the programme. I am writing to Michael Green, head of Radio 4, to remind him that I am always alert to their knavish tricks. They appear to flatter a performer by begging him to tape for a fee. They then sell it around the globe for a much handsomer fee, which they pocket ... I may want to do this again somewhere. Stand-up comics were often ruined, once their routine was put out over a national network and then video-taped.'

If work was plentiful, there was a growing shortage of friends. The obituary columns which he had once savoured became a source of deepening depression. Worse still, many of those with whom Cooke felt most comfortable did not die gracefully, but suffered gradual mental decline – Whitney Darrow, Jerome Weidman, Paul Mannheim. In March 1991 he wrote to Alan Owen from the depths of unaccustomed gloom, 'In this town, there are practically no friends left. I drop in on Paul about once a fortnight to try to cheer him over a drink. His right eye has gone for good. He has to use a mini-respirator to pull the breath out of his one lung. So on and so on. (N.B. DON'T GROW OLD.) We don't have a contemporary friend who is in the pink. We touch wood every morning, and Scotch every evening.' He grew accustomed to sick visits, though he had not always found them so easy.

John Cooke recalled his father's reluctance, back in 1978, to call on Ralph Emerson, Ruth's younger brother and always Cooke's favourite member of the Emerson tribe. Ralph, who lived in Berkeley, was dying of cancer. 'I simply cannot decide whether to go and see Ralph or not,' he wrote to John. 'It might seem so final and funereal.' His son urged him to make the effort and although Ralph was in the terminal stages of mesothelioma, both men seemed to find it a rewarding experience. John thought his father had 'faced a fear, and found that what he feared was not so fearful'. But it never ceased to be depressing, and death, when it came to his long-suffering friends, looked to Cooke increasingly like a release. The novelist Jerome Weidman clung to a half-life for years and when he finally died in 1998, Cooke's eulogy in a *Letter from America* was rich with the sense of relief on behalf of his wife and family. 'Weidman was the Dickens of the Lower East Side,' he wrote. 'He will be rediscovered and revived when many more famous and fashionable American writers – big guns today – are dead and gone forever.'

A few months later the suffering ended for Paul Mannheim, too. Mannheim, Jewish banker and arch-conservative, had been one of Cooke's dearest and quirkiest friends. Once again, it fell to him to compose the farewell speech, which naturally ended with anecdotes from their shared experience of the golf-course: as Mannheim flailed at his ball in a San Francisco bunker, Cooke remembered, his playing partner offered a sympathetic 'Bad luck, Paul'. Mannheim crawled out and muttered, 'What d'you expect, after two thousand years of persecution?' 'I hope I have said enough', Cooke concluded, 'to show that for so many of us to have had so many decades of the friendship of this mischievous, generous, lovable man is no cause for moaning at the bar but surely, today, cause for rejoicing.'

A minority, it seemed to Cooke, were luckier. He heard news of the passing of his Cambridge friend Norrie Davidson in Dublin: a day or so later, a letter from his old friend arrived by airmail, written, as if from beyond the grave, in a typescript transparent with over-use. It consisted of just a single sentence: 'The evening fades, along with the spool.'

He himself just carried on. In a letter of thanks to Graham Greene for a kind review he wrote as early as 1985: 'I miss all my best friends, who are dropping like flies. Shaw said one of the tragedies of old age was that "the knees give out before the brain". In my case, I think it's a dead heat.' As he reached ninety, only a handful of (non-contemporary) friends survived, ready to rally round when the need arose – like Heather Maclean, Jason de Montmorency and the faithful Richard Somerset-Ward, who was always on hand, prepared to offer anything from advice on dealing with the BBC to the mowing of the lawn at Nassau Point, or Ken Pursley, the BBC sound engineer, who was in charge of straightening out all the Cookes' consumer appliances. He was called one day to be informed that the television screen was going purple. 'What should I do?' came the desperate voice.

Pursley said, 'Did you adjust the colour?'

'Yes.'

'How old is your TV?'

'I think it's twenty-five years.' Why buy a new set while the old one was still working? Pursley spent much of the next week helping Cooke negotiate for a modern machine which would work with his video equipment and having lengthy phone discussions from his home in New Jersey with the television engineer. The Cookes ended up with three remote controls: 'Have you ever seen two people in their eighties squabbling over a remote control?' Pursley asked wonderingly.

The routine of the Cookes' lives – as well as the comforting familiarity of Nassau Point and the Huntington Hotel in San Francisco – helped insulate them from the surrounding gloom. Each night in New York has its own immutable pattern. At 6.25 they convene in the study for cocktails with half an hour of news, originally McNeill-Lehrer, but latterly Peter Jennings anchoring ABC's *Evening News*; then an hour of homage to light entertainment – the general knowledge quiz *Jeopardy* followed, as night follows weekday, by *Wheel of Fortune*. This, for Cooke, is a matter of special reverence – not an obvious choice for a couple of such erudition and (in Cooke's case) intellectual pretension, but graced by the presence of an elegant and long-serving hostess, Vanna White, worshipped with only the barest hint of irony by Cooke and any polite visitor who happens to be passing by – talking only being allowed during commercial breaks. Then, and only then, comes a meal cooked by Jane, a surf across the cable channels and bed at around eleven, Cooke often reading for hours as he used to in Blackpool as an insatiable student.

He had started trying to put his affairs in order years earlier, by making arrangements for his papers to be handed over to the Mugar Library at Boston University. This came about only after a long period of courtship by Howard Gotlieb, who had met Cooke while he was the Curator of Historical Manuscripts at Yale in the 1960s. When he was asked by Boston to set up the Department of Special Collections, to store the written records of a wide range of twentieth-century figures, he approached Cooke who politely ignored the request, thinking – privately – the idea ridiculous. 'Howard told me they had some Elizabeth Bowen material, and George Bernard Shaw, D.H. Lawrence, Robert Frost and all the papers of Teddy Roosevelt – and I thought, "So what?" A journalist's papers – how pretentious!' Gotlieb continued to pester him and in due course Cooke agreed to meet him for dinner. His attitude altered somewhat when Gotlieb told him that a document handed over to an approved archive could attract handsome tax relief: 'What's more, he told me it didn't only apply to manuscripts. I could wake up in the middle of the night, jot down "milk – beer – yoghurt for Jane", and send him the piece of paper the next day.' The blandishment worked and Cooke's first offering was his hand-written despatch on the night of Bobby Kennedy's assassination. He was delighted to discover that this was assessed at a notional future value of $700, which he deducted from his next tax bill.

He put off the task of going through his Closet in search of further gems, and that was a mistake. Before any more material had been sent to Boston, there was an outcry over LBJ's plan to present his papers to the Lyndon B. Johnson library in Austin, Texas and claim millions of dollars of tax repayments in advance. The Internal Revenue Service was appalled and Congress moved swiftly to legislate away the loophole. Cooke shrugged, rued the lost fortunes from his laundry tickets and restaurant bills, and forgot about the whole thing. He wasn't the only one. Gotlieb and his counterparts around the country found their sources of supply drying up overnight, and matters were only marginally relieved by the concession that, although writers themselves couldn't claim the relief, their heirs could do so after their deaths.

Eventually, after years of further letters, meetings, phone calls and the massaging of egos, Gotlieb succeeded in re-arousing Cooke's interest in the archive business. Cooke began to ship papers to the Mugar in bulk, without shedding his scepticism about their value to anyone. His refusal to embrace the computer, and his dogged adherence to the portable typewriter, produced a wealth of 'holographs' – pieces in which the process of creation survives for the benefit of researchers. Yale University woke up to this possibility much later – and much too late: the Professor of History wrote in 1998 (expecting the worst), 'I felt that I must ask, for obviously your papers are one of the major sources of information on Anglo-American cultural ties in this century.'

In 1995 the Mugar Library decided to mount a Cooke exhibition. The subject was not amused. This was perfectly in character, but Gotlieb and his assistant Perry Barton were prepared to be very persistent and very patient. They tempted Cooke to Boston, putting him up in his favourite room at the Ritz. In the hope of re-creating the old *Masterpiece* magic, they made sure there was a bottle of Dewars, a box of biscuits, and a rose in a vase to greet him. At the library, Barton had covered a black table with material from the collection.

'These pieces of paper were like old friends to him,' Barton realised. 'He would identify each one and start telling the marvellous stories that lay behind them.' Cooke was hooked, and as soon as he got back to New York he started phoning Barton, often at home in the evening, with ideas and questions. From indifference, to absorption, to the overwhelming desire to control and organise – Barton watched the transformation with fascination. Cooke would ring up in triumph at some new discovery in the Closet and emissaries travelling to or from New York were often diverted to pick up the document or photograph. A copy was made of the portrait of him by Jane which had recently been hung in the National Portrait Gallery in Washington.

It turned out to be one of the Library's most popular shows. Gotlieb believes that – through *Masterpiece Theatre* – 'Cooke introduced more people to what one would call "good literature" than thousands of high-school and college instructors might have done.' The only blot on this sunny landscape was that Cooke, having neglected Mencken's advice on three occasions, remembered it again when Boston University offered him an honorary degree. He turned it down.

Cooke's decision to dispose of his papers to a museum stirred in him a yen to examine the rest of the (more or less essential) detritus of his long life. In November 1992 (the month of his 'total knee') he came to a radical conclusion. 'There is, so far as I can discover, no antonym to "collecting",' he wrote in the newsletter of the auctioneers Sotheby's. 'I have found thirteen synonyms, but nothing to describe the stage that I am now declining into: the need, if not the wish, to shed, dispose of, discard, dispense with, slough off and altogether abandon most of the worldly goods that I have sometimes lovingly, sometimes haphazardly, collected during most of sixty years.' The word he chose to describe this plan of action was 'de-collecting'. Cooke was quite specific about the emotional impact of his experience with Howard Gotlieb and Perry Barton:

When I was now made to face, to expose, the closets and catacombs bursting with thousands of clippings and notes and letters and articles and reviews and phonograph records and audio and video tapes and manuscripts (so called) and other rubbish, I suddenly saw Boston University as the provider of a godsent landfill. All will go. I shall retain a box of compact tapes, of Handel and Gershwin and twelve-bar blues. I shall reduce four thousand volumes to one shelf of books I refuse to be without.

It was an eccentric collection including, after the four main Shake-spearean tragedies, Philip Larkin's *Required Writing*, the *Vintage Mencken*, Richard Asher's *Talking Sense*, a two-dollar *Weather Around the World*, *Bobby Jones on Golf*, William Safire's *Political Dictionary* and Taber's *Cyclopedic Medical Dictionary*.

> I shall have a smooth, empty desk. For the first time in fifty years or more, I shall be a free man. This is the plan, what the politicians call the agenda. Like them, I fully expect to 'implement' it in the next eight to ten years.

The time frame, at least, was realistic, for in only one area did he move quite swiftly to fulfil his own resolution. Cooke had met Peter Mintun on one of his San Francisco visits around 1980. He and Jane were, as always, at the Huntington Hotel, where Mintun played the piano in the bar attached to the Etoile restaurant. He was working through his specialist repertoire of music from the Twenties and Thirties, when Cooke strolled over and leaned on the piano. 'I bet there's one you don't know – can you play Bix Beiderbecke's "In A Mist"?' Without a word, Mintun started to play: he had known the piece for years, and had even included it in a recent concert. Soon, Cooke was back with another challenge. 'Here's one you couldn't possibly know. Richard Rodgers wrote this in London in the Twenties. It's called "I Need Some Cooling Off" – from a show called *One Dam Thing After Another*. Once again, Mintun obliged and the bond between the two was sealed.

Cooke's acclamation could be a mixed blessing. Mintun's job was to satisfy as wide a cross-section of diners as possible and one night – gauging the mood of the assembly – he had concentrated on classics: 'These Foolish Things' and 'Embraceable You'. As he played the opening chords of 'As Time Goes By', Cooke sidled past the piano, shaking his head and muttering, 'This is terrible – it's trash, so common.' But for the most part, it was a perfect rela-tionship between two kindred spirits. Like Cooke, Mintun did occasional radio shows on vintage music and they started to exchange tapes – while on one occasion, Mintun brought a portable phonograph and some of his own records to the Cookes' suite in the Huntington. It took some time for Cooke to pluck up the courage to offer taped evidence of his own performance skills and only once did he presume to play in front of the professional – and then only to illustrate a point he was trying to make. 'It was in the

Etoile one night,' Mintun remembers, 'when all the other customers had gone. He sat down and played me one of his blues tunes.' It was an obscure number which did not figure in his own exhaustive collection – 'Make Me a Pallet On Your Floor'. Mainly, though, Mintun played and Cooke talked, revealing that he was simply 'a great jazz buff', with an encyclopaedic knowledge of the origins of jazz, the blues and show music.

From time to time, the conversation turned to Cooke's own early records, and vague promises were issued to the effect that one day, Mintun could take his pick. There was no evidence that this promise might be activated until 1995 when, partly at Cooke's prompting, Mintun managed to get a job at the Carlyle in New York. After a while, he was invited to the apartment and came away with dozens of records, including some that were completely new to him. Mintun had to keep reminding himself that Cooke had experienced Miff Mole's Molers ('You Took Advantage of Me'), Ethel Walters with 'Miss Otis Regrets' and Edythe Baker's 'Birth of the Blues' (which he'd once played on a punt with Erik Chitty in Cambridge) as contemporary music. When he'd carried the records away, there was a little more space in Cooke's Closet.

That act of de-collecting was the exception. Cooke was comfortable in his study, which had grown around him like a second skin. In a rare act of self-revelation he had allowed the *Observer* newspaper (in 1986) to look around the place for the regular feature, 'A Room of My Own'. And even more rarely, he was delighted with the result. The interviewer, Ena Kendall, was enthralled from the moment she was invited to step along the central corridor with 'its delicate Hepplewhite furniture and thick pale Indian carpet' and intrigued by what she saw along the way: 'Open doors allow glimpses of splendid rooms, the walls hung with paintings.' And then, to the study, which – Cooke told her – had seen some two hundred reporters pass through its portals, almost all of whom referred to it afterwards as his 'red study' or his 'book-lined' room. It was both those things, of course, but he found the repetition tiresome. 'Once, in a spasm of mischief,' he confessed to her, he had removed every picture that was not a nude in the hope that an interviewer from the *New Yorker* would refer to a 'nude-lined' study' – to no avail.

After that piece of pre-emptive advice, he showed her with pride the portrait of Churchill bequeathed to him by Ben Sonnenberg,

Jane's portrait of Susie, the eighteenth-century map of California as an island and the Staffordshire figure with the inscription 'G. Washington'. (This, he explained, was a piece of eighteenth-century conmanship. In reality, the gentleman portrayed was Benjamin Franklin, but English potters realised that no one would know any better if they used the same face for both men.) He told Kendall about his preference for English furniture – the Georgian mahogany wine coolers serving as occasional tables, his beloved Queen Anne padauk chest, the Sheraton barometer – as well as his distaste for anything Victorian. And he pointed out the cushion embroidered by Jane with a spoof family crest – featuring the three cockerels of Jesus College, the lion and unicorn (for the UK) and the eagle (for the US), a golf tee and a radio beam. Only the picture accompanying the article failed to ring true: it showed Cooke on a seat in the corner, his arms thrown high and wide, and a look of unconfined joy on his face. It was a most uncharacteristic pose.

If Cooke's study was too much of a sanctuary to allow radical surgery, there was never any danger either that moving house would do the trick. It wasn't only the *America* annuity, as it became known in the family, that allowed the Cookes to maintain their chic lifestyle. The family finances benefited hugely from New York's rent control system. Every few years there would be a flurry of press attention generated by the fact that Manhattan landlords had no legal right to charge market rates to long-term tenants. In May 1986 the *Daily News* headline screamed its protest: HIGH LIFE AT A LOW RENT. A researcher was offering $50 a time for information about celebrities enjoying what, in his opinion, were indecently generous rents. 'I am morally certain', proclaimed William Tucker, 'that New York's housing crisis is due to rent regulations.' Among the celebrities he'd identified were Alistair Cooke, William Shawn (editor of the *New Yorker*, who lived in the same block) and Mia Farrow.

Tucker learned that Cooke was paying $975.03 a month, and demanded an explanation from Irving Cohen. 'Wow!' the lawyer replied, with what sounds suspiciously like mock amazement: 'His apartment is fabulous. It should cost at least $4000.' Neither William Tucker nor the *Daily News* was convinced. 'Actually,' the report went on, 'a comparable apartment has a market value of between $10,000 and $12,000 a month' and they quoted a real estate broker in support of their figure. Mayor Ed Koch, whose own private apartment was even more of a snip at $350 a month, showed no interest in tackling the problem.

More than ten years later the debate was still rumbling on. Cooke's rent, according to the *Independent* newspaper, had risen – but only to $2078. The new plan was to penalise the wealthiest tenants immediately – those earning $175,000 a year – and allow the rest of the system to wither over time. Since Cohen had by now finally retired through ill health, his partner renewed the fight to ensure that, through a complex reshuffling of the figures, the Cookes could be protected from a dramatic increase. On reading the letter, Cooke himself muttered, 'You'd think there'd be something in the new code about guys of eighty-nine.'

~

Money, in any case, had not been a problem for a long time, but it didn't solve everything, either. Soon after the *America* deal had been struck, Cooke arranged for a regular annual payment (the maximum allowed tax-free) to his two children, John and Susie, each Christmas. In John's case, inevitably, the first gift – in 1973 – was accompanied with a fatherly exhortation: 'I hope you will not blow it on a tape-recorder or other bauble but hoard it (huh?) against maintenance till the 20th Century ship comes in [a reference to a six-month contract as a producer on a Bette Midler film]. Anyway, enjoy it.' This went some way towards offsetting the income Holly and Stephen had enjoyed for so long from their own father's estate. Yet Cooke's relationship with the children, and the grandchildren who followed in regular succession, never attained (or aspired to) that picture-book image of a grey-haired grandfather with twinkling eyes, dandling infants on his knee. He had not been that sort of man in 1940, when Johnny was born, and nothing much changed over the next half-century. Each case had to be taken on its merits. He never established strong links with Stephen, tending his Californian vineyards, and the indifference became mutual. John, by contrast, was a constant source of anxiety and guilt, since – despite deep-seated emotions on both sides – neither father nor son could find a way to build up the bonds between them. Holly, far away in England, was so much her own woman that Cooke found her the easiest of all to deal with: unlike her siblings, she teased him, pricked his vanity and simply trampled over his defence mechanisms. While Susie, the baby of the family, was always loving and supportive – but could not so easily ignore her father's shortcomings as a family man.

As for the grandchildren – ten in all – they provided the sort of tests, from time to time, which kept Jane on her mettle, and had Cooke fretting about the strain on his wife. One disappeared for a month in California on the way back from a world tour and had to be rescued from the Moonies; another came out as gay; a third insisted on tracking round America in the footsteps of the band The Grateful Dead. Or there was the day one young man stayed in the Fifth Avenue apartment, allowed the bath to overflow and did hundreds of dollars' worth of damage to the floor below. Cooke's problem, as he confessed with brutal frankness, was that he lacked a frame of reference whereby he might deal with these alien creatures. It was left to Jane to sort out crises, provide doting attention and keep open the lines of communication to her husband.

It became a little easier when each child approached adulthood. Holly's daughter Josephine Berry, for instance, by the time she reached her twenties, had enough of her mother about her to make Cooke's comprehension easier – though not without alarums along the way. On one trip she decided to follow Jane's advice to avoid bringing the forty-year-old boy-friend she'd picked up on her travels to stay on Long Island. At the time, she resented the idea that her grandfather might not be prepared to 'accept her as she was'. Looking back, she realised that it would have been a horrible mistake. She had already experienced the icy blast of his disapproval when she and her cousin Jake (Stephen's son) were staying at the apartment alone. They ran out of money, had to be re-financed by Cooke's secretary, blew the new funds during a long night in Greenwich Village and were just wondering how they were going to manage the bus-fare to Nassau Point when Cooke, quite unexpectedly, walked in, before they'd had a chance to clear up. The place was a shambles. As the youngsters stood frozen with fear, Cooke appraised the situation, bent down and removed a small white fleck from the floor. 'It was terrifying,' Josephine recalled. 'He didn't lose his temper, but this one meticulous gesture said everything. He told us he was going out to get us some money, and when he came back he expected the place to be clean.'

Apart from these comparatively isolated contacts, 'meeting the grandchildren' was confined to Christmas and other holidays, or family trips to Manhattan or Long Island. Susie soon stopped taking all five of her children (two boys from her first marriage, three girls from her second) to the apartment at once – there were simply too many artefacts to break or damage. For a time the Cookes spent alternate Christmases with Holly and her second husband, Henry Rumbold, at their large country house in Wiltshire. This ritual ended when Cooke started to complain about the damp and the cold, and made it clear that he had no interest in socialising with the locals who came round for a Boxing Day shoot. Instead, he and Jane became annual migrants to Susie's home in Vermont, where Cooke could be sure of being kept warm, despite the sub-zero temperatures outside.

There was one horrible hiatus between Cooke and his daughter – after what she felt was an unjustifiably grumpy Thanksgiving stay. Susie was seriously upset, not least because Cooke seemed not to have realised how cussed he'd been, complaining about everything from the toughness of the turkey to the excessive friendliness of the dog. It took many emotional phone calls before relations were restored to normal. And her tendency to frankness in dealing with her father caused another – far more public – family altercation. In 1996 Susie fell foul of a piece of sharp journalistic practice when she, and to a lesser degree Holly and Stephen, were lulled into talking at length to a reporter from the *Mail on Sunday*. Since the article was scheduled to coincide with the fiftieth anniversary of the *Letter*, all three assumed that they were taking part in a more or less celebratory exercise. Susie in particular let her guard down and among other more benign reflections, offered some anecdotes which did not reflect well on the public face of Alistair Cooke. Those stories, together with Stephen's straightforwardness and selective quoting from an interview with Holly, combined to produce a snide piece headlined, 'TO HIS MIL-LIONS OF LISTENERS, ALISTAIR COOKE HAS THE IMAGE OF A KINDLY FATHER. TO HIS CHILDREN, HE IS A SELFISH AND REMOTE FATHER'.

Stephen's quotes were thoughtful, yet blunt. It had given him no pleasure to remain so distant from a man who was so important to his mother and he tried to offer a rational explanation: 'Alistair is not at ease with children ... Maybe it is inevitable to anyone who remar-ries and who isn't a saint to feel a certain sense of competition with the stepson ... He was jealous of my relationship with my mother ... I don't think Alistair wants anyone to outshine him.' This recital ends with what is clearly an unconsidered jibe: 'Of course, I respect what

Alistair has achieved. But no man is a hero to his valet.' The writer seizes on the remark, and adds, 'Abruptly Stephen catches himself. "That sounds cruel, doesn't it?" ' It was harder to quarry something nasty from Holly's story. The worst she was made to say was that Cooke tended to be possessive and that when she went to England, he didn't want her to be 'better friends with his English friends than he was'. Her 'final verdict' sounded a little tart, but was typical Holly: 'He is egocentric, but he is not really difficult – as long you go along with what he wants to do.'

The really painful blow came in the final three paragraphs, because it was Susie speaking: 'We were never a close-knit family. The children were all shoved away to boarding-school, so we were not home together very much.' That sounded good and cold. The report had her complaining that he didn't like babies and kept them – as he did dogs – at arm's length, a charge which he certainly wouldn't have denied. But the paper obviously decided that it was keeping the best till last. The section had a sub-heading – 'The Daughter Spurned at a Family Reunion': 'About fifteen years ago, we had a large family reunion in New York, when my brothers and sister came and all the grandchildren. And Daddy *left*! It just appalled him. He couldn't bear it and went to play golf somewhere.' It had required something of an imaginative leap to bill this as a daughter being spurned: but it was enough. In an odious tone of moral superiority, the article ended, 'None of this will ever appear on *Letter from America*. But if it did, perhaps Cooke's children – in their different ways – would understand him better.' Naturally, Cooke found out about the piece, suffered acutely and did what Freud would never have allowed – he buried it in the dark places where bad things can be made to disappear. It wasn't that the piece was a lie. It was a half-truth of the most dangerous kind, with just enough elements of reality in it to touch several exposed nerves.

And sometimes, events in the real world of his family conspired to shock Cooke just as profoundly, none more than the news that his daughter Susie intended to become a minister of the Church. Since she had dropped out of college during her more turbulent youth, she first had to resume her studies for a basic degree before beginning her seminary training. For two years, she didn't tell her parents what she was doing, pretending that she was just intending to make up for her lost graduation years. Finally the news had to be broken and it turned out to be just as discomfiting as she'd expected. Given her determination to succeed (which sometimes involved putting the children to bed, driving to Boston, attending evening lectures, sleeping in the car, and being back in Vermont to provide breakfast) there was no possibility that either parent could dissuade her.

Jane converted her trauma into a pragmatic decision to involve herself in theological discussions. 'How can you believe in God and science?' she would demand to know.

'How can you not?' Susie replied.

Cooke's reaction was more painful to behold. But gradually, he trudged from outright reaction, through puzzlement, to a perverse sort of pride in his daughter's commitment and achievement. This was something he could not control – the presence on his doorstep of a Congregational minister of the United Church of Christ: instead he was gradually transmuted into Susie's most enthusiastic promoter. Did he, she wondered, envy her the certainty of her faith? 'He told me once,' she said, 'that hardly a day went by without his remembering a verse of scripture that he learned at the age of eleven or twelve.'

38

SIGNING OFF

As Alistair Cooke passed his ninetieth birthday he could look back on a life of unparalleled professional success. He had become a broadcasting legend. He had fulfilled his youthful ambition by forming a conduit for all that was best about the country in which he'd chosen to live: he had created the *Letter from America* – a unique achievement, which will never be matched – in the face of opposition and adversity and had sustained it, even when the world decided that change for its own sake was an absolute good. On top of that he was recognised as one of the finest newspaper foreign correspondents of his generation, he wrote one of the bestselling non-fiction books of all time, and he became a cultural icon through a medium – American television – in which culture had to be measured by the size of the audience. He was a public speaker who could command five-figure fees when most of his surviving contemporaries were content to live on their old-age pensions: he was an acknowledged authority on an entire era of popular music, and he became one of the most knowledgeable people in America on the subject of golf, even if his own performance never quite matched up to the standards he set himself.

He had been a collector of fine furniture and paintings, a familiar of film stars and actors and a dab-hand with a pan of scrambled eggs. His collection of friends and acquaintances had been broader and more mixed than most people could manage in several lifetimes – and an army of faithful fans spanned the globe. He had been honoured by the Queen, by great universities and by humble communities across rural America. Above all, perhaps, he had been a rare figure of continuity in a period of rapid, and sometimes unpredictable, change. He did not dictate what one country felt about another, but he *was* a sign of something enduring, even if only subconsciously – a reassurance that the gulf created by the Atlantic was, at least, not growing wider.

Freud knew that such external triumphs can make a man con-tented, but not necessarily happy – and certainly not all the time. Cooke was no happier than most. He fretted continually about his family. John, his eldest child, was always there in the back of his mind – the boy he left behind. From the start he knew the risks – that his natural emotional restraint would be hard pressed to grapple with such a complex relationship with an absent child. By his own lights, he tried his best, but it wasn't enough to prevent John being affected by a nagging sense of loss. It might have happened anyway, and John has always been fiercely defensive of his father. His own career – as novelist, scriptwriter, musician, photographer, historian – shows all the signs of a man striving to emulate his father. He started to collect books, and his father wrote (in 1978), 'Dear Captain ... I'm delighted to hear you begin to see the nucleus of a library – it is one of the great pleasures, and I find I no longer deride people who do little else but *collect* books. I hope to have some more for you soon.' This library was destroyed in a fire twelve years later.

Somehow, something always held Cooke back. Just as he had (as far as John knew) never watched him perform on stage in the 1960s, so the publication of John's first novel *The Snowblind Moon* never received from his father the praise which he craved. It had an aus-picious launch, with a handsome advance, good displays at a Fifth Avenue store, and a six-city tour for the author. Not surprisingly, he waited with some anxiety to hear what his father thought. Finally, the judgement was delivered.

> I have been chased by deadlines and much reading. But I have eventually started *Snowblind*. The opening two pages are masterly. The time, the place, the mood, the reasons for anxiety are splendidly set, in a lucid, direct prose. As I've gone along – not very far at the moment – I begin to be a little apprehensive about the amount of research that arrests or overwhelms the narrative. Maybe I speak as a journalist. I once dared tell [the golf writer] Herb Wind – who sees a coffee table in Arnold Palmer's house and then calls off the details of every plaque and medal assembled under the glass top – that 'in journalism research is the part that doesn't show – it's been digested.' I'll let you know more later – not that it's going to help. And I could well be out of touch with this sort of modern documentary novel.

Even for a man who was out of practice – he had stopped reading novels years earlier – it was a half-hearted response to years of effort.

Father and son continued to see each other regularly, if not frequently, in New York, Boston or San Francisco: John attended birthday parties at the Huntington Hotel, where Cooke habitually fled in November to escape the dampness of early winter in New York. The hotel's owner, Newt Cope, paid tribute to his most loyal guest by redeveloping the twelfth-floor 'Alistair Cooke Suite' to Jane's specifications. The decorations included her second large-scale portrait of her husband – 'a happy generous impulse of Newt Cope,' according to Cooke, who announced 'the best way to fill that blank wall is to have Jane paint your portrait, then it will be the Cooke suite even when you're not here'. Cooke's familiarity with the place, verging on a sense that he was at home and beholden to no one, did give rise to some disconcerting moments: on one occasion a new manager, trying too hard to please and overly keen to meet the hotel's celebrity guests, hovered at Cooke's shoulder as he checked in. 'Good evening, sir. I'm the new manager,' he simpered. 'So?' Cooke replied as he walked off, leaving a proffered hand dangling in the air. On another visit, he was travelling up to his room with the legendarily eccentric lift attendant Mary Fraser. After forty years or so, she was no respecter of persons: it was said that Luciano Pavarotti and Placido Domingo would vie hopelessly for her disdainful approval. Cooke was in town to launch a book, and Mary demanded to know whether she was going to get a signed copy. 'No,' Cooke snapped. 'Go out and buy one like everyone else.' Unfortunately, there was a local journalist in the lift and the story spread rapidly.

Just twice, Cooke visited Jackson Hole in Wyoming, to which John had repaired in the first place to complete his book, but to which he became increasingly attached. In 1993 Cooke agreed to give a speech in support of the Jackson Hole Writers' Conference. Sadly, the event – held in a tent overlooking a picturesque bend in the Snake River – was disrupted by the worst summer weather in living memory. The barbecue was a wash-out, and Cooke ended up sipping Scotch in the cab of a pickup truck with the sister of Glenn Close. 'He was a real trooper,' was John's grateful tribute. 'I promised him that if he came on the same day the following year, it would be thirty degrees warmer.' It was just one more piece of bad luck, dogging the noble efforts of two men to find common cause. Cooke never ceased to resent the emotional reserve which had been imposed upon him in his youth – a reserve which (in its more benign aspects) deemed all sentimental films to be 'sloppy', but which also made it hard to say the words 'I love you' and certainly drew the line at family kissing. At some point he remembered John being brave enough to ask him outright how he really felt about their relationship. He managed a stumbling reply about how fond he was of his son, but how articulating those feelings had always been a matter of intense embarrassment – that he himself had never been kissed by his mother or father – and that John should not take it badly that he'd had so little sign of affection.

John remembers the exchange with far more clarity. He had been upset to learn at second hand that Cooke was about to visit San Francisco. Why had his father not warned him in advance so they could arrange to meet as usual? John didn't stop there. In frustration he ploughed on: did his father perhaps consider him a failure? Did he even love him? The reply, according to John, was 'the single most positive step in bringing them closer.' Cooke wrote back that he did not regard his son as a failure and that he did love him, even if it was hard for a 'crusty Lancashire man' to say so. As for Ruth, she proved just as durable as Cooke. She finally inherited the house at Southold and continued to visit the Bungalow, even after it had been sold and she had moved to a retirement home in Pennsylvania – still fit and active into her late 80s. Just once in later life she bumped into Cooke on Long Island and the two conversed for a while. Afterwards it became clear to Jane that Alistair had failed to recognise his former wife.

Apart from these vexatious family matters there were some other sources of regret. Some were jocular: that he hadn't followed the promptings of a Cambridge friend and joined the Gog Magog golf club. There was simply too much going on to indulge what seemed such a trivial pursuit. But if he had started so young . . . More seriously, in old age he admitted that his absence from Britain during World War Two had caused him qualms of conscience: should he have been using his talents in Broadcasting House, London, rather than broadcasting from New York? He also felt that he had never done enough for charity. This self-criticism dated from the war, too, when Jane had been a nursing aide and he had made no parallel effort to contribute to the cause. At the back of his mind there was a memory of his first father-in-law, Haven Emerson. 'When Ruth and I came back to this country in 1937,' Cooke recalled, 'Dr Emerson took me on one side and announced that he was going to give me some advice on domestic finances: "We usually put aside a third of our income for rent, a third for living expenses, and always a tenth for charity." ' This edict was spoken with such solemnity that Cooke assumed that tithing must be a constitutional requirement. He even did it himself, for a while, until hard times made him question, and quickly abandon, the habit.

The charitable instinct lay dormant for many years, and was only revived in earnest years later and almost completely by chance. A businessman friend asked Cooke to speak at a luncheon in Southern California, an event which was supposed to raise money for a hospital in Monterey. He agreed and a large audience of well-heeled patrons turned out to hear the words of a man who was at the height of his *Masterpiece Theatre* fame. As he and his friend flew back to San Francisco, the conversation turned to the amount of money the hospital would make: 'It rather depends on your fee,' his friend said. 'What fee?' Cooke exclaimed, assuming that he was donating his services to a good cause. It transpired that previous speakers, including a celebrated opera singer and a famous black jazz musician, had demanded $10,000. Cooke not only waived his fee, but accepted a further invitation to address a $500-a-plate dinner. These functions raised so much money that the hospital honoured Cooke by naming its new atrium after him – an airy space where patients and visitors could eat, meet and relax. This did a little to assuage his guilt.

When it came to analysing his more personal shortcomings, he sat down one evening in December 1996 and typed out a short paragraph on one of his ubiquitous sheets of yellow paper: 'Character flaw: a lifelong propensity for sarcasm – as a reflex response to stupidity or slowness of thinking. To put it bluntly, I suppose it cannot be said of me that I suffer fools gladly. Unfortunately the put-down habit extends to nice people who are by no means fools but at that moment are slow, or literal, on the uptake.' It was a flaw, he hoped, which had been suppressed more often than indulged in his later years. He could certainly be impatient and intolerant of criticism or advice. When it came to matters of the mind, he was not given much to self-doubt. Even his closest friends testified to his preference, in company, for holding court while others listened.

The one person who could never be railroaded was Jane. Her strength of character and stubbornness were more than a match for Cooke's need to control and organise. He pleaded with her not to tramp about the city in the snow, or to insist on travelling by subway, complaining that a woman in her mid-eighties ought to be prepared to take a taxi once in a while; he fretted when she set out in her frail craft to scull round Peconic Bay in choppy water, he fumed helplessly as she tended her garden through long, hot summer afternoons when he thought she should be resting. It never made any difference. She had been her own woman all along and remained the solid rock in the household. When things went wrong – when, for instance, Stephen fell dangerously ill – she dropped everything and rallied round, leaving Cooke to fend for himself. And when she returned she simply resumed her own routine – always busy during the day, even when she decided she could no longer paint to a standard she found acceptable, then, at six in the evening, rejoining Cooke for cocktails, television and dinner. In very different ways, each came to rely on the other. This did not mean that Jane always suppressed her yawns at yet another outing for one of Cooke's favourite anecdotes: 'Sometimes, in company, he can be boring,' she sighed. 'But never when we're alone together. He is self-centred, but not selfish or conceited. In fact, he's rather shy. I think he knows his value, but he doesn't like to parade it.' Or, as she put it on another occasion, 'He's egocentric, but he's not an egotist.'

Cooke, as the true apostle of Freud, took one other step to tidy up his affairs (as it turned out, long before it was necessary). At about the time of his eightieth birthday he wrote out a piece for a magazine called *Living Philosophies*. It had been seventy years in the writing, he liked to say afterwards. The article was called 'Reflections of a Non-Positive Man', a typically roundabout description of a man intrigued by (but by no means ashamed of) his own inner driving force. It was in this document that, for the first time, he sought to rationalise what he had been – and what he had done. It began with the rationale for choosing a reporter's trade, as the only way he could find of satisfying his inquisitive spirit. Schoolmasters had been censorious, he remembered, about the way he kept so many irons in the fire: 'I was interested in too many things – as a boy, in literature, music both classical and jazz, motion pictures and all games, indoors and out. Later on, I took to history, linguistics, domestic architecture, Western Americana, meteorology, medicine and politics, always politics. Probably I wound up – if not as a jack-of-all-trades – at best as a third-rate polymath never able to focus these curiosities into a commanding "view of life".'

Cooke didn't really believe this – or rather, he did not think there was anything third-rate about these achievements; but he'd been brought up to accept that modesty was a gentlemanly quality, and, after all, people could make up their own minds. These were the characteristics of Isaiah Berlin's fox, were they not? Characteristics shared by such heroes as Aristotle, Chaucer, Mark Twain, and a whole raft of satirical essayists from Hazlitt to Mencken – not to mention Shakespeare. It was in the works of such as these that Cooke felt most at home.

Seen in this way, journalism took on a more respectable air.

> Forty years ago, when psychoanalysis appeared to many New Yorkers to be the remedy of choice for an itching neurosis, the wisest of the local administrators of the Rorschach Test remarked: 'If the ink blots seem to show that your character and your ideas match, that's the best any of us can hope.' I like to think that in choosing a reporter's life, and having the choice resoundingly confirmed down the years, I managed the most effective compromise between my weak character and my strong sense of curiosity.

What it did not do was produce any blinding light of inspiration on the great issues of life and death, and this nagged away at Cooke. Jane might be a comfortable atheist, but he had always used the word 'agnostic'. He was incapable, he often said, of a mystical experience – Susie's ministry notwithstanding. The *Living Philosophies* essay propounds – in a rather conventional way – the problem facing all sceptics: namely, the bewildering range of religious codes, each equally sure of its exclusive right to the absolute truth, and their habitual need to defend that right by force of arms. He preferred to stick with Aristotle: 'Unlike the young, the old have lived long: they have often deceived, they have made many mistakes of their own. . . . they have seen the pain caused by positive men, and so they are positive about nothing. And when they err, they err in all things by extreme moderation.' He explained that he had abandoned, long before, the search for a logical reason to believe in some First Cause, and he stated as a matter of fact that he had never been visited by faith. 'Since I have not a twinge of mysticism in my being, I have never felt the shock, or attained the leap, or heard the voices, and so – in a scarcely known universe of thirty thousand million stars in which we are six billion midgets on one planet – I cannot believe that a personal, presiding God, devoting himself/herself/itself to our affairs, much less than to the affairs of particular sects, can be anything more than a consoling myth.'

He ended this agnostic testament by quoting the old Mencken aphorism – about the prospect of ending up in heaven, and admitting to the twelve apostles that he had been wrong.

Rather less ponderously than in *Living Philosophies*, Cooke gave another 'end-of-term' interview for a book on successful old age: *Going Strong*. The two final questions were on health and happiness.

Do you have any rules about health – a regime?

The only thing I go on is a remark of a friend of mine at Yale who became a distinguished neurologist. He thought more people had died from what they called fresh air than anything else, so I avoid fresh air, except when it's unavoidable, on the golf course. But not my sainted wife! I go in Jane's bedroom in the morning and she has the window open. It's about thirty-four degrees in there! In my bedroom, I never have the window open in winter.

A final word, please, on happiness?

I think happiness – content is a better word – is a by-product of good work and friendship. As you get older, the best thing is friendship. Life would be very miserable without close friends. And the luckiest thing is a good marriage. It is important for me to share my life. There are people who manage not to do it. I marvel at them.

ACKNOWLEDGEMENTS

Many people have helped me with this book. I did more than a hundred interviews in Britain and the US, and I would like to thank all those who spared me their time to talk about Alistair Cooke. But some special votes of thanks are required.

THE BRAINWAVE

Richard Cohen had the original idea for this book, and offered it to me at the suggestion of my old friend, John Coldstream. Both nurtured the idea in its early difficult days, and I owe them both a debt of gratitude.

THE FAMILY

John B Cooke was a regular correspondent throughout, providing me with letters, photographs and ideas about his father. He also cast an American eye over the script, searching for transatlantic oddities. Holly Rumbold gave me many acute insights, never lost her sense of humour about the project, and introduced me to the finer points of Wiltshire country life. Both Susie Kittredge and Stephen Hawkes welcomed me with more warmth than a biographer expects. Kathleen Turner, long-lost niece, has never forgotten her Uncle Alfred – and has a cache of mementoes to prove it. Above all, Jane Cooke treated me and Barbara like old family friends, offering us hospitality without question. She also cooks a mean bluefish.

Not forgetting the incomparable Patti Yasek and her predecessor, Linda Wichtel, who helped keep my letters somewhere near the top of Cooke's in-tray.

THE CORRESPONDENTS

Rupert Hart-Davis postponed his retreat from society and gave me a wonderful afternoon in North Yorkshire as well as a box of treasures. Esme Done helped me re-construct a long and important friendship. Alan Owen's collection of personal letters would have been prize enough – but his filing system also yielded invaluable information about Cooke's music programmes. I had the good fortune to meet Sir Isaiah Berlin before he died: his letters were kindly provided by Henry Hardy, with the permission of the Isaiah Berlin Literary Trust. William Safire dipped into his etymological files and produced a thick batch of illuminating correspondence. And my thanks, too, to Valerie Eliot for allowing me access to Cooke's correspondence with T.S. Eliot in the 1930s.

THE FRIENDS
(in alphabetical order)

Mary Ahern, keeper of the records of *Omnibus*
Lauren Bacall, for showing me the inside of the Dakota Building
Carl and Abby Borders, guardians of Cooke's golf clubs, and generous hosts
Bob Brown, life-saver, and Vera, Cooke's favourite woman golfer
Irving Cohen, who remembered those *America* negotiations as if they were yesterday
David Curnow, not least for a great story of illicit smoking
Norrie Davidson, possessor of the faintest typewriter ribbon in the West
Peggy and Kevin Harrington, with the best number plate in town
Stephen Hearst, who had his doubts but (I hope) overcame them
The Huntington Hotel, San Francisco, which took Cooke to its heart, and looked after me just because I mentioned his name – with special thanks to Cynthia Reid, Jimmy and Newt Cope
Heather Maclean, guide and adviser on many knotty issues
Jason de Montmorency, who made me feel at home at the National Arts Club
Edna and Eugene Rostow, who offered me the fruits of a sixty-five-year friendship, and a copy of the *Harkness Hoot*
Hugh Stuart, whose photograph album conjured up the atmosphere of a Cambridge generation
Eddie Wiltshire CBE, lepidopterist, jazz-instructor, and known to all his friends as James.

THE HELPERS

(in alphabetical order)

Sue Anstruther, who bought some cufflinks and broke a logjam
Alan Bailey, who showed me a map of Edwardian Salford
Colin Clark, possessor of the only known copy of Cooke's favourite film
Elizabeth Crawford, who could find any book
Hilda Curnow, who told me a love story
Rebecca Eaton, who opened the door to the *Masterpiece Theatre*
Freddie Hancock, impresario, and the woman who devised the Bernstein/Galway
    duet of 'Danny Boy'
Sheila Hetherington, tireless collator of her husband's recollections
Kristine Krueger, of the Academy Foundation
Peter Marshall, moving spirit of the Alistair Cooke lectures
Leonard McCombe for his splendid photographs
Karen Sharpe, of KQED San Francisco, for her splendid book
Roy Stevens, who captured the spirit of *Omnibus*
Geoffrey Taylor, who knew how the *Guardian* worked
Ann Turner, who guided me through the maze of *America*
William Whalley, probably the only other survivor of the Blackpool Secondary
    School 1st XV; vintage 1925
And many more besides.

THE READERS

My thanks to the brave few who read the drafts and wielded their scalpels: Barbara
Want, Alan Owen, Pat MacLoughlin, John B Cooke and Maria Trewin

    To the Weidenfeld & Nicolson team for their unquenchable enthusiasm – Ion
Trewin, but also Rachel Leyshon, Ilsa Yardley and Nick Castle

    And to David Miller, for his unsinkable optimism.

THE ARCHIVES

I am particularly grateful to Dr Howard Gotlieb, Director of the Department of
Special Collections at Boston University for his generosity in allowing me unfettered access to Alistair Cooke's papers – and to members of his team who gave of
their time and effort whenever I asked: Perry Barton, Exhibitions Co-ordinator;
Margaret Goostray, former Associate Director (now retired); and Sean D. Noel,

Public Service Administrator. I can recommend their '20th Century Archives' to any scholar...

Also to the staff of the BBC Written Archives Centre at Caversham, where Jeff Walden has handled so promptly and efficiently all my requests, however inconvenient. And to Tony Grant, the *Letter*'s latest overseer...

To Jesus College, Cambridge, and its former archivist John Mills, Emeritus Fellow...

To the *Manchester Guardian* Archive, and in particular Jackie Sen, Head of Collections Management at the John Rylands University Library of Manchester – as well as Peter Preston and Alan Rusbridger, for supporting the enterprise...

To the *Blackpool Gazette*...

To Amanda Lock and afterwards Clare Thorp, who carried out eclectic research tasks with patience and enthusiasm...

To Tom Clarke, probably the only person apart from Cooke himself to have read *all* the *Letters from America*...

And to my wife, Barbara, for sticking with it through thick and thin.

BIBLIOGRAPHY

COOKE BOOKS

Garbo and the Night Watchmen, 1937
Douglas Fairbanks (monograph), 1940
A Generation on Trial, 1950
Letters from America, 1951
Christmas Eve, 1952
A Commencement Address, 1954
Around the World in Fifty Years, 1966
Talk About America, 1968
General Eisenhower on the Military Churchill, 1970
America, 1973
Six Men, 1977
The Americans, 1979
Above London, 1980
The Patient Has the Floor, 1986
America Observed, 1988 (Selected and introduced by Ronald A. Wells)
Fun and Games, 1994
Masterpiece Theatre (Introduction), 1995

INFLUENCES

A Christmas Garland, Max Beerbohm, 1912
On the Art of Writing, Sir Arthur Quiller-Couch, 1923
Collected Poems, William Empson, 1935
The American Language (and Supplements), H.L. Mencken, 1936
Ego, James Agate, 1935 and onwards
I Can Get It For You Wholesale, Jerome Weidman, 1937
A William March Omnibus (Introduction, Alistair Cooke), 1956

PROFESSIONS

Good Evening, Raymond Gram Swing, 1964
The Sugar Pill, T.S.Matthews, 1959
Guardian – Biography of a Newspaper, David Ayerst, 1971
Guardian Years, Alastair Hetherington, 1981
Changing Faces – A History of the Guardian 1956–1988, Geoffrey Taylor, 1993
The History of Broadcasting in the UK, Asa Briggs, 1961–79
Inside the BBC, Leonard Miall, 1994

CITATIONS

Persona Grata, Cecil Beaton and Kenneth Tynan, 1953
Peggy Ashcroft, Michael Billington, 1988
On the Firing Line, William F.Buckley, 1989
A New York Life, Brendan Gill, 1990
Personal History, Katharine Graham, 1997
A Miracle and a Privilege, Francis D. Moore, 1995
The Complete Gamesmanship, Stephen Potter, 1971
Political Dictionary, William Safire, 1978
Broadcasting A Life, Olive Shapley, 1997
Cambridge and other memories, Basil Willey, 1968

JOHNNY

Love Janis, Laura Joplin, 1992
The Snowblind Moon, John Byrne Cooke, 1984

AMERICA

American Jazz Music, Wilder Hobson, 1939
The WPA Guide to New York City, 1939, reprinted 1990
The Penguin History of the USA, Hugh Brogan, 1985

INDEX